HIS SONG

The MUSICAL JOURNEY of ELTON JOHN

HIS SONG

The MUSICAL JOURNEY of ELTON JOHN

Elizabeth J. Rosenthal

BILLBOARD BOOKS

an imprint of Watson-Guptill Publications

NEW YORK

To Stan Shur, my teacher, mentor, adviser,
best friend, soul mate, and husband

First published in paperback in 2004 by Billboard Books
an imprint of Watson-Guptill Publications
a division of VNU Business Media, Inc.
770 Broadway, New York, N.Y. 10003
www.wgpub.com

Library of Congress Cataloging-in-Publication Data
Rosenthal, Elizabeth J.
His song : the musical journey of Elton John / by Elizabeth Rosenthal.
p. cm.
Includes discography and index.
ISBN 0-8230-8892-8
1. John, Elton. 2. Rock musicians—England—Biography. I. Title.

ML410.J64 R67 2001
782.42166'092—dc21
[B]   2001025909

The principal typeface used in the composition of this book was Centaur.

Senior Editor: Bob Nirkind
Editor: Julie Mazur
Designers: Leah Lococo and Jennifer Moore
Production Manager: Ellen Greene

Manufactured in the United States of America

First paperback printing, 2004

2 3 4 5 6 7 8 / 08 07 06 05 04

CONTENTS

ACKNOWLEDGMENTS

MANY PEOPLE DESERVE THANKS for helping to make this book possible. Senior Editor Bob Nirkind believed in this project and brought me on board. Masterful, patient editor Julie Mazur slaved away at the details. Richard Buskin and Wayne Martin provided invaluable insight. Ken Greengrass generously provided encouragement, wisdom, and time.

Linda Bowden, a biographical researcher, uncovered obscure articles. Phil Clarke traded his Down Under material for my American clippings. Of invaluable assistance was the groundbreaking 1993 booklet, *The Complete Elton John Discography*, by Elton scholars John DiStefano and Peter Dobbins. Steven Betts, David Bodoh, David T. Clancy, John Duval, Mark Giles, Alan McCormack, Steven L. Olson, and Jason Stevens also imparted their knowledge of Elton John's recordings as I labored to fill gaps in my discography. Pat White unselfishly gave of her practical skills.

Nannette Bac, Julie Balatico, Lynn Baxter, Normand Bérubé, Gerda Bosscher, Angie Browning, Darla Bruno, Rob Cargill, Sylvio Edgard de Castro, Carla Dinsmore, Anthony Dodd, Sue Duffin, Lorraine Edmunds, Per-Gunnar Eriksson, Morris Farinella, Tim Fitzpatrick, Cheryl Gane, Andy Geisel, Dick Georgeou, Brendan Glover, Leonard Herman, Gina Herring, John Higgins, Leonard Hodgkinson, Jeff Horton, Marilyn Kalfen, Sharon Kalinoski, Julia Knight-Shehata, Pat Koetz, Michael Lehman, Andy Lubitz, Dave Lundy, Lisa Macdonald, Barry Mandell, Lisa Margolin, Dr. Stephen Matlaga, George Matlock, Judy McArthur, Steven McGrew, Jim McKay ("The 22nd Row"), Domenico Mellone, Jeff Nesler, Frank Nieradko, Gloria Noble, Grace Piraro, Pam Quier, Morgan Reinhold, Ann and Jim Richardson, Valeria Rusconi, Sharon Russell, Beth Schulman, Lori Sears, Dave Sigler, Paul Smith, Tom Stanton, Lynn Sykes, Daryl Treger, Edward and Sophia Tsou, Jim Turano, Pip Williams, Doug Wirth, Charlene Young, Jeff Young, and Gary Zeichner shared their friendship, collections, useful tidbits, and/or photos, as the case may be.

The fantastic Elton John fan magazines *East End Lights* and *Hercules* delivered sustenance.

Thanks also to my sister Maddy for her faith in me, to my mother for helping me sharpen my writing skills, to my brother Dan for being himself, to my father for his humor, to my sister-in-law Sharon for her spirit, and to her brother for being the greatest man in the world. Aunt Sabina Lyons and cousin Dr. Irene Shur continue to inspire. Speaking of home, I can still see my favorite English teachers at Nanuet High, the exuberant Mrs. Achille and the provocative Dr. Demarest, coaxing the best from me.

Finally, without Sir Elton, how dull music would have been!

THE PIANO MAN MAKES HIS STAND[1]

CARNEGIE HALL on the night of April 12, 1995 was the site of the annual benefit for Trudie Styler and Sting's Rainforest Foundation. The place was abuzz with anticipation. The musical theme for the night, "It's Now or Never," suggested both Elvis Presley nostalgia and the urgency of protecting South American rainforests.

After a first half that was a basic greatest hits review—Elton John performed "Your Song" and "Can You Feel the Love Tonight," Sting showcased "Fields of Gold," and Bruce Springsteen offered "Streets of Philadelphia" (with Elton) and "The River" (with James Taylor)—the show finally turned to its theme. Bruce Springsteen reappeared with a new composition, "I'm Turning into Elvis and I Don't Know What to Do," then segued into "Viva Las Vegas." Springsteen became Elvis incarnate, much of his performance relying on convincing guitar play. Other performers followed his lead: Billy Joel used a guitar slung around his neck and a microphone stand as props for "Don't Be Cruel"; James Taylor tenderly rendered "Love Me Tender" on a folk guitar; and Sting, all mock sneers and with his knees turned inward in classic Elvis mode, used a guitar to attack "All Shook Up." Display after display of guitar-oriented bravado left one wondering what Elvis songs Elton John would tackle. The only song he had ever done on guitar was Lesley Duncan's "Love Song," a favorite from his *Tumbleweed Connection* album, which he had last played live nine years earlier, in 1986.

Bruce Springsteen announced Elton's return. The Briton grandly emerged from backstage, aflame in a painfully brilliant gold suit. He wiggled his backside at the crowd, then sat at his piano to launch into a spirit-tickling boogie-woogie/rock/jazz rendition of Fats Domino's "Blueberry Hill." Later, in a less-than-oblique reference to his sexuality, Elton smiled and said: "I was going to do 'My Boyfriend's Back' but I decided not to. I'm going to do [Little Richard's] 'The Girl Can't Help It' instead." Bruce Springsteen, Sting, Billy Joel, and James Taylor, all seated on stools near the piano, rocked to the pounding beat Elton extracted from the keys.

That night, Elton John proudly demonstrated not only the piano's importance to his career, but its role in the development of rock'n'roll. Numerous rock pioneers had played piano—Fats Domino, Little Richard, Jerry Lee Lewis, Ray Charles. They were heard alongside guitar stars like Elvis Presley and Chuck Berry. But before long, something happened—maybe it was the introduction of folk music into early rock'n'roll, or Bob Dylan "going electric," or the dominant hold Elvis seemed to have on the early rock'n'roll scene. Or maybe it was all those British youngsters who, weaned on Lonnie Donegan's "skiffle" music on the one hand and old American blues on the other, took up the guitar and quickly embarked on a peaceful "invasion" of American shores. Whatever the reason, the rock'n'roll that became known as "classic rock" obscured the piano's early role. According to Gary Cee's book *Classic Rock*, radio station programmers define classic rock as the "body of electric-guitar–driven popular music that began to flourish in the early sixties."[2]

As a piano player, Elton is now an oddball on the rock scene, just as he was when he played at Doug Weston's Troubador Club in Los Angeles in August 1970. His trio of musicians didn't then include a lead guitar. Within two years, he had added one in the form of Davey Johnstone, and his live bands have not been without a lead guitarist since. Still, Elton's piano has defined his sound from the beginning. Writing for *Contemporary Keyboard* in February 1981, Bob Doerschuk observed that although organists like Keith Emerson and Billy Preston had gained some prominence in the late 1960s, consequently lending a new legitimacy to keyboard playing in rock, Elton had brought the piano "back to the forefront of rock instrumentation. . . .When it revived under . . . [his] hands . . . it had been reinvigorated with a sense of melody and texture unprecedented in the style."[3] Still, Elton's almost single-handed resuscitation of the piano in rock'n'roll has prompted few keyboard players to follow him to prominence.

Despite Elton's unique status, he has been extraordinarily successful. Ever the humble music fan, when he first entered *Billboard's* Top LPs chart on October 3, 1970 at number 156 with his self-titled second album, he didn't expect his career to endure. The thought would have been contrary to his understanding of the fickle "pop" world. Four months later, on February 6, 1971, the twenty-three-year-old Elton and "Your Song" shared the upper reaches of *Billboard's* Hot 100 chart with the Osmonds, the Bee Gees, George Harrison, and the Fifth Dimension. Some sixty-four charted singles hence, on October 11, 1997, the fifty-year-old musician was on top of the Hot 100 with the double-A-sided Princess Diana benefit record, "Candle in the Wind 1997/Something About the Way You Look Tonight," besting twenty-somethings Boyz II Men, Mariah Carey, and the Backstreet Boys, as well as fifteen-year-old country prodigy LeAnn Rimes, and Usher, an eighteen-year-old hip-hop artist with a baby face and ribbed stomach muscles.

Longevity is not all Elton John has accomplished. He has also been remarkably consistent, breaking records and attracting a variety of accolades and honors. He has sold an estimated 200 million records worldwide. He has amassed ten multiplatinum, twenty-four platinum, and thirty-three gold albums in the United States alone. He boasts the best-selling single in the history of the world, the aforementioned "Candle/Something," bringing the platinum and gold singles tally in America to one multiplatinum, six platinum, and nineteen gold. In 1992, he tied Elvis's record for twenty-three consecutive years of Top 40 hits. And by the spring of 1999, Elton could boast of having had a song in the Top 40 every year for thirty years.

Elton and his lyricist Bernie Taupin were inducted into the Songwriters Hall of Fame in May 1992. He was inducted solo into the Rock and Roll Hall of Fame less than two years later. In 1995, he won an Academy Award in the best original song category for "Can You Feel the Love Tonight"—one of three songs nominated from his work on *The Lion King* film soundtrack. He also won a Golden Globe Award for the song that year. He has five Grammys (including one for his vocal on "Candle in the Wind 1997"), twenty-nine nominations, and a Grammy Legend award for his continuing contributions to music. He won a People's Choice Award in 1999 for all-time favorite musical performer, a distinction voted on by the American public, and a Tony Award in 2000 for the score he cowrote with Tim Rice for the Broadway musical *Aida*.

In June 1993, the French government awarded Elton one of its highest honors, naming him an officer of arts and letters for his music and humanitarian efforts. Two years later, Elton shared the Polar Music Prize, presented by the King of Sweden, with cellist-conductor Mstislav Rostropovich. In February 1998, Elton was knighted by Queen Elizabeth in honor of his work in music and for charity.

CHAPTER 1

YOUNG MAN'S BLUES[1]

(1947–1967)

R EGINALD KENNETH DWIGHT was born on March 25, 1947 in Pinner, Middlesex, a London suburb. His father, Stanley Dwight, was an officer in the Royal Air Force and was frequently away. When the elder Dwight was home, he was demanding, disapproving, and difficult to please, exuding a frightening countenance. Reggie's mother, the former Sheila Harris, was strict, but in contrast to her husband was his true mentor, confidante, and confidence booster. Years later, she said that her son grew up "a bundle of nerves."[2] Reggie's childhood was marred by terrible arguments between his parents. But something happened in 1950 that would set his life on an immutable course: At age three, he started playing the piano by ear.

Decades later, the future Elton John credited his maternal grandmother, Ivy, whom he affectionately called his "Nan," for laying the groundwork. She would sit him on her knees at the piano as he "banged away" at the keys. Also influential was the home's general tunefulness. Stanley Dwight had once played trumpet with an American-style big band called Bob Miller and the Millermen. He and Sheila were avid record buyers, exposing Reggie to the music of pianists Winifred Atwell, Nat King Cole, and George Shearing, and to singers Rosemary Clooney, Frank Sinatra, Kay Starr, Johnny Ray, Guy Mitchell, Jo Stafford, and Frankie Laine. One day, Reggie sat at the piano and perfectly reproduced Atwell's recorded rendition of "The Skaters' Waltz." Using the piano to mimic music he had heard in the house only moments before would become a favorite activity.

Atwell, skilled in many musical genres, had several piano hits in Britain during the 1950s and remained a source of inspiration to Reggie. Later, as Elton John, he would reminisce about the two pianos she'd had on stage, a "jingly" upright on one side and a grand on the other. He fondly remembered how she would "stomp across the stage" from the upright to the grand and play a classical piece. As a famous pianist in his own right, he eventually shared tea with her in Australia, where she had settled.[3]

The import of Reggie's newfound talent was not lost on his parents. His mother recalled, "When he was four we used to put him to bed in the day and get him up to play at night for parties."[4] He didn't look back fondly on this habitual enlistment to entertain. "I always liked playing the piano, but I hated being forced to play," he remembered. "My parents always used to do it. . . . I'd just curl up with embarrassment."[5] Nevertheless, Reggie developed a keen sense of stage demeanor. Three years later, he would play at the wedding of cousin Roy Dwight. The hired band was late, so Roy had Reggie amuse the guests by playing piano until the group arrived.[6] By this point, Reggie was taking formal lessons with a Mrs. Jones.

"GIVE ME THAT SWEET GEORGIA PEACH AND THE BOY FROM TUPELO"[7]

IN THE INTERIM between his first formal lesson and the scholarship he won at age eleven to become a junior exhibitioner at the Royal Academy of Music in London, Reggie discovered rock'n'roll. One day in 1956, Reggie was at a barbershop waiting to get his hair cut when he saw a picture of Elvis Presley in *Life* magazine. "I'd never seen anything like it," he later remembered. That weekend, his mother, who had a government job that paid her enough to bring home records each week, came home with "ABC Boogie" by Bill Haley and the Comets and "Heartbreak Hotel" by Elvis Presley. "Oh, mum, I just saw this bloke in a magazine!" he exclaimed, upon seeing the Presley record.[8] By the time Reggie entered the Royal Academy, where course director Margaret Donington regarded him as a student of "exceptional promise,"[9] his musical mind was firmly wedded to rock'n'roll.

Reggie preferred playing by ear. Subprofessor Helen Piena once said that, upon the boy's entrance into the Academy, she'd played him a four-page piece by Handel, which he promptly played back for her like a "gramophone record."[10] Reggie enjoyed playing Chopin and Bach[11] and singing in the choir during his Saturday classes at the Academy, but was not otherwise a diligent classical student. As he remembered decades later, "I kind of resented going to the Academy. I was one of those children who could just about get away without practicing and still pass, scrape through the grades." Sometimes, he would play truant and ride around the tube.[12]

Yet Piena saw Reggie as a "model student." The boy was polite and seemed willing and able to tackle his assignments. In Piena's opinion, it was only toward the end of his tutelage at the Academy that he became a tad careless in his studies.[13] By then Reggie was doing something on the side: playing popular music. His mother had engaged a private tutor for that purpose.

A student at the Academy for five years, Reggie rounded out the little free time he had with a newspaper route and a job at a wine shop on Saturday afternoons after class.[14] At Pinner County Grammar School, he was more advanced musically than his peers, and had an aptitude for songwriting, dashing off good melodies for his composition assignments—although his music teacher, Mr. Stoupe, berated him for approaching his work in a "casual" manner.[15]

Reggie's record collection grew rapidly. He took sustenance in the early rock'n'roll piano pioneers, annoying his father, who wanted him to concentrate on the classics, and frightening his mother with a fascination for music of the sexual, androgynous Little Richard. Reggie gained some notoriety by playing like Jerry Lee Lewis at Pinner County Grammar functions, and even sang.

Though he was taking ginger steps toward future rock'n'roll stardom, Reggie didn't look the part. He was short, rotund, and wore spectacles reminiscent of Buddy Holly's. Despite his claimed disdain for classical studies, he wasn't rebellious. He just wanted to do what he loved. Looking back on these fanciful days, the future Elton John said, "I used to stand in front of the mirror—I was very fat—and I'd mime to Jerry Lee Lewis records, thinking, 'Fuck, I wish this could happen to me.'"[16]

When he was in his early teens, Reggie's embattled parents finally divorced, in the wake of Sheila Dwight's friendship with a painter named Fred Farebrother. The future Elton would recount in later years that his mother had been labeled the guilty party for her relationship with Farebrother, although he believed his father "was doing the same thing behind her back and making her pay for it." He recalled during the 1970s how the ink on the divorce papers had barely dried before his father had remarried, going on to have four children in four years. "My pride was really snipped, 'cause he was supposed to hate kids," he shuddered. "I guess I was a mistake in the first place."[17]

In succeeding years, these bitter feelings would marinate in a stew of growing insecurities, but for now Reggie pursued his musical interests with zest. At age fifteen, with the help of caring father figure Farebrother, he became a weekend pianist at the nearby Northwood Hills pub, playing on Friday, Saturday, and Sunday nights. The crowd was often rough—sometimes an unruly patron would dump a pint of beer into Reggie's piano—and the youngster had to work hard to please them. He played everything from Jim Reeves country songs ("He'll Have to Go") to Irish folk numbers ("When Irish Eyes Are Smiling"), decades-old ditties ("Beer Barrel Polka"), hits of the day ("King of the Road"), and songs that he had written himself. He received a modest, steady income and substantial tips. "During that whole period, I don't think that I ever missed a gig," he said later.[18] A stint with a short-lived group called the Corvettes rounded out his time.

"TOO HOT FOR THE BAND, WITH A DESPERATE DESIRE FOR CHANGE"[19]

NOT LONG BEFORE REGGIE was to complete his preuniversity schooling, he dropped out of Pinner County Grammar, disappointing many of his teachers. Cousin Roy helped him get a job as a tea boy at Mills Music, a publishing company. By this time he had already quit his studies at the Royal Academy of Music, and the

Corvettes had folded. Reggie had a new group, comprised of local boys. They called themselves Bluesology, after a tune by seminal Belgian jazz guitarist Django Reinhardt called "Djangology." Bluesology began as a quartet, with Reggie on organ, Mick Inkpen on drums, Rex Bishop on bass, and Stuart A. Brown on guitar and vocals. The group, while reformulating frequently, devoted itself to the blues, as its name implied.

Bluesology engendered substantially more artistic credibility than the Corvettes. Elton John would later remember: "As a semi-pro group we got quite a bit of work, and we were ambitious and dedicated."[20] Inspired by Otis Redding's brass arrangements, the group soon added trumpet and saxophone players. These new musicians were, according to Elton, older, frustrated jazz musicians. Their presence helped get the group into some discriminating venues (at one of which, one electrifying evening, Stevie Wonder sat in on Reggie's Vox Continental organ[21]). Eventually, Bluesology's manager, a jeweler named Arnold Tendler, won the group a limited recording contract.[22] Philips Records's Jack Baverstock was impressed with a demo tape of a song Reg had written called "Come Back Baby."[23] The two singles the group would record for Philips's Fontana label, however, were flops.

The first single, "Come Back Baby," was recorded in June 1965. During the three-hour recording session, Reggie supplanted Brown as lead singer because the key was too high for Brown's voice. The Royal Academy dropout lent the song a straightforward, balladlike style, his voice clear and sweet, a harbinger of performances to come. And though Reggie typically played organ for the group, an instrument he never mastered because of its intimidating mechanical features, he played piano on this song. His pianism was full-bodied and aggressive, although the song was a ballad. The melody, an acceptable early effort, tugged at the heartstrings a little, but the lyrics were banal: "Come back baby/come back to me, yeah/and you will see, yeah/how I've changed/'cause you're the only love that I ever had."

The B-side, Jimmy Witherspoon's "Times Getting Tougher than Tough," was sung by Brown in his usual husky manner. Reggie's piano playing, reminiscent of Fats Domino's early recordings, stood out. At eighteen, he was a seasoned pianist, seemingly as familiar with the back of a smoke-filled barroom in New Orleans as with London's Denmark Street, the site of Mills Music.

Reggie was thrilled with his first recording. Ten years later, he said, "I can remember sitting in the car and hearing the record being played on Radio Luxembourg and saying, 'Hey, that's me singing, folks!'"[24]

A second Fontana single was released in February 1966. Reggie wrote the music and lyrics to the A-side, "Mr. Frantic," and sang the song. "Mr. Frantic" was a step backward, the music a poor amalgam of the Beatles and Herman's Hermits, the lyrics embarrassing: "When you hold me/when you squeeze me/hey, hey, hey/ Mr. Frantic!/That's my name!"

The group turned professional after agent Roy Tempest saw them perform and asked if they would like to back American soul acts touring England. The prospect thrilled Reggie. "I simply couldn't dream of anything better; I was soul crazy at the time—used to spend all my money on soul records," he later said.[25] Faced with expanded employment by Bluesology, Reg left his job at Mills Music.

Bluesology's first tour was with Patti LaBelle and the Blue Bells, a Tempest act. Despite strict rehearsal conditions imposed by LaBelle and company,[26] the two groups shared a camaraderie. Bluesology members were often found after hours playing cards at the Blue Bells' British residence. LaBelle and Reggie, whose talent she spotted immediately, were especially friendly. She would routinely win all his money, quickly feel sorry for him, and cook him a meal. She also gave him encouraging words for his future. (In the 1970s, after his first successes, the two would reaffirm their friendship.)[27]

Bluesology's gigs were decidedly unglamourous. They even backed the Ink Spots, a singing group whose career reached back decades and whose music was inappropriate for many of the clubs they played. During one especially grueling day on tour, the group played an American servicemen's club in London at 4 P.M., gigs at two ballrooms in Birmingham later that evening, and a show in another London club at 4 A.M. To make matters worse, "we had to load, unload, and set up all the equipment ourselves!" Reg later recalled.[28]

Eventually, Bluesology left the Roy Tempest agency and affiliated with Marquee Artists, which sent the group across Europe. Reg's disillusionment with the group surfaced. "Most of the guys were happy with their thirty quid a week and didn't have any real ambition," he said years later.[29] Still, a high point for Reg and Bluesology arrived at the end of 1966 when the group placed second on the bill at London's Savile Theatre to the finely coiffured Little Richard, Reg's boyhood idol. Unfortunately, they opened these shows to cries of "Off! Off!" from Little Richard's fans, but this humbling experience did not deter Reg from entertaining blissful dreams. As he remembered, "When I saw Little Richard standing on top of the piano, all lights, sequins, and energy, I decided there and then that I was going to be a rock'n'roll piano player!"[30]

A more radical development occurred when blues singer Long John Baldry asked the group to be his official backing band. At six foot seven, Baldry was nearly a foot taller than Reg, and was a veteran of the blues circuit. Baldry wanted to use three vocal frontmen: himself, Stuart A. Brown, and a man named Alan Walker. When Baldry decided to replace Walker, he chose American expatriate Marsha Hunt, not Reg.[31] Although Reg wasn't overly vociferous in promoting his wish to sing regularly for the band, he would later allow that he was beginning to feel buried. His physical appearance was proving a hindrance, and diet pills were little help.

By November 1967, when Baldry had his breakthrough number 1 British hit "Let the Heartaches Begin," a song that established him as a coveted cabaret act and relegated his backing band to the silent sidelines, Reg was testing other waters. Months earlier, he had answered a Liberty Records advertisement for new talent in *New Musical Express*. And so had a seventeen-year-old boy named Bernard Taupin.

"WHILE LITTLE DIRT COWBOYS TURNED BROWN IN THEIR SADDLES"[32]

BERNIE TAUPIN was born on May 22, 1950, somewhere between Sleaford and Lincoln in Lincolnshire. This northern farmland was rustic, mystical, and beautiful, and presented an endless stream of idyllic daydreams and fantasies for the young Bernie. His mother imbued in him a passion for reading, and a love of writing followed. Though he had a vivid imagination and enjoyed English and history, he had little comprehension of abstract subjects like mathematics and didn't qualify for Temple Lord Grammar School as his older brother had. Instead, he was sent to Market Slaten Secondary Modern, which, in his 1988 autobiography *A Cradle of Haloes: Sketches of a Childhood*, he described as the "legendary underbelly of education."[33]

Students at Market Slaten learned the basic subjects as well as gardening, called "agricultural science." The teachers expected little and the children accomplished little, though Bernie reveled in the poetry of Coleridge and Tennyson. Later, with some difficulty, he discovered rock'n'roll through the crackling of an American Forces Network radio signal. Marty Robbins's song "El Paso" convinced Bernie, as he wrote in *Cradle of Haloes,* that "there was a happy medium between rock and the written word." Before long, he was hooked on music and reading gossip magazines to get the latest on his idols of the moment. Eventually, he discovered the blues.

As Bernie's years of schooling wore on, the small, wiry boy with swarthy features realized that he had little prospect of a decent future. He increasingly engaged in heavy drinking with schoolmates. Graduating from school meant a dreary job in the dark dungeon of a newspaper print shop, which he had mistakenly assumed would lead to a reporting job. When he realized this was not to be, he quit. He landed a job at a chicken farm, but left this, too, after having to dispose of masses of dead chickens following an outbreak of disease.

It was the spring of 1967 and, in sharp contrast to Reg's determination, Bernie had no idea what he was going to do with his life. It is ironic that Bernie, the quintessential disaffected young man, seemed a likelier candidate for rock notoriety, even though he had no apparent musical ability. The responsible and proper Reg, after all this time of playing in bars and clubs and traveling around with a band that played music young people liked, didn't seem headed for stardom. He appeared to be a talented youngster who, due to his chunky frame, would be left in the shadows while others ascended to fame and fortune.

Bernie returned to writing in the spring of 1967, and just a few months later spotted the advertisement in *New Musical Express.* He submitted some silly poetry that he would later say was overly influenced by the psychedelic lyrics of the day, one called "Swan Queen of the Laughing Lake," another, "Year of the Teddy Bear."

"BROKEN YOUNG CHILDREN ON THE WHEELS OF THE WINNERS"[34]

REG SHOWED UP AT LIBERTY RECORDS to audition for Ray Williams, the company's young head of A&R. It had been a long time since Reg had sung anything. He could only remember some of what he'd done at the Northwood Hills pub, like Jim Reeves tunes and the Al Jolson staple "Mammy." He performed them for Williams. Elton later recalled that the Liberty Records representatives were not "jumping up and down with glee at this overweight, respectable thing that looked like a lump of porridge singing a Jim Reeves song."[35] Although Reg failed the audition, Williams kindheartedly offered him a batch of lyrics written by a fellow in Lincolnshire who was unable to compose music. Though still dejected, Reg put some of the lyrics to music, including something called "Scarecrow." Williams was impressed enough that he decided to bring Reg to the attention of another company, Niraki, with which he had set up songwriters Nicky James and Kirk Duncan. Fifty percent of Niraki was owned by Gralto, the Hollies' publishing company, and Gralto was jointly owned by the Hollies and the more expansive Dick James Music (DJM).

Reg began surreptitiously recording some of his new compositions in Dick James's two-track recording studio, encouraged by Kirk Duncan and assisted by sound engineer Caleb Quaye (whom Reg knew from his days at Mills Music when Quaye, an employee of another publishing firm, used to tease him about his weight, some of which had now been shed). Reg impressed Quaye with his musical acumen and inspired Duncan with his voice. Although Reg "had lost complete interest in being a performing artist," Duncan saw the youngster as a "real find" and got the Spencer Davis Group to cover a new Dwight/Taupin composition called "One Time, Sometime, or Never,"[36] although it apparently was never released.

By the fall of 1967, Reg had written music to many of Bernie's lyrics, including "Scarecrow" and "A Dandelion Dies in the Wind." Both had strong folk sounds. He had also written songs with Nicky James and Kirk Duncan, and some by himself, including the catchy and fervent "I Get a Little Bit Lonely."

Bernie would later be the first to acknowledge the pretentiousness of his early lyrics. "See my eyes and see my arms/the seagulls say you've gone/it was just a game of let's pretend/and I'll whistle to the waves that lend me tears," he wrote in "A Dandelion Dies in the Wind." Yet they were more interesting than anything Reg could write. Reg's role, meanwhile, involved perching a set of lyrics on his piano and spontaneously spilling chords onto the keys to fit the words. In those days, he scribbled musical notes on the typewritten lyric sheets to remind himself of the melody he'd composed.

For some musicians, the fact that the lyrics were not apportioned between verse and chorus could have been problematic. "There'd just be 115 lines and I'd think 'Where the fuck do I start?'" Reg said later.[37] But Bernie's writing style only inspired his composing.

Bernie eventually took Ray Williams up on his generous "if you're ever in the area please drop by" invitation, showing up one day in London. Ray took Bernie to a recording studio where Reg was doing session work and introduced the two, who then walked around the corner to the Lancaster Grill on Tottenham Court Road for a cup of coffee. Thus did one of the most momentous meetings in popular music take place. Despite some obvious differences in temperament between the two young men, they hit it off. To Reg, Bernie looked "angelic." The Lincolnshire youth was "like the brother I never had." And Bernie was impressed with Reg's musical worldliness. "The radical differences have always been the thing that drew us together in the end," Bernie later reflected.[38] For a time following this meeting, their songwriting was accomplished via the postal system.

Reg was still officially with Bluesology. The group had one final single in October 1967, as Stu Brown and Bluesology. "Since I Found You Baby/Just a Little Bit" suffered the same fate as its two predecessors. Reg was afraid, at first, to leave his steady position, though it had long since lost its luster. He even endured the embarrassment of Long John Baldry's wardrobe standards for live performances. The group had to wear bells, beads, and caftans worthy of Haight-Ashbury. "Overnight we switched from wearing frilly satin shirts to that love-and-peace thing," he cringed in an interview eight years later.[39]

The last straw occurred in November 1967, with Baldry's number 1 hit, "Let the Heartaches Begin," which established him as a cabaret act. "I was so bored with playing cabaret," the future Elton would say. "I've always said that I will not play to people who are eating fish and chips. It's a dead end for musicians."[40] Of minimal consolation to Reg was that a song he'd cowritten with Baldry and Tony Macaulay —"Hey Lord You Made the Night Too Long," a pleasant ballad with equal doses gospel and country—was included as a B-side to the export single of "Heartaches." The small victory was not enough to keep Reg in Bluesology, though, even if nothing of much of note had yet occurred in his work with Bernie.

Reg had already settled on a stage name. He wanted a short, catchy one, taking "Elton" from Bluesology's new saxophone player, Elton Dean, and "John" from his mentor, Long John Baldry. For him, being called Reg "was kind of like a nightmare when I was young. I couldn't wait to be somebody else."[41]

CHAPTER 2

71–75 NEW OXFORD STREET[1]

(1967–1970)

NOT LONG BEFORE ELTON LEFT BLUESOLOGY, Dick James conducted a "purge" of musicians secretly using his recording studios after hours. Somehow, Elton and Bernie were spared the exit door and signed a songwriting agreement with Dick James Music (DJM) in November 1967. James had built his fortune mainly on the Beatles, who had fallen into his lap in late 1962. Luck had led to other successes, with Gerry and the Pacemakers, Barry McGuire ("Eve of Destruction"), the Troggs, the Hollies, the Mamas and the Papas, and others.[2]

What better publisher to work for than the publisher of the Beatles' catalog? This alone portended a bright future for the tunesmith and his new lyricist. And Dick James wasn't just a publisher. His business was holistic, as DJM also created and promoted recordings. As early as 1965 he had incorporated a record label in association with Larry Page (called Page One) and, less than a year before Elton and Bernie were signed, James's son Stephen had established This Record Company (which would sign Elton's recording contract).

Elton's portion of the duo's 1967 songwriting contract included both composing and session work—doing demos for songs written by other DJM songwriters, and playing on recordings. He played piano on demos and recordings of songs written by DJM's Roger Cook and Roger Greenaway, best known for "I'd Like to Teach the World to Sing." He played uncredited piano on the Hollies' 1970 hit "He Ain't Heavy, He's My Brother," and provided backup vocals on two Tom Jones hits, "Delilah" (1968) and "Daughter of Darkness" (1970).

Bernie soon moved in with Elton, his mother, and Fred Farebrother, returning to Lincolnshire on weekends. Meanwhile, Elton's look was changing. He had lost a drastic amount of weight and had begun to grow his hair, trying to look the part of a potential star as the new songs poured forth. Although Dick James encouraged the two to write hits for mainstream recording acts like Engelbert Humperdinck, the work coming from their quarters in Frome Court, Northwood Hills, seemed instead to promise something new. The sprightly "The Angel Tree" honored a tree from Bernie's dreamy Lincolnshire youth. There was also the tearful ballad "Reminds Me of You," the overtly Beatles-influenced psychedelia of "Regimental Sergeant Zippo," and the early excellence of "The Tide Will Turn for Rebecca." "Rebecca" hinted at Elton's growing talent for composing melodies that stealthily flowed in different directions, returning to the source for a seamless, melodic whole.

The rock numbers were few. There were two Elton wrote not with Bernie but with Caleb Quaye: "Thank You for Your Loving" (covered by the Duke's Noblemen in 1968) and "You'll Be Sorry to See Me Go." Elton also wrote two instrumentals by himself, "71–75 New Oxford Street" (actually DJM's address) and "Get Out (of This Town)." Both contained an abundance of crazed organ riffs, suggesting a discotheque—or *Rowan & Martin's Laugh-In*. Elton's growing compositional versatility was also evident in the down-home country twang and lilting piano of "Last to Arrive."

Elton and Bernie were suffering one disappointment after another, with few musicians expressing interest in recording their songs. One exception was "Turn to Me," a song that fit neatly into the British pop vein, as Dick James wished, but was better suited for the Hollies or the Turtles than Engelbert. It was recorded on the Page One label by Plastic Penny (which included Elton's future drummer, Nigel Olsson). In general, though, it seemed that if Elton wanted his songs recorded, he was going to have to do it himself.

By April 1969, Elton had two British singles credited to his new name: "I've Been Loving You," released on March 1, 1968, and "Lady Samantha," released on January 17, 1969. "I've Been Loving You," produced by Caleb, is an ordinary love song. Elton wrote the entire song but credited the lyrics to Bernie because, as Bernie recalled, Elton "felt guilty, and because we'd been working so much together, he felt I deserved credit."[3] A March 2, 1968 advertisement in *New Musical Express* trumpeted, "Hear the greatest performance on a 'first' disc. . . .You have been warned! Elton John is 1968's great new talent." The single flopped.

"Lady Samantha" was produced by Elton's and Bernie's new mentor, Steve Brown, who encouraged the two to write what they liked. A sing-along type of song, "Lady Samantha" depicts the plight of a forlorn, ghostly figure with a tragic past who roams what might have been the Scottish moors. Bernie later remarked that this was the first song to represent the songwriting team's new direction.[4] They were writing to please themselves instead of the marketplace.

Lionel Conway, head of Dick James's publishing division, lobbied for the release of "Lady Samantha," which James did not initially support since it didn't fit his commercial vision for Elton and Bernie. But when Conway got the BBC to make it their record of the week, James acquiesced. The song had some success on the radio, becoming a turntable hit although it barely sold any copies.[5] What it did do, however, was pique the interest of Three Dog Night, a successful U.S. recording act. One of the group's singers, Danny Hutton, became smitten with Elton's demos, which the Briton played for him while the group was touring England in 1969. So "Lady Samantha" was included on Three Dog Night's *Suitable for Framing* album in June of that year. Elton and Hutton kept in touch, and Hutton's transatlantic telephone calls to the young hopeful were rewarded with many more demo tapes. Three Dog Night would record "Your Song," too.[6]

"Lady Samantha" also brought the first live Elton John performance to BBC listeners. On October 28, 1968, Elton auditioned for a BBC panel, performing on piano and organ, with Caleb Quaye on guitar and others on bass and drums. Besides "Lady Samantha," they played "All Across the Havens" (its eventual B-side) and "Skyline Pigeon." Elton's job was to curry favor with the panel and secure future BBC gigs. Alarmingly, the panel's vote was split on his future. A sampling of individual opinions shows naysayers heavy on the nay: "Male vocal in the 1968 feeling—thin, piercing voice with no emotional appeal . . . dreary songs . . . one-key singer . . . pretentious material." But BBC producer Aidan Day was impressed. His reaction? "First class!" A draw awarded Elton the benefit of the doubt. The audition performance was broadcast Sunday morning, November 3, 1968, on the Day-produced *Stuart Henry Show*[7] and, despite the nay-voting panelists, provided a vivid foreshadowing of Elton's live performances in years to come. No matter how good the recording, Elton had a knack for vastly improving the song onstage.

"SAVED IN TIME, THANK GOD MY MUSIC'S STILL ALIVE"[8]

DICK JAMES OFFERED A SONG WRITTEN solely by Elton (but credited to both Elton and Bernie), "I Can't Go on Living Without You," for the Eurovision Song Contest. Lulu, a British singer who had recently scored an enormous American number 1 with "To Sir with Love," was to represent Great Britain in the contest. But first the British entry had to be selected. She performed several candidates on her television show during the first two months of 1969, including "I Can't Go on Living."

This may be the most ghastly song ever attributed to the struggling duo, overloaded with 1960s songwriting clichés and ill-conceived Spanish exclamations. "It was the worst song I've ever heard," said songwriter Bill Martin, who voted on the contest entries. "If he'd won that contest, he wouldn't be the Elton John we know today."[9] "Boom-Bang-A-Bang" won instead, tying for first place in the Eurovision Song Contest and providing Lulu with another hit.

Meanwhile, Elton was putting the finishing touches on his first album, which could have proved impossible had he gone through with marriage to one Linda Woodrow. Elton met Linda at the end of 1967, when he was still in Bluesology. His first romance ensued, and he and Bernie came to share an apartment with her in

Islington. Though the relationship was doomed to failure, Elton, perhaps hoping for some kind of conventional domestic life, proposed marriage. Years later, he remembered that his fiancée had disliked music and discouraged his ambition. "It really destroyed me inside," he said.[10] The prospect of marrying a woman who didn't share his passions, along with his general career frustrations, made Elton miserable enough to create a tragicomical scene of attempted suicide. He turned on the gas in the oven of their apartment and lay on the floor to await his fate. Another failure awaited; he had left the windows open.

Elton had already asked for an advance from Dick James for an apartment and furniture. Then Long John Baldry entered the fray. Elton, Bernie, and a couple of members of a DJM act called the Mirage (including a bass player named Dee Murray) went for drinks at a club, the Bag O' Nails. Baldry showed up. "So he comes rolling up to me and we catch up on things with me telling him I'm going to get married," Elton later remembered. He was unprepared for what Baldry had to say next. "He turns to me and says, 'If you marry this woman you'll destroy two lives, hers and yours.' He knew I was gay and told me I had to get used to it or else it would destroy my life." It would be some time before Elton recognized his sexuality; he hadn't even recognized Baldry's at the time. "I'd spent a long time in his backing band so I knew him pretty well, but I swear I had no idea he was gay," he insisted. "I simply didn't know about those things then. I was, in so many ways, very naive."[11]

Fortified by large amounts of alcohol, Elton told Linda it was over. Bernie and Elton returned to Frome Court, posthaste.

"OUR EMPTY SKY WAS FILLED WITH LAUGHTER"[12]

ELTON RECORDED HIS FIRST ALBUM, *Empty Sky,* in the winter of 1968 and the spring of 1969 at a DJM eight-track studio. Elton was by now boasting a Lennon-ish *Sergeant Pepper*-style coiffure with an immaculately carved set of connected sideburns and mustache. He still tended toward pudginess but kept his weight down. An optimistic photograph shows a t-shirt–clad Elton, beefy arms on piano, leading fellow musicians Caleb Quaye on guitar and Tony (not Dee) Murray on bass during rehearsals. The recording sessions were exhilarating.

Good fortune had already smiled on Elton some months earlier when Roger Cook, a singer himself, had persuaded Dick James to allow him to record and publish "Skyline Pigeon" through Cookaway Music, the company set up by Cook and Roger Greenaway within DJM. Its inclusion on *Empty Sky* boded well for the album's acceptance, and Elton and Bernie regarded it as their first significant composition.

"Skyline Pigeon" represented a first plateau for Elton and Bernie's developing songwriting technique. "Turn me loose from your hands/let me fly to distant lands/over green fields, trees, and mountains/flowers and forest fountains," Bernie wrote about an imprisoned bird yearning for the open skies. Elton, the self-described poor organ player, played organ and harpsichord. His virtual hymn perfectly and gently envelops the lyrics, adding further imagery.

The title song, "Empty Sky," pays tribute to the Rolling Stones, a band Elton idolized. The opening bars feature Caleb Quaye's "Sympathy for the Devil" conga drums. Elton's melody is typical of the better John/Taupin compositions, offering a complex emotional structure. Caleb's lead guitar bursts through Elton's discordant piano playing while the pianist shouts the angry words of a prisoner who, from the shadows of his cell, feels betrayed by a woman who will soon repeat and profit from her misdeeds by "shining [her] . . . eyes on the wealth of every man." A dramatic album opener, "Empty Sky" may have fed future accusations of misogyny against Bernie, but the lyrics merely indicate his penchant for writing stories in which he stands in the shoes of an undesirable character.

The other songs were almost all prompted by Bernie's memories of his youth and a boyhood fascination with mythology. "Val-Hala" fantasizes about the Viking afterlife; "The Scaffold" refers to the Minotaur. In "Hymn 2000," with a set of lyrics that Bernie would later agree are particularly obtuse, he seems to be questioning, among other things, his religious upbringing (Catholic). "Lady What's Tomorrow" is an environmental protest song lamenting the encroachment of the city on the country ("But no one cares/if branches live and die out there") and reminiscing about the beauty of the countryside that filled his childhood. "Gulliver," on the passing of a beloved dog, may include the album's second-best set of lyrics next to "Skyline Pigeon": "Gulliver's gone/to the final command of his master/his watery eyes had washed/all the hills with his laughter."

Rounding out the set are "Western Ford Gateway," which portrays a poverty-stricken, hopeless part of town where drunkenness is both survival and death, and "Sails," the only rock song on the album besides the title track. Elton's music for "Sails" must have surprised Bernie. The lyrics suggest a quiet lunch with a girlfriend amongst the seagulls. Elton turned the song into a bouncing romp, with his electric piano and Caleb's electric guitar competing for attention.

Aside from "Sails," the album's music naturally matches the lyrics, and it portends the future star's virtuosity on an array of keyboard instruments. "Val-Hala," with ancient harpsichord strains (supplemented by piano and organ) and a distant vocal, evokes the mists that surround the mountain from which Thor observes his subjects. Elton's vocal on "Western Ford Gateway" echoes through the nearly deserted, desolate streets portrayed in the song, his organ recalling strains of music emanating from a bar around the corner as neon lights flicker overhead. In "Hymn 2000," Elton's piano serves as a billowy cushion for his reflective folk melody, while the song's introductory chords sport an assertive bass line that would come to be a trademark of his pianism. The musician also proved deft with organ playing, which at times turns into a countermelody. Even better is "Lady What's Tomorrow," with a folkish surface in the vein of Peter, Paul, and Mary that becomes a surprise musical foil to Elton's syncopated piano. The folk melody of "The Scaffold" is buttressed by Elton's electric piano, which again competes with Caleb's guitar, and serves as a subdued encore to the rock of "Sails."

But only one other song on the album comes close to approaching the seeming effortlessness of the well-structured music of "Skyline Pigeon" or the gripping turmoil of "Empty Sky." That song, "Gulliver," is both grief-stricken funeral music and a tuneful protestation of the loss of a treasured pet. Elton's insistent, classically rendered chord style would provide the basic underpinnings of many of his future ballads; "Someone Saved My Life Tonight" has its musical roots here. And the musician's vocal convincingly imitates the wailing of a child who has just learned of his dog's death.

The album concludes with an instrumental, "Hay Chewed," a title most likely inspired by another favorite group of Elton's. But the title is all that reminds the listener of the Fab Four. The music is a jazz/rock fusion of acoustic piano against aggressive tenor saxophone, segueing into a startling aural overview of all the preceding album tracks ("Reprise").

At the time of its release on June 3, 1969, *Empty Sky* portended a star who could boast any style of piano chops, a facile singing voice, and an unselfconscious, natural melodic approach. Besides Elton and Caleb Quaye, other future notables on the album include Elton's soon-to-be regular drummer for live performances, Nigel Olsson, on "Lady What's Tomorrow"; Roger Pope, a member of Hookfoot with Caleb, who played drums and percussion on the other songs and would continue on a few more of the pianist's early albums; and Clive Franks, here a tape operator and whistler, soon to be Elton's invaluable sound engineer for studio and stage.

In July, Elton appeared with Hookfoot members Quaye, Pope, and David Glover on the BBC's *Symonds on Sunday* radio program to play "Lady Samantha," "Sails," and a couple of brand-new songs. In response to David Symonds's question about the possibility of live concerts, Elton responded: "We want to make personal appearances, but there are things to be sorted out at the moment. And also, I've only had six hours' rehearsal with the band. The band at the moment are a band in their own right. . . . But we want to team up together, because I've known the boys for so long." He was so nervous he couldn't even mention Hookfoot's name, nor, at first, Bernie Taupin's. Of his songwriting partnership with Bernie, he said hopefully, "We haven't written a hit yet, but we've been very lucky."[13]

Empty Sky sold only four thousand copies. This was not the star-making enterprise it had seemed at first.

"WRITIN'S LIGHTIN' UP"[14]

BY SUMMER 1969, Elton must have wondered whether he would ever have success, although he was still managing to enjoy himself. He had been sporadically "helping out" at a record shop called Musicland for several months already, just for the thrill of seeing new releases arrive, especially the American imports. (His record collection saw a marked expansion during those months.) He attended a Bob Dylan concert in August on the Isle of Wight and, in September, saw the Who in Croydon. On Monday, October 27, 1969, he wrote the music to "Your Song." It took him ten minutes.

With "Your Song," Elton and Bernie reached another songwriting plateau. Some might argue it never got better than that. Undoubtedly, the lyrics feature a simple sentiment with which almost anyone can identify. A piano and voice demo features this in its barest form, with Elton practically whispering into the microphone and his gentle piano chords clearly providing the framework for the orchestral arrangement to come.

"Your Song" was part of a growing stockpile of songs that Elton and Bernie wrote in the middle to latter part of 1969. A good many were soon ripe for recording. But Steve Brown, who had produced *Empty Sky,* believed he wasn't qualified to produce the new collection of songs, especially since he had found someone, Paul Buckmaster, who was interested in doing orchestral arrangements for the entire album. Brown made an appointment for Elton and Bernie to meet with Gus Dudgeon, an industry veteran who had produced David Bowie's "Space Oddity."

Elton later recalled that, at the meeting, Dudgeon didn't seem especially excited by the John/Taupin compositions presented to him.[15] Brown was annoyed by Dudgeon's seemingly cold reaction, since he was making the sacrifice of stepping down so that a more seasoned producer could take charge. "I could have punched him in the nose," Brown said. Dudgeon has since explained that he had been so thrilled by the material, he hadn't wanted to risk losing the project by appearing *too* enthusiastic. "So I was Johnnie Cool," he noted. In any case, he agreed to produce the songs.[16] Brown coordinated the album.

Dick James granted the project about twelve thousand dollars, a large sum of money for an unknown act. The music was planned note for note, as the hired classical musicians would be an integral part of the effort. "All the notes were written down, even the rhythm notes," Elton said in 1980. "I had to play live with everything. Can you imagine? I mean, they had all these brilliant session musicians standing there . . . and I had to play live. . . . It was a very, very disciplined album for me to make."[17] The recording was completed at Trident Studios in one week in January 1970. An enraptured Dick James launched the final product on April 10, 1970. A mark of his optimism was his reworking of the recording contract originally signed by Elton in early 1968. This new contract was much more lucrative for the young composer.

Meanwhile, in the United States, another record deal was made. In 1969, DJM tried to get an American licensee, Bell Records, interested in "Lady Samantha" and *Empty Sky.* Bell Records passed on the latter, releasing only "Lady Samantha" to no effect. Finally, in January 1970, the president of Uni Records, Russ Regan, was approached by DJM representative Lennie Hodes in Los Angeles. Hodes informed Regan that Elton had just been discarded by Bell Records and, worse, that his then only album, *Empty Sky*, had been rejected by five other record companies. Regan thought at the time, "If five companies have turned him down, he can't be very good." Playing the album, though, prompted him to exclaim, "Somebody's crazy, because this album is really good!" He contacted Hodes, who said that Elton was still available, and that Regan need not pay any money but should just promise to promote him. "I got Elton John for nothing, which is probably one of the best deals ever made," Regan said later.[18]

Despite this deal, it would be years before *Empty Sky* was released in the United States. And according to a different account, Regan was interested in Elton only because DJM threw in a then unknown group called Argosy, which, as fate would have it, would remain unknown. Regan agreed to pay a ten thousand dollar advance for Argosy.[19] If this is true, Regan did not really get Elton for nothing.

Dealings aside, there was plenty to be excited about with the *Elton John* album. It opens with the future musical staple "Your Song," which begins with Elton's voice and piano—much like the demo, although the introduction of an orchestra within a few bars further expands the song's innocent, romantic thoughts.

The next song, "I Need You to Turn To," starts with voice and harpsichord before the strings quietly intercede. It isn't just the harpsichord that gives the song an ancient aura, or the harp played by Skaila Kanga, but also the melody, which could have fit into the "Greensleeves"-filled repertoire of a fourteenth-century troubadour. The quiet beauty of the song belies the anxiety Elton felt while recording the harpsichord live with the orchestra. He had played the instrument on *Empty Sky*, but this was different. "'I Need You to Turn To' was a really nervous moment," Elton remembered some twenty-seven years later. "While the harpsichord looks very similar to the pianoforte, there's a kind of delay to how its mechanism works, so it's very easy to fuck it all up if you're not thinking ahead."[20]

The third song, "Take Me to the Pilot," starts like the first two, with Elton's voice and piano, but even before the orchestra's jubilant entrance the piece hurtles in a different direction. Elton's vocal here is assertive and strong (in the first two, he sounds tender, almost hesitant). The piano seems to herald a raucous, African-American gospel number. By the song's end, the orchestra has completed a rocking, rolling adventure, punctuated by Elton's percussive piano and supplemented by percolating rhythm guitar, Caleb's wailing lead guitar, and spirited backing vocals by six singers, including Roger Cook and singer-songwriter Lesley Duncan.

Bernie's lyrics to "Take Me to the Pilot" are intriguing. "If you feel that it's real/I'm on trial/and I'm here in your prison/like a coin in your mint/I am dented and spent with high treason," Bernie wrote. The speaker in this strange tale then observes, "Through a glass eye, your throne/is the one danger zone" and exhorts his captor to "Take me to the pilot for control/take me to the pilot of your soul." What is all this about? Bernie has claimed since the beginning that he doesn't have a clue. The lyrics possess many elements: betrayal, either political or personal ("treason"); the illusion of danger ("through a glass eye"); and fearlessness toward the unknown ("take me to the pilot of your soul"). According to Elton, this and other songs that emerged from these sessions were inspired by the science fiction books Bernie was reading at the time.[21]

"No Shoestrings on Louise" is next, a down-home country-and-western slice of life and another Rolling Stones tribute. Elton would later joke that every album of his had to have a Stones tribute song on it (a pledge that didn't last long). If the song is Stones-like, it is in Elton's growling faux-Southern vocal, which resembles the one Mick Jagger sometimes adopted. But the brash, ringing piano chords are unmistakably Elton's, conjuring up images of the manipulative "Loo-ays" striding confidently down the dusty main street of town, searching for male prey. Caleb's twangy guitar completes the picture of a dry, gray Western scene.

The next song, "First Episode at Hienton," was a leftover from 1968. In it, a young man looks wistfully back on his schoolboy romance with "Valerie," who has since grown up and moved away. The "first episode" refers to the adolescent main character's first sexual experience with Valerie ("For your thighs were the cushions/of my love and yours for each other"). Bernie's childhood memories dominate, as he links remembrances of roaming the hills or running through castle ruins with fantasies of a fictional love. Elton's melody changes shape in response to the lyrics, which meander in a free-form style.

Side two commences with "Sixty Years On," one of Elton John's most brilliant compositions and the first of his and Bernie's songs about the loneliness of old age to be recorded in 1970 (along with "Talking Old Soldiers" on *Tumbleweed Connection*, recorded later that year). The song depicts a veteran who has gotten little for his role in an unnamed war. His dog is dead, he sees nothing in his future, and he is losing his faith. Elton's touching piano and voice demo of the song is translated on the album into a vehicle for a harp- and cello-dominated orchestra, vividly portraying the veteran's growing isolation. The harp mimics the demo's broken piano chords; the orchestra follows the demo's dark, brooding note clusters. The innocent timbre of Elton's boyish voice lends the story even more poignancy.

"Sixty Years On" is followed by an overlooked gem of a ballad, "Border Song." It contains more than a little gospel; witness Aretha Franklin's cover of the song, an American Top 40 hit early the following year (and the first time a star recorded one of their songs). Typically, Bernie claimed that "Border Song" wasn't about anything in particular. Elton later posited that the song was about the alienation Bernie felt in and about London at the time ("Brand of people who ain't my kind"), and his desire to visit home as often as he could.[22] For those unfamiliar with Bernie's disaffection with British urban life in the late 1960s, "Border Song" seems to be a homily against bigotry, even before one reaches the last verse, penned by Elton himself. (Bernie acknowledged that "the great thing about Elton's last verse was that he tried to put it all into perspective."[23]) Although Elton's words lack imagination, they do not lack in longing for an age of better race relations: "Holy Moses let us live in peace/let us strive to find a way to make all hatred cease/there's a man over there, what's his colour I don't care/he's my brother let us live in peace." These words are far from the banality of his early lyrics for "Come Back Baby" and "Mr. Frantic." The song's plaintive melody has the aura of a spiritual, like "Swing Low, Sweet Chariot." A choir sings during an instrumental break led by Elton's piano, which is itself accompanied by weeping strings that build to a climax, and contributes to its otherworldly feeling.

The next song, "The Greatest Discovery," tells of the birth of Bernie's younger brother. With its lullaby lilt and sweet piano, the melody sensitively portrays Bernie's boyhood "discovery" of his household's newest member.

The album's imagery shifts to the surreal with "The Cage." Elton later claimed that the lyrics, like those for "Take Me to the Pilot," were inspired by the science fiction Bernie was devouring, but this isn't obvious.[24] Bernie's "cage" represents emotional captivity ("I've never loved in a cage/or talked to a friend or just waved") formed by an existence in which dishonest sentiments prevail ("Watched you kiss your old daddy with passion and tell dirty jokes as he died"). Like "Take Me to the Pilot," the music begins with Elton's up-tempo piano, a percussive feast that suggests Aretha Franklin's "Think." Elton snarls his vocals, conveying a dungeon of human nature that is the antithesis of the previous song's family values. The symphonic-sounding piano solo in Elton's demo becomes a moog synthesizer moment in the studio for Diana Lewis, done in French horn style, and furthering the song's surrealism.

The pièce de résistance of the album is its closer, "The King Must Die." The surrealism continues with this song, which some have speculated refers to Martin Luther King, an idea Bernie rejected. But even if the song was not inspired by contemporary events, it speaks to assassination plots dating back to Caesar's time: "And sooner or later,/everybody's kingdom must end,/and I'm so afraid your courtiers,/cannot be called best friends." This tale of secret plans, trust betrayed, and dead dreams becomes more disturbing as Elton's sparse collection of treble piano notes, accented by an ominous intercession of piano bass, seems to warn the listener, showing how completely alone the threatened monarch is among his assumed friends. By the end of the song, when Elton nearly yells the words "The King is dead" and declares "Long live the King" to a thunderous piano conclusion, the listener's psychic insecurities have been dramatically heightened.

Surprisingly, Elton would look back on his *Elton John* album vocals with distaste. "I was just an infant vocally at the time," he said. "Listening now, I sound like a schoolboy with my balls cut off."[25] But in 1970, he was still discovering the potential of his voice. And the *Elton John* album was an exciting musical development in his career.

The first single from the album in Great Britain was not "Your Song," as one might assume, but "Border Song," released on March 20, 1970. It did not chart. It did, however, receive a lot of radio play and secured Elton the chance to perform the song on BBC television's *Top of the Pops.* The single was also significant for the B-side, "Bad Side of the Moon," from the *Elton John* album sessions—another song that, according to Elton, was inspired by Bernie's science fiction passion, and a funky number that would become a live staple.[26] "Border Song" was released in the United States on Uni's Congress label in April, but failed to chart there as well.

A bigger problem was that the album, on which so many hopes had been placed, was not selling as well in Britain as it should have. This situation led to a startling conclusion: Elton would have to tour. He didn't want to; in later years he would point to laziness as the reason. Of course, he had performed on the BBC by himself and with other musicians as early as October 1968, and had shown that he was a good live performer. His rendition of "Sails" on the *Symonds on Sunday* BBC radio show, taped in July 1969, had been fluid and allowed him to show off his flexible voice. But these broadcasts had been infrequent.

In fact Elton had tried out some of his new songs live onstage with Hookfoot,[27] but previous attempts by DJM to get him his own live gigs had been rewarded with performances by an unconfident musician. The eagerness he'd had as a boy to perform had been nearly destroyed by his experiences with Bluesology.[28] One such gig was at the Speakeasy in 1969. Dick James had asked Lionel Conway and Muff Winwood, brother of Stevie, to manage Elton. The two booked him at the Speakeasy, to which they also invited several agents. Conway remembered that Elton "did a very good show," but none of the agents were interested, believing he wouldn't be successful. One agent commented that he always tried to picture an act at Carnegie Hall and he couldn't envision Elton there. In the interest of preserving their friendship with Elton, Conway remembered, he and Winwood declined to manage him further.[29]

But it was now 1970, Elton's second album was out, and he would have to forget earlier indignities. He formed a trio with two DJM-affiliated musicians, Nigel Olsson (drums) and Dee Murray (bass). He didn't arrange for a lead guitar player because he didn't want his band to have a guitar-dominant sound. His piano playing would be at the forefront instead.

Nigel, a small young man with fine, long black hair and a beautiful face, had played with Plastic Penny, the Spencer Davis Group, and Uriah Heep. "As soon as we started to rehearse I knew it was the kind of music I wanted to do because I could play from the heart," Nigel said later.[30] Dee, born David Murray Oates, was taller, with an ordinary but affable look. He had played with Nigel in the Spencer Davis Group, as well as the Mirage. Nigel and Dee had nary an extra ounce on their bodies, in sharp contrast to their new musical leader.

The trio took its fledgling show to continental Europe. In Paris, Elton later remembered, he and his poor compatriots, who were opening for Sergio Mendes and Brasil '66, were pelted with every manner of fruit and vegetable. "We got booed before we even got on stage and people chucked things at us, but we played for forty-five minutes and played bloody well," Elton said.[31] Mendes disagreed, calling DJM's Vic Lewis, who had booked the trio, to complain: "How dare you send us a group like this!"[32] On April 21, 1970, they played a Pop Proms concert date at London's Roundhouse. Acts above Elton on the bill that day included Tyrannosaurus Rex and Heavy Jelly. In ensuing weeks, the trio played the Roundhouse again, along with Fotheringay and Argent, and the Lyceum, in support of Santana.

Elton slowly regained his self-confidence, and his performances became increasingly animated. This is evidenced by BBC radio performances in the spring and summer of 1970. A March 26 performance (with Hookfoot) for a *John Peel Concert* broadcast on April 5 of "Take Me to the Pilot" and "My Father's Gun" (from the to-be-recorded *Tumbleweed Connection* album) revealed a musician enraptured with the continued discovery of his music. The same can be said for August 13 performances with Nigel and Dee of "Border Song" and "Bad Side of the Moon," later broadcast on Bob Harris's *Sounds of the Seventies* show.

But Elton's May 1970 performance on a BBC television special, called "In Concert: the Songs of Elton John and Bernie Taupin," was different. The show's objective was to faithfully reproduce the sound of the *Elton John* album, with Paul Buckmaster conducting a small group of musicians on several numbers. Elton dutifully mimicked the keyboard performances he had set to vinyl and, in deference to the album's arrangements, did not touch the piano on songs like "Sixty Years On." During these moments he stood awkwardly, holding a microphone to his mouth to sing. Clean shaven, with shoulder-length hair and short bangs in a fringe cut, he seemed embarrassed to be there. He still hadn't begun to think of himself as a potential star. Elton humbly introduced Bernie, sitting in the studio audience, as the more important member of their songwriting team, explaining that Bernie wrote the words before he composed the music. The program closed with a severely truncated version of an as-yet unreleased song, "Burn Down the Mission," with Nigel and Dee joining in as the credits rolled.

On May 23, 1970, the *Elton John* album entered the British chart. The album was ultimately on the chart for fourteen weeks, eventually peaking at number 11.

"THE SWEETEST SOUND MY EARS HAVE EVER KNOWN"[33]

THAT SPRING OF 1970, a year that was turning out to be most productive, Elton was at Trident Studios recording his third studio album, *Tumbleweed Connection*. *Tumbleweed* was culled from the same stockpile of songs from which *Elton John* had sprung, and was named after lyrics for which Elton never got around to writing music.[34]

Tumbleweed would not be released in Great Britain until October, and in the United States until January 1971, giving some critics the mistaken impression that Elton had evolved musically or that his style had changed. In fact, *Elton John* and *Tumbleweed* were cut from the same creative cloth. Because the authors were versatile, and Elton's musical tastes and compositional predilections extraordinarily eclectic, *Tumbleweed* successfully reflects Bernie's fascination with the old American West and South, and the tragedies and social strife brought on by the Civil War. It didn't hurt that both Elton and Bernie were big fans of the Band, which married country-and-western music with rock.

The opening number, "Ballad of a Well-Known Gun," is not a ballad but a sizzling mid-tempo rocker built atop Elton's syncopated piano. The lyrics portray a fugitive whose jig is up; Elton's confident vocal radiates resentment on behalf of the apprehended fugitive. Behind his piano are members of Hookfoot. Caleb's lead guitar gives the song a razor's edge, befitting the distasteful character who, until now, had been running from the law. Backing vocals are provided by, among others, Lesley Duncan and Dusty Springfield. (Not long before, Springfield had thrilled Elton backstage at the BBC's *Top of the Pops* by complimenting him on "Border Song.")

The next song, "Come Down in Time," is a haunting number with a sparse Paul Buckmaster arrangement. It has nothing to do with the old American West or South, and may be about nothing more than the missed opportunity of potential lovers. In the end, one of the two is left "counting the stars in the night." Elton sings, accompanied only by harp and oboe. (His piano and voice demo, which may have been recorded at the same time as the demo for "Your Song," featured harplike piano that would have been just as effective on the album as Buckmaster's arrangement.)

"Country Comfort," which attracted some covers, including one by Rod Stewart, follows. Bernie's lyrics include several vignettes of sweet, imagined nineteenth-century country life that hint at impending economic strife. "Grandma" was "really going fine for eighty-four," but needed someone to "fix her barn." There was old, old-fashioned Clay who, observing the plight of the employees at a well, disapproved of the "new machine" their employers favored that would "cut manpower by fifteen."

Elton's version of the song includes every instrument that might conjure up the imagined idyllic peacefulness of rural life. The song begins with gentle piano and is soon joined by Elton's best country voice, then the swelling sounds of steel guitar, violin, and harmonica. The two new touring band members, Nigel and Dee, provide backing vocals, as they would elsewhere on the record.

In later years, Elton would express little affection for this recording of "Country Comfort," saying that it was "sugary."[35] Another reason to look askance at it is that Elton's piano work doesn't come from the live session, but was overdubbed later. Elton was away in Holland for a promotional television appearance when Gus Dudgeon scheduled the recording session. A session pianist stood in for him, Elton overdubbing the playing with his own when he returned.[36]

"Son of Your Father" is next, the tale of a mean-spirited freeloader who takes advantage of "blind" Joseph on an "East Virginia" farm. A gun battle follows, leaving both men dead. The music is as rough and dirty as the fight. Elton sings like a tough farmhand; his piano is as mean as the song's two characters. The recording is a full-blown effort by Hookfoot—with harmonica by Ian Duck—and was undoubtedly drawn from Elton's live work with the group. The same day he had taped the *Empty Sky* track "Sails" (July 11, 1969), he had taped a performance of "Son of Your Father" with Caleb, Glover, and Pope for a July 20 BBC radio broadcast on *Symonds on Sunday*.[37]

In "My Father's Gun," which follows, the setting is the Civil War and the perspective is the South's. (Bernie favored the underdog.) A young man whose father has been killed by the Yankees determines to avenge the death by joining the fighting in New Orleans. The song starts quietly, with tentatively delivered gospel-style piano chords and Caleb's muted acoustic and lead guitars. Elton's vocal begins quietly, too, but before long increases in volume, sounding convincingly angry, like the young man whose father was killed. Backing vocals by Dusty Springfield, Lesley Duncan, and others lend a spiritual righteousness befitting the Civil War setting. The song ends with an extended interplay, reminiscent of New Orleans music, between Elton's voice and those of the backing singers, laced with horns and honky-tonk piano.

Side two begins with the eerie "Where to Now, St. Peter?," a look at passing to the "other side." A soldier has been killed in action. The sensations are odd ("I floated like a leaf/dazzling, dancing,/half enchanted/in my Merlin sleep"). Then his fate sinks in ("I understand I'm on the road/where all that was is gone"). The opening piano notes invoke the soldier floating "like a leaf," a sound that runs throughout the song, even as it reaches rock tempo. Elton's melody also captures the feeling of passage between worlds and provides a challenge, in range and forcefulness, for which he was ready. Nigel and Dee contribute ghostly backup singing.

The next track, "Love Song," written by Elton's friend Lesley Duncan, is another that features him singing without piano. Duncan provides harmony and acoustic guitar accompaniment. The second number on the album alien to the overall Western and Southern feel, it constitutes a welcome interlude after all the shooting and dying in the three previous songs.

Elton had clamored to get his new band on *Tumbleweed* and succeeded with "Amoreena," the next song. This provides the only clue of what it was like to hear the group live then. (Caleb puts in an appearance on understated lead guitar.) The lyrics are a fictional remembrance of a past love affair with a young, energetic woman of the countryside called Amoreena (a "lusty flower" with a "bronze body"). Very nearly an update, with change of venue, of "First Episode at Hienton," the protagonist here is more obviously amorous. The song allows Elton another foray into funkiness, with percussive, syncopated piano pulsating about the lyrics, a trademark of his live performances. He also plays organ on the song, and sings the lyrics in a lower voice than elsewhere on the album. He would later attribute this to Van Morrison's influence.

"Talking Old Soldiers," which comes next, offers one of the most affecting vocals of Elton's career, though his voice was still developing. As the title implies, the song is a dialogue between two old soldiers. "Old Mad Joe" tells of the terrible things he has seen, hinting that these terrors took his only friends from him, though no one understands or cares ("Well do they know what it's like/to have a graveyard as a friend/'cos that's where they are boy, all of them"). Elton's voice and piano performance are heartrending, the piano providing an accompaniment that crescendos with the pain in his voice.

The last song on the album, "Burn Down the Mission," is one of the most musically inventive of Elton's career and has provided him with a hell-raising concert staple. The song includes some of Bernie's most striking imagery: The have-nots ("restless folks") are "getting desperate" and must do more than covet the "fat stock" of the wealthy, proclaiming, "It's time we put the flame torch to their keep." A mob descends on the "mission." After torching it, they hoard what they can ("Take all you need to live inside").

Elton's introductory piano brings to mind a nice, quiet day in the country that, with the chords' increasing speed, gives way to the boiling rage of the populace and a fiery riot. Paul Buckmaster's orchestral arrangement seems unnecessary for the most part, lending too much civility to the recording, but the ending, which features frantic piano chords and an undercurrent of Buckmaster's strings, successfully suggests the ongoing, frenzied efforts of the rioters.

It would be months before *Tumbleweed Connection* was released. Meanwhile, there were other completed projects, frustrations—and planning for the future.

"I'M ON THE BOTTOM LINE"[38]

WITH ALBUMS ALREADY MADE AND BEING MADE, it is surprising that none of the stellar songs rapidly making their way into the can were released as singles, other than "Border Song." Apparently, Dick James wanted a single that would please the masses; "Rock and Roll Madonna," released on June 19, 1970, was the result.[39] Recorded during the *Elton John* sessions in January 1970, the single is a tribute to Jerry Lee Lewis, featuring Elton on piano along with Hookfoot's core. Elton's uncanny understanding of Lewis's piano technique is reflected in his playing, which is the highlight of the song. The corny canned audience applause is not.

The B-side, featuring an early incarnation of "Grey Seal" and recorded contemporaneously with the A-side, is more satisfying. Bernie mused some two decades later, "I hadn't a clue what I was writing about. It was just images."[40] The lyrics recall his childhood, with a curious student asking numerous questions, reflecting on the poor education Bernie received at school ("I never learned why meteors were formed,/I only farmed in schools that were so worn and torn"). The student concludes that education may be obtained without schooling ("I read books and draw life from the eye") and regards the "grey seal," representing any animal living in the wild, as the real world expert.

Elton's music for "Grey Seal" is as odd as the lyrics. Like the questions Bernie asks, the melody seems to have a question mark at the end of each line, with quizzical piano chords following the chorus. Paul Buckmaster's orchestral arrangement lends the song a dreamy feel. But its A-side, "Rock and Roll Madonna," got nowhere.

Throughout this period, Elton also filled up whatever spare time he had by recording cover versions of the day's hits for budget record labels. Elton and the other artists who did this received no credit.

CHAPTER 3

THE
GREATEST
DISCOVERY[1]

(1970–1973)

BACK IN THE UNITED STATES, Uni Records's Russ Regan had gotten a copy of the *Elton John* album. "I played it—and I'd been in the record business twelve years at that time—and I was never more overpowered with an album. . . . The songs were unbelievable. I shut the office down, shut the phones off, called everybody in and the entire company listened to the album twice," Regan later said. At a sales meeting in July, it was decided that the album, which had just been released on July 22, could be effectively promoted by bringing Elton in for a series of performances at Doug Weston's Troubadour club in Los Angeles.[2] Since its opening in 1957, the club had boasted shows by many prominent songwriters, such as Gordon Lightfoot, Laura Nyro, Randy Newman, and Joni Mitchell.

Elton didn't want to go. He believed that his trio was establishing itself as a live act in Britain, however incrementally, and it was too early to travel to America. He also didn't see how an engagement at one venue could "break" his album. "I thought it was going to be a joke. I thought it was going to be a complete hype and I thought it was going to be a disaster," Elton later reflected.[3] But Dick James liked Regan's offer, despite the fact that the Troubadour would only be paying Elton and his band five hundred dollars, and that the group would also be obligated to play at the Troubadour's sister club in San Francisco. Acquiescing, Elton rationalized that at least he could shop in American record stores and add to his flourishing collection of vinyl. Ray Williams, who had become Elton's manager through DJM that spring at the pianist's own behest, was to accompany the band to Los Angeles.

By this point, Elton had a full beard and mustache and relatively short hair that was noticeably thinning on top. He was still keeping his weight down; he would rarely be so thin again. Still, he would have given anything to have a wiry, lithe body like Mick Jagger's. "I've never been satisfied with my body image, ever," he has said.[4] Elton's legs, while well muscled, were short, and his long, hirsute torso still retained traces of chubbiness, even at its leanest. Onstage, the requisite wiriness would have to emanate from his hands, which, though his fingers were small and stubby, were encased in tight webs of sinew. In his favor, too, were a friendly, gap-toothed smile and a bottomless enthusiasm for music.

By all accounts, Elton was a personable fellow whose sense of humor craved and emulated Monty Python-style zaniness. But he also was given to the occasional temper tantrum, a trait that had surfaced in childhood and gained momentum with the ups and downs of his career. So the trip to America was not exactly free of turmoil. Throughout the nine-hour flight to Los Angeles, he was anxiety-ridden, sweating profusely over thoughts of the unknown.[5] Perhaps it occurred to him that he would have to be a success at the Troubadour for things to improve; a rerelease of "Border Song" had finally debuted on *Billboard*'s Hot 100 on August 15 at number 93, but would get no further than number 92.

Upon arriving in Los Angeles, Elton and his entourage were met by a red double-decker bus, seemingly plucked right out of swingin' London, with an enormous banner that read "Elton John has arrived." This was the brainchild of Uni publicist Norman Winter, who explained, "We decided that we had to throw everything we had at the artist, because we believed in the artist, and we didn't realize at the time that the artist himself would . . . gain great acceptance based on his appeal as a performer. We decided to do a lot of things that were very 'hype-y' at the time, above and beyond the norm. . . . In addition to the usual billboards there were posters in all the stores, there was lots of radio time. We treated him as if an Elvis Presley was opening in Vegas, even though nobody had ever heard of Elton John."[6]

At the time, Winter thought Elton appreciated the double-decker bus gimmick. "It just blew his mind. He really dug it," Winter told *Rolling Stone*. Elton later confided to Winter that he would have preferred a low-key limousine: "I'm a great lover of things that are done with taste . . . and double-decker buses don't qualify."[7]

There were some days to kill before Elton, Nigel, and Dee opened at the Troubadour. The sister of Ray Williams's old girlfriend offered to show them around Palm Springs. Everyone was eager to go, except Elton. The thought of leaving his charge alone on the eve of an important engagement did not trouble Williams. He figured they were all just a "group of mates" on a trip. He did not think of Elton as a "star," a strange blind spot for a potential star's manager. So the "group of mates," minus Elton, went on their merry way, leaving Elton to stew in his room and, in the middle of the night, call Dick James long-distance in a state of distress. James had to talk Elton out of abandoning the Troubadour gig entirely.

When Williams and the others returned from their Palm Springs sojourn, it seemed that everything was all right with Elton. Bernie, who had pined over many young women during his short life, had returned madly in love with a Californian, Maxine Feibelman.

Other anxieties were in store. When Elton arrived at the Troubadour, he noticed that, on the marquee, he was the headliner, and cult folk musician David Ackles, whom Elton and Bernie both greatly admired, was second on the bill. In a bizarre case of inverted ego, Elton screamed that Ackles, a "living legend," should have his name first, since he, Elton, was a "nobody."[8] But the billing remained unchanged. Norman Winter's publicity machine chugged onward, distributing press kits that trumpeted Elton's arrival: "ELTON JOHN . . . is making an auspicious debut in the United States on Uni Records via a superb album which simply bears the artist's name and likeness. . . ." The press release quoted enthusiastic reviews by U.S. music trade papers, including the observation by *Cash Box* that *Elton John* was "one of the two or three most beautiful albums released this year."

"REJOICE"[9]

ELTON'S FIRST PERFORMANCE at the Troubadour, on Tuesday, August 25, 1970, attracted all sorts of luminaries, thanks to Norman Winter's endless efforts to alert the music industry to his bearded wunderkind. Neil Diamond introduced him onstage, and the audience included Quincy Jones, Henry Mancini, Gordon Lightfoot, Mike Love of the Beach Boys, Danny Hutton, and one of Elton's old boosters, Roger Greenaway. And Elton did what he had to do. He rose to the occasion.

Paul Buckmaster's arrangements were so prominent on *Elton John,* and the album cover so stark, it would have made sense for the pianist to appear, staid and conservative, for a series of dark, brooding introspective numbers. But it soon became clear that a subdued performance was not to be. Elton wore an outfit designed by London's Mr. Freedom: light-colored bell-bottoms with a huge belt that sported stars and half-moons, and a long-sleeved shirt that proclaimed "Rock'n'Roll." Film footage of Elton's Troubadour debut shows him at his piano, rocking to a flurry of flying chords during "Sixty Years On," a vigorous contrast to the album's cello-dominated orchestral version. But it was the as-yet-unreleased "Burn Down the Mission" that gave many a jaded music industry representative the biggest jolt of all. Elton grabbed a tambourine and urged his audience to sing along as he slammed the instrument against his left hand, finally getting on his knees to play a stirring piano finale.

After the show, Norman Winter introduced Elton to every bigwig he could find, describing him as a "genius." In an August 27, 1970 review in the *Los Angeles Times,* critic Robert Hilburn raved: "Rejoice. Rock music, which has been going through a rather uneventful period lately, has a new star." Hilburn called Elton a "multidirectional talent of the highest order" whose music was so "staggeringly original" that, though it borrowed from a variety of genres, it established a new musical field. "He's going to be one of rock's biggest and most important stars," Hilburn exulted.[10]

Promoter Bill Graham offered Elton five thousand dollars to play New York's Fillmore East the following November, the largest amount ever to have been offered a new act.

On the second night, more stars turned out to see Elton, including piano player Leon Russell. "I nearly died! My knees went to jelly!" Elton mused a few months later. "He was sitting there, with his beautiful silver hair, looking like Rasputin." Russell invited Elton to his home afterwards, and though the Londoner feared Russell would tear his piano playing down a peg or two, they got along well, and even jammed.[11]

Later that week, Danny Hutton, who had met Elton about a year earlier when Three Dog Night was touring England, took Elton to meet Brian Wilson, another source of inspiration. Though at first reluctant to meet, Wilson relented, and even invited Elton to play some of his own songs on the piano. A nervous Elton treated Wilson to what the Beach Boy called the "most impressive string of new material" he'd ever heard. Wilson concluded that Elton was "tapped into the great source" to which he himself had once had access.[12]

"THEY ALL THINK THEY KNOW BUT THEY ALL GOT IT WRONG"[13]

THE NEXT STOP WAS SAN FRANCISCO. Doug Weston had granted the trio a bigger sum of money for this engagement, $750.[14] Robert Hilburn of the *Los Angeles Times*, still excited about his recent discovery, conducted the first in-depth American interview with Elton and Bernie, taken during a sound check before their first show in the Bay Area. Hilburn watched Elton play an hour of old rock'n'roll—including numbers by Little Richard, Wilson Pickett, and Danny and the Juniors—and learned that he was a "human computer of rock and roll," with diverse tastes that ranged from Motown to Frank Zappa. Elton told Hilburn that it only took him about twenty minutes to compose a song. That night, Hilburn wrote, the musician got the San Francisco Troubadour's patrons out of their seats by the third number, and daringly included the Rolling Stones' "Honky Tonk Women."[15] It would become a concert staple.

Someone in the audience that week would soon become central to not only Elton's career, but his personal life, too. A native of Paisley, Scotland, the diminutive, ambitious, twenty-one-year-old John Reid ran the Tamla-Motown label in England, a job he had gotten partly by lying about his age. Elton, the soul enthusiast, sometimes went into his office looking for unreleased singles. Reid later recalled that Elton "wore what I thought then were pretty outrageous clothes: jumpsuits with the zips up in back, bib overalls, and star-spangled t-shirts, and I thought, 'What is this guy?'"[16] Now in San Francisco for a Motown tenth-anniversary celebration, Reid went to see his acquaintance perform. This led to one of the crucial milestones in

Elton's life: He had his first homosexual experience, with Reid, two years after Long John Baldry had implored him to accept being gay.

Elton had at times nursed thoughts of his true sexuality, even confessing to Bernie a crush he had on the lyricist. "He made his affections known," Bernie recalled decades later. "When I started laughing, it sort of broke the ice. . . . He got over it very quickly."[17] But where Bernie had gently rebuffed, Reid reciprocated. Elton later said that their first sexual encounter was "wonderful,"[18] and that it helped him come out of his shell and learn more about himself. Elton's encounter with Reid would lead to an intimate, loving relationship that would last more than five years, during which time Reid would take up the reins of manager and work monetary wonders for his client and lover (though Elton would not disclose the personal side of the relationship for nearly two decades). After the love, a singularly close friendship and productive business arrangement would continue for years to come.

The next stops on the tour were the Playboy Club in New York and the Electric Factory in Philadelphia. By Philadelphia, some Uni executives were beginning to criticize Russ Regan for spending too much money promoting Elton, as *Elton John* still had not made a commercial impact. Elton was being called "Regan's Folly." But the infuriated Regan showed skeptical promoters that his boy was the real thing during the Electric Factory performance in Philadelphia.[19] Elton was thrilled with the Philadelphia audience. They clapped for him as he mounted his grand piano and, in response to a mere wave of his arm, stood for him.[20] By October 3, 1970, *Elton John* finally entered *Billboard*'s Top LPs chart at number 156. On October 31, it moved into the Top 40.

Elton returned to England that fall. After a well-received live performance at the Royal Albert Hall (and praise from London *Times* critic Karl Dallas, who called him a "welcome, fresh, individual voice"[21]), he hunkered down to record the soundtrack to the upcoming film *Friends*.

"I HOPE THE DAY WILL BE A LIGHTER HIGHWAY"[22]

ELTON AND BERNIE had committed to doing the *Friends* project well before their American success. After hearing the *Elton John* album earlier in 1970, John Gilbert had approached the songwriting duo about scoring the film, to be produced and directed by his father, Lewis Gilbert. Bernie and Elton wrote three songs specifically for the film.[23] As Elton recalled later, working on the film score with Paul Buckmaster in between U.S. tours was a high-pressure enterprise. "It was such a panic session," he said. "I would never score a film again, too mathematical."[24]

Elton also had to record the soundtrack album for the movie. "I didn't want them to release a soundtrack album with three songs on it and fill it out with garbage, motorists peeing by lakes, and things like that," Elton later said, so he and Bernie agreed to include two other songs initially intended for a new album, *Madman*

Across the Water, which would not be released until the end of 1971. Recording the soundtrack was problematic. An aborted attempt at Olympic Studios in London was ruined by "film people," as Bernie put it, who kept telling the musicians what to do. A second try at Trident Studios yielded the finished product.[25]

Friends, produced by Gus Dudgeon with executive production by John Gilbert, turned out to be a mixed bag. The soundtrack begins with the title song, which follows the two main characters, teenagers Paul and Michelle, as they experience their first pangs of love. It is sweet, but atypical of the direction in which Elton and Bernie were going by this time. Gentle piano chords give way to a full orchestra; a vocal filled with naive inflections suggests the characters' unsullied spirits. In "Michelle's Song," the best of those written specially for the movie, Bernie's words are filled with images of the Camargue in the south of France, where Paul and Michelle flee by train from their uncaring elders. Wild horses and herons in the region assume supernatural qualities as the youngsters find they were meant for each other. Elton's melody and vocal, backed by Buckmaster's arrangement, take on the bright optimism shared by the teenagers. "Seasons," a merely charming ballad written for the film, is similar in mood to "Friends," celebrating the transformation of Paul and Michelle from friends into lovers.

The other original songs on the album are the interlopers from *Madman*. "Honey Roll" is a joyful up-tempo number, a showcase for the bubbly, inviting, piano bass line that was an integral part of Elton's live performances at the time. Elton said the song was his tribute to Fats Domino, apparent in the Briton's affected drawl of the word "honey" ("HAW-neh"). "Can I Put You On?," primarily a vehicle for Elton, Nigel, and Dee to show how well they interacted, steals the album's spotlight, with generous chunks of Elton's hair-raising rock piano. The album also contains an orchestral revisiting of "Seasons," "Friends," and "Michelle's Song," and eleven minutes of somnolent music composed by Buckmaster.

The *Friends* album would not be out for six months, but in the meantime, on October 30, 1970, another completed album was finally released in Britain: *Tumbleweed Connection*. At the launch party at London's Revolution Club, Elton told the crowd that the album had been a team effort: "It's Steve Brown as much as me, Gus Dudgeon as much as me, Paul Buckmaster as much as me."[26] *Tumbleweed* would not enter the British album chart until January 16, 1971.

"MORE! MORE!"[27]

THE *ELTON JOHN* ALBUM, now climbing the *Billboard* chart, would be pushed higher thanks to Elton's next batch of live American shows in fall 1970, and to the release on October 26, 1970 of the second single from the album, "Take Me to the Pilot/Your Song." Though "Take Me to the Pilot" was Uni's official choice for the follow-up A-side to "Border Song," disc jockeys preferred the reflective "Your Song," which thus became the single by accident.[28]

As "Your Song" was garnering interest from a growing number of platter spin-ners across the country, Elton began the tour that would continue to enhance his reputation as a live performer. It started in late October at the Boston Tea Party. The irony of this gig to the English invaders must have been obvious.

The trio was often second on the bill to established acts, but still managed to attract the attention of the Band and Bob Dylan, who made a point of meeting Elton and Bernie backstage at New York's Fillmore East. In New York and Anaheim, Elton shared the bill with his piano mentor, Leon Russell. But on November 15, Elton headlined at the Santa Monica Civic Center, the result of a buy-out of his contract for a remaining Troubadour commitment. Elton credited his agent, Howard Rose, with the idea. The pianist recalled Rose telling him, "You are going to be big and you ought to invest in yourself." Elton added, "We felt the momentum would justify the move."[29]

The Santa Monica show also heralded Elton's deepening affinity for garish apparel and striking physicality. Wearing a top hat, cape, overalls, and a purple jumpsuit, Elton thrashed the keys with a starry silver boot. He played with one hand while balancing himself on the floor with the other, defied gravity with handstands on the piano keys, and executed giant bunny kicks in the purple tights to which he eventually stripped down, all to the delight of the audience. He maniacally shook his head, and was in constant motion—moving his legs on an imaginary conveyor belt, leaping in the air—as he hit the piano keys with astonishing accuracy.

Elton's performance drew mixed reviews. The clothing and antics did not amuse Eliot Tiegel, a *Billboard* reviewer, who asked, "Does he abandon his valid musical skills in favor of being a 'stage freak' using unnecessary physical tricks?"[30] But Fred Kirby, another *Billboard* writer, didn't let the pianist's unusual clothes bother him. "John, gaudi-ly attired, is a magnetic performer in blues, boogie and rock," he wrote, adding, "only a performer as brilliant as [Leon] Russell could have followed."[31] Writing for the *New York Times*, Mike Jahn observed that Elton's melodies were complemented by his "rich" pianism, "laced with strains of Beethoven and Gershwin."[32]

Bootleg albums of Elton's performances would soon surface, but no piece of recorded live music from the waning days of 1970 could match the sheer excitement of the trio's performance on November 17 at Phil Ramone's A&R Recording studio in New York, played before an audience of about a hundred and an unknown number listening at home to the live WABC-FM broadcast. Elton, Nigel, and Dee played their usual numbers, alongside the new "Indian Sunset," a song about the fate of Native Americans that Bernie had written after visiting a reservation while in the United States the first time. During his studio patter, Elton noted that Rod Stewart had already recorded "Country Comfort" for his *Gasoline Alley* album, and that Aretha Franklin, whom he called the "Lady Soul," had just recorded "Border Song," which he jokingly redubbed "Boredom Song" because he and his band had played it so often.

Showstoppers abounded during the radio performance, not the least of which were the ferocious up-tempo numbers. "Burn Down the Mission" drove the studio audience into a lather, with bloodcurdling screams heard as Elton pounded out furious chords. He teased his audience by descending into abstract jazz improvisation, subtly supported by bass and drums, and then picked up the pace again with surprise renditions of a lesser-known Presley hit from 1956, "My Baby Left Me," and the Beatles's "Get Back." (Songs making cameos during other performances that autumn included Junior Walker and the All Stars's "Shotgun" and Sly and the Family Stone's "I Want to Take You Higher.") As "Get Back" ended, Elton returned to the barn-burning chords of "Mission" and proclaimed that he would "burn it right on down" to the hoots and cries of his studio audience. The concert proved an important exhibition of Elton's developing vocal skills. His voice was thickening, gaining a robustness that approached the tireless joie de vivre he brought to his shows. Though his band mates' backing vocals usually blended well, particularly on "Honky Tonk Women," they were sometimes off-key, and were perhaps more effective just playing their instruments.

In the months following the broadcast, a tidal wave of bootleg records flooded the United States. Some included the entire show, others only portions. All capitalized on the pianist's expanding reputation as a performer. Among others, there were *Knockin' Em Dead Alive* and *Live E Jay*; several incarnations of something called *Radiocord*; *Very Alive* on lustrous gold vinyl; and *Superstar: Live*. Unbeknownst to Elton, there was also a legitimate taping of the concert, arranged for by Steve Brown. No immediate plans were made for its release. That would change.

"BURN IT DOWN TO STAY ALIVE"[33]

ELTON HAD BARELY FINISHED his first full-fledged U.S. tour when *Time* magazine speculated that he might be the musical "superman" the younger generation needed to succeed the supergroups of 1969. *Time* lauded his songwriting, calling him a "one-man music factory," and found that he displayed both a "natural stage presence and timing worthy of a veteran stand-up comic." The article recognized that Elton played the piano "in a field where once no composer worth his suede jacket would be caught dead without a guitar," attributing the acceptance of his guitar-less persona to the encroachment of jazz and blues on rock and to Elton's search for compositional versatility.[34] Elton himself was a bit more skeptical about being the new musical messiah: "Something new's gonna come along soon," he said a few months later. "I hope there is, anyway, because I think everybody needs a shot in the arm. . . . I'm looking forward to seeing who it is."[35]

British music magazine *Disc and Music Echo* reported in its January 2, 1971 issue that Elton had been voted by BBC Radio One disc jockeys as the act making the "most impact in pop during 1970."[36] The question, though, was whether the promise of 1970 would be fulfilled in 1971.

Tumbleweed Connection was finally released in the United States on January 4, 1971; within a month, it had reached number 5 on *Billboard*'s Top LPs chart. Meanwhile, the *Elton John* album had just peaked at number 4 on the strength of "Your Song," a number 8 hit by January 23rd. A similar story was playing out in Britain, where *Tumbleweed* peaked at number 6. "Your Song," released in that country on January 7, 1971, reached number 7.

Tumbleweed became one of the fastest selling albums in America early in 1971 and was well received by the critics. Calling the album "exciting," *Rolling Stone* magazine critic Jon Landau welcomed its stripped-down sound, after the string-laden *Elton John*, and hoped the next studio album would be even more musically naked.[37] Robert Hilburn exuberantly labeled *Tumbleweed* "that near-perfect album that artists often spend a whole career trying to produce."[38] There was some grousing from critics like *Life*'s Albert Goldman, who preferred to ignore the album in favor of simply characterizing Elton's music as "meretricious copycatting."[39] Though concerned about critics' views, Elton was more interested in just doing what he enjoyed. "I don't want to be what people want me to be; I want to be a complete opposite of what people want me to be," he said.[40]

The British leg of the tour commenced at the start of 1971 and continued through March, although Elton did cancel some dates on medical advice. In between gigs, he managed to get in some recording for his fourth studio album and a coproduction with Rod Stewart of *It Ain't Easy*, an album by John Baldry (who had recently dropped the "Long" from his name).

Elton must have rued that last year in Bluesology when he was so ungenerously kept out of the limelight, but over the years has expressed nothing but warm feelings for Baldry who, Elton said, treated all his band members kindly and had been there for Elton during the break-up of his marriage engagement. "John is one of those people I'd swim a lake full of piranha fish for because he was great to me," Elton said.[41]

Meanwhile, elsewhere in the music world, a young folk guitarist named Davey Johnstone had just left Noel Murphy's Draught Porridge to join medieval music aspirants Magna Carta. Davey had already played on one of Magna Carta's albums, *Seasons,* but fellow Magna Cartan Glen Stuart knew their group wasn't necessarily the end of the line for Davey. "The thing is that Davey might go on from us later on," said Stuart. "In fact, he probably will."[42] Stuart's words were prescient. Within a year, Davey would be a full-fledged member of Elton's band.

"SLOW DOWN, JOE, I'M A ROCK'N'ROLL MAN"[43]

IN FEBRUARY, Elton received his first American gold record for *Elton John*, signifying more than one million dollars in shipments. In March, the feat was repeated with *Tumbleweed Connection*. It was also in March that Elton made his first live appearance with an orchestra (a session orchestra) at London's Royal Festival Hall.

"I've always said that I'd like to get an orchestra together on stage just for one gig," he said later.[44]

The *Friends* soundtrack was released on the Paramount label on March 5 in the United States, in anticipation of the film's opening March 25 in New York, and in April in Britain. The album's minimal commercial impact was a shock. In future years, *Friends*, which only made it to number 36 on *Billboard*'s Top LPs chart, would be on prominent display in the cut-out bins. The U.S. single, which included the title track backed by "Honey Roll" and was released simultaneously with the album, fared little better. The story was worse in Britain, where neither soundtrack nor single, released on April 23, 1971, charted at all.

Elton's next album did not even go gold, though it should have. Released in Britain as *17-11-70* (in April 1971) and in the United States as *11-17-70* (in May), the album was done for a number of reasons, but mainly to acquaint music listeners with the live Elton John. "I'm very anti-live album," Elton said in 1973, but remarked that the spring of 1971 "was a time when people were coming to see me and people were buying my records and the two of them weren't getting together." He also wanted Nigel and Dee to get some exposure, as well as to receive money for a complete album's worth of work. He was proud of *11-17-70*, too, as it was taken from one live performance rather than the usual handful from which most acts create live albums.[45] But record buyers, particularly in the United States, may have been reaching their saturation point with Elton John. *11-17-70* was the fourth Elton album in American record stores in ten months, and the third in four months!

To be fair, the album, produced by Gus Dudgeon, may have lost a marked number of sales to the bootlegs that had deluged thirsty record buyers months earlier. Also, it included only half the songs performed live on the radio, and in shuffled order. This may have been done to avoid harming sales of the albums from which the songs were derived. More important was the goal of showing all the world the spine-tingling freneticism of Elton's live work, since all but one of the album's songs were fast-paced. Regardless, the point Elton was trying to make—that he was a live performer of note—never reached most people, as few bought the album. The British version charted on May 1, 1971 and stayed for only two weeks, stopping at number 20. The U.S. version charted on May 29, 1971 and eventually reached number 11; it stayed on *Billboard*'s Top LPs for several months, mostly on the chart's lower end.

Elton soon realized that his saturation of the marketplace made a poor commercial strategy. "We had only just happened, and six months later we were blowing it," he said in 1976. "I became extremely unhappy with the whole situation."[46] He needed a manager to, among other things, control the stream of product. Ray Williams was long gone. Dick James had ripped up his contract after the previous summer's Palm Springs debacle. Elton had asked John Reid, with whom he was now living, to be his manager, but Reid needed several months to wrap up his obligations at Tamla-Motown. In the meantime, Dick James was "managing" Elton. This precarious situation would change by August 1971, when Reid finally came on board at DJM as Elton's in-house manager.[47] It was a professional union that mirrored their personal bond; Elton trusted Reid implicitly.

"YOU AIN'T SEEN NOTHIN' TILL YOU BEEN IN A MOTEL, BABY, LIKE THE HOLIDAY INN"[48]

ELTON RETURNED TO THE UNITED STATES IN APRIL 1971 for a tour that would crisscross the continent and take him through June. Here was the first real opportunity for a good cross section of the country to sample Elton's stage show.

On tour that spring, Elton exhibited both a flair for fashion and an assortment of facial expressions, which he explained to *Rolling Stone* writer David Felton by saying, "I bang the piano a lot. It's hard work." His hands had bled every night at the start of the spring tour, but now they were hardening up. He showed Felton some of his nails, which were splitting. "My hands, by the time I go home, will be ruined," he worried. But Elton continued to play the piano as loudly as he could—he had to, as, unlike electric guitars, the piano hadn't been lavished with attention to amplification technology. But Elton's hands were not the only parts of his body to take a beating during performances. He even bruised and soiled his knees.[49]

As for fashion, the pianist's hair was now short. His stage attire included small white boots sprouting wings—fitting props for his piano handstands, in which he appeared to be in flight over the piano keys. He was also known to wear shirts with cartoon characters and striped shorts out of which his strapping legs bulged, as if he were some innocent schoolboy on half-effective steroids.

After completing the U.S. tour in June, Elton's schedule took him to Scandinavia, then to headline the "Garden Party" at London's Crystal Palace. Several acts were slated for the "party," including blues guitarist Rory Gallagher. Elton fretted, "How can I follow the blues? Look, they're leaving—they only came to see him [Gallagher]."[50] All of the success he had had during the first half of the year could not eradicate his feelings of insecurity. According to Michael Wale of the London *Times,* Elton need not have worried. Performing in a red tracksuit with cohorts Nigel and Dee, he ran through a substantial amount of the new material that would comprise his upcoming album, *Madman Across the Water.* Elton would later describe this performance of unfamiliar songs as "dying a death,"[51] but Wale reported that the musician brought the crowd to its feet by the blazing grand finale, Jerry Lee Lewis's hit "Whole Lot of Shakin' Going On," which Elton had begun playing in the spring. Actress Barbara Windsor attended the show and would later fondly reminisce, "[The group] Yes were on the bill, but nothing could compete with Elton. I sat on the grass and got totally lost in the music."[52]

Elton returned to the United States again in August for a week each on the east and west coasts and a short stay in Las Vegas.[53] His sold-out week at the Greek Theater was his fourth Los Angeles–area appearance in one year.

The pianist had now taken to wearing denims held up by suspenders. On the denims he wore a large white button that read, "Bitch Bitch Bitch"—perhaps a response to critics who were still carping about the number of albums he had come out with that year. Some suggested that Elton's career was already waning.[54] That summer he told Nik Cohn of the *New York Times*, "Now that I've made it, it's become very hip to put me down. When I was nowhere it was hip to call me a genius, but now the same critics sneer at me. They won't share me with a mass public—the snobbery in rock is amazing."[55]

In fact, one of the perennial problems for Elton's image, from the perspective of many critics, has been that he does not personify a movement or an idea. Stories about the fat, myopic Reggie who dutifully practiced classical piano for hours and toiled during his pubescence to make something out of his musical talent—rather than get into fights or plot how to bed girls—do not make good proletarian fodder. "A solid pro, thrifty, industrious, he seems to know where his head is at, but he isn't telling us," wrote the astute Margaret English for *Look* magazine.[56] Over the years, Elton has occasionally dropped clues about his personal political views. A fan of Tony Blair and Al Gore, he has numerous times expressed affinity for Britain's Labour Party, although he grew up in a Conservative household. One of his earliest pro-Labour expressions occurred in the spring of 1979 when he endorsed the Labour Party in upcoming elections.[57] But ultimately, for Elton, music was music and politics was politics, and never the twain shall meet. "It's power that runs and changes any country and you can't change things overnight with a hit song," he once observed.[58] He sang Bernie's lyrics, of course. Both songwriters took great enjoyment in using snippets of life and emotions in their songs. In recent years, Elton has finally been able to explain that his emotions have always formed the basis of his melodies.

"FROM A TERMINAL GATE TO A BLACK LIMOUSINE"[59]

BY THE FALL OF 1971, Elton still had not made much of a commercial impact outside the United States and Britain. Though he was the biggest DJM recording artist in Finland, his albums sold steadily in Scandinavia, and he was also rating some attention in France,[60] he was not yet the superstar he would be in Europe by the late 1970s. He plodded on, embarking on a six-date tour of Japan and then toured Australia from October 16 through 31, where his venues were primarily tennis courts and racetracks.

The Australian tour garnered some press attention. Elton created a small fuss upon flying into Sydney when Australian authorities took umbrage at certain four-letter words and a sexually suggestive symbol that decorated a few of the 150 badges on his denim outfit. Oz officials warned that some of these could be "damaging" to Australian society. "I told them I certainly couldn't help their society," Elton later boasted to an Australian journalist, coming as close as he ever would to being an authority-tweaking rock'n'roll rebel. "To save a stupid, needless hassle I stuck a few Band-Aids over them [the offending badges]." The authorities, still not convinced that the musician was not a troublemaker, asked him if he smoked marijuana (he answered "no") and searched the luggage of those in his party.[61]

Otherwise, the Australian stay was mostly smooth sailing. Ian "Molly" Meldrum, a prominent Australian music journalist who, over time, would become one of Elton's good friends Down Under, had the privilege of accompanying the entourage for the whole tour and chronicling this first visit by the Britons.

Elton impressed his audiences with his humorous taste in clothing. He would emerge from backstage wearing a cowboy hat with stars beneath the brim, a black or blue velvet cape, and those winged boots. Later, he would expose the strangely coordinated garb underneath: shorts, striped knee-highs, and a long-sleeved shirt with a large image of lips.

Much more thrilling was the music. In Perth, the crowd "forced" the band to return from their cars after the show had ended to do an encore. At the last Australian concert, in Sydney, Elton displayed a knack for overcoming adverse conditions when, during a terrible storm, the canvas tent under which he and the band had been performing came crashing down, forcing the show to be temporarily stopped. Before the stage could be set aright, Elton comforted the crowd with an instrumental version of an Australian standard, "Waltzing Matilda," to which everyone happily sang along.[62]

Before leaving Australia, Elton made sure to acquaint himself with that country's own pop music. He raved about a group called Daddy Cool and bought extra copies of their current album to distribute to friends and acquaintances.

"THEIR TINY MINDS AND SACRED COWS JUST FAKE IT"[63]

THOUGH DUE FOR A VACATION, Elton had British tour dates in November and December 1971, scheduled to coincide with the release of his next studio album, *Madman Across the Water*, which was to become available in Britain on November 5 and in the United States on November 15. His new manager, John Reid, could not immediately halt the cramped concert scheduling or flow of new product. For one thing, he was just learning the ropes. For another, Elton was bound to complete two albums per year under his DJM recording contract. Since he had released only one album for James in 1971, *11-17-70* (*Friends* was a separate arrangement), another album was expected. Workaholic Elton was only too happy to oblige.

To an extent, *Tumbleweed Connection* had been recorded in between concert dates, but the songs had been written months earlier, away from the pressures of live performing. By contrast, *Madman* was written and recorded in snatches, mainly from February to August 1971. The time constraints under which Elton recorded are exemplified by the fact that he performed at the International Song Festival of Vilar de Mouros in Portugal on August 8[64]—one day before three songs were placed on tape.

By now, Nigel and Dee should have had a prominent role in Elton's studio recordings. Instead, the album would mark Hookfoot's last Elton John hurrah. Paul Buckmaster returned for the orchestral arrangements which, though brilliant, weighed more heavily on several of the songs than his arrangements had on *Elton John*. Gus Dudgeon would recall that he had wanted to do another well-planned album, unlike *11-17-70* and *Friends*, and had thus returned to his old recording approach.[65]

With the brief periods of time available for recording, Elton and the others felt a pressure that had been absent from the other non-soundtrack studio albums. In particular, Paul Buckmaster did not take well to the stress. "Buckmaster, at that point in time, was spilling ink spots over the score with eighty string musicians sitting in the studio and it was nail-biting time," Elton remembered.[66] Despite these problems, the end product would be a compelling work, if not the musically bare approach that does Elton's songs the most justice.

Madman opens with a song that would become an Elton John standard: "Tiny Dancer." Bernie wrote the lyrics for wife Maxine, for whom his passion had not dulled, and dedicated the song to her. The lyrics contain some of his most famous lines: "Blue jean baby,/L.A. lady, seamstress for the band./Pretty eyed, pirate smile, you'll marry a music man./Ballerina. You must have seen her, dancing in the sand." They tell not only of his love for Maxine, but also of her work with the band. She *was* a seamstress for the band, did accompany Bernie to Elton's shows ("Piano man/he makes his stand/in the auditorium"), and enjoyed them like any other audience member ("Looking on/she sings the songs/the words she knows/the tune she hums"). After a show, they might leave in a limousine, exhausted and cuddling ("Hold me closer tiny dancer,/count the headlights on the highway./Lay me down in sheets of linen,/you had a busy day today.").

Recorded on August 9, 1971, the music to "Tiny Dancer" is as beautiful as the lyrics. Elton took inspiration from Bernie's "dancer" theme and his description of Maxine as a "ballerina." The music begins quietly and simply, with just piano accompaniment recalling the sound of a music box. By the second verse, a supporting cast of musicians helps to give the song an ambience of epochal proportions, with pedal steel guitar by B. J. Cole, tasteful electric guitar by Caleb Quaye, and unobtrusive acoustic guitar by a new name, Davey Johnstone. Heavenly backing vocals by familiar voices, including Lesley Duncan, Roger Cook, and even Nigel and Dee, add to the recording's otherworldly quality. Buckmaster's arrangement on this song, unlike some others on the album, tenderly uplifts without overwhelming Elton's composition.

"Tiny Dancer" is the first of several songs on *Madman* that feature multiple musical sections. The music-box approach gives way to measured, staccato piano chords by the fourth verse (a demo of the song has Elton excitedly explaining that this is where the song "builds"), paving a path toward a climax ("Hold me closer Tiny Dancer") that includes flashy, concerto-style piano chords.

Elton has said many times over the years that he dislikes his *Madman* vocals, but the album presents a milestone in his development. "Tiny Dancer" marks his first significant use of falsetto (the high use of the voice outside the normal range). Elton had experimented with this technique on *Tumbleweed Connection* in "Where to Now, St. Peter?" and even on *Empty Sky* in the title track and "Sails," but here he relies on it to help shape the melody. He would do so again many times in the coming years, establishing a subset of the Elton John "sound."

The album's next track, "Levon," would become another signature Elton John song. Bernie's sad story about the son of "Alvin Tostig" has been the subject of much speculation among fans. Some have seen religious overtones in the song, and indeed the lyrics do contain some biblical phrasings. Levon is born on Christmas Day as the *New York Times* declares, "God is dead and war's begun." As an adult, he carries his war wound proudly and tries to fulfill his father's wishes to be a "good man . . . in tradition with the family plan." But although Levon becomes a successful businessman, who sells "cartoon balloons in town" and provides well for his family, he ails, and his son, Jesus, just wants to get away from him.

Music reviewer Thomas Ryan characterized the piano introduction to "Levon," recorded on February 27, 1971, as "enough all by itself to guarantee immortality for the song," proclaiming that it "contains some of the most hauntingly beautiful and evocative piano chords ever recorded."[67] Like "Tiny Dancer," the music boasts multiple sections, but instead of representing distinct parts, they evolve in accordance with the song's lyrical pattern. Buckmaster's arrangement would become an integral part of "Levon" in live performances with the full band, although the orchestra sound comes close to jeopardizing the simple grandeur of the melody and Elton's chord progressions. One must peel away many layers of orchestration before appreciating the countermelody Elton plays on piano during the song's lengthy coda.

The next track, "Razor Face," reverts to a band-oriented sound. This is another of Bernie's strange stories, set in an America that he now knew from personal experience. The tale is about a homeless old man whose tough life and heavy drinking have excessively weathered his countenance (hence the name "Razor Face"). Recorded the same day as "Tiny Dancer," "Razor Face" exudes the energy of a live performance. Elton's vibrant vocal sports numerous slips into falsetto. Infectious piano chord progressions are punctuated by Elton's powerful bass notes, so generously featured in his live work. Guest star Rick Wakeman, playing the organ, contributes a "country-ish" atmosphere. (Despite successfully tackling the instrument on *Empty Sky* and

Tumbleweed Connection, Elton believed he wasn't much of an organ player,[68] preferring that Wakeman fill that bill on this album.)

The title track, actually written in 1970, follows. The lyrics are again set against multiple musical sections, and paint a surrealistic portrait of mental disturbance. The "madman across the water" is a psychotic individual who utters fascinating non sequiturs: "I can see very well./There's a boat on the reef with a broken back/and I can see it very well./There's a joke and I know it very well,/it's one of those that I told you long ago."

The recording highlights a spooky Buckmaster arrangement that tends to overwhelm the song, but makes for intriguing listening. Recorded on August 14, 1971, "Madman" begins with Davey Johnstone playing concise acoustic guitar licks. Elton's tentative syncopated phrases follow; then he begins to sing. His piano, which indulges in a considerable amount of tremolo, is accented by Arp synthesizer, giving the song a little jolt before the strings become evident. Buckmaster's orchestra enters via sweeping interludes, offering a view of the dark maelstrom in the mind of the "madman." Besides Davey Johnstone, one other new musician plays on this song who would figure prominently in Elton's career before long: percussionist Ray Cooper.

The song that begins side two, "Indian Sunset," is the most perfectly recorded song on the album, completely faithful to Elton's live treatments since its October 1970 writing. Like so many other tracks on the album, it contains several distinct musical sections. Recorded on the same day as the title track, "Indian Sunset" tells of a warrior who is ordered by his chief to lay down his weapons. It begins with Elton singing a capella; his piano then enters, faintly audible, until the conclusion of this first musical section, which ends with heightening fury in Elton's voice ("And now you ask that I should watch the red man's race be slowly crushed!"). This verse leads to a musical interlude in which Elton pounds out piano chords resembling the sound of Native American drums, with Buckmaster's strings emphasizing the more dramatic portions of Elton's solo. The pianistic wrath recedes to reveal lyrical piano playing to introduce the next musical section, in which the young Iroquois flees, his will fading as he learns of a hero's death. The final section, heralded by premonitory piano and strings, sees the warrior, faced with either disobeying his chief or facing the eventual death of his people, commit suicide. Bernie was influenced in this instance by the spaghetti westerns of his youth.[69]

Next is the lighthearted "Holiday Inn," a reflection on touring the United States that focuses on a motel chain that Elton and his entourage must have availed themselves of quite a bit. "Holiday Inn" is told more from Bernie's perspective, suggesting that the lyricist had little to do with the successful staging of any of Elton's shows, save the occasional cameo onstage in which he shook a tambourine.

Recorded on August 9, 1971, the song doesn't boast one of Elton's better melodies. While the music is spirited and his vocal gripping, the song's importance lies primarily in Davey Johnstone's performance, which eventually convinced Elton to make the first major change in his band since he started touring in the spring of 1970. Davey's mandolin and sitar lend the song a folk sound not otherwise present in Elton's symphonic piano chords or Buckmaster's rather understated orchestral arrangement.

The next track, "Rotten Peaches," is a more interesting song. Another slice of Americana, it looks at the sorry life of an ex-drug addict who has found religion while fleeing from the law. In prison, he had picked "rotten peaches," symbolic of his life's dreary quality. Recorded on August 14, 1971, "Rotten Peaches" is a marvelous sing-along song. Elton's lively, tireless, honky-tonk chords fuel the seamless folk melody, and the lyrics themselves are also rhythmic, containing an irresistible chorus that begins with "rotten peaches, rotting in the sun."

The next-to-last song, "All the Nasties," has the feel of nineteenth-century Americana about it, but the subject matter could not be more modern. Officially, the song strikes back at rock critics who had been taking potshots at Elton since it became apparent that, with a sense of humor and corresponding sense of outrageousness that was only starting to blossom in 1971, he did not embody the serious side of popular music that those critics preferred. It is said that Elton asked Bernie to write a response to them, and he obliged: "But I know the way/they want me,/in the way they publicize./If they could turn/their focus off,/to the image in their eyes."

These and other lyrical segments work better with another interpretation that, five years later, Bernie would offer as the song's true meaning. *Rolling Stone* writer Patrick Snyder asked Bernie in 1977 whether he and Elton had planned to write a "gay song." The lyricist responded, "There was one once, 'All the Nasties,' on *Madman Across the Water*, that no one picked up on. That was a song for Elton when the press was really crucifying us. It says something about, 'if they asked, maybe I would tell them, then they would understand.'"[70] The quote that Bernie was referring to reads: "If it came to pass/that they should ask,/what could I tell them?/Would they criticize/behind my back,/maybe I should let them."

Unfortunately, the recording of "All the Nasties" on August 11, 1971, is not as effective as the basic composition and pure reading that Elton would give the song in concerts later that year. If there is one song on *Madman* that should be rerecorded, this is it. While Elton's vocal is sincere, it is too wispy. He had been experimenting with falsetto at the time of the recording, but was still not accustomed to singing high, and this song requires a substantial amount of upper-register singing. Another drawback is its overproduction, which includes monklike chants and echoing church chamber singing by the Cantores in Ecclesia Choir, directed by Robert Kirby.

Fittingly, the album closes with "Goodbye," a brief, melancholy ballad about unrequited love, recorded on February 27, 1971. Elton's vocal is accompanied only by his piano and a lovely but unnecessary string arrangement.

British music critics were particularly unenamored of *Madman*. "The press was resentful that I spent more time in America than I did in England," Elton posited in 1976, explaining that he had to spend more time touring the United States since it was so big.[71] Some critics were also still troubled by the quantity of new product that Elton was offering on both sides of the Atlantic, even though there had been six months between his last release, *11-17-70*, and *Madman*. "Opinions differ as to which is the real dregs, but there is a general consensus that his apparent crisis of overproduction made for rock bottom," wrote Mike Flood Page and Chris Salewicz in 1973.[72]

In Britain, where no singles were released from the album, *Madman* did poorly, only charting on May 20, 1972 for two weeks and peaking at number 41. In the United States, however, the "apparent crisis of overproduction" did not hurt the album's commercial success, and it became Elton's first Top 10 since *Tumbleweed*, entering *Billboard*'s Top LPs chart on December 4, 1971 and going gold in January before hitting a high of number 8 on February 5, 1972, right behind Carole King's *Tapestry*. The album was assisted by FM airplay, which his other studio albums had also received, and two singles: "Levon," which was released on November 29, 1971 and reached number 24 on the Hot 100 on February 5, 1972, and "Tiny Dancer," which wouldn't be released until February 1972.

Although most of Elton's good fortune was emanating from the United States, he remained undaunted, and filmed two BBC television appearances in Britain. In late 1971 he appeared on the *Old Grey Whistle Test*, performing "Tiny Dancer" and "All the Nasties" alone at the piano. Both benefited from the solo interpretations— the rich fabric of his playing buttressed by his increasingly soulful voice. Following the music, Elton and Bernie gave a short interview. "During the year, I had my own fair share of bitchiness, which I really can't stand," Elton said about the critics' onslaught. He paraphrased one comment on his involvement with Lesley Duncan's *Sing Children Sing*: "Even though Elton John is on the record it still manages to be quite good." "All the Nasties" was the response to these critics, he said.[73]

A second BBC television appearance was filmed in December but not aired until late April 1972—when Elton had already completed his next album and was thinking of yet another one, to be recorded in June. Elton's appearance on *Sounds for Saturday*, which featured Elton, Nigel, and Dee performing most of the songs from *Madman*, may have been partly responsible for the album's British chart life, however abridged. A highlight was Elton's Keith-Jarrett-meets-Fats-Domino rendition of the title track, in which manic note clusters delivered in syncopated rhythm superbly illustrated the "madman's" confusion. The studio audience also witnessed a brilliant contrast between this now-famous Elton John and the Elton John who, in May 1970, had so uncertainly stepped into the television limelight with his *In Concert* special. Now confident and poised, yet dressed relatively conservatively, he showed that he knew he had something significant to offer.

BY THE END OF 1971, Elton had proven that the first flush of renown he had received in the summer and fall of 1970 had been no fluke. Now he was ready to reach new levels of popularity—and sartorial outrageousness. He had just legally changed his name to Elton Hercules John ("Hercules" being the horse on a favorite childhood television program, *Steptoe and Son*). Amazingly, friends, family, and associates had still been calling him "Reg," which must have put a damper on the public fantasy he was living as "Elton John." With his name change, there would be no more "Reg"; his given name would become a distant memory.

Elton was ready for another recording project, and a new lead guitarist. Davey Johnstone, Elton's new recruit, hailed from Edinburgh, Scotland, and was a blonde telephone pole of a man, nearly as tall as John Baldry, with firm roots in the British folk circuit. It was odd that, after steadfastly refusing to add a lead guitarist and developing his live music through the imagination of his pianism, Elton would change his mind. "I think that if we hadn't gotten Davey, the band would have broken up," he later said, dramatically. "[W]ith no lead guitar I was having to play the same things; and we'd gone as far as we could go."[75] The addition of Davey opened up new avenues for Elton, Nigel, and Dee. And, with Davey's folk background, he was likelier than a guitarist reared on rock'n'roll to augment, rather than take over, Elton's sound.

With a new band member in the wings, at least a couple of new songs written, and the *Madman* album and "Levon" climbing the charts in the United States, Elton and company tried something different, retreating in January 1972 to the Strawberry Studios at the rustic Chateau d'Hierouville in France.

Practically speaking, recording outside England served as a tax shelter and was becoming common practice. Artistically speaking, the group could record without any distractions. "The atmosphere was fantastic, sort of a luxury campout where everything you could think of was at our disposal," Elton later recalled. All those ensconced at the Chateau luxuriated in apartments decorated in antiques. Each studio within the complex offered a fully staffed kitchen, and everyone ate together in communal fashion at a long refectory table.[76]

Most significant about the recording of this next album, though, was Elton's use of his band on all the songs. One wonders how he managed this victory after fighting, with limited success, to get Nigel and Dee on previous albums. The signing of Davey Johnstone could have been a factor. But it is telling that Elton was finally able to use his band—and achieve a more basic sound—on *Honky Chateau*, the first album made under the watchful managerial eye of Elton's prime booster, John Reid.

Something else transpired at the Chateau that had not happened before. "It was like a Motown hit factory," Elton later marveled. "Literally, Bernie upstairs, me downstairs, and the band playing. . . . I couldn't believe how everything began to flow."[77] Maxine would transport freshly inked lyrics down the stairs from Bernie's work area and plant them on Elton's piano. The pianist would then begin composing and have music for a song within, on average, half an hour. The band would join in, arranging the musical parts. Elton's songwriting had always been an immediate, spontaneous flow of feelings from mind to keyboard, but at the Chateau this method gelled into a veritable assembly line of hits.

What resulted was the most playful Elton John album recorded to that point. Completed in three weeks, it sparkled with Elton's piano front and center—his silky vocals marrying the soul stylings of Al Green and Marvin Gaye to English music-hall humor—and the natural combination of band members feeding off each other's instincts. At the time, Elton had been reading books about Noël Coward and Ivor Novello, and a "nostalgic kick" for the 1920s shows on several tracks.[78] Innovative French jazz musician Jean-Luc Ponty guests on two of the songs, a collaboration that Elton would later remember as "probably the most exciting moment of my musical career."[79]

The album's first song, the merry "Honky Cat," could have been conceived and recorded in New Orleans, where the L'il Abner–type main character longs to find his fortune. The lyrics may also allude to Bernie's decision to leave the Lincolnshire farming community of his youth for the bright lights of London ("They said stay at home, boy, you gotta tend the farm,/livin' in the city, boy,/is gonna break your heart"). Elton takes the listener on a tour of Dixieland jazz with syncopated attacks on acoustic and electric pianos. His harplike broken chords at the start are grin-inducing, and Davey's banjo accompaniment offers the perfect hillbilly depiction of the "honky cat." Gus Dudgeon's brass arrangement for the French guest musicians provides extra New Orleans flavoring.

The savory "Honky Cat" portends an album full of treats. The next track, "Mellow," reflects on Bernie's romance with Maxine in their recently acquired Lincolnshire manse, "Piglet-in-the-Wilds." Here Elton maintains the New Orleans atmosphere with shimmering honky-tonk piano flourishes, peppered by imaginative rhythms by Nigel. Toward the end, Elton's organ solo and Ponty's sharp electric violin combine to depict the happy couple's bedtime bliss. Elton was probably still dissatisfied with his talents on the organ, but the relative seclusion of the Chateau, without a multitude of session musicians on hand, forced him to explore other keyboard instruments, including the organ.

The next song, "I Think I'm Going to Kill Myself," continues Elton's adaptation of New Orleans–style jazz with an amusing ditty about a disillusioned but manipulative teenager who wants to shoot himself because his parents won't let him use the car or stay out late. Elton's vocals during the catchy chorus take on a Rudy-Vallee-with-megaphone quality; "Legs" Larry Smith of the Bonzo Dog Doo Dah Band tap-dances as the piano exults in joyous music-hall sound. Rounding out the 1920s flavor is Dee's tuba-like bass playing.

"Susie (Dramas)" follows, painting an old-time vignette of the infatuation of an "old hayseed harp player" with "pretty little black-eyed Susie." Elton turns the song into a tight, funky romp with rock undertones and honky-tonk nuances. Davey gets in some of his first electric guitar licks, contributing a rough edge to the already simmering music.

The last song on side one, "Rocket Man (I Think It's Going to Be a Long, Long Time)," would soon become one of Elton's signature tunes, along with "Your Song" and "Tiny Dancer," as well as the source of his first pop nickname. This song might never have happened but for Bernie's sighting in the quiet English countryside of either a shooting star or an airplane. He started thinking about astronauts, who were no longer heroes but incumbents in what was rapidly becoming (to him) an "everyday occupation."[80] These thoughts filled his mind as he drove along a dark road, and the first lines of the song came to him as if planted by some extraterrestrial force: "She packed my bags last night/pre-flight,/zero hour, nine A.M./and I'm gonna be high as a kite by then." He rushed home to transcribe the words and, the next day, finished the lyrics, borrowing the song title from an obscure number by Tom Rapp, who had, in turn, been inspired by the writings of Ray Bradbury.[81]

What new insight can possibly be made about the sonic sweetness of "Rocket Man"? It is impossible to find fault with this recording. Everything about it conjures up the loneliness of space, from Elton's plaintive piano and voice opening and Dee's equally plaintive bass playing, to Davey's multifaceted guitar work, guest Dave Hentschel's Arp synthesizer accents, and the backing vocals, notable for cementing the blending of Davey's, Dee's, and Nigel's voices.

"Salvation," a pretty number with white gospel leanings, begins side two. The song is a commentary on how the quest for religious "salvation" can negatively affect people's willingness to solve the world's problems themselves. The areligious Elton creates a pleasant hymn and sings like a true believer. His arpeggiated piano playing and uncredited carpet of organ music, and Davey's weeping guitars, further the song's image of Bible Belt Americans at a tent revival meeting.

Bernie returns to his fascination with nineteenth-century Americana in "Slave," with obvious references to slavery in the South and the coming Civil War. The music reveals the main character's slow-burning fury, tempered only by the South's humidity. Its relaxed pace accentuates the melody, which Elton delivers with characteristic delicacy for one of the best vocals on an album filled with superb vocal moments. His piano is missing, though, the brunt of the instrumentation being provided by Davey's stringed threesome of acoustic guitar, electric guitar, and banjo.

"Amy," the next song, finds an oversexed adolescent pining over an older woman, which gets him into trouble with both his father and roughnecks on the street. It is, among other things, another Rolling Stones tribute song, evident from the "Jaggeresque" slyness of Elton's vocal. "Amy" is a joint onslaught of fast-paced, percussive piano and the squealing of Jean-Luc Ponty's electric violin, a combination that gives voice to the diabolical mischievousness of the main character.

A return to introspection marks "Mona Lisas and Mad Hatters," a secular hymn that would become one of the best-loved of Elton's more obscure songs. A response to a shooting in the streets of New York beneath Bernie's hotel room window, the poignant words were penned in castigation of the inhabitants of America's largest city: "While Mona Lisas and Mad Hatters,/sons of bankers, sons of lawyers,/turn around and say good morning to the night,/for unless they see the sky,/but they can't, and that is why/they know not if it's dark outside or light."

That Elton latched onto music appropriate for a hymn in a song about those who live life without any hint of spirituality may be surprising, but with *Honky Chateau* Elton revealed an affinity for matching a seemingly incompatible melody to lyrics, giving life to an alternate meaning. Though "Honky Cat" sounds joyous, the lyrics reveal a farm boy frustrated with his life on the farm and discouraged from bettering himself. "I Think I'm Going to Kill Myself" is about a disheartened teen willing to snuff his life out, but Elton's gleeful music fleshes out the absurdity of the teen's expectation that something positive could come from suicide. In "Salvation," Elton's reading is pious though the song is critical of religion. And in "Mona Lisas and Mad Hatters," he criticizes the myopia of the people he watches while, through the spirituality of his honeyed melody and imploring piano playing (aided by Davey's flowery mandolin), attributing a potential spirituality to those he chides.

The final track, "Hercules," lacks any quality that could be characterized as spiritual. Purportedly about Elton in honor of his new middle name (and the name of the new home he shared with John Reid in Virginia Water, Surrey), the lyrics have nothing to do with him. The protagonist is a sexist man who jealously watches as his dream woman walks away with "Hercules." An irreverent union of New Orleans piano flourishes and 1950s doo-wop choruses, this festive song had room even for Gus Dudgeon on backing vocals.

All in all, little about *Honky Chateau* is serious, other than inspired musicianship, memorable melodies, and Elton's most lustrous vocal performance to that point. Elton could also proudly refer to the album as a marked change in direction. "[N]obody can turn round and say, 'Oh, it's Elton John and his bloody one hundred-piece orchestra again,'" he beamed.[82] But, as usual, he would have to wait months to enjoy the fruits of his labors.

"BOY, I MUST HAVE BEEN GREEN"[83]

BY FEBRUARY 1972, Elton was back on the road in Britain, this time with Davey as the lead guitarist. On February 5, he revisited his 1971 orchestral experiment by playing a concert at London's Royal Festival Hall, featuring the Royal Philharmonic

Orchestra. Elton and the band were alone for the first half, playing several new songs, including "Mona Lisas and Mad Hatters," "Honky Cat," and "Hercules." The orchestra, conducted by Paul Buckmaster, joined in for a second half devoted to veteran songs, including "Burn Down the Mission" and "Take Me to the Pilot." Nigel, Dee, and Lesley Duncan provided backing vocals from a balcony behind the orchestra. In center stage was the disheveled Ray Cooper, sitting in with his assortment of percussion instruments. Elton seemed inhibited, in his glistening tails and top hat, and for good reason. Most orchestra members resented their assignment.

"I felt so tense because I was uncomfortable playing with them," Elton said later that year. "It was all snide remarks during rehearsal, like Paul Buckmaster would say to them, 'Can I please have a bit of quiet?' and someone would say 'Well, if you got your fucking hair cut perhaps you could hear quiet,' and it was all down to that sort of scene."[84]

William Mann, writing a review for *The Times* (London), paid Elton a small compliment in observing that the union of rock'n'roll and symphony orchestra was less objectionable than other collaborations involving rock or jazz acts. But he had a point when he suggested that "Elton's songs are basically natural and only need him to sing and play them. . . ."[85] Indeed it is puzzling, given the more basic direction his recordings were taking, that Elton chose to give live voice to Buckmaster's arrangements. Thereafter, Elton put only his revised band on display.

Later in February, Elton played two charity concerts for the National Youth Theatre, a large drama club for young people. On one of the evenings, Lord Snowden and Princess Margaret, the latter of whom would become a loyal fan of the musician, were in the audience. (Elton, with John Reid, had first met the princess at a dinner organized by friend Bryan Forbes,[86] which had eventually led to other royal invitations and hobnobbing with the Queen Mother.) Again, concertgoers received a sneak preview of *Honky Chateau*. Michael Wale of *The Times* (London) was impressed with the fresh material, lauding "Honky Cat" and "I Think I'm Going to Kill Myself." Although Elton continued to have a penchant for unusual clothing and laughing at himself, Wale wrote, it would be a mistake to dismiss him as "all fun," since "his songs have a way of purveying the sadness of life as well. Therein lies his strength."[87] The grateful National Youth Theatre made Elton a vice president, and he determined to see as many of their plays as he could.

Elton now had a new American single, "Tiny Dancer," released on February 7, 1972. It debuted on *Billboard's* Hot 100 on March 4 at number 85, the same day as Roberta Flack's "The First Time Ever I Saw Your Face." Flack's song spent six weeks at the top of the chart, but "Tiny Dancer" couldn't even squeeze into the Top 40, peaking at number 41 on April 8. This unremarkable chart performance did not portend the almost hallowed stature "Tiny Dancer" would eventually be accorded. And though it did poorly as a single, it had received a lot of airplay as an album track before the single's release, which may have caused it to run its course on the Hot 100 earlier than it should have.[88]

As the band toured with Davey as its newest member, it successfully avoided turning into the wailing guitar group that Elton had avoided when first on the road with Nigel and Dee. Davey, schooled in folk, didn't control Elton's sound, but supplemented the band's piano-based music with appropriate flourishes, choosing the right stringed instrument for each song—banjo on "Honky Cat," mandolin on "Mona Lisas and Mad Hatters." Davey also supported the natural crescendos in Elton's music. "He has this subtle sort of control over his musicians," the guitarist said of Elton. "He doesn't actually tell you what to play but you get to know what he wants and he forces the best out of you."[89] On "Madman Across the Water," Davey contributed eerie, understated licks and traded off spooky solos with Elton, whose own soloing on the song reached epic proportions.

In keeping with his growing stature, Elton had taken to wearing luxurious, colorful, satiny outfits onstage. In Chicago on May 8, 1972 (during a U.S. tour that had started in April), he wore a glittery jacket with black velvet lapels. "You want a superstar, Elton John gives you a superstar," gushed reviewer Lynn Van Matre.[90]

At the end of May, Elton, dressed comparatively modestly, appeared with Rod Stewart on the BBC's *Top of the Pops*, to support John Baldry by promoting a single, the Elton-produced "Iko Iko" off Baldry's *Everything Stops for Tea*. At the post-show party, Baldry reflected on the commercial success of his two students. "I always knew that Rod [a pre-Bluesology band mate] was going to become something very, very special," Baldry said. "But how could one predict that a boy with an overweight problem . . . I mean, he is a bit broad across the beam, our Reg. . . . Who would have thought that this strange boy with his myopic lenses and fat arse . . . could turn out to be one of the pop sensations of all time?"[91]

"I THINK IT'S GONNA BE A LONG, LONG TIME"[92]

BY APRIL 1972, Elton had amassed a nice assortment of American singles, most of which had done well, and a little pile of albums, many of which were popular, especially in the United States. But that month his commercial standing took a dramatic upturn. "Rocket Man" was released as a single in the United States on April 17, 1972, and later that month in Britain.

In Britain, "Rocket Man" charted on April 22, peaked at number 2, and spent thirteen weeks on the chart. (It was during this phenomenon that Baldry, with some bewilderment, had commented on Elton's fame.) In the United States, "Rocket Man" entered *Billboard*'s Hot 100 at number 80 on May 6, in the middle of Elton's U.S. tour. (Coincidentally, while stopping in Houston for an April 28 concert, Elton and the band paid a lengthy visit to NASA headquarters, where they watched the splashdown of *Apollo 16*.[93]) By May 27, "Rocket Man" had hit the Top 40, where it stayed for fifteen weeks, peaking at number 6 in mid-July. It was Elton's first Top 10 single since "Your Song."

Even more exhilarating was the chart success of *Honky Chateau*, released in Britain on May 19, 1972 and in the United States on May 26. *Honky Chateau* was welcomed by critics who'd been looking forward to a band-oriented Elton John album. Writing for *Rolling Stone*, Jon Landau found the songs much more straightforward than those on earlier albums. This collection of songs "rewards each additional playing with increased enlightenment and enjoyment," he wrote.[94] Robert Hilburn predicted the album would be Elton's "most popular."[95]

It certainly was Elton's most popular offering until then. *Honky Chateau* spent twenty-three weeks on the British chart following its June 3 entry, climbed to number 2, and was the second best-selling album there in June.[96] In the United States, it only debuted on *Billboard*'s Top LPs at number 110 on June 17, but took just two more weeks to reach the Top 10, spending five midsummer weeks at number 1, becoming the first chart-topper of his career.

"I'M GONNA GRAB MYSELF A PLACE IN HISTORY"[97]

WHILE OPTIMISTICALLY TRACKING the fate in June of his nearly six-month-old work that had finally charted, Elton returned to the Chateau d'Hierouville to record yet another album. It seemed, at first, that he was not in any shape to do it. He had glandular fever and was generally worn out from constant activity. But the final product, *Don't Shoot Me, I'm Only the Piano Player*, has an even more celebratory, life-affirming sound than *Honky Chateau*, and contains no intimation of his poor physical and mental states. It is also noisier and less funky. "It's got more balls," Elton observed.[98]

While he had been fairly nostalgic about the 1920s and, to an extent, the 1950s during the *Honky Chateau* sessions, Elton delved into his well of knowledge about specific 1950s and early 1960s pop acts for much of *Don't Shoot Me*, its overall theme even more supremely nostalgic than that of *Honky Chateau*. Of the new album, Elton would later wisecrack, "The whole record's a total rip-off."[99] Over the years, many critics would dismiss much of Elton's work as derivative. It is fairer to say that *Don't Shoot Me, I'm Only the Piano Player* (and much of his other music) was inspired by, rather than derivative of, his musical idols. Elton absorbs the music around him as a writer might a neighborhood milieu in preparing to write a novel. Filtering it through his web of emotions and experiences, Elton defines his musical milieu in the context of all other music he has heard, cooking up a unique mix of old and new ingredients with the all-natural flavoring of his melodic gift.

Don't Shoot Me is another band album, with *Honky Chateau*'s French brass section returning for three songs. Paul Buckmaster, who at the time was turning up on some other recordings of note (Nilsson's "Without You" and Carly Simon's "You're So Vain"), also returned for two songs. In deference to Elton's band,

Buckmaster contributed restrained orchestral arrangements responsive to the essentials of the songs.

Buckmaster had no role in the first song, "Daniel," a soon-to-be standard for which the arrangement was apportioned solely among the band members (and the album's engineer, Ken Scott). "Daniel" pays necessary homage to Bernie's obsession with Americana. It is also the only John/Taupin song to refer to the Vietnam War—not expressing an opinion on the conflict, but instead looking at its toll on American combatants through Daniel's one eye. Daniel has returned from overseas a hero but, to his younger brother's disappointment, prefers to flee to the anonymity of Spain, where he can nurse his painful memories in peace.

Bernie based his lyrics on an article he had read in bed one night, telling the story of a veteran who couldn't accept the adulation he'd received upon returning to Texas.[100] Predictably, Bernie initially made light of the song's theme. "Daniel's nobody," Bernie said. "I don't have any set idea on who he is. I just started the song with that corny rhyme, 'plane' and 'Spain.'"[101] It was easy for him to obfuscate the lyrics' meaning as Elton had struck the last verse, which explained the song's premise and is now lost to the ages. Ultimately, "Daniel" avoids an overt political statement while effectively humanizing a horrific American initiative. Arguably, the song's portrayal of everyday folk makes a more compelling statement than less artful political sloganeering. Besides, Elton liked to keep the public guessing. The last verse, he said, made the song too obvious. "If you don't tell people what they [the songs] are about, sometimes they're more mystical."[102]

Elton had rarely used the electric piano as the lead keyboard instrument, but here his light electric chords further the song's intimacy. His measured use of the mellotron, to create the butterfly-flutter flute effect, adds further poignancy to the picture of Daniel's younger brother watching his elder's airplane ascend, bound for Spain. Nigel's steady maracas, Davey's pleasant, coffeehouse-style acoustic strumming, and Ken Scott's Arp synthesizer solo all help convey the feelings of the song's main characters. Rising above all the instrumentation is Elton's sensitive vocal rendering, featuring more of the falsetto for which he was then becoming known.

The next song abruptly changes pace. "Teacher I Need You" is a merry uptempo number that looks back at the purportedly more innocent school days of the 1950s, when it was easy to develop a schoolkid crush on the teacher. Elton has said that his echoing vocal was inspired by 1950s teen idol Bobby Vee, popular for such songs as "Take Good Care of My Baby." This inspiration is also evident in Elton's gleaming harmonies, although he reaches deeper into his vocal register than Vee. Elton evokes the sound of Jerry Lee Lewis, too, with some manic, lightning-quick chord sequences, but defines the song by his more cultured broken chords in the opening.

The nostalgia in the next song, "Elderberry Wine," doesn't refer to a definable era but to the lost carefree days of a now wifeless, joyless man. The symbol of happier days is the elderberry wine he and his wife shared through the seasons, now just a memory ("How can I ever get it together,/without a wife·in line"). Like much of *Honky Chateau*, the music for "Elderberry Wine" examines the flip side of its obvious meaning: The music's merriment is the antithesis of the protagonist's current loneliness. It is also an aggressive showcase for the compatibility of the band's members, punctuated by another Gus Dudgeon brass arrangement that marks the return of *Honky Chateau*'s reliable French session players.

Don't Shoot Me then revisits the pent-up emotions of "Daniel" in "Blues for Baby and Me," in which a young couple hops a Greyhound to escape their troubles and "go west to the sea." The song features Elton's lower register, which lends an air of authority to the boyfriend, who reassures his girlfriend that their fortunes will improve.

Elton's ballad-style piano would have worked just fine by itself as the instrumental accompaniment, but the music is well supplemented by Paul Buckmaster. His sweet orchestral arrangement gingerly makes itself known as the band joins in the song's chorus. Unassuming but expansive, it reinforces the image of the couple traveling west, full of hope.

The album shifts gears with "Midnight Creeper," a tune about a creep who alternates between cruel perversion ("Long-haired ladies well they look so fine,/ locked in my cellar full of cheap red wine") and remorseless, two-timing habits ("I still don't know why you hate me so,/a little bit of fun never stopped no show"). Like "Teacher I Need You," this song's gleeful rock'n'roll rhythms harken back to the 1950s and early 1960s. Elton contributes his most commanding vocal yet, from roaring twists of verse to creamier chorus phrasings. His frisky electric piano chords, which mimic the stealth of the "midnight creeper," Gus Dudgeon's punchy brass arrangement, and Davey Johnstone's mischievous electric guitar licks move the song along at a brisk, entertaining pace.

"Rotten Peaches" is revisited in "Have Mercy on the Criminal," a dark portrait of wardens' hunt for escaped prisoners. The story is vividly told by an onlooker who has seen more than one desperate convict trying to escape, and who sympathetically pleads: "Oh, there must be shackles, on his feet,/and mother, in his eyes, stumbling through the devil-dark,/with the hound pack in full cry." Elton responds to this serious theme with a forceful, emotional melody evocative of 1950s Tin Pan Alley. Raised on records by Rosemary Clooney and Jo Stafford, he was bound, at some point, to reflect their inspiration.

An upper follows: "I'm Going to Be a Teenage Idol" is a jaunty tribute to the young who covet rock stardom, and to Elton's then new friend Marc Bolan, the glitter rocker and prime mover behind the group T. Rex. At the time, Bolan was a major teen idol in his native Britain. Elton had already assisted Bolan on a BBC *Top of the*

Pops appearance the previous year, playing piano on "Bang a Gong (Get It On)." In his tapered, poodle-decorated jacket, Elton had looked more tasteful than Bolan, who sported a huge, frizzy, dark mop of hair, mascara, and stray bits of glitter pockmarking his face. In 1980, Elton fondly remembered Bolan, who died in a 1977 car crash, remarking, "We wrote that song about him because that's what he wanted to be, and he was living his part to the full and enjoying it, and meant no harm to anybody. Great tragedy that he's gone, because he was one of the few people that would come out with the most outrageous statements."[103]

Little did Elton know at the time he recorded the song, when he was a darling of the college circuit, that he would find himself in the embarrassing situation some months hence of being surrounded by teen screamers. The song would become an ode to himself, a musical route, via contagious melody and honky-tonk chords, to a place of ecstatic abandon.

The scene then shifts to Texas for the satirical "Texan Love Song," in which rednecks get an unsympathetic ribbing. The song's narrator, a Texas native, spews vitriol over the the long-haired, free-living rock'n'rollers strolling into town and contaminating its moral fiber. This enjoyable sing-along features just the four band members. Elton affects his best southern drawl while easing his way through a stint on harmonium (reed organ).

Nostalgic sentiments again arise with "Crocodile Rock," a tribute to the hit songs of Elton's and Bernie's childhoods. The narrator looks hazily back from a vantage point many years later, longing for a youth he cannot recapture. Elton turned "Crocodile Rock" into a tribute to recording acts of the late 1950s and early 1960s—so many, in fact, that it is nearly impossible to distinguish them in his seamless compositional approach. In 1973 he said that the music encompasses the Diamonds' "Little Darlin'," Neil Sedaka's "Oh, Carol," the Beach Boys, and Freddy Cannon.[104] Although Elton never said he regretted writing and recording the song—and releasing it as a single—he was irked that rock purists cited it as a musical sellout. Worse, Elton's high-pitched "la la la" chorus caused the authors of Pat Boone's 1962 hit "Speedy Gonzales" to file suit, claiming the song infringed on their copyright.[105] Although Elton and Bernie ended up settling, the two songs are really dissimilar, with "Crocodile Rock" paying only brief homage to its predecessor.

Don't Shoot Me closes on a somber note, with the romantic "High Flying Bird," a reflection on the passing of a troubled young woman ("My high-flying bird has flown from out my arms,/I thought myself her keeper,/she thought I meant her harm"). Through the voice of the young woman's spurned lover, one hears of a prematurely ended romance. Elton's melody wraps around the listener like a soft, warm blanket as he digs again into the lower end of his vocal range. The band's backing vocals lend further warmth to the song.

Don't Shoot Me, knee-deep in 1950s and early 1960s nostalgia, would not be released until late January 1973. It would help usher in a wave of nostalgia for the music, fashions, and caricatures of that time, exemplified by the movie *American Graffiti* and the television show *Happy Days*.

JOHN ELTON AND MARX GROUCHO: "I'VE SEEN THAT MOVIE TOO"[106]

STILL SUFFERING FROM GLANDULAR FEVER, Elton rewarded himself with a July 1972 vacation in a rented Malibu, California house. John Reid, Bernie, Maxine, and numerous invited friends took up residence there that month, including Bryan Forbes, his wife Nanette Newman, and their two young daughters. Forbes and Newman were Virginia Water neighbors of Elton and John Reid. Forbes also had a strong Hollywood connection; besides having acted in such movies as *The Guns of Navarone*, he had produced and directed numerous films (his weird, suspenseful *The Stepford Wives* was still to come). Starstruck Elton thus had his ticket to a completely different universe, and while in Malibu took advantage of opportunities to meet elderly former screen stars who, decades after their popular peak, were still household names.

Of the old Hollywood era, Elton once told Eric Van Lustbader, "I would have loved to have grown up in that era, 'cause to me it's magic. It seemed so full of excitement at that time—in the thirties and forties—it was just a hive of industry, people were creating things all the time. Nowadays," Elton dejectedly noted, "it's just plodding along, all the magic has gone out of it."[107] The symbol of old Hollywood who made the biggest impression on him was Groucho Marx, or "Marx Groucho" as the mustached, acerbic comedian called himself to counterbalance his inversion of Elton's name to "John Elton." "Elton John" sounded wrong to Groucho, to which Elton retorted, "Don't shoot me, I'm only the piano player." The phrase was a play on the name of François Truffaut's 1960 movie, *Shoot the Piano Player*, and was identified as the ideal name for Elton's upcoming album. Not surprisingly, vestiges of the old Hollywood would begin cropping up in Elton's stage act that fall.

But first, another single from *Honky Chateau* was in the offing: "Honky Cat," released in the United States on July 31, 1972. The single realized much of its promise as a successor to Elton's then most popular single, "Rocket Man." Debuting on the Hot 100 on August 12, "Honky Cat" took six weeks to reach the Top 10, where it stayed for two weeks, peaking at number 8. But music listeners at home didn't take as well to "Honky Cat." It debuted in Britain on September 9, peaking at only number 31. Still, the song marked his third charted single at home. In Britain and America, Elton was now neck and neck with his competitors.

After the end of his limited British tour in late summer and during the beginning of his more extensive U.S. tour in the fall, Elton and some friends and associates came up with a plan designed to help promote other acts, including Davey Johnstone, who needed a record label for an album he wanted to record. The plan was to found a label and name it after Elton's biggest hit. Hence, Rocket Records. This was the perfect idea for Elton, the quintessential starstruck music fan. He could help bring unknowns from obscurity to renown, giving them a fair deal in the process. "The idea that started Rocket was simply that record companies don't want to give a new artist a decent deal," Elton said later. "They sign them for three to five years at a really low percentage, and if the act should happen within a year, it just means that they've got four years of being screwed to look forward to."[108]

Elton wanted Rocket Records to employ only those he believed could sympathetically develop new acts—himself, Bernie, John Reid, Gus Dudgeon, and Steve Brown. "We all know something about music," Elton explained to Robert Hilburn. "I won't have anyone working for us who doesn't understand music. I'm trying to get away from the Dick Jameses of the world."[109]

This was one indication of Elton's growing disenchantment with DJM. Granted, James had generously supported Elton and Bernie throughout their lean years. But those years might not have been as lean if the duo hadn't been pressured to write the wrong kind of songs. More recently, Elton's skyrocketing career had been in disarray behind the scenes until he had convinced John Reid to manage him, albeit in an in-house arrangement scheduled to begin early in 1973 when DJM's management contract with Elton expired. There would be more cause for dissatisfaction with James in the coming months.

"IT KIND OF MAKES ME FEEL LIKE A ROCK'N'ROLL STAR"[110]

ELTON'S FALL TOUR IN THE UNITED STATES solidified his reputation as a flamboyant stage act—with staging to match. His earlier stage getups were, by contrast, merely eccentric. Typically, he appeared before audiences in a brilliant red, white, and blue lamé suit with matching top hat and toweringly tall silver platform shoes, the right one sporting a red "E," the left a red "J." His prescription eyeglasses had grown larger, with colorful tinted lenses; a favored pair had big white hexagonal frames with orange-tinted lenses. This outfit was just the beginning for a show with hilariously vaudevillian tendencies.

During "I Think I'm Going to Kill Myself," Elton and the band were joined by "Legs" Larry Smith, who had tap-danced on the record. Smith danced live during the song, wearing a crash helmet and wedding cake decoration atop his head, and a long bridal train, which at Carnegie Hall in New York and the Forum in Los Angeles was held up by two tiny men whose outfits were described variously as befitting South American dictators, doormen, or sailors.

In another number, Elton would ask the audience to please be patient while he and his band members left the stage for a minute. To the taped strains of strings from the 1952 film *Singin' in the Rain*, the band would reappear, with Elton and "Legs" Larry in raingear and tour manager Marv Tabolsky, in tails, taking his seat at Elton's piano to mime to the music. Elton would ask, "Have you got a light, Mac?" Legs would shout "No!" and, to laughter in the audience, they would embark on a singing and dancing rendition of the film's title song. (Elton had taken hoofing lessons just for the occasion.[111]) The two added silly lines to the song, such as, "We walk down the street, with warts on our feet," and, in the tradition of yesterday's theater acts, engaged in lighthearted dialogue as each cheerily expounded on the benefits of possessing the other's talents. During the extravaganza, Elton might toss lollipops to fans, Bernie might emerge with chocolate kisses for the crowd, and Maxine Taupin sometimes appeared to sprinkle glitter over Elton and Legs. At Carnegie Hall and the Forum, a line of female dancers was in tow for the number, and they, along with others onstage, were showered with confetti.

For the rest of the show, however, it was the music that mattered. "I know it is the music that counts, but I also like it when someone puts on a good show," Elton said. "Ninety percent of my act is music, the heart of it is music, but the ten percent theatrics is fun. For me and for the audience."[112]

While it had become apparent by the spring of 1972 that Elton's shows were already career retrospectives, this tour also included songs that were recent ("Levon" and "Tiny Dancer"), current ("Honky Cat" and "Rocket Man"), and even still unreleased ("Daniel," which he performed alone, and "Crocodile Rock," which featured sound engineer Clive Franks on organ). And Elton was now closing his shows with a hot twenty-minute combination of "Whole Lot of Shakin' Going On" and "Hercules." During the latter, he usually did a camp impersonation of strutting Mick Jagger, stripping down to a sweat-soaked shirt, short pants rolled to the knees, and a pair of winged boots.

Some performances on the tour were especially memorable. At the Scope Auditorium in Norfolk, Virginia, Elton blended myriad keyboard attacks for a "Levon" that followed in the footsteps of "Madman Across the Water," convincingly exploring moody jazz ponderings. Beginning with barrelhouse chords that segued into gospel progressions, Elton intensified the song's early drama, with heavy piano bass lines bellowing from his left hand. No sooner did this sonic mountain burst forth than it receded into a jazz reflection with occasional angry crescendos, creating an ebb and flow of musical temperament. Happily, a couple of bootleg albums, one titled *Scope 72*, the other *Apple Pie*, appeared on the market to immortalize parts of this concert, including a portion of "Levon."

It couldn't have been easy for Elton to continue at length on "Levon," or any other song. He was still hitting the piano keys so hard that his nails split and bled.

In a Los Angeles dressing room, he presided in pain over one finger that had erupted like a geyser. He doctored it enough to go on with the show, and played just as well as he had elsewhere. Making light of his discomfort before twenty-two thousand concertgoers, he asserted from his piano, "Even if I had only one finger left, I'd play for you."[113]

This time, critics realized that the stage antics and costumes did not detract from the music. A review of one of the Carnegie Hall shows in *Variety* dubbed the band "excellent instrumentally" and found Elton's playing and singing "exciting."[114] Nat Freedland, writing for *Billboard* about Elton's Forum appearance, said: "Elton got over a half-dozen standing ovations because of musicianship, not freakiness." He added, "Elton is now able to consistently play it for kooky laughs, while making music that is spectacularly better than ever."[115]

"THE BIGGEST KICK I EVER GOT"[116]

ELTON'S STATURE ON THE AMERICAN CHARTS was nothing short of gargantuan for the next three years, starting with "Crocodile Rock," which was released toward the end of 1972. It may not have endeared him to critics, many of whom were looking for a reason to pan his music, but it did win over the public. Elton saw "Daniel" as the single, and didn't want to be categorized as a musician who typically performed songs like "Crocodile Rock," but he recognized that the latter song helped dispel the notion that "Elton John is a slow record singer."[117]

In Britain on October 30, Elton launched publicity for "Crocodile Rock" on the "Royal Variety Show," a televised charity event held at the behest of the royal family that necessitated an interruption in his fall U.S. tour. Elton was competing with many celebrities for attention that night, including the Osmonds, the Jacksons, Jack Jones, and Liberace. The older, flamboyant pianist stole the show, Elton believed, but the younger pianist's performance of "I Think I'm Going to Kill Myself" with "Legs" Larry got a fair amount of attention, too, as "farting" balloons were released into the air. "The audience was full of the most dreadful people imaginable, and all these balloons were going 'pffft, pfft, pfft,' all over the audience and they were all sitting there in their tiaras going 'Ooooh! Ooooh!'" Elton later laughed.[118]

"Crocodile Rock" was released in Britain on October 27, and charted there on November 4, 1972. It peaked at number 5 and logged fourteen weeks, spending more time on the singles chart than any of his prior singles. In the United States, where Elton's music was now released on MCA Records, Uni's parent company, the single came out on November 20, 1972 with thrilling results. It entered the Hot 100 on December 9 at number 73, the highest debuting single. By February 3, 1973, it was the first number 1 single of Elton's career and, shortly, his first gold single. "Crocodile Rock" stayed on top for three weeks.

As "Crocodile Rock" climbed the Hot 100 in the United States, Robert Hilburn reported that *Madman Across the Water* was 1972's tenth best-selling album according to *Billboard* magazine (with *Honky Chateau* outselling it but not factoring significantly in the results because it had been released much later than *Madman*). *Record World* magazine tied Elton with Neil Young as the top selling male album artist, and the pianist was named the seventh best-selling male singles artist by *Cash Box* magazine.[119] Meanwhile, "Crocodile Rock" was lifting Elton to new levels of popularity, and he was close to working on another album—with *Don't Shoot Me* still to be released.

"YOU'RE A STAR IN THE FACE OF THE SKY"[120]

DON'T SHOOT ME GOT A SECOND prerelease boost in Britain in January 1973 with another single, "Daniel," which had only narrowly made the cut. "We are releasing 'Daniel' as a single solely because of pressure from Elton," Dick James protested. "It is untrue to say I don't like 'Daniel.' It is a beautiful, fantastic number—one of the best Elton and Bernie Taupin have written." But since two songs from the album had already been released ("Crocodile Rock" and the B-side, "Elderberry Wine"), he believed releasing a third track from the album two weeks before it was to be shipped was poor marketing strategy. He had already budgeted what he considered a lot of money to promote *Don't Shoot Me,* and only if the single reached the Top 10 would he reimburse Elton for the musician's out-of-pocket promotional costs.[121]

Maybe James figured Elton would back down. But Elton believed in the song, and it was released. "I was very bitter about that," Elton said later. "It was a ludicrous position for an artist to be in."[122] The death knell was beginning to sound for his professional association with DJM, even though James made good on his promise to back up the promotional expenses. Entering the British singles chart on January 20, 1973, "Daniel" reached number 4.

Close on the heels of "Daniel," *Don't Shoot Me* was released in Britain on January 26, 1973, four days after its U.S. debut. Its cover strikingly captures the album's late 1950s, early 1960s musical theme, subtly tipping a hat to Elton's growing immersion in Hollywood fantasy. Here, Elton is the movie star. The front and back covers blare the album's name and its star attraction on a movie-house marquee, hanging over a bobby-soxer and a greaser buying tickets to this latest smash hit of filmdom. The only likeness of Elton is on a movie poster outside the theater. Dwarfed to its right is an anachronistic poster for the Marx Brothers' 1940 film *Go West,* referring to lyrics in "Blues for Baby and Me" ("We're gonna *go west* to the sea"). Elton thus affectionately paid tribute to Groucho, his idol and Malibu companion. Inside the album, the grinning visage of little Reggie Dwight sits in knee pants at his trusty King Brothers upright piano. The cherubic schoolboy had made it.

Don't Shoot Me did what it deserved to do. It climbed to the top of the album charts on both sides of the Atlantic, becoming Elton's first transatlantic number I album (and a number I album in both Britain and the United States for the month of March 1973[123]) and another gold album in America.

"WE'RE ALL HAPPY IN JAMAICA"[124]

WELL BEFORE THE ASCENSION OF *DON'T SHOOT ME*, Elton wrote twenty more songs in, of all places, Jamaica. Bernie had spent two weeks in December 1972 writing lyrics for the songs but, come January, Elton had learned that the Chateau d'Hierouville was temporarily closed. He noticed that the Rolling Stones had just completed *Goats Head Soup* at Byron Lee's Dynamic Sounds Studios in Jamaica, and liked the idea of a remote complex that, like the Chateau, could function as both a working and living community. He figured he and his crew might as well try it.

It was just after the George Foreman–Joe Frazier fight in Kingston. Elton and his entourage encountered difficulties at their first hotel in the city; among other problems, the pianist caught a case of crabs from a toilet seat.[125] The group quickly moved to the Terra Nova Hotel, where Elton found the post-fight atmosphere anything but comforting. (When the band decided to take off for a mini-vacation while he wrote, he was too afraid to leave his room.) In the midst of this sense of unwelcome, Elton wrote the music for twenty songs in about two days on a Fender Rhodes electric piano.

Elton and the band were soon ready to try recording the songs, but problems intervened. The studio adjoined a record plant where striking workers would shoot crushed fiberglass through blowpipes at Elton and the others as they entered. "Half an hour later we'd all come out in rashes," he remembered.[126] There was also a lack of suitable studio equipment. "First, the piano didn't materialize," Elton said afterwards. "Then, the mikes didn't arrive and we couldn't get any Dolbys. Ken [Scott, the engineer] and Gus went into the studios for three days with Dee, Nigel, and Davey to try and get a rhythm section sound but they couldn't get it together." Consequently, although they rehearsed all the songs Elton had written in the confines of his hotel room, they recorded only one, "Saturday Night's Alright for Fighting." "When we played it back in the studio, it sounded like it had been recorded on the worst transistor radio. . . . God knows how the Stones got an album out of there," Elton later mused.[127]

It wasn't long before Elton realized that *he* wasn't going to get an album out of there. They would have to return to their charmed hideaway, the Honky Chateau. That wouldn't be until May.

CHAPTER 4

TEENAGE IDOL[1]

(1973–1975)

B Y LATE FEBRUARY 1973, when Elton started another British tour, the "screamers" had arrived. As a headline on the front page of *Melody Maker* screamed, "Now Elton's a Teen Idol!"[2] At the Edmonton Sundown Theatre, where Elton performed right around his twenty-sixth birthday, the front third of the venue was filled with teenage girls, many of whom clambered onstage and had to be carried off.

Even in the midst of this new commotion, Elton offered a quality show. He appeared onstage in a flowing cape decorated with raised palm trees, which he ceremoniously doffed, revealing a sparkling green tuxedo-style suit and a pair of platform shoes from his never-ending supply. Visible were locks of thinning hair awash in pastel colors. Piano handstands were plentiful. Backing vocals were provided by two new Rocket Records signings: Longdancer, a group that included Dave Stewart (future founder of the Eurythmics) and Nigel Olsson's brother Kai; and the former Pauline Matthews, now called Kiki Dee, a white soul singer who had been seeking recognition for years. This ad hoc pairing added luscious vocal vibrato to "Rocket Man." Elton also premiered two songs at Sundown: "Candle in the Wind" and "Love Lies Bleeding."

It was a festive week. Elton hosted a combination birthday and Rocket Records party in a boat dubbed the "Sloop John D," which floated in its mooring on the Thames as Rod Stewart, the Faces, Paul Simon, Ringo Starr, and others celebrated into the wee hours. The official launching of the Island Records–distributed Rocket Records Company in Britain occurred afterwards, on April 30, with a party held on a train specially chartered for a couple of hundred music industry types.

Just as "Crocodile Rock" was fading from the charts in the United States, "Daniel" was released, on March 26, 1973, earning the highest chart debut for the week of April 7 at number 77. Weeks later, it was in the Top 10, and on June 2, peaked at number 2. Though it couldn't dislodge "My Love," the big hit by Paul McCartney and Wings, from the top spot, over the years it has proved more indelibly etched in the public mind. Oddly, though, "Daniel" would not officially go gold until September 1995, a full twenty-two years after its release.

"I SET MY OWN PACE BY STEALING THE SHOW"[3]

AS "DANIEL" CLIMBED THE CHARTS IN THE UNITED STATES, John Reid, through the recent incorporation of John Reid Enterprises, officially became Elton's manager. Elton and company returned for a third time to the enchanted old chateau in France. Things went swimmingly. Elton wrote a few more songs to add to the Jamaica stockpile, and recorded *Goodbye Yellow Brick Road* in two weeks. (The album was almost called *Talking Pictures, Silent Movies,* but "I thought that tied in too closely with the cinema on the cover of *Don't Shoot Me,*" Elton later explained.[4])

Bernie once said that the album does not encompass a particular concept.[5] In fact, it comprises an overview of the songwriting duo's entire career through the spring of 1973—and then some. It was "the ultimate Elton John album—it's got all my influences from the word go," Elton told Eric Van Lustbader. "It encompasses everything I ever wrote or sounded like."[6] On it, Del Newman replaced Paul Buckmaster for a handful of string arrangements.

There are three ballads on *Goodbye Yellow Brick Road,* the first being "Candle in the Wind," another of Elton's flawless hymns. Elton and Bernie have often said that this song perfectly marries lyrics to music. Soon, it would be a concert standard, ripe for sing-alongs with "Your Song" and "Daniel."

An ode to Marilyn Monroe, who had tragically died eleven years earlier, "Candle in the Wind" could just as easily apply to other stars of old Hollywood. "Goodbye Norma Jean," the song's opening line, could have been "Goodbye Frances Gumm," for Judy Garland ("They set you on the treadmill/and they made you change your name"). Garland's spirit pervaded the album anyway, with its *Wizard of Oz*–inspired title track. But it was Monroe Bernie thought of when he heard the phrase "candle in the wind" used in tribute to the late Janis Joplin.

Elton delivers a lonely vocal to tell the story of a star whose life has ended too soon but who conducted herself with dignity ("You had the grace to hold yourself/while those around you crawled."). The band's naturally blended backing vocals are among their best, and every instrument comes through sharply—Elton's lilting arpeggios, Dee's complementary bass lines, Nigel's precise drum beats, Davey's guitar accents. Interestingly, the distinctive, trill-like guitar line heard between verses was Elton's idea.

A second ballad, "Roy Rogers," sounds like the ideal county fair song for a Southwestern audience, with the cry of Davey's steel guitar like a cat wailing on a distant fence. Elton harmonizes with himself in an overt attempt to sing à la the

Everly Brothers, thus revisiting *Don't Shoot Me*'s nostalgia for the 1950s and early 1960s. But, like his other tributes to some of his musical idols, such as Bobby Vee and the Stones, the song is still entirely his own. The waltz tempo is framed by Elton's chords, which ascend and descend like a hammock swaying in a backyard breeze outside the trailer where the song's protagonist reflects on how little he has— except for the television, on which he can watch Roy Rogers and Trigger.

The third and final ballad, "Harmony," is a strange love song. At first glance, the lyrics suggest a straightforward love story, symbolized by the relationship's "harmony." But "Harmony" could also be the story of Elton's courtship with music.

"Harmony" closes the album, expressing Elton's lifelong love affair with music in only two minutes and forty-six seconds. The brief time frame is packed with luscious indicators of the harmony to which he avows his undying devotion. Elton's piano and Nigel's drumming, perfectly in sync here, and Del Newman's orchestral arrangement, provide a cushion for the pianist's affectionate melody and vocal. The band's backing vocals lend the music a fanciful quality and, in the last, drawn-out note, further illustrate how Elton and harmony are for keeps.

The album also has two up-tempo ballads, soft songs that are faster paced, though not fast enough to cause an onset of dance fever. The first, "This Song Has No Title," is a woeful reflection by Bernie on the apparent meaninglessness of life. "Take me to the garrets where the artists have died,/show me the courtrooms where the judges have lied," Bernie writes. "Let me drink deeply from the water and the wine,/light colored candles in dark dreary mines." The contradictions of life make the world a directionless place—hence, "This Song Has No Title."

Elton whispers the verses with an intimacy not heard since his "Your Song" demo. During the chorus, he sings with himself, urging the world to turn faster so that some conclusion may be reached ("If we're all going somewhere let's get there soon"). "This Song Has No Title" contains the folkiness of "Hymn 2000" and "Lady What's Tomorrow" from *Empty Sky*, but sounds more basic, since Elton plays every instrument: acoustic piano, farfisa organ (also heard on "Crocodile Rock"), electric piano, and mellotron. Elton would look back proudly on his keyboard versatility here. His mellotron, which he explores with more depth than in "Daniel," accompanies the narrator as he witnesses the inexplicable travails of humanity.

The second up-tempo ballad is "Grey Seal," a re-creation of the B-side to "Rock and Roll Madonna." In Bryan Forbes's documentary of Elton John, still in progress at the time, we see Elton at his piano at the chateau, fooling around with the broken chord exercises that quickly turn into the new opening for this song. Here again, Elton experiments with multiple keyboards, though his band also contributes to the rollicking tempo that almost qualifies "Grey Seal" as a rock number. Together, they thrash their way through this essentially introspective song. The new, raucous conclusion, which was tacked on and not part of the original

1970 version, successfully celebrates the omniscience of the seal, who knows more about life than the frustrated student who "farmed in schools that were so worn and torn."

Goodbye Yellow Brick Road also contains a number of panoramic ballads, each painting a broad, sweeping musical landscape. Elton had written such ballads for past albums: *Elton John* has "First Episode at Hienton," *Madman Across the Water* has "Tiny Dancer" and "Indian Sunset," and *Don't Shoot Me* has "Blues for Baby and Me." It is only right that *Goodbye Yellow Brick Road*, which sums up Elton's musical accomplishments to this point, would also include four highly memorable panoramic ballads: the title track, "I've Seen That Movie Too," "Sweet Painted Lady," and "The Ballad of Danny Bailey (1909–34)."

Bernie once remarked that the album's title track contains references to himself and Elton.[7] Listeners must figure out exactly what he meant by that. The song tells the story of a young hopeful's disenchantment with a promised "Emerald City"—a land of opportunity, a town where troubles wash away. Instead, the youth is exploited for his talents and decides to abandon this place of vanquished dreams by taking the "yellow brick road" back home, where his future really lies. The song finds him telling off the person who triggered this profound disappointment: "You know you can't hold me forever,/I didn't sign up with you./I'm not a present for your friends to open,/this boy's too young to be singing the blues."

"Goodbye Yellow Brick Road" contains numerous reference points. Bernie certainly had more than his share of disappointments prior to meeting Elton. During their earliest days together, he and Elton were unhappily trying to be Engelbert Humperdinck–style commercial songwriters. The song is also a thinly veiled reference to Judy Garland. Intriguingly, an album by an artist who had not yet gone public about his sexuality contained songs about two icons for the gay community: Marilyn Monroe and Judy Garland. (True, heterosexual Bernie wrote the lyrics, but he often wrote with Elton in mind.)

As with the melodies for many of Elton's greatest songs, this one is strikingly visual. Like some graceful winged creature, it glides over the scene of the malcontent who retreats to the yellow brick road, finally swooping downward as descending chords portray his grudging steps homeward. This melody, so ably interpreted by all the band's instruments, the orchestration, and the singular backing vocals, makes for an unexampled musical sojourn.

The second panoramic ballad, "I've Seen That Movie Too," is a different sort of reference to Hollywood, the lyrics supplanting the popular saying "You can't pull the wool over my eyes" with a similar admonition, "I've seen that movie, too." Here, a romantic relationship has gone sour because of a partner's infidelity. The wronged lover knows what's going on ("You can tell by the lines I'm reciting,/that I've seen that movie too"). The music is chilling. Elton's jazz-lounge piano seems to emanate from some nightclub with a cutting draft, his melody an arctic criticism of the unfaithful lover, his vocal so cold that icicles could hang from it.

The third panoramic ballad, "Sweet Painted Lady," is set in a port city, where sailors on leave search for a good time. The proprietor of a boarding house announces to the delight of the hormonally charged young men, "If the boys all behave themselves here/well there's pretty young ladies and beer in the rear." Although this and other songs on *Goodbye Yellow Brick Road* would encourage charges of misogyny, Bernie sympathetically portrays the prostitutes. A young sailor admits, "Many have used her and many still do."

The music for "Sweet Painted Lady" looks at the flip side of the story Bernie tells, as do so many of Elton's compositions. The lyrics seem to recount the ostensibly meaningless, hapless lives of the prostitutes, but the music's cheery, jazz-hall demeanor and creamy vocal emphasize the hope that some of the sailors have affection for their brief mistresses. Maybe there is something to be gained all the way around.

Another tale of the illicit is the foundation of *Goodbye Yellow Brick Road*'s final panoramic ballad, "The Ballad of Danny Bailey (1909–34)," in which Bernie brought his fascination with the American West and South closer to the present time. "Bailey," a fictional Kentucky bootlegger and remnant of the waning days of Prohibition—loosely based on the exploits of Pretty Boy Floyd—got into trouble with the law, and a lot of other people, too. A hero in the Kentucky hills until he was killed by "some punk with a shotgun," his admirers sadly acknowledge that whatever glory he once had is now a thing of the past ("We're running short of heroes/back up here in the hills/without Danny Bailey/we're gonna have to break up our stills").

The music begins quietly, as Elton proclaims Bailey's death in voice and doom-laden piano bass notes. The drums, bass, guitar, and some ingeniously odd backing vocals join Elton's honky-tonk piano chords and, enveloped in a tempo emulating the ebb and flow of Bailey's own fortunes, the singer recounts the local legend and the sad ending to Bailey's short-lived fame. Residents of the hills seem to be paying their respects to their hero in the lengthy instrumental finale. Elton's sprightly rolled chords and syncopated rhythms accompany the funeral procession as a breathy orchestral arrangement suggests an aerial view of the mourners.

A third group of songs on the album can be characterized as eccentric, up-tempo songs—non-ballads that catch the ear with their picturesque individualism but are not fast enough to be considered rock'n'roll. Of these, one stands out as another unprecedented musical exploration and among the most fervently anticipated of Elton's concert staples: "Bennie and the Jets."

"Bennie" just doesn't sound like anything else Elton had done before or since. Bernie has explained that it is about a futuristic rock'n'roll band made up of identical-looking female David Bowie types. Elton has said that it's a "send-up of the glitter rock thing."[8] But who really cares about the lyrics? They may as well be gibberish. The music still encourages frightening paroxysms of joy with its opening notes, and what follows is a phantasmagorical musical experience.

"Bennie" resembles a classical march, but veers sharply off the beaten path. Starting with taped applause creatively inserted by Gus Dudgeon, the applause merges into an infectious, single clap, stressing the syncopated beat that Elton has set up with a teasing piano chord, which itself takes on continuity. Backed by a brew of perky drumming and smooth bass lines, Elton shouts the melody as it alternates between Tin Pan Alley, big band humor à la "Chattanooga Choo Choo" or "Three Little Fishies," and sweaty 1960s soul, the latter particularly evident in the funny falsetto he adopts toward the end. Numerous submelodies fight for attention: the syncopated jazz piano solos in the middle, the ricocheting piano chords at the end during the extended falsetto "Bennie" chorus, and the electronic duel between Elton's organ and Davey's electric guitar during the same chorus.

Less musically distinguished, but just as idiosyncratic, is "Jamaica Jerk-Off." After it was written, Elton and Bernie wondered if they should change the title to "Jamaica Jerk" or "Jamaica Twist." "People would probably take it ['Jamaica Jerk-Off'] the wrong way and think we're having a go at Jamaica," Bernie worried.[9] But the original name stuck. It portrays Jamaicans as carefree, a dichotomy between travel brochures and reality that was probably the point of the lyrics. In Bernie's satire, written with Jamaican inflection in mind, all the local people do is dance to music.

Elton had never written a calypso tune before "Jamaica Jerk-Off." He linked the melody to Caribbean rhythms, yielding a festive, sunny romp built on carousel-style organ chords (which he called "putrid"[10]) and a rhythm section that proved as flexible as its pianist. Added to the joyous instrumentation are his taut upper-register vocalizing and inane "vocal interjections" by one Prince Rhino, undoubtedly Elton himself.

The final song from this category is "Social Disease," which, with its 1920s vaudevillian melody and New Orleans jazz elements, would have been just right for a *Honky Chateau, Volume II.* The song is a musical party, with Elton's saloon piano and Davey's hillbilly banjo, although, judging from Bernie's words, Elton could just as easily have written a depressing blues song. The lyrics tell of an alcoholic who pays his rent with sexual favors and liquor. As the song begins, we hear the sound of birds singing and a dog barking, painting a picture of economic decay that recalls the trailer park in "Roy Rogers," but could as easily be a low-income neighborhood in the English countryside ("I get bombed for dinner time and tea"). Here again, Elton's music examines the other side of the lyrics' overt meaning. What a desolate life this carrier of a social disease has—yet he manages to live it up and squeeze the few ounces of pleasure out of it that are available.

Goodbye Yellow Brick Road also has four rock'n'roll rave-ups, something Elton hadn't done as much of in past years. During the seminal, post-*Empty Sky* phase of

Elton's career, he was unlikely to write straightforward rock in light of Bernie's moody, introspective lyrics. Heavy orchestration on such albums as *Elton John* and *Madman,* and the country-and-western theme on *Tumbleweed,* also made this sort of rock unlikely. But after the advent of Elton's more band-oriented sound, he was likelier to record raucous rock numbers (witness "Hercules" and "Elderberry Wine") that capture his live performing prowess more effectively than most of his Buckmaster-era recordings.

The first of the album's rock'n'roll rave-ups is "Dirty Little Girl," a song that continues the tradition of Bernie's interest in malcontents and misfits. It is another song that provoked claims of Bernie's misogyny, though, as in other songs with distasteful characters, the voice isn't Bernie's but that of a loathsome man who despises a possibly homeless woman who hangs around outside his house. Whatever the reason for her poor appearance and bad luck, the man just wants her to disappear.

Elton's music, a clanking cacophony executed in lively fashion by all the band members, is as unkind as the man, so protective of his property and delicate sensibilities. With Elton's rough-throated rendition of a harsh melody, his abrupt mellotron solo, and the dissonant hard-rock vibrations of Davey's guitar, the song would grate on the eardrums if not for the undeniable groove initially set up by the leaping, "Leslie" speaker-distorted piano chords and the lively vocal tidbits ("Oh, she do!" and "Dirty, dirty, dirty!") that Elton throws in, coaxing the listener to sing along.

The second rock'n'roll rave-up is "All the Girls Love Alice," which follows "Dirty Little Girl." The song reflects on the short life of "Alice," a sixteen-year-old private school student (Bernie writes "spawn of a public school," but in Britain, a public school is the same as an American private school), who was "raised to be a lady by the golden rule." She found that she "couldn't get it on with the boys on the scene," and began keeping company with lesbians, soon managing to lure "young girls" away from their husbands and into her bed.

Bernie's lyrics approach homophobia at times. "It's like acting in a movie when you've got the wrong part," for example, suggests that lesbianism is "wrong." When he asks, "Who could you call your friends down in Soho?/One or two middle-aged dykes in a Go-Go," he disparages the character of her companions. And the teenage Alice ends up dead, a fate that some commentators believe has too often been dealt gay characters in popular fiction. Assuredly, Bernie did not intend this reading. After all, his songwriting partner was gay and he would not have countenanced anti-gay lyrics.

Behind the rock energy in "Alice" we see Elton's different reading of the girl's predicament: as a victim mixed up with shadowy figures who prey upon fearful, desperate young rebels. The song begins with one of Elton's most unforgettable piano riffs, adapted by Davey for his electric guitar, some booming bass by Dee, and the rattlesnake tambourine technique of a returning musician, Ray Cooper. Elton's hortatory melody segues into a baleful chorus into which Dave Hentschel's Arp synthesizer intervenes with a deep-throated horn effect, suggesting brewing danger. Kiki Dee makes her first guest appearance on an Elton John album, taking up backing vocal duties, her spirited "hey, hey, hey" segments signaling Alice's uncertain but outwardly brave facade. Special effects run rampant in this song; Nigel is responsible for car noises.

The third of the album's rock'n'roll rave-ups, "Your Sister Can't Twist but She Can Rock'n'Roll," immediately follows "Dirty Little Girl" and "Alice," telling of a blues-obsessed youngster turned on to rock'n'roll by a friend's sixteen-year-old sister. This song is the heir apparent to "Crocodile Rock," harkening back to late 1950s, early 1960s, fun-loving rock'n'roll. But distinguishing it from the music of that period, and even from "Crocodile Rock," is its rushed tempo. "It's so ridiculous," Elton said, cheerily. "Eric Lustbader said he didn't think we'd played it, that it was speeded up, but it wasn't."[11] "Your Sister Can't Twist" also doubles as a surfing song, as the Beach Boys's Bruce Johnston suggested.[12] Elton made a surprise replacement, subbing in the word "surf" for "twist" toward the end.

He played farfisa organ on the song, just as he had on "Crocodile Rock," and acoustic piano. "I can't play organ, I'm the worst," Elton still insisted. "I just love messing around with shitty organ sounds and things like that. I mean, the organ sounds like pure Freddy Cannon 'Palisades Park.'"[13] And, in fact, he does lift a line from that well-known organ riff mid-song.

"Your Sister Can't Twist" segues into the marginally slower "Saturday Night's Alright for Fighting." This concert staple has gotten closer than any other of Elton's songs to that libidinous ideal that every rock band seeks to achieve. It is also the first quintessentially English song that Bernie ever attempted to write, an English drinking song ("It's seven o'clock and I want to rock/wanna get a belly full of beer"). In general, he had in mind the aimless youth of the English working class ("I'm a juvenile product of the working class/whose best friend floats in the bottom of a glass").

Elton recently admitted that "Saturday Night's Alright" is not a "typical piano number." He remembers that it was "so hard to record. . . . In the end the band played it first and I put the piano on afterwards. It was the first song I'd ever done standing up, I actually sang the number just leaping around the studio going crazy."[14] Nevertheless, one only has to hear Elton perform this song by himself, as he did later in the 1970s, to acknowledge that though it may not be a "typical piano number," he not only wrote it as a piano number but makes it one in his live performances.

Many have said that "Saturday Night's Alright" owes its sound to the Stones, although on the 1991 *Two Rooms* tribute album it was the Who—not the Stones— who performed it in tribute to Elton and Bernie. In the accompanying video, Roger Daltry said that it's a Who kind of song. Writing in *Circus* magazine in December 1973, Steve Demorest remarked that the song imitated the music of English glitter rock group Slade[15], known for songs like "Take Me Bak 'Ome," "Mama Weer All

Crazee Now," and "Gudbuy T'Jane." But "Saturday Night's Alright" can't be an imitation of the Stones, the Who, *and* Slade. If it sounds like all three, then it doesn't really sound like any of them, and is just a great Elton John rock number.

Any Elton John album can boast diversity of material, and *Goodbye Yellow Brick Road* is no exception, ranging from the irreverently un-serious "Saturday Night's Alright" to the grieving twofer "Funeral for a Friend/Love Lies Bleeding," which opens the two-record set. The twofer actually started out as two songs. "Funeral for a Friend" was written as an instrumental dirge. "I got very down one day," Elton said in 1976, explaining that he wrote music he would have liked at his own funeral.[16] "I'm hung up on things like that," he said. "I really like tearful, plodding music."[17] More notable than his affinity for sad music was his sudden desire to write music without lyrics, something he had only rarely attempted since his first days with Bernie. Ultimately, it seemed an appropriate coupling, attaching wordless music about the permanent loss of a friend to "Love Lies Bleeding," a unique rock number that tells about the loss of a love through the vagaries of the rock'n'roll lifestyle.

The two-part musical odyssey starts with Dave Hentschel's most distinguished contribution to Elton's music: the Arp synthesizer opening that begins with the dull sound of wind broken by a lonely, fog-enveloped train whistle, perhaps a background aural experience for someone at a sparsely attended graveside service. Hentschel's synthesizer then transforms into a musical instrument, integrating the melodies of several songs on *Goodbye Yellow Brick Road*—"Candle in the Wind," the title track, and "The Ballad of Danny Bailey." As this fades, Elton's piano introduction to "Funeral for a Friend" emerges, with three distinct musical sections probably representing the gamut of emotions felt by mourners at the service.

"Funeral for a Friend" leads into the bitter "Love Lies Bleeding," an unparalleled feat of rock'n'roll: an adult rocker. The jilted rock'n'roller in the song only has words of stunned misery for his runaway love. "The roses in the window box/have tilted to one side," he cries. "Everything about this house/was born to grow and die." This could easily have been a bluesy, weepy ballad, but instead Elton composed an ultramelodious rock number.

Elton has always had a knack for assigning notable melodies to loud rock riffs. On "Elderberry Wine," he took this a step further with an aggressively up-tempo but sweet commentary on a happy past. The melodically more complex "Alice" establishes a bridge between the maturing "Elderberry Wine" and the mature "Love Lies Bleeding," but misses the mark of an adult rocker with its gossipy lyrics and sly but repetitive chord patterns. But on "Love Lies Bleeding," the melody cuts deeply into the lyrics and underlying instrumentation. One of many high points is Elton's piano interlude, a waterfall of notes met with a flutelike synthesizer solo by Hentschel. "Love Lies Bleeding" is not a rock'n'roll fist-raiser, but a solemn, if noisy, reflection, and the perfect companion to "Funeral for a Friend."

The seventeen songs on *Goodbye Yellow Brick Road* represent another milestone in Elton's career, both summarizing all that had gone before and breaking new ground. If it had been a single album instead of a double, it might not have achieved this dual feat. And in fact, the album almost wasn't released as a double. As early as the spring, Elton was toying with the idea of two records coming out simultaneously.[18] "I must say I was sort of worried," Elton said a year later. "Not that the stuff wasn't good, but about whether people would be ready for a double album from me. I was worried about the price."[19] MCA Records convinced him that the two-record set was the way to go,[20] a decision that would be vindicated many times over.

"GONNA SET THIS DANCE ALIGHT"[21]

BRITISH MUSIC FANS got their first taste of the new album when "Saturday Night's Alright for Fighting" was released as a single on June 29, 1973. "Daniel" had been off the singles chart for a couple of months, and British listeners needed something new to keep their interest piqued in the latest teen idol.

It would be another Top 10 hit for Elton in Britain, entering the chart on July 7, 1973 and peaking at number 7. On the down side, its nine-week chart life was the shortest of all his British charted singles except for "Honky Cat," which never got near the Top 10. In the United States, since "Daniel" would remain in *Billboard*'s Top 10 until almost the end of June, it would not have been wise to release another single so soon; MCA waited until "Daniel" had been out of the Top 10 for three weeks. On August 4, 1973, "Saturday Night's Alright" debuted at number 74, and entered the Top 40 the following week. Notably, it never made the Top 10, stalling at number 12 and becoming Elton's first single since "Tiny Dancer" to fall short of expectations. Hard as it may be to believe today, "Saturday Night's Alright" was likely too combative a rock'n'roll song for Top 40 radio.

The summer of 1973 was also filled with other activities. Elton and his coproducer, sound engineer Clive Franks, were putting the finishing touches on Kiki Dee's debut album for Rocket Records, though the Rocket onslaught had already begun. The August 16, 1973 issue of *Rolling Stone* featured a full-page advertisement for three new Rocket Records releases: Mike Silver's *Troubadour*, Longdancer's *If It Was So Simple*, and Davey Johnstone's first, and only, solo album, *Smiling Face*.

Recorded over a period of nine days in April and June 1973, and mixed in August, Kiki's *Loving and Free* should have been the springboard for a promising talent. The former Pauline Matthews and Bradford, England native was nineteen days older than Elton but had received only sporadic recognition. She was discovered at age sixteen by Dusty Springfield's manager, who helped her obtain a recording contract with Fontana Records. Initially, she was to be Kinky Dee, sort of a combination of "Kookie" and "Sandra Dee," but her promoters settled on Kiki to give her a Continental mystique. She recorded an album and some singles for the label, and was made to sound just like Dusty Springfield, but didn't make a name for herself with Fontana.[22]

In 1969, Kiki got what seemed a real break, and an acknowledgment of where her talents lay. She signed with Tamla-Motown, the London branch of which John Reid would soon be heading. But success was still far off. An album, *Great Expectations*, did not commercially live up to its title. A single for the label, "Love Makes the World Go Round," spent three weeks on *Billboard*'s Hot 100, peaking at number 87 on March 20, 1971.

Kiki's Elton connection actually went back a few years, to a time when they were both struggling for recognition and performing odd musical jobs. "I was in an elevator when I met him for the first time," she said later. "He was doing some backing vocals on a show I was doing—it was a bunch of people doing oldies."[23] She had other, real meetings with Elton, at John Reid's Motown offices following the musician's first big success. Later, Kiki brought Elton demo tapes of the first two songs she had written, "Loving and Free" and "Sugar on the Floor." "Usually, the first two are so embarrassing that you never want to hear them again," Elton mused, but he believed Kiki had nothing to be embarrassed about.[24] It was only natural, after all this, that she be among the first to sign with Rocket. "It was his belief in me that got me started in '73," she recalled.[25]

Loving and Free is a good folk-rock album with exemplary Kiki Dee vocals. Dee wrote four of the tracks (Elton and Bernie contributed two), including those first two songs she had ever written—the Anne Murray-ish title track, and the eloquent "Sugar on the Floor," which Elton would later record himself. *Loving and Free* is occasionally reminiscent of Elton's early efforts. He plays on seven of the songs, and one or more members of his own band can be heard on all ten.

The album's pastoral "Amoureuse," cowritten by Gary Osborne, of MCA recording act Vigrass & Osborne, would be Kiki's first hit anywhere. On November 10, 1973, it entered the British singles chart and peaked at number 13, with a strong chart run of thirteen weeks. It was Rocket Records' first triumph.

"ELECTRIC BOOTS, A MOHAIR SUIT"[26]

THAT SUMMER, Elton and his Rocket Records business partners launched the new label in Los Angeles, at Universal Studios' Western set. Still fresh-faced and with barely a release to its name, Rocket Records' party was attended by MCA executives (Rocket recordings were being released through MCA in the United States), and personalities as diverse as Al Kooper, Wolfman Jack, Bobbie Gentry, and the recently signed Hudson Brothers.

Meanwhile, Elton was already planning some of the visuals that would greet concertgoers for his summer/fall U.S. tour and, in particular, the lucky sixteen thousand or so who would be attending his Hollywood Bowl concert on September 7.

Part of these visuals would be his burgeoning collection of unusual eyewear. By the spring of 1973, Elton owned about twenty-five pairs of glasses, none of which were that outrageous. The frames were larger than average, sporting interesting shapes with tinted lenses in one or more colors, but they didn't obscure his face, nor were they the most eye-catching part of his wardrobe. By the summer/fall tour, that had changed. Elton was a client of a Los Angeles-based shop called Optique Boutique, and began establishing himself as entrepreneur Dennis Roberts's most inventive customer. One new pair had windshield-wiper frames that required a special battery pack; another had flip-down window shade frames. Elton requested one pair with lenses sandwiched between two sets of teeth that would open and close like mouths. The newest addition was about twice as wide as his head, the frames spelling out "Elton" in colored capital letters, with fifty-seven lightbulbs designed to blink on and off. One of the ever-needed prescription lenses, a square one, was between the "L" and the "T"; a round one rested inside the "O." "This is the most unique pair of glasses ever made in the entire history of the world," Dennis Roberts gloated. "They are optically perfect. They are a masterpiece of electronics and engineering." Roberts said that Elton wanted glasses that reflected what he was—flamboyant.[27]

The wider Elton's audience became, the more he challenged it with his vibrant fashion sense. One could attribute this flamboyance to an ego ballooning out of control, but more likely it was simply that no one could hold him accountable. Elton was the naughty schoolboy who would never be punished for his pranks. His flamboyance was his own humorous brand of rebellion. "Unfortunately, the more people said to me you can't do things, the more I did them," Elton once said.[28]

Elton's fashion aesthetic was also informed by a basically libertarian fashion philosophy (in Bryan Forbes's film, he explained that the reason he liked to color the odd lock of hair was that, quite frankly, people should be able to present themselves as they saw fit), as well as a reaction to his negative physical self-image. "I wasn't the thin rock singer that stood up at the microphone, I was the cuddly person on the piano who was tongue-in-cheek, really," he reflected some fifteen years later.[29] Writing about his August 24, 1973 concert for the *Chicago Tribune*, Lynn Van Matre noted that, underneath the layers of flashy trappings, Elton looked "about as charismatically captivating as the late Wally Cox."[30]

For the summer/fall U.S. tour, Elton emphasized the grand entrance. At most venues, he greeted his screaming legions in one of his capes—maybe a glittery, ruffle-necked number that read "EJ" on the back, or one with enormous musical notes splayed over its flowing folds, his nose weighted down by the blinking "ELTON" glasses. Having made his grand entrance, he would exchange the hefty optical marvels for more comfortable frames and remove his cape to reveal one of many favored outfits, such as a two-piece, glistening red leatherette suit with black and white braid along the seams and musical notes from top to bottom. There was also a light green leatherette suit that announced his first name across the front of the zippered jacket and his middle name, "Hercules," down the left pant leg. Whatever costume he wore, before long it would be zipped down to his waist so that fans could get a full view of his matted body hair.

"LADIES AND GENTLEMAN, PLEASE WELCOME THE BIGGEST, GIGANTIC, MOST COLOSSAL . . ."[31]

AT THE HOLLYWOOD BOWL concert on Friday night, September 7, 1973, John Reid told Robert Hilburn, "He [Elton] has been looking forward to this show for weeks. He wanted it to be a big party for everyone."[32] *Deep Throat's* Linda Lovelace acted as master of ceremonies; uptight before a crowd of sixteen thousand that included plenty of Hollywood glitterati, she explained that the purpose of the evening was to inject glamour back into show business. Elton must have somehow anticipated the wave of nostalgia for the lavishness of old Hollywood that would be unleashed by 1974's *That's Entertainment!* Behind Lovelace was a 65- by 28-foot backdrop of a caricatured Elton, unmistakably clothed in Fred Astaire's trademark attire of top hat, tails, and cane. The extravagant stage set offered five pianos, each painted a different color, as well as palm trees and a stairway that cried out for tap dancing. Lovelace introduced myriad "celebrities" (really celebrity impersonators) who made entrances down the stairway: Queen Elizabeth, Groucho Marx, Elvis Presley, Mae West, the Beatles, Frankenstein's monster, and others.

"Ladies and gentlemen," Linda Lovelace then shouted, with all the Hollywood grandeur she could muster, "Please welcome the biggest, gigantic, most colossal . . . Elton John!" With the odd assortment of faux celebrities looking on, Elton appeared at the top of the stairway, opened his arms wide as if to catch the audience's delirious reaction, and trotted down the stairs. This he did with some difficulty in light of his chosen costume for the night, a brilliantly white cowboy suit with silver around the waist and collar and a large matching hat. Feather boas bobbed from his shoulders, the seams of his pant legs, and even the rim of his hat as he made his way across the stage. At the same time, all five piano lids opened, displaying the letters of his first name and liberating four hundred white doves. Finally at his piano, Elton, now joined by his band, commenced "Elderberry Wine."

After the show, even Bernie Taupin experienced the adulation reserved for teen idols. As he walked toward his limousine, hundreds of girls ran in his direction. "I was looking behind me to see who they were looking at and just walked straight into them," he said. "Then suddenly I was getting grabbed and kissed. . . . It was all very strange and I was very scared, and by the time I drove away I was dazed and wondering, did I enjoy that or didn't I?" The answer was yes.[33]

On this night, as on other nights during the tour, Elton and his band really cooked as a musical unit. On such songs as "Honky Cat," "Daniel," and "Crocodile

Rock," they played as if united by some force that lifted the music onto a higher plane. On the other hand, Elton's piano playing had become less adventurous. It was still muscular, but he took fewer improvisational chances. Subconsciously, he may have been responding to his new audience of teenage fans, who would not have had the patience for extended piano ruminations.

Elton did acknowledge his older fans on a number that he must have trotted out to please himself. Breaking from the otherwise hit-laden, up-tempo shows, he allowed for an ambitious "Madman Across the Water" interlude. Typically engendering only polite applause, and probably taken by the teen screamers as an opportunity to use the facilities, "Madman" teasingly opened with a kaleidoscopic classical introduction that worked its way into the more familiar opening chords heard on record. From there, he traveled great musical distances, surveying percussive phases, George Shearing–style lyrical phrases that included ticklish waterfalls of notes, staccato jazz-club rhythms, rock'n'roll tempos, and classical marches. It was everything that Elton's teenage fans did not come to hear. And there was no telling how long these piano explorations might take: The version of "Madman" played at October's Bloomington, Indiana concert lasted twenty minutes.

Two other piano highlights on this tour were provided by, oddly enough, "Saturday Night's Alright" and "Honky Tonk Women." In Bryan Forbes's film, Elton is illuminated in a ghoulish light during "Saturday Night's Alright" as he plays his chunky, brisk chords while perched on his knees at the piano. As he pounds the ivories, back arched, head thrown back, and mouth agape in the dimly lit shadows, he looks like a character from a science fiction movie. The tour's "Honky Tonk Women" finale was every bit as exciting—a hair-raising, Little-Richard-meets-"Burn Down the Mission" kind of number that should have pleased Elton's old and new fans alike.

Even amid the music and spectacle of this tour, Elton was not above feeling overawed himself. One night in October, he boarded *Starship One*, the chartered jet used for travel from city to city, to find a surprise guest waiting for him in the lounge—Stevie Wonder, who had just finished recovering from injuries sustained in a near-fatal car accident. "There were a lot of people going up to Boston with us, and all I really wanted to do was to rest in the front of the plane," Elton remembered. "Someone kept telling me that I had to go into the back to listen to this terrific cocktail pianist who'd come aboard. That was the last thing I wanted to listen to." He even suggested that the "cocktail pianist" be removed, but was finally persuaded to enter the lounge.[34]

It was not the first time he and Stevie Wonder had met, though it was the first time they had greeted each other as peers. But despite the fact that Elton was now a musician among musicians, he was still reverential when they shook hands. At Elton's Boston concert, Wonder joined him onstage with another set of keyboards for the final encore, which included "Honky Tonk Women." Not long afterwards, Elton said the piano sound had been much fuller during the show's encore and that this demonstrated a need for, of all things, another keyboard player in the band.[35]

Elton's U.S. tour that season was not all flights of fancy and dumbfounded wonder. At his September 30, 1973 show in Baltimore, Elton got into trouble when trying to win for his fans the right to get up out of their seats and dance where they pleased, telling security "You should be home minding your babies."[36] The guards then disappeared from sight, resulting in about five hundred concertgoers, as Elton later put it, joining the band onstage. In 1980, during his only appearance on Johnny Carson's *The Tonight Show*, Elton remarked that he could understand the need for security at concerts, but wished the guards wouldn't enjoy exercising their power quite so much. It would not be his last run-in with concert security personnel.

"I WAS PLAYING ROCK'N'ROLL AND YOU WERE JUST A FAN"[37]

ON SEPTEMBER 7, 1973, "Goodbye Yellow Brick Road," the single, was released in Britain, providing yet another preview of an album that still had not been shipped. The single charted on September 29, 1973, cresting at number 6, and spent sixteen weeks on the chart, the longest of any of his singles. It was released on October 16 in the United States. The top debut on *Billboard*'s Hot 100 on October 27, 1973 at number 62, it eventually occupied the number 2 spot for three weeks, a stint that ended on December 29 when it slipped to number 5. The single spent seventeen weeks on the Hot 100, taking the song's ubiquitous presence on American Top 40 radio well into 1974, when, in January, it became Elton's second gold single (platinum certification would come twenty-one years later).

The long-awaited release of *Goodbye Yellow Brick Road*, the album, in between the release dates of the British and American singles and during Elton's popular summer/fall U.S. tour, solidified his place in the highest popular music echelon. He had already teased British audiences with selections from the album during his winter/spring 1973 tour, and had been tantalizing U.S. audiences with some of its songs for nearly two months. It was time for the real test.

Released on October 5, 1973, the album garnered many critical accolades, although as with his earlier albums the acclaim was not unanimous. In *Rolling Stone*, which had seldom applauded his records, writer Stephen Davis called the album "too fat to float" and "artistically doomed by pretension." He declared "All the Girls Love Alice" and "Saturday Night's Alright for Fighting" the only keepers, suggesting that the album might be salvageable as a single record.[38] Robert Christgau graded the album a "C plus" and asserted that it was "at least three sides too long."[39] Years later, while defending the album's length, Elton stopped short of characterizing it as his best record. "It was a high in the sense that it was a double album that succeeded," he said in 1980, adding that the album could have spawned ten hit singles. But Elton rejected the suggestion that it represented his artistic apex. "As a high point in my career as a musician, I would probably say no," said the artist who eschewed looking backward.[40]

Elton soon found that the album wasn't too long for the public: Fans snapped it up like they had never snapped up an Elton album before. Debuting on *Billboard*'s Top LPs chart on October 20, 1973 in the United States, it went gold within one week of release and went on to be the top seller in November and December, spending eight weeks at number 1 as Elton's third chart-topping album in a row. The album also spent forty-three weeks in the Top 40 of the Top LPs, and nearly two years in total on the chart. In Britain, it entered the album chart on November 3, becoming Elton's second chart-topper in that country, and spent eighty-four weeks on the chart altogether.

"THANK YOU FOR THE YEAR"[41]

THE YEAR 1973 WAS SHAPING UP as an incredible one for Elton. With four hit singles and two spectacularly successful hit albums, he was leaving his competitors in the dust. Despite this success, he still jumped if someone needed him to do a session, as Jackson Browne did. "I think there are probably better session pianists around than me," Elton had said with characteristic modesty the previous spring. "My name is valuable, but there's always Billy Preston, and if I was Ringo Starr I'd rather have Billy Preston playing on his record than me. I'd rather have Nicky Hopkins, probably, because . . . [he's] so good. They can fit in so easily."[42]

When the publishing contract Elton and Bernie had with DJM ended, the two launched Big Pig Music on November 10, 1973.[43] Dick James would thenceforth have no right to their new compositions, and Elton's DJM recording contract would only last another two years. However, one song that made it under the wire for DJM was the Christmas single "Step into Christmas," Elton's first and last of that genre. It was written and recorded in November at London's Trident Studios and released on November 26, 1973 in both Britain and the United States. Elton said, cheerily, "We were going to make a semi-joke single and give it away like the Beatles used to do, but then Taupin said why don't we make a good one and spoilt everything."[44]

Elton and Bernie intended "Step Into Christmas" to be a thank-you card for the great year their fans had given them. "Welcome to my Christmas song/I'd like to thank you for the year," it starts. "Take care in all you do next year/and keep smiling through the days./If we can help to entertain you,/oh, we will find the ways." Elton has said that the music recalls Phil Spector's Ronettes, and his vocal does have that honey-sweet, chimes-tinged sound that characterized their style. But mostly, the music recalls the holiday season. The sound of sleigh bells is heard throughout, and even Elton's piano chords are touched by holiday tinsel.

The single was a minor success in Britain, entering the singles chart on December 8, 1973 and peaking at number 24. In the United States, it debuted on *Billboard*'s Christmas Singles chart on the same day and reached number 1 later that month. Singles on this chart received no Hot 100 recognition; if they had, Elton surely would have had another Top 40 hit. "Step into Christmas" has been a radio staple every holiday season since.

"IT'S NICE TO HAVE YOU HERE"[45]

AS "STEP INTO CHRISTMAS" dominated holiday airplay on both sides of the Atlantic in December 1973, Elton and the band toured Britain. With them was percussionist Ray Cooper. A purportedly mild-mannered man offstage, Ray had a gaunt face and piercing eyes. Onstage, he looked like some kind of deranged creature, and moved like a lunatic. But his mastery of all percussion instruments ensured that he was not there just to command the visual element Elton claimed to have relinquished.

Despite his obvious talents, Ray had had difficulty finding a niche. A stint in repertory theater had led nowhere, though it must have influenced his dramatically unsettling stage bearing. He had played in jazz ensembles, with such notables as Maynard Ferguson, as well as in theater orchestras, session work (including work on several of Elton's albums), and had eventually joined the group Blue Mink. Finally, Elton invited him to join his band. "I was very, very surprised—indeed, shocked—to be asked to join the band," Ray later said.[46]

Kiki Dee also joined the tour, as a supporting act with her own five-piece band. The tour was relatively limited, with just over a dozen concerts, most notably at London's Hammersmith Odeon, which boasted three evening shows and an afternoon engagement that had been hastily added to quench the public's thirst for Elton John tickets.

In the middle of the tour, Bryan Forbes's documentary film about Elton, *Elton John and Bernie Taupin Say Goodbye Norma Jean and Other Things*, premiered on Britain's ITV network (ABC broadcast it in the United States on May 12, 1974). Forbes's motivation in making the film was apparently to show the outside world what an unusual, impressive character his friend and subject was. The final product captured the star in all manner of poses, activities, clothing, and philosophical moods, with generous helpings of live footage and candid shots of the writing and recording process behind *Goodbye Yellow Brick Road*.

Out of the glamour, multicolored glasses, explanations by Bernie, and testimonials from Mum, Dick James, and members of the band emerged a portrait of an eccentric of seemingly limitless talents and energy who bore an exceedingly earthy view of himself. Forbes, who narrated the film, described Elton as a "one-off, a true original" and the "legend he [Elton] has always wanted to become." The filmmaker juxtaposed the latter phrase against Elton's self-effacing comment that he would like to become a legend but doubted he ever would. Rather than lay claim to a branch of music, Elton believed his music was an ever-developing phenomenon. To him, it was not what he had done that was important, but what he would be doing. "I'm only twenty-six," he said in the film. "My best work is yet to come." He added, "I'm more interested in the songs I've just written," and declined to trumpet his musicianship.

When Forbes offered, "You can be a superb classical pianist when you want to be," Elton held up his undersized hands and retorted, "They're not pianist's hands, they're midget boxer's hands." He recalled that at the Royal Academy of Music he could barely stretch an octave. He tried to convince Forbes that he could no longer read music. Then he admitted that he could read chord sheets. Finally, he allowed that he could read music, but didn't need to. Even as Elton's popularity approached the stratosphere, he felt compelled to demystify his talents to the point of ignoring their existence.

In fact, Elton's excessive humility started to become a self-fulfilling prophecy during his dozen-odd shows in Britain that November and December. His status as a teen dream was continuing to affect his pianistic aspirations; in Britain, he didn't even fall back on a lengthy "Madman" to please his own musical tastes. An "old" song could barely be found in the set list.

Critic Tony Wilson detected the growing deficiency in Elton's playing in a review of his November 29, 1973 Manchester concert, holding that Elton's current compositions failed to mark an artistic progression. Amid glib comments he managed to notice the real problem: The performance of Elton's songs rarely deviated from their recorded versions. He lauded those rare moments in Manchester when Elton performed songs alone at the piano, an approach that harkened back to the early days of his fame.[47] An incensed fan from Blackley, Manchester later wrote a letter to the editor, rebuking Wilson's assessment of the show: "Elton played for two hours and left Belle Vue in uproar—no one wanted it all to end."[48]

Elton was giving the fans what they wanted, a trend that continued with the Hammersmith Odeon shows. First, he awarded them a visual treat. The piano and stage (decorated with a Christmas tree) were laden in crimson, against the huge backdrop of Elton as Fred Astaire. Neon lights above read "Watford," Elton's favorite soccer team (of which he was an honorary vice president). He paraded in several of his most colorful, sparkly, two-piece outfits, all of which exposed the requisite amount of body hair.

Of the four Hammersmith Odeon shows, it was the second, on December 22, 1973, that was taped by BBC television, to be broadcast Christmas Eve from 10 P.M. to midnight, thus attaining immortality, however undeservedly. The broadcast would lead to scores of unauthorized recordings, countless rebroadcasts on both British and U.S. radio, and misled acceptance of the concert as an exemplar of Elton's performing prowess. Not that the show didn't have its high points. Elton sat alone at the piano for a convincingly emotional "This Song Has No Title." And on "I've Seen That Movie Too," his voice rose to the challenge, and he and Davey Johnstone joined forces for a shivering denouement that surpassed the panoramic quality of the original. But overall, the show was another example of Elton's less-than-adventurous approach to playing, exacerbated by a terrible cold that affected his voice and sapped his energy considerably. During an instrumental of "Rudolf the Red-Nosed Reindeer," an ideal pub number if there ever was one, Elton's playing more closely resembled that of Bent Fabric, the Danish pianist who made "Alley Cat" famous in 1962, than the unique combination of New Orleans back-room piano, fire-breathing barrelhouse, and classical elegance that he had first brought to the United States less than three and a half years earlier. He joked, "I'm available for weddings, Christmas parties. . . ."

Numerous unauthorized two-record sets sprang up after the radio broadcast. But much better listening, overall, resulted from Elton's Christmas Day Radio One appearance on John Peel's *Top Gear*. Elton was invited to do comedic pub-style takes on popular Christmas songs, playing on an upright "jangle" piano. Recalling this hilarious session some thirteen years later on Radio One's "Elton John at the Beeb," *Top Gear* producer John Walters said that he had initially thought inviting Elton on the show for this purpose would be "inappropriate," since he was seen as a "serious artistic figure." But when Walters watched Forbes's *Say Goodbye Norma Jean*, he learned of Elton's early pub piano roots. "This is his real culture. Not open skylines, or ballads of Jesse James," Walters said.[49]

The producer found, to his delight, that Elton was "very adaptable." Walters procured drinks, and he and the others involved with the program stood around Elton and the upright "as one would do in a pub." After the Christmas songs, and against a background of chuckling from his "pub" companions, Elton began a medley of pub standards, then spoofed his own music. Said Walters, "Elton took his most sensitive songs and destroyed them himself."[50] He purposely adopted an obnoxiously nasal voice to sing "Daniel" and "Your Song" in as vile a manner as possible, over a humorously overbearing saloon-style piano accompaniment. Elton still excelled at putting a persuasively different spin on his music, and the music of others. He was still ripe for a musical dare.

One could not be certain in December 1973 whether one would get "Elton John the Inventive Musician" or "Elton John the Teen Idol," but either way, he had racked up impressive sales numbers by year's end, especially in the United States. He, Helen Reddy, and Stevie Wonder were named the most popular recording artists of 1973 by music trade publications *Billboard*, *Cash Box*, and *Record World*. Although Wonder was the top album artist in two of the three publications, Elton was voted the top singles artist by all three magazines.[51]

"I'M GROWING TIRED AND TIME STANDS STILL BEFORE ME" [52]

IN THE FALL OF 1973, Bernie had the title for Elton's next album: *Stinker.* The name didn't stick, but was presciently fitting.

Within days of the Hammersmith Odeon engagement and his appearance on *Top Gear,* Elton and entourage, including new band mate Ray, traveled to Colorado for their first attempt at recording in the United States. The studio was at the Caribou Ranch, owned by Chicago creator and Blood, Sweat, and Tears producer Jim Guercio. It offered fresh Rocky Mountain air and other blessings of nature that should have relaxed Caribou's occupants and brought out their best. That didn't happen.

Elton's schedule was no longer as hectic as it had been before John Reid became his manager, but still left little room for error. He had about ten days in January 1974 to write and record the new album before he and the band were to take off for the Far East; upon his return, he had British and European tours scheduled. Any rest was months down the line. And the childlike enthusiasm he had harbored for music-related activities during his first three years of success had evaporated, at least for now.

The stress Elton was under hindered his ability to act constructively. His mood swings, which he'd had since the beginning, were particularly intrusive at Caribou. "I went through a weird one after writing all the songs, so we lost three days of recording," he said. Also, he and the band had difficulty adjusting to the studio's monitoring systems.[53] In defense of what would become *Caribou,* Elton later posited that the album was meant as a sort of palate cleanser,[54] a kind of pleasant, unassuming sorbet between two spicy main courses—*Goodbye Yellow Brick Road,* and one that was already being cooked up in the minds of the songwriting duo, the autobiographical *Captain Fantastic and the Brown Dirt Cowboy.*

Ironically, part of the blame for the very existence of *Caribou* lay with its immediate predecessor. Elton had hoped that *Goodbye Yellow Brick Road* would count under his DJM contract as two albums. After all, he had toyed with the possibility of releasing it as two collections of songs but had been talked out of the idea by MCA. Since James accepted it only as one album, Elton had to write and record another in quick succession to honor his contract.[55]

Producer Gus Dudgeon made no excuses for the final product. "*Caribou* is a piece of crap, the sound is the worst, the songs are nowhere, the sleeve came out wrong, the lyrics weren't that good, the singing wasn't all there, the playing wasn't great, the production is just plain lousy," he seethed.[56] Dudgeon added some of the album's signature sounds after Elton and the band departed, bringing in the Bay Area rhythm and blues group Tower of Power for horn work, and some vocal luminaries for a little backup singing. Tower of Power was mostly misused; the heat the ensemble generated, rather than keeping the aural atmosphere at a low but persistent boil, nearly burned down a couple of songs, which were weak at the outset.

It is possible to overstate the album's problems. *Caribou* does offer some radiant examples of Elton's and Bernie's best songwriting. Two of its songs—"The Bitch Is Back" and "Don't Let the Sun Go Down on Me"—have, since their recording, barely gotten a rest on the radio or in concert, and deservedly so. And "Don't Let the Sun," the next-to-last song on the album, is arguably the greatest one Elton and Bernie have ever written.

Though there have been better marriages of lyric and melody among Elton's and Bernie's traditional ballads—the tightly written "Candle in the Wind" and, later, "Nikita"—"Don't Let the Sun" carries on in the grand tradition of the Elton John panoramic ballad. Here, he takes the genre steps further with music that sweeps the listener effortlessly along, from the hurtful despair of the opener to the brave, declarative, hopeful chorus. The song's bare parts, purely heard during the verses, delicately brush the listener. Nigel's cymbal complements Elton's opening piano notes, which plead in heartsick descent. Within seconds, the individual notes join for the rumble of prefatory descending chords, and Elton delivers a sweet, lonely vocal of pure misery to match his melody of unbridled sadness. Backed by some chirping acoustic and electric guitar strokes by Davey, Elton sings to someone he has helped and from whom he is now experiencing rejection ("I took a chance and changed your way of life/but you misread my meaning when I met you/closed the door and left me blinded by the light"). The chorus swells into one of the most recognizable anthems, becoming a symphony supported by Del Newman's horn arrangement and the notable backing vocals of the Beach Boys' Carl Wilson and Bruce Johnston, and Toni Tennille. The voices combine with well-timed percussion accents from Ray Cooper and surreptitious mellotron from Dave Hentschel for a collective musical catharsis, a virtual emptying of the soul.

Elton's vocal almost didn't make the final cut untouched. He had not gotten over the funk that had almost prevented him from recording anything at all, and was unusually uncooperative in his first attempts. Dudgeon didn't like his singing and was later tempted, after Elton and the band were gone, to alter it. Fortunately, he changed his mind.

The pianist had apparently had the Beach Boys in mind when he wrote the song, even though, apart from the backing vocals, it sounds nothing like the group's sun and fun. "It is my Beach Boys tribute," Elton told Robert Hilburn years later. "I was always so much influenced by them, especially Brian Wilson."[57] The song is another example of the pianist translating a musical inspiration into his own harmonic language.

The second significant song on *Caribou* is the album's first track, "The Bitch Is Back." The lyrics are among the least focused of Bernie's career, although they do prompt an initial image of a rung climber whose behavior is less controllable the higher on the ladder he gets. "I get high in the evening/sniffing pots of glue," he boasts, but later confusingly claims that he is "stone cold sober as a matter of fact." That the lyrics in "The Bitch Is Back" aren't really about anything isn't surprising;

they are a generalized reference to the man who wrote the music. Bernie later revealed that his then wife Maxine coined the song's recurring phrase in response to one of Elton's notoriously bad moods. "Oh God, the bitch is back!" she exclaimed.[58] The song, in essence, was born. All Bernie had to do was flesh it out.

"The Bitch Is Back" is a testament to Elton's ability to poke fun at himself. He understood that he was the "bitch" and reveled in this role during live performances. Some segments of the gay community have taken the song as a signal of his sexuality. Adam Block, writing for *Ten Percent* two decades after the song was written and recorded, argued that "The Bitch Is Back" and, intriguingly, "Your Song" both functioned during the 1970s as winks in the direction of gay listeners.[59]

"Bitch" also stands as Elton's only song that critic Dave Marsh deemed worthy of inclusion in his book, *The Heart of Rock and Soul: The 1001 Greatest Singles Ever Made.* Otherwise unimpressed with Elton's music, and sloppily misstating Elton's record label and the song's lyrics, he was nevertheless right to describe "The Bitch Is Back" as a "shivering rock and roll brag."[60] "Bitch" isn't an adult rocker like "Love Lies Bleeding," but does have the contagious patterns associated with some of Elton's other rocking melodies, like "Elderberry Wine" and "Crocodile Rock." His deliberately raspy vocal is a perfect companion to Davey's versatile guitar and the strange bleats of Dee's phased "pignose bass." Tower of Power and the backup singers (including Dusty Springfield and Clydie King, a former Raelett) were wise additions to the song, despite the already overwhelming mightiness of its instrumentation.

The promise exhibited by "The Bitch Is Back" and "Don't Let the Sun" spills onto "Ticking," the album's closer. "Ticking" is a fictional account of a young man, strictly brought up by adults unaware of his inner turmoil, who ends up taking the customers in a New York bar hostage, killing fourteen of them. It contains some of Bernie's most engaging lines. He peppers the lyrics with quotes from the boy's elders who had, through the years, continuously missed opportunities to help him: "He's unconcerned with competition, he never cares to win" and "Grow up straight and true blue/run along to bed." While he commits mass murder, the man hears in his head many of these utterances by his parents, his teachers, his priest. When, disarmed, he finally surrenders to police, they shoot him to death ("Oh, you danced in death like a marionette on the vengeance of the law").

Elton's stark arrangement includes only his lead vocal, his overdubbed backup singing, a small amount of Hentschel's Arp synthesizer, and piano playing that gives the term "piano accompaniment" a whole new meaning—lyrical as he sings about the boy's misguided upbringing and the voices in his head, presciently percussive as the drama unfolds. As the situation worsens, Elton unleashes a torrent of notes that puts the listener on edge. He also demonstrates further vocal development with this song, especially in backing vocals that range from squeaking at the upper reaches of his register to bellows from the bottom.

Amazingly, Elton recorded both the lead vocal and piano for "Ticking" at the same time. He later said of trying to record the piano part alone, "I would think so much about the voice that I wouldn't play the piano right." This predicament prompted the unconventional approach of recording both, simultaneously.[61] He played the song as if at a live show, encouraging hope that he was not permanently focused on giving the fans only what they expected of a teen idol (although to be fair, Elton's "solo" playing has always proved infinitely richer than that with a band. The fewer musicians, the more pressure he places on himself to replicate a band sound, and the more splendid his playing becomes).

Only one more song on *Caribou* even remotely measures up to "Ticking," "Don't Let the Sun," and "The Bitch Is Back": "I've Seen the Saucers," an amusing commentary on UFO sightings powered by Elton's manifold melody, lovely singing, and portentous chord progression. Ray's congas and gong, which sounds like an extraterrestrial spaceship alighting on earth, provide extra sparks.

After that, the rest of the album is all downhill. The chief appeal of the remaining songs lies in the charm of Elton's vocals that, by this time, coupled a candy-coated resonance with more technical control than ever before. "Pinky" is a lyrical follow-up to "Mellow," Bernie's exultation of a cozy breakfast in bed with Maxine while the temperature outside their Caribou Ranch cabin plummets. It is romantic, with a vocal by Elton as intimate as a whisper in the ear, although Hentschel's synthesizer, which had worked so well on many of Elton's greatest songs, abrasively intrudes here.

"Grimsby" is a near miss, an unlikely tribute to the inglorious English city of Grimsby. The joke has probably been lost on most non-British listeners, who may have taken literally such lines as "Grimsby, a thousand delights/couldn't match the sweet sights/of my Grimsby./Oh, England you're fair/but there's none to compare/with my Grimsby." Elton usually excels at such tongue-in-cheek efforts, but the melody is hidden by the band's clamorous accompaniment, particularly an over-reliance on Davey's electric guitar, which drowns out Elton's piano. On a July 1974 appearance on BBC television's the *Old Grey Whistle Test*, viewers learned how the song should have sounded. Elton played the song's distinctive chord pattern with a jocularity missing from the recording. Even his booming, rhythmic bass line was funny, assigning a strength and nobility to the unfortunate Grimsby that, according to the composers, the place does not really possess.

Blatantly comical on record, without much else to commend it, is "Solar Prestige a Gammon." Written in a language wholly contrived by the lyricist but based on English words, it strikes back at critics who had been grouchy about Bernie's lyrics in the past. "This is one of my bright ideas that Bernie is going to get crucified for," Elton said, explaining that his idea was inspired by the Beatles' song "Sun King," which includes Italian-sounding nonsense words. "I thought it would be great to write a song with English words that didn't mean a thing, but that sounded fantastic when put together."[62] Thus, Bernie came up with such lines as "Hair ring molassis abounding/common lap kitch sardin a poor floundin."

The musicianship on "Solar Prestige" is superb. Laid over an Italian-style melody, Elton's chummy chords, Dee's thudding bass, and Ray's pealing vibes combine for a lively rush of musical notes. Also significant is Elton's faux operatic singing, coaxed from years of vocal trial and error. Still, "Solar Prestige a Gammon" functions as the musical equivalent of a tasty confection, containing more air than substance.

The silly premises of "Grimsby" and "Solar Prestige a Gammon" give way to a John/Taupin essential, the country-and-western song, a bit of which is present on nearly every Elton John album. *Caribou* has "Dixie Lily," an affectionate look at a Louisiana riverboat on its way to Vicksburg, Mississippi. Though he does award the song some of his most fluid, sunny, honky-tonk piano playing, Elton nevertheless misses the obvious New Orleans cue and fails to sweep the music into the kind of Dixieland encomium that makes songs like "Honky Cat" such treasures.

"You're So Static" is disastrous. Intended to be a "send-up of groovy, trendy, American ladies," as Elton put it,[63] it has a dull, mid-tempo melody superimposed over an incongruous rock'n'roll rhythm, punctuated by Elton's flamenco-esque piano chords. Tower of Power's horns screech indiscriminately over the two mismatched musical parts, splattering brass sounds like enormous paint blots on a canvas. This song, and "Stinker," for which the album was almost named, do not belong on *Caribou* at all.

Elton conceived of "Stinker" as a traditional blues number with some added rock'n'roll vigor. It is entertaining, with the musician's gruff vocal and straightforward blues piano, Davey's scorching blues guitar solo, the loudest bass pumping by Dee yet heard on record, and organ accents by Tower of Power's Chester Thompson. But it fits in too neatly with traditional blues. Elton's music has worked best when it takes components of other musical genres and reworks them into compositions that can exist independently to express his own melodic language. "Stinker" is not born of this compositional approach, and does not succeed.

"BENNIE MAKES THEM AGELESS"[64]

IN THE UNITED STATES, the chart standing of "Goodbye Yellow Brick Road" (the single) had begun falling in January 1974, following its peak of number 2 at the end of 1973. Elton assumed the next single would be "Candle in the Wind," a song of which he was especially proud. And in fact "Candle in the Wind," with "Bennie and the Jets" as the B-side, was released as the single in Britain and elsewhere.

But in North America, the then individualistic spirit in radio programming intervened. According to one account, the Windsor, Ontario AM radio station CKLW added "Bennie and the Jets" to its playlist on its own. CKLW was also heard in Detroit, and the Motor City's soul stations latched on to "Bennie," elevating the song as an album track to the number 1 soul record in town.[65] In another version, told by WJLB-Detroit programming director Jay Butler, WJLB's night disc jockey, Donnie Simpson, broke the song. Just as Simpson was oozing enthusiasm for it, Butler noted that the source album was selling in black record shops. He gave Simpson the go-ahead, and within three days, "Bennie" was the most requested song on WJLB.[66] According to MCA executive Pat Pipolo, it was only then that CKLW picked up the song.[67]

While recording *Caribou* in Colorado one day, Elton received a call from Pipolo, who suggested that "Bennie" be the third single. "I beg your pardon?" was the soul enthusiast's initial response to hearing of its status on Detroit soul radio. He only acquiesced to the release of "Bennie" because of the ego boost of having a number 1 black record, and warned Pipolo that if "Bennie" failed as a single, it would be on his head.[68]

On February 4, 1974, "Bennie" saw its American release. By February 16, it had the highest chart debut for that week, number 69. Terry Jacks's corny "Seasons in the Sun" and Blue Swede's "oogga-chugga" love song, "Hooked on a Feeling," were among the predecessors to "Bennie" at the chart's apex during its nine-week climb to the top. Finally, on April 13, "Bennie" was number 1. Pipolo's judgment had been right.

Although the single would go on to sell, by Elton's own conservative estimate, 2.8 million copies,[69] in the days before the Recording Industry Association of America's platinum certification was reflected on the *Billboard* charts, "Bennie" simply became his third gold single—a mere "million-seller" (due to belated sales recognition afforded pre-platinum era releases, the single would not be certified platinum until September 1995).

By the time "Bennie" fulfilled its chart promise in the United States, "Candle in the Wind" was a British hit, charting on March 2, 1974 and peaking at number 11. For the next two years, Elton's British singles would mostly fail to make the Top 10, while he thoroughly dominated *Billboard*'s Hot 100 in the United States.

"I CAN BITCH THE BEST AT YOUR SOCIAL DO'S"[70]

ELTON'S FEBRUARY 1974 JAPANESE DATES put him on the cover of the book-sized Japanese magazine *Music Life*. But it was his return to Australia, and his first-ever stop in New Zealand, that brought out the headlines.

Despite the success of his October 1971 Australian tour, Elton had, in interviews since then, engaged in some partly good-natured public grousing about some of the unfortunate mishaps that had plagued him there both on- and offstage. In an open letter to Elton published in January 1973, his new Australian friend Ian "Molly" Meldrum refuted the musician's claims of how bad it had been there the first time around: "Everywhere throughout your Australian tour you had almost capacity houses and . . . the audiences time and time again gave you incredible receptions. Well, we'd love to have you back because if you judge popularity on record sales then you are one of the most popular artists in this country."[71]

So Elton returned, and he and Meldrum resumed their friendship. Elton played tennis courts, racecourses, and soccer grounds, much as he had in 1971, but to far larger crowds. The reaction to these shows, both critically and commercially, was cause for nothing but celebration. Elton's spirits rose after the difficulties he had encountered at the Caribou Ranch, and he not only entertained thousands of Australians but, with Meldrum often by his side, himself, too. He scouted lions at Perth's National Lions Park and, ever the music fan, made sure to attend shows by the enormously popular English group Slade.[72]

Elton's Australian tour garnered enormous attention. He had taken to opening his shows with "Funeral for a Friend/Love Lies Bleeding" and closing them with an encore of "Crocodile Rock" and "Saturday Night's Alright for Fighting." In between, he and the band would play a generous offering of other selections from *Goodbye Yellow Brick Road*, also unveiling "Don't Let the Sun Go Down on Me." Not to be heard were many of his "old" songs[73]; the crowds were there to hear the new hits he was churning out at a seemingly unstoppable pace. And if Elton's pianism had lost some of its adventurousness, no one seemed to notice. One reviewer, writing about the February 21 show at the South Melbourne Football Ground, gushed that Elton's "piano playing is comparable to the venom of Jerry Lee Lewis, with at times the delicate touch of a classical pianist."[74]

In endless competition with his own flamboyance, Elton introduced Australian audiences to at least two new feathered outfits. One was his tribute to Josephine Baker, the American star of European cabaret during the 1920s and 1930s. Comprised of a zippered jacket and trousers, the outfit was green on the right, red on the left, and covered with puffs of matching feathers. Accompanying the suit was an elaborate head covering sporting a sequined green net veil that flowed from a wide-brimmed green hat decorated with red pheasant feathers.

But no costume he wore on that tour could top the black Lurex jumpsuit covered with numerous dangling fluorescent balls. The collar and accompanying skullcap were even more stunning, with additional balls that, in the dark, appeared to hover about the musician's head (but were actually attached to the Lurex with lengthy piano wires). Elton's glasses were usually white-rimmed with tinted lenses, though he did shock the crowds midway through some shows with his blinking "ELTON" spectacles.

Elton drew a record-breaking 14,500 concertgoers to his opening show in Perth. In Melbourne, he played for 19,000. At Sydney's Randwick Racecourse, 25,000 came, the highest grossing crowd ever at that venue. Not long before, David

Cassidy had played the same venue, drawing only 12,500.[75] The final stop, on February 28, was Auckland, New Zealand, for a show that was shaping up to be another record-breaker.

In Auckland, Elton made an impromptu appearance at a David Cassidy concert on February 26, at which Cassidy, in a fit of competitiveness, shout-sang himself into laryngitis.[76] The pianist also had two parties to attend on February 27, the night before his only concert there.

Things began unraveling at the first party, held by Festival Records, Elton's regional record distributors. A depletion of wine and liquor led to an argument between Reid and a Festival Records representative named Williams. This argument drew the attention of Williams's friend, a model named Judith Anne Baragwanath. She later claimed she only called Reid a "rotten little bastard," but Reid insisted that she labeled both him and Elton, who was not present for the exchange, a "couple of poofs" ("poof" being a derogatory term for a gay man). Reid, who was not averse to using his fists in support of his gentle client and friend, allegedly punched Baragwanath in the face.

Later, at a party for David Cassidy, Reid heard a report that some men were waiting to pick a fight over the earlier incident. Reid gathered his group and said they would have to leave. Elton made his manager tell him why. When he did, the Pinner pianist quickly reentered the party and, mistaking reporter David Wheeler for the source of the threats, collared Wheeler and asked why he and his tour party were being threatened. Reid, close behind, eyed the scene and allegedly decked Wheeler, kicking the reporter as he lay on the floor. The incidents led to the arrest of John Reid on two counts of assault on the day of Elton's Auckland concert, a fact that was kept from Elton until after the show.

The concert, held at Western Springs Oval, was a resounding success, attracting thirty-four thousand fans. But the next day even Elton was charged with assault, although the most he did was grab Wheeler by the collar. Following a New Zealand court hearing, in which it was determined that Elton's treatment of Wheeler had been precipitated by a misunderstanding, he was ordered to pay prosecution costs of fifty dollars (Australian) and released. Reid wasn't so lucky. In addition to being ordered to pay substantial civil damages to Baragwanath, he was convicted of assault and ordered to serve twenty-eight days in jail. His sentence was stayed over an extended weekend while the high court entertained, and rejected, an appeal.[77]

It got worse. Plastered on the cover of the March 16, 1974 issue of the normally lighthearted music magazine *Go-Set* were these awful headlines:

ELTON JOHN SCANDAL

MANAGER JAILED ON ASSAULT

PUNCHES N.Z. MODEL

KICKS N.Z. REPORTER

Embarrassingly, Elton had just taken out full-page advertising to commemorate the conclusion of the Australian tour. "Elton John and John Reid wish to thank the audiences of his tour of Australia for their incredible response and Act One International for their superb organization," it happily read.

Elton left New Zealand without his manager and intimate friend, though he did not leave empty-handed; he had spent hundreds of Australian dollars on the music of indigenous acts. Now he pondered whether to honor his British and European concert dates.

"I'VE DONE THE WORK OF TEN TO FIFTEEN MEN"[78]

THE COMBINATION OF JOHN REID'S month-long imprisonment and Elton's fatigue from months of touring and recording prompted him to cancel his spring 1974 British and European tours. This didn't mean he was taking a break from work, however. That April, just as "Bennie and the Jets" was reaching the summit of the Hot 100, he recorded a brilliant cover of the signature song from the rock opera *Tommy*, "Pinball Wizard," at Rampart Studios in London.

Initially, filmmaker Ken Russell had approached Elton to accept the role of Uncle Ernie in the film version of *Tommy*, slated for release in 1975. Elton knew he wouldn't have the time and declined the offer. Russell then approached Rod Stewart, offering him the part of the Pinball Wizard. Stewart had originated the role in a London stage production some years earlier. He called Elton and asked what the pianist thought. Elton pointed to the unpleasantness Stewart had had with the stage production. Stewart rejected the offer.

Later, Elton was offered the Pinball Wizard role for himself and, after much cajoling from Pete Townsend, accepted it. Elton reasoned that the part was small, would only involve three days of filming, and was a way to return Townsend a favor. "Pete has always been a very big supporter," he recalled in 1990. "I remember Pete sitting out there when I first started, and I'm a great believer that if people have done you great favors or have been supportive, you should do things back for them."[79]

Unsurprisingly, Stewart was angry to learn that Elton had taken the part. "He was really furious," the pianist said, "and quite rightly so." But it was a good career move for Elton, and his friendship with Rod was strong enough to withstand the setback.

Elton and the band recorded "Pinball Wizard" under Gus Dudgeon's guidance. "We knew we had the best song," Dudgeon said.[80] Whereas the Who's original version is dominated by Pete Townsend's guitar, Elton's remake places the piano at the forefront. In place of Townsend's rhythm chords, Elton created a unique opening for a song that no one imagined could be so passionately reinvented. Even as Davey Johnstone's own guitar vibrates throughout, and especially during the instrumental interlude (intended to lengthen the song to fit the film footage), the tingling of Elton's cascading piano notes and the ranting of his power chords provide irresistible magnets for the listener. Elton's singing may not equal Roger Daltry's wild savagery, but it is as ferocious as any of his own rock vocals, delivered with a sneer of mock anger at his fictional pinball competitor, the young Tommy.

"THE LADS IN GOLD AND BLACK"[81]

ALTHOUGH ELTON CANCELED HIS BRITISH AND EUROPEAN TOURS, he had not forsworn live performances. These were still his favored way to reward fans or assist a cause in which he believed. In the spring of 1974, Elton became a member of the Watford Football Club's board of directors. Watford was a poorly financed team, forty thousand pounds in debt. Elton agreed to perform a benefit concert that, if it drew the expected crowd of thirty thousand at a ticket price of two pounds apiece, would net the team enough money to pay off its debts.

"I am doing this concert in spite of canceling my British tour because I have supported Watford ever since I was a kid," he said. "I wouldn't like to see them go under, and for this reason I will do everything in my power to save them."[82] Rod Stewart, another avid football fan, agreed to appear with Elton. Prior to the major event, the pianist made three smaller-scale benefit appearances at Watford, sans band.

One might have thought these solo gigs would have made Elton pine for the days when it was just him, Nigel, and Dee, or would have inspired him to perform even more solo shows. But he was immensely happy with his energetic band. "One-man shows are boring," he declared, referring to those distant days when he, Nigel, and Dee had had to fend for themselves in the untested wilderness of lead guitar-less rockdom. "I'll never do that again. I mean, who wants to see one guy up there for two and a half hours?"[83] For now, it was still Elton and the band.

On May 5, 1974, Elton, the band, and Rod Stewart staged the Watford benefit, drawing forty thousand people to the Vicarage Road facility. Elton wore a special outfit just for the football fans—a reasonable facsimile of a hornet, in honor of the team name. And a real surprise was one of his song choices, a cover of the Beatles' "Lucy in the Sky with Diamonds."

"I CAN BITCH, I CAN BITCH, 'CAUSE I'M BETTER THAN YOU"[84]

THAT SPRING OF 1974 saw Elton still embroiled in a struggle between teen idol showmanship and adult musicianship. It also saw substantial progress in his commercial success and brought him to the cusp of greater artistic achievement. The late spring and summer of 1974 was a time that, in many ways, matched the spate of activity and growing recognition of Elton's talents that had occurred in the spring and summer of 1970. It didn't hurt that the first single from *Caribou*, "Don't Let the Sun Go Down on Me," was continuing the string of huge hits, particularly in the United States, that had commenced with "Crocodile Rock" about a year and a half earlier. "Don't Let the Sun" was released during the latter half of May in Great Britain and charted on June 1, 1974, making it to number 16.

In the United States, the song's success was more impressive. Released on June 10, 1974, while "Bennie and the Jets" was still in the Top 40, it reached the Top 10 after only four weeks. On August 10, the song's two-week stay at number 2 ended. It could not oust John Denver's "Annie's Song" from the top spot, nor resist the onslaught of Paper Lace's "The Night Chicago Died." But a number 2 pinnacle meant another hit that would become a must-play song for audiences everywhere. By September, it would become the musician's fourth gold single.

Caribou, released on June 24 in the United States and June 28 in Great Britain, was another number 1 album, charting in both countries a week apart: on July 6 and July 13, respectively. Its performance in both nations could not rival the eye-popping chart longevity of its significantly superior predecessor, *Goodbye Yellow Brick Road*, which was still in the Top 10 in the United States. However, *Caribou* did best the two-record set's U.S. showing in one important respect, debuting on *Billboard*'s Top LPs at number 5. Only four other albums had debuted in the Top 5 since *Billboard* had begun publishing charts in 1955—George Harrison's *All Things Must Pass*, the Woodstock soundtrack, the Beatles' *Hey Jude*, and *Led Zeppelin III*.[85]

At MCA, anticipation was lent to Elton's expected re-signing with the company. Until now, he had been bound to MCA for his U.S. and Canadian releases via a strange deal engineered during the first half of 1970 by Russ Regan, which involved a one-year contract with options for additional years.[86] John Reid, fresh from his stay in a New Zealand jail, worked to better that deal. Initially, he made the rounds to different record companies to test the waters. An informal chat between Reid and David Geffen, then the president of Elektra-Asylum Records, caused Geffen to effuse: "I've signed Bob Dylan. Next, I'm going to sign Elton and then we're all going to take over the world." Geffen would have to wait six years for his turn, as Reid decided Elton should stay with MCA. Elton wanted to stay anyway, partly because of the success of "Bennie and the Jets" on black radio.[87]

Reid and Mike Maitland, president of MCA Records, worked out a deal with Dick James whereby MCA would continue to distribute all of Elton's records in the United States and Canada. Without this agreement, DJM could have sold its rights to Elton's back catalog to another company, which could have then released singles from Elton's old albums that would compete with his new product.[88] Dick James did get to keep a consolation prize. In Britain, Europe, and elsewhere in the world, he could release old Elton John product in any number of creative packages.

The deal with DJM done, Reid and Maitland turned to negotiating a new MCA contract for North America. Although Reid refused legal assistance, he was bargaining from a position of considerable strength. MCA didn't want negotiations to break down. Maitland told Robert Hilburn that the "emotional effect of my having to tell the staff that we had lost him would have been tremendous. We would have survived, but it could have crippled us for a while."[89]

This was a telling admission from a record company executive who wielded substantial power in his own right. The twenty-four-year-old Reid took ample advantage of his negotiating position and, during four days in early June, demonstrated brains and savvy in working on a daunting, fifty-five-page document that, he later claimed, became the industry standard.[90] Although the exact terms of the contract were not disclosed, the signers dropped enough hints that news organizations were able to deduce some terms. It was reported that the contract guaranteed Elton at least eight million dollars over five years and six or seven records, although Maitland told *Billboard* that that dollar figure was "slightly low." It was estimated that Elton's royalty rate would approach twenty percent per album (with some later estimates putting the rate at twenty-eight percent). The usual rate for a superstar was no more than fifteen percent.[91]

Elton signed the contract on June 13, 1974. On the eve of the signing, Reid got MCA to agree to take out full-page advertisements in *The New York Times* and the *Los Angeles Times* to announce the new contract. "I was endeavoring to make a lot of statements in one simple way," said Reid. "It made a statement to the public, to the financial community, to the record industry, and for myself."[92] The advertisements appeared in the June 19 issues of both newspapers. Elton would later come to regret this ostentatious move. Being less enamored of the business side of things, he realized that the advertisements set a new standard for industry hype.

It was the contract itself, however, that really upped the ante. It may not sound like much in this age of one hundred million dollar deals, but Elton's figure set a record, exceeding the estimated four to five million dollar record-breaking deal signed by Neil Diamond with Columbia Records in 1972.[93] In fact, Diamond's deal was dwarfed by Elton's, since the contract for the composer of "Sweet Caroline" covered the world, not just the United States and Canada. Stevie Wonder's reported seven-year, thirteen million dollar Motown deal, signed in 1975, appeared to best Elton's North American numbers, except that, like Diamond's, Stevie's agreement was worldwide.

Elton's good news would keep him waiting for a while. The terms of his contract would not begin until the original leasing agreement between DJM and MCA ended in 1976.[94]

"FROM THE END OF THE WORLD TO YOUR TOWN"[95]

WITH A NEW MCA CONTRACT TAKEN CARE OF, Elton returned to the Caribou Ranch for another album. Some time earlier, Elton and Bernie had discussed a possible album concept. Bernie later recounted, "We came up with a science fiction concept, but we thought, 'No, people have done that, David Bowie—yawn, yawn. . . .'"[96]

Bernie finally suggested an autobiographical theme and a title, *Captain Fantastic and the Brown Dirt Cowboy*. This would be their only intentional concept album until 1989's *Sleeping with the Past* (*Tumbleweed Connection* was a concept album by accident). "I thought we might be accused of being conceited because writing about yourself is a bit off, but I just wanted people to get the idea of what really happened," Elton later noted.[97] He explained that it was about the dues he and Bernie had paid. Relevant to every artist, the story also meant to show that he and Bernie were not all "sheen," or robotic musical purveyors. "We are human beings," Elton said. "We're not machines like everyone else thinks we are."[98]

They decided the songs would be presented in roughly chronological order. Bernie spent extra time on the lyrics. Elton worked on them during his five-day July voyage, with friend Tony King, on the final excursion of the SS *France*, from Southampton, England, to New York. On the ship, Elton tried and failed to book the music room. "An opera singer had it booked the whole time except for when she scarfed her lunch for two hours," he recalled. "So every two hours at lunchtime I used to go in there and nip out to the piano, and wrote the whole of the *Captain Fantastic* album."[99] (Years later, he admitted that he had actually only written three to four songs on the ocean liner.[100])

Once in New York, Elton and King visited John Lennon, who was recording *Walls and Bridges* at the Record Plant. King, who had been a DJM "song plugger" before joining the Beatles' Apple Records as an executive, had been fostering a friendship between the two musicians for about a year. As King said in 1976, "They're both fabulously warm, sympathetic, intelligent people. I felt that they would have a lot in common."[101]

As an idolizer of the former Beatle, Elton was elated to have a "John Lennon session." The original purpose of his visit to the Record Plant was to contribute backing vocals,[102] which he did for two songs, "Whatever Gets You thru the Night" and "Surprise, Surprise (Sweet Bird of Paradox)." Just as important was his instrumental contribution to the former.

Lennon remembered some months later that he had been working on "Whatever Gets You thru the Night" when the two seafarers from the SS *France* showed up. "I was fiddling about one night and Elton John walked in with Tony King of Apple—you know, we're all good friends—and the next minute Elton said, 'Say, can I put a bit of piano on that?' I said, 'Sure—love it!' He zapped in. I was amazed at his ability. . . . I knew him, but I'd never seen him play. A fine musician, great piano player. I was really pleasantly surprised at the way he could get in on such a loose track and add to it and keep up with the rhythm changes—obviously, 'cause it doesn't keep the same rhythm. . . . And then he sang with me. We had a great time."[103]

Elton's playing is featured prominently on the track, giving it a supple, jazzy brawn that acts as a counterpoint to the rock vocals and the gritty rock of Bobby

Keys's tenor saxophone. Elton also added organ. "Me playing organ on someone's record? I mean, really," Elton commented, predictably. "That's disgusting because I'm the worst organist. But we put that on and it was over and done with in five minutes."[104] Elton's bright harmony vocal is prominent; he and Lennon sang together at a lone microphone for this performance, which, Elton said, didn't take long. His harmony vocal on "Surprise, Surprise" is less audible. Elton later claimed that it took him three and a half hours to get that one right, after finally becoming accustomed to Lennon's unique phrasing. "People were leaving the room!" he laughed a few months later. "Razor blades were being passed out!"[105]

Elton made Lennon promise that the ex-Beatle would join him onstage during his upcoming fall U.S. tour. This promise has been described variously as depending on whether "Whatever Gets You thru the Night," "Lucy in the Sky with Diamonds" (yet to be recorded by Elton), or Lennon's album *Walls and Bridges* reached number 1. As all three did, the bet would have worked either way.

"THE CAPTAIN AND THE KID"[106]

SPANNING JULY AND AUGUST, the recording of *Captain Fantastic* took a whole month. The album didn't closely resemble anything Elton had previously done. He had entered the realm of musical theater.

Gus Dudgeon didn't have any complaints about the creative process this time. "It's the best that they've [the band] ever played, it's the best that he's [Elton] ever played, and it's the best collection of songs," he exclaimed. "There's not one song on there that is less than incredible."[107]

This album meant more to Elton and Bernie than any other, with the exception of *Empty Sky*, because it represented a story that they wanted to tell, and tell well. It also was the first one with which Elton could personally identify. Instead of doing the usual—painting a musical landscape with his own oils and colors but using a brush and canvas stored in the imagination of another—here he set to music stories in which his own life and feelings were at front and center.

On the album, Elton and Bernie fondly remember their innocent first days together, working the path to fame and fortune. It all started with their boyhoods, which, as Bernie hints at in the title track, did not presage rock stardom but instead nurtured an infantile wonderment at what lay ahead. Bernie dubs Elton "Captain Fantastic" and himself the "Brown Dirt Cowboy" to bring to mind cartoon characters who could be the heroes of a tale that begins in mundane fashion. Reggie, as Captain Fantastic, was "raised and regimented." He was "hardly a hero, just someone his mother might know." Unassuming but talented, he was "very clearly a case for corn flakes and classics." Back in the north of England, Bernie, the little Dirt Cowboy, basked in the fresh air of the farmlands, delighting in "sweet chocolate biscuits, and red rosy apples in summer."

As the boys grew to their teens, the two were evidently far from realizing their potential. Documented are Bernie's jobs of drudgery ("For cheap easy meals/are hardly a home on the range") and Reg's Bluesology days ("Too hot for the band/ with a desperate desire for change"). Disappointments littering the trails of their still unfolding destinies led to the momentous meeting between them, and their union as a sort of superhero team—"Captain Fantastic and the Brown Dirt Cowboy, from the end of the world to your town."

The music for the title track finds Elton's unaffected singing marking the tabula rasa beginnings of the dynamic duo. The only hint of things to come is the steady progression of the melody, which moves through the dreaminess of childhood, the weariness of early disappointment, the years of determination, and, finally, the realization that they, as a team, had the chance to attain personal fulfillment. In testament to the Brown Dirt Cowboy, the musical backdrop is vaguely Western, with Elton's understated electric piano reflections and Davey's acoustic guitar and mandolin providing a sunny, breezy accompaniment fit for a mighty warm day down on the ranch.

The album's next two songs, "Tower of Babel" and "Bitter Fingers," find the superheroes battling what might as well be kryptonite. Both Elton and Bernie have said that "Tower of Babel" was inspired by the "sharks" of the publishing industry. In the song, the songwriters are "attempting to climb to the stars," said Bernie years later,[108] but instead find "sharks in the doorway, nipping at our heels." For Elton, the Tower of Babel is a vortex of meaningless activity punctuated by the misplaced interests of an ostensible benefactor. "We'd signed a contract with Dick James and there wasn't anyone within his organization to give us even a little bit of help, not even a *little* bit of thought or encouragement," Elton bitterly remembered.[109]

"Tower of Babel" is an angry ballad. Bernie doesn't let the inhabitants of the wobbly structure off lightly; using numerous biblical references, he attacks the phoniness of the music industry. Elton's melody glows with the irony of this sordid little tale. Punctuated by arpeggiated piano and sparse but effective use of the band, it evolves from leisurely and conversational to a more fast-paced, snide critique of the industry whose true face became more evident each day.

"Bitter Fingers" continues the theme of disenchantment. Elton and Bernie had not forgotten that, initially, they were pressured to compose for such singers as Tom Jones and Cilla Black. "I'm glad that happened," Elton later admitted, "because without the struggle, you don't appreciate anything."[110] In the song, the Captain and the Kid learn how hard it is to "write a song with bitter fingers." For now, though, they have to make do. "There's a chance that one day you might write a standard lads," they are told. "So churn 'em out thick and fast."

The hybrid music in "Bitter Fingers" begins as if to accompany a 1950s documentary about how members of an "average" American family were to comport themselves. This guidance usually ignored reality, and so did the expectations placed on the Captain and the Kid. By the chorus, the music has transformed into a hostile, mid-tempo affair, allowing the duo to freely express their feelings. The musical tension between the verses' pre-rock'n'roll, 1950s docileness and the chorus's lit-fuse aggression illustrates the double lives Elton and Bernie were leading in their first days writing together, when they had to do one thing but dreamed of doing another.

The two songs that follow and close side one of the album, "Tell Me When the Whistle Blows" and "Someone Saved My Life Tonight," depict the superheroes' private lives. "Tell Me When the Whistle Blows" has the Brown Dirt Cowboy pining for the Lincolnshire countryside. "I was still fresh from the sticks, and I still had tremendous ties to my friends back home in Lincolnshire," Bernie said years later. He couldn't wait to get home on weekends.[111]

Elton had Marvin Gaye in mind when he composed the music for "Whistle Blows."[112] He recruited Gene Page, arranger for disco star Barry White, to do a string arrangement, and Page summoned up a sweeping, blues-flavored landscape. Elton furthers the smokey vocal work he had begun refining with *Honky Chateau*, his voice nimbly wafting through the strings' lovely haze and the gurgling airiness of the piano and band ensemble. A highlight is the combination of the pianist's electric piano and clavinet, which mimics the gliding of a train over tracks as heard through sleepy ears.

Elton's near-marriage is the subject of the song that closes side one, "Someone Saved My Life Tonight," one of the most moving, powerful songs that he and Bernie have ever written. The song had to be that way. If he had married Linda Woodrow, Elton said much later, "That would have been goodbye to the music scene for me. I would have been down working in Barclay's Bank or something."[113] Bernie covers this ground with the distinct imagery and judgmental tone that characterize all his lyrics on the album. Woodrow, already nearly six years out of the picture, doesn't get off lightly. She is "sitting like a princess perched in her electric chair" as Elton and Bernie return from the Bag o' Nails, full of beer ("And it's one more beer,/and I don't hear you anymore"). Elton explains to her, "someone saved my life tonight, sugar bear," referring to John Baldry's sound advice. "You nearly had me roped and tied," Elton says, "altar-bound, hypnotised." He hadn't realized before how much he'd dreaded getting married ("A slip noose hanging in my darkest dreams"). Marriage would be akin to death: "I would have walked head on into the deep end of a river,/clinging to your stocks and bonds,/paying your H.P. [credit] demands forever." He was "saved in time" by Baldry's words. "Thank God my music's still alive," he sighs.

Elton admitted to David Frost in an interview broadcast almost two decades after writing this song that his classical training came in handy here (as it did for so many of his songs). Referring to the song's thunderous chord sequences, he told

Frost, "There's an A-flat chord with an E flat in the bass, which is something one would have never done without musical training."[114] This combination infuses the song with drama, illustrating the barrage of thoughts and feelings going through Elton's head as he pondered whether to get married.

Even just singing the song brought back difficult memories for Elton. Gus Dudgeon didn't know what the song was about as he coaxed the vocal out of Elton in the studio. Elton seemed upset as Dudgeon had him sing the song over and over again. Finally, Davey Johnstone took the producer aside and told him of the song's meaning. "I made him sing the most unbelievably personal things over and over again to get a bloody note right or get a bit of phrasing together!" Dudgeon later exclaimed, incredulously.[115]

"Someone Saved My Life Tonight" is also an example of one of the richest uses of the band on record. Elton's electric piano injects bell-like flashes to his booming acoustic piano declarations. His synthesizer successfully emulates a string section that rises above the fray as the song's orchestral tendencies emerge toward the end. Nigel and Ray add drums, shakers, and cymbals that accentuate Elton's dark chords and the crescendo of emotion that develops. Davey's "Leslie" speaker-distorted guitars introduce an extra dramatic relish. And the backing vocals by Dee, Nigel, and Davey stand as the epitome of their singing experiments.

The album's second side opens with "(Gotta Get a) Meal Ticket." On one level, the song refers simply to the difficulties of getting paid only ten quid (then about twenty dollars) a week. On a more general level, it refers to any struggling act's situation. This is the only real rock song on the album. With his raw, almost raspy vocal, Elton sounds determined to succeed, to beat the odds. The driving rhythm of his piano and Davey's blaring guitar give the song a ravenous sound, bringing to the fore the Captain and the Kid's hunger for that still elusive meal ticket.

Images of hopelessness pervade the lyrics in "Better off Dead," though the song is supposed to be a memento of the happy nights that followed recording sessions for the *Empty Sky* album. Elton and Bernie would go to a place called the Wimpy Bar to drink and watch through the windows as London's less fortunate trudged by or got into trouble with the law.[116] The title of the song refers to the unhappy people of the streets, and less obviously to the struggling duo. The hopelessness of the drunks, whores, and others whom they watch helps them recognize all they have to be thankful for. By the song's close, they realize that if they can't handle small misfortunes in the course of an otherwise fulfilling life, they are probably "better off dead" ("If the thorn of a rose is the thorn in your side/then you're better off dead if you haven't yet died.").

Bernie was surprised at the music for this song. He had been expecting a folk number, but the staccato rhythms of a Gilbert and Sullivan-esque light opera emerged instead.[117] Elton's empathetic but machine-gun delivery of lines like "as-the-flickering-neon-stands-ready-to-fuse/the-wind-blows-away-all-of-yesterday's-news" brings to mind theater revivals of *The Pirates of Penzance* and *H.M.S. Pinafore.* This spirit is equally evident in Elton's declaratory staccato piano chords and Nigel's decisive, vibrating drum beats. Ray adds some comical touches, always an important part of a Gilbert and Sullivan production, with a triangle solo. The joviality of the music carries on in the grand tradition of Elton finding alternate meaning in Bernie's lyrics. Like that of "I Think I'm Going to Kill Myself" and "Sweet Painted Lady" before it, the music for "Better off Dead" takes a less obvious interpretation of the lyrics—optimism—and makes this the dominant theme (here, with the song's buoyant, staccato rhythms).

"Writing," the next song, is more obviously optimistic. Years after writing the lyrics, Bernie reflected fondly on the days of 1968 and 1969, when they were first refining their new craft. "We were never so close as we were in those days," he said. They walked the streets of London in a blissful fog, sharing daydreams.[118] Day after day, following each productive recording session for the *Empty Sky* album, they would ask each other if it would be as good tomorrow ("Will the things we wrote today sound as good tomorrow"). Thus the superheroes fend off the last bits of kryptonite.

The melody in "Writing" is a blithe survey of those contented days, when Elton and Bernie received support, however tentative, to do what they wanted. Grins and satisfied expressions seem glued to the chord progressions as Elton and Davey glide along on electric piano and acoustic guitar, respectively; Ray turns to precise congas and triangle ringing for more sounds of contentment. After the negative feelings and the doubt expressed elsewhere on the album, this music utters ultimate triumph for the Captain and the Kid. They may not have any hits yet, but they are writing what they like. Life is better. If, in the lyrics, the two are ridding their environs of the last bits of kryptonite, the music casts aside all doubts: The kryptonite is gone.

Captain Fantastic could easily have ended here, but Bernie wanted closure. The last two songs on the album, "We All Fall in Love Sometimes" and "Curtains," put everything into perspective. For Bernie, "We All Fall in Love Sometimes" is a sign for the duo of great things to come. "It means we all find something sometimes, whether it's success, a relationship that works out," he explained years later. "It's really a song that says there's something tomorrow."[119] Elton sings of the songwriting chemistry that had developed between the two. Their early failings are reviewed ("Naïve notions that were childish/simple tunes that tried to hide it") and acknowledged as temporary ("And only passing time/could kill the boredom we acquired/running with the losers for awhile"). The song also contains the only actual reference to the album *Empty Sky,* which had provided a glimmer of hope in the worst of times, and which would soon open the floodgates of success ("But our Empty Sky was filled with laughter/just before the flood,/painting worried faces with a smile").

For Elton, the lyrics to "We All Fall in Love Sometimes" invited another interpretation. For him, the song documents his friendship with Bernie. "He said everything in that lyric that I felt about our relationship, and it still exists today," he said.[120] The lyrics also infer his real love for the lyricist, although Elton and Bernie never had a physical relationship. His strong feelings for Bernie in those days were at least a subtle indication of his sexuality, years before the pianist ever met John Reid.

Elton has described the music for "We All Fall in Love" as right for French balladeer Charles Aznavour.[121] His first experiment with the Continental sound, it reeks of a sadness that belies the intended message of optimism. Here again, the music portrays the flip side of the lyrics' obvious meaning, ignoring the exhilaration that the duo had found by the time *Empty Sky* was recorded and reflecting instead on the hard times before their songwriting collaboration fell into its proper place, as well as on Elton's unrequited love for Bernie. Lurking behind the doleful melody may also be the realization that their early struggles housed a spiritual innocence they would never recapture. Contributing to the melancholy are Elton's flute-style mellotron playing, reminiscent of that found on "Daniel," and the return visit of Dave Hentschel for a French horn imitation executed with his trusty Arp synthesizer.

"We All Fall in Love Sometimes" segues into "Curtains," in much the same way that "Funeral for a Friend" becomes "Love Lies Bleeding." "Curtains" is an intriguing puzzle, with its clever references to Elton and Bernie's early songs. "Scarecrow," one of their first demoed songs, is paid affectionate tribute ("I used to know this old scarecrow/he was my song"), as is "A Dandelion Dies in the Wind" ("I held a dandelion, that said the time had come/to leave upon the wind"). Bernie apologizes for his pretentious early lyrics ("Beneath these branches/I once wrote such childish words for you"). As Elton said later, "That was a comment on our early songs because Bernie's lyrics were really . . . like flower-power, very much in that garden of taste. As we say later in the song, 'That's okay. There's treasure children always seek to find, and just like us, you (meaning everybody) must have had a once upon a time.' Everybody has a dream, and we had a dream."[122]

The music for "Curtains" begins quietly, but builds to a crescendo that ends in a musical onslaught by the entire band. Amid the commotion of Elton's expansive Tchaikovsky-esque piano chords, Nigel's thunderous drums, and Ray's brilliant bells, Elton's vocal "lum-de-lums" take Captain Fantastic and the Brown Dirt Cowboy to the horizon, where the superheroes, of such humble origins, ride off into the sunset.

The recording of *Captain Fantastic and the Brown Dirt Cowboy* was a milestone. Elton found himself in the rare position of singing about himself. When the album was finally released, about nine months after the last notes were played at the Caribou Ranch, it artfully showed the two's humanity. They were as susceptible to crushing failure as anyone else, and had had to work hard for several years before receiving their due. They were not the invincible automatons some might have thought.

Musically, the album was the first to showcase the strengths of Elton's five-man band. *Caribou* had failed to do that. And for the first time, the record-buying public would hear the advantages of having Ray Cooper in the lineup. The pointed physicality, not to mention personality, of his percussion sharply frames every last note, adds sheen to Nigel's drumming, and generally offers all sorts of quirky surprises on all ten songs.

But if *Captain Fantastic and the Brown Dirt Cowboy* thus marked the rightful beginning of one musical era, it marked the end of another. This would be the last Elton John album with Nigel and Dee until 1980.

"THE WHIPPOORWILL OF FREEDOM ZAPPED ME RIGHT BETWEEN THE EYES"[123]

IN BETWEEN SESSIONS for *Captain Fantastic*, other notable songs were recorded. John Lennon stopped by the Caribou Ranch to record "Lucy in the Sky with Diamonds." Said Gus Dudgeon, "Everybody adored him, he got on so well with the band." The only problem was that Lennon couldn't remember the chords to "Lucy in the Sky"—Davey had to remind him.[124]

On *Captain Fantastic*, Elton sang about questionable attempts to write and record flower-powerish songs. Here, he had his chance to record a bona fide theme for descendants of the halcyon days of Haight-Ashbury, and to leave his musical imprint on it. If the original version seemed spaced-out, distant, and in a different cognitive dimension, Elton's version was firmly planted on the ground. Plucking his bass as if under water, Dee helps drag the song to earth, where Davey waits with his electric guitar and exotic sitar and Ray rolls out a bevy of eccentric instruments—a gong that ripples like water rings around a newly fallen pebble, a rattlesnake tambourine, and uncredited crunchy shakers and shimmering bells for good measure. Lennon is at the ready during the "reggae break" with his "reggae guitars," officially attributed to "Dr. Winston O'Boogie." But it is Elton's adventurousness that holds this unique recording together. As with all of his best musical efforts, his keyboard interpretations, sense of melody, and facile singing are paramount in making the recording work. The throbbing percussiveness of his piano, the idyllic sounds of his string/flute arrangement for mellotron, and his stubborn adherence to a melody that is not nearly as discernible in the original, make the song gel.

Even more significant than this homage to Lennon was an unlikely love song, written as an outgrowth of a blossoming friendship between Elton and tennis star Billie Jean King. Elton had met King in 1973. He was himself a fierce, if not stellar, tennis player, having spent time playing tennis while a young DJM signee. In fact, his love of tennis (and soccer) would, for a time, counterbalance the aftereffects of a now growing weakness: his periodically excessive drinking.

Elton had graduated from being an occasional social drinker with the younger but veteran Lincolnshire imbiber Bernie, during their early songwriting days, to taking swigs on the concert stage as he reveled in being a teen idol. Yet he prided himself on having control over his "body systems." He could, he said, stop whenever he wanted.[125] Still, the drinking, combined with a love of eating and a natural tendency toward stockiness, had resulted in extra poundage that Elton determined to shed at the first opportunity. In the spring of 1974, he trained with such tennis stars as Jimmy Connors and King at the John Gardiner Tennis Ranch in Arizona. While there, he said, he won the mixed doubles two weeks in a row, and lost about forty pounds.[126] A couple of months later, he played an exhibition match at the Spectrum in Philadelphia with Bill Cosby, whom he beat, six games to three.[127]

Elton once told journalist friend Paul Gambaccini that "Philadelphia Freedom" is the only song he ever consciously wrote as a single.[128] The song is a tribute to Billie Jean King and her World Teamtennis team, the Philadelphia Freedoms, and to the Philly Soul sound epitomized by the Delfonics, the production duo of Kenny Gamble and Leon Huff, and Thom Bell, among others. Elton had told King he would have Bernie write lyrics for her, then asked Bernie to write lyrics called "Philadelphia Freedom." "I can't write a song about tennis!" Bernie had protested.[129] And he didn't. The words bear no relationship to tennis, nor even to Philly Soul, though they loosely acknowledge soul music. The first line echoes the Temptations' "Papa Was a Rolling Stone," with "I used to be a rolling stone."

Though probably just a coincidence—as Bernie claims that the lyrics mean nothing—"Philadelphia Freedom" also served as a flag-waver, just in time for the American Bicentennial. The words hold a little Horatio Alger, Emma Lazarus, Mark Twain: "Philadelphia Freedom took me knee-high to a man/Yeah! Gave me peace of mind my daddy never had." And: "If you choose to you can live your life alone/some people choose the city,/some others choose the good old family home."

Elton recorded a rough mix of "Philadelphia Freedom" at the Caribou Ranch. He presented it to King in Denver, where the Philadelphia Freedoms were playing. "He was so nervous that I wasn't gonna like it, but I loved it . . . ," she has said. "It's just so thoughtful that they wrote a song and dedicated it to me. It meant a lot."[130]

Gene Page's string arrangement wouldn't be added for several months, but the song's heavy beat, punctuated by Dee's bass plucking and wrapped inside Davey's slick guitar work, had enough soul punch to last until Page provided his finishing touches. Elton's barrel-chested lead vocal suggests some Teddy Pendergrass, some Four Tops' Levi Stubbs. His chirpy backup singing was meant as a tribute to falset-to-charged soul groups like the Stylistics, and offsets the near-baritone he mustered for the lead.

"Philadelphia Freedom" represented a challenge for the album-oriented rock stations of the time, not used to playing anything that remotely approached disco.

Once classic rock radio took hold years later, rock snobbery kept the song off some stations' playlists. The song proved a courageous step for Elton in an industry in which he already didn't fit.

"THE FEVER'S GONNA CATCH YOU"[131]

"SOME RADIO STATIONS IN AMERICA are more puritanical than others," Elton once said. "I used to get bleeped quite a lot."[132] He was referring to the treatment of his late summer 1974 single, "The Bitch Is Back," which, for many American Top 40 radio stations, contained a forbidden word. Since the unmentionable noun was prevalent throughout the song, bleeping over it substantially affected the song's listenability.

Some stations wouldn't play it at all. Other stations would play the song only during certain hours. John Biggs, a disc jockey who worked at WIFN, a station in Franklin, Indiana, thirty miles outside Indianapolis, recalled that although the song wasn't banned, many local disc jockeys were self-conscious about announcing its title. At his own station, the then music director was reluctant to add the song to the playlist, only acquiescing after endless badgering from the phone request lines. Even then, the music director would only permit it to air after 7 P.M. Midway through this controversy, Biggs was promoted to music director, ousting his conservative superior and, in his first proud act, he removed the 7 P.M. restriction on "The Bitch Is Back."[133]

The single was released on August 30, 1974 in Britain and days later in the United States. In Britain, it took two weeks to chart and peaked at number 15. In spite of, or perhaps because of, the controversy, the single ignited in the United States, where it became Elton's ninth, and fourth consecutive, Top 10 single. It entered *Billboard*'s Hot 100 four days after its release, at number 63, just as "Don't Let the Sun" was slipping out of the Top 40. After six weeks, "The Bitch Is Back" reached the Top 10, peaking at number 4 on November 2 (but not certified gold until September 1995). Meanwhile, Elton's duet with Lennon, "Whatever Gets You thru the Night," leapt to number 6 in the United States, eventually reaching number 1 on November 16; in Britain, it peaked at number 36.

At the same time, Rocket Records recording act Kiki Dee was enjoying unprecedented American success. Just a couple of months earlier, this would have been hard to fathom. Another single from her *Loving and Free* album, the John/Taupin-penned "Supercool," only got as high as the Bubbling Under singles chart. But her new single, the fiery "I've Got the Music in Me," from a new Gus Dudgeon-produced Rocket album of the same name, charted one week after "The Bitch Is Back" and peaked at number 12 on November 30. The single reached similar heights in Britain, when it peaked at number 19. The album as a whole didn't chart in Britain, but became Kiki's first to do so in the United States, where it reached number 28.

Kiki's title track, and the only hit from the album, had caused her difficulties in the studio. Dudgeon enlisted Elton's help. While she attempted to tap into the song's spirit, Elton sneaked into the studio through a back door, hid behind a screen to disrobe, and "streaked" past her.[134] Judging from the vocal, Elton's immodest act did Kiki a world of good.

Elton also had a hand in the success of another Rocket recording act that fall. Fellow classically trained pianist Neil Sedaka had had a string of bubblegum hits in the early to mid-1960s in both the United States and Britain. By the 1970s, he was an unknown quantity in the United States, but in Britain was enjoying a commercial renaissance. Two British hit albums and seven British hit singles followed before friend and admirer Elton learned that Sedaka lacked a U.S. recording contract.

Elton had been to numerous Sedaka concerts in Britain. The two had even had meals together. One evening in 1974, after a Sedaka concert at the Royal Festival Hall, Elton and John Reid retreated with Sedaka to the latter's London residence. There, Sedaka offered them his recordings for release in the United States. He didn't want an advance, just a note on the sleeve of his first Rocket album and heavy promotion.

"We couldn't believe our luck," Elton remembered, joking, "We sort of ran into a corner and laughed, and said the guy must be an idiot!"[135] Sedaka recalled, "They fainted. It was kind of a mutual respect with Elton and I. I had always loved his work and he had told me he was influenced by many of my early things."[136]

Years later, Sedaka told Dick Clark that he may have helped launch Rocket Records, but that Elton was responsible for his comeback. He cited Elton's enthusiastic personal promotion of his music.[137] Elton did give his all for Sedaka, partly in his capacity as "EJ the DJ" at different U.S. radio stations. "There's too much musical snobbery around," he said of Sedaka's naysayers in November 1974, while playing disc jockey on WNEW in New York. "Anyone who dismisses Neil Sedaka for 'Calendar Girl' should just go out and get the album [*Sedaka's Back*] and see what he's doing now."[138]

When Elton made this declaration, "Laughter in the Rain" had been in the Top 40 for two weeks. On February 1, 1975, it finally reached the top of the Hot 100. And just a week after Elton's appearance on WNEW, *Sedaka's Back*, a compilation of songs from his two recent British hit albums, finally charted on *Billboard*'s Top LPs, eventually going gold. This was only the second Sedaka album ever to chart in the United States, the first being a compilation of his early singles, *Neil Sedaka Sings His Greatest Hits.*

Elton also tried transferring some of his golden touch in 1974 to fellow stars Rod Stewart and Ringo Starr, with less success. For Rod's album *Smiler*, Elton and Bernie wrote "Let Me Be Your Car," which remained an obscure album track. For Ringo's *Goodnight Vienna*, the duo wrote "Snookeroo." The latter song made it to number 3 on the Hot 100 as one half of a double A-sided single on April 3, 1975, but it was the other half, "No No Song," that got all the attention.

"IT'S THE WAY THAT I MOVE, THE THINGS THAT I DO"[139]

ELTON'S U.S. TOUR THAT FALL, the most wildly anticipated one yet, was one party after another. "I start getting a little hyper late in the afternoon before a concert, and it keeps building up," he told the *Chicago Tribune*'s Lynn Van Matre. "You get to the dressing room and you hear the crowd and you finally step onstage, and it's like Christmas Day and opening your presents. And then it's over, and there's this feeling of release and also a definite letdown. I mean, I never go out after a show's over—what could I do that wouldn't be a drag after performing?"[140]

The speed with which his concert tickets flew from the hands of ticket agents into the hysterical palms of fans would have been unfathomable even a year earlier. It was all the more remarkable considering that, at the time, many music fans were staying away from the concert scene, and big names like George Harrison and Stevie Wonder sometimes couldn't fill arenas.[141] But tickets to Elton's concerts sold out as quickly as they were available. Three shows at Los Angeles' 18,700-seat Forum sold out in six hours. In two more hours, a hastily added fourth show sold out. In Detroit, so many fans were waiting in line that the box office opened two hours early. Tickets to the two Detroit shows were gone in five hours.[142] The mind-boggling popularity of Elton John grew ever more feverish. It was on the move like wildfire.

On September 24, 1974, as "The Bitch Is Back" reached the Top 30, Elton and his growing entourage left Los Angeles for New Orleans on *Starship One*, the chartered luxury jet that would take him to each of the tour's forty-four stops. MCA Records had already thrown him an elaborate tour-launching party that featured a carnival.[143]

The tour would take him from California to Boston, ending in Philadelphia. Kiki Dee and her new group, the Kiki Dee Band, were to be his opening act, performing a forty-five-minute set that included her current single, "I've Got the Music in Me." The four-member Muscle Shoals Horns was also along for the last third of Elton's set, to provide the brassy wallop that recalled the Tower of Power's better moments on *Caribou*.

Of his costumes for the tour, Elton said, "They're all absolutely stupid, I mean absolutely ridiculous. They've gone over the top this time, and I'm really pleased. I've got one that is a giant chicken outfit with huge feathers everywhere, which makes me look like the moron of all time."[144] He also unveiled, for the first time anywhere, costumes that seemed better suited for aliens on *Star Trek* than a purveyor of some of the most popular and inspired music of a generation.

One getup saw Elton in a jewel-studded white scarf, long-waisted topcoat, satin pants with yellow-green and violet stripes, and a violet top hat from which lengthy violet and black quills streamed. Then there was a flared-leg yellow and orange jumpsuit, decorated with diamanté and minute mirrors and with matching cuffs, choker, and ornate skullcap—all topped off with a kingly cape trimmed with white marabou feathers and more diamanté and mirrors. Another costume included a black jumpsuit with openings at the front that exposed his hairy chest and abdomen. Completely open in the back, in the style of a woman's one-piece bathing suit, the outfit featured panels down the centers of the pant legs covered in sequins and small mirrors and, along the inner pant legs, pink and white bugle beads, which also adorned his tinselly jacket. The accompanying sequined and mirrored black hat, from which white and pink ostrich feather boas seemed to be growing, could have doubled as either a giant punch bowl or a friendly UFO.

The eyeglasses were similarly outrageous. One pair had orange-tinted lenses encased in diamanté-encrusted frames that covered nearly half of Elton's face. On another pair, pink-tinted lenses were surrounded by mother-of-pearl- and rhinestone-decorated frames covered with curlicues of feather puffs. A third set had pink-tinted lenses with mink linings. And an especially notorious set boasted purple- and yellow-tinted lenses in frames larger than the blinking "ELTON" spectacles. Two rhinestone bejeweled wires spiraled outward in concentric circles from three points on each mother-of-pearl frame, seemingly poised for a scientific display of the atom's inner workings.

Herein lay the paradox of Elton's concert persona. The hottest musician in the United States was using unearthly garb to deflect attention from what he believed were his physical shortcomings, but succeeded only in drawing attention to his willingness to thwart all preconceived notions of fashion. Meanwhile, he told Robert Hilburn, "Forget about the costumes and staging, it's the music that counts."[145]

Elton's musicianship was actually on the road to recovery. Although still shying away from the sort of wild musical chances he took during those first couple of years on the road, this tour saw Elton more mindful of his musicianship than he had been a year earlier. He was still a teen idol, with a stature growing larger each day, but he knew what was important, and he tried to find a balance between the fans' needs and his own.

For each show on the tour, an intermission followed Kiki's opening set, allowing the crew to transform the stage into Elton's multi-level colorfest. During the makeover, large video screens showed a short cartoon entitled *I'm Going to Be a Teenage Idol*, with Elton standing atop a stack of records as a starstruck teenage girl falls into the horn of a gramophone playing the title song. A heart replaces her on the screen. An acknowledgment to his devoted teen following, the cartoon also heralded Elton's grand entrance onstage.

The first number was "Funeral for a Friend/Love Lies Bleeding," played to cheers that reviewers found more frenzied and delirious than anticipated. Whatever the venue, Elton was hungrily greeted with thunderous applause. A review in *Variety* of one of the four shows at the Los Angeles Forum reported: "Audience explodes with his appearance to a deafening, screaming ovation with many of the eighteen thousand standing on seats, crying, stomping, and lighting sparklers. John is undoubtedly at the peak of his career."[146]

In Los Angeles and elsewhere, as Elton slowly unfurled the opening notes to the somber "Funeral for a Friend" on his glitter-draped piano, his full name flashed in blue neon lights nearby. The first names of the other band members flashed in yellow neon. Even the Muscle Shoals Horns got star billing when they made their entrance, two-thirds into the show. Every song was greeted with screams of joy.

Along with all the stage distractions, Elton managed to slip his fans many memorable musical moments, some approaching his early 1970s adventurousness. He turned "Take Me to the Pilot" into a battle between the combination of his rock-tinged, gospel-style vocal and deft, climactic piano accents on the one hand, and Davey's blues-influenced guitar on the other. "Grey Seal," already a swift mover in its second incarnation on *Goodbye Yellow Brick Road*, gained lightyears onstage, especially during the instrumental conclusion. Ray Cooper, usually content to add percussive embellishments to Elton's songs, here had the chance to prove his mettle with an impressive fingernail-conga solo tacked onto the end. In a foreboding "All the Girls Love Alice," Elton engaged in shadowy interplay with the Muscle Shoals Horns. Even two of the songs that had proved disappointing on *Caribou*—"Grimsby," which was badly recorded, and "You're So Static," which was badly written—took on new life. "Grimsby" had the whimsy missing on record. And "You're So Static," which Elton sometimes told audiences was a tango, was delivered with enough verve, and almost excruciatingly loud Spanish piano stylings, to overcome the uninspired melody.

Elton was sometimes subjected to criticism for wearing costumes that contrasted sharply with the sobriety of some of his music. *Billboard*'s Jack McDonough was offended by the juxtaposition of Elton's fluorescent-ball bodysuit against "Funeral for a Friend/Love Lies Bleeding" at one of two shows at the Oakland Coliseum. The outfit, said McDonough, "made him look like a psychedelic porcupine and the ludicrous effect of the costume was incongruous with the emotion contained in the lyric of 'Love Lies Bleeding,' the first number."[147]

The show reached new levels of camp humor in the encores, "Crocodile Rock" and "The Bitch Is Back." Elton played up a heterosexual female/homosexual male erotic fantasy by riding on the sinewy shoulder of his bodyguard, Mr. America Jim Morris, who wore a sparkling loincloth that showed off a plethora of rippling, ebony muscles. Morris acted as a human rickshaw, returning his regally feathered employer back to the stage and the screaming legions.

During the first of his four nights at the Forum in Los Angeles, audience hysteria provoked overzealous security guards. After watching them hurl concertgoers out of aisles and order those standing on their seats to sit, he exacerbated the situation by defiantly beckoning his fans forward, yelling, "This is your concert, come down!" Afterwards, the musician pleaded with Forum manager Jim Appel to restrain the guards for the remaining three nights at the venue. Instead, security forces doubled. Elton told *Circus Raves* magazine that Appel threatened to arrest both agent Howard Rose and the musician if Elton made any more such comments from the stage. "Just let him try. I would have loved to have been arrested on stage," sniffed the pianist. "I would have ground him into the floor."[148]

"MY GIFT IS MY SONG, AND THIS ONE'S FOR YOU"[149]

IN THE MIDST OF THE BIG 1974 U.S. TOUR came a new single, "Lucy in the Sky with Diamonds," as well as the new *Greatest Hits* album. Released on November 15, 1974 in Britain, "Lucy" charted by November 23 and peaked at number 10, Elton's highest-charting British single since "Goodbye Yellow Brick Road." Released on November 18, 1974 in the United States, just as "Whatever Gets You thru the Night" and "The Bitch Is Back" were slipping, the single debuted at number 48 on November 30, the highest debut for that date and in Elton's career thus far. "Lucy" reached number 1 in the United States by January 4, 1975, Elton's third single to reach the top, where it stayed for two weeks. (It also shared the Top 10 for four weeks with Neil Sedaka's American comeback single, "Laughter in the Rain.") A month later, "Lucy" became Elton's fifth gold single. While its Beatles identification probably made it especially desirable to record buyers, there was also, by that fall, a definite attraction to buying anything by the hotter than hot Elton John.

Caribou was still a current hit album in its own right, but sales of the new *Greatest Hits* not only dwarfed all prior Elton John album releases, including *Caribou* and *Goodbye Yellow Brick Road*, but has to this day continued to dwarf all subsequent albums, too. *Greatest Hits* arrived in U.S. record stores on November 4, 1974; four days later, the album was ready for British consumers. It was an enormous hit on both sides of the Atlantic, reaching number 1 in Britain in its first week of release and following suit in the United States by its second. In the United States, the album sat atop *Billboard*'s Top LPs for ten weeks (eleven in Britain), and became Elton's ninth gold album, selling an estimated five million copies in its first year (an amazing feat, as *Caribou* was still doing well and another major hit album, *Captain Fantastic*, would be released in only six months).

Greatest Hits had all the music Elton's fans were looking for on one record: "Your Song," "Daniel," "Honky Cat," "Goodbye Yellow Brick Road," "Saturday Night's Alright for Fighting," "Rocket Man," "Bennie and the Jets" (in Britain and elsewhere in the world, the track was "Candle in the Wind" instead), "Don't Let the Sun Go Down on Me," "Border Song," and "Crocodile Rock." "Border Song" wasn't a hit, but a sentimental favorite of Elton's, as the first single from his first hit album, *Elton John,* and his first song to chart in the United States.

There were some notable omissions from *Greatest Hits*: "Tiny Dancer" and "Levon," both concert favorites, and "Friends," which had briefly struck a chord with the public. Also not included were the near A-side from 1970, "Take Me to the Pilot," and anything from *Tumbleweed Connection,* an album that admittedly had yielded no singles, much less hits. But by the time *Greatest Hits* was released, and as fans bought it during that first blockbuster year, another fact was glaringly obvious—it was outdated. It didn't include the fall 1974 hit "The Bitch Is Back," or the up-and-coming hit "Lucy in the Sky with Diamonds," or another song that was awaiting release, "Philadelphia Freedom." The Elton John musical steamroller just kept rolling along.

"GOOD EVENING, NEW YORK(HAPPY THANKSGIVING)"[150]

THE 1974 "ELTON JOHN TOUR" also kept rolling along, conquering every city it invaded. But no concert that fall was as special to Elton and the band as the one that took place in Madison Square Garden on Thanksgiving night, November 28, 1974. Earlier, John Lennon had accompanied the tour to Boston to decide whether he would honor his pledge to join them onstage. "I came on in a chocolate box outfit. It was just a heart with, like, a bikini, and John said, 'So that's what it's all about,'" Elton remembered.[151] Two nights before the first Madison Square Garden date, Elton, the band, and John Lennon held a rehearsal at the Record Plant in New York, running through "Whatever Gets You thru the Night" and "Lucy in the Sky with Diamonds." Elton wanted to do more than two songs together, suggesting "Imagine" as a third. Lennon preferred to do something up-tempo. They agreed on "I Saw Her Standing There," which Lennon had never sung live.[152]

Elton has claimed that, on the evening of November 28, it was he who was nervous and Lennon who was perfectly composed, but many have recounted how Lennon was throwing up backstage before his three-song set. Meanwhile, Yoko Ono had come to the show with a friend, and had sent a white gardenia and an encouraging note backstage to both Elton and her then estranged husband.

To cries of "I love you!" from young female fans, Elton and the band began as usual with "Funeral for a Friend/Love Lies Bleeding." But when the show was nearly over, Elton had some news for the audience. "Seeing as it's Thanksgiving, we thought we'd make tonight a little bit of a joyous occasion by inviting someone up with us onstage," he said. "I'm sure he will be no stranger to anybody in the audience when I say, it's our great privilege, and your great privilege, to see and hear . . . Mr. John Lennon!" The audience, according to one witness, "bounced politely off the ceiling."[153] Fortunately, Lennon had recovered from his backstage jitters and greeted the cheers wearing Yoko's gardenia. They raced through a lively version of "Whatever Gets You thru the Night."

Elton has described "Lucy in the Sky with Diamonds" as "one of the best songs ever written." It probably got a better live treatment here than anywhere else on the tour. Elton sang with a special self-assuredness, achieving just the right balance between his ringing piano chords and Davey's psychedelic guitar. And Elton and Lennon jovially traded off singing the title phrase prior to the song's climax.

Before the last number, it was Lennon's turn to make an announcement. "I'd like to thank Elton and the boys for having me on tonight," he said. "We're trying to think of a number to finish off with so I can get out of here and be sick, and we thought we'd do a number of an old, estranged fiancé of mine, called Paul. This is one I never sang, it's an old Beatles number, and we just about know it." After a joyously rowdy "I Saw Her Standing There," the duets were over.

The show continued, with more emotion in store. During a rendition of "Don't Let the Sun," Elton closed his eyes for a time, only to see, upon reopening them, a sea of lighted matches. "A little tear did run down me eyes," he reflected later. "It's impossible not to be touched by that sort of thing."[154] Several songs and encores later, at 11:45 P.M., the show, which Elton to this day cites as his career's most memorable, was over. The night, however, was not, as Elton and numerous friends, including Lennon and Neil Sedaka, congregated in the grand ballroom at the Hotel Pierre for a party that ran into the wee hours.

"YOU CAN STILL SAY HOMO, AND EVERYBODY LAUGHS"[155]

DURING ROBERT HILBURN'S TRAVELS with Elton and the band during the U.S. tour, he read, along with an incredulous Elton and Bernie, a review of one of the first fall shows. The reviewer, who may have been thinking of David Bowie, expressed relief that Elton's act was devoid of "supercharged sexual overtones—particularly bizarre sexual overtones." Bernie laughed, asking whether the reviewer was familiar with "All the Girls Love Alice."[156]

That was probably beside the point. Despite the feathers, the bugle beads, and the punch-bowl hats, Elton was not perceived as threatening, and few seemed to imagine that he might not date women. Lynn Van Matre asked Elton during the tour what he thought of the young female fans who were "dolled up" and lying in wait for him in a strategic spot downstairs. "That doesn't really upset me," he answered, probably not the response Van Matre was expecting. "It's just that sometimes you say hello to someone and are friendly and they take that as an invitation and expect more."[157]

Elton's sexuality wasn't a secret to the editors and writers of *Rolling Stone*, who had begun dropping hints about it in various articles. Although he had been the subject of two excellent cover story interviews, in 1971 with David Felton and in 1973 with Paul Gambaccini, the honeymoon had ended by the fall of 1974. Suddenly *Rolling Stone* seemed bent on "exposing" Elton's sexual leanings. In one article, writer Ben Fong-Torres referred to the recent incident in New Zealand in which Reid had reacted violently to being called gay. He also described an incident involving an MCA listening party for *Goodbye Yellow Brick Road*, when a tape had malfunctioned, prompting one of Reid's famous temper tantrums. Elton "clomped out of there with his friends," stopping only to call the sound engineers "bloody cunts." Fong-Torres made sure to point out the "insinuating reminder" that Elton and Reid shared a house in England (in the article, Elton insisted that Reid was just his manager) and noted that, at Elton's rented Los Angeles home, all the houseguests were men.[158]

This article was followed by a January 2, 1975 story that purportedly covered John Lennon's historic appearance onstage with Elton the previous November. But over half the piece, written by Ed McCormack, was about an incident that had allegedly occurred at the post-concert party at the Hotel Pierre, where the wife of a local disc jockey had reportedly called Elton a "fag," prompting angry responses from both Elton and John Reid, who had ejected her and her husband from the party. McCormack described the efforts of Reid and others to make sure that the two really were leaving, with "Elton John suddenly appearing on the fringe of the crowd, waving a finger like Truman Capote playing the Godfather. . . ."[159] The inference was clear—famed author Truman Capote was gay, often the target of impressionists on comedy shows who enjoyed emphasizing his effeminate mannerisms. Why this incident, and the attendant description of Elton, needed such extensive airing in a rock magazine is puzzling, unless one concludes that *Rolling Stone* had developed a keen interest in "outing" Elton John.

"WE ONLY RECORDED IT TO POINT OUT WHAT A GOOD SONG IT WAS"[160]

ELTON AND THE GROUP OF MUSICIANS he was now calling the "Elton John Band" closed out 1974 with a series of Christmastime concerts at London's Hammersmith Odeon, between December 21 and Christmas Eve. The BBC televised part of his final concert of the year on a special December 24 edition of the *Old Grey Whistle Test* (simulcast on *Top Gear*, John Peel's BBC Radio One program). Viewers saw an Elton John in love with his audience and live performing. On display were the tinselly, bugle-beaded outfit (without the punch bowl hat) and several pairs of spectacles, including the fluff-and-rhinestone and rose motif sets.

Also on display was Elton's trademark humility, when he responded to critics and Beatles purists who had suggested that he should not dabble in such works as "Lucy in the Sky with Diamonds." One anonymous Beatles fan had written a vitriol-filled letter to the editor of *Record Mirror* that fall, saying, "Fair enough, the Beatles as a group are dead, but it does not give Elton John or any other recording artist any right to ruin one of their best numbers."[161] Elton didn't disagree, telling his audience, "We only recorded it to point out what a good song it was."[162]

Viewers were entertained with Elton's trademark physical antics. In "Honky Cat," he picked out a piano solo with his right hand and cupped his chin in his left, leaning against the piano and facing his audience as if to say, "Who could top this?" And during "Saturday Night's Alright for Fighting," he attacked the piano on his knees, his back arched in a near-backward jackknife. The show ended with Rod Stewart and rocker Gary Glitter assisting on vocals for an up-tempo "White Christmas," as polystyrene snow and colorful balloons with Elton's likeness fell on the audience.

The Hammersmith concerts were a nice way for Elton to professionally end 1974, another dream year. The *Los Angeles Times* reported that according to three music trade magazines—*Billboard, Cash Box,* and *Record World*—Elton had tied with Helen Reddy and John Denver as the best-selling record artist of the year. *Billboard* also named *Goodbye Yellow Brick Road* the top album of 1974, while *Record World* named Elton the top singles artist.[163] Robert Hilburn named Elton the pop music artist of 1974. Although Hilburn acknowledged distinguished efforts by David Bowie, Jackson Browne, Bob Dylan, the Eagles, Stevie Wonder, and others, he believed that "no one reflected the pulse and spirit of pop music as continuously during 1974 as the colorful English singer-composer-pianist," citing not only *Caribou* (a stretch, to be sure), but Elton's appearances on others' albums, his string of hits, and his fall tour, which, Hilburn said, was a "marvelously entertaining combination of rewarding music and engaging manner."[164]

"SHINE THE LIGHT THROUGH THE EYES OF THE ONE LEFT BEHIND"[165]

THE START OF 1975 was nothing like the start of 1974. Elton was no longer being pulled in different directions by a demanding schedule. He had another album and a soon-to-be-released single in the can. Now he had time to attend to other interests—the Watford Football Club, playing "EJ the DJ" on BBC radio, thinking.

He also appeared on the inaugural episode of Cher's new American comedy-variety show, reportedly lured on by David Geffen, with whom Cher had taken up residence after her divorce from Sonny Bono. Elton sang his current hit, "Lucy in the Sky," duetted with Cher on "Bennie and the Jets," and collegially joined in on some numbers with the host, Bette Midler, and Flip Wilson. He also made his comedic debut in a sketch in which he and the others played themselves as residents of an old-age home, fifty years into the future. As a glamorized version of Arte Johnson's "Dirty Old Man," he rode in a computerized Art Deco wheelchair, asked his "senior citizen" chums whether anyone remembered how to have sex, and promptly fell asleep. He seemed to relish the self-mockery; when Cher attempted to wake him, he emerged, disoriented, from the depths of slumber, momentarily forgetting who he was. "Elton? Where's *Elton?*" he said in a Python-esque voice. "I *love* 'im! 'E's my *favorite!*"

Although Elton's schedule of appearances was relatively unhurried, the same could not be said for his album release schedule. In the United States, at least, albums were being released like it was May 1971 all over again. On January 13, 1975, MCA finally issued *Empty Sky* in the United States. It became the third Elton John album to come out since June, but this was as good a time as any. *Greatest Hits* was still number 1 in the United States (and Britain), and the release of *Captain Fantastic* was more than four months away. *Empty Sky* was a fitting hors d'oeuvre to *Captain Fantastic*, as much of the latter album concerned those halcyon days of winter 1968–69, when *Empty Sky* was being recorded.

Buttressing this sense of history and nostalgia were the liner notes by early Elton John supporter Eric Van Lustbader, who recalled how, as album editor of *Cash Box* magazine in June 1969, he had been so taken with an *Empty Sky* import that he had been moved to write about it in the magazine. Like the fan he still was, Van Lustbader heaped glowing praise on the album and its creators. "In those days the name 'Elton John' comprised only Elton and Bernie and in that sense this album offers a brilliantly clear insight into what they were like as people. There was no image, no ornate production, nothing in fact except the remarkable melodies, the remarkable lyrics, and that remarkable voice." Van Lustbader compared the album to the charming crudity of the Beatles' American debut, *Meet the Beatles!*

Unlike *Meet the Beatles!*, *Empty Sky* never reached number 1. It debuted on *Billboard*'s Top LPs chart on February 1, 1975, peaked at number 6, and stayed on the chart for eighteen weeks, missing a gold certification. This was only Elton's second album since *11-17-70* to meet this fate, although as the primary function of *Empty Sky*'s belated U.S. release was to set the table for *Captain Fantastic*, this wasn't so terrible.

In February, Elton became the twenty-fourth member of the *Playboy* Jazz and Pop Hall of Fame, which inducted only one musician into its ranks per year.[166] And during the last week of February, "Philadelphia Freedom" became the single of a new entity called the Elton John Band. A small inscription on the A-side read "With love to BJK and the music of Philadelphia." The B-side was the live performance of "I Saw Her Standing There" on which John Lennon had guested.

Elton was still on a chart roll in the United States. Debuting at number 53 on March 8, "Philadelphia Freedom" reached number 1 by April 12, staying there for two weeks. In May, it became Elton's sixth gold single (and was certified platinum in September 1995). The British were still a bit intransigent with their native son, allowing him the pleasure of peaking only at number 12, a solid enough outcome.

"THE LESS I SAY THE MORE MY WORK GETS DONE"[167]

IN FALL 1974, Elton had made the decision to remain a British resident, despite a tax burden that tempted many other musicians and entertainers to resettle in the United States or elsewhere. He decided that he had too many ties to his home country to leave it. "I can't imagine going to live in Geneva," Elton remarked. "There is nothing there but people who've gone to Geneva."[168] And the United States was no place to feel a sense of normality, even though he loved Americans. Hero worship there was taken to extremes, he said. "England to me is sane," he told talk show host Michael Parkinson on BBC television in late spring 1975.

Elton's passion for the Watford Football Club played no small part in his decision to remain in Britain. His work as a director, he said repeatedly, brought him down to earth. That he was treated as a pariah by some board members of other clubs because of his rock star status gave him a sense of perspective. He was ejected from one boardroom in the north of England for this very reason. Another time, a board member who had had too much to drink started making fun of him, saying "'Oh, look, he's a pop star and he can read! Miracles! Miracles!'" Elton had to tell himself, "It's for the club. You've got to keep your temper for the club."[169] Ultimately, he showed that he wasn't seeking entry in football boardrooms across England because he was a rock star, but because of his love for the game.

Elton's quest for normality left him with a confusingly bifurcated existence. His decision to remain British didn't stop him from buying a million-dollar mansion in Los Angeles's Benedict Canyon for when he was visiting or working in Southern California. The home had once belonged to a powerful old-Hollywood producer, David O. Selznick; mysterious film star Greta Garbo had once lived there as well.[170]

With the April 1975 premiere of the film *Tommy*, for which he attended gala openings in Melbourne and Sydney, Australia, as well as in New York and London, Elton became a movie star, too. In his much-heralded five-minute cameo as the Pinball Wizard, he was unceremoniously unseated by the deaf, dumb, and blind Tommy, played by Roger Daltry. The three-foot-high Doc Marten boots, which Elton mounted with the assistance of six stagehands,[171] were probably the strangest gear he had worn yet.

Although "Pinball Wizard" was not released as a single that year in the United States or Britain, it got enough American airplay right around the time "Philadelphia Freedom" was topping the charts to have given Elton another number 1 had it been commercially available.[172] Airplay of his music had reached saturation level.

It was against this background that Elton decided to make a radical change in his band. Following Christmas 1974, he said, he had felt "empty." After "brooding like a hen" for months, he realized he had to make a change. "It's something I honestly felt in my stomach," he said. "I had the urge to play with somebody else."[173] He decided to fire Nigel and Dee. Years later, he admitted, "I had to tell them over the phone, which was an extremely awful way of doing it, and I regret that intensely."[174]

Besides being badly communicated, the decision itself was odd in light of his efforts to give the entire band more recognition of late. In the fall, he had introduced his band mates as the Elton John Band, the name of each displayed prominently in neon lights. At the time he had said he was "constantly having battles with people who just don't recognize this is a unit. They still think it's Elton John and a backing group, which is something I fought against for a long time. . . . It is gradually coming around, it takes a long time. Nigel was voted second-best drummer in the rock magazine *Circus* so that's a step in the right direction."[175] "Philadelphia Freedom" was the Elton John Band's first single, and was still high on the charts when Elton gave his drummer and bassist the fateful news.

"Dee is not so happy," Elton said about a month later. "I haven't had a chance to see him, so I think he feels currently very bitter about the whole situation."[176] Nigel, though stunned, was eager to pursue a solo career, so took it well at the time.

While at the Caribou Ranch recording *Captain Fantastic,* Elton had encouraged the drummer to take tentative steps toward a solo outing. Although Nigel had had an album out in 1971, *Nigel Olsson's Drum Orchestra and Chorus,* he hadn't promoted it. But in the summer of 1974, Elton had said to him, "I know you've been wanting to record, so while we have the spare time, let's do it." With Gus Dudgeon producing, Elton and the band recorded the Bee Gees' "Only One Woman" with Nigel singing lead. The song charted on *Billboard*'s Hot 100 on March 1, 1975, peaking at number 91. So Nigel was receptive to Elton's encouragement. "He gave me the push to get me out there and said, 'Now's the time for you to make it,'" Nigel said.[177]

"BREAKING UP'S SOMETIMES LIKE BREAKING THE LAW"[178]

As the fallout from his dismissal of Nigel and Dee continued, Elton basked in flattery. The May 3, 1975 edition of the Los Angeles-based *Soul Train* television show saw host Don Cornelius standing in front of a grand piano made of glass. "This is especially for a very, very gifted young man," he announced, "who has combined absolute genius as a musician/composer with a sort of psychedelic outlook on life, which causes everybody that comes near him to be thoroughly entertained." With Elton's entrance in a striped black and white suit, a glittery black derby with black plumage, and black-framed, rhinestone-decorated glasses, *Soul Train* had its first white guest star.

"I never did *American Bandstand,* but I did *Soul Train,* and I was so chuffed with that," Elton told late night talk show host Conan O'Brien some years later.[179] On *Soul Train,* he took questions from some of the show's dancers—about where he got his "funky" glasses (Optique Boutique), what his favorite song was (that was always changing), and when he had started to sing ("I'm just learning to sing," he responded). Then he performed "Philadelphia Freedom" and "Bennie and the Jets" to a taped backing track, as the dancers moved to *his* grooves.

Just days later, *Captain Fantastic* was released—on May 19 in the United States and in Britain four days later. The old band would have its last day in the sun for a time, featured in both the vinyl grooves and the album's extensive packaging, which included an *Alice in Wonderland*–style cover illustration, consistent with Bernie's conceptualization of the Captain and the Kid as cartoon characters.

In the United States, with an advance sale to retailers of 1.4 million copies,[180] *Captain Fantastic* became the first album in album chart history to enter at number 1 in all three trade magazines, *Billboard, Cash Box,* and *Record World* (going on to spend six more nonconsecutive weeks at number 1). It didn't even have a hit single yet, but many radio stations willingly played tracks from the new album. Meanwhile, "Philadelphia Freedom" and "Pinball Wizard" were still getting substantial airplay.[181]

The story was not quite as good in Britain, where the album entered the chart on June 7, peaking at number 2. This was probably because DJM Records had stuck an exorbitant price on the album of three and a quarter pounds. It was the most expensive one-record album in the history of British recordings to that date.[182] Dick James's son Stephen didn't take kindly to criticism over the album's high price. "I've never known the public not to moan about the price of records. You should compare the price of albums in Britain with the price on the Continent," he argued. "The new album has a very costly packaging, and two sixteen-page booklets and a poster. When you add up the real cost of those, they're actually getting them cheap."[183]

As usual, reviews were mixed. Robert Hilburn, while acknowledging that the album lacked an "immediately accessible blockbuster single," wrote that the "arrangements, vocals, and lyrics are as controlled and finely honed as anything they've yet done."[184] Greg Shaw, writing for *Phonograph Record,* praised the "remarkable process by which Elton John transforms mere lyrics (however sophisticated) and mere musicians (however brilliant they may be—and certainly are) into a gestalt that defies analysis."[185] But Dave Marsh, in a nationally syndicated *Rolling Stone* review, proclaimed that Elton John "has never made a great or even consistently worthwhile album," and *Captain Fantastic* didn't change this perception.[186] But however mixed the reviews, fans were buying Elton's records at an unprecedented pace, and the pianist was riding high.

"SWEET FREEDOM WHISPERED IN MY EAR"[187]

ASSEMBLING A NEW GROUP of musicians to play with the remaining band nucleus of Davey and Ray was Elton's next project, and an urgent one. He was scheduled to play in an all-star Wembley Stadium concert on June 21.

Choosing a drummer was the easiest. Elton grabbed the unassuming, bearded Roger Pope for the job. Pope had played with Hookfoot and, more recently, the Kiki Dee Band. Elton hired the leprechaun-ish Kenny Passarelli as his new bass player on Joe Walsh's recommendation (Passarelli had cowritten the rock radio staple "Rocky Mountain Way" with him). For a second lead guitar player, he had two candidates in mind: Jeff "Skunk" Baxter of the Doobie Brothers, who could be on hand only for Wembley, and Caleb Quaye. To Elton's surprise, both guitarists said yes, giving him three guitarists (including Davey) for the Wembley show.

Selecting a new keyboard player was the most intimidating detail. Elton's agent, Howard Rose, recommended a twenty-three-year-old dabbler in new keyboard technologies, James Newton Howard. The serious-looking James's "audition" turned out to be a meeting with Elton, during which the latter played the *Captain Fantastic* record. Elton, who had already made up his mind, then offered James the job.

James, an accomplished pianist in his own right, wasn't surprised at the choice. Much of Elton's music was heavily orchestrated, and there was a trend in popular music toward electronic support. "I think Elton was intelligent enough and aware enough to realize that," said James,[188] who recognized Elton's own piano artistry. "He's one of the finest pianists I've ever worked with, and I didn't know how good he was 'til I worked with him."[189]

The new group began rehearsing for Wembley in a sweltering Amsterdam heatwave, without air conditioning. Rehearsals lasted ten hours a day.[190] Three days before the concert, London's *Evening Standard* ran a special edition with a headline extolling the achievements of its esteemed native son: "Bound for Wembley—the world's No. 1 rock star: KING JOHN THE FIRST!" On the day of the big event, the *London Times* ran a feature on Elton's career, fondly looking back at the nondescript origins that somehow led to a musical phenomenon. He was, said writer Geoffrey Wansell, "the most popular single performer in the ephemeral history of rock'n'roll, Britain's true successor to the Beatles." By then, Elton had sold seventy-five million records (presumably worldwide), but his mother and stepfather had never left his side, living just "two doors down" from his Virginia Water home. Stepdad Fred Farebrother still helped his boy with painting and decorating.[191]

With so many heights already scaled, the Wembley date looked to be another triumph. Elton hoped his new band would be the novelty he believed his fans now needed. "An album coming straight in at number 1 in America is unheard of," he had told a BBC radio interviewer the week before the show. "It makes me think that I've really got to work hard to sustain a level. . . . That's what I'm trying to do with this band. My albums will always sell well because of my name, but I've really got to try hard to make things sound a little different and better."[192] Among other things, he intended to perform all ten songs from *Captain Fantastic* live, in running order.

Elton was donating his personal share of the Wembley proceeds to the Watford Football Club and other good causes, including the British Heart Foundation, the Royal National Institute for the Blind, Help the Aged, the Lady Hoare Trust for Physically Handicapped Children, and the organization that had first piqued his interest in charitable work, the National Youth Theatre.[193] Preceding him in the all-day, eleven-hour concert was a handpicked lineup, including the Eagles and the

Beach Boys. The Beach Boys' ninety-minute set came just before Elton, and was especially warmly received by the 120,000-strong crowd. After being fed the Californians' brand of infectious, harmony-laden hits, the audience was expecting hits from Elton, too.

Elton did give them hits, and well-known album tracks, for the show's first half, opening with "Funeral for a Friend/Love Lies Bleeding." The change in the band's sound was immediately evident with the addition of James's synthesizer, which closely approximated Dave Hentschel's contribution to the two-part composition on *Goodbye Yellow Brick Road*. Later, during a premiere performance of "Philadelphia Freedom," James convincingly mimicked Gene Page's string arrangement. Two Rocket Records acts, Brian and Brenda Russell and Donny Gerrard, supplied backing vocals.

About seven songs into his show, Elton tipped his hat to the Beach Boys with a new composition, "Chameleon." He and Bernie had actually written the song for the Beach Boys who, to the songwriters' great chagrin, had turned it down. Elton, who ordinarily took between ten minutes and half an hour to compose music to Bernie's lyrics, had labored over this one for six months.

Having three lead guitar players meant that each had the freedom to do more of what he wanted. For Davey, this meant playing the Scottish folk music he loved. One could almost envision a sea of kilts flapping in a country jig as he rhapsodized on mandolin in a prelude to the countrified "Dixie Lily." But it was the band's performance on "The Bitch Is Back" that solidified the impression that no longer was the piano most important in Elton's live sound. He had wanted a different sound, and he got one—a veritable wall of sound. Getting James Newton Howard "gives me more freedom to play less," he said. "I can play much better when I play less."[194] For all intents and purposes, Elton's band had become a guitar band.

This change was not as evident on the *Captain Fantastic* songs, reached midway through the set list. They demanded a more delicate touch overall. The performances were true to the originals, with some artful twists. Elton's buoyant jazz lines on "Tell Me When the Whistle Blows" gave the song an exhilarated air, not the sleepiness exuded by the recording. "Someone Saved My Life Tonight," aided by Ray's timpani, was full of more fire and brimstone than on vinyl. And the optimistic "Writing," a smiley, up-tempo ballad on record, became more of a mid-tempo rocker in concert.

Many of the concertgoers didn't take kindly to the unleashing of so much new material. This, combined with the length of the all-day affair, reduced the crowd to about seventy thousand. Philip Norman, not an Elton John admirer, proclaimed him a loser. "I reasoned that, when he offered to perform the whole of his amusingly titled new album, the slight dwindling in the crowd must be a figment of my own indifference," Norman wrote. "Then I went outside. Hundreds of people were streaming off down the avenue, into the Wembley sunset."[195]

Would this affect the British success of the new single, "Someone Saved My Life Tonight"? Charting there on June 28, 1975, it peaked at number 22—his least successful single in Britain since "Step into Christmas," which had been just a seasonal release. True to form, the American single, released on June 23, was the highest debuting song on *Billboard*'s Hot 100 on July 5 when it entered the chart at number 51, even while "Philadelphia Freedom" was still in the Top 40. After four weeks on the chart, it was in the Top 10, eventually peaking at number 4. In September, it became Elton's seventh gold single.

"I THOUGHT IT WAS TIME TO THROW IN MY HAND FOR A NEW SET OF CARDS"[196]

AFTER THE WEMBLEY LETDOWN, recording another new album should have been just the thing to brighten the band's spirits. In Oakland, California, on June 29, Elton jammed onstage with the Eagles and the Doobie Brothers. Then he and the new band retired immediately to the Caribou Ranch to record what would become *Rock of the Westies*.

"It was a bit tricky because we were dealing with a different bunch of people," Gus Dudgeon said later.[197] There was infighting, which no doubt increased the music's noise level. Even without the infighting, however, Elton's new band represented a change in artistic direction, while a growing reliance on illegal substances in his private life also influenced his art. Elton wouldn't admit until the 1990s that, by the time he began work on *Westies*, the polite and proper former Reggie Dwight was more than just a casual user of cocaine, and often returned to the influence of liquor.[198]

Elton was not the only one relying on drugs. As Bernie later remembered, "That period of time is a little foggy because we were all at the high point of abusing ourselves to the max." At the Caribou Ranch, he said, "It was Jack Daniels and lines on the console, and for some reason, we got it [the album] done. I don't remember anything about the sessions and I don't think anybody in that band will remember them either, but for some reason, it paid off. Luckily, we're all still alive to tell the tale."[199] Elton later explained that substance abuse was a way of fending off his insecurities. The costumes were only a stopgap measure. "If I had a drink in my hand, I'd feel a little safer," he told David Frost in 1991. "And I thought after I took drugs, that broke down all my barriers because I thought, 'Well, I can really communicate now.' . . . I felt that I was part of a gang. I felt I'd really arrived when I started taking drugs. 'Yeah, . . . I take drugs so I'm finally accepted. I'm one of the in-crowd.'"[200]

The prevalence of drugs during the sessions, along with the infighting that Gus Dudgeon remembered, helps to explain the anarchic sound of *Westies* (nearly titled *Bottled and Brained*). It's not that Elton didn't approach *Westies* with the same sense of purpose he had on other albums, or with the same need to excel. As James Newton Howard later said of him, "I think we stimulate each other. When I first joined the band I think it was good for his playing because he's an incredibly competitive person, and I was sort of a kick in the ass for him. But he was certainly a kick in the ass for me. . . . [During the *Westies* recording sessions, Elton devised] a piano riff in triads starting up on A-D-F and going down in sixteenth notes, all the way to the bottom of the piano. He developed the riff, then turned around at the piano, looked at me, and said something like, 'Check that one out!'"[201]

Gus Dudgeon later recalled how, on the morning after he arrived at the ranch, he had thought everyone else was asleep. Suffering from a severe case of jet lag, he tried resting, but found Elton was wide awake in the cabin the pianist shared with Davey Johnstone, pounding the ivories.[202] Naturally, Davey couldn't stay in bed under these circumstances, and added his guitar to the flood of piano riffs. Soon, two new songs were completed—probably "Medley (Yell Help, Wednesday Night, Ugly)" and "Grow Some Funk of Your Own," the first ones to bear Davey's name as cowriter.

The recording schedule was swift, as usual. In less than a month the album was complete, with backing vocal contributions from Davey, Caleb, Kenny Passarelli, and Elton, too, in his alter ego of "Ann Orson." Remaining were a small amount of overdubbing and additional backing vocals (by Patti LaBelle, Kiki Dee, and even sound engineer Clive Franks) to be recorded in Los Angeles's Sound Factory.

"Medley (Yell Help, Wednesday Night, Ugly)" is a medley of three short songs that manage to get entangled in one another. Bernie's disjointed lyrics lay the groundwork for the final product's barbarism, an orgy of sexism combined with testosterone-driven hell-raising. The bridge of the song is an uninteresting four-line ode to loneliness on a Wednesday night, followed by a crude rhapsody about ugly women.

There are only three appealing aspects to this medley, which is devoid of any discernible melody or cohesiveness. First is Elton's ambitious vocal, which shows advances in tonal control, alternating between the voice of a self-possessed country charmer, the cloudiness of a woman's voice à la Olivia Newton-John, and a gravel-throated, sensory impaired drunk. Second is the musicianship of the band members, as versatile as the music and lyrics are meaningless. And third is LaBelle's chesty backing vocals, which lend the recording some rhythm-and-blues spunk. Never before in Elton's career had so much talent been lavished on something of so little consequence.

"Grow Some Funk of Your Own," the other song written with Davey, is marginally better. The tale is coherent, but its basic ingredients are predictable rock-'n'roll fodder. A group of young men travel south to a "border town" to enjoy the "local sounds" in a cantina. One of them gets into trouble with a big, angry Mexican for attempting to flirt with a "señorita." The band's wall of sound is in full bloom as Elton barks out a near melody, banging out his trademark percussive piano. But unlike his chords for *Goodbye Yellow Brick Road*'s "Dirty Little Girl," which serve to cushion Davey's grating guitar licks, his percussive attacks here can't soften the song's harshness. The only real dignity accorded "Grow Some Funk" is Ray's well-timed work on castanets, bell-tree, and, especially, the vibes.

All of the other songs on *Westies* were written by Elton and Bernie alone. Two, "Street Kids" and "Billy Bones and the White Bird," take advantage of the band's wall of sound but have little melody and none of the sonic pleasures usually associated with Elton's gemlike, symmetrical compositions. The lyrics to "Street Kids" seem a follow-up to "Saturday Night's Alright for Fighting," which explains and laments the aimlessness of working-class British youth. The kids in "Street Kids" are in the same demographic, but are less interested in having a good time on a Saturday night than in proving their collective manhood as "East End" gang members. Also, the lyrics aren't as effective, thanks to Bernie's ill-considered combination of movie-esque dialogue ("And if you think you've seen gasoline/burnin' in my eyes/don't be alarmed/tell yourself/ it's good to be—it's good to be alive") and rock'n'roll clichés ("I'd like to break away from the rut I'm in/but beggars can't be choosers/I was born to sin").

The feedback-filled music to "Street Kids" evokes the kids' fury, but the wall of sound is so thick that, unlike "Saturday Night's Alright," there is no ebb and flow in the song's aggression. "Street Kids" just harangues. Strangely enough, some of Elton's best playing of the album is featured here, with collections of vibrant chords that reach through the wall of sound like lightning flashes, probably a variation on the sixteenth-note riff that had so impressed James Newton Howard.

"Billy Bones and the White Bird" is little better, its lyrics nearly as incoherent as those for "Medley." Throughout, Bernie intersperses puzzling exclamations of "check it out," which become the centerpiece of probably the most annoying music Elton has ever composed, even amid an appealing electric piano solo by James and powerful timpani accents by Ray.

There are glimpses of Elton's old, melody-driven approach elsewhere on *Westies*. On the lower end of the melodic scale is "Dan Dare (Pilot of the Future)." The song is a tribute to comic-book superhero Dan Dare, to whom Bernie bids a tired adieu, having finally outgrown Dare's brand of courageousness. Though silly, the song makes up for its insouciance with some funky musicianship. The kaleidoscopic jazz of Elton's piano chords, the combined "wah-wah" of Davey's "voice bag" and James' clavinet, and a guitar solo by Davey that could have been at home in a Sly and the Family Stone recording, all lend the song a meatiness that saves it from being completely disposable.

More impressive is "Hard Luck Story," a song originally written for Kiki (for a failed 1974 single) by Elton and Bernie alter egos Ann Orson and Carte Blanche, respectively. The success of this version owes nothing to the lyrics, which are confusingly skewed to represent the perspective of the husband, who returns home to his wife after another rough day at the factory. Elton sings to a wife whom he admits is unjustly embattled, yet he, in the guise of the exhausted laborer, is the one who wants to leave. The song would have worked better as a duet between Elton and Kiki, with each playing a spousal combatant.

It is the music, however, that works. Elton's vocal is impassioned and soul-inspired—providing the only soul on the album, besides LaBelle's backing vocals on "Medley"—and Kiki dominates the backing vocals. Where "Street Kids" lacks the ebb and flow of a well-constructed song, and "Billy Bones and the White Bird" reaches for decibel where an understated chord sequence would have been better, "Hard Luck Story" alternates volume and texture, and features a rewarding choral climax.

The following song, "Feed Me," is a preview of the infinitely more visionary music that would characterize Elton's next album. Its lyrics could be "Madman Across the Water" revisited. Images abound of the madness of a junkie aching for his next fix. In light of the drug-driven album sessions, the subject matter is apropos.

Elton's doesn't play on "Feed Me," but envelops the melody in an airy chord pattern—played on electric piano and vibes by James and Ray, respectively—that presages Chuck Mangione's Top 10 contemporary jazz hit, "Feels So Good." But the music is not all about airy good feelings. Elton makes the listener grasp the junkie's pain with a melodic crescendo that soars over the percolating sounds of the band.

More of the new band's aptitude is present on the album's only ballad, "I Feel Like a Bullet (in the Gun of Robert Ford)." Described by Bernie as a "knife in the back love song,"[203] this is the tale of a man guilt-ridden over heartlessly breaking up with his girlfriend, a lyrical premise that allows Bernie to return to his old fascination with the American Wild West. The protagonist's guilt is symbolized by the bullet in Robert Ford's gun that killed outlaw Jesse James: "I feel like a bullet in the gun of Robert Ford/I'm low as a paid assassin is/you know I'm cold as a hired sword./I'm so ashamed we can't patch it up/You know I can't think straight no more." He cogently observes that "breaking up's sometimes like breaking the law."

Elton modifies the lyrics to make these words slide off the tongue, assigning hope to a seemingly futile situation. Instead of singing "we can't patch it up," he asks: "I'm so ashamed, can't we patch it up?" The song is lifted by the billowy combination of his arpeggiated piano and a despondent melody that teeters between resignation and desperation as he makes facile use of his falsetto. All the while, the band engages in an instrumental slow dance.

The only other praiseworthy song on this album is also its only well-known song, "Island Girl." Written in Caribbean-style English, the song is about a Jamaican prostitute in New York City who, while exploited by the "racket boss," holds her own by getting even with the clients. The band members provide the song's tropical flavor, even if they don't all stick to Caribbean stylings. Davey's song opener smacks of Hawaii, not Jamaica, while James Newton Howard's synthesizer and mellotron solo offers a generic Caribbean flavoring. But what defines the sound of "Island

Girl" defines too little of the rest of the album—Elton's pianism, here a hardy show of chord muscle and submelody that weaves through the song, serving as the glue that holds the other elements together.

Rock of the Westies sounds like no other Elton John album recorded before or since, in part because Elton had retreated from the melody-making that had helped make him a star, and also because he misused the talents of his new band members, deferring too much to that wall of sound. Perhaps because of the infighting, the drug-taking, and the often hackneyed lyrical style Bernie disturbingly embraced, Elton misused the new band's potential—although he did share with a reporter the generous but ominous insight, at the height of his popularity, that the band could serve as a career springboard for both Davey and Caleb.[204]

"A MOTIVATED, SUPERSONIC KING OF THE SCENE"[205]

JUST AS "SOMEONE SAVED MY LIFE TONIGHT" was peaking on the Hot 100, Elton cohosted with Diana Ross the first ever Rock Music Awards, in Santa Monica. The show was telecast on Saturday, August 9, showing a fairly sartorially subdued Elton in the omnipresent rhinestone-lined, orange-tinted glasses, a glistening yellow-orange suit with flared lapels, and a low-cut shirt from which thick, curly chest hair was visible, contrasting with his ever-thinning pate.

The awards were distributed based on votes from a panel of rock critics and disc jockeys. Stevie Wonder was named best male recording artist and Joni Mitchell best female recording artist, while Elton was named outstanding rock personality of the year.[206] This made sense. In the year leading up to the awards, Elton had amassed a startling five Top 10 hits, two of which had reached number 1. The previous month, Elton had been the subject of a *Time* magazine cover story, a testament to the impact he was making on the American consciousness.

"Elton John the Hit Machine" was also "Elton John the Newly Skinny," as a *People* magazine cover story reported the week after the awards show. One picture showed him in a room-sized closet, surrounded by two hundred pairs of shoes and rows of clothing, proudly showing off his flat stomach.[207] He would maintain his trim figure for several months, the entire length of his fall West Coast tour.

The summer of 1975 was filled with celebration. In commemoration of the fifth anniversary of his career-making debut at Doug Weston's Troubadour club, Elton and his new band played six shows there over three nights, on August 25, 26, and 27. The bespectacled musician donated the $150,000 in proceeds to UCLA's Jules Stein Eye Institute.

Journalist Robert Hilburn was present for the first night's rehearsal and sound check, finding a slender Elton, fresh from the Robert F. Kennedy Pro Celebrity Tennis Tournament in New York, where he had played tennis with Billie Jean King, and sporting a several days' growth of beard. Elton, who had had a full beard for his

Troubadour debut in 1970, denied that the stubble was a sign of superstition about playing at the club that had launched his career. "Just coincidence," he laughed, which seemed to imply that it wasn't.[208]

Wearing only a black, rhinestone-studded jumpsuit for the first show, Elton was introduced to the audience by Neil Diamond, just as he had been on August 25, 1970. But the nineteen-song set, presented in roughly chronological order, failed to ignite the crowd, a cross section of older music industry types and associates of Jules Stein (a founder of MCA), who'd paid $250 apiece for the benefit. An exasperated Elton mischievously introduced one song by saying, "Here's one you can all tap your wheelchairs to," which, fortunately, was lost on the already lost concertgoers.[209]

The chemistry was different for the second show that night, also a benefit. Elton toned down his garb, wearing a short-sleeved Esso gas station attendant uniform from which tufts of chest hair sprouted. He attacked the keys aggressively, seemingly pent up from months of being deprived of a live audience. This time the audience, a much younger mix of celebrities and musicians like Cher, Ringo Starr, Helen Reddy, and Joe Walsh, gave him the reception he craved. Nigel Olsson was there, too, and seemed to be harboring no ill will. "Now I know he's the greatest," he told Hilburn. "I've never been able to see him from here before. It's weird being out here rather than on stage, but he's just fantastic. Fantastic."[210]

The four shows spread over the following two evenings were strictly for Elton-hungry fans, who had sent in a total of one hundred thousand postcards in July for the chance of being one of the lucky thousand to purchase a twenty-five dollar ticket. Elton's music and positive attitude at the shows drew high praise. *Billboard* noted how Elton had, at the first show, humbly commended key players in his career, from Russ Regan to Pat Pipolo.[211] Promoter Bill Graham latched onto the talent and potential in Elton's new band. "That's the best band I've ever seen in support of a vocalist," he said. "Its fullness is something you just never get outside of a studio. It was an absolutely brilliant set. He is number one." Robert Hilburn believed the shows demonstrated the musical force Elton John had become. "Watching the two shows, it was easy to see . . . the growth in John as both a writer . . . and as a performer," Hilburn wrote. "He has not only created a major body of work but his light, good-natured manner on stage has helped kick much of the pompousness out of rock."[212]

Still, the Troubadour shows couldn't quite recapture the excitement of Elton's 1970 debut. Hilburn admitted the band was too loud for the small venue. And its full sound was not a substitute for the more basic sound of the trio that had played there in 1970, when Elton had been forced to rely almost completely on his improvisational imagination. The significance of these new Troubadour dates lay not in Elton's artistic advancement or in the pianism that had made him unique, but in their confirmation of Elton's lofty stature in the music and entertainment worlds.

"ISLAND GIRL" was released in Britain on September 19, 1975. It charted on October 4, peaking at number 14, a respectable enough result considering the relative failure of its predecessor, "Someone Saved My Life Tonight." In the United States, the story was different; Elton competed with himself for the number 1 spot. Neil Sedaka's highly catchy "Bad Blood," from his upcoming Rocket Records album, *The Hungry Years,* featured Elton on such prominent backing and harmony vocals that, although his contribution was uncredited, the song was practically a duet. Debuting on *Billboard's* Hot 100 on September 13, it was number 1 by October 11. Meanwhile, Elton's "Island Girl" was released in the United States on September 29, a preview of *Rock of the Westies* and a send-off of sorts for his same-named West Coast tour, which commenced the same day.

The single was a good send-off. Two weeks after "Someone Saved My Life Tonight" had run its course, and the same week "Bad Blood" began its three-week perch at the top of the Hot 100, "Island Girl" was the highest debuting single on *Billboard's* Hot 100, at number 49. On November 1, its fourth week on the chart, it leapt to number 1 for a three-week stay, bumping "Bad Blood" in the process. The Christmas holiday season had already taken hold by the time "Island Girl" became Elton's eighth gold single. ("Bad Blood" would become Sedaka's first gold single; "Island Girl" would finally be certified platinum in September 1995.)

As "Island Girl" rose on the charts, Elton could watch with pleasure the success of some of his Rocket Records acts. Neil Sedaka was the prized star. After his early 1975 comeback hit, "Laughter in the Rain," Sedaka had had two more Top 40 hits from *Sedaka's Back*: the arresting ballad "The Immigrant," about John Lennon's troubles with U.S. immigration authorities, and the up-tempo "That's When the Music Takes Me." Before long, Sedaka was back in the number 1 spot with "Bad Blood," and another hit album, *The Hungry Years,* reached number 16, his highest charting album ever. It was only right that Elton was instrumental in Sedaka's resurgence. Both men were the products of classical backgrounds, had a gift for melody, and possessed sweet, natural singing voices.

CHAPTER 5

THE
CAGE[1]

(1975–1977)

T HE *ROCK OF THE WESTIES* TOUR opened in the United States on
September 29, 1975, at the San Diego Sports Arena, just as "Island Girl" was filling
the airwaves. Ticket sales, like those for the 1974 tour, reached fever pitch. Eleven
thousand tickets for the October 14 Portland, Oregon, show were sold in ninety
minutes.[2] For the October 2 show at the Las Vegas Convention Center, scalpers took
advantage of high ticket demand by charging up to one hundred dollars a ticket,
accounting for some empty seats at the venue.[3]

On July 5, Robert Hilburn reported that Elton John was to become the first
rock act since the Beatles to be booked into Dodger Stadium. The security nightmare that had marred the Beatles' 1966 concert at the stadium had meant that no
rock act could ever play there again—until now. John Reid and agent Howard Rose
had been besieged by concert promoters proposing that Elton play an outdoor stadium in the Los Angeles area. Because they thought Dodger Stadium was off-limits,
contenders had included Anaheim Stadium and the Rose Bowl. But Rose took the
brave step of contacting Peter O'Malley, president of the Los Angeles Dodgers,
who became convinced that Elton's act would be safe after receiving positive security
reports from other venues where he had performed, and being assured that the concert would take place after the close of baseball season. One show was announced,
for Saturday, October 25. Tickets were available by mail only. Publicity surrounding
Elton's return Troubadour engagement in August led to the addition of a second
show, on October 26. In all, 110,000 tickets were sold.[4]

It became clear that, despite the band's volume,[5] the three-hour show, bifurcated
by a half-hour intermission, offered fans an effective balance of purely rendered ballads and elastic rock'n'roll. Like the recent Troubadour engagement, the tour represented a broad overview of Elton's career, broader than his set list had been in some
time. This was largely made possible by the extra hour he played.

Elton continued to tone down his visuals—in comparison to his last tour, that is. He still shimmered, thinning hair shielded by a glittering derby, here in a white jumpsuit, there in an aqua-colored jumpsuit covered with piano keys. Meanwhile, Ray added to his onstage collection of percussive instruments, even squeezing in an extra drum set so that, at times, he could play in relative unison with Roger Pope. Elton also added the strong backing vocals of Jim Haas, Cindy Bullens, and Jon Joyce.

The concerts began promisingly with Elton alone at the piano for "Your Song" and "I Need You to Turn To," both demonstrating that his ability to communicate and redevelop the pristine power of his simple ballads had not diminished. Ideally, these first numbers should have led to more solo piano interpretations. This didn't happen, but his muscular playing—and increasingly ambitious singing—were still crucial in lifting most songs to a higher plane, even if he often deferred to band members to fill in textures.

"Dan Dare" was an early treat. Elton broadened his vocal horizons and, despite the song's lack of innate spirituality, inserted some gospel piano chord progressions that made the song uplifting, rather than simply funky, as it was on record. The obscure fan favorite "Levon" took on a more poetic aspect; a balance between piano and guitar actually slowed the tempo enough for audiences to savor the song's structure. In the more obscure "Empty Sky," Elton displayed some of the most magnetic playing since his early days, although, true to his current habit, he let the song become an extended jam among his band mates before returning to the magnetic riffs of his opening.

The "Empty Sky" jam worked well. The jams that resulted in exceedingly long band endings for "Hercules" and "Meal Ticket" didn't, although they did permit Elton to cavort about the stage. But just when it seemed that his music was getting lost behind the wall of sound, or that no more "bare" musical renderings would be forthcoming, he shifted gears again. Wedged into the wall's gaps were a warm "Harmony" and imaginative versions of several *Captain Fantastic* songs. With "We All Fall in Love Sometimes," Elton nearly returned to the genuine simplicity of his solo "Your Song," and "Curtains" became a rock band symphony that metamorphosed into a driving rock number, buttressed by Elton's rapid-fire piano.

"I SHALL DIE WITHIN THE HOUR"[6]

ELTON'S MOOD has always tended to take nosedives without warning. He can go from a sense of profound well-being to great despair. During his peak commercial years in the mid-1970s, he readily admitted that his success was as likely to encourage dark moods as elation. "I sometimes get depressed for no reason whatever, just stay in bed and get really miserable," Elton said. "Usually, they're one-day jobs, just out of the blue. It's quite frustrating. I just say, 'Oh, Christ, let's get on to tomorrow.'"[7] Recently, he acknowledged that the drug habit that he eventually conquered exacerbated these mood swings. Coming down from cocaine, he said, caused "massive depressions."[8] In fact, just as he should have been basking in the glow of his Dodger Stadium engagements, his cocaine use, coupled with a perverse response to his continued success, nearly ended his life.

The week he was to play Dodger Stadium was Elton John Week in Los Angeles. He was to get his star on the Hollywood Walk of Fame in front of Grauman's Chinese Theater, and had arranged for a large group of friends and family to fly in from England and help him celebrate. Film footage shows Elton greeting his smiling loved ones at the airport with hugs and kisses.

Elton tackled the Walk of Fame ceremony with aplomb, style, and good humor, arriving at the wheel of a gilded golf cart that showed his name framed by light-bulbs. His white, gilt-edged suit was decorated in Walk-of-Fame motif, buttons with his name evenly distributed among those with the names of movie legends like Pola Negri, Broderick Crawford, and Dick Powell. His white, gilt-edged derby and star-shaped glasses completed the picture. "I declare this supermarket open," he said, upon exiting his eccentric mode of transportation and trotting toward the dais past a cheering crowd of five or six thousand.[9]

The Dodger Stadium concerts were a love fest for the fifty-five thousand people who attended each night, and Elton could forget his troubles for the eight hours or so it took to stage the two shows. The only evidence of his depression was in his physical appearance. He was emaciated, his body barely discernible inside the sequins of his specially made Los Angeles Dodgers blue and white baseball uniform.

The shows began at noontime with opening acts Emmylou Harris and Joe Walsh, virtually ignored by the throngs who preferred to picnic, lob beach balls, and wait for the arrival of a certain Englishman. When Elton took the stage, his seeming frailty gave way to the stamina of yore. He hurled hats and piano stools about, jumped on and off his blue-carpeted piano, and played and sang tirelessly. The unauthorized live album, *West of the Rockies*, is the lone vinyl testament to the high-voltage ambience of the two shows, with six songs from the October 25 performance (and three songs from the tour's opening show in San Diego). The electricity in the air is audible, from the eager time-clapping of thousands of fans enveloped in the percussive blasts of "Island Girl," to the crowd's fervent clapping to "Pinball Wizard." The album also reveals that Elton remained a fan; when introducing "Pinball Wizard," he told concertgoers to buy the Who's latest album, *The Who by Numbers*, which he hadn't heard yet but was sure would be "worth investigating." Altogether, the two concerts grossed more than $1.1 million.[10]

Elton's mother was worried about him even before the shows had begun. "It was a terrible, terrible time, those days," Sheila Farebrother remarked twenty years later. "I wouldn't want to go through them again. It's an awful thing to see someone you love unhappy. . . . There were the drugs, which he denied frantically, but I'm not daft. I knew he was taking the drugs." After arriving in Los Angeles for Elton John Week, she didn't see him for days, until visiting backstage just before the first show. She watched him apply NuSkin to his hands, as his nails were cracked "from playing the piano so hard," but could only think about how worried she was about his health. She wept later, watching her son from the stands as he performed "Your Song."[11]

After the concerts, Sheila's first fears were realized. As friends and family lounged by the pool at Elton's Benedict Canyon home, her son appeared in a ter- rycloth robe and announced, "I have taken eighty-five Valiums. I shall die within the hour." He threw himself into the water, then struggled to come to the surface.[12] Caleb Quaye later remembered the arrival of an emergency medical team to pump the pianist's stomach.[13] Oddly, Elton has pointed to this episode as an example of the lev- eling influence his family has had on him. After his suicidal dunk, his grandmother remarked, with feigned nonchalance, "I suppose we've all got to go home now."

"SHE BURN LIKE FIRE"[14]

ELTON'S CAREER continued as though nothing had happened. *Rock of the Westies* was released on October 4, 1975 in Britain and sixteen days later in the United States. In Britain, it charted on November 8, reaching only number 5, and had a life of just twelve weeks, the shortest for any of his albums since the brief tenures of *11-17-70* and *Madman Across the Water*. In the United States, too, *Rock of the Westies* had a shorter than usual chart tenure. Of the previous twelve U.S. Elton John albums, only the hitless, recently issued *Empty Sky*, the equally hitless *11-17-70*, and the near- ly hitless *Friends* soundtrack spent as little time on the charts. Of course, *Westies* did still debut at number 1, Elton's second album to enter all three American album charts at the top, and also the second album ever to do so in chart history. It stayed at number 1 for three weeks and sold far more than any of Elton's other briefly charted albums.

Critic Robert Christgau finally found an Elton John record he was completely happy with, dubbing it the musician's "best album." Unaware that Elton had adopt- ed a pseudonym for the record, Christgau specially commended Ann Orson for "her" work on "Hard Luck Story." But he still bestowed upon the musician all sorts of less flattering names while ostensibly writing a positive review—"garbage process- ing plant," "mechanical," and "our tabula rasa." Buried among his rants was one rea- son why he (and other critics) had had problems with Elton since the musician's 1970 debut. ". . . [H]e is not a child of the '60s the way I am," Christgau sighed. "He threatens me, and like most people I know I tend to fear and distrust him, so I write him off all the time."[15]

Another critic, while arguing that Bruce Springsteen was the best hope for rock fans, unwittingly elaborated on the queasiness expressed by Christgau and others. Springsteen should be a superstar, wrote Peter Delacorte for *Modern Screen*, "because there's an awful lot of trash passing itself off as popular music for the last few years, because someone like Elton John, who's good but not *that* good, has by virtue of a near vacuum suddenly become the symbol of what's happening (which, of course, is nothing), because millions of sets of ears are waiting for something to happen."

Delacorte explained some of Springsteen's virtues: He "neither dyes his hair green nor wears ten-inch platform heels. He does not, as far as I know, have any bizarre sexual aberrations, or any other fashionable habits."[16] Central to Springsteen's attraction was his machismo, something that Elton didn't offer but that was, and continues to be, the dominant force in rock'n'roll, regardless of technological trends or a genre's geographic center. Although Elton hadn't said anything about his sexuality by the end of 1975, there were probably plenty of critics and popular music watchers by this time who suspected he wasn't heterosexual. Rock'n'roll rebellion never embraced the rebellion embodied in New York's 1969 Stonewall uprising.

Whatever the murmurings in some circles about his sexuality, Elton still wasn't ready to be frank. *Playboy* tried getting a confession from him without success. First, he was asked whether groupies were a nice fringe benefit to stardom. After evading the topic, he said the only women he attracted were "bus spotters and stamp collectors." When asked about the "bisexuality scene," he turned his discussion to cold theaters and foggy tennis courts.[17]

In this and other interviews, Elton frankly acknowledged that he wasn't a cultural behemoth like some of his popular peers. On the eve of his Wembley Stadium performance the previous June, he had remarked that he was not a hero, like the Stones, or loved by everyone, like the Beatles. "With me, you loathe me, actually utterly loathe me, or you love me. I've got the hard core fan, or people who despise me."[18]

"WE'D PAINTED TOO MUCH OF THIS TOWN"[19]

AT THE END OF 1975, *Billboard* reported that Elton John was the first solo artist to sell more than a million albums on audiocassette in Britain, at a time when vinyl was still overwhelmingly favored by music buyers.[20] By February 1976, he was the "biggest earner in pop music history," grossing more than the Beatles had at the height of their popularity. During the previous fourteen months, more than sixty million dollars had been spent on Elton's records and concert tickets.[21]

In light of this success, it was all the more surprising when Elton's next single, the double A-sided "Grow Some Funk of Your Own/I Feel Like a Bullet (in the Gun of Robert Ford)," did disastrously in Britain and disappointingly in the United States. In Britain, the single was released on January 9 and didn't chart at all, the first of his singles to be snubbed since "Friends." In the United States, the new single was released on January 12, debuting on *Billboard*'s Hot 100 on January 24 at number 55. It had a fast start, leaping to number 31 in its second week, and number 22 in its third week. But it peaked by February 28, at number 14. The next week, it was number 42!

Confused promotion of the single may explain its brief chart life. Initially, "Grow Some Funk" was the A-side. Rick Sklar, program director at the influential AM Top 40 station WABC in New York, declined to put it on the playlist. Then Elton sent Sklar a huge cake with a message that said, "Give Elton a shot. 'Feel Like a Bullet' is the hit." The cake, however tasty, didn't help. "We still didn't play it," Sklar said. "We were skeptical." The name of the other A-side probably didn't lend itself to typical AM programming; "I Feel Like a Bullet (in the Gun of Robert Ford)" had the lyrical cadence of a "Don't Let the Sun Go Down on Me," but was not easily recited and, after all, contained a hopelessly obscure reference to a little-known historical figure. The following week, Elton sent another cake with a different message: "Disregard first cake. 'Grow Some Funk' is the hit."[22]

Judging from the single's performance, Sklar wasn't the only radio programmer who declined to play the single. Some would interpret radio's resistance to this record as a signal that the tide was turning against Elton's dominance of Top 40 radio. Perhaps, but the rise and fall of "Grow Some Funk/Feel Like a Bullet" on the Hot 100 bore a striking resemblance to the chart performance of "Saturday Night's Alright for Fighting," released more than three years earlier toward the beginning of Elton's chart reign. The latter song, a shouter, though still more melodious than "Grow Some Funk," appears to have met resistance due to its harsh sound.

While Elton was monitoring the progress of his latest single, his personal life was undergoing changes. His intimate relationship with John Reid had ended (Elton later said Reid was "more unfaithful than I liked"[23]), although Reid remained his friend and manager. With that change came the necessary residential move. Elton bought the centuries-old Woodside in Windsor, near London, and became a neighbor of the Royal Family. Reid bought a large house in London.[24]

"MOVE THAT MUSCLE AND SHAKE THAT FAT"[25]

IN MARCH 1976, Elton joined his band in Toronto, Canada, at the Eastern Sound recording studio. It was time for another album, the first of his albums to be released on Rocket Records (through MCA in the United States and EMI almost everywhere else). Elton had several songs left over from the *Westies* sessions and, as of late 1975, envisioned the album as another double.[26]

Perhaps it was the band, still fresh and raring to go, that inspired Elton to do something he probably never thought he would, or could, do. He wrote several melodies before Bernie had the lyrics. Going a step further, Elton even contributed some lyrics. Like two *Westies* songs, several of the songs on *Blue Moves* come from jam sessions. Unlike *Westies* songs "Medley" and "Grow Some Funk," however, the *Blue Moves* songs coauthored by band members adhere more to Elton's compositional approach and melodic sense. They are complete Elton John songs that offer ingenious instrumental contributions by Davey, Caleb, and James, but can also exist independently of them.

Blue Moves is notable on several levels, one being the instrumentals written by Elton. Paul Buckmaster was also back, taking turns with James to do the string arrangements. Unlike some of Buckmaster's earlier work, his arrangements don't overwhelm these songs, instead serving as unusual flourishes to a few already unusual songs.

These string arrangements, as well as other aspects of the album's recording, demonstrate that this was not a back-to-basics effort. The album's long list of credits hails, among others, Toni Tennille, Daryl Dragon, Bruce Johnston, Randy and Michael Brecker, David Sanborn, David Crosby, Graham Nash, the Cornerstone Institutional Baptist and Southern Californian Community Choir directed by the Reverend James Cleveland, the Gene Page Strings, the Martyn Ford Orchestra, and the London Symphony Orchestra. These diverse contributors were recorded as far away as London, Santa Monica, and Los Angeles.

Another unique aspect of this two-record set is that Bernie's lyrics are intensely personal. Although earlier lyrics had been outgrowths of his feelings, experiences, and interests, no other collection had been as emotionally straightforward. Bernie's marriage to Maxine was in a shambles, and he was pouring his anguish onto paper. Some lyrics were so personal and acrimonious that Elton did something, in the making of *Blue Moves*, that he had never done before—rejected them.

One might expect that the lyricist's wounded plaints might make for an album of drone-like, miserable monotony, but this isn't the case. *Blue Moves*, like *Goodbye Yellow Brick Road*, functions as a summary (and forecast) of Elton's musical achievements, talents, and tastes. He is more adventurous than ever, with abstract jazz experiments in some songs, funk grooves in others—following the lead of "Feed Me," on *Westies*. And Elton's singing sprawls all over the vocal map, unfurling ever greater wonders with each succeeding song.

The multifaceted, pliable *Blue Moves* is far removed from the rancorous *Westies*. Elton has said that *Blue Moves* is his favorite album. "We were all weary, feeling the pressure and needed a break," he remarked years later, speaking more for himself and Bernie than for his new band members. "Out of those situations comes rawness, and some of the lyrics are real desperate. I just love the album."[27]

The most familiar song on *Blue Moves* is "Sorry Seems to Be the Hardest Word," one of its three traditional ballads. Written months before the album sessions, while Elton was in Los Angeles aching over an unrequited love, "Sorry" falls squarely within the album's predominant lyrical theme of heartbreak and lovelorn loss. The musician not only composed the music for the song without having words in front of him, but also wrote most of the lyrics himself. "I was sitting out there in Los Angeles and out it came, 'What have I got to do to make you love me?'" Elton recalled.[28]

The lyrics may contain more than Elton and Bernie's brainstorming. Early in the song, Elton sings, "What do I do when lightning strikes me/and I wake to find that you're not there?" Ever the rhythm and blues enthusiast, Elton may have sub-consciously drawn from the 1962 Ray Charles single "Born to Lose," in which Charles sings, "Born to lose/oh, it seems so hard to bear/when I awake and find that you're not there."

The music for "Sorry" ranks among the most heart-wrenching of Elton's superbly lachrymose melodies. Almost just a piano and voice recording, its ample arpeggiation is couched in gently descending chords, with James's accordion and string arrangement and Ray's tender, piano-tracking vibes lending restrained support.

"Cage the Songbird" is another of the traditional *Blue Moves* ballads. Surprisingly, "Songbird" emanated from the *Westies* sessions, although it bears none of the anarchic or drug-induced mania that laces, and sometimes strangles, the album's other songs. A tribute to Edith Piaf, the French songstress whose image was similar to those of Monroe and Garland, "Songbird" is a kind of "Candle in the Wind." It, too, complements the double album's theme of lost love. Bernie has Piaf committing suicide backstage after she learns of her love's infidelity.

Davey Johnstone shares the songwriting credit on "Songbird," presumably in appreciation for the acoustic guitar work he did during the jam session that pro-duced the song. An assortment of stringed instruments (acoustic guitar by Davey and Caleb, and Davey's dulcimer), electronic supplements (James's synthesizer and mellotron), Ray's percussive embellishments, and backing vocals by David Crosby and Graham Nash, lend "Songbird" a folk quality. But at the same time it is quintes-sential Elton John. He doesn't play on the recording, but his vocal skims over the accompaniment, carrying a melody similar in style to some of the songs on *Elton John*, such as "First Episode at Hienton" and "The Greatest Discovery."

The third traditional ballad on *Blue Moves* is "The Wide-Eyed and Laughing." This doesn't seem at first like a traditional Elton John ballad; its instrumental accompaniment is full of sounds of the Far East. Almost half the band—Caleb, James, and Davey—shares the songwriting credit. The three provide a musical pat-tern of ancient strains that suits Bernie's mystical reflection on the disintegration of his relationship with Maxine. Elton only sings here, mustering a tenor that, along with the sitar, acoustic guitar, and synthesizers played by his coauthors, paints a pic-ture of miracles and enchantment gone awry. Backup vocals by Crosby and Nash add to the song's supernatural aura.

These traditional ballads are joined by two jazz ballads, "Idol" and "Chameleon." "Idol" was born of a "technical breakdown" in the studio. Not being a technical sort, Elton passed the time by coming up with a chord sequence, which led to music for a new song—in fifteen minutes.[29] Bernie was faced with the rare challenge of fitting his words to his partner's music. A seamless melody entwined with the jazz form became a sad homage to a music superstar whose life and career had entered a troubled phase.

The song caresses the listener's senses. Elton's thoughtful piano is backed by sweeping, brushed drums and a brass coating of varying hues. Suspended above these sensitive musings is his voice, conveying both an innocent bystander watching the Elvis-like star fall ever further into hopelessness, and a jaded fellow who's been there before. Elton's singing on this and other *Blue Moves* songs reveals the special confidence he had in his vocal ability by 1976.

Bernie's lyrics to "Chameleon" relate the story of a childhood romance, brought back to life by the specter of the narrator's long-lost love, who plays a sort of "chameleon." Instead of changing colors to blend in with her surroundings, however, the love-interest-as-chameleon changes the perspective and feelings of the protagonist, who finds himself transported back to "those lazy summer days" when the two "were alien to all outsiders," engaging in private flights of fancy. This is the song that was written for, and rejected by, the Beach Boys, its soaring melody reminiscent of the group's characteristic rising and falling harmonies. And in fact, one Beach Boy, Bruce Johnston, and the sometime Beach Boys backing vocalist Toni Tennille, are featured on backing vocals. But the song also meshes Elton's gospel-inspired, jazz-lounge piano with Caleb's blurry guitar effects and Ray's soft vibes. It ends with a gospel call and response between Elton's lead vocal and his own layered, Marvin Gaye-inspired backing vocals, hinting at the gospel leanings elsewhere on the album.

Another of Elton's genres, the gospel ballad, showcases the important place in his compositional repertoire occupied by spiritual songs. "Skyline Pigeon," "Border Song," and even the seemingly secular "Candle in the Wind" sound as though they were conceived in a house of worship, despite their composer's lack of conventional religiosity. "When in doubt, write a hymn," Elton has said. "If you want a poignant song that will touch people, I mean, there's nothing more poignant sometimes than a hymn."[30]

The lyrics to "Someone's Final Song," one of the gospel ballads, are maudlin, again reflecting Bernie's lovelorn misery. This is the second song on the album to address suicide. But Bernie doesn't just hint at it, as he so craftily does with his farewell lines in "Cage the Songbird." Here, he comes right out with it ("He died when the house was empty . . . "). Elton could have relegated these lyrics to the rejection heap, but he must have believed he could salvage their excessive desperation. And he did.

"Someone's Final Song" is more nakedly interpreted than even "Sorry Seems to Be the Hardest Word" or "Idol." It relies solely on Elton's voice and piano, some cautious support from James's electric piano and synthesizer, and a bare backing vocal arrangement by Bruce Johnston and Curt Becher. Around the maudlin words, Elton sculpts a lament so private it begs to be let alone. Sung with a voice saturated in despair, his melody searches for the answers a believer might seek in church. These answers, however, remain hidden, and the song leads into the other gospel ballad, "Where's the Shoorah?"

Before asking *where* the "shoorah" is, one may ask *what* it is. At least two popular rhythm and blues songs have contained the nonsense word. One is "Shu Rah," cowritten by Fats Domino, a mild American hit in 1961. Reggie Dwight, already in the throes of rhythm and blues mania by age fourteen, would have gravitated toward "Shu Rah" like a moth to a flame. "Shu Rah" is short, celebrating life's simple pleasures à la the nursery rhymes of Domino's youth: "Here comes my baby, shu rah/How ya doin', shu rah/Glad to see you, shu rah."[31]

A second rhythm and blues song that includes the word was written by another formative influence on Elton, Allen Toussaint. Like Domino, Toussaint hailed from New Orleans, and actually played on some 1950s Domino recordings. It isn't surprising, then, that Toussaint would pen a song called "Shoorah! Shoorah!" Recorded by soul singer Betty Wright, "Shoorah! Shoorah!" never made the Hot 100, but reached number 28 on the rhythm and blues chart in 1974—and number 27 on the regular British singles chart in January 1975. In this up-tempo, brass-flavored song, a woman tells her lover that she finally has him figured out. She isn't going to let him take advantage of her anymore ("Shoorah! Shoorah! I can see you comin'/Shoorah! Shoorah! But you won't catch me"). Here, "shoorah" expresses not the simple pleasures of life, but self-awareness and empowerment.

The "shoorah" in "Where's the Shoorah?" functions as both an affirmation of carefree life and a celebration of self-determination. The problem is, there is no "shoorah" to be found in "Where's the Shoorah?"; hence, the question that permeates the song. Bernie's lyrics (likely written with Elton's soul obsession in mind) are simple, perhaps too simple. This may be because the song emanates from the *Westies* sessions. He may have been expecting another irreverent, high-octane treatment of his lyrics. Instead, Elton infuses the song with spiritual wonderment.

Elton plays piano and a churchy harmonium on this song, accompanied only by Kenny Passarelli on bass and the Reverend James Cleveland's choir on lush backing vocals. Like the music for "Someone's Final Song," the music for "Where's the Shoorah?" focuses on the search for some greater understanding—in this case, of why some important elements of life are missing. Every musical line ends with a question mark; every musical phrase drips with doleful dissatisfaction. "Where's the Shoorah?" carries on in the grand tradition of the sad Elton John song, harkening back to "Sixty Years On," "Funeral for a Friend," and "Don't Let the Sun Go Down on Me." "Where's the Shoorah?," along with several other songs on this album, shines as one of Elton's more perfect sad songs.

Three other sad ballads on *Blue Moves* sport upbeat, up-tempo music. In "Shoulder Holster," Bernie indirectly mourns the demise of his marriage with the story of Dolly Summers, "a simple girl from a Midwest family," who had a stucco house, a Ford Mustang—and an unfaithful husband. Dolly decided she was going to hunt down husband and girlfriend, with the aid of her Mustang and "a pistol in her shoulder holster." When she locates the couple, she realizes her husband isn't worth the fuss ("And as she looked back on the chances/that she'd passed up at home,/ well, she quietly dumped her pistol in a ditch/and she headed home alone").

The synergy of Elton's rhythm section is palpable. Their tight playing, coupled with Elton's piano hybrid of gospel and honky-tonk chords, and the brash brass of the Brecker Brothers, Barry Rogers, and David Sanborn, make for a foot-stomping instrumental. Elton gives Bernie's lyrics a country-and-western melody that he sings with "yodelly" inflection. The result is an up-tempo, good-natured ballad that mocks Dolly's misguided obsession with vengeance.

Another up-tempo ballad, "Between Seventeen and Twenty," refers to the respective ages of Bernie and Maxine when they first met. The lyrics express the anger and jealousy Bernie felt upon learning that his wife had been unfaithful, sleeping with a friend of his behind his back. It was later revealed that the friend was Kenny Passarelli.[32] (Amazingly, Kenny played on "Between Seventeen and Twenty" and other similarly tortured songs on *Blue Moves*. Despite the bassist's involvement with Maxine, Bernie and Kenny remained friends.) "Between Seventeen and Twenty" also reveals the real reasons for Bernie and Maxine's problems: He hadn't been there for his wife, and he knew it.

The music, whose foundation of mandolin and electric guitar awarded Davey and Caleb co-songwriting credits, is defiant, even as sorrow oozes from the lyrics. The bass, drums, electric guitar, mandolin, congas, and organ create a flowing mixture of optimistic bravado. Elton's melody is even more dauntless, his high tenor pulsing with sleek muscle.

The third up-tempo ballad on *Blue Moves* is also the least interesting song on the album, a failed satirical experiment intended to poke fun at overly pious songs. A favorite soul group, the Chi-Lites, had recorded a song called "There Will Never Be Any Peace (Until God Is Seated at the Conference Table)," which, though Elton loved the Chi-Lites, he found to be overblown. He asked Bernie to write a set of "tacky" lyrics to mimic, in good fun, this type of song.[33] A good idea on paper, "If There's a God in Heaven (What's He Waiting For?)" never reached its potential. The faux sentiment is appealing enough, as the lyrics rail against poverty, war, and needless death, and offer a tongue-in-cheek attack on the selfishness of wealth when the song's authors were among the wealthier men on the planet. Mostly, though, the words are tired clichés. "They need the handouts/to hold back the tears,/there's so many crying/but so few that hear," wrote Bernie.

"If There's a God," which again bestows a co-songwriting credit on Davey, recalls late 1960s, early 1970s efforts at sensitive rock piety, such as the Youngbloods' 1969 Top 10 hit, "Get Together." Two elements save it—the spirit with which the music is played, and Elton's impressive, confident singing.

Despite their wide range, the ballads on *Blue Moves* don't define the album, though they do enrich it. Also on tap are some real surprises, including three contemporary instrumentals that break up the pace of the already sophisticated musical terrain. One of these, composed by Caleb, opens the album. Appropriately entitled "Your Starter For . . .", this is a simple, pleasant tune, adorned not only by the stringed instruments played by Caleb and Davey, piano by Elton, and synthesizer by James, but glockenspiel and marimba by Ray, who was as versatile on percussion instruments as Davey was on stringed instruments.

A more substantial instrumental is the quaking, jazzy "Out of the Blue," composed by Elton, which raises the listener from the melancholy "Sorry Seems to Be the Hardest Word." It is chunky music, bustling with diverse ideas that usually peacefully coexist but sometimes playfully collide.

The third instrumental, "Theme From a Non-Existent TV Series" (destined to win Elton an Ivor Novello songwriting award for best instrumental in 1977), is a funny tune that succeeds satirically where "If There's a God in Heaven" fails. Elton's electric harpsichord and James's electric piano and synthesizer toot and bleat their way to an imaginary finish line.

Jazz defines some up-tempo songs with lyrics on *Blue Moves,* too. "One Horse Town" is one of these, another song in which the music came first. For some reason, Bernie transforms the song into a snapshot of life in a poor Alabama town. "Nothing much doing of an afternoon," he has Elton sing, "unless you're sitting in a rocking chair just picking a tune." The music is more momentous than one would expect for a song about a sleepy old town in the South, but one line provides an explanation for the seeming dichotomy: "I just can't wait to grow out of this one horse town." There is at least one person in town with a lot on his mind.

A one-song extravaganza defying easy categorization, "One Horse Town" has a vital modern jazz element, exemplified by the song's unorthodox tempo shifts. It's a bumpy ride, as Elton's eccentric chord progressions result in the unlikely but blissful union of cultured strings and savage guitar licks. His vocal alternates between frustration at confinement to his "one horse town" and elation, portrayed by his soaring falsetto, at the thought of what lies beyond.

One up-tempo, contemporary jazz number that has received a bit more attention is the strange "Crazy Water." The lyrics are among Bernie's most inspired on *Blue Moves,* containing some of his most enigmatic references to marital discord. He likens his separation from his wife, the result of a rock lyricist's unsettled life, to the separation between "shoreline widows" and "missing whalers." Hence, the "crazy water" that comes between two who should have been together.

Elton has often grabbed a conceptual hook in Bernie's lyrics and used it as the premise of his music. In "Tiny Dancer," he latched onto the word "ballerina," and made his song sound like a life-sized music box. "Indian Sunset" became a rhythmic testament to the spirit of the Native American. "Captain Fantastic and the Brown Dirt Cowboy" centered musically on the image of the "brown dirt cowboy," with its vague country-and-western leanings.

Here, Elton latched onto the word "crazy" and composed music that can only be described as demented. The song's insanity is evident from its opening notes, as Elton's piano appears on the sonic horizon and, like the sun, gets brighter and hotter with time. As he sings, his piano chords and thundering bass line provide haphazard boundaries that barely contain the melody, its limbs struggling to punch through gaps in the music. The band follows Elton's lead with light, witty guitar strokes, James's menacing clavinet, and Ray's facile congas. Daryl Dragon's backing vocal arrangement is, as Gus Dudgeon later described it, "peculiar,"[34] a combination of resonant "oohs," "aahs," and mutterings of "crazy water" hacked into asymmetrical, illogical syllables.

A third foray into up-tempo contemporary jazz, this one bathed in rhythm and blues and gospel, is "Boogie Pilgrim." Another jam-session product, it credits Davey and Caleb with some of the songwriting. "Boogie Pilgrim" is an exposition on the dreary life of a ghetto dweller. The music is loose and liberated, just like the restless "boogie pilgrim." The abrupt timing of Elton's gospel chords moves the song along, like a car caught in a traffic jam that hastily jerks forward whenever possible. The misty sound of Elton's chords and Davey's frayed slide guitar are unlikely but friendly collaborators as Kenny offers some oily bass plucking and James even gives the music a little "retro" flavor with some late 1960s-style organ work.

The most satisfying treat in "Boogie Pilgrim" is Elton's vocals. On so much of *Blue Moves*, Elton plays with his voice to create sounds marginally, sometimes radically, different from his standard vocals. Nowhere is this more evident than on "Boogie Pilgrim." He varies his singing from a gritty, mid-range tenor to a high-altitude silkiness to a smooth, deep-throated testifier with plenty of thoracic heft.

The jazz, gospel, and rhythm and blues of "Boogie Pilgrim" aren't present in *Blue Moves*'s two-part musical odyssey. Like "Funeral for a Friend/Love Lies Bleeding," "Tonight" is a reflective, emotional piece with two distinct sections. Unlike its antecedent, "Tonight" was not written as two separate compositions, nor does it have rock elements.

The lyrics to "Tonight" are not nearly as elaborate as the music. They chronicle the self-destruction of Bernie's marriage through imagery and symbolism ("Tonight,/ do we have to fight again/tonight?/I just want to go to sleep/turn out the light"). Elton begins "Tonight" with a nearly three-minute introduction—just his piano, accompanied by the London Symphony Orchestra. With the modulated, disciplined tones and tempos of a classical pianist taking a four-part journey through the lands of Introspection, Defiance, Anger, and Grief, Elton communicates his collaborator's torment long before he sings a note. The music that follows, as he delves into Bernie's lyrics, unveils one of the pianist's more intricate melodies. "Tonight" sounds as natural as any of his ballads—from "Daniel" to "Candle in the Wind"—but is also unpredictable, representing a logical extension of Elton's melodic gifts.

"Bite Your Lip (Get Up and Dance!)," the song that closes *Blue Moves*, offers neither introspection nor melancholia. The album's lone rock'n'roll rave-up, it is, in essence, an update of such marvelous Tin Pan Alley ditties as "Get Happy." Bernie's lyrics recall great songs of more recent vintage, like Martha and the Vandellas' "Dancing in the Street," with his references to American locales—Chicago, Los Angeles, and Santa Fe.

The music to "Bite Your Lip" is a successor of sorts to "Saturday Night's Alright for Fighting," but where the latter is a rough-and-ready tribute to youthful rowdiness, the former is also spiritually cleansing. At first, it's just Elton and the band, throwing themselves into their respective grooves and creating a ruckus. But the extended ending really turns this song into a rock'n'roll "Tarantella."

Gus Dudgeon said later that the song wasn't originally supposed to have a "ninety-five-year fadeout," as he put it. In fact, "Bite Your Lip" was not supposed to turn out at all the way it did. Elton and the band had just recorded "Between Seventeen and Twenty," and the studio sound was still set for that song. The musicians decided to do a run-through of "Bite Your Lip," but didn't want to stop there. "Roll the tape!" they declared. Dudgeon never had the chance to change the sound, and couldn't turn off the performance, which kept going and going.[35] The lengthy chorus allowed the choir led by the Reverend James Cleveland, and James Newton Howard's half-disco, half-Gershwin-esque string arrangement, to shine. If there is a problem with the sound, it isn't evident.

The ambitious, adventurous *Blue Moves* was put to bed in the late winter, early spring of 1976. Its unbridled energy, channeled toward the exploration of varied musical avenues, made it an artistic milestone, like *Goodbye Yellow Brick Road*. But because of the direction Elton's career would soon take, *Blue Moves* was destined to become an outer bookend to a collection of albums, and an overlooked one at that.

"HE'S A PINBALL WIZARD"[36]
ON MARCH 7, 1976, Elton became the first rock star since the Beatles to have his likeness immortalized in Madame Tussaud's Wax Museum in London. On March 12, in Britain, where Elton's DJM contract was nearly over, DJM Records released a two-year-old recording, "Pinball Wizard." When it reached number 7, Elton was rewarded with his first Top 10 hit in Britain since late fall 1974, when another cover, "Lucy in the Sky with Diamonds," had peaked at number 10.

In May, Elton embarked on his first British tour in more than two years. As he readied himself for the six-week undertaking, yet another album was released—the live *Here and There*. The five songs on side one ("Skyline Pigeon," "Border Song,"

"Honky Cat," "Love Song," and "Crocodile Rock") were taken from a May 18, 1974 Royal Festival Hall charity performance before, among others, Princess Margaret. The four songs on side two ("Funeral for a Friend/Love Lies Bleeding," "Rocket Man," "Bennie and the Jets," and "Take Me to the Pilot") were taken from the November 28, 1974 Madison Square Garden concert at which John Lennon had guested. Lennon's numbers weren't included on the album, as Elton had asserted, "I wasn't going to let them use any of that on *Here and There*. No way. It would have been taking advantage of John who did the gig as a favor."[37]

That was just as well. Somewhere between the live shows and Gus Dudgeon's production, the vivacity of these performances had disappeared. Only a colorless sound remained. For the inside narrative, Paul Gambaccini wrote passionately of the Garden performance: "When the crowd stomped to rockers like 'Bennie and the Jets' and 'Take Me to the Pilot,' limousines backstage bounced up and down as if clumsily attempting the bump. When Elton sang ballads like 'Rocket Man' to the light of a thousand matches, an ethereal tranquility descended on the hall." Unfortunately, none of this translated to record.

Elton hadn't wanted this album released, but allowed it to fulfill the rest of his DJM contract. Bitter feelings against his soon-to-be former label continued to mount. He had felt badly enough about the two-LP *Goodbye Yellow Brick Road* counting as only one album, which had meant he'd had to go back into the studio again six months later to compose and record more material when he wasn't ready. "But the thing that really destroyed me was putting *Here and There* out as the last one on DJM," Elton said a year later. "It was 'Either release this album or, if you don't, we'll put it out later anyway.' Which would have meant them getting *Blue Moves* as well [because it would count as the final album]."[38] Elton wanted to break from DJM as soon as possible, and release *Blue Moves* on his own label. (In the end, it was actually a second volume of greatest hits released in 1977 that finally convinced Dick James that Elton had fulfilled his contract.[39])

Here and There was released in Britain on April 30, 1976. It charted on May 15 and peaked at number 6, but spent only nine weeks on the chart. In the United States, *Here and There* was released on May 3, debuted on *Billboard*'s Top LPs on May 22, and reached number 4. It had more staying power in the United States than in Britain, remaining on the chart for nearly half a year, just in time for *Blue Moves*. It also became his twelfth gold album, commercially besting his other, infinitely superior, live album, *11-17-70*.

"YOU PLAY PIANO LOUDER THAN CONCORDE!"[40]
ELTON HAD LONG BEEN A KIND OF COURT MUSICIAN to the Royal Family,[41] often invited to teas and asked to play for whichever Royal was in the mood. One day, not long before launching his 1976 British tour, he was having tea

with Princess Margaret when she put a new spin on the musician's playing. "You play piano louder than Concorde!" she exclaimed. Elton liked her observation enough to name his tour after it, coupling it with a self-deprecating remark for the "Louder than Concorde (but Not Quite as Pretty)" tour.

April 29, 1976 saw the commencement of the twenty-nine-date British tour. The logo for the tour, a sharp-nosed Concorde jet slipping across a set of piano keys, seemed to symbolize the course the musician's life had taken over the last six years. Despite grabs at normality, exemplified by his work with Watford and his commitment to raising money for charities, Elton's home in Windsor remained a springboard for an endless whirlwind of activities—recording, touring, even the odd unveiling of a foreign soccer team like the Los Angeles Aztecs.

Despite the band's high-decibel output, the focus of this British tour was on small venues in small cities. Also simplified was Elton's wardrobe. He now eschewed both the monstrous get-ups that had weighed down his body and the simpler (though showy) jumpsuits in favor of jacket-shirt-suspenders-sweatpants-socks-sneakers combos. Every imaginable kind of stripe was put to use—fat horizontal stripes on the fatter lapels of his jacket, skinny horizontal ones on his Popeye shirt, razor-thin horizontal ones on his socks with similar vertical ones on his suspenders and sweatpants. Most of the glitter was on his sneakers and the stuffed fruit he wore around his neck. He went with white-framed, clownish spectacles that, in obscuring a good part of his face, pressing against his nose and constricting his nostrils, replaced the outrageous costumes of yesteryear in discouraging audiences from taking him too seriously.

Reports from various tour stops suggest that Elton took further advantage of his band's versatility by playing even less and using the stage as a giant living room in which to romp, mug, throw his piano stool in any suitable direction, and mischievously taunt his band mates into playing their solos. It seemed that Elton's desire to please the young crowds had emerged victorious once again. This capitulation to the lowered expectations of the masses signaled a change in his outlook. In two months, he would explain what was on his mind.

In Elton's personal life, his natural father, Stanley Dwight, who'd divorced his mother in 1961, was a new source of difficulties. Although father and son had resumed contact in the early 1970s and Elton had spent time with his half-brothers and lavished gifts on the family, Elton had abruptly terminated the contact without explanation. In interviews like the one he gave to *Playboy,* he didn't hesitate to criticize his father's treatment of him, opining that Dwight had never really wanted or loved him.

Then, in May 1976, Dwight talked to the press. He denied any ill-treatment of his ex-wife or son, whom he still called Reggie. In quoting from pre-1976 conversations with his son, whose statements the elder Dwight had taken seriously, he unwittingly revealed that Reggie, being fundamentally uncomfortable with him, had lied to him, claiming that Elvis Presley was one of his best friends. His son had also told him that he had had no time for girlfriends. Dwight took some potshots, too. Of the piano skills of a son, Stanley, Jr., from his second marriage, he said, "He's so much more advanced than Reggie was at that age. I don't think Reggie's all that good even now."[42]

"WHEN I WAS DOWN I WAS YOUR CLOWN"[43]

THROUGHOUT THE UPS AND DOWNS of his personal and professional lives, Elton continued to oversee the chart success of his Rocket Records acts. Over the winter, Neil Sedaka had enjoyed another Top 10 hit with a slow, torchy remake of his 1962 single "Breaking Up Is Hard to Do." In the spring, Sedaka had a Top 20 single, the disco ballad "Love in the Shadows" from his new album *Steppin' Out*. The album charted on May 1, reaching number 26, and featured several current and former Elton John band members; Elton himself contributed backing vocals on the title track. The single "Steppin' Out," which peaked at number 36, would be Sedaka's last Top 40 hit until 1980, and the last time the two would sing on a record together.

Another Rocket Records single, a duet released just as Elton was launching the U.S. leg of his "Louder than Concorde" tour in summer 1976, brought the musician his sixth U.S. number 1 hit and fourteenth Top 10 hit. "Don't Go Breaking My Heart" was written under circumstances similar to those that produced "Idol"—as a response to a technical breakdown.[44] "I was messing around in the studio . . . on the electric piano and came up with the title line," Elton said. The melody surfaced, as well as a chunk of lyrics. "I made a hasty phone call to Barbados [where Bernie was staying] and said, 'Write a duet,' and Taupin nearly died 'cause he'd never done one."[45]

What resulted was a tip of the hat to the legacy of Marvin Gaye and Tammi Terrell that dominated the soundtrack to summer 1976. The song was originally recorded in its entirety without Kiki, whose vocals were spliced in later, as was an orchestral arrangement by James Newton Howard.

Released on the Rocket label on June 21, 1976 in both the United States and Britain, "Don't Go Breaking My Heart" was not only a number 1 hit in the United States, but Elton's first number 1 in Britain. There, it charted on July 3 and stayed around for a healthy fourteen weeks, longer than most of his other British singles (it was number 1 for six weeks). "When I heard it was number 1 [in Britain] I rang everybody I knew to tell them," Elton said. "They were pretty annoyed but, hell, it got me excited again. It really did."[46] In the United States, it debuted on *Billboard's* Hot 100 on July 4, reaching number 1 just days before the pianist's record-breaking seven-night stand at Madison Square Garden. The single stayed on top for four weeks, longer than any of his other number 1 hits, and was certified gold at the end of August.

The success of "Don't Go Breaking My Heart" was a more significant boost for Kiki. Until 1976, she had had only mixed fortunes and no number 1 hits. In Britain, she had managed two Top 20 hits with "Amoureuse" and "I've Got the Music in Me," and a 1975 Top 40 hit with "(You Don't Know) How Glad I Am." In the United States, she had made even less of a commercial splash, with only one song, "I've Got the Music in Me," nearing the Top 10. It must have been frustrating for her that, after all Elton's efforts on her behalf, she would owe her fame to this duet. But if she felt this way she didn't say so. Instead, she pointed to how she enjoyed recording with Elton: "I like working with him because he just makes me feel comfortable, at ease."[47]

"RIGHT FROM THE START, I GAVE YOU MY HEART"[48]

THE THIRTY-ONE-DATE, stadium-dominated U.S. tour leg, which began on June 29, 1976 at the Washington, D.C.-area Capital Center, was a major summer event. But Elton cast a long shadow over most of it with talk of taking time off. He had been spooked before the tour even started when he took his mother and stepfather to see an Elvis Presley concert in the D.C. area and met Presley backstage. Officially, it was a wonderful time for all. Sheila Farebrother recalled how, back in the 1950s, she used to buy Elvis records for little Reggie. "That's how he got started," she said proudly, adding of Presley, "He's just as good as he was then, but a little fat around the middle."[49] Elton, on the other hand, didn't like what he saw. Years later he told David Frost in hushed tones, "I looked into his eyes and there was nothing there."[50] Here was a message for the former Reggie, who had laid eyes on a much more vibrant man twenty years earlier in the *Life* magazine article he'd seen in a barber shop.

Elton decided that this tour, with four of the shows yielding the highest concert grosses of the season,[51] would be his last for a long time. But how could this be true? He seemed to attack everything with the same gusto as before. Offstage, he was everywhere. In D.C., he created a stir by showing up at a Keith Jarrett concert at Constitution Hall, and also showed support for old friend Lesley Duncan at Georgetown's Cellar Door.[52] He was often seen at discos and mingling with other celebrities. In Pontiac, Michigan, he made the day of star Detroit Tigers pitcher Mark "the Bird" Fidrych when the two exchanged sporting gear. In New York City, Elton sang a duet with a favorite singer, the then struggling Bonnie Raitt, at the Schaefer Music Festival in New York's Central Park. And at Madison Square Garden, he shared a laugh backstage with Leonard Nimoy, Freddie Mercury, Shirley MacLaine, and Frankie Valli. Valli presented him with a pair of "Four Seasons" spectacles as a thank-you for his comment that he owned all of the Four Seasons's albums. "My eyes adore you," Elton quipped.[53]

In Atlanta, Elton was received by Mayor Maynard Jackson. And in Philadelphia, he was given the key to the city by the controversial, embattled mayor, Frank Rizzo, ostensibly in honor of "Philadelphia Freedom" and the positive thoughts Elton had uttered about the City of Brotherly Love. It was speculated that Rizzo really launched Philadelphia's "Elton John Day" to generate desperately needed political capital. How could he lose by patting the back of a musician who generated so much excitement and heady good feelings?

Familes attended Elton John concerts in droves. It seemed that every family member could appreciate Elton. A dad might profess to liking the "beat" and muse that the show was good family entertainment. A daughter might describe Elton as "cute" and a son express his approval of the musician because he "acts crazy."[54]

The Elton John experience often shaped the family experience. One Chicago dad pleaded to Bernie for his empty Coors beer can, insisting that the whole family tended to sit together in the living room of an evening to listen to John/Taupin songs.[55] The pianist was considered the safest of rock acts.

Elton's band for this tour had changed marginally since the West Coast shows a year earlier. Replacing backing vocalist Jim Haas was Ken Gold, the songwriter for new Rocket act Cliff Richard. Kiki Dee was on hand to sing "Don't Go Breaking My Heart" with Elton and "I've Got the Music in Me" by herself. Ray Cooper was sick and would miss most of the tour.

On stage, Elton's blue carpet-topped piano was surrounded by a sparkly molding, making his instrument resemble a streamlined object not unlike a Concorde jet. A control unit allowed him to switch the lighting on the piano between magenta and blue. His outfits were more glittery than in the spring. In New York, he greeted the crowd dressed as the Statue of Liberty, complete with book, torch, crown, and flowing gown, which he quickly doffed to reveal a relatively less showy ensemble. Another time, he modeled a sequined 1920s Pierrot's suit. Where stripes of every ilk had predominated in the spring, now it was ice cream sodas on a hot pink background, or a grinning Carmen Miranda on a rich green background, or sizeable sunflowers against shiny green, or, in honor of the American Bicentennial, red, white, and blue sequins. Fruits and vegetables were still main props; parents caught up in the wholesome festivities may have failed to notice that the giant carrot Elton wore around his neck was so long its tip bounced against his crotch or that, sometimes, he put the carrot in his mouth.

It was so much fun and so silly that it seemed Elton was having as good a time as always. But veteran Elton watcher Lynn Van Matre, who previewed the tour in Philadelphia, noticed something amiss. "I was struck with the uncomfortable sensation of watching a man going through the motions," she wrote, "seeing a performer whose act has begun to weary him and become far more work than fun."[56]

The musician tried his best to shield his discomfort. The opening number, "Grow Some Funk of Your Own," with its repeated guitar chord patterns, allowed him time for an energetic romp around his giant stage-cum-living room before he took a seat at the piano and added flashy, combustible chords that made the song much more musical than on record. But in general, amid the sometimes deafening claps of the audience, Elton's vocals were more distinguished than his playing. Taking his cue from the British spring tour, he rarely challenged himself on the piano. Overall, it was the band that stood out, as it stretched out on some songs for so long that, even though the shows lasted about three hours, there was little room for much of Elton's back catalog and no room at all for the new songs he had just recorded in March, save the Kiki Dee duet.

Elton gave the masses mainly what they had come to see—him—and very little of what they were not clamoring for, which was his inspired musicianship. The piano-based songs held up well whether they were interpreted with or without the best efforts of their author, but the range of emotions that Elton's playing had brought to other tours was largely absent.

The U.S. tour was not without its emotionally satisfying moments. New York's Madison Square Garden shows were, fittingly, the most memorable. Elton was the first rock act to ever sell out seven nights at the arena, with tickets going to 137,900 people. The shows featured the return of Ray Cooper and his percussion warehouse; also on hand were the New York Community Choir and drag queen Divine, who lent more camp to a show already full of double entendres. Elton still enjoyed tossing piano benches into the offstage pit, which usually destroyed the small, pin-cushioned seats and cost the tour two hundred dollars apiece. He hadn't stopped doing his famous piano handstands. And, as usual, he mounted his blue-carpeted piano lid to coax his audiences into a frenzy.

But despite the Garden's celebratory atmosphere, the pianist was in a poor frame of mind and was less able than usual to tolerate post-show criticism. He bristled at an August 12, 1976 review by *The New York Times'* John Rockwell, who had no complaints about the August 10 opening show but plenty about the very fact of Elton's monumental success. "Those of us who write about the arts are used to dealing with popular performers who aren't particularly popular with us. We treat them as fairly as we can," Rockwell wrote, "delineating their strengths and weaknesses as we see them, report on the crowd's reaction and call it a day." He praised the show's professionalism, then confessed: "Mr. John's music provokes an indifference in this listener so complete as to preclude any trace of hostility."[57]

On August 13, the day after the review, Elton was a guest on Scott Muni's radio show on WNEW-FM, armed with a couple of bottles of Dom Perignon and some words for John Rockwell. "If you're listening, you asshole, come down here now and I'll destroy you," he warned Rockwell. "I'll rip you to bits on the air."[58]

Months later, a more sober Elton offered a calmer response: "I don't mind bad reviews at all. I always get them, in fact. I'm used to them. But . . . [i]t was more like an edict: 'You mustn't like Elton John, because I don't think he's very good.'

Everyone at the concert should have been home listening to Linda Ronstadt's albums. It was very condescending."[59]

"SO DON'T MISUNDERSTAND ME"[60]

ELTON WAS DESPERATE to get out of what he viewed as a vicious cycle. Though his touring and recording schedule was nothing like it used to be, he wanted to escape what he had become. "I did go through a period in '75 and '76 when I was very depressed," he said two years later. "I knew that I had to come off the road to cure my depression. I also knew it was time to quit because it was getting to be too much of a routine."[61] It was this routine, he believed, that had harmed his musicianship.

"Towards the end, I was fucked," Elton said in 1986. "My piano-playing had suffered."[62] Instead of riding on an endless conveyor belt of high-profile activity, he was interested in pursuing quieter passions—producing other Rocket acts, acceding to the chairmanship of Watford, just being home for a change. Elton was also desperate to talk openly about his sexual orientation. He probably should have consulted movie hunk Dirk Bogarde before doing so, though. In the 1961 film *Victim*, Bogarde had said "I love you" to another man, a movie first. "Overnight, I didn't have a single fan left," Bogarde remembered.[63] But Elton apparently saw sexual frankness as a way to do what he wanted—step cleanly off that endless conveyor belt. He had never been more right about a means to an end.

Over the years, certain aspects of Elton's stage show may have provided hints of his sexual orientation: among other things, "Legs" Larry Smith tap-dancing in a wedding dress to "I Think I'm Going to Kill Myself" in 1972; the bugle-beaded, rainbow-colored, feather- and quill-laden wardrobe of his 1974 shows; and, most recently, Divine's guest appearance at his New York shows. But it was during his appearance on Scott Muni's talk show on August 13—the same one on which he'd disparaged John Rockwell—that some comments made all in fun would give away more than hundreds of campy concert gimmicks.

"Welcome to WNEW, the only transvestite station in New York," Elton had said, insisting that Muni was wearing an Yves Saint Laurent dress. As "EJ the DJ," he offered to play disco "for all you people out there who are straight." He apologized for not making it to record company executive Clive Davis's bedroom.[64]

Rolling Stone magazine, which had demonstrated an unseemly interest in "outing" him for some time already, finally scored the coup they'd been searching for during that record-breaking week at Madison Square Garden. Cliff Jahr, whom Elton has since said was fair and accurate, was the lucky interviewer.

Jahr wrote a sort of preview piece for *Rolling Stone* in the September 23, 1976 issue, just before the one that would contain the big interview. In it, he described Elton's guest appearance on Muni's radio show. He also fueled speculation about Elton's sexuality by throwing in some innuendo from other sources. Jahr quoted an obscure presidential candidate as saying that summer that "homosexuality has been sighted in America. . . . Stay away from Elton John."[65]

But it was Jahr's next story, in the October 7, 1976 issue of *Rolling Stone*, that would quell speculation. After all, Elton had never actually said he was gay on Scott Muni's radio show, nor in his many magazine interviews. He had avoided the subject during a *Playboy* interview earlier in the year. And he had nearly said nothing of the kind to Cliff Jahr.

The interview had started off innocuously. Jahr, recovering from the pianist's "bone-crushing handshake," noticed how shy he was. Averting his eyes, Elton cited some record sales figures, defended his remarks concerning Rockwell, and explained his thoughts on retirement. As if Jahr were not already poised to ask *the* question, Elton made it easier, mentioning that he didn't really go out after his shows in New York, except for a visit to 12 West, a members-only gay disco. The door thus opened a mite, Jahr peeked inside, turning to David Bowie's recent remark that Elton was the "token queen of rock." Elton closed the door. "I think he's a silly boy," he said of Bowie. But before long, the pianist opened it again. He needed intimacy, he said, and hadn't met anyone with whom he would want to settle down. Jahr asked him if he was bisexual. Defensively, the musician said, "There's nothing wrong with going to bed with somebody of your own sex. I think everybody's bisexual to a certain degree. I don't think it's just me. It's not a bad thing to be."[66]

Talk of his sexuality led to a hasty retreat. He was only "bisexual." He might still settle down with a woman someday.[67] But in later interviews, he usually referred to this interview as an acknowledgment of his homosexuality. And that is how the public took it, too.

"WHAT DO I SAY WHEN IT'S ALL OVER?"[68]

"EVER SINCE I GAVE THAT INTERVIEW . . . it seems twice as many people wave at me in the street," Elton joked to London's *Daily Mail*, referring to the reaction of the British public to his "bisexual" statement.[69] He got letters from gay people in small towns who had gained encouragement, in their isolated worlds, from his bold words.[70]

The reaction in the United States was different. "America's supposed to be the great liberated free-minded society—which, of course, it isn't," he said, after the fallout had settled. "Everyone goes 'peace and love man,' but it'll never happen because hatred is rammed into kids by their parents and hate makes much more money."[71]

News of Elton's "confession" fell like a torrent on the ears of Middle America's kids. If they didn't read his interview in *Rolling Stone*, they saw a synopsis of it in the local paper, or heard about it on the radio. It was, as one writer observed, a slow news week, and Elton had provided news organizations with a human interest segment made to order.

Across the country, kids turned their backs on Elton John. Boys who habitually bought his latest releases didn't anymore. Kids just becoming acquainted with their own sexuality struggled to come to terms with that of their favorite rock star. To add insult to injury, they were forced to fend off callous remarks from peers. Many kids turned to other rock stars for escapism, to preserve their sensibilities or their social standing, and especially to avoid being labeled "faggots."[72]

Until then, *16 Magazine* had been presenting Elton to its young, mainly female readership as one of the day's premier bachelors. It had put out special issues that featured or were completely devoted to him, including one that presented, among other things, Elton's physical dimensions (neck, 15 $\frac{1}{2}$ inches; chest, 42 inches; thighs, 22 inches . . .), source unknown. Another issue had analyzed his moods and "philosophy of life," offering such tidbits as "The Truth about Elton!"

For some time, *16* had been getting more mail about the musician than any other "teen dream," and now his statement in *Rolling Stone* generated even more. Teenage girls begged the editors to, essentially, "say it ain't so." The editors asked his fans to support him in his time of need, but, faced with the news that Elton was, indeed, "bisexual," his fans abandoned him. The deluge of Elton John fan mail came to a screeching halt.[73]

Before the *Rolling Stone* interview hit the newsstands, and as his temporary retirement took hold, Elton began the process of reconstructing his live musicianship. On September 17, wearing a leisure suit with pinched shoulders that put him in a perpetual state of shrugging, he gave some fortunate Scottish youngsters at Edinburgh's Playhouse Theatre (and BBC radio and television audiences) a two-hour surprise, closing a local music festival with his first-ever solo show for public consumption. It was also an exhibition of public drunkenness, though he may have been the most charming drunk his audience had ever seen. Pouring a glass of tomato juice and vodka from a hefty pitcher, he grinned, "I don't want the people at home to *think* I'm an alcoholic, I want them to *know* I'm an alcoholic."[74]

Elton sat surrounded by good luck charms, mementos to remind him of home. Animal statuettes were placed around his opened-lid grand piano to watch him play, their stony but benevolent stares supporting him through many songs he had rarely, or never, performed live. A grandfather clock stood nearby, as did a fully stocked liquor cabinet. Listeners and viewers got what had been missing from his live shows of late: the genuine, bare-bones, often electrically charged treatments of songs that had made him a star six years earlier. He surveyed most of his recording career, neglecting only *Madman Across the Water* and the *Friends* soundtrack.

Some watching the show may have forgotten about or never been witness to Elton's early concerts, at which he shifted with ease from the somber reflection of "Sixty Years On" to the funny rantings of "Honky Tonk Women" to the blazing fury of "Burn Down the Mission," relying almost exclusively on his piano for sonic embellishments. Now, he nimbly alighted on diverse numbers and, just as Princess Margaret had said, challenged the noise of the Concorde, possibly splitting a few more fingernails and even busting a few piano strings, as he has been known to do.

By evening's end, Elton had had several glasses of tomato juice and vodka. He thanked everyone associated with the show, and chortled, "But most of all, I'd like to say how pissed I am."

"WHAT HAVE I GOT TO DO TO MAKE YOU WANT ME?"[75]

ON SEPTEMBER 9, 1976, nearly a month before "Sorry Seems to Be the Hardest Word" was issued in Britain as Elton's second Rocket Records single, Dick James followed up the "Pinball Wizard" single from March with another song to which he had the rights, "Benny and the Jets" (the spelling of "Bennie" mysteriously modified), previously released as a B-side to "Candle in the Wind."

"Benny" only reached number 37. It was not exactly a new song to those who had bought its source album or seen a few Elton John concerts. And it was a distraction from his new product.

Elton had been having a hard enough time breaking into the Top 10 in Britain lately, and having "Benny" on the airwaves didn't make the success of "Sorry Seems to Be the Hardest Word," released on October 10, any easier. The lead single from *Blue Moves* took a full month to chart in Britain. It peaked at number 11, not really a bad result considering the competition DJM had presented and the earlier, disappointing performance of such songs as "Philadelphia Freedom" and "Someone Saved My Life Tonight." "Sorry" did better in the United States, where it was released on November 1 and took two weeks to chart, reaching number 6. It stayed in the Top 10 for six weeks and achieved gold status by February 1977.

In just viewing the latest single's chart placing, it might seem that Elton's *Rolling Stone* interview hadn't harmed him in the United States. But "Sorry" would be his only Top 20 single from the upcoming *Blue Moves,* and his last Top 10 single and last gold one for three years. Further, the commercial performance in the United States of the adventurous *Blue Moves* album was disturbing and disappointing. Some may point to the fact that *Blue Moves* was his first platinum album as evidence that his commercial standing had not been affected. But it was his first platinum album only because the platinum certification had just come into being in May 1976.

Blue Moves peaked at number 3 in both Britain and the United States, released in both places during the last week of October 1976. In Britain, where it charted on November 6, this was a good result. *Rock of the Westies* had only gotten to number 5 there, *Captain Fantastic* to number 2. *Blue Moves* fell squarely within the range of success to which Elton had become accustomed at home.

Elton's "confession" did affect his public image in Britain, but not as one would expect. The album cover featured a painting he had recently bought, depicting men in various states of repose, some shirtless, all picnicking together and gently conversing. London's *Sun* newspaper was set to use the album as a contest prize until its editors saw the cover. "They rang us to say they couldn't do it because of the painting," Elton said, incredulously. "Silly, isn't it?"[76]

It was in the United States that the impact of Elton's "bisexual" statement on the album was more obvious. True, *Blue Moves* had followed on the heels of two studio albums that had entered the album charts at number 1 and stayed on top for a few weeks. But Elton had to look to 1971 to find a new studio album that had not topped the charts. Moreover, the album, which charted on the same day as the lead single, was released only two months after the hottest tour of the summer—his tour—that had packed arenas and stadiums alike, prompting public officials to take notice and evoking rapture from teens, even whole families. The public's response to news of Elton's sexual orientation was edging its way into stores and cash registers.

"BITE YOUR LIP, GET UP AND DANCE"[77]

IN DECEMBER 1976, Elton attended to his responsibilities as Watford's new chairman. He met with his directors to strategize how to get their players out of the fourth division, the lowest ranking a soccer team can have. His first significant act as chairman was to convince his directors to hire manager Graham Taylor. Taylor, who had gained an impressive reputation working with higher ranked clubs, signed on in May 1977.

Elton had faith in the future of Watford. "I'm always optimistic. I think we'll do very well," he told Tom Snyder. "But football is a very hard game. You just can't be successful overnight. It takes a matter of two or three years to get something together. You're dealing with individuals that will have to make up a team. . . . We're in the fourth division, but I want us to end up in the first division. So I've set my sights on that. It's something to aim for. We'll get there in the end."[78]

Also, as planned, Elton and sound engineer Clive Franks returned to the recording studio to produce other Rocket Records acts. Elton's first project was Kiki Dee's new album, *Kiki Dee*. He would also coproduce, with Clive Franks, albums for the Scottish light-rock group Blue, and for a group called China, comprised primarily of Elton John Band veterans—Davey, James, and Roger Pope.

Neither China nor other Rocket acts, such as the Foster Brothers, Radiator, Solution, and Brian and Brenda Russell, had any chart impact. Rocket was still a young company but, especially with the departures of Neil Sedaka (to what he thought were greener pastures at Elektra Records) and producer Gus Dudgeon, the outfit was beginning to show signs of trouble.

Even so, Elton must have gotten some satisfaction from helping create albums. "I like most sorts of music," he once told David Frost who, as an Elton observer of long vintage, couldn't have been surprised. "There is something to be picked up in all art forms that can be pleasant."[79] His broad tastes, and the knowledge that he could have a part in popularizing any sort of music that tickled his fancy, maintained the driving force behind his involvement in Rocket Records.

Elton's exile from touring didn't spill over into the area of new music; in January and February 1977, he had two singles released. In Britain it was the demented "Crazy Water," which stopped at number 27. "Crazy Water" continued a trend that would endure for years: Just as several singles in a row would get no higher than double digits, a maverick would vault into the Top 10. Then the pattern would begin anew.

In the United States, the single was "Bite Your Lip (Get Up and Dance!)," released on January 31. Elton thought American Top 40 had exhibited an interest in "Bite Your Lip," and Tony King, now a Rocket Records executive, believed that, in that case, the song could do with a bit of remixing. They enlisted Tom Moulton, a well-known disco remixer, for the job.[80] The remix yielded a crisper sound, with both Elton's piano and Davey's electric guitar shining more brightly than on the album. Just as important were Elton's manic vocal interjections, inaudible on the album version, that burst with rock'n'roll joy in the remix. The single debuted on *Billboard*'s Hot 100 on February 12 at number 56, stalling at number 28 four weeks later. All told, despite imaginative and hopeful promotion by Rocket, it spent only six weeks on the chart, the briefest tenure of any single since Elton's grand Hot 100 debut nearly seven years earlier with "Border Song."

A new era on the Hot 100 was on the horizon, with acts like Fleetwood Mac ("Go Your Own Way") and the Steve Miller Band ("Fly Like an Eagle") coming into their own, and acts like the Bee Gees ("Boogie Child") on the cusp of a hot streak. The negative reaction to Elton's personal candor had created a void, and others were rushing to fill it. By July, the talk was that Elton's demographics had changed. A radio consultant, Lee Abrams, pooh-poohed the "conventional wisdom," that Elton was popular with teens under the age of eighteen. "We found that Elton is most popular with the twenty-three-to-thirty-year-old group, and the songs they request are his older songs. His current material just is not making it," he said.[81] But when Abrams expressed this opinion, in summer 1977, Elton didn't *have* any new product out. The song request lines would have, of necessity, been filled with requests for his "old" songs. And the claimed shift in demographics would have been jarring to anyone who had seen the musician less than a year earlier at Madison Square Garden, when he bid farewell to tens of thousands of fans, many of them young teens.

June 3 marked the musician's final 1977 British single, "Bite Your Lip." The song shared an A-side designation with Kiki Dee's "Chicago." Both recording artists received credit for the Top 30 hit (actually, number 28) that resulted. But a month earlier, Elton had done something more significant. He had reacquainted himself with his artistic roots, returning to the concert stage to pick up where he had left off in September 1976.

"IT'S A LIFE AND A LIVING"[82]

ELTON SHOWED OFF HIS NEWFOUND CONFIDENCE at a college social on June 17, when he got some students at nearby Shoreditch College out of a jam and played at their Valedictory Ball after another, lesser-known musician canceled his appearance. The college's vice principal marveled at the pianist's solo performance. "I was astonished by how intimate the show had been, and how well he could communicate without any props or lights," he said.[83]

In fact, Elton had already played a series of semi-solo shows May 2 through 7 at London's Rainbow Theatre, where he was accompanied only by Ray Cooper during the second part of each performance. Not long before, in an interview for Australian television, Elton had told Molly Meldrum that "Ray doesn't know whether [the shows' concept] is gonna work. We'll only know when we rehearse if it's gonna work or not. If Ray doesn't do it, I'll just do it on my own." The rehearsals obviously piqued Ray's interest. Like the Edinburgh performance the previous September, these shows were cultured, reflective, and passionate—even approaching "classy cabaret," as a reviewer for *Variety* put it[84]—and certainly not the type of concert fans would expect from a rock star.

The staging was simple. Elton, Ray, and their instruments were perched atop platforms with rounded edges (Elton's was piano shaped). The two were surrounded by potted plants carefully placed in remote spots. A liquor cabinet sat innocently at the far end of Elton's nine-foot grand.

The first show was a benefit for the Queen's Silver Jubilee Appeal, and attracted luminaries of the rock world as well as royalty in the form of Princess Alexandra. As he had done in Edinburgh, Elton chose songs that could most obviously benefit from solo piano interpretations—not just the stalwarts, but also "The Greatest Discovery," "Cage the Songbird," his own expression of "I Heard It through the Grapevine," "Border Song," and, for the first time anywhere, "Roy Rogers." Ray Cooper made his dramatic entrance one-third of the way through a unique coupling of "Funeral for a Friend" and "Tonight," attacking his timpani just as "Funeral" gathered heroic momentum. He then used sundry instruments—congas, the vibraphone, and the tambourine—to tastefully supplement Elton's piano meditations.

Occasionally sipping wine from a long-stemmed glass, Elton expanded on the experiment he had found so delightful months earlier. During each show's first half he toyed with the melody in "Daniel," added a chord-heavy, percussive finale to "Rocket Man," gave "Dan Dare" a rowdy, backroom bar feeling, and transformed "Take Me to the Pilot" from the rock'n'roll rave-up it had been in the early 1970s to a rambunctious fusion of classical and jazz insights.

Following Ray's entrance, audiences were treated to virgin performances of "Idol" and "I Feel Like a Bullet," and a mirthful, saloon rendition of "I Think I'm Going to Kill Myself." But it was "Crazy Water," the number 27 single, that confirmed Elton's return to his early 1970s rock'n'roll raver form. The song gave Ray the chance to break free on the congas, and allowed Elton the freedom to be as maladjusted on the keyboard as the composition was on record. The pianist played the song as if propelled by a high wind that forced his hands into rapidly paced, unlikely chord positions. At once unnerving and exhilarating, the music resounded like thousands of sharp, gleaming darts hurled from varied directions into the pitch black of a predawn sea.

Elton John also achieved something he had never before accomplished on the road: He played for 150 minutes straight, without any of the antics away from the piano for which he had been known in 1975 and 1976. But, even as Elton regained confidence in his musicianship, he remained as self-deprecating as always. "Thank you for splashing out a lot of money to see a piano player with a receding hairline in a ridiculous suit," he told his audience the first night.[85]

The pianist's stamina intrigued Princess Alexandra, with whom he had an audience after the first show. "How do you play for two and a half hours at a stretch?" she asked. "Do you take cocaine?" Elton related to reporters later, "I couldn't believe it. Of course when I recovered, I told her that I don't take cocaine before I go on stage—which is the truth."[86]

"YOU CAN WORK ON A SPELL AND WEAVE YOUR MAGIC SO WELL"[87]

BACK IN 1974, Elton had told Eric Van Lustbader, "I'd like to do an album with just things like 'Ticking' on them. Just piano, voice, and the odd Moog thing somewhere. I'd like to go back and do an ultra-heavy album with Buckmaster, and a whole album of up-tempo dance numbers, soul things."[88]

The unrealized voice and piano album is a project Elton talks about to this day. Only his live performances offer what he has, over these many years, hoped to accomplish on record with just voice and piano. As for working with Paul Buckmaster, another collaboration was not long in the offing. And Elton's ambition to make a danceable soul album was realized during his quietest year.

Elton couldn't wait to work with producer Thom Bell,[89] a Philadelphia native who had collaborated with Kenny Gamble and Leon Huff on recordings by Harold Melvin and the Bluenotes, the O'Jays, and the dreamy Philly strings of MFSB. Bell had also produced hits for the Stylistics and the Delfonics, and now was riding a wave of prosperity with the Spinners, for whom he was writing, arranging, and producing.

"I just loved the way his records sounded," Elton said years later. "Very dry sounding records."[90] The pianist contacted Bell through the Spinners, after visiting the group backstage in London. Bell determined to study his subject before recording with him, and spent a few days at Woodside to learn what made Elton tick. Before long, the verdict was in. "I believe I can do a good job for you," Bell told him.[91]

Working with Bell, though, meant that Elton would have to surrender the creative independence he'd cultivated over the years. Unlike Gus Dudgeon, or the production team of Elton John and Clive Franks, Bell controlled every aspect of the recording process. The sound of the Spinners was the sound of Thom Bell, pure and simple.

Perhaps Elton just wanted to throw himself into Bell's world and see what would happen. He was such a fan that the idea of simply being *on* a Thom Bell record must have sent shivers up his spine. So, on Friday, October 14, 1977, the Thom Bell sessions were born when Elton arrived in Seattle for work at the Kaye-Smith Studio, Bell's new home base. Instrumental tracks for six songs were recorded on Saturday and Sunday; Elton recorded vocals for these on Monday and Tuesday.[92]

Playing on the songs was the identical cast from such Spinners singles as "Sadie" and "Heaven on Earth (So Fine)": Thom Bell on keyboards; Bob Babbit on bass; Charles Collins on drums; Larry Washington on percussion; and Bobby Eli, Tony Bell, Leroy Bell, and Casey James (the latter two recorded as Bell and James) on guitar. Added later at Philadelphia's Sigma Sound Studios were MFSB on strings and horns, and backing vocals by a veritable army of people, including Bell and James, and the Spinners themselves.

Only two of Elton's compositions were used in the project, "Nice and Slow" and "Shine on Through." "Nice and Slow," cowritten with Bernie and Bell, was a pleasant but inconsequential song with a lighthearted, surprisingly lightweight melody. The lyrics are filled with thinly veiled references to sexual arousal and intercourse. Bell's MFSB arrangement gives the song most of its unobtrusive disco sensibility. Most appealing about the recording is Elton's self-assured vocal, which comfortably sweeps from Philly Soul falsetto to sensible tenor grittiness, and back again.

"Shine on Through" is a more substantial song, one of Elton's fabled hymns and one of his first collaborations with lyricist Gary Osborne. Osborne, who had written lyrics for Kiki Dee's *Loving and Free*, as well as for her most recent album, *Kiki Dee*, was also a friend. "Though Elton's known as a loner, he's quite fun to be with and we had lots of good laughs with him," Osborne recalled later. He was afraid to press the tantalizing thought of their writing together, since he didn't want to jeopardize a friendship he so valued.

As fate would have it, Elton was fooling around on his piano one day and Osborne was throwing out lyrical ideas. In twenty minutes, a song they called "Smile That Smile" emerged. It was never recorded, but Elton may have realized that this was a strangely attractive way to work. He was thus spurred to play Osborne a melody he had recently composed. Osborne taped it, and returned the following day with lyrics. The result was "Shine on Through."[93]

On the version recorded with Bell, Elton reached further into the depths of his vocal range than ever before. The most obvious song to receive similar treatment was "Philadelphia Freedom," in which the entire lead vocal seems to originate from the bottom of his lungs. Another of these pleasing efforts is found on *Blue Moves'* "Boogie Pilgrim," though the impressive heft he achieves there is a teaser, since he returns to falsetto for the song's chorus. So when on "Shine on Through," following the main part of the heart-rending hymn, Elton commenced several minutes of vocal improvisation (as Bell often encouraged his artists to do), it was clear something was happening. Elton was still attracted to the vocal leap, but his slithery range also slipped neatly, and more frequently, onto a lower level. While there, his voice acquired additional bands of sound. His singing was firmly on a new trail, thanks to Thom Bell.

"He was the first person that ever taught me about my voice," Elton remembered. "He said, 'You don't use your lower register enough, and you don't breathe properly.' I thought, 'Oh, fabulous, we're going to get on really well.' Well, he was right."[94] Consequently, the Bell- and James-penned "Mama Can't Buy You Love" favors a measured, more masculine tenor, as do two other songs, "Are You Ready for Love" and "Three Way Love Affair." Only "Country Love Song" acceded to Elton's familiarly sweet, boyish voice, but Thom Bell couldn't have minded. The song's "shoop-doo-doop" chorus that Elton chirped with relish is irresistible.

When Elton heard Bell's final mixes of the six songs, he decided to put them away for a while. "It was too saccharine," Elton said three years later. He especially had misgivings about "Are You Ready for Love." He had asked Bell to have the Spinners add backing vocals to the song. "When his mix came through I only sang one verse and they did the whole lot," Elton laughed.[95]

A highly anticipated second round of recording with Bell, planned for early 1978,[96] became a casualty once Elton realized that Bell's finished product didn't live up to his expectations. The first twelve-inch single, originally planned for release by the end of 1977, didn't come out anywhere for a year and a half. An ABC-TV documentary, which would have included playback session footage, was shelved.

"THE TIMES HAVE CHANGED"[97]

WHILE ELTON WAS BUSY IN SEATTLE, another album was already out, one that had not required any new work. This was *Elton John's Greatest Hits Volume II*, issued on September 13, 1977 in Britain, and October 1, 1977 in the United States. Its release was precipitated by the settlement of a dispute as to whether the DJM recording contract really had been satisfied.[98] It also drew renewed attention to Elton's recorded output, even with no singles released in support of the effort—as Elton had had enough hit songs to fill the second volume, only three years after the first. Its contents should have made a coveted package for the coming Christmas season.

The American version differed from that released elsewhere in the world in that "Levon" was included in place of the misspelled "Benny and the Jets." The other songs on the album represented the 1974–1977 period. The first *Greatest Hits* had come out at a time when new Elton John hits were rolling out as rapidly as fans were buying the album. "The Bitch Is Back" and "Lucy in the Sky with Diamonds" had both just missed being included on the first volume, and now received their due on volume two. The remaining songs—"Sorry Seems to Be the Hardest Word," "Don't Go Breaking My Heart," "Someone Saved My Life Tonight," "Philadelphia Freedom," "Island Girl," "Grow Some Funk of Your Own," and "Pinball Wizard"—provided a reminder of Elton's former radio primacy.

Record buyers in the United States were only mildly interested. *Elton John's Greatest Hits Volume II* was certified platinum but, in peaking at number 21 and barely spending a quarter of the time on *Billboard*'s Top LPs that *Greatest Hits* had, it had the smallest impact on the charts since *Friends*. In light of its contents—number 1 songs previously unavailable on any album and, in the case of "Pinball Wizard," a song played so often on the radio it could have been number 1 had it been commercially available—the album's chart performance was surprising. The growing reluctance of Americans to buy Elton's music was now patently obvious. In Britain, the compilation did better, reaching number 6. Although hits in Britain were not that easy for Elton to come by, he was still able to offer up a Top 10 album.

Elton's appearance with Bernie in New York to promote a new picture book chronicling the 1976 American and British tours, *Elton: It's a Little Bit Funny*, created a stir, and hope for the future. Bernie had written the narrative, as well as a prefatory poem, "On the Road," which wistfully looked back on what may have then seemed the songwriting duo's last year of glory.[99] But hysteria reigned behind barricades at Sam Goody's, where a book signing took place, as young women shed tears and screamed. It was evident that, even with the *Rolling Stone* interview fallout, Elton still had a solid core of loyal fans.[100]

"THERE'S A LOT MORE TO ME THAN PLAYING ON THE ROAD"[101]

THAT FALL, Elton became the first rock star to be inducted into the Madison Square Garden Hall of Fame, following four years of sellout shows at the venue and the record-breaking seven-night stand in August 1976. Now his likeness hung alongside boxing greats Muhammad Ali and Sugar Ray Robinson, and circus pioneer P.T. Barnum.[102]

On November 3, 1977, Elton and a reshuffled China (with Ray Cooper providing the necessary percussive touches) presented a two and a half hour charity concert at the Empire Pool, Wembley, in North London. Elton was suffering from depression again, and hadn't enjoyed rehearsals. "The thought of getting a band together for another concert really filled me with gloom," Elton explained later to a Home Box Office audience, just before parts of the concert were aired on television. "I didn't have the feeling for it anymore." He made up his mind the night of the show that this would be his last concert.

Elton had a new look for his audience—shoulder-length hair topped by a black beret, a black leather jacket traversed by zippers, a sensible pair of dark sunglasses. He began by playing solo. Besides interpreting such numbers as "Better off Dead," "Daniel," and "Roy Rogers," he unveiled "Shine on Through." There was no hint yet of Elton's mood. His performance was charmingly engrossing. Then China joined him for a percolating version of "I Heard It through the Grapevine" and a surprise rendition of the blustery "One Horse Town." By now, the pianist was playing with intensity but singing less ardently. He looked unhappy, even during the many moments when he smiled at the seven-thousand-strong audience. Then, he made an announcement.

"It's very hard to put it in words, really. But I haven't been touring for a long time," he began, hesitantly. "It's been a painful decision whether to come back on the road or not [the crowd cheers] and I've really enjoyed tonight, thank-you very much [more cheers]. I've made a decision tonight—this is going to be the last show, all right? There's a lot more to me than playing on the road, so this is the last one I'm gonna do."[103] The cheers were rapidly replaced by a great, incredulous murmur, interspersed with cries of "No! No!"

Writing a review for *Melody Maker* after the show, Colin Irwin observed that the musician was "something of a conjuror with emotions." Elton, once rid of the weight on his shoulders, "launched into a blistering, mountainous finale that quickly lifted everyone from their brooding." The encores included a fifteen-minute version of "Bite Your Lip," for which he brought out from the wings none other than Stevie Wonder. Having been so moved by the show's conclusion, Irwin wrote, "The loss of Elton John is considerable."[104]

Afterwards, all those associated with Elton scrambled to make sense of the announcement and fend off questions from the press. "That just shattered me," said sound engineer Clive Franks. "My last five years had been on the road with him. Amazing. So emotional. I used to have trouble at times mixing [at concerts] because everything was so emotional. I used to shake."[105] "I've got to discuss this whole thing with him," a nonplussed John Reid told reporters.[106]

CHAPTER 6

RESTLESS[1]

(1977–1980)

JUST THREE MONTHS after announcing his retirement from live performance, Elton got the studio bug again. Fresh from a vacation in Rio, he did something he hadn't done since the spring of 1974: He recorded songs in England. That was where he planned to be for a long time. The studio of choice was the Mill, in Cookham, Berkshire (owned by Gus Dudgeon). Clive Franks was along to coproduce. The initial objective was to record a leftover song, "Ego."

Elton viewed "Ego," a rare collaboration in which the music came first, as a commentary on bloated show-business vanity of the type embodied, he said, in the careers of David Bowie and Neil Diamond.[2] "I'm not in it for the bread, I'm in it for the gravy, honey," read Bernie's lyrics. "I'm not in it as an extra, I'm in it for the killing." With tumbling notes leading into the locomotive pull of dark, clanging chords, it is an eccentric number—not a ballad, not quite rock, or jazz, or soul, or gospel. The melody alternates between a robotically linear concoction befitting the egotism at the song's center and a soft, dreamlike sequence recalling the tough days before success beckoned. Synthesizer touches develop the robotic sections, the most intriguing of which creates the sound of liquid dripping on metal. Metal also makes its way into Elton's noticeably deeper, post-Thom Bell voice, which produces an aluminum polish worthy of the song's imagined star.

Elton was convinced that "Ego," released in March 1978, would be a hit. He was so interested in promoting it that he made one of the first music videos, filmed on March 13, 1978 and produced by John Reid for movie theater consumption. It was given the grand Hollywood treatment. A premiere was set for the first week in April at the National Theater in Westwood, a similar premiere to follow in London. MCA Records gave "Ego" as much of a push as possible, inviting radio personalities, the press, and other music-industry types to the five-minute Westwood showing and party afterwards. "It's a unique opportunity to put this much energy behind a single," said Bob Siner, MCA Records vice president of advertising and publicity. "Cost is not important."[3]

As significant as the fanfare surrounding the film was the new look of its star. Gone was any trace of spectacles—no oversized frames, no tinted lenses, not even a pair of sensible sunglasses. Just contact lenses. His eyebrows, theretofore concealed by some form of "face furniture," were given a rare airing. Normally bushy, they were trimmed and brushed for the occasion. His right earlobe was pierced with a jeweled stud. And he wore a dapper sky-blue felt fedora covering closely cropped hair, with a matching sky-blue suit that seemed to hang on him, creating the illusion of height and litheness he'd been seeking all his life.

The five-minute movie star sang into a microphone against a backdrop that read "Elton Ego," as if to apply the point of the song to himself. The fleeting dramatic scenes seemed to support this theme, tracing the progression of a young boy from the self-consciousness of prepubescence to the self-assured megalomania of superstardom, not unlike, his critics might have said, the blossoming of Reggie Dwight into Elton Hercules John.

But Elton's grimaces and the negative images conveyed by this pioneering video didn't make for pleasant viewing. Nor did the single do well in either the United States, where his brief tenure on his own label had ended, or Britain, stalling at number 34 in both countries. Its tepid performance in Britain kept Elton off BBC-TV's *Top of the Pops*. He questioned the reliability of the British Market Research Bureau's (BMRB's) information, on which the BBC relied, since other sources showed the single doing better than 34.[4] "Everybody in the business knows it's ridiculous. But far too few people have had the courage to say so," he protested. He pulled Rocket Records's advertising from publications in which the BMRB tabulations were featured.[5]

Elton must have believed "Ego" was his ticket back into the spotlight. Although his retreat into the shadows had been self-imposed, with two retirement announcements within a year and a half and damage purposefully self-inflicted through a frankness the American public wouldn't accept, he had never meant to take a back seat to other recording acts, and was trying to edge his way to the front again. As much a fan as he was of others, Elton had grown accustomed to the status he had worked so hard for and was loathe to relinquish it.

Some six months later, cooler tempers prevailed. "'Ego' was an unusual type of song for me to come out with," Elton told *Billboard*'s Ed Harrison. "I did the film, which was slightly weird and spooky. But I'm proud of it. . . . I don't think people were ready for it. They like to cubbyhole an artist and would like for me to come out with jewel glasses again."[6] At around the same time, he admitted to Robert Hilburn that having to work for hits was undoubtedly better for the creative process. "At one point, I could have sung the national anthem and it would have gone to number 1," he said. "Creatively, it's better that it isn't always like that."[7]

"EVERYBODY'S GOT A SONG TO SING"[8]

As "Ego" disappeared from the singles charts in spring 1978, Elton was already at work on a larger project. The day he recorded the doomed single he had also recorded another version of "Shine on Through." And a dangerous thing happened between takes. Without warning, the music for about twenty-eight new songs burst from his fingertips onto the piano keys, a case of "writer's diarrhea," he said later. Bernie was unavailable for consultation as he was working on an album (*From the Inside*) with Alice Cooper in Los Angeles (although he had previously given Elton some new lyrics). Bernie's collaboration with another musician halfway around the world didn't bother Elton, who insisted that he had been pushing Bernie to write with others for years. "Because he's a sweetie and very loyal, he didn't want to do it, afraid of a new venture that might go wrong," Elton said. "He was so reliable in our relationship. I wish he'd push himself more. Perhaps this little breakup will be good."[9]

Later, both he and Bernie would contend that there never was a "breakup," though after all the recording was over, Bernie's lyrics would be conspicuously absent from the new songs. Instead, Elton enlisted the services of Gary Osborne, who was nearby, to write words for the music that had poured forth in the recording studio. The pianist had ideas for most of the song titles and some of the lyrics, but he needed Osborne to flesh out the words. Once Osborne came through, Elton was, to his surprise, ready to record a whole album's worth of new material.

Since there was no rush—no tours on which to embark, no deadlines to meet—recording sessions stretched out over months. Elton had no band. With the exception of the return of Ray Cooper for percussive flair, and coproducer (with Elton) Clive Franks's turn on bass guitar, session musicians were used: Steve Holly, who had played on Kiki Dee sessions, on drums; Tim Renwick, formerly of the Sutherland Brothers and Quiver, on acoustic and electric guitars (with one cameo by Davey Johnstone on electric guitar); Herbie Flowers, who had played on *Tumbleweed Connection* and *Madman Across the Water,* on acoustic bass; and B.J. Cole, another *Madman* veteran, on pedal steel guitar. With Paul Buckmaster returning for orchestral arrangements, it was like old times.

Still, some important things distinguished these sessions from those distant, naive days. Not only were Bernie's lyrics largely absent (they were used on B-sides), but Nigel and Dee weren't around to play on the solitary track permitted them by Gus Dudgeon ("Amoreena" on *Tumbleweed* and "All the Nasties" on *Madman*), and Hookfoot was nowhere in sight. But the biggest difference between these sessions and, say, the *Madman* sessions was the quality that would make the name of the new album, *A Single Man,* so apt—the simplicity with which each song was interpreted.

In between sessions for *A Single Man,* the musician picked up a British music trophy, winning best male singer at the Capital Radio Music Awards. Proving his flamboyance intact, he accepted the award in a red jacket with wide white lapels, a red bow tie with large black polka dots, a flat red cap, and a red stud in his right ear. He might have resembled a comical life-size doll but for the beard fuzz covering his face and neck. Afflicted by a case of acute humility, he announced that Elvis Costello should have gotten the award. "I really hadn't done anything during that year [1977] to warrant it," he said afterwards. "It seemed a bit farcical for me to pick up the award."[10]

Back at the *Single Man* sessions, Gary Osborne's role was limited, mainly filling in gaps in Elton's lyrical ideas. Osborne's words didn't make a good read, as Bernie's usually had. They didn't, for the most part, have a life apart from the music, but seemed wedded to it, like an instrument played through the voice of Elton John. This made sense, given Elton's limited lyrical abilities and Osborne's straightforward approach.

"Shine on Through," the album's first song, is a hymn in the vein of "Candle in the Wind," bidding farewell to a love affair whose embers could still turn to fire if stirred sufficiently. The song comes through purely as a gospel-flavored piano and voice number with modest orchestral involvement, a far cry from the Thom Bell version that takes Elton's singing through unprecedented gyrations. This doesn't mean Elton's vocal on "Shine on Through" is insignificant; to the contrary, it is the first on an entire album of songs featuring the more textured, layered sound that had become a part of the musician's vocal signature, thanks to Thom Bell.

The album's next song, "Return to Paradise," is meant to be a satirical look at British vacationers in Spain. But with no trace of irony in either the music or lyrics, and with words that don't adhere naturally to the music, "Return to Paradise" stands as *A Single Man*'s sole failure. This is a shame. On its own, the melody is an affecting Latin conceit set against Elton's music-box piano stylings, with a gleaming arrangement by Buckmaster that features Herb Alpert–influenced trumpet by guest musician Henry Lowther, tidy acoustic guitar plucking by Tim Renwick, and restrained marimba strokes by Ray. The song is also the only one on the album in which Elton gravitates toward his upper register.

"I Don't Care," the third song, is a celebration of the life-sustaining qualities of love in the face of adversity ("I got bills piling up in the hall/I got paint peeling off of the wall/I got you, I'm a happy man"). Elton's playing on this joyous up-tempo song, a happy union of puissant bass notes and convex chords at once soft and brittle, signals a new style that would, with considerable embellishments, take him through a world tour in 1979 and noticeably infect his piano approach on his next important studio album. The only element in this song that makes as much of an impression as Elton's piano is Buckmaster's orchestration. Consistent with many of his post-1971 arrangements for the pianist, this one is a buoyant outgrowth of Elton's playing rather than a completely separate composition.

The supporting musicians and backing vocalists have a bigger role on the next song, "Big Dipper." This is also one of Elton's funniest, raciest songs. Having come out as a "bisexual," Elton couldn't resist delving musically into homosexual attraction. "Big Dipper" is the story of a "cute little slip of a sailor" who discovers, with the help of a horny stranger, that he likes gay sex ("He's got his own big dipper/but he's got his eye on yours").

The fictional episode in "Big Dipper" may not have been that far off from some of Elton's own sexual escapades at the time, as by his own admission he was going through more boyfriends and one-night stands than he could count. His habits stemmed from his love of cocaine. "I used cocaine basically for sex," he said years later. "My sexual fantasies were all played out while I was on cocaine."[11] He'd see a "fabulous" busboy in a bar and fantasize a whole relationship with him before they'd even met. Then he'd use his pickup line: "Would you like to come back to the house and have some drugs?" Afterwards, he'd snort coke for hours, waiting for the busboy to get off duty.[12]

But in "Big Dipper," Elton was not just telling a bawdy tale. The story also offers a taste of wisdom, a sort of variation on the oft-uttered "different-strokes-for-different-folks": "Everybody's got a song to sing/everybody's got to do their thing." The lyrics are wrapped in a hybrid of musical cousins—Dixieland melody and brass meshed with Elton's ragtime piano—to approximate what Al Jolson might have sounded like had he teamed up with Leon Redbone. Here, jazz music is used to express the original meaning of "jazz" (from "jass"), copulation. Despite the sexually taboo subject matter, Elton was able to recruit members of the Watford Football Club to sing backing vocals, along with a group dubbed the South Audley Street Girls' Choir, which was actually made up of female staff at Rocket Records. The company was then located on South Audley Street in London.

The song that closes side one, "It Ain't Gonna Be Easy," tells of someone's slow-boiling fury after learning of a lover's infidelity. At more than eight minutes long, trimmed from twelve,[13] the song moves the listener along like the ocean's undertow when a hurricane far offshore churns up the waves. Beginning as a mild current, the music builds into a tidal wave of anger, commencing with Elton's whisper of a vocal, some hesitant piano lines seemingly left over from "Big Dipper," speckless electric guitar picking by Tim Renwick, and the hiss of Ray Cooper's tambourine. As the song progresses, Elton's playing changes from the musing of ragtime to forceful convex chords, his voice increasing in volume to match the protagonist's rising anger and tamed only by Ray's vibraphone and Buckmaster's orchestral arrangement. As the song fades, Elton showcases the growing elasticity of his voice, taking considerable liberties with the melody and lyrics.

The song opening side two, "Part-Time Love," is a curious counterpoint to "It Ain't Gonna Be Easy," with sentiments favoring free love. "I've got someone at home, but she's got a love of her own," Elton sings, "Because you, me, and everybody got a part-time love." "Part-Time Love" is a merry song with an irreverent melody that mocks the very thought of the fidelity so prized in "It Ain't Gonna Be Easy." Davey Johnstone makes his sole *Single Man* appearance here, with a sonorous lead guitar that heightens the melody's irreverence. A Buckmaster arrangement hums politely in the background, unleashed with circus-like fanfare at strategic points (as when Elton sings, "Love, well, it ain't no crime"), adding to the humor. A backing vocal ensemble, including Gary Osborne and Davey, does some righteously spiritual singing, accentuating the mirth with which the song embraces free love.

The next song, "Georgia," is a toast to the idyllic American countryside as symbolized by one Southern state. Coincidentally, the song, with its yearning for the simplicity of bucolic life found, according to the words, in the state of Georgia, could have functioned as a theme song for Elton just over a decade later, when he established his American residence in Atlanta. "Oh Georgia take me to your Southlands, I sometimes feel that life has passed me by," he sings.

The lyrics for "Georgia" were inspired by one of the musician's favorite musical forms, the hymn. A warm gospel chord progression welcomes the listener, with harmonium and church organ brushing the ears as parishioners extol not the wonders of God, but the enjoyment of nature and quietude that they hope will not be obliterated by progress. The Watford Football Club and the South Audley Street Girls' Choir are the parishioners being led in song by their areligious musical mentor. The music of "Georgia" thus epitomizes, along with such compositions as "Border Song," the paradox of Elton's professed impiety in the face of his fascination with spirit-cleansing melodies. It is also testimony to a tug-of-war within his psyche, between the sexual daring of songs like "Big Dipper" and "Part-Time Love" and the more conventional emotions of "Georgia" and "Shine on Through."

This paradox returns as early as the next song, "Shooting Star." One of Elton's most sensuous melodies, "Shooting Star" is a jazz ballad that he considered melodically similar to "Idol," inspired by his trip to Brazil for Carnivale.[14] The song's bedtime intimacy ("I'm still in love with you, oh, shooting star") is furthered by the misty sounds of a tenor sax and an acoustic bass against the twinkling of Elton's Fender Rhodes piano.

Elton moves from sensuous whispers to indignant classical flourishes with "Madness," a commentary on the futility of terroristic acts committed in the name of political change. The words are both powerful ("They hide inside a smoke filled room/to hear at last the blast of doom/and so the deed is done") and redundant ("And it's madness—every time the bullets start/there is madness—burning in a poor man's heart/and it's madness—something that we can't control"). The music begins with mighty broken piano chords played as a scales-type exercise, punctuated by decisive bass notes that continue through much of the song until they periodically mushroom into symphonic chords. Over this backdrop, accented by Ray's congas and timpani and a stimulating undercurrent of strings, Elton wails his surging melody like someone fleeing the scene of a disaster.

As if mourning the tragedy depicted in "Madness," the subject turns to death with two final songs, both instrumentals. The first is "Reverie," described by the pianist as a "very wistful death thing."[15] It features just him on piano and Buckmaster on Arp synthesizer for a simple, desolate melody just under a minute long that functions mainly as an introduction to the funereal "Song for Guy."

"Song for Guy" was not written with the other melodies that make up the bulk of the album. Elton had been at the piano at Woodside one Sunday when thoughts of death overwhelmed him. Prevalent in the news at the time was the Shroud of Turin, the garment that appeared to bear the outline of Jesus' body. "It's amazing. Even an old cynic like me was moved," said Elton.[16]

The pianist probably didn't need a newspaper story to remind him of death, given his morbid interest in capturing feelings of death in music, such as in "Funeral for a Friend." Elton enjoyed any kind of sad music; hearing Sir Edward Elgar's "Enigma Variations" would leave him in a flood of tears.[17] So on that Sunday, he was consumed with morbid thoughts and imagined himself dying, his spirit leaving his body as he looked down on it.

"Song for Guy" has both sad and hopeful elements; Elton has described this as an "optimistic" death song. Its danceable rhythm, which suggests a discovery that there really is life after death, interchanges with sad, sluggish chords, possibly a reminder of the end of one's corporeal existence. A convincing electronic arrangement uses synthesizers, Ray's wind chimes and shakers, and a self-supporting wonder of musical technology, the rhythm box, which provides a firm backbeat. Elton inserts the lone words of the song, "life isn't everything," at the end, which he sings over and over until the words shorten to "life" and the music halts, the out-of-body experience completed.

The title, "Song for Guy," didn't come to Elton until the day after he wrote the song, when he learned that Guy Burchett, a seventeen-year-old messenger boy for Rocket Records, had been killed on his motorcycle that Sunday, the very day on which the musician had composed his music about death. "Song for Guy" turned into a tribute to Burchett.

Five or six other songs were left off the album, which could have been released in August 1978 except that Rocket Records was in the middle of changing affiliations outside the United States and Canada, moving its allegiance from EMI to Phonogram.[18]

The outgrowth of the *Single Man* sessions was an album that broke no new ground but reaffirmed Elton's commitment to melody. It also revealed a man struggling with an inner conflict. This might not have been evident had Bernie been the lyricist, but as Elton was responsible for the themes and many of the lyrics on

A Single Man, the songs took on a personal bent. He craved the emotional intimacy and commitment possessed by the poverty-stricken fellow in "I Don't Care" and lost in "It Ain't Gonna Be Easy." He was also obsessed with sexual gratification—hence, "Big Dipper" and "Part-Time Love." And his innate spirituality surfaced several times, including in the songs "Georgia" and "Song for Guy."

"I GOT EVERYTHING A MAN COULD NEED, BUT IT STILL ISN'T QUITE ENOUGH"[19]

A *SINGLE MAN* WAS RELEASED IN OCTOBER 1978, in both the United States and Britain. Elton was determined that the album should be successful, so determined, in fact, that he freely gave interviews and made countless public appearances on the album's behalf—something he hadn't done much of in recent years. Although he concentrated on press and radio stations in New York and Los Angeles, he willingly talked at length with disc jockeys in smaller markets and made himself available to lesser-known writers and publications, such as Daisann McLane of *Feature* magazine and Mike Greenblatt of *Aquarian Weekly.*

And that was not all. Elton's pledge to forgo the rigors of live performance, announced at the Wembley Pool charity show in November 1977 while he was suffering from one of his "moods," was showing signs of wear. While in Los Angeles, where he gave about twenty interviews in a seven-hour period,[20] he treated MCA executives to a surprise ninety-minute solo performance. The musical seeds planted at the May 1977 Rainbow Theatre concerts were starting to push through the soil. Elton not only played a retrospective of hits, but also his "custom-made" (as Robert Hilburn described it) version of "I Heard It through the Grapevine," a boogie-woogie reworking of Elvis's "Don't Be Cruel," and six songs from *A Single Man.*

"The adrenaline was really pumping. I was really nervous," Elton said later that evening. "When I sat down at the piano, my knee was shaking so hard I put it on the pedal to stop it, but it just kept shaking." He even made mistakes. But before long, he was aiming wisecracks at various MCA executives.[21] A press photograph shows the musician crouched over the keys with knees bent and face contorted, as in days of yore, having just kicked over the piano bench. The show seemed to motivate the troops, one of whom enthusiastically proclaimed "Part-Time Love" a sure-fire number I.

Elton then took his campaign to Europe, where his star had risen in the last couple of years, in contrast to what was happening in the United States. In particular, France had embraced him in 1976 following the release of *Blue Moves,* a wildly popular album there.[22]

A solo performance in France some days after he'd thrilled MCA executives in Los Angeles also proved electrifying. If his Rainbow Theatre shows had seemed like manna from heaven to ears starved too long for his delicious improvisations of the early 1970s, his solo venture in Paris that October 1978 had to seem a sumptuous meal from heaven. "Bennie and the Jets" finally received the funny, expansive treatment that had always been hiding behind the recording's syncopated rhythms, with jagged chords leaping like sparks from the keys, and cries of "Bennie!" from Elton and his admiring French audience.

But no matter how spectacularly the musician performed for select audiences, or how available he made himself to the press, he couldn't ensure good reviews. As usual, reviews of *A Single Man* ranged from gushing praise to near vilification. *The New Orleans Times-Picayune* called the album "one of . . . [Elton's] most brilliant efforts."[23] Britain's *Melody Maker* found "Song for Guy" the "most elegant piece of music that Elton has ever recorded," and viewed the album as proof that "Elton John is alive and well."[24] But harsh words came from *Rolling Stone*'s Stephen Holden. Hurling epithets like "garbage" and "junk," Holden fumed, "If John and Taupin's final collaboration, *Blue Moves,* was a disastrous exercise in inflated pop rhetoric, *A Single Man* is an equally disastrous exercise in smug vapidity."[25]

Music fans in the United States were as lukewarm to the new album as many critics. Debuting on *Billboard*'s Top LPs on November 11, 1978, *A Single Man* only reached number 15, although it did become Elton's third platinum album, after *Blue Moves* and *Greatest Hits Volume II.* But, like the reissued *Empty Sky, A Single Man* spent only eighteen weeks on the chart. Unlike *Empty Sky,* this album did not have to compete against other new or recent Elton John releases; it also had a couple of singles that should have bolstered sales.

The first single in both the United States and Britain was "Part-Time Love." In the United States, the song charted at the same time as the album, peaking at number 22. In Britain (where the album reached number 8), it peaked at number 15. This may not seem cause for celebration, except that it was Elton's first British Top 20 single since "Sorry Seems to Be the Hardest Word." And, with thirteen weeks on the chart, it had greater chart longevity than any single since "Don't Go Breaking My Heart."

The success of "Part-Time Love" in Britain owed much to a collapse Elton suffered at Woodside on November 7, which some initially feared to be a heart attack, as he had complained of chest pains. After the musician was admitted to Harley Street Clinic in London's West End, it was learned that the collapse had been triggered by exhaustion, itself caused, some said, by the hectic schedule Elton had maintained in support of his new album.[26] That Elton had reportedly played both an exhibition tennis match with Billie Jean King and a charity soccer game on the same day, just two days before he was stricken, couldn't have helped.[27]

Elton's status in Britain as a favorite son finally worked to his advantage. His collapse helped sell "Part-Time Love," pushing the single to number 15 and extending its life on the singles chart. "If any of you artists want to sell more records," Elton laughed, "just have a heart attack scare and go into hospital, because your sales go up immediately."[28]

But it was "Song for Guy" that gave Elton his first Top 10 British hit since 1976 and proved a worldwide sensation outside North America. Released in Britain on November 28, 1978, it charted on December 16 and reached number 4. While undoubtedly helped by the momentum created by "Part-Time Love," some of this positive response must have been due to the song's somber but gorgeous melody.

In the United States, "Song for Guy" never had a chance. Just months after the solo show that had supposedly stirred MCA executives, trouble began brewing between the record company and the musician. More than a year earlier, MCA had announced it would no longer press Rocket Records releases, which hadn't been selling well.[29] By the summer of 1978, RCA Records had replaced MCA as Rocket's distributor.[30] Even so, perhaps MCA would have been more interested in promoting "Song for Guy" if the musician had been on a hot streak, as he was when he'd put his name to the eight million dollar contract. Though it was demonstrating tremendous hit potential everywhere else, MCA decided that the single didn't have any in the United States.

The problem, as MCA saw it, was that there was another immensely popular instrumental on the American charts during the winter of 1979, precluding the success of a second. This was Frank Mills's "Music Box Dancer," a Polydor single that, by April, was in the Top 10 and certified gold. But although the song had some piano music in it, its cheery theme could hardly be compared to the funeral chord progressions of "Song for Guy." MCA released "Song for Guy" in March but declined to do anything for it. As a result, it only got as far as number 110 on *Billboard*'s Bubbling Under chart.

Chart watcher Joel Whitburn would later cite "Song for Guy" as one of the one hundred singles to have "bubbled under" the Hot 100 that should have been a national hit.[31] Elton agreed. He never forgave MCA for its slight to a single that meant so much to him.

Fortunately, as "Song for Guy" languished, untouched in American record store bins and unplayed by American disc jockeys, Elton was able to put his mind to other things. He was already two months into a major world tour that, for him, would prove he was still a good musician and a good singer, and was capable of improving, too.

"YOU MAY HAVE SEEN ME AT THE EARLY SHOW"[32]

THE YEAR 1979 was one in which Elton John almost became a movie star. This had also almost happened in 1970, when he'd been offered the role of Harold in the film *Harold and Maude*. He had turned down the opportunity (although he probably looked even more like the death-obsessed Harold than the eventual star, Bud Cort) because, at the time, his fledgling music career was fiercely taking off. With a gift for mimicry and a sharp wit, as demonstrated in a guest stint on British television's *Morecambe and Wise*, the idea that he could have become a successful comedic actor is not at all far-fetched.

Toward the end of 1978, Elton and Rod Stewart considered making a comedy together, along the lines of the Hope-Crosby *Road* films, tentatively titled *Jet Lag*. The leads were to be two rock stars who avoided paying taxes by flying around the world in their private jets.[33] But Rod was in the middle of a tour until mid-1979, so filming couldn't commence until after that. And by that time, Elton had reembraced the concert stage. This movie was not to be.

But Elton did manage to get in some *Road* movie–style licks in real life, anyway. He and Rod had already acquired a reputation for jokingly "having a go" at each other in the press. A year earlier, Rod had told the London *Evening Standard* that he doubted Elton had been "born to be a rock and roll star," suggesting that the pianist's place was with Watford and that he was beginning to *look* like a chairman of the club, too. In retaliation, Elton asserted that he could be both a rock star *and* chairman of Watford, and that he'd sold more records than Rod. "Anyway, he should stick to grave digging [one of Rod's first jobs as a boy] because that's where he belongs—six feet under," Elton added.[34]

More good-natured ribbing occurred at Christmastime 1978. Rod, on his way to Olympia Hall for his first London show that season, found an enormous banner hanging nearby on Hammersmith Road that played with the title of his current hit album and used the two friends' female nicknames, "Phyllis" for Rod and "Sharon" for Elton. It read, "Blondes have more fun but brunettes have lots more money. Happy Christmas Phyllis. Love Sharon." Rod recruited roadies to tear the banner down and replaced it with another, referring to Elton's pursuit of hair plugs, that read, "Blondes may have more fun, but brunettes have more transplants."[35]

By 1979, Elton had moved on to thoughts of being onstage again. This was also the year that his soccer club, Watford, advanced to the second division. The team's ascension was another example of its chairman's determination to taste victory despite any obstacles. He declared, "If I had a broken leg or a broken arm, I'd still go play tennis against somebody just to prove I could still beat them. I've had abuse hurled at me everywhere I go. Sometimes there'll be bleachers full of people, twenty thousand people, all singing 'Elton John's a homosexual, la la la.' And the only way you can answer them is by winning the bloody match!"[36] This was the same determination to win that had made Elton a star, and was the driving force behind his return to standing ovations.

For the first time ever, Elton would start a tour at the end of paths not so well traveled. It would also be his first genuine world tour, a sign of his increasing stardom in Europe's distant corners. He declined to take a band with him, Ray Cooper being his sole accompanist. The tour was aptly named, "Elton John, a Single Man in Concert, Plus Ray Cooper."

The venues were to be small. Elton said, at one point, that he didn't want to play before more than two thousand people, though crowds tended to reach upwards of five thousand. The tour began on February 5 at the Stockholm Concerthaus. The rest of February saw him sweeping the continent.

For this tour, Elton dressed in nothing gaudier than a sweatshirt, baggy pants, boots, an Andy Capp–style cap, with shoulder-length hair curled under in Dutch boy fashion, and sometimes a long, dark, zippered jacket. He continued to eschew eyeglasses in favor of contacts. Typically, he would quietly appear onstage, take a modest bow, walk over to his grand piano at stage right and begin playing the first number, "Your Song." As in the 1977 London shows, Elton played the first hour or so by himself and was joined midway through "Funeral for a Friend" by Ray on timpani. Also like the London shows, many relatively obscure songs graced the program, including "Sixty Years On," "Skyline Pigeon," "Roy Rogers," and "Better off Dead." There was also room for plenty of hits, as well as near-misses like "Ego" and "Crazy Water."

Elton sometimes paid tribute to the place where he was performing. At the Théâtre des Champs Élysées, for instance, he played "I Love Paris in the Springtime." He also played covers: "I Heard It through the Grapevine"; "He'll Have to Go," a staple of Reggie Dwight's nights at the Northwood Hills pub; and "Be-Bop-A-Lula," "Don't Be Cruel," "Hound Dog," and "Whole Lot of Shakin' Going On"—all of which Reggie had lapped up as a preteen.

"Grapevine" had passed through several stages since Elton had first experimented with it at the Rainbow Theatre in May 1977. Performed on the electric piano at stage left, it began with a tremolo played in almost staccato fashion, and was overloaded with sharp-edged brazen chords as likely to unleash a percussive storm as an avalanche of notes gripped in coiled tension. "Don't Be Cruel," characterized by the pianist's rumbling, strident left hand, was less a Presley tribute than a homage to Jerry Lee Lewis. Elton gave other songs a less predictable flair. "Daniel" had a Latin rhythm, "Take Me to the Pilot" combined steamrolling gospel with classical chord progressions, and "Rocket Man" possessed a weightlessness not expected from acoustic piano. He took chances with his voice, too, sometimes abusing one of his perfectly constructed melodies for fun, or singing scat as sound engineer Clive Franks multiplied his voice several-fold, transforming this "single man" into an eerie chorus.

Ray used his theatrical background to good effect, riling up the crowd with a mischievous gesture of the arm, a silly face, a toss of a drumstick, or the slam of a gong. Even in his conservative bank manager's clothing, he provided more visual flash than did Elton, whose flamboyance was now primarily reserved for his playing and singing. Elton had turned back the clock to the days of Reggie Dwight. He was the pub pianist again, this time playing to adoring throngs.

To the relief of fans at home, most of April was devoted to England, with six consecutive nights at London's Theatre Royal Drury Lane and dates up and down the country. May was reserved for more untested waters.

"GUNS AND GATES NO LONGER HOLD YOU IN"[37]

IN EARLY MAY 1979, Elton and Ray performed in Israel, a national event since the tiny country attracted few rock acts. But even more newsworthy were the eight shows they played in the Soviet Union. No act of Elton's caliber had ever before toured the superpower. Fleetwood Mac, the Beach Boys, Santana, and Joan Baez had all been met with roadblocks in their bids to do the same.[38] Elton figured he was being permitted to bring his tour because he was "safe." After Vladimir Kokonin, deputy director of the official Soviet concert agency, Goskoncert, attended one of Elton's April shows in Oxford, the tour was approved for Russian consumption.[39] The only stipulations were that Elton not kick over his piano bench, and that he not sing "Back in the USSR."

Although most of the concert tickets were sold to Communist officials, the audiences in Leningrad (now St. Petersburg) and Moscow included large numbers of young people. Many had purchased tickets on the black market for up to $150 each in Leningrad and up to $225 each in Moscow, although the regular price was only about eight dollars. Elton, aware of ticket scarcity, realized that if he had insisted on open sales, Goskoncert would have forbidden the tour and he would have accomplished nothing. When asked how he could go to Russia in view of the Soviet Union's mistreatment of dissidents and Jews, he declared that he had toured other places, like Northern Ireland and Israel, where "there are political things happening that one might not particularly agree with." He added, "I'm not going to say I'm not going to tour the States because I don't like [anti-gay crusader] Anita Bryant and how popular she is."[40]

Elton was to make only one thousand dollars a concert, an infinitesimal fraction of his usual take. The tour was expected to cost promoter Harvey Goldsmith, all told, twenty-five to forty-five times that. It was the movie that film producer-director Ian LaFrenais was making about the Soviet trip that was expected to bring in the real money later. One version was to be shown in British movie theaters, another on Britain's ITV network, a third on American television, yet another adapted for Soviet and Western European audiences, and a final one for home video.[41]

"Twenty-five years after Elvis Presley first excited American teenagers, rock'n'roll officially arrived in the Soviet Union and ignited immediate sparks," were Robert Hilburn's first words about the visit.[42] He was the only American journalist invited to travel with Elton's entourage, which included the musician's mother and step-father. Hilburn was right—young Russians were starved for Western rock. Access to such music had to be achieved with Cold War stealth, as the official government record label, Melodiya, pressed few albums of Western music and Soviet radio stations played little of it. Soviet soldiers stationed in East Germany taped music off Western radio stations, then brought the songs home, where other Soviet youth would tape them by placing two tape recorders next to each other. This would happen again and again, so that they often had songs several generations removed from the originals. It was also possible to get some Western albums on the black market, including Elton John albums.

Of course, Elton was not bringing typical rock music to Russia, since his shows consisted of just himself and Ray. The duo couldn't have met the expectations of some, based on the searing electric guitar licks present in much of Elton's recorded work. This was a different kind of rock'n'roll.

Elton, Ray, and the rest of their party boarded an Aeroflot jet and flew from London to Moscow on Sunday, May 20, 1979. The traveling had only begun—they still had an eight-and-a-half hour train ride from Moscow to Leningrad, where the first concerts were to take place. Robert Hilburn noticed that the 3,800-seat theater where Elton and Ray were to play in Leningrad, the Bolshoi Oktyabrsky Concert Hall, stood in a sharp contrast to the large collection of bleak-looking gray buildings surrounding it. The hall was as lavishly appointed and as technologically advanced as any concert hall in Los Angeles. The concertgoers, too, didn't resemble people he'd observed on the street, evidence that those with tickets were among the privileged few. Most wore fashionable Western-style outfits.

Before each show at the Oktyabrsky, an announcer read short biographies of Elton and Ray to the audience. Then Elton appeared onstage wearing a "modified Cossack outfit," as Hilburn put it. The audience that first night reacted politely to what Elton assumed was mostly unfamiliar music. Initially, there was little movement among the crowd, especially in the first few rows, which were occupied by older officials. But a flaming performance of "Grapevine"—during which he moved mid-song from the electric piano to his grand piano without missing a note—brought a roar of approval from the audience. A group of young people seated toward the back began responding to Elton's overtures to them in increasing numbers until, by the encores—when the pianist played "Saturday Night's Alright for Fighting" with an interpolation of "Pinball Wizard"—the youngsters jammed the aisles and surged toward the stage. This prompted him to break into "Back in the USSR," a no-no.[43] "It just came to me, and I was singing it before I realized I didn't know any of the words," Elton later told *Chicago Tribune* reporter Jim Gallagher in his dressing room. "So I just sang 'Back in the USSR' over and over again."[44]

There were more young people at the remaining three Leningrad concerts although, on another night, Elton and Ray found the crowd unmoving, even during "Bennie." To provoke a physical reaction from the audience, Elton worked some Russian folk music into the song, which, in his hands, flawlessly assumed the syncopated rhythms of "Bennie." Ray banged his tambourine, stomped, waved his arms at the audience, and yelled, "Come on! Come on!" Audience members looked pleased, but remained motionless. The performers later learned that when anyone tried to get up, they were pushed down by security personnel. This excessive caution by Soviet officials may have been in response to the audience's almost anarchic reaction the first night, and possibly to crowd-control problems that developed in the streets after the show.

Every night after a show, hundreds of young people would run from the Oktyabrsky to the street below Elton's third-floor dressing-room window, trying to catch another glimpse of the Western superstar. They would shout, "El-*tone!* El-*tone!* El-*tone!*" He would throw them flowers presented to him during the show.

Elton's lifestyle while in Russia was markedly unhealthy, although it probably differed little from his lifestyle at home. He would stay up until the wee hours of the morning drinking and, he insisted, listening to the Sex Pistols, and would not arise until noon. True to form, he never allowed this habit to adversely affect interpersonal relations or foreign diplomacy, and was as likely to be entertaining passersby in his hotel with an impromptu concert as listening to a punk band.[45] Upon arising at noon, Elton would sightsee, accompanied by producer-director Ian LaFrenais and the film crew.

May 24 saw the last Leningrad show. A train trip back to Moscow followed, for four shows at the three-thousand-seat Rossiya Concert Hall, set for May 27 through 31.[46] The May 28 show was broadcast live over BBC radio, the first such broadcast ever between Russia and Great Britain and the brainchild of BBC radio producer Jeff Griffin. The idea created a whole series of technical dilemmas. New, untried BBC equipment was set up to send a signal from Moscow to the Ukraine, where a satellite dish would beam the signal to a satellite, which would then transmit the sound to London.

Elton, who later proudly called this broadcast "creating a bit of history," had to be relied on to spend no more than two and a half hours onstage, the time allotted for the radio program. Griffin said that no one but Elton, who was "so professional," could have been expected to comply with this restriction. "Elton had promised me if I gave him signals all the way through, especially the last half hour, he would come out on time," remembered Griffin. "On the last but one encore, we were running very tight on time. So instead of staying off the stage for about a couple of minutes like an artist usually does while the applause builds and builds, I had [an engineer tell Elton] . . . 'You've got to go straight back on!'" In five seconds, Elton left the stage, ran around the back, and came right out on the other side. The audience had barely started cheering before the musician was back and had begun his last number. He had just enough time to make his closing acknowledgments.[47]

Elton took away bittersweet memories from the tour. Wherever he went in Leningrad and Moscow, he was besieged by fans asking for autographs—so afraid to impose they often snatched the paper he was writing on before he was finished— or showering him with flowers, candy, and stuffed toys. Upon returning to London, he spoke affectionately at a press conference of his experiences, and expressed hope for more cultural exchanges between East and West.[48] Just as he got home, talks began between concert promoter Harvey Goldsmith and Goskoncert about bringing other major Western acts to the Soviet Union.[49] Sadly, the Soviet invasion of Afghanistan just months later nixed further progress.

For the time being, Soviet officials were happy with this cultural exchange. The official record label, Melodiya, issued the album *A Single Man* under a new name, *Poet: Elton John.* The only catch was that "Part-Time Love," with its admonitions against monogamy, and the racy "Big Dipper," were omitted. The September 1979 issue of an official entertainment and cultural magazine, *Krugozor,* contained a blue "flexi-disc" recording of "Shooting Star" and "Madness," along with a small feature article that celebrated Elton's recent visit.

"DADDY DON'T NEED YOU"[50]

WHILE ELTON WAS ON TOUR, setting new boundaries for the fusion of jazz, rock, and rhythm and blues on both acoustic and electric piano, and exploring his voice's rubbery elasticity, some older music was being released to radio and record stores under his name. On April 30, 1979, an EP called *Thom Bell Sessions '77* came out in Britain, with three of the songs from those October 1977 Seattle sessions— "Are You Ready for Love," "Three Way Love Affair," and "Mama Can't Buy You Love." Elton and Clive Franks had remixed these in January 1979 to reduce the sugariness in the mixes and to practically erase the Spinners from "Are You Ready for Love," the first British single from the sessions.

"Are You Ready for Love" was an ill-chosen follow-up to the sublime melancholia of "Song for Guy." British record buyers weren't drawn to it as they had been to the ode that had brought Elton closer to his first solo number 1 than any song since "Daniel." The new single entered the chart on May 12, 1979, rising no higher than number 42, and became his worst-performing British charted single up to that time.

The EP itself didn't appear on any British chart. The mistake of releasing "Are You Ready for Love" as the lead single in Britain became all the more evident after Elton reaped notable success in the United States with the most appealing, radio-ready of the three EP songs, "Mama Can't Buy You Love."

Released in June 1979, following the conclusion of the first leg of Elton's tour with Ray, the untitled EP's *Billboard* album placement of number 51 may not have seemed like a reason to celebrate, until one looked at the chart strength of the single. "Mama Can't Buy You Love" was Elton's first Top 10 hit in the United States since "Sorry Seems to Be the Hardest Word" in December 1976. The new single took all summer to climb to the Top 10, further evidence that an Elton John single was no longer a certain chart blockbuster. It peaked at number 9 on August 25, and was certified gold. A gold single still meant a million-seller. It was also, like "Bennie," a crossover soul hit, bringing the musician his twelfth Grammy nomination, this one for best rhythm and blues vocal performance, male. Although it would be more than half a decade before Elton finally brought home a Grammy, the nomination was a distinction, as the category was virtually reserved for African Americans.

The summer of 1979 served as a break between tour legs, and a time to record. Sessions in August 1979 led to three more studio albums, the first of which would have been better left in the can—forever. To be charitable, *Victim of Love* could be regarded as one of the last projects that Elton had fantasized about back in the days when he'd been putting out two albums a year and had never had time to fool around. Now was his chance. He was, after all, a disco fan. And just as Elton had thrilled at the thought of playing on a John Lennon record, or reviving Neil Sedaka's career, or recording with Thom Bell, he wanted to experience the rush of having a disco album of his own.

Producer Peter Bellotte made it easy. Elton had met Bellotte in Hamburg, Germany, in a nightclub called the Top Ten Club, when the musician was with Bluesology and Bellotte was a member of another group sharing the bill. They lost touch, until Elton noticed Bellotte's name on a Donna Summer record. Bellotte went to see one of Elton's shows in London in April 1979 and broached the subject of doing a disco album. Elton agreed, but asked that the producer take complete charge of the project, much as the pianist had allowed Thom Bell a free hand at the Seattle sessions. In August, while Elton was writing and recording songs for two future albums, he took a day off to record this disco venture, flying to Munich and spending eight hours laying down vocals on seven songs at Musicland Studio.[51] Six of the songs were cowritten by Bellotte and a few German disco songsmiths; the seventh was Chuck Berry's signature tune, "Johnny B. Goode."

Those who eventually bought *Victim of Love* probably found that playing it was dangerous. One must be ready to dance for the record's entire length, as each song leads directly into the next. That quality, and the opening track, "Johnny B. Goode," provide the album's only charm. Although Chuck Berry was never known for writing challenging chord progressions or uplifting melodies, his 1958 hit seems brilliant compared to the songs that follow. It also coaxes the best vocal performance from Elton on the album—a more virile, saltier sound than he had ever managed before. But the rest of the songs don't measure up to the massively popular disco tunes that had been saturating the airwaves during the late 1970s. Alicia Bridges' "I Love the Nightlife (Disco 'Round)," Evelyn 'Champagne' King's "Shame," and Taste of Honey's "Boogie Oogie Oogie" all exude the gusty physicality that made the best 1970s disco songs work, with their clever band arrangements and effective melodies. The remaining *Victim of Love* songs only capture a modicum of that quality with their dominant common element—a driving beat—since the melodies are, at best, pedestrian.

It is hard to imagine Bellotte presenting those songs to Donna Summer. And before this album came out, the thought of Elton recording such songs was unimaginable, too. Elton would claim for a time, during the early 1980s, that people would have to expect a few self-indulgent things like this album once in a while, but a self-indulgence in any number of other musical directions would have been more welcome. The critics had a rare good excuse to pan something he had done. Lester Bangs of *The Village Voice* was perplexed, positing, "There's no getting around it, Elton's got problems."[52] Bob Claypool of the *Houston Post* was all too happy to get in some jabs: "Rock and roll never deserved Elton's empty babbling, and neither does disco. . . . [P]erhaps old Elton will simply shut up and fade away. . . ."[53]

Released in October, *Victim of Love* couldn't have done worse, eventually selling only 381,000 copies worldwide. In Britain, the disco recording, with its peak of number 41 and chart stay of three weeks, was Elton's worst-selling album since *Madman.* In the United States, the new album fared only a little better, peaking at number 35 and spending ten weeks on *Billboard*'s Top LPs. Unlike every other Elton John album before it, with the unfortunate exception of *11-17-70*, it was not certified gold.

Elton managed to squeeze into the American Top 40 with the album's lead single, "Victim of Love." It debuted on the Hot 100 at number 76 on September 29, 1979, less than two weeks after Elton had begun the U.S. leg of his tour with Ray Cooper. "Bennie" might have taken six weeks to reach the Top 10, but "Victim of Love" took five weeks just to reach the Top 40. In mid-November, it stalled at number 31, managing to reach a peak that the infinitely more satisfying "Ego" couldn't do in the spring of 1978. By Thanksgiving weekend, "Victim" had plummeted to number 64.

After this indulgence in disco fantasy, the record-buying public was justifiably suspicious of new Elton John product. Whereas the material released after his "confession" to Cliff Jahr suffered from the intolerance of former American fans, he could now blame only himself for disappointing the fans who had remained loyal during his commercial downturn. Unfortunately, not enough people could see Elton's tour of small venues to know that, despite some poor decision making, he was as vital an artist as ever.

In Britain, "Mama Can't Buy You Love" was pressed and ready for shipment in August, in response to its hit status in the United States that summer, but was then unwisely withdrawn in favor of "Victim of Love," to be released September 14.[54] "Victim" failed to chart.

"BACK IN THE USSA"[55]

MANY CRITICS half expected Elton to do one or more disco numbers during his fall U.S. tour with Ray—wasn't he supposed to be plugging his new album?—and were sometimes surprised when he didn't. But they were missing the point. Elton had put out *Victim of Love* because he'd wanted to, and was doing a world tour with his percussionist because he wanted to. There needn't have been any relationship between the two endeavors. His fall tour of the United States was not the *Victim of Love* tour, but the "Back in the USSA" tour, dubbed so in honor of his recently completed stint in the USSR. The name was also a sly reference to the end of his absence from the U.S. touring scene—it had been three years since he'd toured the East Coast, four years since he'd toured the West.

The "Back in the USSA" tour lasted nearly two months, opening in Tempe, Arizona, on September 19 and closing in Houston, Texas, on November 11. In between, there were dates in fifteen other cities, with lengthy stretches in Los Angeles and New York.

Elton's attire for this tour was his simplest yet. He wore a crinkly suit—on some nights red, others gold, still others pink or yellow—plus a simple shirt and a narrow tie. He still wore contacts, but avoided hats. His hair transplants were taking for now,[56] and his natural hair was shorter than it had been in well over a year. He'd never looked so conservative.

But audiences didn't come to see Elton for his looks, or because he was "in." He was no longer "in," and, with the exception of his summertime Thom Bell hit, was not played all over the radio anymore. Judging from the nightly response, people came to see him because they knew they would be hearing some of the best, most beloved music of the decade.

The songs Elton and Ray played were, for the most part, the same ones they'd performed in Europe. They added "Mama Can't Buy You Love" to the set list, which worked unexpectedly well without the MFSB horns or other trappings of a Bell production. One could hear the horn arrangement and backing vocals in Elton's playing. He proved once again that he could replicate such divergent sounds on the piano.

Another song new to the set list was "Elton's Song," written and recorded over the summer with lyrics by Tom Robinson, a British singer-songwriter who, with his eponymous band, had had three Top 40 hits in Britain since 1977. One non-hit written by Robinson was the anthem "Glad to Be Gay." Although it wouldn't become apparent for some years that "Elton's Song" also had a gay theme, Elton wasn't shy about reminding his audiences that he wasn't heterosexual. On opening night at Los Angeles's Universal Amphitheater, he asserted, "Since you've seen me last [1975], I don't care anymore."[57]

But Elton did care about wringing as much zeal, humor, and spunk as possible from his instrument, and his audiences rewarded him with noisy ovations. At an October 13 performance in West Lafayette, Indiana, a thirteen-minute version of "Grapevine" took Elton and the crowd through a universe of musical styles, fans hooting and hollering throughout. In many shows, "Bennie" took on more of the attributes that would enjoy further ornamentation in succeeding years, becoming a generous mix of witty ragtime romps, rapid-paced classical chord exercises, and touches of boogie-woogie. And humor wasn't limited to his piano improvisations. As the weightlessness of "Rocket Man" floated to great heights, he would, at some shows, cut through the depleted oxygen levels with cries of "I'm just a fuckin' rocket man!"

For anyone wondering, as Princess Alexandra had back in May 1977, how Elton could maintain his high energy level for three hours a night, the pianist noted half-jokingly at one Los Angeles show: "It's only taken me fifteen grams of coke and twelve quaaludes tonight. There's self-confidence for you!"[58]

"A GENIUS WITH GUTS"[59]

ELTON'S LATE NOVEMBER 1979 arrival in Sydney for his "Down Under '79" tour marked the third Australian tour of his career, this one scheduled to begin in Sydney on November 25 and to wind up during the first week of December in Perth. Many were disappointed with the tour's limited geographic scope. He was bypassing South Australia and Queensland (as well as New Zealand) due to logistical problems, including the absence of suitable indoor venues in those areas.[60]

Elton rolled up to a Sydney reception held in his honor (the Watford colors on prominent display) in a wheelchair pushed by John Reid. From his seated position, the pianist explained that during his recent Hawaiian vacation he had imbibed innumerable cocktails, leading to an excessive number of arm-wrestling bouts and a pinched nerve in his back. He was sure he would be able to perform.[61] With just a few days to recover before the first show, somehow he was. "A Genius with Guts," read the headline after his first Melbourne performance, where he played through extreme humidity and had to towel off his face and head after every other song.[62]

A couple of nights later, a taped appearance was broadcast on Molly Meldrum's *Countdown* television show. The taping allowed for some sanitizing, as the musician's quips were often a bit saucy for tender ears, and Meldrum was sometimes seen raising his hands for a halt to filming. "Do it again straight, mate, please," he asked Elton more than once.[63] Meldrum was gay,[64] but his sexuality—or that of his guests—was not to be fodder for national television. Elton refused to be stifled. When Meldrum presented him with a yellow bouquet topped with two canaries, Elton grinned at the camera, caressed the beak of one canary, and said, "First bird I've been out with for years."[65]

This was likely the television appearance in which Elton got "legless" on more than half a bottle of scotch. By concert time that evening, he was out of his mind, and performed a twenty-five-minute version of "Rocket Man" that included negative comments about the Ayatollah Khomeini. Eighteen years later, he would point to this performance as one of his career's most embarrassing.[66]

That concert aside, Elton's tour of Australia would have been a nice way to close out 1979, as well as the decade. But there was still the business of prolonging the last labored gasps of *Victim of Love*. Another single was released, "Johnny B. Goode," which should have been the lead single, ahead of "Victim of Love." But a jaded public had no interest in a follow-up, and nothing came of it in either Britain or the United States.

As if prompted by mediocre chart success, Elton's substance abuse continued. On Boxing Day (December 26) 1979, after being up all night and "looking the worse for wear," he went to a Watford home game against Luton. Watford manager Graham Taylor noted his uncharacteristically shabby look and beckoned the pianist to his office. "So I go in," Elton later recalled, "and he's holding a bottle of brandy and he's going, 'Here you are, fucking drink this. It's what you want, isn't it? For fuck's sake, what's wrong with you? . . . Stop doing this to yourself!' He frightened the fucking life out of me."[67] For a time after that, Elton stopped drinking.[68]

"TOGETHER THE TWO OF THEM WERE MINING GOLD"[69]

IN JANUARY 1980, on the tenth anniversary of the recording of the break-through album *Elton John*, Elton was at Sunset Sound Studios in Los Angeles putting the finishing touches on his first album of original material since *A Single Man*. The pianist had traveled light-years since his make-or-break effort in January 1970. Images of frenzied fans the world over had been the stuff of dreams when he'd set "Your Song" and "Take Me to the Pilot" to tape. Ten years later, he was an established star, though the depths of his fandom had thinned following his sexual candor, and he had, in effect, shot himself in the foot with the uninspired *Victim of Love*. Finishing up another album was no grand event; it was just something someone of his stature was expected, and wanted, to do.

But Elton was more interested in a different milestone. At some point before the release of this album and after his thirty-third birthday on March 25, 1980, he realized that the new record would be his twenty-first release. (It was really his twentieth album, but the two separate times *Empty Sky* was issued—in Britain in 1969 and in the United States in 1975—brought the album total to twenty-one.) Elton was obviously taken by this impressive achievement, enough so to name his new album after it. Hence, his twenty-first album, coproduced with Clive Franks, was called *21 at 33*.

Elton actually did the bulk of work on *21 at 33* when he was thirty-two, in August 1979 between tour legs. Virtually all of the songs were written in Grasse, on the Riviera. Most were recorded that same month at Superbear Studios in Nice, although overdubbing wasn't done until the first quarter of 1980 in Los Angeles.

Making appearances on the album were newcomers Alvin Taylor (bass) and Reggie McBride (drums), both veterans of Leo Sayer's band.[70] Richie Zito was on hand for lead electric guitar parts, along with Toto's Steve Lukather from the best-forgotten *Victim of Love* sessions. But the *21 at 33* recording sessions also included some old familiar faces. Elton gave James Newton Howard free rein with electronic keyboards. And, five years after they had last appeared on an Elton John album, Nigel and Dee returned to play on a couple of tracks. Dee even sang backing vocals on one song. Conspicuously missing from the sessions was Ray Cooper. "People just see me as Elton John's percussionist," Ray had said during the 1979 Australian tour. He saw how large a shadow Elton's fame had cast over supporting musicians. "They don't realize that things like this tour are projects on which we work and then go our separate ways."[71]

Elton generously spread his songwriting bug, collaborating with no fewer than four lyricists on the album. Two of them he had never worked with before—friend and gay-rights activist–songwriter Tom Robinson, and Rocket Records recording act Judie Tzuke. The other two were Gary Osborne and the Brown Dirt Cowboy himself, Bernie Taupin.

The reunion of Captain Fantastic and his renowned sidekick began tentatively. Elton invited Bernie and the lyricist's new wife, Toni Russo, to Grasse, where the songwriters came up with about ten new songs. In agreeing to this working vacation, Bernie was taking a break from writing lyrics for his second album (the first being a 1971 poetry record), for which recording would commence in October. Although only three of the songs that Elton and Bernie wrote together would be used on *21 at 33*, their Grasse re-pairing apparently freed the steam needed to revitalize their personal and professional relationships.

When Elton had declined to use any of Bernie's lyrics on *A Single Man*, and Bernie had remained in the United States to embark on an effort at cowriting lyrics with Alice Cooper, it had seemed that the Captain and the Kid were sending signals that they had tired of each other, though they never said so publicly. Now they each celebrated their long overdue reunion in separate statements to the press. "I realized that I really did have fun writing with him," Bernie said of their time in Grasse.[72] Elton firmly rejected any notion that unpleasantness had existed between them. "There was never any feud," he asserted. "It's the typical thing you read in the papers—just because he lived in America and I had an album out and he had an album out with different people, the tongues started to wag."[73]

Elton and Bernie's reunion was celebrated in song on *21 at 33*. "Two Rooms at the End of the World" rejoices in the differences that drew Elton and Bernie together, placed a wedge between them, and then brought them together again. Bernie once explained how the differences in their respective lifestyles went beyond the issue of sexuality. "My friends are shitkickers, Elton's are much posher," he had said in 1976. "You can tell the difference between a party Elton gives and one of mine. Elton's parties are elegant and very, very Hollywood. At one of mine people are liable to arrive on horseback in cowboy outfits, and there's beer instead of the champagne Elton serves."[74]

In "Two Rooms," Elton sings of their shared struggles and triumphs ("Well we've both ridden the wagon, bit the tail off the dragon/borne our swords like steel knights on the highway"), their eventual separation ("Door to door they would whisper, will they ever get together"), and their reunion. The title refers to the two being never really that far apart ("For where there is one room, you'll always find another/two rooms, at the end of the world"). It also refers to the songwriting method they famously employed—rare in the world of popular music—of composing in separate rooms.

The celebratory music of "Two Rooms" manages to couple the naive, sunny optimism of "Honky Cat" with the worldly sounds of big band jazz. Although Elton's mid-tempo melody, which vigorously ascends a challenging incline, is the same from verse to chorus, it is never boring. The instrumentation builds. Brass is added by the third verse, thanks to an arrangement by Jim Horn that exists in harmony with Steve Lukather's punchy electric guitar. Elton's Yamaha electric piano surfaces halfway through, engaging in amusing interplay with the brass. His keyboard soon wins out, with a waterfall of notes that transforms into a fountain of convex chords of the type Elton had been fashioning around "Bennie" live in 1979. His backing vocals are actually more exciting than his bold, vibrato-tinged lead. Overdubbed countless times to create the effect of a roomful (or maybe two rooms full) of men and women of varying vocal ranges and timbres, his backup vocals add to the song's sophisticated big-band sense.

Another John/Taupin composition selected for 21 at 33 was "Chasing the Crown," a close lyrical cousin to the Rolling Stones's "Sympathy for the Devil." (Both are engaging puzzles in which the listener is invited to identify a culprit who has caused conflict and misery.) The phrase "chasing the crown" refers to this villain's goal of securing the highest prize—the obliteration of peace—for wreaking havoc everywhere.

Elton took the lyrics, a litany of victories for evil, and did what he had done many times before: invert them to find new meaning. Here, he dresses them in a robe of gospel fervor, awash in the loud colors of rock aggression. His piano, a scaled-down adaptation of some of the peppery chord patterns he had incorporated into "Grapevine" during his 1979 world tour, sets a driving tempo, as the melodious screeching of Steve Lukather's guitar sifts through the chords. Giving "Chasing the Crown" its predominantly gospel spirit is Elton's melody, a deliberate collection of phrases, each delivered with an exclamation point, as if part of a sermon designed to stir the unfaithful.

The third song cowritten with Bernie is "White Lady White Powder," which re-forms the original Elton John rhythm section of Nigel and Dee. Also significant are the song's backing vocalists—Eagles members Don Henley, Glenn Frey, and Timothy B. Schmit. When Elton wrote the music for this song in Grasse in August

1979, he instinctively felt that it would be perfect for some of the Eagles to sing on, and waited to record it in Los Angeles early the following year, when the Eagles returned for their engagement at the Forum.[75]

"White Lady White Powder" is another tale of the forbidden. As the title implies, this is a drug song, about a substance well known to both lyricist and composer. Bernie itemizes the reasons Elton himself had grown fond of the drug: "Shock waves to a tired brain/send that hungry lady to my door again/she's my shelter from the storm when I feel the rain/entertaining white powder." Elton makes "White Lady White Powder" another exercise in irony, turning the song into a jolly nursery rhyme, complete with happy piano chords just right for frolicking children. Backing vocals on the song are provided by Henley, Frey, and Schmit.

The album goes from the wit of "White Lady White Powder" to the frustrating banality of "Dear God," one of three songs Elton cowrote with Gary Osborne. Since Elton was still writing with Osborne the conventional way, with the music preceding the lyrics, and as the musician offered up a line or two of lyrics and possibly a title, too, Elton is as much to blame for the trite verbiage of "Dear God" as Osborne. The lyrics are a bunch of clichés ("Dear God, I hope and pray/you'll lead us to a brighter day. . . . Love is the answer/so light up our way Dear God"). Also, being aware of Elton's religious skepticism makes it hard not to cringe when listening to him sing these words. "Dear God" sounds not only right for church, but as if it had already been played to death in church for decades.

Better is another John/Osborne song, "Take Me Back." This pleasing country concoction with a natural yet variable melody could have been inspired by Elton's performance of Jim Reeves's "He'll Have to Go" during his 1979 shows. Elton sings with his best cowboy voice, complete with minute vocal flips and the pointiest country twang probably ever heard in Nice. He converts the friendly cushion of a Wurlitzer electric piano into a set of notes fit for a saloon. Session man Byron Berline's fiddle completes the song's hayseed moxie.

The third song with Osborne, "Little Jeannie," would become the album's only hit. It was born the usual way for a John/Osborne tune, with Elton writing a melody and thinking up a title and a couple of lines for Osborne to work around. One of these was "I want you to be my acrobat,"[76] which could have been taken as either an inspirational expression of love or a sexually suggestive request. But "Little Jeannie" is about love of a higher order, sung from the perspective of a man without the most pristine values, whose life has been transformed by the pure and idealistic young Jeannie.

The sad melodic core of "Little Jeannie" is at odds with Gary Osborne's reassuring words, but the tension between the two elements adds to the song's mysterious aura. Elton sings as if the song were a tragic love song and the protagonist had hurt Jeannie instead of welcoming her into his life. The only flaw in "Little Jeannie" is its dangling secondary melody, which bears no smooth connection to the song's core. On the recording, James plays this as an introduction. It also serves as a coda, sung by Dee, among others ("You stepped into my life from a bad dream/making the life that I had seem/suddenly shiny and new"). Elton realized, after the song had become a major hit, that a good portion of this dangling melody was nearly identical to the primary melody of a 1977 number 1 hit, Leo Sayer's "When I Need You." He even worried that he would be sued, but nothing happened.[77]

As ambitious as the core melodic concept of "Little Jeannie" is, Elton doesn't play on the song's recording. He had James use the Fender Rhodes because he believed James had better technique on the instrument.[78] James's work with that and with a Yamaha CS80 synthesizer recalls the song's progenitor, "Daniel." So does the self-sustaining Rhythm Ace, which makes the shaker sound Nigel had created on "Daniel" with maracas. Also similar is the prominent sound of acoustic guitar strumming. In the absence of Davey Johnstone, Richie Zito filled the bill.

The song that would become the second single from *21 at 33* is "Sartorial Eloquence," with lyrics by Tom Robinson. Here the heterosexual imagery of the songs written with Osborne, like "Little Jeannie" and "Take Me Back," is replaced with expressions of homosexual longing, the object of affection a stylishly dressed, emotionally unrevealing man, who prefers to leave an intense affair for other pleasures down the road.

Starting simply, with just Elton's despondent voice and mournful piano, the music evokes the disappointment of the man left behind. The song grows in volume and despondency with the introduction of supporting musicians and backing vocalists, finally reaching the chorus of "Don't you wanna play this game no more?" Then the music ends suddenly, like the departure of the well-dressed man for untapped wells of excitement.

The second Robinson song, "Never Gonna Fall in Love Again," seems at first to be about someone half-seriously lamenting an overabundance of careless infatuations with members of the opposite sex. The female pronoun is prevalent, and the song's oversexed protagonist apologizes for being "sexist." But the clincher is the clever lyrical twist in the second verse, which uncovers the sexual orientation of the protagonist's infatuations: "Cos everywhere there's lots of foxes/and every cat I meet's a tom." Elton delivers these, and all the other lines, as if singing a tender love ballad, despite the protagonist's mischievous lecherousness. The intimate but slippery melody is, however, violated by a production too similar to that of a song with a larger vision, "Little Jeannie," and relies too heavily on James's electronic keyboard touch.

"Give Me the Love," Elton's collaboration with Judie Tzuke, closes *21 at 33* and gets a more expansive interpretation. Tzuke's lyrics aren't original, but appealingly suggest a mini love epic in musical form ("For I am an eagle, but my wings are all tied up/you got the power to fly me again, so. . . . Give me the love, baby/give me the key to your heart"). This is the sort of song that Elton should have written for that disco album. Like "Philadelphia Freedom," "Give Me the Love" combines the lilt of soul with the infectious beat of a disco number and the immediacy of rock. Gene Page and MFSB are absent, but the supporting musicians (including Steve Lukather) and arrangers (David Foster on strings, Jerry Hey on brass) masterfully recall the "sound of Philadelphia" beneath the pianist's urgently confident melody. A bonus is Elton's echoing, overdubbed piano, which seems to be coming from the jazz lounge next door to where the disco drama is playing itself out, lending the recording an enchanted quality.

In 1984, Elton would say of *21 at 33*, "I think that's one of my best albums. There are a lot of really good songs on it."[79] It is also one of his most underappreciated albums. As with his work on *A Single Man*, Elton didn't break any new ground here, yet the songs fall within the grand tradition of some of his earlier signature compositions—"Daniel," "Honky Cat," and "Philadelphia Freedom." He was continuing to write lively, irresistible melodies, and some songs, like "White Lady White Powder," feature the irony that has infected much of his best work. Happily, too, Elton and Bernie had re-formed their songwriting partnership.

April 1980 saw a friendly side project with popular French singer France Gall, Gall's husband Michel Berger, and Bernie Taupin. That year, France Gall had released her album *Paris, France*, which included a song written by Berger with the intriguing title "Il Jouait du Piano Debout," roughly translated as "He Plays the Piano Standing Up." The song was a tribute to Elton—his individuality, his complete fidelity to music as the ultimate truth in life, and the joie de vivre of his performance style, as epitomized by the freedom with which he attacked the piano keys.

"Il Jouait" wasn't the first French-language tribute to the pianist. In 1972, Québec singer Diane Dufresne had recorded "En Écoutant Elton John," or "Listening to Elton John" (lyrics by Luc Plamondon, music by François Cousineau) for her album *Tiens-Toé Ben J'Arrive!* Dufresne sings, "Don't talk about love/but just make it to me/while listening to Elton John/talking about love in stereo."[80]

The idea for Elton and France Gall to record a duet had been conceived the year before in St.-Tropez, France, where Elton had met Gall and Berger for the first time.[81] In April 1980, the two recorded at Los Angeles's Sunset Sound Studios, producing "Les Aveux" ("Avowals"), cowritten by Elton and Berger, and "Donner Pour Donner" ("Giving for Giving"), by Bernie and Berger.

"Les Aveux" had an English-language predecessor, "Reach Out to Me," which Elton had demoed as a country-style expression of yearning for love. For the duet, Berger wrote a new set of lyrics. Like the earlier English words, these also express love, but in the context of a couple sharing thoughts of the strength they expect to gain by their union. The former "Reach Out to Me," with its towering chorus, was converted perfectly into a Continental tune fit for schoolchildren to sing in the

French countryside. "Donner Pour Donner," with introductory English-language lyrics by Bernie, is folksier and allows more interplay between the two singers.

Despite the participation of Gall and Berger, these sessions were practically an extension of the *21 at 33* sessions, with Elton and Clive Franks producing, Nigel and Dee on their respective instruments, Richie Zito on guitar, James on keyboards (Elton's piano is heard only on "Les Aveux"), and arrangements by Marty Paich. Elton and Gall couldn't have known at the time that their duets would top the French charts when the songs were released as a single in February 1981, with six hundred thousand copies purchased by French fans.[82]

"YOU TAKE IT WHERE IT STRIKES AND GIVE IT TO THE LIKES OF ME"[83]

21 AT 33 DEBUTED ON BILLBOARD'S TOP LPS on May 31, 1980, reaching number 13 and becoming Elton's highest charter since *Blue Moves* and his sixteenth gold record. (Bernie's first, and labored, rock album, *He Who Rides the Tiger*, cowritten with a former member of the Buckinghams, Dennis Tufano, came out at the same time as *21 at 33* but didn't chart.)

Although *21 at 33* didn't have the commercial impact in the United States most of Elton's 1970s albums had, its success there was an encouraging start to the 1980s. Things were less encouraging in Britain, where the album peaked at number 12. Only one of Elton's new studio albums since *Honky Chateau* had missed the Top 10 in Britain: *Victim of Love*. Not unlike during Elton's commercial heyday of the mid-1970s, then, the United States again seemed to hold the brightest commercial promise, despite the loss of many a fan after his "bisexual" statement of 1976.

Even more encouraging was U.S. acceptance of the album's lead single, "Little Jeannie." It debuted on the Hot 100 on May 3, 1980 at number 65 and entered the Top 40 by its second week. By June 7, it was in the Top 10, where it stayed for eleven weeks, a longer stay in the Top 10 than any previous Elton John single. All told, the single charted for twenty-one weeks, tying with "Philadelphia Freedom" for the longest-charting single of Elton's career. With its peak at number 3, "Little Jeannie" failed to best Billy Joel's "It's Still Rock and Roll to Me," which edged it out for number 1, but the single dominated the soundtrack to the summer of 1980 and was certified gold by the end of August, in time for the beginning of Elton's next U.S. tour.

In Britain, "Little Jeannie" made less of an impact. Charting on May 24, it stalled at number 33. British music fans had other "new" Elton John releases to contend with. "I know what the world doesn't need now is another Elton John album," Bernie had said in 1976 about *Here and There*. "[W]e know Dick James is still going to put out tracks he's compiled, like *Best of, Volume 300*. We get upset because people go 'Oh shit, not another Elton John album,' and it's so maddening because it's not our fault."[84] Bernie had foreseen the avalanche of Elton John rereleases undertaken by DJM in 1979 and 1980.

Even before the March 1980 release of *Lady Samantha* (a compilation album), there were other "new" Elton John albums. DJM repackaged *11-17-70* (or *17-11-70*, as it was known in Britain) with *Here and There*, a terrible combination of live recordings, for a double album entitled *The Elton John Live Collection*, released on February 5, 1979. That August, a five-LP set of hits and diverse album tracks was unveiled to make up Elton's first boxed set. In October 1980, six months after *Lady Samantha* was released, another compilation appeared—*The Very Best of Elton John*. All but two of the songs on *Very Best of* were from the Dick James era. It did much better than *Lady Samantha* had, peaking at number 24.

To be fair, some of these albums were also available in other countries, but this saturation of the British marketplace with old Elton John product, while generating more royalties for DJM's publishing arm and providing some nice packages for budding Elton John collectors, didn't do much to advance Elton's career at home.

A second single released from *21 at 33* in August 1980, "Sartorial Eloquence," was renamed for the United States by MCA as "Don't Ya Wanna Play This Game No More?" (with "Sartorial Eloquence" in parentheses), condescendingly catering to what were perceived to be the less literate minds of the American record-buying public.

This confusingly titled single was destined to shiver in the United States, unattended, under the humongous shadow of "Little Jeannie." It charted on August 9, 1980 at number 82 while "Jeannie," after four weeks, was still number 3. It took two months for the new single to edge into the Top 40. By September 27, when Elton was in the middle of his U.S. tour, it had reached its apex of number 39. (It reached number 44 in Britain.) By then, Elton could be happy that he had had one of the biggest U.S. hits of the summer. He was getting used to the more modest pattern of his U.S. chart achievements since 1976. And, he was attracting crowds again with his new band.

"YOU MIGHT SAY I'M A SCREAMER"[85]

ON AUGUST 25, 1980, Elton and MCA Records celebrated ten years of the musician's success in the United States—not at Doug Weston's Troubadour club in Los Angeles, but at Tommy Thomas's Palomino Club in North Hollywood, a place known for country music. The impact he made that night wasn't as seismic as it had been on August 25, 1970—how could it be?—nor as ear-splitting as on August 25, 1975, when he had premiered his revamped band. On this night, he appeared with four musicians from his new band and a couple of members of the house band for several numbers, including Jim Reeves's "He'll Have to Go." Elton was presented with a plaque commemorating the twelve gold singles accumulated during his ten years of stardom. "This means more to me than the Troubadour [anniversary] show," Elton said about the party. "I guess that's because I always figured that I'd be around for five years, but there were times when I wondered if I'd make it through for ten."[86]

Elton had indeed made it through ten and, in what seemed like further celebration of this anniversary, brought the two original members of his band back for the upcoming tour. It had occurred to him when Nigel and Dee joined the album sessions in January that he'd like to play with them again. Just a year earlier, Nigel had hoped for this very thing. "I would love to—and I haven't mentioned this to anybody but Dee and Davey, seeing that the band split up before we could tour *Captain Fantastic*—go out with Elton on tour," he'd said. "[I]t would be incredible. Just one more major tour."[87]

Since Nigel's and Dee's 1975 dismissal, Dee had toured with different acts, including Procol Harum, Alice Cooper, and even Kiki Dee. Nigel, who'd been pursuing individual stardom in those years, now had a fourth solo album to promote, *Changing Tides.*

Joining Nigel's and Dee's bass-and-drums nucleus in the new band were James Newton Howard, with his usual array of keyboards and synthesizers, and two recent Elton John recording sessions alumni, guitarists Richie Zito and Tim Renwick. Opening for Elton was Rocket Records act Judie Tzuke and her band. Tzuke, who had had a measure of success at home in Britain, was touring for the first time in the United States.

With a draining two-and-a-half-month schedule, the tour began on September 4 in Madison, Wisconsin, and would snake through the United States before closing in Honolulu in mid-November. Conspicuously missing from the itinerary were Philadelphia, Boston, and a conventional New York venue.

Set mostly in arenas, the tour was not a consistent sell-out—a dose of reality that showed Elton he was still burdened with the marred image he'd had since 1976. Robert Hilburn noticed that radio stations were no longer climbing over themselves to provide Elton John coverage in advance of his shows, or even playing much of his music. Whereas Bruce Springsteen's concerts in Los Angeles prompted heavy coverage, Hilburn heard only one Elton John song on the radio during his forty-five-minute drive to the Anaheim Convention Center for a November 1 show. When the journalist arrived, however, he found fans in rapt anticipation. One twenty-six-year-old woman said, "I was thrilled when Elton's 'Little Jeannie' was a hit because I didn't want him to think people had forgotten about him. We still love him."[88]

Elton rewarded still-substantial crowds with some of the most manic performances of his career, his piano bench doubling as a springboard for physically exhausting playing. He had a renewed confidence and no longer catered to the teenybopper set. The new ensemble was as big as his 1976 band. James was available for synthesized flourishes, but Elton kept most of the musical initiatives for himself. He had taken to wearing interesting outfits again, too.

Although he didn't return to the eye-popping outrageousness of 1974, the sleek jumpsuits of 1975, or the campy silliness of 1976, Elton still had a taste for color and humor. His outfits, styled mainly in more conservative jacket, cap, and pants combinations, sported strange designs and markings. One suit had piano keys swelling from the front of a police cap, with more keys on his jacket. These merged into a pattern that draped around his shoulders and hung down his back, an ivory tribute to the yellow brick road. Other outfits resembled modern paintings, one with a haphazard checkerboard pattern interrupted at the midriff by polka dots and random lines, another a blue, black, and yellow suit with yellow chrome mirrors swarming around his upper arms, down his pants, and circling his collar—all topped off with a white cowboy hat.

Though the shows were shorter than those on his tour with Ray, lasting about two hours, the song selection was nevertheless imaginative, representing all eras of his ten-year-old career. He delved into familiar songs while also dusting off rarities such as "All the Girls Love Alice," "Harmony," "Ego," and "Have Mercy on the Criminal." For a good part of the tour, three *21 at 33* songs were in the set list, "Little Jeannie," "Sartorial Eloquence," and "White Lady White Powder."

The tour's climax came early, only a week and a half into the schedule. It happened on Saturday, September 13—a free afternoon concert on Central Park's Great Lawn, with about seventy-five thousand dollars of the proceeds from memorabilia sales slated for rebuilding and restoring parks and other city landmarks. For two days beforehand, while Elton and his band were gearing up for their Providence, Rhode Island show, music fans had been trickling onto the Great Lawn. By the night before, several hundred people were camped out.[89] When Judie Tzuke took the stage at three o'clock in the afternoon on the big day, there were, by cautious police estimates, four hundred thousand people on the lawn, the largest mass Central Park had ever seen. "They all came to see Elton John!" WNEW's Scott Muni exclaimed on the radio.[90]

In many respects, the show wasn't much different from others on the tour. Wearing his chrome-yellow mirror outfit, Elton opened with "Funeral for a Friend/Love Lies Bleeding," then worked into "Tiny Dancer" and "Goodbye Yellow Brick Road." But much also distinguished this show. Most of the hundreds of thousands of people were uncomfortably crammed together in Woodstock fashion, with some acrobatic souls dancing and swaying atop friends' shoulders. Others were perched in trees. It was not unknown for a wily fan to bribe fellow concertgoers with a can of beer for a better view.[91] Elton, feeling a charge from the throng, turned up his energy level a few notches. His padded sneakers had more bounce; he seemed to hover above the piano keys he flogged with his hands. "Bennie" became a sensual exercise in hip-undulating inflections and Scott Joplin examinations. Songs like "Philadelphia Freedom" and "Sorry Seems to Be the Hardest Word" had unstoppable consistencies that took on lives of their own.

"Well, they're packed tonight in Central Park," he sang during "Saturday Night's Alright for Fighting." When introducing "Imagine," the lyrics to which he had already been taking liberties with during the tour (singing "you might say I'm a screamer" instead of "dreamer," and nearly doubling over in laughter), he acknowledged Central Park neighbor John Lennon. "He hasn't made a record for ages, but he's doing one at the moment," Elton said. An emotionally draining "Someone Saved My Life Tonight" drew a bold, toothy female fan to the stage, where she planted a kiss on the pianist's cheek and was granted the exceedingly rare privilege of sitting next to him as he finished the song. She then proceeded to wave at her friends on the lawn, pointing at Elton's head and yelling, "I made it!"

But nothing could outdo the chutzpah of the pianist's fashion proclamation toward the show's end. Although most of his tour outfits possessed a modicum of dignity, Elton hadn't relinquished his desire for the outrageous, so when designer Bob Mackie had asked if he would like a Donald Duck outfit for Central Park, he had happily acquiesced. Leaving the stage for the first encore, then, his mission was to get into this clumsy suit as quickly as he could.

The time spent backstage turned into the "longest costume change in history," he told Tom Snyder a few days later.[92] It was the task of Bob Halley, his personal assistant of some years, to help him into the ungainly mass of material. "I put my legs in the armholes and arms in the leg holes, and I'm saying to Bob, 'They're going to go,'" he reminisced later.[93] But they didn't.

Elton strode onstage to many a gaping mouth and incredulous eye. What four hundred thousand people saw was a bulbous, human Donald Duck, complete with sailor hat (sporting a pair of eyes and wobbly yellow bill) and what appeared to be a blue sailor jacket attached to a puffy white lower torso from which protruded a huge creampuff tail. Rounding out this getup were fat yellow leggings and the floppiest flippers ever to stomp a Central Park stage. The musician may have looked ridiculous launching into "Your Song," as the bill on his sailor hat nodded along with the music, but this was no worse than playing "Funeral for a Friend" in 1974 as he sprouted feathers and mother-of-pearl. During the final encore, "Bite Your Lip," Elton crouched behind the piano, using his white "bum" for some disarmingly funky wiggling, and used his flippers to cavort about the stage.

Some two months later, Los Angeles audiences at the Forum were treated to a Minnie Mouse outfit, also designed by Bob Mackie. But that performance couldn't diminish the raw splendor—duck bill and all—of the afternoon on the Great Lawn.

"I USE A LITTLE MUSCLE TO GET WHAT I NEED"[94]
BACK IN 1964, an ambitious Brooklynite named David Geffen had gotten his first important job as an agent with the William Morris Agency, four years later switching to Ashley Famous Talent Agency, where he became a successful music

agent. His interest in a then-unknown songwriter, Laura Nyro, whetted his appetite for the money music could make him; he became her manager and cofounded a music publishing company with her. As her manager, he renegotiated her Columbia record contract and sold her publishing company to the label, striking gold. Before long, Geffen had started his own management firm with partner Elliot Roberts, inheriting Roberts's association with Joni Mitchell, Neil Young, and Crosby, Stills, and Nash. In 1971, his discovery of Jackson Browne prompted him to form a new label, Asylum, under the Warner Communications, Inc. (WCI) umbrella, alongside Atlantic and Elektra. Geffen told Browne and the other new signees that the label's purpose would be to afford them artistic freedom. Asylum became a haven for California-based folk-rock and soon Browne, a new group called the Eagles, and Joni Mitchell were churning out hit after hit for Asylum.

Eventually, trouble brewed within the fledgling company. Original acts like the Eagles began to resent the expansion of the label's roster to include acts like America and Linda Ronstadt. Just as Asylum was going somewhere, Geffen sold it for a profit to Warner Brothers Records, another WCI company. This resulted in the pairing of Asylum with Elektra; as part of the deal, Geffen was assigned to run the hyphenated label. The Eagles felt betrayed, despite Geffen's continued involvement, and eventually viewed his total control of their interests (initially not unlike Dick James's approach) as a conflict of interest. This prompted a break from Geffen's management and a lawsuit in which they won control of their publishing. Crosby, Stills, and Nash, also under a Geffen-Roberts management contract, broke up due to Stephen Stills's differences with Geffen, reuniting only when David Crosby and Graham Nash acquired new management. Bob Dylan, lured by Geffen to Elektra-Asylum from Columbia, returned to Columbia after two albums.[95]

Geffen left the record business in 1976, after having made untold millions, but decided to return in the spring of 1980, announcing a new company, later named Geffen Records. Along with the Warner Brothers, Elektra-Asylum, and Atlantic record companies, Geffen Records was to come under the WCI umbrella, with publicity, marketing, and promotion handled by the more established Warner Brothers Records. Geffen offered an admirable vision for his new label, which sounded reminiscent of his original goal for Asylum. "What we'll be offering that's different will be intelligent, sensitive people who understand the process and who'll do a good job for people," he said. "I think that's what artists want from a record company; they're not looking for someone to tell them how to make records or whether or not they should use a bass player. I think that I have a long history of being involved with the most creative, intelligent and productive artists, and I believe people will be attracted to what that's all about."[96]

Donna Summer, who had recorded some of the most popular music of the late 1970s, was by this time embroiled in a lawsuit that affected her relationship with Casablanca Records, and became Geffen's first signing in June 1980. Then John

Lennon and Yoko Ono joined Geffen. *Double Fantasy* was to be their first release, in November. Before Elton's new tour was a month old, the musician had followed suit, signing with Geffen for a reported ten million dollars. (Elton also renewed the Rocket Records-Phonogram affiliation elsewhere in the world.)

Discussions for terms of a new contract with MCA had commenced in August 1980 without success. It is doubtful that money was Elton's issue. He was still angry about MCA's failure to promote "Song for Guy," as well as its general inattentiveness. Geffen would have to wait a while longer for Elton's first album—the second album completed while working on *21 at 33* was owed to MCA—but he was obviously pleased with his acquisition. "Elton is going to be a superstar for many years to come," he said. "I expect to see him touring all around the world every year."[97]

In November 1980, two more Elton John singles were released in Britain. Neither charted. On November 1, it was another DJM reissue, "Harmony." The other single, and the last from *21 at 33*, was "Dear God," which had been released in both a regular package, with one B-side, and a deluxe, with two more. As it turned out, the B-sides upstaged "Dear God": "Tactics," a solo instrumental that presaged the theme to *Chariots of Fire;* "Steal Away Child," a spare lullaby with Osborne lyrics; and the Latin-seasoned "Love So Cold," with lyrics by Bernie and a tinny piano break completed by Elton in ten minutes while waiting for others to get the right steel drum sound.[98]

Any one of the B-sides would have been better than "Dear God" on *21 at 33*. However, "Love So Cold" was originally intended for the follow-up to *21 at 33*.[99] The fact that it showed up much sooner as a B-side to "Dear God" was the first indication of differences between Elton and his new record label. Although the *21 at 33* follow-up was owed to MCA, Elton had presented the new material to Geffen, who had rejected more than half the songs, including "Love So Cold." One of the others in the batch of rejections was "The Retreat."[100]

"The Retreat," written in Grasse in August 1979 and recorded in Nice, with finishing touches added in Los Angeles the following year, could have been a *Tumbleweed Connection* outtake, with Bernie's lyrics revisiting the Civil War devastation of "My Father's Gun" and "Where to Now, St. Peter?" Like the "white sails on the water" for the wounded who are honored in the song, Elton's melody, cushioned by expressive piano arpeggiations, bobs and weaves among the imagined waves. "The Retreat" would be used in the next couple of years at least twice as a B-side, an unjust fate for a tune worthy of a great deal more attention.

"LOVE'S SO COLD WHEN IT SHOOTS THAT ARROW THROUGH YOUR HEART"[101]

"THIS WEEK, the worst thing in the world happened," Elton said, introducing "Imagine" to his audience in Melbourne, Australia, on December 11, 1980. "This is a song written by an incredible man." After performing "Imagine," the pianist took temporary refuge backstage, where he was consoled by stagehands.[102] He had just learned, while in flight from Brisbane to Melbourne, of John Lennon's murder. Disembarking with his parents at Tullamarine Airport to the flash of cameras, he said, from behind dark glasses, "I'm just too upset," then walked quietly with head down, lips pursed, past the press as he clutched the hand of Fred Farebrother.[103] That night, he got very drunk.

The tour had begun in New Zealand not long before. Elton had then arrived in Sydney for a press conference dressed, true to form, in something ridiculous—a green-, white-, and purple-striped blazer with matching cap, and a gray-striped tie. This suit may not have rivaled the fluorescent ball outfit he'd premiered in Australia in 1974, but it was still silly. As one reporter put it, Elton "looked quite the overgrown public school boy." Also true to form, he talked of serious subjects from within his self-mocking threads.

"I have greater things within me than writing a four- or five-minute pop song," he declared. "I want to write a really long, good, instrumental piece of music, and you just cannot sit down and write that in ten minutes." He added, "To do something more creative, you have to take about one and a half to two years out and that's exactly what I intend to do after this band has terminated its life."[104] Elton later tried to explain that last statement, which was quickly misinterpreted to mean that the tour was his last: "All I said was I probably wouldn't be back with the present band. . . . I change my act and style. For instance, when I was here last year I had a totally different show to the present one."[105]

The tour Down Under was not too different from the U.S. tour, although "Bennie" was just as likely to contain bits of "Pinball Wizard" and "Waltzing Matilda" as Scott Joplin references. Also, Elton added "Song for Guy" to the set list. Offstage, Elton visited his good friend Molly on the December 7 *Countdown* show. Wearing a multiplicity of head toppings, including a police cap, a hat with a flimsy hand pasted to its front, a unicorn head covering, and a woman's wig with plenty of flowing hair, he couldn't resist embarrassing his host again with some quips for adult ears only.

It was nearly Christmas Day when the Australian tour ended. Security at London's Heathrow Airport probably overreacted upon receiving a report from Rocket Records that an anonymous fan had called three times to ask when Elton would be arriving. But in the wake of Lennon's death at the hands of a deranged fan, it was deemed better to be vigilant. Airport officials searched and questioned all the fans assembling at Heathrow to greet Elton, and the pianist and Bob Halley were kept waiting for twenty minutes after their arrival so they could be whisked safely away. "I am so tired after the tour and the long flight home," said a rattled Elton, "that I shall have mince pies and drinks with my football team, Watford, and then spend Christmas Day in bed."[106]

Piano prodigy Reggie Dwight, about the time he discovered rock'n'roll. ©Photofest

The summer of 1970. Elton doesn't know it yet, but stardom isn't far off. ©Photofest

The November 28, 1970 issue of the UK magazine *Melody Maker*, showing Elton at his U.S. debut performance. Elton was now "with it."

Image of magazine by Lori Sears

The January 9, 1971 issue of the UK magazine *Record Mirror*. Rock's hottest trio—(left to right) Dee Murray, Elton John, and Nigel Olsson—proudly pose on the cover.

Image of magazine by Lori Sears

"I remember when rock was young": on the cusp of his first U.S. number 1 single, late in 1972. ©Photofest

Opposite, "Captain Fantastic" plays the entire album of the same name at Wembley Stadium in England, June 21, 1975. ©Photofest

November 1973. Watford Football Club's newest vice president takes a dip with the help of some Watford players. ©Photofest

Picture sleeves from 1960s and 1970s French singles. Clockwise from top left: "Philadelphia Freedom," "It's Me That You Need," "Island Girl," "Friends," "Honky Cat," and "Daniel." Image of picture sleeves by Lori Sears

By the mid-1970s, Elton was the talk of teenage girls and was constantly on the cover of *16 Magazine*.
Photo courtesy of Primedia Youth Entertainment Group

Elton joins Kiki Dee for a rare fall 1977 performance of their number 1 hit, "Don't Go Breaking My Heart."
©Jeff Mayer/Star File Photo

Showing off his Carmen Miranda jacket as he plays his "louder than Concorde" piano. Madison Square Garden, **August 1976.** Photo courtesy of Michael Lehman

On the football pitch for charity, England, 1978.
Photo courtesy of Brendan Glover

Percussionist Ray Cooper works his tambourine magic
in Dallas, November 1979. ©Ann and Jim Richardson

Some of the album compilations of Elton's early material that competed with his newer songs of the late 1970s, early 1980s. Clockwise from top left: *The New Collection* (1983), *The Album* (1981), *The Live Collection* (1979), *Lady Samantha* (1980), and *Candle in the Wind* (1978).

Image of album covers by Lori Sears

Wringing meaning from the keys in Manchester, England, April 1979. ©Robert Cargill

Opening a show in Tulsa, Oklahoma, with "Funeral for a Friend," July 1982.

Photo courtesy of Steven W. McGrew

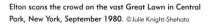
Elton scans the crowd on the vast Great Lawn in Central Park, New York, September 1980. ©Julie Knight-Shehata

Elton's classic boater look on full display in Oklahoma City, September 1984. Photo courtesy of Steven W. McGrew

With Sir John Gielgud at a charity performance at London's Theatre Royal Drury Lane, December 1984.
©Paul Smith, www.eltononline.co.uk

Fooling around with "Bennie and the Jets" in his "Ruritanian general's outfit," Hammersmith Odeon, London, Christmas Eve, 1982. ©Robert Cargill

Elton with wife Renate on a happy occasion toward the end of their marriage, 1988.
Terry McGough/Pictorial Press Limited

Strutting for fans in a New Year's Eve wig at the turn of 1986, Bournemouth, England. ©Wayne Martin

One last feather-laden hurrah, Houston, fall 1986. Photo courtesy of Jeff Young

CHAPTER 7

I'M STILL STANDING[1]

(1981–1983)

IN JANUARY 1981, Elton was back at Los Angeles's Sunset Sound Studios, this time with a new producer. The musician probably would have liked a break after finishing his last tour so close to Christmas, but David Geffen had rejected several of the songs Elton had chosen for his next album, and had asked for replacements.

"You want people to be honest with you," Elton later observed. "But it's tough at times, especially when you know deep inside that the music's not quite there."[2] He told Geffen that he would agree to record more songs if Chris Thomas, a former classmate from the Royal Academy of Music, could produce.[3] Geffen granted the wish, and Elton and Thomas reaffirmed their ties from the early 1960s. In the intervening years, Thomas had produced albums for an eclectic group of acts, including Procol Harum, Badfinger, Pink Floyd, the Sex Pistols, Pete Townsend, and the Pretenders.

The new album that emerged, *The Fox*, was recorded over a longer period of time and at more studios than any previous Elton John album. The process had begun in August 1979 in Grasse, where Elton wrote the music for three of the songs, and at Nice's Superbear Studios, where he had laid down the basic tracks for them with Clive Franks's assistance, and then at Los Angeles's Davlen Studios, where Elton recorded the piano for an instrumental segment. The recording of the instrumental spilled over to EMI Studios at Abbey Road in London, where the London Symphony Orchestra did its part on New Year's Eve 1979.[4] Recording resumed early in 1980, as finishing touches were being placed on *21 at 33* at Sunset Sound. Elton was now returning to Sunset Sound to work on his replacement songs, this time with Thomas at the helm. Backing vocals for three of the songs were recorded at Village Recorders in Los Angeles. Considering the disjointed timetable, it is remarkable that the album offers such continuity.

The musical and lyrical team appearing on *The Fox* wasn't much different from that on *21 at 33*. Bernie, Osborne, and Robinson provided lyrics. Reggie McBride and Alvin Taylor played bass and drums on songs surviving the Geffen purge. Nigel and Dee returned for other songs. Richie Zito, Steve Lukather, and Tim Renwick contributed lead guitar, and James Newton Howard lent synthesizers and orchestral arrangements. *The Fox* also had a connection with the *Blue Moves* sessions: Working on an Elton John album for the first time in five years was the Reverend James Cleveland, with his Cornerstone Baptist Church Choir.

The continuity of *The Fox* is derived from its centerpiece, a collection of four melancholy pieces linked together for maximum impact. Most of the other songs serve as musical moons, orbiting this four-part centerpiece, their intrinsic sadness thus surfacing to become the album's dominant theme.

The centerpiece is comprised of three reflective instrumentals—"Carla," "Étude," and "Fanfare"—and one ballad of excruciating misery, "Chloe." Although Elton wrote "Carla" and "Étude" separately, once he linked them it was as if they had been joined forever. In fact, their unity belies the geographic expanse that marked their recording; Elton's piano was recorded in Los Angeles, the London Symphony Orchestra in London. "Carla/Étude" is a simple piano lament, accented by James's delicate use of strings, French horns, and flutes, which, with its soaring phrases, sports just the slightest hint of optimism. "Carla/Étude" then segues into "Fanfare," James's pre-New Age synthesizer adaptation of some of the elements of "Chloe," written as the bridge between "Carla/Étude" and "Chloe."[5]

Gary Osborne's lyrics for "Chloe" aren't nearly as miserable as the music. This is good, as the words dilute, ever so slightly, the saturated torment in Elton's tune. Osborne's "Chloe" is about a man both inspired and puzzled by the loyalty of his lover, which never wavers, no matter how badly he treats her. For Elton, who, as always when writing with Osborne, wrote the music first, the focus is not the man who wonders about Chloe's tolerance but the unfortunate Chloe, with her pain and wounds laid out for all to see.

Many ingredients contribute to this recording's perfection. James's twinkly Fender Rhodes piano suggests the man's worn-out, frayed nerves; the string arrangement on which he collaborated with Marty Paich wafts sadness between the melody lines. Half-country, half-blues guitar picking makes "Chloe" right for a close dance. But it's Elton's melody and vocal delivery that lay bare Chloe's damaged insides. Alternating between light, porous tones and dark, thick ones, he sings without any glimmer of happiness. The mood is ensured by descending melody lines, and Elton's throaty utterance of Chloe's name at the end of each verse. While not as anthemic as "Don't Let the Sun Go Down on Me" or as shapely as "Sorry Seems to Be the Hardest Word," "Chloe" delves intimately into the bottomless pit of human emotion that Elton was so adept at exploring.

The melancholy of "Elton's Song," another that Geffen permitted Elton to retain, is found in a thread that wends its way through the song's structure. This is the one song from the Grasse-Nice sessions that Elton premiered during his fall 1979 "Back in the USSA" tour, and also the only one on *The Fox* to include Tom Robinson's lyrics, which makes its title all the more fascinating. Robinson, who wrote songs from gay perspectives, handed Elton a set of lyrics with the pianist's name on it, as if to imply that the lyrical sentiments of the song were Elton's. In a radio interview, the pianist allowed that "Elton's Song" was about "male hero worship,"[6] but the words go much further than that. Set in a school, the scene is of one boy in love with another. He says at first: "It's hard to grin and bear/when you're standing there/my lips are dry/I catch your eye and look away." He finally wishes: "I would give my life/for a single night/beside you."

The recorded "Elton's Song" is mostly a solo outing for the musician, who treats both the piano accompaniment and the melody as a classical étude not far removed from the piano expression in "Carla/Étude." But whereas the latter implies a modest glint of happiness, "Elton's Song" offers only despair and the isolation that attends a secret, unrequited love.

The final track that missed Geffen's axe is "Heart in the Right Place," the first blues song Elton had written since the misguided "Stinker" from *Caribou.* Unlike "Stinker," "Heart in the Right Place" shies away from clichés. Instead, the usual blues lines are transformed from a musical narrative of what it is to be down and out, into a perverse glorification of mean-spiritedness, achieved with unexpected melodic shifting in both verses and chorus.

Osborne's lyrics, among the most arresting he would write for Elton, tell the story of a bloodthirsty hack journalist who delights in maligning the reputations of celebrities ("If you're doing fine boy/you got my vote/but step out of line boy/and I'll go for your throat"). Osborne has rarely come closer to Bernie's technique of expressing drama in increasingly greater increments (witness "Indian Sunset" and "Ticking"), slowly but steadily revealing the intentions of this "queen of the sly line."

Between Elton's steely vocal and tingly blues chords, the evil fluctuations of James's synthesizer, and Reggie McBride's foreboding bass picking, the heartless journalist's image comes to the fore. Although the doldrums of a traditional blues song are absent, the mood is still solitary. Amid the journalist's aggression is the awareness that she has painted her victim and herself into an uncomfortable corner.

The remaining songs on *The Fox* were commissioned by Geffen and produced by Chris Thomas. "Breaking Down Barriers" opens the album and features another set of Osborne lyrics. Its melody is the unlikely product of a BBC-TV interview with Elton conducted by Paul Gambaccini at Woodside during the summer of 1980. During the interview, Elton claimed he could write music to lyrics in a matter of minutes. Gambaccini, calling the musician's bluff, handed Elton the John Donne poem, "No Man Is an Island." To his embarrassment, Elton was forced to make good on his boast. As the camera rolled, he promptly found some suitable chords on the piano, and, as he played them, sang the poem from top to bottom without a break, almost instantly identifying the chorus from among the ancient stanzas. Within five minutes, or as long as it took to sing the poem, with chorus, he was done. Elton's on-camera exercise came into use months later, when Geffen required him to record more songs for *The Fox*. Osborne wrote new lyrics, and the song was set to tape with only minor alterations from the version he had composed in his living room at Woodside.

The main difference between Elton's John Donne melody and the version on *The Fox* is that, in the former, the melody's pace was more deliberate, the approach more contemplative. In "Breaking Down Barriers," the music has blaring bravado, nearly reaching rock proportions. The protagonist is, after years of living within a mental fortress, finally in touch with his feelings, unafraid to let love enter his mind and heart. Rapid piano arpeggiations herald the song's start, announcing his new bravery. Elton's vocal, sung as if through a barrel-sized chest, conveys pride and confidence, even as he slips into a rare falsetto for extra flair. The song flows swiftly along, lifted by the iron support of some of Elton's trademark rhythm chords, with Nigel and Dee on bass and drums and a powerhouse backing-vocal entourage that includes Stephanie Spruill, Venette Gloud, and Bill Champlin.

The last song on the album that Osborne cowrote, "Nobody Wins," was born in the summer of 1980, though Elton had nothing to do with the music. While on vacation in the Riviera, he heard a song called "J'Veux d'la Tendresse," sung by Janic Prevost. As Elton later explained, "[I]t's a record I heard driving out of town in St.-Tropez in a traffic jam and it just suddenly came on. . . . [I]t just sent shivers up and down me spine even though it was sung in French. . . . I would love it to be a hit in England. In French, probably it wouldn't be, maybe it would need an English translation, but it's got a special thing about it, I don't know what it is."[7] The words and music of "J'Veux d'la Tendresse" were written by Jean-Paul Dreau, his lyrics describing the search for happiness in life. Osborne adapted the French lyrics for the English-speaking world.

Osborne's penetrating words—like those for "Heart in the Right Place"—are among the best of his career with Elton, transforming the song into a view of Reggie Dwight's broken home.[8] Portrayed are Reggie's pain as he listened to his parents argue ("I used to hide beneath the sheets/I prayed that time would find a way/but with the passing of the years/I watched as laughter turned to tears") and the indelible imprint of these episodes on his psyche ("It's the innocent who pay/when broken dreams get in the way").

The simple production for "Nobody Wins" includes James's programmed percussion and synthesizers. Elton's splendid singing is a sublime example of his increasing mastery of his lower register. In interpreting the melody's European angst, he extracted from the typical Continental melody more edges, textures, and tonal qualities than he could have ever mustered during his commercial heyday.

The remaining songs on *The Fox* show further evidence of Elton's growing vocal potential. Cowritten with Bernie, they are also a welcome return to the mini-screenplays the lyricist was known for. The first of these is "Just Like Belgium," in which alcohol-soaked vagabonds try to recapture a trace of the glamour of their younger days in Belgium. Elton and Bernie had originally written the song for Rod Stewart, who turned it down, claiming the melody and lyrics were incompatible. The pianist was all too happy to keep it once he learned he would have to record six more songs for the new album.[9]

Does the melody for "Just Like Belgium" match the lyrics, or was Rod right? Both sport Continental themes. On a comfortable bedding of bass and drums, Elton places chunky, sun-washed piano phrases that evoke life in bohemian Europe. Adding to the Continental ambience are synthesizer interjections from James and the French whispers of one Colette Bertrand. Atop these is Elton's vocal, sung with an attitude that embraces the future rather than mourns the past. The only suggestion of melancholy—found in most of the song-moons orbiting the album's centerpiece—is in his elongated "ohhh" toward the end, which seems to emphasize nostalgia for a happier past.

Melancholy turns to bitterness with "Fascist Faces." Rarely has Bernie used such a blunt title, but in these lyrics he expressed both his and Elton's disdain for right-wing reactions to current events. Elton was especially concerned with "fascism" hiding beneath the guise of evangelical religion, which he identified as a growing problem in the United States,[10] but Bernie's words more blatantly attack anti-Communist hysteria. The protagonist, a seeker of information the establishment is reluctant to reveal, resents being accused of Communist sympathies ("But some journalist got his mug shot kit/and his briefcase on his lap/but I'm tired of being linked with the K.G.B./and all that political crap").

Elton turns "Fascist Faces" into a rock-gospel protest song. With a slow but assertive beat set by his piano bass notes and Dee's bass, the pace suggests a goose-stepping army. Elton at first sounds distant, but the volume of his singing, and the aggressiveness of the instrumental backing, markedly pick up with Richie Zito's blazing guitar chords. By the chorus, the song is a confrontation between the opposing forces of justice and repression. Over the tempo, Elton and the Reverend James Cleveland and his choir sing with outrage ("When I see your fascist faces/then I know I've had enough/trying to trace it or erase it/is it foolproof or a bluff"). Elton adds a deliberate piano solo of equal parts reflection and tension.

Much more peaceful, and without any anger, is "Heels of the Wind," the story of a person willingly living a life without purpose, motive, or dreams. Elton gives the slacker a light musical treatment that mimics his contentment and the swift passage of his inconsequential days. Elton's in-flight piano and James's happy-go-lucky synthesizer unite in a harmonious satisfaction that somehow seems disconcerting coming on the heels of "Chloe" (which it follows). But "Heels of the Wind" still succeeds in evoking the solitary feeling that a ne'er-do-well might sense as he or she slowly follows the footsteps of those more attuned to thought and action.

The album's final song, and the one least affected by the melancholy of the album's centerpiece, is its title track. Geffen had asked Elton to think of a name for the album. The musician thought of the fox, an animal whose cunning seemed a symbol of the way he had conducted his own life, and of his own nationality, too, as the fox was central to the traditional sporting life of the English aristocracy. Elton asked Bernie to write lyrics for a song named after the crafty mammal, and Bernie obliged.

So Elton became the "fox," a creature who had, through talent and shrewdness, survived countless personal attacks and near-derailments of his professional career. His skills allowed him to turn the tables on his enemies ("the snowfall leaves the tracks that catch a few/if you're wily, you will leave them lying/snared up in the traps that they set for you"). Over the objections of rock critics, Elton had had a number I hit with "Crocodile Rock"; his costumes were the antithesis of his sensitive songs; and after he had said he was "bisexual," he had used the resulting negative energy to do what he'd wanted—becoming chairman of Watford, recording with a soul producer and, especially, reintroducing himself to the unlimited potential of his pianism. Through it all he had continued to compose and record music of note. To his critics' dismay, he wasn't going to disappear any time soon ("I'm always gonna be there running over the rock").

The music for this biographical sketch combines the tough muscularity of Elton's gospel chord progressions with a matter-of-fact melody that tells it like it is. He sings his declaration of survival through a growing intimacy with his voice, occasionally delving into those additional bands of sound discovered under Thom Bell's tutelage. The only prominent instrument in the song, besides Elton's piano and voice, is a harmonica, a testament to the bramble-patched countryside of the fox's home.

The overarching theme of The Fox is one of sadness and disappointment. But as both the closing title track and the opener, "Breaking Down Barriers," are the furthest from the melancholy of the album's centerpiece—the former self-determined and tough, the latter an expression of emotional triumph—we are left with an impression of Elton as strong and sure of himself as ever.

"I AM THE FOX, LIKE IT OR NOT"[11]

AT THE END OF APRIL 1981, Geffen Records released the first single from The Fox, the album following in mid-May. But behind the scenes, legal battles were being waged. The album after 21 at 33 was supposed to be Elton's last for MCA, to satisfy his eight million dollar contract. But disenchantment with the label had prompted him to give *The Fox* to Geffen.

Elton still had to satisfy his MCA contract. On March 13, 1981, he delivered to MCA all six songs recorded with Thom Bell in 1977, even though MCA's 1979 Bell EP contained alternate mixes of three of the songs, and a rerecording of "Shine on Through" had already appeared two and a half years earlier on *A Single Man*. Elton demanded the $1.3 million due him for delivery of an album. Five days later, MCA refused to either accept the songs or pay the money.[12]

On March 19, Elton, John Reid, and the musician's production company, Sackville Productions Ltd., filed suit against MCA. They charged breach of contract for MCA's refusal to pay for the final album and to "use its best efforts" to distribute and market it. They alleged that the contract permitted an album to include previously released singles, and afforded Elton the discretion to decide an album's content. They demanded money due along with ten million dollars in exemplary damages because MCA had "acted maliciously, oppressively, and in bad faith." The record company countersued, asking the court to define what constituted an album and claiming that the six songs Elton had delivered did not meet the definition as contracted.[13]

The situation got nastier shortly before the release of *The Fox*. MCA sued not only Elton, Reid, and Sackville, but also the Geffen and Warner companies, charging that it was entitled to *The Fox* and asking for a temporary restraining order to prevent its release by Geffen Records. MCA was aware that Elton had commenced work on the album in August 1979 and had continued to work on it through early 1981; it argued that he had been legally committed to MCA until the end of March. In a countersuit, Elton swore that he had begun work on *The Fox* on April 1, 1981, by which time his MCA contract had expired. Warner said it had already paid Elton nearly $2.5 million as a nonreturnable advance against royalties from the album, and had run up production and promotional expenses. A Federal District Court judge denied MCA's application for a restraining order, reasoning that the record company would not suffer irreparable harm if Geffen released *The Fox*, as it could still win damages if it prevailed in court.[14]

This decision cleared the way for Geffen's release of the album. After the dust settled, Elton was freed of his contract with MCA, which is what he'd wanted all along. Although MCA didn't release the six Thom Bell tracks in 1981, it did so eight years later, following the musician's return to the MCA fold. In light of the company's belated gesture, maybe the collection was not the "piece of junk" their attorney had called it after Elton filed his initial suit.[15]

"THINGS WERE ALREADY GOING WRONG"[16]

"WE FEEL THIS IS ONE OF THE FINEST ALBUMS we've had in a long time," said one Geffen Records executive of *The Fox* during an early April 1981 teleconference. The teleconference was a business meeting held before a studio audience comprised of the Los Angeles branches of Warner-Elektra/Asylum-Atlantic (WEA) and Warner Brothers, and WEA home office staff. The meeting was also being beamed to twenty Holiday Inn locations throughout the United States and Canada, where other record company staff had gathered for the cheerleading and entertainment.

The teleconference's format was like a talk show, with Elton as "host" and various Geffen and Warner Brothers representatives as "guests." Even Bernie dropped by, to excite enthusiasm for their "reunion." The show was very nearly a dull, uneventful event, saved only by the rantings of the host, who, in between swigs from a beer can, gave the show a zany, disheveled quality that made it worth watching.

At times during the show, Elton was serious, as when he promoted "Fascist Faces" as an FM-friendly track. "It's very important for me to get FM play back because a lot of stations gave up when 'Crocodile Rock' came on," he said, also acknowledging the detrimental effect *Victim of Love* had had on his image among FM programmers and listeners. He added, "If they can play Dan Fogelberg, they can bloody well play me!" He also had nothing but praise for the Geffen-Warner team. "You can get all the money in the world, but all the money in the world doesn't make up for someone showing a bit of interest," he said.

But the show's most memorable lines were those Elton delivered about his sexuality. When Geffen executive Ed Rosenblatt welcomed the representatives of WEA (pronounced "WEE-uh") Canada, the musician asked with mock curiosity, "Did you say *queer* Canada?" Later, he rhapsodized that a "faggot" was really an English sausage. When a teleconference participant asked who "the fox" was, he replied that *he* was, elaborating that, after Bernie had written the lyrics for the title track, "we changed the [album] title from *The Female Impersonator* to *The Fox.*"[17]

Despite the elaborate planning for *The Fox*, its commercial performance in the United States was decidedly dismal. This shouldn't have been entirely unexpected. By the album's release, and just as "Nobody Wins" was advancing on *Billboard*'s Hot 100, Geffen Records was knee-deep in litigation. It was in their best interest to make *The Fox* a less commercially attractive product to fight over, in the hopes that MCA would agree to settle. And in the event that MCA won the suit, it would have laid claim to the album's profits anyway, another reason keeping them down could have seemed the thing to do.

Always a realist, Elton expected barbs from rock critics to continue unabated following the album's May release. It had been fashionable since 1976 for critics to describe his career as on the wane (before that, they had just shaken their collective heads at the steamroller effect his hits created). "I know people will look at this record, once more, as a comeback for me. In fact, David [Geffen] and I laughed about that," Elton told Robert Hilburn. "If the record is a huge success, people will give him credit for launching my career again."[18]

Indeed, *The Fox* was treated to mixed reviews that leaned toward the lukewarm. "Precious, finely crafted, sentimental, catchy, impeccably tuneful, and grandiose . . . all the characteristics that made you weak at the knees/rush to the lavatory in the first place," wrote Colin Irwin for *Melody Maker*.[19] The *Los Angeles Times*'s Steve Pond remarked that Elton was now "Corporal Pretty Good" rather than "Captain Fantastic."[20] Writing for *The New York Times*, Robert Palmer called *The Fox* "flawed and uneven" but "with some potential hit singles that are more finely crafted than much of today's AM radio fodder."[21] And a review in *The Washington Post* chided: "This former enfant terrible refuses to age gracefully, or to learn discipline."[22]

The latest offering of the "former enfant terrible" arrived nearly stillborn in the United States. Debuting on *Billboard*'s album chart on June 6, it stopped at number 21. Although it lasted nineteen weeks on the chart, it would not go gold. In Britain, the story was a little better. The album's performance was comparable to that of *21 at 33*, peaking at number 12 and staying on the album chart for twelve weeks, a respectable, though not spectacular, performance.

In keeping with Elton's smashed hopes for a major hit album was the botched release of an accompanying full-length video nearly eighteen months later, in October 1982.[23] So belated was this video's release that naming it after the album that inspired it would have made little marketing sense—especially since by that time Elton had another album to promote. The video was thus dubbed *Visions*. The premise of the five hundred thousand dollar film, directed by Russell Mulcahy in 1981, was that mesmerizing glass fragments, found by a lost boy searching through an abandoned house, provide visions in the form of video clips. The clips, most starring Elton, feature the songs on *The Fox*.

Visions made little news, except for the minor "scandal" that broke in Britain when the headmaster of the public school where the clip for "Elton's Song" was filmed expressed mortification at its true subject matter (a boy's homosexual crush on another boy), learned during a private screening. Director Mulcahy later admitted he hadn't been candid with the school's officials about what he'd intended to portray. The small brouhaha resulted in the deletion of the "Elton's Song" clip from the British version of the video.[24]

Long before this "scandal," "Nobody Wins," *The Fox*'s first single, was released. In the United States, it got more attention than the *Visions* video would later, but not much. Charting on May 9, 1981, it had a promising start, leapfrogging through the Top 40. But on June 27, it stalled at number 21, then fell from sight. This disappointment had its roots in the litigation over Elton's record label switch in the United States.

The British chart performance of "Nobody Wins" was worse. Maybe Elton should have recorded it in French for British release, after all. His troubles there were unrelated to his legal problems as a new Geffen signee; he hadn't had a British hit since "Song for Guy" made the Top 5 in December 1978. A DJM single released in tribute to the late John Lennon, the Elton/Lennon duet "I Saw Her Standing There," from their joint 1974 appearance, peaked at number 40. Similarly, "Nobody Wins" stalled at number 42.

The French version of the single was another story. Elton was inspired to record the original song, "J'Veux d'la Tendresse," for inclusion on the French release of *The Fox*, following the notable success of his duets with France Gall earlier in the year.[25] The synthesized backing track was retained, as were Elton's English-language backing vocals. But Jean-Paul Dreau's rhythmic French words set a different tone, expressing the universally felt love of blue skies ("J'veux du ciel bleu toujours"), children ("J'veux des enfants plein ma maison"), guitars, laughter, and songs ("Des guitares des rires des chansons"). Chosen as the single in France, "J'Veux" yielded Elton another French hit.

More likely casualties of Geffen's veto power were turning up as B-sides. For "J'Veux" and "Nobody Wins" it was "Fools in Fashion," a Taupin collaboration. For the U.S. release of "Chloe" it was "Tortured," also with Taupin lyrics. In Britain, a delightful slice of country pie written with Gary Osborne, "Can't Get Over Getting Over Losing You," was the flip side to "Just Like Belgium."

"Chloe" was the summer 1981 single in the United States. It debuted on the Hot 100 on July 25, took seven weeks to reach the Top 40, peaked at number 34, and then tumbled off the chart. One of Elton's most gripping tales of misery barely had the opportunity to touch a nerve among Americans. The days when Elton's commercial success had rebounded a bit, with "Mama Can't Buy You Love" and "Little Jeannie," must have seemed distant by this time. On the other side of the Atlantic, the intransigence of British record buyers was proved again with "Just Like Belgium," released in early July. It didn't chart at all.

"IMAGINE, HE'S THE MAN WHO NEVER DIED"[26]

DESPITE THE DISAPPOINTMENTS that were beginning to surface about his Geffen contract, Elton maintained a forward-looking attitude that would stand him in good stead through numerous 1980s setbacks. "A lot of people have stood in my way, funnily enough, about doing it," he told Scott Muni, regarding his ambition to record an instrumental album. "I've had tremendous pressure not to do it."[27] It wasn't that anyone doubted his ability, but something he did had to be commercially viable, to yield a hit. Since 1976, he had racked up only nine hits each in the United States and Britain, compared to his first six years of fame, when he had scored twenty-two in the United States and eighteen in Britain.

By the middle of 1981, when Elton told Scott Muni about his interest in doing an instrumental album, he was no longer talking about taking that year and a half off to compose, as he'd announced in Australia the year before. It is hard to imagine

David Geffen countenancing such a protracted effort. In fact, it is hard to believe Elton ever countenanced such a protracted effort.

Nothing about Elton's compositional technique was protracted. If his music didn't come almost instantly, it was not going to come at all. By the summer of 1981, the lofty ambition had been cast aside in favor of a project more consistent with his spontaneity. He now had plans to work on an instrumental album in Paris—all keyboards—with James Newton Howard accompanying him. One of James's jobs would be to encourage Elton to play more keyboards. "I'm a lazy keyboard player," Elton told Muni. "I kind of shy away from doing things on electronic keyboards because I always say I can't understand things."[28]

The only important activity to come before these sessions was a June 20 private performance at Windsor Castle, for Prince Andrew's twenty-first birthday. The musician played for an hour before four hundred guests, including Queen Elizabeth, Prince Charles, and Charles's fiancée, Lady Diana Spencer. The festivities shifted to a disco afterwards, where Lady Di invited Elton to do the Charleston, and he danced to "Rock Around the Clock" with the Queen. It was then that Elton's friendship with Lady Di commenced. After the party, she wrote him a "lovely letter," he recalled years later. It was the first of many letters he would receive from her. "She was very quick," Elton said. "You went out to dinner with her and there was always a letter the next day."[29]

Following the party, Elton left for Paris. The sessions there didn't lead to the masterwork Elton coveted. "We sort of ground to a halt halfway through," he said a few months later.[30] The sessions abruptly converted to work on his next Geffen studio album. Perhaps this change was due to the influence of some lyrics he had just received from Tim Rice, the famed lyricist of *Jesus Christ, Superstar* and *Evita*, which happened to fit a complex melody Elton had just written. The lyrics were called "Legal Boys," and soon another non-instrumental Elton John song was born.

Elton later said he still hoped to someday use some of the instrumentals he had written during the aborted Paris sessions. "I still have the melodies of the songs, so I'll probably get 'round to it," he said not long afterwards. "The classical stuff is still there—it's just got to be recorded or re-recorded, one of the two. There's one song . . . that I will definitely keep. It's called 'The Man Who Never Died.'"[31] He had written this one with John Lennon in mind. Though he hadn't seen Lennon regularly since the mid-1970s, he had always considered the ex-Beatle a close friend. He was also godfather to John and Yoko's son Sean, born in 1975. Seven months after Lennon's murder, Elton was ready to mourn through his music.

"The Man Who Never Died," coproduced by Elton and Clive Franks, is of the same ilk as "Song for Guy." Like "Guy," it is stark, with stabbing piano chords and simple synthesizer accents set against a backdrop of programmed percussion. But unlike "Guy," "The Man Who Never Died" isn't an "optimistic" death song. It is more mournful, more aware of the loss than of what might come afterwards. Its only upbeat qualities are the bridge, which seems to celebrate Lennon's life, and the coda, in which Elton repeats the mantra, "Imagine—he's the man who never died." Also unlike "Guy," this song didn't inhabit an important spot at the end of a full-length studio album. "The Man Who Never Died" would only see the light of day as a B-side in 1985.

"I FOUND AN EMPTY GARDEN AMONG THE FLAGSTONES"[32]

"ELTON JOHN'S SECOND GEFFEN RECORDS OFFERING, *Jump Up!*, is named for a West Indian expression—the essence of parties and good times, and an appropriate title for the album that was inspired so much by the atmospheres of Antigua and Montserrat," said a Geffen press release around the time *Jump Up!* was issued in 1982 and another world tour was underway. True, the album was recorded primarily at George Martin's AIR Studios in Montserrat in the British West Indies, but it had been conceived by accident in Paris. "Paris wasn't conducive to recording so we went to Montserrat [in late 1981] and that's where we got everything together," Elton said. "I wrote all the songs in Paris, but when it came down to recording we sort of were bashing our heads against a brick wall."[33] Once again, Chris Thomas produced. And sandwiched around the sessions were Elton's tennis matches, played in nearby Antigua.[34]

Other than "Empty Garden (Hey Hey Johnny)," the songs on the new album came about with melodies first, even those written with Bernie's lyrics.[35] Elton once said that *Jump Up!* marked for him a new enthusiasm for recording.[36] This has to be true; as successful artistically as *The Fox* was, the prolonged process of its completion couldn't have been pleasant. But Elton's renewed enthusiasm also signified a distinct lack of musical focus. *Jump Up!* presents a motley assortment of styles and concepts. It is a sparkling but disjointed collection of tasty morsels thrown together willy-nilly.

After all this time, Elton still didn't have his own band to use in the studio. In the *Fox* "teleconference," he'd discussed the possibility of touring again at the end of 1981. He expected to have essentially the same band used in 1980, with the exception of a "different drummer." This tour didn't come into being, but the departure of Nigel did. In his stead, Toto's Jeffrey Porcaro was enlisted following a limited role on *The Fox*. Richie Zito was back on lead electric guitar, and Dee was on bass. As always, James provided the synthesizer and electric piano treatments that, after some goading in Paris, could not seem to be shoved into Elton's "lazy" lap. Backing vocals were provided by a few hardy souls already on hand— Elton, Gary Osborne, and Dee.

The lyricist lineup was modified only slightly. Lyrics by Bernie and Osborne were plentiful; missing was Tom Robinson, who had been replaced by a significantly different writer, Tim Rice. No longer during the 1980s would any of Elton's songs sport a gay theme.

"Blue Eyes" is the one song on *Jump Up!* that proves Elton wasn't just treading water. It is more than just one of the many pleasingly seamless ballads that Elton continued to churn out the way Pete Rose got hits. "'Blue Eyes' features . . . some of the most sophisticated chord sequences that Elton John has ever written," observed Thomas Ryan in his book *American Hit Radio.* "With a progression steeped in complex jazz changes and a melody that resonates with blue notes, it's anything but ordinary for early-'80s pop music. . . . Unlike much of its competition, it seems destined to become an evergreen among a field of annuals."[37]

Many of Elton's seamless ballads have become evergreens, but "Blue Eyes" is something more—a twist of sadness housed in the wise cadences of jazz and set against a gentle landscape of unobtrusive, countrified blues. Osborne's words are subsumed in the music, as well they should be, since Elton had started the ball rolling. "Blue eyes, baby's got blue eyes," he'd cooed as he composed the music.[38] Osborne had taken it from there, with the musician throwing in another line or two, entrapped in the song's jazz cadences. Although Elton later mused that, before getting it right, he'd kept singing the song like Dean Martin, what finally emerged was not Dino's debonair, whiskey-laced voice but a new Elton John sound. Instead of the sophistication of his singing on "Idol" or the sensuousness of "Shooting Star," "Blue Eyes" gets the balladeering of someone no longer interested in playing lovers' games. The singer caresses the melody in a protective coating of honest intimacy, girded by deep-note delving.

The other songs Osborne cowrote on *Jump Up!* are like "Blue Eyes" in that, following Elton's lead, Osborne reverted to his method from the *Single Man* era of penning words that attach themselves directly to the melody. "Princess," with a message of goodwill to Diana, the new Princess of Wales, was written as an ordinary love song whose real focus was lost on many foreign fans, particularly Americans ("You are my princess/you make me smile"). "Dear John," the album's opener, is a corny lament about those famous "good-bye" notes to lovers—even though, in this case, "John" was merely beaten to the punch ("We could not go on/living like we were/I was just about to write/a Dear John note to her"). "Ball & Chain" speaks of a burdened relationship, described with as many clichés as Osborne could muster ("I got a heart so true/you got a heart of ice").

As ordinary and predictable as Osborne's words are, the music that inspired them is anything but. The silky sounds of "Princess" are delectably fluid, as sincere an expression of devotion as the words are unimaginative. The music for "Dear John" is swift and fun, with plenty of Jerry Lee Lewis–style rhythm chords and glissandos, and an affirmative melody that belies the separation of "John" from his love, though it seems less disconcerting when one realizes that the story has a happy ending.

The upbeat, countryish music for "Ball & Chain" is harder to reconcile with the lyrics, which describe the dejection of one carrying a weighty burden. The only keyboard sound is James's synthesizer—not the first time an Elton John country song had been devoid of piano. "Slave" and "Texan Love Song," both from the early 1970s, relied on Davey Johnstone's plucking for their hillbilly flavors. But "Ball & Chain" has a less sweaty, more contemporary country flavor. It is also more of a hybrid. The dominant acoustic guitar strumming is from none other than Pete Townsend. Elton's reverberant vocal is reminiscent of Buddy Holly; his airy melody, with its facile shifting, is a throwback to the multipart melodies of *Madman Across the Water*. The music, however, sheds no light on the protagonist's sorry situation.

After Osborne's songs, the quality of the lyrics could only improve. "Legal Boys" boasts the services of Andrew Lloyd Webber's former lyricist, Tim Rice. Lloyd Webber and Rice were, during the 1970s, the John and Taupin of musical theater. Like Elton and Bernie, they were young and inexperienced, but they were fresh talents that couldn't be ignored, going on to become goliaths of a genre in dire need of reinvigoration. For Elton and Bernie, it was popular music; for Lloyd Webber and Rice, it was musical theater. Unlike Elton and Bernie, however, Lloyd Webber and Rice developed irreconcilable differences following their mammoth success. There would be no "Two Rooms at the End of the World" for them.

The impetus for Rice's contact with Elton isn't certain, although Rice had an exceptional passion for popular music. Back in the 1960s, he had had his eyes set on the rock scene. His attention was diverted with the (then) happy confluence of his path with Lloyd Webber's. Later, Rice's appearances on British television and radio and his coauthorship of books on British hit albums and singles helped establish him in the world of popular music. He went on to collaborate with songwriters as diverse as Paul McCartney and Freddie Mercury.[39] Besides, Rice admired Elton. While still partnered with Lloyd Webber, Rice had commented on the John/Taupin songwriting approach. "I have occasionally written lyrics—though only very rarely—as it were, on their own. But I don't like doing that," Rice had said. "And, I think, obviously with one or two exceptions (such as Elton John or Gilbert and Sullivan) on the whole you'll find the best songs are those in which the words follow the tunes."[40] Unbeknownst to Rice, in the summer of 1981 Elton was using the very "music first" method the lyricist preferred.

The lyrics Rice sent Elton were, unsurprisingly, a decidedly theatrical batch of words. In fact, "Legal Boys" was a Lloyd Webber reject.[41] A more complex take on marital dissolution than "Dear John," "Legal Boys" opines that lawyers and accountants make the situation worse than it has to be, while profiting handsomely from it. The lyrics are filled with the melodramatic irony one finds in musical theater ("Your accountant called this morning/there was springtime in his heart/he couldn't wait to tell me/how he'd pulled our lives apart"), as well as delightfully witty asides ("I would rather call you darling/than defendant in the case").

"Some of the finest songs I've written have gotten ignored," Elton said three years after that productive summer in Paris, referring specifically to the music that would become "Legal Boys." "I thought it was an exceptionally fine song."[42] The music Elton paired with Rice's lyrics challenges the listener's train of thought, with two melodic sections in the verse that carry subparts, and a climactic mood shifter in Elton's staccato piano chords that signals the choral lamentation—which provides a third, distinct melody. The song is a classical rhapsody calling for the space and majesty a theater could provide.

It is fortunate that Elton recognized how perfectly Rice's lyrics matched his music. And it is unfortunate that, as Elton later noted, the song would be ultimately underappreciated. Happily, this one-song songwriting partnership avoided being a mere asterisk in their careers, as it foreshadowed a much more lucrative partnership to come in the 1990s.

The songs Elton wrote with Bernie on *Jump Up!* are no less interesting. In "Spiteful Child," Elton shapes descending chords and ascending broken chords into a catchy pattern that coaxes the listener into a gingerly downward spiral. Despite the catchiness of the music, it conveys a mild anger well suited to Bernie's story of vengeance ("Breaking the spirit in me, only added to your conceit/playing you at your own game, is going to make it complete"). In "I Am Your Robot," Bernie attaches the story of a man whose strings are being pulled in high-tech fashion by his girlfriend ("You went and flipped the switch and turned me positive when I was negative/I've been stumbling around like a metal man, on the graveyard shift") to Elton's mechanistic rantings, full of elongated, unnerving notes. Supplementing the musician's android-esque melody are sci-fi robot noises, probably courtesy of James's keyboards, and Steve Holly's synth drum. "Robot" is also one of Elton's most unusual vocal efforts, in which he moves from a tittering basket case to a robotic caricature, amid exaggerated breaths.

Nostalgia is the theme for "Where Have All the Good Times Gone?," which may be regarded, like "Give Me the Love" on *21 at 33*, as a follow-up to "Philadelphia Freedom." But the melody of "Good Times Gone" is markedly different—much more romantic, swollen with desperation, and obsessed with significant loss. Bernie's words play into these feelings like a perfectly fitted glove: "Young enough to chase our dreams/we were captured by romantic things/touched by love until it made us cry/how our hearts could fly without wings." James faithfully emulates the smooth string sound of Philly Soul. Elton's vocals are purposefully streamlined until the music's emotional breaking point, when he works into a final fade-out of raw, Thom Bell–inspired ad-libbing that questions the cruel passage of better days.

Inspired by Erich Maria Remarque's German World War One novel of the same name, Bernie's "All Quiet on the Western Front" was also prompted by the weary sound of surrender heard in one of Elton's most beautiful melodies. "Feel the pulse of human blood, pouring forth/see the stems of Europe bend, under force," Bernie wrote. In a rare editorial mode, Elton demanded one deletion from Bernie's lyrics for this song. As he later remembered, "There was one line which said, 'thin white men in stinking tents.' And I said, 'Bernie, I can't sing "thin white men in stinking tents." It's not an attractive line to sing.' And so we changed it."[43] (Though this line would be deleted from the album, it was sung in performances late in 1982!) There was plenty else to conjure up images of senseless carnage. The tragic draining of human life takes on musical dimensions, as Elton sings with a sigh against a dirge-like tempo. Fireworks of violence explode in the song's culmination, as Elton's weary melody turns strident, wrapped in James's electronic keyboards and Jeffrey Porcaro's thunderous drumming.

"All Quiet," which closes the album, isn't the first song on *Jump Up!* to address senseless loss. Bernie had surprised Elton with lyrics called "Empty Garden" while the musician was in Paris writing melodies. "It said everything I wanted to say [about Lennon's death] without sounding too cloying," Elton remarked later, while on tour in 1982. "I thought it was so perfect for me that I just sat down and wrote the song immediately. The song came out straight away. I looked at the words and there was the melody coming out."[44]

Bernie had written the lyrics within a few days of Lennon's death, while he was still reeling from the loss.[45] "I don't remember writing it. It just fell on the page," Bernie said about a decade later.[46] The lyrics question why someone so important to so many had to be taken away. A passerby walking past a New York brownstone asks, "What happened here?" and "Who lived here?" as he tries to make sense of the desolation he sees. He slowly deduces the tragic events that have caused him to stop, as Bernie has him liken Lennon to a "gardener that cared a lot, who weeded out the tears and grew a good crop." The passerby notices the toll the gardener's disappearance has taken on the garden, which is now "empty," ravaged by murder ("it's funny how one insect/can damage so much grain"). The lyrics' imagery abruptly shifts focus during the chorus, when the passerby, seemingly replaced by a child, looks for Lennon but can't find him ("And I've been knocking but no one answers/ . . . . /Oh, and I've been calling oh, 'hey hey Johnny'/can't you come out to play"). Someone later told Bernie that these words might have been subconsciously influenced by the Beatles' "Dear Prudence." "They said, 'Oh, you were taking lines from different Lennon songs, "Dear Prudence/won't you come out to play,""'" Bernie said years later. "I never thought about that when I was writing it."[47]

It is impossible to read these lyrics, or listen to the final song, without shedding a tear. The music of "Empty Garden" may not trample a path to the future the way "Blue Eyes" does, but it evokes a sense of tragedy in a way that George Harrison's 1981 Lennon tribute, "All Those Years Ago," does not. Whereas "All Those Years Ago" seems like a musical reworking of two other Harrison singles, "Crackerbox Palace" (1977) and "Blow Away" (1979), the music of "Empty Garden" reflects the uniqueness of its subject. It begins as a persistent question, Elton's vocal suggesting disbelief over what he fears has happened. By the chorus, when the child knocks "but no one answers," reality sets in. Elton's voice becomes a resentful shouting, transforming the child's near tantrum into an anthem of psychic torture. This child hasn't lost a playmate for the day, but for a lifetime.

On February 24, 1982, Lennon posthumously shared with wife Yoko an album of the year Grammy for their 1980 album *Double Fantasy*. According to Elton, this prompted Geffen to insist that "Empty Garden" be the first single in the United States and Canada from the as-yet-unreleased *Jump Up!* [48] Less than a month later, on March 20, 1982, the single debuted on the Hot 100 at number 79. By June 5, it had peaked at number 13, bested by several permutations of blandness that had managed to creep into the Top 10—Tommy Tutone's "867-5309/Jenny," Paul Davis's "'65 Love Affair," Toto's "Rosanna," and Asia's "Heat of the Moment."

Though Elton hadn't made the Top 10, "Empty Garden" was still his highest-charting single since "Little Jeannie." He had to be pleased. It was also the first U.S. hit cowritten with Bernie since 1978's "Ego."

Elton's single in Britain was "Blue Eyes," which charted on March 27. It did even better than "Empty Garden" had in the United States, reaching number 8 and lingering on the singles chart for ten weeks, the longest tenure for an Elton John single there since "Song for Guy" in 1978.

"BLUE EYES LAUGHING IN THE SUN" [49]

ELTON BEGAN HIS 1982 WORLD TOUR IN AUSTRALIA, where it was called, fittingly, "*Jump Up!* Down Under," in honor of the new album "rush released" there in late March. Early reports showed the album selling at a fast clip. "Australia has always been my most loyal market," Elton told one reporter. His star was still on the rise there, and making Australia and New Zealand his first stop (as opposed to his 1980 tour, when they were his last) showed how keenly he hoped to build on fan support in the two countries.

Elton seemed content. He had played a substantial amount of tennis in Antigua, and had lost weight. Watford was nurturing his sense of normality; a recent project with the club entailed making soccer more attractive for families and less so for "hooligans." The team had continued its deliberate climb from soccer's basement, and was now a first-division contender. Also, his passion for the latest in popular music hadn't abated, leading to an interest in new Australian bands, including Men at Work, Mental as Anything, the Church, and his opening act during this part of the tour, Moving Pictures. "[In Australia,] it's all so fresh," Elton enthused. "In America, it's the same old stuff on the radio all the time." [50]

Elton had originally anticipated having a six-piece band for this tour, just like in 1980. But James and another musician pulled out of the arrangement because of other commitments. Elton was left with Nigel and Dee, and a familiar but long absent face, Davey Johnstone. Since 1976, Davey had played with China and on *A Single Man*, as well as with Alice Cooper and Stevie Nicks, sometimes rejoining his old band mates for the odd gig, such as a surprise appearance at Elton's November 6, 1980 concert at Los Angeles's Forum during the "Bite Your Lip" encore.[51] When Elton called, Davey had just returned from an unsatisfying tour with Meat Loaf, in which, following management disputes, no one had gotten paid. "He [Elton] said he was thinking about getting the old band together again," Davey said. "I was really excited because it had always been a dream of mine to reform the band."[52] Ray Cooper was still in exile, but the original quartet was back together. The Elton John Band diaspora had effectively ended.

Australians and New Zealanders were lucky enough to see the rebirth of this phenomenon first. With all of Elton's professed misgivings about playing synthesizers himself, he seemed unconcerned about James's absence and played even more ferociously than he had in 1980. True, Davey willingly reproduced on guitar some of the synthesizer lines that had previously been James's responsibility, but nothing the band did could override Elton's chunky, vociferous piano approach. In this tour, more so than others in recent memory, Elton really lived up to Princess Margaret's observation from the mid-1970s that his playing was "louder than Concorde." In 1982, it was also at least as pretty.

Sartorial outrageousness from Elton's past was returning. On opening night in Australia, he appeared onstage for the solemn first notes of "Funeral for a Friend" in what was described as modified Carmen Miranda apparel.[53] Nestled on his head was a gilded turban. Down below were green and yellow sandals and yellow satin pants, his torso covered by an ocean scene. Myriad silken fruits—including a whole pineapple, a bunch of grapes, apples, oranges, and bananas—surrounded his shoulders, supported by a pair of palm tree trunks that rose from Elton's midsection like a set of suspenders. About to sing "Empty Garden," he eyed the fruit surrounding his neck and remarked, "I feel so inappropriate singing a song like this."[54] But hidden among the bananas and oranges was a message that maybe this wasn't such a bad way to deal with grief.

Throughout the tour, Elton's voice continued to develop. On "Someone Saved My Life Tonight" and "Blue Eyes," his hardwood timbre took on a sweet, lacquered cherry finish. In "Rocket Man," Elton used his voice to extend the song's ending, sending the melody floating into space. Davey's deft plucking brought to mind flashes of interstellar light as Elton, classical rolled chords in full force, began emitting reverberant, inhuman vocal sounds in his tribute to the nine-to-five astronaut.

Elton's piano added its chops in all sorts of areas one might not have predicted. Besides the inevitable boogie-woogie-cum-Beethoven mélange that surfaced in the middle of "Bennie," his playing was central to the forward movement of some other songs—"Meal Ticket" and "Ball & Chain," in particular—whose recorded versions seemed more guitar-based. And the live version of "Where Have All the Good Times Gone?" received the driving rock piano belligerence normally reserved for such barn-burners as "Saturday Night's Alright."

The musician's soft use on "Chloe" of electric piano—played for only a limited selection of songs—made one question his decision to rely so much on James for *The Fox*. But James was definitely missed during "Nobody Wins," which, in his absence, Elton sang against a taped backing track. In any case, the predictability of the taped backing forced concertgoers to concentrate on Elton's voice, in its own right a compelling instrument.

Fortunately, the presence of many a "screamer" at these shows no longer deterred Elton from challenging himself at the piano. He had long since lost his teen idol persona in the United States and Britain, and, judging from his determined performances Down Under, was not about to permit its return anywhere else. One review of the first Sydney concert raved, "Elton Hercules John proved to critics and fans alike what is now an indisputable fact . . . that he doesn't need to prove ANYTHING!"[55] Days later, Elton celebrated his thirty-fifth birthday with the help of thousands of fans, who were prompted by a local radio station to sing "Happy Birthday" to him.[56]

At thirty-five, Elton had a new twenty-three-year-old boyfriend, Australian Gary Clarke, who, with his fair complexion, long eyelashes, and pouting lips, resembled a male Kim Basinger. Elton didn't seem to notice that Clarke wasn't attracted to him, nor particularly concerned about the musician's feelings or frailties, despite accepting Elton's invitation to come live with him in England. As Elton would admit years later, this was one of many relationships he had at the height of his substance abuse in which his young love interest was whisked from home and given a new, Eltonian identity. These never worked out. Even as he pursued these relationships, he engaged in risky sex with multiple partners, with or without his latest love.[57]

"SOME SAY HE FARMED HIS BEST IN YOUNGER YEARS"[58]

IN BETWEEN ELTON'S DATES in the South Pacific and the commencement of his European tour, *Jump Up!* was finally released outside Australia and New Zealand. In the United States, the album charted on May 8, 1982. It bested *The Fox*, peaking at number 17, and lasted thirty-three weeks on *Billboard*'s Top LPs. In Britain, the album did about as well as *The Fox* and *21 at 33*, rising to number 13 with a chart life of twelve weeks. But the album spawned only one major hit there—the first single, "Blue Eyes," which reached number 8. The follow-up in Britain was "Empty Garden," the successful American lead single. British fans once again proved how unsentimental they could be: After their lukewarm response to Dick James's issuance of the Elton/Lennon duet "I Saw Her Standing There" just three months after Lennon's murder, "Empty Garden" stalled at number 51 following its June 12, 1982 chart debut.

In the United States, by contrast, Elton's commercial fortunes were looking up. "Blue Eyes" debuted on *Billboard*'s Hot 100 on July 10, 1982 at number 82. In mid-October, the single ran out of steam after a three-week stay at number 12. The song was bested by, among others, "Who Can It Be Now?," the first American hit for Men at Work, a group that Elton had touted while in Australia in March.

Elton had other things on his mind when he, Davey, Nigel, and Dee opened their first European tour as a unit in Stockholm on April 30, 1982. On May 9 at Brussels's Vorste Nationale Centre, Elton and the band excited and flattered their Belgian audience when they played the perfectly titled "Just Like Belgium." In Brussels, Paris, and Avignon, Elton joined "J'Veux d'la Tendresse" and "Nobody Wins" to form an appealing English-French hybrid. He sang in French of a desire for blue skies and happy songs, and in English of unhappy memories of parents at extreme odds. French audiences lapped it up, although Elton recalled Parisians booing his use of a backing tape.[59]

After a grueling month in Europe and a short break, the tour arrived in Denver on June 12 for a two-month survey of North America with opening act Quarterflash, a fellow Geffen group.

By now, some critics were distancing themselves from the notion that Elton was still struggling. Lynn Van Matre was ecstatic that he was, in her estimation, back to his old rock'n'roll raver self. "His rock and roll spirit, which apparently was flagging for some time, seems relatively rejuvenated these days," she wrote with relief about his July 10 show outside Chicago.[60] Writing for *The Washington Post*, Richard Harrington observed, "John finds himself on the upswing in a decidedly cyclical career."[61] A little farther up the East Coast, *The Philadelphia Inquirer*'s Ken Tucker expected good things of Elton's July 27 show at the Mann Music Center, not only because of the original band's reunion, but because of *Jump Up!* "After a few years of divorce and reconciliation with Taupin," he wrote, "each reconciliation yielding mediocre results, their collaboration on a song like 'Spiteful Child' is exhilaratingly good."[62]

Ken Tucker reveled in the suspicion that the gaudier Elton's attire, the better his new music. Indeed, Elton's flamboyance was making a huge comeback. For these shows he made his grand entrance in a costume that was variously described as a South American dictator's outfit, a Ruritanian general's uniform, or, mischievously by Elton, the habiliments of a Fascist leader. It was a mock military uniform that included a blood-red, gold-braided jacket with gold-fringed epaulettes; a royal blue sash set diagonally across his chest from which faux medals dangled; gold-braided white jodhpurs tucked into knee-high black patent leather boots, each sprouting a gold tassel; and a cap that, despite its gold braid and visor, resembled a chef's floppy white bonnet.

Elton sometimes began the show with one of two other costumes. Anticipated in many quarters was the matador outfit, with black jacket in gold braid and an abundance of pink—notably in the cummerbund, necktie, and majestic cape. Another outfit was described as a seventeenth-century "French fop" costume.[63] Satiny blue, it had a gold-fringed jacket with frilly white cuffs and collar; a flowing, thigh-length cape; knee-length trousers; matching shoes; and a feather-plumed hat— the latter three further adorned with giant buttons made of blue ribbon. This was also the only costume in recent memory to display, from within skin-tight white leggings, the musician's still-muscular calves.

No matter what Elton played in the U.S. shows, his approach was more feral than it had been in Europe or Australia, and the band responded in kind. Most songs, even the ballads, tended to move at a swift pace. The weeping "Empty Garden" was executed with salty-teared vigor. The desperate plea—"watcha gonna do about me"—of the guilt-ridden victimizer in "Chloe" was laced with strands of sinew. And Elton's ringing piano phrases in "Goodbye Yellow Brick Road" gave the song a more defiant tone than originally suggested.

The rock and up-tempo numbers were also thrilling. On "Saturday Night's Alright," Elton banged his piano as he had in his hair-raising performances circa 1971, even attacking the keys while on his back from underneath the instrument. "Bennie" proceeded with its fascinating evolution: The witty argument between Scott Joplin, Fats Waller, and Beethoven gave way to an even wittier rapprochement in which light, jolly piano phrases disarmingly segued into the grand finale, marked by the band mates collectively packing one last punch as cries of "Bennie!" filled the air.

The American tour had its share of "events." Large parts of the Kansas City and Saratoga, New York, shows became syndicated radio broadcasts. In St. Louis on July 5, as part of a holiday weekend fair, Elton and the band played a free afternoon concert on the Mississippi River, under the Arch known as the "Gateway to the West." To escape the gawkers watching for him in every passing limousine, Elton cooperated with a St. Louis police security plan in which he dressed as a police officer, rode in a patrol car, and slipped unnoticed through the fair's throngs, even fooling some of his own entourage.[64]

The first of three nights at Madison Square Garden provided the tour's most memorable moment. It had been almost eight years since John Lennon had joined the Elton John Band onstage at the Garden—and more than a year and a half since Lennon's murder in the same city. Such thoughts were likely racing through Elton's head as he sat at the piano in his South American dictator's outfit to perform "Empty Garden," about a third of the way into the August 5 show. It seemed as if all twenty thousand concertgoers were holding lit matches. When the song ended, Yoko Ono and six-year-old Sean emerged to greet the boy's godfather. "I just folded," Elton said later. "The old eyes went."[65] The three hugged. Yoko told the audience amid a five-minute ovation, "I want to thank you. I really feel you are all my family."[66]

A MONTH LATER, in September, "Blue Eyes" was still crawling up the chart in the United States. In Britain, the last traces of "Empty Garden" had been razed and "Princess," the homage to Princess Diana, became the new single. If British record buyers were relatively unmoved by the musical eulogy to Lennon, they were less moved by Elton's expression of affection for Princess Di. The single failed to chart.

Elton, Bernie, Chris Thomas, and the band returned to Montserrat for more recording. The idea for these sessions had begun germinating before the start of the North American tour, while Elton was visiting Bernie and the lyricist's second wife, Toni, in their Southern California home. They spoke about working on a whole album together, as in the old days. Bernie was busy cowriting songs with Rod Stewart, the Motels, a newcomer named Bruce Hornsby, and others, but the attraction of working as a team was stronger than ever. "I think it was at that time that we both realized how much we wanted this," Bernie told reporter Paul Grein about a year later.[68] Early in the tour, the plan jelled. "We're going to lock ourselves away for a few weeks and work on the album—just like we did with *Caribou* and *Yellow Brick Road*," Elton said at the time.[69]

For this next album, Elton and Bernie would be the only songwriters (with some tangential help from Davey), and the core ensemble of Elton/Davey/Dee/Nigel the only band, though guests and other helpers, all familiar and often central to the life and career of Elton John, were also on hand. James was back for a couple of string arrangements. Kiki lent her voice to some backing vocals. Ray dropped in for a little percussion. Skaila Kanga, whose work with Elton dated back to January 1970 when she played on "I Need You to Turn To" and "The Greatest Discovery," returned with her harp. One of Elton's idols, Stevie Wonder, contributed harmonica work. And a woman who would help Elton give the newspapers unexpected headlines in less than a year and a half, German-born recording engineer Renate Blauel, assisted with tape operating.

Elton set a tough deadline for himself: two weeks. Such discipline shouldn't have meant much, given the brevity of many 1970s album sessions. All of *Elton John* was recorded in one week. Elton wrote nearly everything for *Goodbye Yellow Brick Road* in just over two days. And he had had a ten-day window for *Caribou*. But in recent years, Elton's almost instantaneous composing had tended to float in neat clumps within much larger pools of time. Now, for the first time in ages, an album was conceived and born in the closed quarters of one studio in a remote geographical area, with only touch-ups left for a later date. *Too Low for Zero* was the result.

Elton's timetable was impressive, given his determination to shake his fear of synthesizers with a user-friendly Yamaha, which he used to write and play most of the album's tracks. "I've never really consciously gone in to set new trends, except on this new album I really wanted to try and get away from the piano sound," he said.

"I wanted to play synthesizer. I was just hoping they would invent one that I could understand."[70]

Some of the motivation for Elton to venture into this "dangerous" territory may have come from his admiration for the rising star Prince, whose recordings were synthesizer-heavy, but synthesizers had also been an integral part of the New Wave sound going back to the late 1970s. Even before A Flock of Seagulls had their first hit in 1982 with "I Ran," Blondie, Devo, and Gary Numan—all of whom enjoyed success on the British charts before gaining American recognition—had forged paths in "synth-pop." Elton, the quintessential music fan, had long been absorbing all this. His decision was also a pragmatic one: "It's hard to write up-tempo songs on the piano. It's a different technique to writing on guitar," he explained. "It's very hard to be simple on piano and write four-chord songs. And that's what the best sort of rock'n'roll songs are."[71]

Bernie, too, was writing most of his lyrics differently. Gone were Danny Bailey, Old Mad Joe, Dolly Summers, Bennie (rock star of the future), Alice (so popular with the girls), even the Captain and the Kid. Gone, too, were tales of war and its aftereffects ("My Father's Gun," "The Retreat," "Sixty Years On," and "All Quiet on the Western Front"), as were examinations of insanity, discontent, and evil ("Madman Across the Water," "The Cage," and "Chasing the Crown"). In their place were sober reflections of adulthood—spousal estrangement, battles with depression, missed opportunities, avowals of love. Bernie was thirty-two and settled down.

The album's opener is "Cold as Christmas (In the Middle of the Year)." Inspired by the paradisaic surroundings of Montserrat, Bernie set this song in an unspecified Caribbean locale, where a husband has taken his wife to pursue mended fences and regain lost passion. Unfortunately, the husband's strategy doesn't work.

In Elton's hands, "Cold as Christmas" becomes a cottony, synthesizer-fringed ballad of the type he was, and still is, so good at composing. His keyboard arrangement, which was chosen over one written by James, features hesitantly rhythmic acoustic piano, outlined in the halo effect of his newfound electronics. Above this is a mellifluous melody that takes the musician from studied soft tones to the highest falsetto, decorated by his trusty Yamaha with sporadic wintry "whooshes," spicy interjections, muted penny whistles, and spangly undercoatings. In truth, even if Elton wouldn't admit it, he had done similar arrangements for such songs as "Lucy in the Sky with Diamonds," "Someone Saved My Life Tonight," and "Song for Guy." Lending the song added touches of grace are some tambourine shaking by Ray, a few well-placed harp accents by Skaila Kanga, and backing vocals by Kiki, Davey, Dee, and Nigel.

The album's second song, "I'm Still Standing," wasn't meant to be an anthem symbolizing Elton's defiance of adversity, but it turned out that way. Within a year, when trouble with Geffen had grown, the song would become a figurative nose-thumbing at the company.[72] Later, it would assume a more general meaning of triumph against the odds, a salute to the pianist's staying power. "I'm Still Standing" started out as an anti-love song, not much different in theme from the Gloria Gaynor hit "I Will Survive." "Once I could never hope to win,/you starting down the road/leaving me again,/the threats you made/were meant to cut me down/and if our love was just a circus/you'd be a clown by now," Bernie wrote. "I'm still standing/after all this time,/pickin' up the pieces of my life/without you on my mind."

Elton delivers the words in a rhythm and blues cadence—toying with them, allowing them to slide off his tongue ("Once I never could-a hope to win")—within the framework of a jubilant, triumphant melody. The music is a minor tour de force. The Yamaha gives Elton an electric guitar sound for the opening riffs and intermittent interpolations as he sings of "looking like a true survivor, feeling like a little kid." Underneath, hot rays of percussion emanate from Elton's acoustic piano. The other band members shine, too. Davey unleashes a swaggering guitar solo mid-song, peppered with hoots and yells from his band mates. And he, Dee, and Nigel memorably blend their voices for the most attractive string of "yeah, yeah, yeah"s in years.

The album goes from victory to capitulation with the title track, "Too Low for Zero." The song's protagonist is worried and depressed, can't sleep and can't get up. The lyrics are a prime example of Bernie's masterful combination of rhythm, rhyming, colloquialisms, and simple imagery, in this case to portray a loser's doldrums: "Six o'clock alarm/I get the wake up call/let that sucker jingle-jangle/ring right off the wall/I'm too low for zero/I'm too tired to work."

Elton has said this song is "atmospheric,"[73] and it is. It demonstrates that synthesizers can be used in a strikingly emotive manner—by one whose songwriting is almost religiously dominated by melody. It is also nearly a solo effort by Elton, his synthesizer punches, piano ruminations, and Ray Cooper-esque drum machine pounding supplemented by only his band mates' backing vocals. Elton's voice is weary, dry, and cracked, as if he were uttering his first few words after a sleepless night. The perpetual cloud under which the protagonist languishes is sounded in synthesizer humming, with bright but pessimistic piano chords heralding the story line. Later, a piano solo expresses the dreary listlessness in which the protagonist is entrapped, the synthesizer voicing a sympathetic, whispering harp. All the while, the versatile synthesizer buffets the melody with a gentle rhythm, even as the drum machine goes full throttle.

The next song, "Religion," attacks the hypocritical conduct of many who profess piety. According to Elton, it is Bernie's "go against born-again Christians," although if Elton had written the words it would have been even more critical. "I wanted it to be a bit more blatant on the religion aspect, but Bernie wouldn't have it," he said. "I would have made it a little bit stronger. America is so conservative, so religious-minded. . . . Everybody's got their own church."[74] But since Bernie wouldn't change the lyrics, the song wasn't so much an indictment of certain Christian institutions as a series of down-home vignettes of downtrodden people in the Bible Belt who get religion, even as they continue to sin. There's the gambler who feels better about his gambling once he realizes "somebody up there likes me," the alcoholic who can't remember his binges but sees the light in a parking lot and becomes a drinking believer, and the prostitute who receives money but no appreciation until it finally comes in the guise of an omnipotent force.

Little synthesizer can be heard on "Religion." The Yamaha sounds like a harmonium, which is just as well since the song is about religion. Musically, "Religion" works as a superior follow-up to Caribou's "Dixie Lily," with all band members showing their respective strengths in a country-and-western–flavored setting. Elton purposely overstates this flavor, bellowing like a flush-faced Southern used car salesman who tries to attract customers according to the spiritual advice of the "holy guide." His melody tells the story as if he really believes that the gambler, the alcoholic, and the prostitute are now on the right path, even as they still, respectively, gamble, drink, and sell sex for money. That's the joke.

"I Guess That's Why They Call It the Blues" is the last song on side one, and the last of the ten Elton wrote and recorded in Montserrat. Bernie's words are those of a man totally consumed by love for his wife Toni. Written as a love letter from afar (he was in Montserrat), he tells her that he will be back home soon, asking her to think of what they will do when he returns ("Laughing like children,/living like lovers/rolling like thunder under the covers") and to remember his devotion to her in the meantime ("Wait on me girl/cry in the night if it helps/but more than ever I simply love you/more than I love life itself").

Davey has a cowriting credit on this song because an exhausted Elton, who had put himself under so much pressure that he had nearly had it, dragged Davey into the room where he was composing to help him begin the last tune. "I was so drained by the end," he later explained.[75] Neither Elton nor Davey has said what Davey did to facilitate the process, but it is likely that his guitar strumming provided the jump start Elton needed for one last song.

More than any other track on Too Low for Zero, "Guess That's Why" showcases the band's synergy, their collective imagination rivaling their best work from the 1970s. The song's gradual start, with Elton's florid piano introduction buttressed by Dee's bass playing, is similar in mood to the start of "Rocket Man." Davey's guitar layers are as clever as his playing on "Rocket Man" and as pleasingly folkish as his work on "Daniel." The backing vocals by Davey, Dee, and Nigel revive and perhaps even surpass their grand tradition, filled with heightened levels of flair and enthusiasm. The melody, sung with less sexual passion and more sentimentality than Bernie might have intended, travels naturally in a self-propelled carriage, with some lively roller-coaster lines to change the carriage's direction on occasion.

Elton recorded his luxuriant piano accompaniment for "Guess That's Why" in one take. Years later, music journalist Chris Salewicz noted how awed Chris Thomas had been by this feat, saying, "Chris Thomas said he's never worked with such a brilliantly accomplished musician." Elton, his humility in momentary repose, responded, "Well, musicians know it. I think the general public don't consider me as the number one pianist. Well, I'm not the number one pianist, but I'm a fuckin' good piano player."[76]

Another well-respected musician played on "Guess That's Why," too—Stevie Wonder, whose harmonica solo has become a trademark of the song in concert, when its tones are replicated by, of all things, a synthesizer.

Side two of the album opens with "Crystal," the story of two friends whose comradeship is threatened by their love for the same woman. Fortunately, Bernie doesn't stoop to clichés; like the words for "Too Low for Zero," these lyrics employ appealing colloquialisms and simple imagery to bring the story to life. "We're caught up in a web you and I," Bernie has Elton, the unlucky loser in the match, sing. "Since Crystal came between us, the knots of friendship seem to be untied." Crystal, whose name describes her fragility ("Handle her with care/don't hurt little Crystal"), is only wished the best in pursuing her newfound love ("The world is your oyster,/you're a pearl/but he's a jewel, and my friend").

Elton again opted for a drum machine over Nigel's organic abilities. "[W]hen we tried it [Nigel's drumming], it didn't have the same feeling," Elton said. "The machine was actually better than the drummer."[77] Davey's acoustic and electric guitars and Dee's submelody on bass were squeezed in, but are nearly indistinguishable from the all-encompassing swirl of synthetic sounds. As atmospheric as "Too Low for Zero," "Crystal" boasts some of the same, if sparser, synthesizer tricks. Most of the melodic accompaniment and percussive elements—outside of the drum machine's thick clapping and Dee's bass—are courtesy of the Yamaha's humming. Yet "Crystal" still has a full, rich sound, as if labored over by many more personnel. This is due in no small way to Elton's industrious use of the Yamaha and to his melody, which turns Bernie's words into an endless string of anxious thoughts.

The next song, "Kiss the Bride," is another of Bernie's stories of romance gone awry. A man dutifully attends the wedding of his former girlfriend, but all he wants to do is stop it. When the preacher asks if anyone present objects to the marriage, he has his chance, then cowers ("I should have stuck up my hand/I should have got up to stand/and this is what I should have said/I wanna kiss the bride, yeah!").

With this song, more than any other on the album, Elton may have succeeded in creating the kind of rocker he believed he needed the Yamaha to inspire, though it wasn't exactly the one he'd been pursuing. It has a shouting chorus ("I wanna kiss the bride, yeah!"), the pulverizing beat of Nigel's drums, and an irresistible chord pattern that the Yamaha, masquerading as strings, shares with Davey's guitar. But it also has something most straightforward rockers don't: a strong melody that can stand on its own. Characterized by feelings of disappointment in the marriage and the ex-boyfriend's cowardice, the song's high volume is the one quality that betrays its rock message.

The funny "Whipping Boy," which follows "Kiss the Bride," has a thirty-something man involved in an illicit affair with a much younger woman ("I could do time if they found out/look out, San Quentin, here I come"). Another rocker, it moves along at warp speed, but suffers from the same "infirmity" as "Kiss the Bride"—it has a strong, loping melody, albeit without the emotional peaks and valleys of "Bride." The Yamaha doesn't get much of a workout, either. Elton uses it conventionally as Davey whips up an appropriate guitar frenzy.

The last two songs are a pair of "Bernie Taupin ballads," as Elton later put it.[78] "Saint" is a rousing song about a young woman who jealously protects her individualism. Over an active, unpredictable melody that uses both Elton's falsetto and his lower register, the musician supplies another keyboard arrangement. While not as sweeping as those devised for "Too Low for Zero," "Crystal," or "I'm Still Standing," this arrangement still taps into the Yamaha's versatility, layering synthesized horns and organ-like spurts over a carpet of soft-hued ambience.

The last song, "One More Arrow," marks the only appearance of James Newton Howard on the album, with a romantically old-fashioned string arrangement. Like "Guess That's Why," "One More Arrow" is mainly a piano ballad—so much so that the band doesn't intercede until the song is half over. Bernie tells of a young man whose hopes and dreams are unrealized because of his untimely death. The song marks one of the last uses of Elton's falsetto on record. He uses almost nothing else here, as if he knows it won't be featured on an album again for years. In taking his singing up to a vocal precipice, he sounds as if he will never find his way down—but perhaps to illustrate the once "strong will" of the young man in the song, he lands on lower, solid ground, only to confound the witnesses and fly upward again.

Too Low for Zero proved a few things. First, no matter how hard he tried, Elton still couldn't write a simple melody. Second, he couldn't take a complete hiatus from the piano. And third, he was perfectly able to use a synthesizer to build on his hopelessly melodic songwriting precepts. The songs that are especially dominated by synthesizer sounds are not symphonies of flailing sheet metal—so prevalent in synth-pop circles—but compositions whose moods are tastefully shaped by unorthodox yet satisfying sounds. As a result, there is nothing synthetic about Too Low for Zero.

Elton's experiment would be vindicated by the album's success. It would go on to yield several worldwide hits—"I'm Still Standing," "Kiss the Bride," and "I Guess That's Why They Call It the Blues." The title track would be well received in some territories, and "Crystal" would become a major hit in Australia, helping to propel the album to quintuple platinum status there. Elton was perhaps reaping good karma from his return to full-time work with Bernie and the original band.

In the fall of 1982, however, *Too Low for Zero* was still an unknown quantity, and the karma was not good on all fronts. At the time, David Geffen was a major financial backer of Andrew Lloyd Webber's new Broadway musical, *Cats*.[79] On October 7, *Cats* opened to what was then the largest advance ticket sale in Broadway history. Geffen fervently wanted Elton to attend the premiere. But the timing was poor, as Elton was rehearsing for his upcoming November–December British tour following completion of the new album, and he didn't show up. According to English show-business manager Barry Krost, Geffen was so incensed that he "torpedoed" the remaining albums Elton owed the company.[80]

"STRING THE HARPS TO VICTORY'S VOICE"[81]

NOVEMBER 1982 was not a good month for Elton's music in either the United States or Britain. Although *Jump Up!* was finally certified gold in the United States— oddly, a good six months after its release—another single, "Ball & Chain," failed to chart. In Britain, the choice was "All Quiet on the Western Front," which did so badly Elton later commented, "It's the worst-selling single in Phonogram's history."[82] Whether that is true or not is beside the point. The fact is, it didn't chart, either.

Elton's sole recorded success in Britain that November was a compilation of his recent love songs, aptly titled *Love Songs*, featuring selections from *Blue Moves*, *A Single Man*, *21 at 33*, *The Fox*, and *Jump Up!* The album only reached number 39, but it stuck around for thirteen weeks, one week longer than *Jump Up!* Elton was finally able to compete with the spate of DJM-related releases of his early material.

The musician's first British tour with a band since the spring of 1976 met a different reception than his last three British singles. The tour opened on November 2 in Newcastle, making its way north to Scotland. There was even a stop at the Edinburgh Playhouse, where Elton had wet his feet as a solo performer in September 1976. Later in the month, the tour returned to England and continued on into December, finishing in London, where Elton and the band set up shop for a two-week stay at the Hammersmith Odeon.

A splitting headache didn't keep him from the stage one late November night in Manchester. He downed aspirin and water and kept going. After the show, Elton returned in a private plane to Woodside, where he spent the next day recuperating, returning dutifully the following night to thrill another Manchester audience.[83] During his stint there, headache or not, he still managed to occasionally play the piano from underneath, sprawled awkwardly on the floor, a look of childish mischievousness on his face, gold medals and tassels splayed in every direction.

The fourteen nights at the Hammersmith Odeon made the most news. Taking up residency there on December 9, Elton prepared for the shows in characteristic lavish fashion by paying $12,800 to have the outside of the Odeon decorated as a giant Christmas present. Neon Christmas trees decorated the Odeon's entrance, and in the foyer stood real, two-story high Christmas trees. Concertgoers found other decorations inside—ribbons; crêpe paper; and arrangements of blue pine, berries, and pinecones.[84] Garishness was in evidence onstage, too. Neon lights once again trumpeted the name of each band member.

Elton's stay at the Hammersmith wasn't all goodwill and cheer. One night during the first week, Nigel took sick and didn't show up. Elton felt obligated to perform with Davey and Dee as an unlikely trio, all the while fighting off a rotten mood. After the opening number, he announced, "We still expect him to turn up, and nothing's happened, so we're in the dark as much as you."[85]

If Elton was angry because he thought Nigel's absence marred the live performance, or damaged the overall sound, he was wrong. His playing, which never needed accompaniment to achieve a complete song interpretation, easily filled in the gaps. Also, Dee's bass playing was more pronounced in the sound mix. During "Better off Dead," Elton and Dee teamed up effectively on rubbery, staccato chords. But in introducing the song, the pianist said its title "could apply to Nigel Olsson if I get my hands on him at this very moment." Upon reaching Nigel's drum set during the introduction of the band members, he uttered a simple "humph" as the audience laughed. But it was during "Bennie" that things turned serious.

Throughout 1982, Elton had often marked one of the many climaxes in "Bennie" by hurling his piano bench in the audience's general direction but letting it go toward the back of the stage. This time, he threw it forward, into what he thought was an open orchestra pit. The pit, however, was covered, and the bench slid along, hitting a woman in the shoulder, unbeknownst to Elton. "Bennie" marched on. Elton stopped his typically savage barrelhouse pounding when he noticed a commotion in the front rows. Possibly not believing that anyone could have been harmed by his runaway piano bench, he unleashed an ugly, runaway display of bad temper—unusual for a public appearance. "Listen, I'm very sorry I threw the piano stool," Elton said through his microphone. "If you're *that hurt*, go and see an RSPCA [Royal Society for the Prevention of Cruelty to Animals] man. . . ." While others could be heard asking the woman whether she was all right, Elton seemed more concerned with explaining his conduct. "I didn't throw it at you, I meant to throw it *there*," he said desperately, gesturing toward the covered orchestra pit. Finally, he said that she should leave "if you're *that hurt,* and you're keeping up *such a fuss.*" The musician played a few more notes on the piano and then abruptly ended "Bennie." A lengthy intermission ensued.

"I was so distraught, I was in tears," Elton remembered years later. He finally ensured that the piano bench victim got medical attention and looked for his manager. He found Reid and Bob Halley in the dressing room sharing champagne with guests. Enraged at their jollity while he, Elton, had a crisis on his hands, he headed for his limousine and rode around for ten to fifteen minutes. Only a traffic jam prompted him to return.[86]

He came back to face Davey, Dee, and the waiting but appreciative audience for an abbreviated final set. After the last encore, which included the now legendary medley of "Whole Lot of Shakin' Going On," "I Saw Her Standing There," and "Twist and Shout," he apologized to the crowd. The woman who had been hit by the bench was brought backstage and apologized to, Elton presenting her with a leather jacket and a bottle of champagne, and offering to buy her a dress. He arranged for a staff member to take her shopping the following day.[87]

This episode evidenced a disturbing development in Elton's disposition. In the old days, he might have been annoyed by overzealous arena security guards, but he was never unkind to his audience. Affectionately calling his Hammersmith audiences "Messerschmidts" and acknowledging the cheers of concertgoers in the shadows ("I can't see you, but thank you") were more his modus operandi. Back then, he was used to handling adversity—even being hit in the head by an object suspiciously dropped from a balcony was not enough to ruin his mood. He would never have told an injured fan to go to the RSPCA. One had to wonder whether Elton was in the throes of another post-cocaine-use depression.

The remaining Odeon shows passed without incident. The second half of the final show, on Christmas Eve, was simulcast on BBC television and radio. Elton was jovial and fun-loving. The camera revealed that he had gained weight, but this didn't prevent him from doing a now rarely seen handstand on the piano keys. His hair, or what could be seen of it from underneath the South American dictator's cap, was longer—sweaty and stringy by the time the broadcast joined him for "The Bitch Is Back." As usual, he wasn't shy about referring to his sexual preference, dedicating "Blue Eyes" to "all you gorgeous hunks out there." Later, he playfully changed some of the lyrics to "Crocodile Rock," singing, "Susie went and left me for some Choc Ice guy," a reference to one of his alter egos, Lord Choc Ice. Then Kiki Dee joined the band, singing with Elton on, among others, "Don't Go Breaking My Heart." Thus did the musician's 1982 world tour end.

"DID YOU THINK THIS FOOL COULD NEVER WIN"[88]

THROUGHOUT 1982, David Geffen signed one established recording act after another. In late spring, Neil Young joined; in the fall, Geffen's friend Joni Mitchell, who had been an Asylum artist since the 1970s, followed suit. It was a lean year for many record companies, but Geffen had managed to come out on top—no thanks to Young or Mitchell, or Elton or Donna Summer for that matter. The eponymous debut of the Geffen group Asia—which spent nine weeks at the top of *Billboard*'s Top LPs—was one of the year's two biggest sellers. Another big debut album for Geffen, *Quarterflash*, went platinum, and the Geffen soundtrack to the Broadway musical *Dreamgirls* reached number 11 and went gold. These successes put Geffen Records in the lead among its competitors.[89]

But Mitchell's first album for Geffen, *Wild Things Run Fast*, peaked at number 25 and didn't go gold. Geffen rejected the album Donna Summer recorded with Giorgio Moroder for 1982 release.[90] Summer's next Geffen release, *Donna Summer*, was produced instead by Quincy Jones. Like the singer's first Geffen album, *The Wanderer*, it was certified gold and produced one Top 10 hit. These achievements were good, but a far cry from her successive number 1 albums for Casablanca Records. (Tellingly, Summer's first Top 10 album since 1979, 1983's *She Works Hard for the Money*, would not be for Geffen, but for Mercury.)

The year 1983 would be a fairly good one for Elton, even if his standing with Geffen Records was questionable. It started quietly. He vacationed in Australia in January while Thomas supervised overdubs on *Too Low for Zero* in Los Angeles. On February 23, the musician attended his first Grammy Awards ceremony, at Los Angeles's Shrine Auditorium. He had received his thirteenth and fourteenth Grammy nominations that year—best pop vocal performance, male, for "Blue Eyes," and video of the year for *Visions*—although he still hadn't won a Grammy. He may have thought the time was finally ripe. If so, he was wrong. He watched as the two awards went to Lionel Richie for "Truly" and Olivia Newton-John's *Olivia Physical*, respectively.

On the eve of *Too Low for Zero*'s release, Elton was again contemplating Hollywood and films. The idea of doing a movie with Rod Stewart had resurfaced. He envisioned it as a bit like the uproarious 1959 Tony Curtis/Jack Lemmon comedy *Some Like It Hot*, with Rod and Elton dressing in drag. Elton expected filming to take place in the first quarter of 1984. More definite plans were cited for a romantic comedy, tentatively called *Hang-Ups*, to be directed by Blake Edwards, that Elton was sure he would begin with Liza Minelli in September. "It's a dual part—an English guy who works in New York and adopts an American alter ego," he explained. "I had to go to Hollywood to do a screen test for it and I was absolutely petrified. I threw up and everything."[91] He had been disappointed with the other movie roles he'd been offered. One would have paid him one hundred thousand dollars for four lines and two nude scenes. "With my body, you're not going to chance that," he joked, adding that the scripts he'd been getting until now were for "high-heeled, transvestite football chairmen." "Well, I'm not having it!" he declared in mock anger.[92]

Another of Elton's well-publicized aspirations was touring with Rod Stewart during the summer of 1984. Like the movie with Liza, this seemed a "sure thing." Almost exactly ten years earlier, Elton had contemplated a one-time charity show with Rod, when the raspy-voiced singer was still the Faces' front man,[93] but the concert never happened. Elton had instead launched Rocket Records in the United States and had helped Kiki finish recording her debut album for the label. Maybe it would be different this time.

In the immediate future, Elton was looking forward to a May–June trip to China with the Watford Football Club, which had advanced to the first division. As expected, Elton took comfort in China's unfamiliarity with his celebrity.[94] One of the players remarked during the trip, "I've never seen Elton looking so happy. It was a holiday for him. For a change, he wasn't mobbed like a pop star so he was able to relax."[95]

Watford played and won three matches against the Chinese national soccer team. By the end of the visit, Elton, who had told the press before the trip that he was going to China for the cause of soccer and not to perform, succumbed to his inclination to entertain. "That night, with eyes like two lumps of sweet-and-sour pork, Elton mastered his exhaustion and took to the piano to crown the farewell shindig," wrote author Martin Amis. "When Elton sang (not for a multitude but for his team) you felt the force, and proximity, of his talent; you didn't want it to end."[96]

"I'M A COMIN' BACK AGAIN"[97]

IN THE SPRING OF 1983, the first singles from *Too Low for Zero* were released in the United States and Britain. "I'm sure a hell of a lot of people don't care, but I think this is one of the best records we've ever made," Bernie Taupin said. "In the early days, it was easy for us to sell records, whether they were good or bad. Now we have a lot more to prove; the competition is very strong. But it's fun to put the gloves on and step back into the ring."[98] Elton was equally enthusiastic: "[T]here have only been a few times I've ever been totally confident about an album—*Yellow Brick Road*, maybe *Captain Fantastic*. And I've got that feeling again with this one," he said.[99]

In Britain, the lead single for the album was "I Guess That's Why They Call It the Blues." The first of two Top 10 hits in a row for Elton at home, "Guess That's Why" debuted on the singles chart on April 30 and reached number 5, enjoying a greater longevity, with its chart life of fifteen weeks, than any British single since "Goodbye Yellow Brick Road." In the United States, the single was "I'm Still Standing," debuting on May 7 at number 56 and making the Top 40 in its second week, the most played new record on the radio.[100] On July 9, the single reached its U.S. peak of number 12—admittedly doing no better than "Blue Eyes" or "Empty Garden," but the public was hearing a different side of Elton, one that rarely got played on the radio.

The videos for the two singles were directed by Russell Mulcahy in three to four days in the South of France. Apart from the innovative long-form video for *Visions*, Elton had done nothing until now to acknowledge the exponentially increasing power of MTV. His earlier videos for "Blue Eyes" and "Empty Garden" had only shown him sitting docilely at the piano, the only difference between the two being the backdrop (for "Blue Eyes" the South Pacific off the coast of Australia, for "Empty Garden" a brownstone facade with a few blowing leaves). But his two new videos were more innovative.

Mulcahy's "Guess That's Why" tells the touching story of the separation of a teenage couple during the 1950s due to the boyfriend's enrollment in military school. There, the teenage boy suffers a close-cropped haircut and loneliness as he and his girlfriend dream separately of each other. Elton is the narrator, appearing as a boater-topped serenader on an empty sound stage, and as a wig-wearing entertainer of bobby-soxers at the local dance. The video for "I'm Still Standing" was even better; it had him moving and mugging for the cameras, surrounded by attractive French dancers cavorting in body paint.

In Britain, the second single from *Too Low for Zero* was "I'm Still Standing"; it bested its immediate predecessor, peaking at number 4 following its chart debut on July 30. A third single, "Kiss the Bride," was released close on its heels on October 15 but only reached number 20.

In the United States, the second single was "Kiss the Bride," which did less well than in Britain. After an August 6 debut on the Hot 100, it peaked on October 1 at number 25. But regardless of the numbers, "Guess That's Why," "I'm Still Standing," and "Kiss the Bride" were still among the most exciting Elton John singles ever released.

The relatively lackluster performance of "Kiss the Bride" in Britain was not as disappointing as its performance in the United States. Elton had already drawn two Top 10 British singles in a row from the new album, but he had been waiting for another Top 10 single in the United States since 1980. The dichotomy between his British and U.S. successes was further accentuated by the stellar chart performance of *Too Low for Zero* in Britain. Debuting on the album chart on June 11, it peaked at number 7, becoming his first British Top 10 album since *A Single Man*. With a chart life of a whopping seventy-three weeks, it demonstrated almost as much staying power as his two most popular British albums of the 1970s, *Greatest Hits* and *Goodbye Yellow Brick Road* (with eighty-four weeks each). *Too Low for Zero* sold and sold and sold.

The story was different in the United States. As usual, the album met with mixed reviews. Elton's stature among critics, on the rise during his 1982 tour of North America, was still on the upswing in the spring–summer of 1983, but compliments were couched in qualifiers. For the supportive Robert Hilburn, *Too Low for Zero* was Elton's best album since *Blue Moves*. For *Hit Parader* magazine, the new album possessed a "consistency" absent from his last few collections.[101] Some reviewers, intent on minimizing his past accomplishments, pushed back the clock on the date of his last good album—for *People* magazine, *Too Low for Zero* was Elton's best since 1971's *Madman*.[102] For *Rolling Stone*, no album, including *Too Low for Zero*, was as consistent as Elton's second album, *Elton John*.[103]

Did David Geffen "torpedo" *Too Low for Zero* in the United States? The album peaked at number 25, following a June 11, 1983 chart debut. It wasn't certified gold for seven months. Its last American single, "I Guess That's Why They Call It the

Blues," may be what gave it new life, spurring it on to chart for a full fifty-four weeks. Still, Elton waxed nonchalant about his American record sales. "No matter how your records sell, if you're good on stage, people will come to see you. In the end, if people say you were a great performer, the records or the songs don't matter. That's all I ever wanted to be—a great performer."[104]

"THINGS CAN ONLY GET BETTER"[105]

"THE THOUGHT OF THE TWO OF THEM on the one stage together is nothing less than awesome," gushed Australia's Molly Meldrum about the possibility of an Elton–Rod Stewart tour. "They have been behind some of the major chart successes throughout the world in the past ten years and both of them are top performers." Meldrum reported that Elton was due to arrive in Australia in mid-January 1984 for a vacation, with Rod following by the end of the month for rehearsals.[106] Late February would see the kick-off for the joint tour.

Later in 1983, Meldrum had other news—the tour was off. "That's a great pity," he mourned. Rod had canceled. Meldrum thought the reason for Rod's backing out was a fear of being "upstaged" by Elton. As Meldrum put it, Elton had taken the "mickey out of Rod" during a joint television interview conducted just before the release of Rod's latest single, "Baby Jane."[107] During the interview, Elton's machine-gun delivery of zingers had allowed his friend only the meager duty of chalking up the witticisms. Concerning Rod's latest release, Elton had quipped that if it didn't do well, people could ask, "Whatever happened to 'Baby Jane'?"[108] Elton was disappointed with Rod's decision—and that Rod had relayed it impersonally, by telex.

Elton and Rod had just done a trial run of the show in South Africa's Sun City. Though now of little use, the trial run did lead to the reinsertion of "Candle in the Wind" in Elton's repertoire, and the introduction of an effortless segue from "Blue Eyes" to "I Guess That's Why They Call It the Blues" into the set list, where it would remain for the next three years.[109] The shows also led to trouble with opponents of apartheid. Elton's decision to go to South Africa may have been questionable, but in maintaining that it was no different from going to China, the Soviet Union, or any other country with political and economic oppression, he had a point. Politics and music don't mix, he insisted. But there were soon rumblings that he might be banned—along with Rod, Cliff Richard, Frank Sinatra, Barry Manilow, and Dolly Parton, among others—from certain British concert venues for having appeared in South Africa.

The Sun City shows also signaled that the movie *Hang-Ups* with Liza Minnelli was off, since filming would have been around the time he was in South Africa. The film with Rod Stewart was also canceled.

As Christmas approached, another single from *Too Low for Zero*, "Cold as Christmas," was released in Britain. But just as "Kiss the Bride" had been a relative commercial disappointment, so was this one. Charting on December 10, it peaked at number 33.

Greater fortune greeted the album's third U.S. single, "Guess That's Why." Americans took to it. Debuting on the Hot 100 on October 29, it slowly crept up the chart, nearing the Top 10 by Christmas Eve. Finally, on January 28, 1984, it peaked at number 4, during a six-week stay in the Top 10. The single was kept from rising further by the Romantics' "Talking in Your Sleep," Culture Club's "Karma Chameleon," and Yes's only number 1 hit, "Owner of a Lonely Heart." No matter. After three and a half years of waiting, Elton had his second American Top 10 hit of the 1980s.

"TURN ON THOSE SAD SONGS" [110]

ELTON HATED CHRISTMAS, a "bah humbug" attitude that seemed an outgrowth of his substance abuse. He decided to work on his next album at Montserrat's AIR Studios over the holidays. Bernie, Chris Thomas, and the band joined him again on this second artistic retreat in the space of little more than a year. The songwriting-recording method revitalized with *Too Low for Zero* was repeated, this time for an album to be called *Breaking Hearts*. It was an assembly line again. Elton would wake up early and begin working around 8:30 A.M., setting Bernie's lyrics to music on a Yamaha synthesizer accompanied by a drum machine. Bernie would continue to write and relay lyrics to his songwriting partner. By midday, the other band members would appear and recording (with Renate Blauel operating the tapes) would begin on Elton's new compositions. The process continued like this each day until about 8:00 P.M. [111]

Elton had great anxiety about recording *Breaking Hearts*. He knew what a success *Too Low for Zero* had been, and still was. "The pressure on me this time was unbelievable," he said months later, intimating that he might have run away from the project had he had the chance. [112] Instead, he opted for extra songs so he could easily decide which deserved to be on the album. [113]

The major difference between *Breaking Hearts* and *Too Low for Zero* was that, whereas the synthesizer had shaped most of the songs on *Too Low*, Elton frequently allowed Davey's electric guitar to take over on *Breaking Hearts*. Depending on one's perspective, this could be good or bad, but the ingenious mood sculpting in such songs as "Too Low for Zero" and "Crystal" was impossible once Elton left it to Davey to interpret the pianist's original synthesizer concepts. Elton's playing was mostly buried and, with only a couple of exceptions, the experimentation present on *Too Low* was mostly lost.

The first track on *Breaking Hearts* was "Restless"—which nearly became the name of the album. It had been a while since Elton had recorded a Rolling Stones tribute and this one seemed to fill the bill. "It sounds like something the Stones could be proud of," he said later.[114] It was also a track Elton could be proud of; it was a one-take number. For Bernie, "Restless" spoke of the state of the world, an indictment of American complacency in the face of supreme social challenges. "Well we could be children from the way we're acting/we feed ourselves lies and then we scream for action," Bernie, by this point a long-time resident of the United States, laments. "We just breed and we lose our nerve."

"Restless" may not rush by with herculean force like Elton's best-known rocker, "Saturday Night's Alright," but it is just as neatly carved and symmetrical, at a slower, rollicking tempo. Following the choppy patterns of Elton's synthesizer, which can be heard with some difficulty, Davey responds with identical patterns translated into hard-bitten guitar language, Dee supporting this musical toughness with an agreeable round of "ba-rump-a's" on the bass. Then Elton's voice enters, displaying his mastery of the rhythm and blues dialect with shadings not unlike those found in the overlooked "Chasing the Crown" from *21 at 33*. In suitably chafed tones, he roars a melody of disgust at the state of the world.

The next song, "Slow Down Georgie (She's Poison)," is a letdown. The lyrics are filled with trite phrases about sexist notions of women who sleep their way to success. The story is told from the perspective of a friend who tries to warn "Georgie" away from a scheming woman ("She's got you hypnotized, with her big brown eyes/and a body that could stop a clock"). Bernie may have meant to do what he had often done so well—step into the shoes of a distasteful character for an interesting first-person vignette—but the lyrics just sound obnoxious.

This would have been a perfect opportunity for Elton to dress Bernie's lyrics, and therefore hide them, in radically different music, but instead he applies a friendly, back-slapping melody to the words, compounding the insult. The band does a workmanlike job on the song, Elton's synthesizer disappearing after the first few bars, but Davey, Dee, and Nigel's backing vocals are schoolboyish and corny. The song's saving grace is Elton's lead vocal, a benchmark for the rest of the album, as adult and authoritative as the lyrics and melody are immature. He was moving ever so gradually away from the last vestiges of youthfulness in his voice; the muscle it carried was increasingly that of a man who could use his sinew with facility and wisdom.

Next, "Who Wears These Shoes?" is notable for more than just Elton's vocal. In a twist on Alfred Hitchcock's *Rear Window*, Bernie tells of a man who knows his girlfriend has been unfaithful because he's seen the whole thing through a lit, shadow-reflecting window. He wants to know who the man is.

This song is a precursor to the utterly thrilling dance-rock number written about four years hence, "I Don't Wanna Go On with You Like That." Elton's voice travels through "Who Wears These Shoes?" as rhythmically as a bass guitar, nimbly shifting between melodic plateaus and enunciating every last syllable in magnetic rhythm and blues sophistication. His scat-style ad-libbing, heard as the song fades ("I wanna know, wanna know, who wear these shoes? I got the blues, oo-hoo, I got the blues"), is the icing on an already tasty cake. Most of the instrumental duties are performed by Davey, Dee, and Nigel, but the effect is better than the instrumentation on "Slow Down Georgie." Davey's plucking is more conservative, and the overall structure of the song compensates for Elton's instrumental self-effacement. Live performances of the song during the upcoming world tour would more properly shine the light on some driving honky-tonk piano playing.

The fourth song on *Breaking Hearts* is its first ballad. On the surface, "Breaking Hearts (Ain't What It Used to Be)" sounds reflective, but a closer look shows it mocking the song's narrator mercilessly. A womanizer finally gets his comeuppance when he notices that the same women he used to take advantage of are now turning their backs on him ("Can't say I blame them all for being hurt/after all I treated each and every one like dirt"). Elton performs the farcically tragic melody alone at an acoustic piano with a light, classical touch. Adding to the amusement are the exaggerated, angelic backing vocals of the band. "Breaking Hearts" gets its point across.

The last song on side one, "Li'l 'Frigerator," suffers from many of the defects found in "Slow Down Georgie." The misogyny of the character Bernie creates may have been written as a springboard for that perfect rock song, but the lyrics would be better sung by a heavy-metal band than by Elton John. Again, someone is warning a friend to stay away from a cold, calculating woman. In the pedestrian melody, Elton finally found the simple rock song that had been eluding his grasp. Only the surreptitious vocal references to Jerry Lee Lewis and Little Richard, and a sax solo by Andrew Thompson of the Australian group Moving Pictures, keep this song from being a wasted effort.

Happily, the album gets better. The opener for side two is "Passengers," Elton's answer to critics of his South Africa sojourn. The lyrics are among Bernie's most intricate, sporting a dual metaphor. On the one hand, the "passengers" are black people of South Africa who are literally passengers on a train, traveling from desolate "homelands" to their jobs. On the other, these same people would prefer to be passengers on a symbolic train to freedom, but are held back by fear, repression, and inertia. "Company conductor/you need the salt of tears/falling on a ticket/that no-one's used in years," Bernie wrote. "The spirit's free, but you always find/passengers stand and wait in line."

Over a simple folk tune written by a South African, Phineas McHize, Elton—with some input from Davey—constructs an enjoyable sing-along that is part calm observation, part urgent awakening. McHize's tune is heard throughout via Elton's synthesizer, first clothed in the shininess of a penny whistle, then in the more traditional wrappings of the harmonium, as the song transitions from matter-of-fact storytelling to nervous admonition, with some delightful call and response segments ("Wanna get on, wanna get on/he wanna get on, he wanna get on"). The listener can hear the tragedy of racism in South Africa as experienced on a mundane, day-to-day level, and as met with the courage of community and the faintest hope that things would change.

The next song, "In Neon," is about broken dreams of a more personal nature, telling of a starstruck woman who leaves her home in the countryside to search for her fortune. "Behind a counter she stares out the window/up at the billboard that's like a reminder in neon," wrote Bernie. "Maybe a stranger could walk in and see her in neon." Musically, "In Neon" is in some ways a successor to "Roy Rogers" from *Goodbye Yellow Brick Road,* with its waltz structure and a melody that plays like a cool breeze from the countryside. Davey adds a mellow, country-influenced acoustic guitar to Elton's pessimistic instrumental refrain. Elton performs the latter on acoustic piano, but a bevy of other keyboard sounds, heard mostly as under-the-breath utterings, abound—electric piano, harpsichord, synthesized strings, and organ—in one of his most notable keyboard arrangements.

Disillusionment of another type is the subject of "Burning Buildings." A partner in a relationship now recognizes it as a "burning building" that he (or she) will have to leap from at his or her peril. An ominous piano introduction—outlined in synthesized horn with Davey adding some Spanish-flavored guitar—repeats between verses, suggesting waning romance. The band joins mid-verse for an early climax that, by the chorus, finds Elton belting out the desperation of the disillusioned lover, trying to escape fire and smoke as the flames lick at his (or her) clothing. Elton delves back into the Tin Pan Alley sound of the 1950s for this slowly heightening drama, as the band raises the volume with brushes of guitar and commanding drumming that bring the song to the present.

The next song, "Did He Shoot Her?," tells of an ex-boyfriend whose former lover has just been jilted by someone else. Feeling vengeful, the ex-boyfriend is ready to mete out justice. Of course, the "shooting" is not really a shooting, but a symbol of the devastation the new lover has wrought: "Did he shoot her/with his compromise/. . . /or did he hang her in a noose/on the telephone line?" Elton's music is full of fury. Choice slices of angry piano and synthesizer pairings, set against Latin rhythms and melody lines and an epochal guitar solo, evoke an impending shootout of words between imaginary cowboys.

Most of the numbers on *Breaking Hearts* are based on sad premises, and the last song on the album ties the whole package together. Coincidentally, "Sad Songs (Say So Much)" was born not of sadness, but of a fit of pique. Elton liked a country-and-western number he'd just written called "Here Comes Miss Hurt Again," and wanted it on the album. The prevailing view was that it didn't fit. He was in a "snotty mood," he later said, and angrily took another set of Bernie's lyrics to work on.[115] As he sat at his synthesizer, he laid eyes on a universal truth: "Guess there are times when we all need to share a little pain/and ironing out the rough spots/is the hardest part when memories remain/and it's times like these when we all need to hear the radio/cause from the lips of some old singer/we share the troubles we already know." Bernie, who "wrote [these lyrics] feeling a commercial element," had left Elton in the studio as the musician first saw the lyrics. Five minutes later, as Bernie entered his residence on Montserrat, he heard the telephone. It was Elton. The song was done. Bernie could barely contain his excitement upon hearing the music. "This is going to be number one all over the world!"[116]

Chris Thomas had wanted Elton to record fast-paced music for the lyrics,[117] but what emerged instead was a buoyant, mid-tempo celebration. Over a bedding of broad piano chords and chiming piano accents, with occasional interjections of some of the more unusual sounds the Yamaha could form, Elton sings his joyous tribute to the world's melancholy music, to which he had already contributed a sizeable portion. "Sad Songs" isn't sad, and that's the idea. Sad songs bring diverse groups of people together to communally share their grief. They learn they are not alone. "If someone else is suffering enough to write it down/when every single word makes sense/then it's easier to have those songs around."

At the time, Elton was more excited about the up-tempo numbers. "The up-tempo songs are the best things I've ever done," he said, upon arriving in Australia for overdubs and tour rehearsals. "I'm writing better songs, stronger songs."[118] It might have been more accurate to say that, despite some lapses in judgment, his songwriting was as strong as ever. Unfortunately, many of the tracks on *Breaking Hearts*—like many on *Too Low for Zero* and a good sampling of those on most of his other albums—would get buried, if they hadn't already, under the collective weight of Elton's overstuffed oeuvre. After momentary blips on the musical radar screen, or no blips at all, deserved attention would fade from such songs as "Breaking Hearts," "In Neon," and "Burning Buildings." All Elton could do was set his sights on another album.

CHAPTER 8

LONELY MAN[1]

(1984–1986)

IN NOVEMBER 1996, as Rosie O'Donnell and Elton John gabbed on her talk show, attention turned to Michael Jackson's second marriage, to Deborah Rowe, in Australia. "I got married in Australia," Elton recalled, and, unable to resist a dig at Jackson and himself, added, "All the loonies get married there!"

How Elton got married anywhere is a puzzlement for many, including him. "It was basically dishonest," he said. "I was so unhappy, I thought that any sort of change. . . . When you take a lot of drugs, and you're out to lunch half the time, you think a change of scenery . . . I'll get another house, I'll move to another country."[2]

Elton was adept at keeping his private hell private. "I thought at the time that he was a happy person and it turned out he wasn't," Rod once said. "I mean, I can drink and do my drugs but he could go all night, twenty-four hours, and I'd be like, 'Fuck, Elton, I'm going to bed,' and he's going, 'No, you're not, you're coming to Watford with me, we're playing Liverpool.' He'd go and have a shower, change, and come out as Mr. Director. I had an early warning system and he didn't."[3]

Despite the plethora of newspapers, magazines, and television and radio shows filled with Elton's daring post-1976 quotes about his sexual orientation, he got married. Eight months earlier, he'd jokingly told WNEW's Scott Muni that he lived in Britain because so many men there wear kilts: "And they don't wear anything under them, either!"[4] Years earlier, Elton had complained to David Frost that *People* magazine had given undue credence to his flippant statement about how often he had sex. He had said three times a week, and mostly with women. He was shocked that writer Fred Hauptfuhrer printed this—and, especially, that Hauptfuhrer had actually believed Elton mostly had sex with women.

True, he had sometimes engaged in a kind of fantasy of heterosexuality. "To be honest," he said in 1978, "I don't believe that I'm 100 percent gay, because I'm attracted to older women and therefore I can't dismiss that side of my character."[5]

But in a 1990s interview, when asked when he'd started "phasing" women *out of* his life, he said that, with Renate in 1984, he'd phased a woman *into* his life.[6]

Elton's trip to Sydney, Australia, in January 1984, to finish off *Breaking Hearts* and rehearse for his upcoming world tour, started normally enough. He was to remain there for three weeks to take care of business before flying to New Zealand to start the tour. Upon arriving in Sydney, he held a press conference for about a hundred reporters in a bar at the Woolloomooloo Bay Hotel. Wearing the requisite boater, a luxurious dinner jacket, and sparkling in diamonds, he enthused about his nearly completed album and strong working relationship with Bernie, and discussed prospects for a sixteen-year-old Australian, Jason Polak, just signed to Watford.[7]

But just after midnight on February 10, a week or so before the start of the tour, Elton dropped a bombshell. He was getting married on Valentine's Day—to his sound engineer! Before this, it had seemed to onlookers that he and Renate were friendly, but that was about it. The musician's Australian publicist, Patti Mostyn, was sitting with John Reid, Bernie, Australian promoter Kevin Ritchie, and a few others in the lounge of the Sebel Town House hotel when in walked Elton and Renate. The two had just eaten at an Indian restaurant.

"I was just getting ready to go home when Elt and Renate came in around midnight with their arms around each other, wandered over to us, and announced they were getting married," Mostyn later told a reporter. She and John Reid were "stunned." Bernie figured it was a prank. "He said, 'Oh yeah,' and went to bed," said Mostyn. When Ritchie telephoned his wife about the news, she advised him to "stop drinking immediately and come home," Mostyn recalled. They all realized something was really up when Elton and Renate retired to their separate rooms to telephone family and friends about the impending ceremony. Mostyn broke the news to the wire services at four A.M.[8] She had already had to arrange for the transport to Britain of a vintage 1928 green Melbourne tram, long since retired from service, which Elton had taken a fancy to and bought. And now this!

Elton and Renate left so little time for planning that they had to invite everyone they could by telephone, including their parents. Any friends who couldn't be reached weren't invited. A bigger hurdle was a little-known New South Wales (NSW) law, the Commonwealth Marriages Act, which required couples to wait a month following their engagement before marrying. The law sought to discourage hastily planned marriages between immature individuals. Elton and Renate applied for an exception. Elton was about to leave for New Zealand, and Renate had recording commitments elsewhere. The situation looked so precarious that Elton thought of having an offshore wedding, outside the reach of NSW authorities. Finally, on February 13, NSW Attorney General Paul Landa approved the wedding, saying the couple had given "good and cogent reasons" for an exception to the law.[9]

The press had a field day. Rumors that Elton still had a male lover led to speculation in the tabloids about sometime boyfriend Gary Clarke, who was with the musician's entourage. "I really don't think I should say anything," was all Clarke said.[10] But the press gave Renate ample opportunity to gush about her fiancé. "He's the nicest guy I've ever met," she said. "He's got a great sense of humor. He makes me laugh and he's very considerate." As for all the fuss about his sexuality, she responded, "I've heard of all sorts of stories about Elton and that he's supposed to be bisexual, but that doesn't worry me. I'm just feeling fabulous."[11] The German-born Renate seemed the antithesis of the rock star wife, with her girl-next-door looks and quiet demeanor. And, unlike some of Elton's past paramours, she was clearly smitten with him.

Elton's family was tickled. "He has had time to sow his wild oats and knows enough about what he wants out of life," his mother rejoiced. "He's got a lovely home in Old Windsor and everything that goes with it and now he's got a woman to go and live with him in it. I think he can start enjoying himself and enjoying life."[12] Elton's natural father, Stanley Dwight, said he was "delighted." But due to the short notice, neither Sheila and Fred Farebrother, nor Renate's parents, still living in Germany, could make the wedding. Nor could Rod Stewart, who was beyond reach in Hawaii.[13]

The excitement mounted outside St. Mark's, an Anglican church outside Sydney, on Valentine's Day afternoon. The wedding was set for six o'clock in the evening. About two thousand people of all ages gathered behind the barriers. The authorities had feared the crowd would be larger, but it wasn't, thanks to the rain. All was peaceful, despite one fan's boom box that kept blaring "Kiss the Bride," "Crystal," and "I'm Still Standing," and Watford fans waving the club flag.

It was still drizzling when Elton arrived twenty minutes early in a white tailcoat, horizontally striped shirt, lavender bow tie, and boater with lavender and yellow ribbons. Just in time, Renate pulled up, freshly adorned in white lace and baby's breath, and a heart-shaped pendant made of sixty-three diamonds that Elton had just given her. Inside the church, Kevin Ritchie stood in as Renate's father and gave her away. Reid was best man. Toni Taupin and Patti Mostyn were bridesmaids.

Upon emerging from St. Mark's, the newlyweds kissed as bulbs flashed and onlookers watched. As they boarded a white Rolls Royce dressed in ribbons, the crowd, straining for a glimpse, broke the barricades, some fans even sustaining injuries. Miles away, the Sebel Town House was the site of a reception for nearly one hundred guests, including Olivia Newton-John, Molly Meldrum, and comedian Barry Humphries (who, as his character Dame Edna, had once performed a song called "Every Mother Wants a Boy Like Elton"). They enjoyed an evening of gourmet food, French champagne and wines, a five-tier wedding cake, and the pre-jazz age music of the Edwardian Palm Court Orchestra. Roses, carnations, and lilies had been imported from New Zealand for the affair, and the letters "E" and "R," in honor of Elton and Renate, made an impressive ice sculpture.[14]

Elton provided much of the revelry at the reception (he later admitted to snorting lines of cocaine behind the scenes). As he and Renate stood together, he dashed off a series of one-liners that had everyone in stitches. At one point, he pretended to read a telegram, purportedly sent from Michael Jackson, which said, "I had to burn my hair to get on the front page, you only had to get married."[15] He also related a curious incident. As he'd left the church that evening, a man waiting outside had yelled, "Good on yer sport, you old poof, you've finally made it." Present was London *Sun* reporter Nick Ferrari, who dutifully noted the story. Shortly thereafter, Ferrari led his story in the *Sun* with the following headline:

GOOD ON YER, POOFTER![16]

A furious John Reid confronted Ferrari in a hotel lobby after the headline appeared, yelling, "Why did you do it? Why did you do it?" According to Ferrari, he tried to explain that the quote "caught the amusing and entertaining side of Elton's wonderful speech." A scuffle ensued. A description of this, too, appeared in *The Sun.*[17]

A week after the wedding, the dean of the Anglican church in Sydney was asked whether he'd known Elton was "bisexual." The dean suggested that Elton had probably put his homosexuality behind him.[18] London's *Sunday Mirror* tracked down the only other woman to whom Elton had been engaged, the former Linda Woodrow (now Sawford), who said Elton was "lousy in bed."[19] Another tabloid took to manufacturing innuendo about Renate who, until about February 10, had been an unknown. The *News of the World* found her male ex-roommate in London and quoted him as saying that they had shared an apartment for several years but had never slept together.[20]

For now, though, none of these mean-spirited whispers mattered. Elton John and Renate Blauel were now Elton and Renate John. Personal business taken care of, the musician could ready himself for the tour.

"THE WORLD IS YOUR OYSTER"[21]

ELTON'S *TOO LOW FOR ZERO* TOUR in New Zealand was met with protests by a local antiapartheid group that advised concertgoers he had been to South Africa in the face of a boycott. Protests followed him around Australia later in February and through March.[22] Nevertheless, ticket sales, finalized late the previous year, had been so brisk that these protests had negligible impact. In Sydney, three shows set for mid-March—with a total of twenty-eight thousand seats—sold out in twenty-four hours, with eighteen thousand tickets selling in Melbourne the same day for shows on February 28 and 29. Within five days, three more Sydney shows were added, bringing ticket sales in excess of fifty-five thousand; soon, another two shows were added. Three more concerts were added in Melbourne, and other March dates were set for Perth, Adelaide, and Brisbane.

The tour saw the addition of a new band member, Toronto, Canada native Fred Mandel. Mandel was a tall, thin fellow, not unlike James Newton Howard in his earnestness and the bushiness of his dark hair, as well as in his knowledge of keyboard electronics. Unlike James, he played guitar, too. Mandel had had extensive experience in rock circles since the mid-1970s, recording with former Guess Who member Domenic Troiano and later touring with Alice Cooper, Queen, and Supertramp. In testament to Elton's "elder statesman" status among rock'n'rollers, Mandel regarded him as an influence.

The predictably celebratory concerts, designed as retrospective surveys, had Renate dancing backstage—sometimes with Reid. Elton and the band opened with beloved "oldies" and a real rarity, "I'm Going to Be a Teenage Idol." Other treats included a whole line of tailcoats in different colors, with suspenders underneath to hold up baggy pants, bow tie–adorned striped shirts, and a series of color-coordinated boaters. Any tailcoat Elton chose had pinched shoulders and tapered tailoring to ingeniously hide his chubby frame, revealed only during "Bennie" and "Saturday Night's Alright" when, enthralled by the music, he would doff his jacket. With tails hanging neatly behind him on the piano bench as he played, and a boater covering his head, Elton's new image was that of Maurice Chevalier gone berserk. He promoted this image with bouts of premeditated insanity, "cured" only by going to the microphone at center stage to implore the audience into chants of "Bennie! Bennie!," or by participating in crawling contests with his guitar players. He would return to his piano from beneath, assaulting it while on his back, and climb atop it to goad on the crowds.

In Melbourne, members of the African National Congress Support Group and the Campaign Against Racial Exploitation picketed outside the shows. Protestors found him again in Adelaide, as well as in Perth. When asked by a reporter at Adelaide Airport to respond to charges that he shouldn't have gone to South Africa, he retorted, "I do not have anything to say on that. They are entitled to their opinion. I respect that opinion."[22]

In Brisbane, concert hysteria reached mid-1970s American proportions. "Whatever he did was rewarded with roars, cheers, gasps, prolonged and powerful applause, and the odd scream of approval," wrote Peter Dean. "Swaying arms and bodies moved in time to the pounding beat and the newlywed pop star had only to play a few notes of 'The Wedding March' to draw a thunderous reaction."[23] In Sydney, Elton was awarded a gold key to the city and a boater with a City Council hatband by the Lord Mayor Doug Sutherland.

Renate, who had left Australia for London after the Melbourne shows, returned for the long Sydney stint. The final show at the Sydney Entertainment Centre, performed on the eve of Elton's thirty-seventh birthday and dubbed his "Thank You, Australia" concert, was televised across Australia and simulcast on radio. It was such an anticipated event that it forced the popular television show *Hey Hey It's Saturday Night* forward an hour and a half. A record-breaking six million viewers tuned in, so many that one newspaper columnist surmised they were the cause of a power surge that night. The Nine Network's Mike Walsh, who hosted the concert on television, noted that Elton had already played to more than three hundred thousand people in Australia during the tour, with another twelve thousand at the Entertainment Centre that night.[24]

Late in the evening, the twelve thousand fans sang "Happy Birthday" to their favorite British star. Molly Meldrum, in his finest Outback cowboy hat, joined Elton onstage for "Crocodile Rock," and even took a turn at the microphone for some "wa-wa-wa's" (instead of the song's "la-la-la's"). After the show, Elton jumped into a limousine where Renate, already inside, covered his face in kisses. The tour would arrive in Hong Kong shortly.

"HE MUST HAVE SENSED ADVENTURE"[25]

AFTER TOURING HONG KONG and putting the last touches to *Breaking Hearts* in Britain, Elton slipped behind the Iron Curtain for visits to Yugoslavia, Hungary, Czechoslovakia, and Poland. Although his trip to South Africa had been lucrative, his visit to Eastern Europe a half year later, where the tour began on April 17 in Sarajevo, was not. It was, however, rich in experience gained while furthering his mission: to bring people together through music.

While in Gdansk, Poland, Elton had an exclusive visit with Lech Walesa, leader of the Solidarity trade union, the populist opposition against Communist rule that had captured the imagination of the world. A flock of reporters followed Elton into Walesa's apartment. The musician nervously waited in the living room for his host; the idea of secret police interfering with the meeting had crossed his mind. When Walesa appeared, all fears vanished. "For me, it's a great honor to meet someone who's won the Nobel Prize," Elton announced.[26] He let Walesa wear his Stetson. They exchanged autographs. This was all the reporters saw; they were excused before the two men engaged in private discussions. Walesa later said they spent an hour talking about soccer.[27]

Walesa attended Elton's show in the Olivia Hall, site of the 1981 Solidarity Congress, where he took a seat near the stage, courtesy of Elton. "Long live Walesa," chanted supporters before the concert started. When Elton appeared, he flashed the Solidarity symbol, "V" for "victory," in tribute to his special guest. After the performance, Walesa said of his meeting with Elton, "I liked him, I tried to put him at his ease." About the show he was more circumspect. "It has been marvelous—but I think I have very sensitive ears—I can still hear a loud buzzing noise in my ears."[28]

After the dates in Poland, the "European Express" tour, as it was now called, took off in Western Europe, hitting major cities in Sweden, Italy, Spain, Germany,

Switzerland, France, Austria, Ireland, and Britain, with a final blast set for Wembley Stadium on June 30. "Really, what we've been doing is consolidating ourselves in Europe," he explained, "because up to '76 we only played in the USA, Australia, Japan, and Great Britain."[29] A highlight of the shows was "I'm Still Standing," which latched onto a frenetic run-as-if-your-life-depends-on-it sequence that had Elton combining pastoral—if musclebound—reflections with saloon piano statements and Jerry Lee Lewis flourishes as the band frantically throttled their instruments.

The tour was not without incident. At one of the Italian shows, Elton walked in the pitch blackness to what he thought was the stage's edge to say hello to someone. Walking too far, he fell down twelve feet. The ensuing bruises and fright didn't keep him from the encores. "I was extremely lucky," Elton later remembered. "I didn't break anything!"[30]

The tour was also injected with another kind of excitement: Elton's Watford Football Club had made it to the FA Cup Final—the English Superbowl of soccer.

"SUCH CRUEL SPORT FOR YOUR KICKS"[31]

FOR SOME TIME NOW, everything had been looking rosy for the Watford team. Back in February 1984, right after Elton's wedding, it had made the quarter-finals. By the time Elton and the band were playing in Eastern Europe, Watford had emerged from the semi-finals with an important win that landed it on the road to Wembley for the FA Cup Final, and Coach Graham Taylor had agreed to an extended contract.[32]

The rival for the final match was Everton. Shortly beforehand, Elton was interviewed backstage at an amphitheater in Berlin for BBC-TV. "This has been the longest week of my life," he said anxiously. He was glad that he hadn't been home in the days leading up to the match, as he'd have been besieged by the press. "I've been fortunate—I've been out of the country, so I've been able to dodge everybody," he observed with relief, as he walked through a tunnel leading to the stage—followed by cameras. Before his bows, he sent this televised message to British viewers: "All best wishes to the Everton team and their supporters, because they've had a marvelous season."[33]

Elton interrupted the tour to return to England for the big match on May 19. Sharing the Royal Box at Wembley Stadium with Renate, he wore a striped double-breasted suit and a Stetson for the occasion. For the traditional singing of "Abide with Me," he removed the Stetson, so moved by the song that day that he wept. When the game was over, the day was more special for Everton. Watford lost, 2–0.

"IT FEELS SO GOOD TO HURT SO BAD"[34]

"SAD SONGS" CHARTED IN BRITAIN ON MAY 26, days after Everton walked away with the FA Cup. It peaked at number 7, becoming Elton's third Top 10 British hit in the span of one year. The last time that had happened at home was between November 1972 and October 1973, when he had had four Top 10 hits with "Crocodile Rock," "Daniel," "Saturday Night's Alright," and "Goodbye Yellow Brick Road." "Sad Songs" stayed on the singles chart for twelve weeks, placing it firmly in a league with his other major British hits.

In the United States, "Sad Songs" debuted on the Hot 100 at number 49 on June 9, 1984, Elton's highest debut of the 1980s. Whereas it often took weeks for one of his singles to break into the Top 40, this one did so in its second week. Perhaps the success of "I Guess That's Why They Call It the Blues" had given him chart momentum, or maybe some radio programmers were reacting to the mainstream vibes of Elton's recent marriage. Whatever the reason, "Sad Songs" was in the Top 10 by July 21. On August 11, it peaked at number 5. It couldn't catch up to Ray Parker, Jr.'s "Ghostbusters" or the red hot Prince's "When Doves Cry," or Elton's fast favorite, Tina Turner's "What's Love Got to Do with It," but he now had his second Top 5 single in a row in the United States. The last time that had happened was 1975, at the height of his popularity there.

"IT'S TIMES LIKE THESE WHEN WE ALL NEED TO HEAR THE RADIO"[35]

IN THE WEEKS LEADING UP to the Wembley finale on June 30, Elton and the band were all over the British Isles. The Wembley date—called the Summer of '84 Concert—would mark Elton's first live appearance at the stadium since 1975. There were similarities between the two appearances. The Wembley show of 1975 had had an extensive lineup of acts that began taking the stage in late morning, well before Elton. In 1984, too, a large lineup was scheduled to lead into Elton's performance— Wang Chung, Nik Kershaw, Kool and the Gang, and Paul Young.

But this time, none of the supporting acts would do what the Beach Boys had done so surprisingly in 1975—upstage the headliner. Elton wasn't planning to devote half the show to a new album. In an interview more than a month earlier in Munich, he'd been asked whether playing the stadium would be especially nervewracking. "Yes, I think so. And that's why I love doing them [these kinds of concerts]," he said. "In every tour you have to do a prestige gig because it lifts you."[36]

The Wembley show was indeed a "prestige gig." BBC Radio One had extensive coverage planned from one o'clock in the afternoon on, with a veritable army of broadcasters in tow. At 7:30 P.M., it was time for Elton. Dressed in a black and white tailcoat and trousers, a white-banded boater, white shirt, black bow tie, and white shoes, he was the very picture of night and day, and appropriately so, as he would be starting in daylight and ending in darkness.

The show began backstage, as Elton—surrounded by an entourage, including his manager—nimbly jogged toward his piano from the wings, seemingly every bit as fit for a musical round as a boxer for the next bout. Although Elton and the band began as always with "Tiny Dancer," it was anything but a usual performance. Controlled by the music, Elton's body rocked as he played, his face a bottomless reservoir of moods—glee, mischievousness, concentration, mock anger, intense exertion. During "Rocket Man," he added the plaint, "I'm spending my life spinning around in circles," followed by concentric piano patterns in dialogue with Davey's guitar, followed by a rocking interlude with Elton and Fred trading off piano and organ quips. Later, Elton sang "Don't Let the Sun Go Down on Me" as if he expected the sun to go down on him (as the real sun set), while providing an expansive piano treatment that more completely than ever evoked the pivotal crossroads the protagonist in the song faces.

The performance of "Bennie" was a concert in itself. Elton projected a stylish, nightclub attitude that became a rock-club sneer as he sang: "You know I'm talkin' 'bout Bennie! And there ain't no one better than Bennie and the Jets—no, no!" Some songs later, the pianist, drenched in sweat, readied himself for his "Kiss the Bride" exertions. Seated, he leaped high into the air after each cry of "I wanna kiss the bride—yeah!" until his knees were level with the piano's top. He made each jump look easy.

The sun had long since set when the encores began. For these, Elton shed the black and white tails for a red tailcoat. "Your Song," dedicated to the thousands of concertgoers with a plaintive new solo piano introduction, surprised them. Soon came the frightening machine-gun pounding of "Saturday Night's Alright," which subsided into a fairy-dusted "Goodbye Yellow Brick Road," but returned with some artful ducking and dodging for the medley of "Whole Lot of Shakin'," "I Saw Her Standing There," and "Twist and Shout." Then Elton perched a leg on the piano, mugged victory, and was gone. The musical boxing bout was over, his seventy thousand sparring partners having loved every minute of it.

"HE WANNA GET ON"[37]

BREAKING HEARTS entered the British album chart at number 2 on June 30; in Australia, it entered at number 1; in the United States, it peaked at number 20. Americans didn't embrace the album the way their counterparts overseas did, although they did buy enough copies of it to prompt a gold certification in less than two months, the only time this would happen for Elton while under contract to Geffen.

The hits kept coming. By midsummer, Elton had a second British hit from *Breaking Hearts*: "Passengers," which charted on August 11 and reached number 5. The single may have benefited commercially from a Simon Milne–directed video as innovative as the "I'm Still Standing" clip. Russell Mulcahy's video for "Sad Songs" was good, with Elton playing everything from a raincoat-wearing bringer of good tidings to desolate streets, to a cherubic, red tailcoat–clothed singer in an empty club, to a hobo in ripped garments seated in a garbage-strewn alley inhabited by homeless violinists. But the "Passengers" video was better. Its antiapartheid message suggested the transplantability of different races into diverse cultures, with dexterous dancers in half-black, half-white faces poised and on the move in grasshopper stances, ready to adopt yet another set of alien mores. Elton, boater cocked, was the cross-cultural facilitator, leading the strange dancers down an old European street.

"I FEEL LIKE AN OLD JUKEBOX" [38]

ELTON TOOK ADVANTAGE of a month and a half break between British and American tours to rewrite "Sad Songs" with Bernie in St.-Tropez. Sasson Industries had agreed to sponsor Elton's North American tour, and the fashion-conscious pianist thought "Sad Songs" and Sasson were a logical pairing. A commercial was the thing to do. "The thing that grabbed Elton was how easily the song lent itself [to promoting Sasson]," publicist Sarah McMullen explained. "He wasn't thinking about selling out." [39]

A television commercial and a promotional gimmick tied Sasson purchases to Elton John concert tickets. In certain regions, Sasson jeans sales went up by 300 percent. In Tampa, where shoppers at a Maas Brothers store were told that a thirty dollar purchase of Sasson items would yield a free ticket, fourteen hundred pairs of jeans were purchased in ninety minutes. [40]

While in St.-Tropez, the music-fan-cum-jingle-writer met a pair of young English musicians who had been taking Britain by storm since 1982. Collectively, they were known as Wham! Separately, they were George Michael and Andrew Ridgely. As Wham!, they had already amassed five Top 10 singles and a number 1 album in Britain. They also held feelings of awe for the Pinner pianist. George Michael would later recount how, when he was barely in his teens, he would rush to buy the latest Elton John album on the day of release and, when he got home, play it again and again. [41] Elton, too, felt a charge in meeting Michael and Ridgely. He thought the two youngsters possessed the "vitality" he and Bernie had had at their age. [42]

Meanwhile, the man who lived to perform was harboring misgivings about the punishing two-and-a-half-month North American schedule that loomed large from August 17 through early November. It seemed as though Elton would be everywhere, including five nights in faraway parts of Canada. As he had during a confused period in 1977, Elton began making noises about coming off the road for good. On opening night at Arizona State University, Elton blurted that the tour would be his last. [43]

Elton clarified this rash statement for Robert Hilburn in his San Diego dressing room two nights later. "I think by the end of these shows I'll have had enough," Elton said. "The band and I have been on the road since the beginning of the year, and it has convinced me that I ought to move on. I want to break away from the rock'n'roll cycle. Instead of spending months on the road, I'd like the freedom to do a few shows with an orchestra or maybe work with just one other musician." [44]

But there was more on Elton's mind than that. There was that Broadway musical he hoped to write, though in 1981 he had sung a different tune, insisting that musicals were of little interest to him. "I can't stand them," he had told Scott Muni, adding that he had found *A Chorus Line* a colossal bore. But the changeable Elton had changed his mind. He also told Hilburn he had approached impresario David Geffen about a part in the movie version of *Little Shop of Horrors.* And finally, he hinted that working on his marriage was an important goal. "Renate and I haven't been able to see much of each other," he admitted, "but we knew it'd be like this because I had this tour planned and I don't think the road is a nice life for anybody." She would be joining him for the Los Angeles shows a couple of days later.[45]

San Francisco Chronicle rock critic Peter Stack didn't buy the retirement rumblings. "I definitely never trust popular singers when they say they're going to retire just before they come to town to give a concert," he snorted.[46] Certainly, the quality of Elton's performances didn't betray an alternate plan. He seemed just as motivated as he had for other tours. He unveiled more outfits, looking positively radioactive in a Day-Glo, rainbow-colored combination of windbreaker, trousers, and military cap, and sporting a Vegas-y rootin' tootin' cowboy getup in gold lamé with a ten-gallon hat.

The set list changed a little. "Levon" was back for the first time since the 1970s. "He shall be Levon!" became the mantra as Elton's full-bodied pianism excavated the song's underlying melodic layers, Davey's guitar reinterpreting the old Buckmaster arrangement. "Li'l 'Frigerator," which varied little from the record except for Elton's 1950s-style piano playing, joined "Restless" and "Sad Songs" as the selections from *Breaking Hearts.* "Who Wears These Shoes?" (the new American single) was a welcome addition midtour, bringing the *Breaking Hearts* track count to four.

"Who Wears These Shoes?" debuted in the United States on *Billboard's* Hot 100 on September 8, 1984, while "Sad Songs" was still in the Top 40; the following week, they traded places. On November 3, just as the tour was winding down, "These Shoes" peaked at number 16. Elton didn't get that third U.S. Top 10 hit in a row—something he hadn't had since 1975—but how could he complain? Until recently, he wasn't getting any Top 10 hits at all.

The sold-out tour had critics nearly united about some things, such as his voice. In reviewing the first of three shows at Los Angeles's Forum, Iain Blair of *The Hollywood Reporter* reported that Elton's "vocals sounded stronger than ever."[47] Wrote Boo Browning for *The Phoenix Gazette,* "Elton wowed a packed house with pure charisma and a voice so taut and sinewy it sounded like Sylvester Stallone had given it a workout."[48] As for Elton's playing, Blair found it "crisper."[49] *San Francisco Chronicle* critic Peter Stack was unrestrained in his compliments, effusing, "What I like most about the guy is that he's a piano man, the best rock and roll piano man that ever lived. . . . He went at it as though he were half Elvis and half Jerry Lee, and then added a whole other half that drew from the entire history of blues, gospel, and boogie."[50] Elton was also becoming known again for some retrospective antics, like demolishing his piano bench and handing audience members the pieces.

As usual, the tour was not all smooth sailing. Aspects of Elton's private life were bound to catch up with him. Besides the substance abuse, from which he sometimes took a hiatus, there was his biggest secret, bulimia, a disorder that would hold him captive for years. Elton had never been able to shed doubts about his physical appearance and, since it was widely known that he read his reviews, these feelings must have been exacerbated by some critics' comments. In 1980, one reviewer observed that Elton "would change into a blue cowboy hat, running shoes, and a satin-like exercise suit that showed, far too clearly, his excess poundage, both fore and aft."[51]

In October, the musician was stricken with a terrible case of the flu and had to postpone shows in Charlotte, Tampa, and Miami, something he had never done before. "I couldn't stand up, let alone go on stage," he remarked a couple of weeks later. These shows would be made up later in November.[52] When the week arrived for his stint at Madison Square Garden, from October 23 through 26, he was obviously still sick. One night, following a performance of "Restless," Elton knelt on the stage as he sometimes did, to catch his breath and take in the ovation before the next number. But this time, he failed to stand up and was administered oxygen for half a minute before the show resumed.[53]

The pianist needed more than oxygen to perform on the next night. That afternoon, he showed up at New York's Hard Rock Cafe for WNEW's seventeenth birthday celebration, hosted by Scott Muni. It was apparent to listeners that the musician should have been far away, resting in bed. He sounded drained and his voice was so muted that his usual garrulousness was missing. When asked about the status of Rocket Records, which had had few successes beyond Elton's foreign recordings, he mumbled, "When I die, that [Rocket Records] folds. It's been kind of winding down. I don't really have the time to take an interest in it. I've been busy enough for the last three to four years." He played a limited "EJ the DJ" role, introducing three songs he loved that would not ordinarily have fit a WNEW playlist— Wham!'s "Wake Me Up Before You Go-Go," Chaka Khan's Prince-penned "I Feel for You," and Tina Turner's "What's Love Got to Do with It." Then he murmured, "I kind of feel like I'm going to pass out any second." After the commercial break, he was gone. That night he was a no-show at the Garden.[54]

By his last scheduled concerts at the Worcester, Massachusetts Centrum in early November, Elton was fully recovered. Singing through the flu mustn't have harmed his voice, which seemed as vibrant as ever. He was back to his old self, smashing his piano bench and handing out pieces like treats to the audience and, as one reviewer put it, "jumping on top of his piano, heaving his coat into the front seats, and dancing around like a caged bear running amok."[55] The following month, as if to cap off an amazing twelve months for Elton, the cable channel Showtime broadcast a 105-minute version of the June 30 Wembley show (which would be split up into two videos and sold commercially within the next two years).

Meanwhile, a universe away, Jeanne White of Kokomo, Indiana, learned that her thirteen-year-old son Ryan, a hemophiliac, had a disease called AIDS.

"THE TOUCHES OF GLAMOUR" [56]

WHILE ELTON WAS IN THE UNITED STATES simultaneously playing to sell-out crowds and fighting off the flu, a third single from *Breaking Hearts* was released in Britain, one that would be his worst-selling single there since the non-charting "All Quiet on the Western Front." "Who Wears These Shoes?," which had gotten a fair reception by Americans, got virtually none at home. The single charted on October 20, 1984 and peaked at number 50.

A fourth British single from the album did worse. The title track was released in honor of Elton's one-year wedding anniversary, but a chart debut on March 2, 1985 yielded a peak of only number 59. Still, Elton had already had two Top 10s from *Breaking Hearts,* something the album, like *Too Low for Zero* before it, had been mysteriously unable to do in the United States. A third U.S. single from *Breaking Hearts,* "In Neon," managed only to crack the Top 40 at number 38 on January 12, 1985, seven weeks after its debut on the Hot 100.

By January 1985, Elton was at Woodside, thinking about his next album. In four days, he wrote eighteen songs in his home recording studio. He had been looking forward to a break but, as he admitted, "I can't sit still for very long."[57] As Elton pondered his career's direction, he took time out to honor George Michael on March 13 at the Ivor Novello Awards in London. This was also his chance to unveil a new, rather grotesque look. With a black coat, a white carnation-adorned black hat, large dark sunglasses in blue frames, and, strewn about his neck, a floppy red ribbon and what looked like a dozen strings of pearls, he resembled a sibling of Morticia Addams—a jolly, flamboyant undertaker.

"George is the greatest songwriter of his generation," Elton bubbled as the presenter for Michael's best songwriter award. "It's very rare that one meets a major songwriter in the tradition of Paul McCartney and Barry Gibb. He deserves to win this award and I'd like to work with him in the future."[58] Elton had been very impressed with the twenty-one-year-old George Michael who, as the songwriter and lead singer in Wham!, already had three years of hits behind him. Thinking back to his early days when a successful record seemed but a dream, Elton mused, "At twenty-one, I was a hopeless mess." He effused about Michael's singing, too, asserting, "His voice, technically, is way ahead of mine."[59]

"DO YOU COUNT THE STARS AT NIGHT?" [60]

IN A MAY 1985 INTERVIEW WITH SCOTT MUNI, broadcast live from London as a treat for New York-area listeners, Elton said, without elaborating, "I've had my problems with Geffen Records." Perhaps to avoid further controversy, he added, "And they've had their problems with me." Muni didn't ask for an explanation, but this omission could be excused. Elton may have been a bit stingy with words during their last interview in October, when he was flu-stricken, but he was back to his old self now. The disc jockey could barely get a word in as Elton expounded upon the relative musical merits of David Bowie, Bryan Ferry, and Madonna, the generosity of John Lennon, Yoko Ono's influence over his godson Sean, and more. He also talked about his new album. Eighteen tracks were recorded already, a new single was on the verge of release, and he wanted to write another few songs. He was bursting with excitement over the songs and his new musicians.[61]

Nigel and Dee were gone again. During the last tour, Nigel had said of touring, "It's like brothers and sisters traveling together."[62] He had spoken too soon; the family ties were cut when the restless head of the brood wandered in search of a surrogate unit. Elton's thinking was that the musical sameness of a certain pair of "brothers" had contributed to his tiring of live performance by the time the tour hit American shores. "It was time for a change from Nigel and Dee, rhythm section-wise," he said. "They're great guys, but I needed another rhythm section."[63] Inspired by Tina Turner's *Private Dancer*, a favorite recent album that employed several rhythm sections, Elton believed that he needed not one, but a few, new rhythm sections. From these, he settled on a drummer and bass player he liked enough for his new touring band, since it was just a matter of time before he reneged on his vow to cut back live performances.

The rhythm sections on the album that would become *Ice on Fire* were diverse. One included drummer Charlie Morgan—who had played with Air Supply, Cyndi Lauper, and French pianist Richard Clayderman—and bassist Paul Westwood. Another had drummer Dave Mattacks, of Fairport Convention, and bassist David Paton, recently a member of the Alan Parsons Project (and who had had success in the 1970s as a member of the Scottish band Pilot, which had an American Top 10 single with "Magic" and a British number 1, "January"). A third rhythm section had Queen's Roger Taylor and John Deacon. The fourth rhythm section included Mel Gaynor, the drummer for Simple Minds, and Deon Estus, a bass player for Wham! (Elton loved that bass line on "Wake Me Up Before You Go-Go").

Ice on Fire marked the return of Gus Dudgeon. Chris Thomas wasn't available. He was about to fly to Australia to work with INXS. Elton then asked producer Trevor Horn, who was interested, but busy. "So I ended up with Gus," Elton bemusedly told Muni.[64] He sensed it was just like old times, despite the involvement of different rhythm sections and a multitude of guest musicians.

Kiki and sometime solo artist Pete Wingfield were along for some backing vocals, as was Sister ("We Are Family") Sledge. The latter was corralled by Elton and spirited into the studio when he learned the group was performing in England. Raunchy soul singer Millie Jackson was recruited the same way. Avowed Elton John fan Nik Kershaw, who had been on the bill at Wembley the previous June, played some guest guitar. "He [Elton] doesn't believe me, but the first record I ever bought was 'Your Song.' So he's always been a hero of mine," said Kershaw.[65] Onward International Horns, comprised of David Bitelli, Paul Spong, Raul D'Oliveira, and Rick Taylor, were on hand for some biting brass work. James returned for string arrangements. As Elton hoped, George Michael dropped by. And Davey and Fred, retained from the "old" band, also left their mark. Missing was Renate. Instead, Stuart Epps did the recording.

These various guests were more than session musicians. After two band-oriented albums, Elton returned to the concept of elaborate ensembles, the use of different combinations of musicians carefully calculated to achieve certain musical effects.

Out of the great stew of talent present for the *Ice on Fire* sessions came an unexpectedly unified musical theme. Some songs are funky, some fun, some introspective, some campy, but they all share a jagged-edged streetwise soul, in this, Elton's first genuine soul album of the 1980s. The album may lack panoramic ballads, cleverly synthesizer-laced melancholia, sentimental jazz balladeering, or gut-wrenching tragedy. It may also lack rock'n'roll rave-ups. But *Ice on Fire* makes the foot tap uncontrollably, and the heart beat in time to Elton's percolating rhythm and blues melodies.

The most notable song on *Ice on Fire*, "Nikita," is a musical sequel to that most divine of Elton's symmetrically beautiful ballads, "Daniel." The song makes a compelling case against the Cold War by examining its impact on the ordinary Soviet citizen. At the time, Ronald Reagan had just been sworn in for a second term as president of the United States. He dubbed the Soviet Union the "evil empire," although not everyone shared this view. Elton had toured the Soviet Union in 1979 and had experienced the warmth of the Russians firsthand, "evil empire" notwithstanding.

"Nikita" is popularly regarded as a love song to a Soviet woman, and the video portrays Nikita as a female love interest. But "Nikita" is a male Russian name. He ("I saw you by the wall/ten of your tin soldiers in a row") needs some companionship and understanding ("Just look towards the west and find a friend"). Most appealing is the lyrics' illumination of the appellation "Cold War." "Hey Nikita, is it cold in your little corner of the world?" asks the song's Western dreamer. "You could roll around the globe, and never find a warmer soul to know." The Westerner notices Nikita's eyes, "that looked like ice on fire," and his heart, "a captive in the snow."

This ballad bears the same markings that made its predecessor, "Daniel," and close relative "Little Jeannie," instantly special. The gem-like but changeable melodic pattern sounds, at first hearing, as familiar as a centuries-old song. A wistful synthesizer solo sums up the pain of the isolated Nikita. Unlike "Daniel," however, "Nikita" lacks Elton's falsetto. This song, and the others on *Ice on Fire*, are marked by a different sort of Elton John voice altogether. "I think I'm a better ballad singer," he remarked after the album's completion, "but I think I'm becoming a much better singer, per se, anyway."[66] Evident on the songs are a huskier timbre and more impressive control of his range's lower end.

Also distinguishing "Nikita" is its buoyant tempo, aided by Nik Kershaw's bubbly electric guitar phrases, intelligent bass guitar commentary by David Paton, Dave Mattacks's up-tempo drumming, and Elton's wind chime–inspired broken chord accents on the "GS piano"—plus a well-hidden drum machine. Also different from "Daniel" are the backing vocals. On "Daniel," Elton backed himself alone. On "Nikita," his backing vocals are joined by the voices of George Michael and Davey, the former providing the soaring, sweet accompaniment Elton was no longer doing.

The second song on *Ice on Fire* with the Paton-Mattacks rhythm section is "Tell Me What the Papers Say," an irreverent, toe-tapping ditty about the tabloids' obsession with the latest scandal. Elton, a voracious newspaper reader, marveled at how often he read stories about himself that weren't true. "Basically, [the song says] that most newspapers are lying bastards," Elton explained.[67]

Unlike *The Fox*'s "Heart in the Right Place," which marries Elton's bitter blues to Gary Osborne's appropriately angry lyrics about bloodthirsty gossip columnists, here Elton takes Bernie's cynical words about the press, adds the musician's penchant for irony, *et voilà!*, a mocking, good-time party tune is born. With Elton on acoustic piano throwing out an amalgam of Jerry Lee Lewis and Little Richard riffs, Fred synthesizing a humorous, big-band horn arrangement on electronic keyboard, and Paton and Mattacks battling for the more pronounced celebratory percussive statements, the music is exhilarating and addictive. Backing vocals parked midway between Las Vegas and Memphis are skillfully rendered by Kiki and Davey, along with Pete Wingfield, Katie Kissoon, and Alan Carvell.

The last Paton-Mattacks pairing on *Ice on Fire* is "Candy by the Pound," Bernie's lyrics describing the sweetness of a new relationship. Although he wasn't one to write upbeat love songs—"Who wants to hear a happy love song?" he once asked[68]—he also disliked mundane song titles that might read "My Heart Got Broken" or "I Love You."[69] So "Candy" takes the ordinary, upbeat love song one step further ("You can tell everybody that this girl of mine/is sweeter than the grapes hanging from the vine/love like wine honey drinkin' till I drown/keep it comin' baby like candy by the pound").

Elton thought "Candy" reminiscent of an old Miracles song.[70] But he didn't sing it in the high, warbly voice for which Smokey Robinson was known. Singing the skulking melody instead in a deep, weathered voice, Elton suggests that this vaunted love affair may not be for everyone. The clicking and popping of the Paton-Mattacks rhythm section and the sophisticated glow of the Onward International Horns informs the song's lack of innocence.

Mel Gaynor and Deon Estus appear on three *Ice on Fire* tracks: "Soul Glove," "Satellite," and "Act of War." Like "Candy by the Pound," "Soul Glove" celebrates a passionate affair, using a tight-fitting glove to illustrate the compatibility of the happy couple ("And slip into my soul glove/pull it on we got a tight fit/oh never take it off"). The song's title also provides a clear musical direction for Bernie's songwriting partner. This was to be a *soul* number, as if Elton weren't so predisposed. The song was originally written for Kiki, but Elton decided to keep it. "How generous!" he later joked. "And then she sang [backing vocals] on it! It's called 'torturing your friends.'"[71]

The melody for "Soul Glove" is more well-adjusted than that for "Candy." Here there is no slinking around, just an open declaration of mutual affection, heralded by the announcement of the Onward International Horns. Rather than click and pop, the Gaynor-Estus rhythm section adds a softer texture.

"Satellite" is a soul song with a different message, the "satellite" an inadequately responsive lover who keeps tempting the protagonist, then pulling back, as if in an orbit of her own making ("Are we there/is this love/is this a space race/that we're both part of"). "Satellite" is delectably funky. It begins with a bubbly Kershaw guitar riff chopped off by blasts from Elton's synthesizer that segue into a chiding vocal, punctuated by Dudgeon's echoing effects. A bumpy ride ensues, propelled by Gaynor's jittery drumming and space-age sounds from Fred's keyboards and Davey's synth guitar.

The third song on the album on which Gaynor and Estus played is "Act of War" (only included on the original CD and cassette versions of *Ice on Fire* as a bonus track), a belligerent update of the *Rock of the Westies* tune, "Hard Luck Story." But unlike "Hard Luck Story," "Act of War" is a duet. The husband comes home drunk after being out all night; his wife is furious, calling his conduct an "act of war." Since the husband refuses to change his ways ("Well I'm a man of convenience I work a long hard day/after twelve long hours ain't I got the right to play"), his wife renounces her faithfulness to him ("Well if that's your game then honey two can play/I'm going on the town tonight and have some fun my way").

Elton and Bernie had Tina Turner in mind as the duet partner, but she declined. "She wanted to sing more 'up' lyrics, which is perfectly understandable," Elton reflected. He found a substitute, Millie Jackson, who went on to "out-Tina" Tina Turner. Elton had known Jackson was coming to town for some concerts and arranged to have a rough tape of the song ready for her at the airport. She was immediately interested. "I'll do it no matter what key it's in!" she exclaimed.[72]

"Act of War" isn't pretty, nor is it possessed of a sense of lost romance. The music adheres closely to the violence of the lyrical message; Elton and Millie yell at each other within the contours of a percussive, minimalist melody. Kershaw, Davey, and Fred unleash aggression with their electric guitars, while Dudgeon provides machine-gun bursts and explosions with Simmons drums. Elton is credited with playing a Yamaha TX81C; Fred, a Yamaha DX7 and a Jupiter 8. Between the two of them, electronic embellishments produce a picture of chaotic armed conflict.

The third rhythm section, Queen's Roger Taylor and John Deacon, only appears on "Too Young," the album's least distinguished song. Another song called "Too Young" had given Nat King Cole a number 1 hit back in 1951, later remade with plenty of saccharine by Donny Osmond in 1972. On the John/Taupin "Too Young," the lyrics represent a lapse for Bernie, coincidentally or not reading like something Osmond would have sung. They tell the cliché-ridden story of an older man in love with a woman who is not just young, but "too young," and whose parents object strenuously to the illicit relationship.

Thankfully, the music takes the song out of Osmond's realm, although it also takes the song out of Elton's. He viewed the finished number as a 1960s "torch song," written in the style of a Righteous Brothers tune, and indeed, "Too Young" does seem influenced by "You've Lost That Loving Feeling." Otherwise, the melody is frustratingly uninteresting, saved only by Elton's rousing lead vocal that builds to a tingling climax by the time he and his backing vocalists blurt out, "Baby!" for that coup de grace.

The last rhythm section, Charlie Morgan and Paul Westwood, plays on three *Ice on Fire* tunes, the first two of which, "This Town" and "Cry to Heaven," open the album and set its tone with a spicy mixture of bustle and grief. With its imagery of unemployment and bread lines, "This Town" is Bernie's take on the decline of the U.S. "Rust Belt": the barroom escapes from the specter of layoffs ("Staring in their glasses/looks like another layoff at the yard") and the powerlessness of organized labor ("Yesterday I heard the union hall come down/they hit it with a wrecking ball").

Despite these images of despair, a throbbing beat defines the music. Elton's speedily portentous piano pattern, tracked by Fred's synthesizer and heard throughout, is like volcanic lava churning and bubbling underground, which, like the discontent brewing in the old coal-mining and steel-forging towns, may suddenly explode to the surface. Charlie Morgan's corpulent drumming and Paul Westwood's cunning bass playing maintain the rumbling below as Elton rhythmically growls his way through a stern lecture on "this town." All this is bracketed by Onward International Horns' defiant phrasing, conjuring up images of laid-off workers who have finally decided to defend themselves. As the song picks up steam, the mood changes, the union of the assertive voices of Sister Sledge with Elton's growling disaffection evolving into gospel interchanges more fit for church than the angry streets.

The next song the Morgan-Westwood rhythm section appears on, "Cry to Heaven," constitutes an abrupt change from "This Town." In "Cry to Heaven," there is no fear—just desolation. Set in a nameless wartorn location, the people have surrendered. The children, lamented as the saddest victims amid the physical destruction ("Shattered glass before their eyes/there's a mad dog barking/in a burned out subway/where the sniper sleeps at night"), have nothing to hope for but "bricks and stones" and their "father's flags" that first started the conflagration.

Elton sized up his melody as Continental, the kind Welsh balladeer Shirley Bassey would sing. "It's got atmosphere and emotion written all over the song," he beamed proudly.[73] His vocal, which has a new raggedness, emotes the waning power of a community, a spare arrangement furthering the sense of despair and desolation. Commanding in its meekness, the instrumentation goes further than any over-wrought combination of instruments could, with Elton's playing melodically questioning the future of the children with "dirty faces"; the lonely percussion of Morgan-Westwood that begins mid-song; and Fred's synthesizer accents (such as the 1940s horror-movie organ sound behind Elton's moan, "I saw a black cat/tease a white mouse/until he killed it with his claws").

The third number bearing the Morgan-Westwood rhythm imprint, "Wrap Her Up," is one of Elton and Bernie's silliest and most jocund collaborations. According to Gus Dudgeon, Elton had wanted to record a Roy Orbison song called "Dream Baby."[74] After they recorded the backing track for "Dream Baby," Elton, at George Michael's suggestion, wrote an original tune. Charlie Morgan recalled, conversely, that although Orbison's "Dream Baby" worked itself into what would become "Wrap Her Up," it all really started with a jam session.[75] But Elton remembered the genesis of "Wrap Her Up" being Dudgeon's suggestion to do a "dance track."[76]

As a dance track, "Wrap Her Up" is loads of fun. Elton rewarded the jamming musicians by giving them songwriting credit. George Michael, originally planned for backing vocals, gained some of the glory when he became a duet partner, with Elton taking the low notes and George the high ones. Alas, the lyrics could be construed as sexist and, like the words to "Slow Down Georgie" and "Li'l 'Frigerator," lack any redeeming literary purpose. Bernie's words celebrate, for all their noncerebral, puberty-laden faults, the joys of admiring the female sex in much the same way that "A Pretty Girl Is Like a Melody" did in a more innocent time.

For all of the fun of "Wrap Her Up," Elton's forte is songs that can be stripped to their barest components and still sound meaningful. "Shoot Down the Moon," on which none of the four rhythm sections played, is one of these. Elton and Bernie wrote "Shoot Down the Moon" for a James Bond movie. The song was rejected, since Duran Duran's "A View to a Kill" had already been accepted as the latest Bond theme. Elton was forced to keep it. He almost saved it for the next album, but George, who apparently had some influence in the *Ice on Fire* sessions, convinced the pianist to use it now.[77]

Elton really did see "Shoot Down the Moon" as perfect for Bond, with its many references to bullets ("You put a gun to my head/a bullet through my brain"). The lyrics also capture some of that Bond enigma ("I never say more than I need/the mystery runs deep/the danger's buried below/the secrets that you keep"). The verses contain a melodic descent that matches the observation, "the mystery runs deep"; the Fred Mandel/Gus Dudgeon faux string synthesizer arrangement and yawning bass picking by guest Pino Palladino add to the mystique. Yet most of the melody has more of an Elton John signature than a Bond trademark, with its delicate, classically tinged chord progressions.

"Shoot Down the Moon" would close *Ice on Fire* on vinyl. Before the album was finished, it was time to promote the new single, "Act of War."

"WE MIGHT SURVIVE THIS ACT OF WAR"[78]

THE CAMPY, Simon Milne–directed video for "Act of War," in which the "marital spat" between Elton and Millie threatens worldwide conflict bordering on nuclear disaster, wasn't the song's first airing. That was the lip-synched performance at the televised Montreux Pop Festival in Switzerland in early May 1985. This showing saw Elton in the black garb he'd been wearing lately, sans sunglasses, pearls, and black hat. A fez, this time with tassel, made its first appearance, and replacing the pearls was a silvery brooch. Millie looked like a 1920s flapper. Bright, layered sequences of beads quivered with every ferocious step she took against her "husband" as Elton scowled, stuck his tongue out, and shook his microphone at her. They both looked ridiculous. How could the live Montreux audience not laugh at this mock fury?

Few people in Britain, where "Act of War" was first released, took the song seriously, despite its ticklish tinderbox of vigorous rhythm and full-throated protestation. Charting on June 15, it peaked a week later at number 32. The situation was much worse in the United States. David Geffen didn't want to release the single at first, contending it would not be a Top 40 record.[79] Geffen was right, although his lack of faith may have had something to do with the single's failure to chart. The poor showing of "Act of War" was, as Elton put it, a "terrible disappointment."[80]

"THIS IS ONE OF MY FAVORITE TRACKS OF ELTON'S"[81]

"YOU HAVE ELIMINATED ALL THE STAR BULLSHIT," Elton told Live Aid organizer Bob Geldof.[82] Never before had such an enormous assortment of stars gathered for a cause. If an act later on the bill bested the earlier performers, the runner-ups had no choice but to accept it with grace. The reason for Live Aid was the Ethiopian famine.

Bob Geldof had become interested in raising money for the starving people of Ethiopia in the fall of 1984, while Elton was touring the United States. Geldof collaborated with Midge Ure of the group Ultravox on "Do They Know It's Christmas? (Feed the World)" and, on November 25, they managed to attract an interesting collection of mostly British acts to record it, including Phil Collins, Paul Young, Sting, Boy George, Bono, and Kool and the Gang's "J. T." Taylor.

Thus, the ad hoc Band Aid came into being, and "Do They Know It's Christmas?" became a Top 20 single in the United States while topping the British chart. Not to be outdone, Michael Jackson and Lionel Richie cowrote "We Are the World" for a massing of American stars, including Bruce Springsteen, Cyndi Lauper, Billy Joel, Tina Turner, and Ray Charles. This union was known as USA (United Support of Artists) for Africa, ostensibly formed to fight hunger in Africa and America. The song rose to number 1 on both sides of the Atlantic in the spring of 1985.[83]

Soon, Geldof thought of organizing a benefit concert. Elton was one of the first artists to express interest, the two having met at the Ivor Novello Awards in March, where Geldof had won a statue for the "Do They Know It's Christmas?" single. Geldof broached the subject of a concert and Elton immediately promised his participation. Thereafter, John Reid offered assistance in organizing the event and Geldof suggested he contact other artists' managers to advise them of Elton's involvement.[84]

The July 13, 1985 benefit concert, beamed all over the world as a marathon telethon, was bigger than anyone could have imagined. It had a British side, at the mecca of big events, Wembley Stadium, and an American side, at the ghostly, fifty-nine-year-old JFK Stadium in Philadelphia, a ninety-thousand-seat relic of the U.S. sesquicentennial and one-time regular site of Army-Navy football games. At Wembley, Queen, David Bowie, Elton, and many others were received by the Prince and Princess of Wales, who would be watching the concert from the Royal Box.

More than eight hours after the first British act opened the event, it was time for Elton's entrance. He appeared quite grandly in Moroccan motif, with a black plumed fez and a frock covered in bright rust-colored circles, golden emblems, platinum traces, and emerald green knitting. His manner was as electric as it had been at Wembley more than a year earlier, as he tore through "I'm Still Standing," "Bennie," and "Rocket Man" before bringing Kiki on for a duet of "Don't Go Breaking My Heart."

By now, the Elton mavens among the millions watching must have realized something was amiss. Most noticeable was the absence of familiar faces among the large group Elton had with him. Davey and Fred were there, but in place of Nigel on drums was a curly-haired, wiry Englishman named Charlie Morgan; in place of Dee on bass was the diminutive, doll-like David Paton. The Onward International Horns could barely stay out of the spotlight even though they stood in a back corner. And Ray Cooper was back.

So it wasn't so much Elton John's performance that was newsworthy, but the surrounding circumstances. Kiki, Elton's erstwhile protégée, acted as if the Wembley crowd was hers as she cavorted about the stage in white lace to her only number 1 single. Then George Michael and Andrew Ridgely, who had grown up on Elton's music, appeared at his beckoning, starstruck and surrounding their musical idol with boyish wonder. Ridgely joined Kiki and the backing vocalists, and his Wham! partner announced, "This is one of my favorite tracks of Elton's." George launched into "Don't Let the Sun Go Down on Me" as Elton proudly, and with extra flourish, accompanied him on the piano. Later, George would say, "It's the most nerve-wracking thing I've ever done. When you've written a song like that which you perform so well on your own, for him to have given me that opportunity was very generous."[85]

After the encore, a cover of the 1963 Marvin Gaye hit "Can I Get a Witness?," Elton was finished. The U.K. grand finale of "Do They Know It's Christmas?" brought the entire cast together for an inspiring exercise in humanity and humility.

"CAN I GET A WITNESS?"[86]

IN THE YEARS since Elton had severed his ties with Dick James, DJM Records had released numerous compilation albums surveying the hits, album tracks, and B-sides of the DJM years. The company had also issued a coupling of *11-17-70* and *Here and There* as *The Live Collection,* and a five-record box set. Other compilation sets were unique to various foreign countries, including *Historia de la Musica Rock,* a 1982 Spanish album with staples like "Rocket Man" and "Candle in the Wind"; *The Most Beautiful Songs of Elton John,* a 1981 Dutch record with such beauties as "Your Song" and "Border Song"; *Star Gold,* a 1979 two-LP German set that chronicled Elton's career from 1969–1975, focusing mainly on album tracks; and two early 1970s song collections released in 1981 and 1982 in France, *Portrait* and *Elton John's Rock Album.*

The release of these various records may not have bothered Elton, Bernie, and John Reid, but it was clear that DJM was milking everything it could from Elton's early work, even though the regular back catalog was already available for marketing and earnings. But what Elton, Bernie, and Reid *were* bothered by was DJM's payment of album earnings and royalties, and its continued ownership of master tapes and early 1970s song copyrights.

Following a High Court victory for Gilbert O'Sullivan in 1982 over similar issues, Elton and Bernie sued their former benefactor. They claimed that the 1967 songwriting contract and 1968 recording contract, both of which were considered standard at the time they were signed, had been obtained under "undue influence" and were an "unreasonable restraint on trade." The songwriting contract had guaranteed a fifty-pound (eighty-dollar) advance for each, a modest weekly retainer, and, for most uses of the songs, fifty percent of the proceeds.[87] The recording contract had initially guaranteed Elton twenty percent of the recording income earned by This Record Company (which really meant twenty percent of the ten percent earnings reaped from its manufacturing licensee, Philips Records, and, later, from DJM Records, for a total of two percent). The 1970 reworking of the recording contract changed this figure to sixty percent of ten percent, or six percent of the proceeds.

Elton and Bernie argued that they had been underpaid and sought control of the early copyrights and master tapes. They insisted that these songs and albums had earned about £200 million (about $350 million) worldwide. DJM countered that earnings were but a fraction of that.[88] The lawsuit was set for trial in June 1985, but broke for recess in July, resuming in October.[89]

The trial involved an enormous amount of testimony, including six days on the stand for Dick James and four for Elton. Finally, on November 29, 1985, the judgment was in (Elton was already on tour in Britain, but Bernie and Reid were in court). The songwriting duo got little of what they'd wanted. The court found the contracts at issue "unfair transactions," and that Dick James had taken "unfair advantage" of Elton and Bernie but, in view of the tremendous success the two had enjoyed since those early days, decided against setting aside the agreements. DJM would retain the disputed copyrights and master tapes. As for the international publishing and licensing arrangements, the court found that Elton and Bernie had been "deliberately underpaid in royalties." The press estimated that damages to be paid ranged from £500,000 to £5 million (about $800,000 to $8.4 million). The issue remained of who would pay the legal costs, estimated at £1.5 million ($2.5 million).[90]

Elton and Bernie were pleased. "It's been very satisfactory to us," Bernie said to television reporters outside the court. Elton was located backstage in Edinburgh for his reaction: "I'm much better off now. It's a shame we didn't get the copyrights back, but I think the judge was very fair in his comments. It was a great moral victory, anyway."[91] It wouldn't be until early 1986 that the damages would be settled. Since Elton ultimately agreed to pay the legal costs, the lawsuit turned out to be decidedly unlucrative.

On February 1, 1986, Dick James died of a massive heart attack. Although Elton didn't regret filing suit, he did regret the unpleasantness it had created. He never forgot that James had been the first to give him a chance, and that instead of banishing him when he'd learned Elton was making unauthorized tapes at DJM Studios, he'd signed the bespectacled boy and his writing partner to a contract. "[W]e were really lucky," Elton said years later. "He was like a father figure."[92]

"YOU WILL NEVER KNOW ANYTHING ABOUT MY HOME"[93]

NEW JOHN/TAUPIN TUNES—and new Taupin lyrics offered to other artists—continued to hurtle down a never-ending conveyor belt of activity. The new Taupin lyrics found their places in songs by Starship (formerly Jefferson Airplane) and Heart, which were hugely successful on the American Hot 100. In September 1985, it was "We Built This City" by Starship, cowritten with three others, including Martin Page. The song hit number 1 in the United States by mid-November, Starship's first record to do so and Bernie's first number 1 for another act. In January 1986, it was "These Dreams" by Heart, which Bernie had also cowritten with Page.

Again, Bernie's touch was magic; the single was the first number 1 in the United States for Heart.

Just as Bernie was enjoying a new kind of success in the United States, the place he was now calling home, his lyrics were getting wide circulation on the new Elton John album and a couple of new singles, released in what seemed like rapid succession. *Ice on Fire* was shipped to stores in November.

In Britain, the album peaked at number 3 following a November 16, 1985 chart debut—becoming Elton's third Top 10 album in a row there—and stayed on the charts for twenty-three weeks, as long as *Breaking Hearts*. Although *Ice on Fire* had slightly greater longevity in the United States, with twenty-eight weeks on *Billboard*'s Top 200 Albums chart, it didn't get anywhere near the Top 10. Elton still had to look to 1976 and *Blue Moves* for his last Top 10 album there. More disturbingly, *Ice on Fire* would become his worst-charting album in the United States up to that time. Following a November 30, 1985 debut, it peaked at a shockingly awful number 48. Barry Krost's "Theory of Elton John's Torpedoed Geffen Albums" (that Geffen had decided not to promote Elton's albums in retribution for the musician not attending the 1982 Broadway premiere of *Cats*) was gaining greater credence. Still, despite its disappointing chart performance, the album was certified gold seven months later. It is hard to figure out how, though, since Elton's first Geffen album, *The Fox*, had peaked at number 21 but never went gold.

The Torpedo Theory is all the more convincing when the success of the album's singles is considered, since successful singles usually translate into album sales. The singles did substantially better in Britain than in the United States, which may be evidence that Elton wasn't getting the kind of promotion his music deserved in the latter market.

One of the American singles was "Wrap Her Up," which debuted on the Hot 100 at the promising position of number 53 on October 26. In its second week, the single was at number 40. But after that it took its time, crawling up to its crest of number 20, reached on December 7.

It was "Nikita" that gave Elton his first Top 10 American single since the summer of 1984. Ken Russell's video showed him as a lovelorn foreigner pursuing a Russian female border guard from behind guns and gates, his only time playing the romantic lead. After a January 18, 1986 debut, the single peaked at number 7 on March 22, while Heart's "These Dreams," with Bernie's words, was number 1.

"Nikita" was a major worldwide hit. In Britain, where it was released before "Wrap Her Up," it peaked at number 3 after an October 12 chart debut. "Wrap Her Up" did well there, too, peaking at number 12 after first charting on December 7. "Wrap Her Up" thus equaled the British success of "Philadelphia Freedom" and fared better at home than had other concert favorites, like "Don't Let the Sun," "The Bitch Is Back," and "Someone Saved My Life Tonight."

Elton was matching Bernie in doubling up on the charts. In a situation not seen since the mid-1970s, he was competing against himself, singing in a little single called "That's What Friends Are For." The song was written by Burt Bacharach and his songwriting partner and wife, Carole Bayer Sager, for the film *Night Shift*, and sung by Rod Stewart. Now, Sager suggested that Dionne Warwick record her own version of the song, and Warwick in turn proposed she sing it with Stevie Wonder. On the day Stevie was scheduled to record his part, AIDS activist Elizabeth Taylor happened to drop by. It dawned on Sager that the song should benefit the American Foundation for AIDS Research (AMFAR). Warwick and Wonder suggested including Gladys Knight, and, finally, Clive Davis proposed Elton as a fourth.[94]

There were probably better songs that this exciting foursome could have sung, but they all belted their hearts out against the soothing tones of Stevie's harmonica. Elton was given the honor of singing the climactic last chorus. Many, weaned on the more delicate voicings of "Your Song" and "Rocket Man," may not have recognized him. Deep in the recesses of his vocal cords he had found a booming resonance that transported him light-years from his early singing.

As Dionne Warwick and Friends, the foursome found themselves on the Hot 100 on November 9, 1985, just as "Wrap Her Up" was slowly crawling up the Top 40. On January 18, when "Nikita" debuted, "That's What Friends Are For" reached number 1, where it stayed for four weeks. In its third week at the top, it was certified gold, Elton's first gold record since 1980's "Little Jeannie." It was also the biggest single of 1986 and (for a time) the biggest single of Elton's career, even if he didn't write it and only shared the lead vocal. In Britain, the song didn't do nearly as well, peaking at number 16. But here again, he saw himself up against both "Nikita" and "Wrap Her Up."

It was now starting to seem as though the only way Elton could get an American number 1, or a single of comparable success to many of his 1970s releases, was by sharing the limelight. (He had long since resigned himself to the impossibility of achieving a solo number 1 at home.) If this concerned him, he didn't say so. But the new year saw Elton against new backdrops. One was the battle against AIDS. The other was the heterosexual setting of the "Wrap Her Up" and "Nikita" videos, which put a different face on him, while he awkwardly talked of his marriage and often made light of it. When Paula Yates of the British television program *The Tube* asked him in November 1985 if he was "romantic," he said he sent Renate flowers "every year." Domestic life, he added, involved company. "We have a lot of friends over to do the washing up," he teased.[95]

The Paula Yates interview occurred a week before the British/Irish leg of Elton's latest world tour, commenced in the middle of the triumph of "Nikita." Renate understood his need to tour and just wanted him to be happy, Elton said.

"SOME THINGS NEVER CHANGE"[96]

ELTON HAD SPENT PART OF CHRISTMAS DAY 1984 with BBC's Terry Wogan, chatting about his young marriage, changing tastes in clothes, and current view on touring. He hadn't shed his disdain for the long concert trail since returning home. "I'm not going to do ten-week tours again," he asserted. "It's going to be in smaller doses."[97] But now, eleven months later, he couldn't contain his excitement about his new band. Appearing on *The Tube* with Paula Yates, Elton gave British television audiences a preview of the tour, scheduled to begin the following week, on November 14 in Dublin. With Alan Carvell, Shirley Lewis, and Helena Springs on backing vocals, the band played four songs, including two from *Ice on Fire*. "This Town" featured a skin-tingling piano melding of modern jazz and primitive rock; "Nikita" was more percussive than on record. The band, despite being Elton's biggest, was well balanced, with an unusually tactile sound. Unlike the 1984 lineup, which boasted an exhilarating cohesion, this band embodied musical crosscurrents that, upon intersecting, lifted the songs to a level of suppleness rarely heard in rock.

In some ways, this band was a time machine back to the 1970s. Elton hadn't toured with backing vocalists since 1976, nor had he had a brass section since the Muscle Shoals Horns toured with him late in 1974. But the new backing vocal trio, with its strong, vibrato-tinged accents, also signaled Elton's appreciation of his own voice. Carvell, Lewis, and Springs were better suited to the increasing vocal prowess of the bandleader than were Davey, Nigel, and Dee. Also, the brass players of Onward International Horns lent the songs a new versatility. On one song, they sounded like a big band. On another, their staccato playing suggested James Brown.

"Birds fly, fish swim, and rabbits multiply. Elton John puts on a good show. The sun also rises," read a review in Ireland's *Hot Press*. "The man is a trouper, a showbiz phenomenon, a perfectionist in an area of the business where the personality and the performer cohabitate. . . . A good show? He probably can't conceive of any other."[98] More than just a "good show," the 1985–86 British/Irish tour featured two-hour reviews of many lesser-known songs that had either not been played in years, had never before been played with a band, or had rarely been played, *period*.

The songs dug out of deep storage included "Honky Cat," which would prove one of the many highlights of the tour. With the return of Ray's duck quacks, this feast of New Orleans revelry had the horn players mimicking some of Elton's carefree arpeggiations. The underappreciated *Blue Moves* also had a belated renaissance. "Tonight," theretofore played only by Elton and Ray on the 1979 world tour, was performed a tad fast, but still captured the desperate intimacy of the stripped-down version.

"Blue Eyes," whose jazz-soaked chord progressions bubbled and boiled where they had once lightly steamed, and "I Guess That's Why They Call It the Blues," were linked with Leon Russell's "A Song for You," the first time Elton had paid homage to, as he put it, "one of the biggest influences in my whole career." Elton also unveiled four songs from *Ice on Fire*. Besides "This Town" and "Nikita," there were "Shoot Down the Moon" and, of course, "Wrap Her Up," done as a duet with Alan Carvell.

Rarities like "Tonight" and the *Ice on Fire* selections functioned as the shows' bookends, the solid middle filled with old friends. But the old friends disappointed. As vigorously, interestingly, and devotedly as Elton pounded the piano, his playing was often swallowed by his enthusiastic, orchestral band. This was especially obvious on "Rocket Man," which was only half as long as it had been in 1984. As soon as he began ad-libbing "I miss my wife, I miss my kids, I'm so alone, I wanna go home," and the horns entered the mix, the song ended. Perhaps Elton was looking for ways to cut back on the show's length while still featuring more songs. As exhausted as he had been in the summer of 1984 thinking about the then forthcoming American tour, he may have hoped that these shortcuts would prevent a new exhaustion from setting in.

Another cause for concern, though not too noticeable yet, was that Elton's voice was beginning to sound worn. His voice seemed to be changing, like an adolescent boy's. The huskiness heard on *Ice on Fire* often gave way to a porousness that threatened to enervate some of the power that, paradoxically, his voice was also increasingly exhibiting. At this early stage, however, these problems didn't detract from the general pleasure of hearing him sing, nor did they prevent the show's closer, "Can I Get a Witness?," from being a hands-in-the-air celebration that would have burst any African-American church at the seams. Elton's voice slid comfortably into a baritone as he opined, "Lord, I wanna testify!"

For the first time since the 1979 tour with Ray, Elton performed "Candle in the Wind" solo. The only other sound heard besides Elton's voice and piano was the sheen of a JX8P synthesizer linked to, and triggered by, the piano via a MIDI hookup. More important was what the pianist did with "Candle," transforming it from a dainty ballad with hymn-like undertones into a full-fledged, fleshy hymn. The original melody that had seemed so perfect on *Goodbye Yellow Brick Road* seemed skeletal after one listen to this solo version.

By now, Elton had long since tired of the fairly tame tails and boaters that had been his trademark in 1984. Hats were out for now. Glasses were back. The outfits of choice were variations on tails, one set described as "flowery,"[99] another as "daft," with "teddy bears patterned all over it." For his final encore at Wembley on opening night, he came out with a "two-foot high bouffant hairpiece flashing 'Merry Xmas.'"[100] And on opening night in Dublin, he wore a fluffy, pastel-flecked yellow garment that resembled a cross between pajamas and a piñata.

In Dublin, more antiapartheid protesters gathered outside the RDS Stadium. Elton responded in a short, preshow press conference backstage: "I went there [South Africa] because I wanted to see for myself what conditions were like," he said. "I went to Russia and Poland for the same reason." He added, "I won't be going again." When informed of Elton's announcement, the demonstrators dispersed.[101]

"YOUR RAG DOLL SITS WITH A PERMANENT GRIN"[102]

SOCCER ATTENDANCE WAS DOWN IN BRITAIN, and the hard numbers were especially hard on Watford. It was so bad that, although Elton had already committed £1 million (about $1.6 million) of his own money toward a £3 million ($5 million) "ground improvement project" that he'd been seeking for years, he suddenly nixed the arrangement. "If we built it now the stand would be like a noose around our necks. We would be back in the third division," he protested. "We wouldn't have the fans to put in it!" He was angry at the Football Association for soccer's attendance problems.[103]

Perhaps this tirade improved Watford's fortunes. On February 24, 1986, Elton was able to announce that the new grounds were on their way; the club had a deal that would cost a million pounds less than first expected. Months later, he would reveal that he had paid for his share of the project from the proceeds of what would become his year-long tour.

Elton had wound up the first leg of his 1985–86 world tour more than a month earlier. Around that time, he and Renate separated. The musician matter-of-factly explained that his wife had thrown him out because the kitchen at Woodside was being redone. "I'm not going to have you getting up at seven o'clock in the morning, with the builders here, being grumpy," she was supposed to have said.[104] While in exile in London's Mayfair Hotel, he wrote a new song, "Paris," from a set of Bernie's lyrics. "I class it in the 'Daniel'/'Nikita' type mold," he said later. "The melody was written practically all the way through without a break."[105] Months before it was recorded, the song would be added to the set list for the European leg of the tour, to commence in Madrid on March 1.

Before returning to the road, Elton was in line for some awards. The first was a British Phonographic Industry (BPI) trophy for his 1979 Soviet tour, an award Elton considered an embarrassment. At the televised February 10 ceremony, in which Wham! was also honored for going to China in 1985, Elton appeared to have little interest in being honored. George Michael felt differently. With Elton, his hair pulled back in a modest ponytail, nearby on the podium, George breathlessly expounded on the need for international understanding. When it was Elton's turn to speak, however, he said only, "I'd just like to say, it's very easy to go to Russia. All you have to do is phone the foreign office up and they'll fix it up for you. I mean, I couldn't believe it!"

Two weeks later, Elton was a guest on *Wogan*. "It [the BPI award] was seven years too late," he opined. Worse, he said, was that Cliff Richard, who had been sitting right in front of him in the BPI audience, had gone to the USSR first. Some suggested Elton received the award because he would likely lose to Phil Collins for best male vocal (which he did). Regardless, he said, he could have done without the ceremony. "It kind of seemed to be a trumped-up award."[106]

The April 7 Ivor Novello Awards ceremony in London was different. Elton and Bernie received statues for "Nikita," cited as the best song musically and lyrically. Elton was alone lauded for his outstanding contribution to British music. Renate by his side, he announced, "We've been back together for two months and this time it's for good," thus suggesting that their separation earlier in the year hadn't been their first.

By this time, Elton's third and last single from *Ice on Fire*, "Cry to Heaven," had slipped from the British charts. Debuting on March 1, it had peaked at number 47. Elton didn't know it then, but he would have to wait nearly two years for another British hit.

The European tour saw some changes in the band. Backing vocalist Helena Springs was replaced by Gordon Neville. Ray Cooper, again conquered by wanderlust, was replaced by Jody Linscott, a slight, attractive woman billed as "one of the few female percussionists in the world." She may not have had Ray's way with a tambourine or his theatrical stances, but she did show he wasn't the only one who could whip kettledrums into shape.

Elton's voice had an increasing tendency during the European tour to veer off in unplanned directions, although any concerns about his singing were kept under wraps. Audiences showered him with affection. Especially touching gestures accompanied "Song for Guy." In Germany, audiences clapped along. In France, they *sang* along to this largely wordless tune, nearly drowning out Elton's solemn playing. But occasional solemnity didn't stop him from surpassing the pajamas and piñatas from the recent British tour with a new passion—mohawks, constructed with specially made headdresses.

During a break from touring, Elton's jet-setting lifestyle continued unabated. The end of April found him in New York meeting with Bob Mackie, of Donald Duck and Minnie Mouse costume fame, to discuss the next line of outfits. "I'm going back to being outrageous," he offered.[107] Elton then hurried back to England to guest on Wham!'s next (and last) album, *Music from the Edge of Heaven*. He also divulged plans for an aerobic workout at a Florida tennis camp in preparation for work on his next album.[108]

Thereafter, live appearances were scattered. On June 20, in London, he played master of ceremonies at a Prince's Trust charity event (for disadvantaged youth), participating in a "supergroup" of Eric Clapton, Sting, Mark Knopfler, Phil Collins, and a resurfacing Ray Cooper. Rod Stewart, whom Elton introduced sincerely as "one of my best friends," also appeared. It was Rod's turn to get in a dig. "It's so nice to have Elton in my backing band at last," he kidded. Rod's pianist was in top form, in control of his voice and, in typical concert fashion, creating dizzying shapes in the air with his body as he played.[109]

"THE KING AIN'T DEAD, HE'S JUST ASLEEP"[110]

SUMMER 1986 STARTED WITH A HAPPY EVENT, the marriage of Prince Andrew and Sarah Ferguson, the Duchess of York. Elton entertained at Prince Andrew's bachelor party, while Renate, in the royal inner circle by virtue of her marriage, helped Fergie and Princess Diana "crash" the celebration. Later, Elton and Renate occupied spots in Westminster Abbey's front pew at the wedding. Elton was further honored by the royal couple's request of BBC Radio Two to play his music on the morning of the big day. He later reciprocated by presenting them with a recording of a song specially written for them along the lines of "Song for Guy," since Fergie adored the hit instrumental.[111]

Early summer also saw Elton working on an album destined to become his most maligned since *Victim of Love*. *Leather Jackets* was at least as commercially disastrous (except in Australia), sharing with the disco album the distinction of being his least remembered work.

Like *21 at 33*, *The Fox*, and *Jump Up!*, *Leather Jackets* was done in stages. This needn't have been a bad thing, as the quality of the earlier albums will attest. The problem lay in Elton's mental state. He'd intended to simultaneously finish both *Ice on Fire* and what was to become *Leather Jackets* in 1985, but instead chose to delay completion of the *Ice on Fire* follow-up so that he could rework some tracks from the 1985 sessions and write more songs. "Paris" was done, but he found himself writing seventeen additional songs in three days for the newest sessions, slated for the early summer of 1986 at Wisseloord Studios in Amsterdam, with Gus Dudgeon producing and, excluding Onward International Horns, his new band playing.[112]

All this work was corrupted by Elton's cocaine abuse. "Very butch, but a total disaster," Elton said candidly of the album, years later. "I was not a well budgie. . . . [I]t was just one bag of coke after another."[113] "There was a chance he could polish himself off," recalled Dudgeon later. "He'd go out and do some coke, and it'd be all over his mouth, his nose would be running, and I'd go, 'Oh god, this is just awful.'"[114] Elton's impairment is palpable upon a listen to many of the tracks written specifically for the *Leather Jackets* sessions.

The poor quality of the more recent songs on the new album, among the least melodic since *Rock of the Westies*, was exacerbated by an overuse of synthesizers. On *Too Low for Zero*, Elton had catered to his fantasy of writing songs with a synthesizer, ostensibly to compose better rock songs. Thankfully, he succeeded instead in shaping unusual but tasteful compositions as melodic as their predecessors. And despite the overabundance of electric guitar on *Breaking Hearts*, which gave many of the better songs a more ordinary quality than they deserved, the album still offered the melodic insights for which Elton was known and some pleasing use of synthesizer was still evident. For *Ice on Fire*, experimenting with synthesizers wasn't a priority, and they were chiefly handled by Fred Mandel, who succeeded as well as James Newton

Howard had before him. But *Leather Jackets* represented a turning point. The synthesizers, like the cocaine, were a crutch, used without regard for their effect on the contours or mood of a given song.

One aspect of his work ethic hadn't changed. Elton had an unquenchable thirst for writing. Months later, he recalled that when he had used up all of Bernie's lyrics, he referred to some of the lyricist's leftovers from 1982, including something called "Love Rusts." The musician scuttled thoughts of using his new song when Bernie suddenly remembered he had already given the lyrics to Starship, who'd used them on their album *Knee Deep in the Hoopla*. "I'll have to call it something else—'Rust Loves,' or something like that," Elton joked.[115] Ultimately, the song didn't appear anywhere. No matter. Elton turned to Gary Osborne for lyrics, and a short-lived alliance with Cher yielded several songs, one of which found a place on the album.[116]

Of the songs Elton wrote for *Leather Jackets*, only "Paris" possesses the melodic flair he used to show in such abundance. Its lyrics are the romantic reminiscences of a protagonist aiming to recapture a long-ago youthful romance in Paris. While he waits all night in an airport lounge for a flight to the city of his lost youth, he dreams of what he'll do when he arrives: "We'll paint all our portraits/in brushstrokes of yellow/and christen the canvas."

Despite the by now uneven strength of Elton's voice, "Paris" paints the portrait successfully. Like "Cry to Heaven," the melody has a Continental flavor, but is characterized by a savoir faire, split in tone between the anticipation of the dreamer awaiting his flight and his euphoric flights of fancy to the Paris he expects to reach. This euphoria is also conveyed by Elton's confident piano solo. Jody Linscott adds castanets and crashing cymbals, which help spur the protagonist's visions. Fred's synthesizers insert unobtrusive commentaries beneath and beside Elton's voice and piano.

If only the other songs written for these sessions—what may be dubbed the *Leather Jackets* specials—had been so elegantly rendered. "Go It Alone," Bernie's simple, bitter plaint over an imagined, failed relationship, is far from an exemplar of Elton's songwriting, with its atonal melody. Also, Fred's programmed sequences and electronic percussion deliver the flailing sheet-metal sounds Elton had steadfastly avoided in previous 1980s albums. Only Davey's guitar flares and Elton's silent movie–era acoustic piano chiming lend the song any sincerity.

"Heartache All Over the World," another *Leather Jackets* special, initially seems like a lyrical successor to "Wrap Her Up," but lacks the latter's blamelessly mindless celebration of the female form. Instead, Bernie latches onto the overused "it's Saturday night, and I ain't got nobody" theme: "And everybody's got a date/and the ones that ain't are tired/what the hell do you do on a weekend honey/when your heart's on fire."

The musician barely improves "Heartache" with his music. The result is vacuous entertainment, like *Caribou*'s "Solar Prestige a Gammon." But where "Solar

Prestige" has a faux Italian charm and Elton's faux operatic voice, "Heartache" is an exercise in synthesizer overkill with a modicum of melody. The musician doesn't even play on "Heartache," leaving the synthesizer symphony to Fred and the flailing sheet metal to Dudgeon and mixer Graham Dickson. And the endless chanting of "Girls! Girls! Girls!" by the backing vocalists is juvenile—and feels dishonest. True, over the years Elton had given voice to many a Taupin rumination, desire, and fabricated character. After all, "Wrap Her Up" is all about the virtues of the opposite sex, too. But knowing Elton's sexual history—despite his being a married man of two years—the credulity of the listener is stretched to uncomfortable lengths as he sings about searching for "Girls! Girls! Girls!"

"I Fall Apart" is Bernie's last *Leather Jackets* special to make the album, his words a no-frills version of "Don't Let the Sun." The lyrics wallow in self-pity, ranging from vaguely interesting observations ("Without you I no longer swim upstream") to boring protests ("This house can get so lonely/when the day grows dark/and it seems to be the nighttime/when I fall apart"). None of the music is interesting. This may be the most disappointing song of Elton's career; a blotchy vocal effort does nothing to help. In an unfortunate twist, Elton's new band contributes its most understated performance of the album here, a sadly wasted effort.

Little better is "Don't Trust That Woman," with lyrics by Cher, who had sent them to Elton to come up with music. That they were composed by a woman is notable because they are more misogynistic than anything Bernie had ever written. The "woman" in "Don't Trust That Woman" is cruel, conniving, sex-driven ("You can rear end her oh it'll send her"), and sadomasochistic ("You can beat her but don't mistreat her"). It is easy to see why Cher decided to leave this song off her album, although not why Elton decided it should have a place on his.

Elton gave half the songwriting credit on this song to an alter ego of his, Lady Choc Ice, spurred by Cher's insistence that the credit read "Cher/Elton John." "If you're going to take that attitude, it's not going to be Cher/Elton John, it's going to be Cher/Lady Choc Ice," Elton later remembered thinking.[117] The music contains some hints of modern jazz, in Davey's electric guitar noodling and Elton's light, witty JX8P keyboard touch, but otherwise leaves scant impression.

"Memory of Love," Elton's sole collaboration with Gary Osborne for *Leather Jackets* (and their last collaboration to date), avoids tarnishing the female image but is dull both musically and lyrically. It is a run-of-the-mill love song with typical love song words ("Take love for better, take love for worse/but never ever take love for granted") and a typical love song melody. Elton's vocal, however, is not typical; despite difficulties, he manages a muscular baritone, the song's sole enticement. But all in all, "Memory of Love" is a pitiful ending to an otherwise fruitful songwriting partnership.

The remainder of the songs on *Leather Jackets* come from the *Ice on Fire* sessions. Bernie's lyrics to the title track examine the mind-set of people obsessed with long-dead rock icons. Elvis Presley ("The King ain't dead, he's just asleep") and Buddy Holly ("Can you talk to Buddy's bones/when you spin a forty-five?") get the bulk of attention, as Bernie name-drops Holly songs ("Not Fade Away" and "That'll Be the Day") and examines Presley's cult-like stature ("Is Memphis real or just a song/three thousand miles from home").

Imitating a musical style has never been Elton's habit, and he avoided writing a 1950s tune to match the lyrics. He opted instead for a rough-edged, jaundiced look back at the good old days, with his increasingly coarse voice convincingly bumping along the music's crags, insensitively mocking those worshipers of past glory. The weaknesses of the recording reflect when it was recorded—in drug-dampened 1986, instead of the more lucid 1985. Buried in Fred's programmed sequences and the electronic percussion of Dudgeon and Dickson, it never achieves the haughty tones contemplated by its melodic structure.

Fortunately, the other *Ice on Fire* leftovers were mostly recorded in 1985, with only finishing touches left for Wisseloord. The best of these—and among the best John/Taupin compositions ever—is "Slow Rivers," a duet with Cliff Richard. Bernie analogizes a dying romance to a sluggish river ("Slow rivers run cold/shallow waters never sank so low") and a frigid winter ("The bitter wind just bites through me like a wild dog/I still see your eyes tonight like headlights through the fog"). The song features one of Elton's most mystical melodies, unlike anything he has composed before or since, laden with the kind of restrained pain only an adult well-schooled in the lessons of failed relationships could sing. The voices of Elton and Richard are an offbeat but pleasurable blend of toughness and tenderness. It probably wasn't necessary to add Richard to the mix, but Elton, a diehard fan of robust singing, wanted to sing with him as he "has probably one of the technically best voices in the world."[118]

Everything else on the track jells, too. James's string arrangement stealthily encroaches on Elton's music. The Charlie Morgan/Paul Westwood rhythm section provides an adroit subtext, and the vibrations of Fred's tinny synthesizers suggest a river drained of life, or a romance drained of passion. What never jelled was this song's legacy; it was destined to sink with the fatally flawed mother ship.

"Hoop of Fire," another *Ice on Fire* leftover, looks at romance from a different angle. Bernie's narrator is a man living on the edge who wants to take his timid would-be girlfriend there with him ("You feel pressure all around you, mistrust in strangers' faces/but don't pretend you wouldn't spend some time in a hoop of fire"). The music builds like a 1960s Phil Spector song. This style is also heard in the steady timekeeping of the Mattacks/Paton rhythm section, jagged castanets, and contrarily smooth backing vocals. But the similarities stop there. Unlike the shiny-faced innocence of a Spector recording, the melody in "Hoop of Fire" dips when one would expect it to keep rising; it bravely bellows where a Spector recording might have meekly pined. The song is obviously not a Spector imitation, a fact brought home by Elton's contemplative piano solo midway through. And Elton's vocal, unaffected by the problems that would begin to take shape late in 1985, provides a heartily piquant ride through his melody.

"Gypsy Heart," the next-to-last *Ice on Fire* extra included on *Leather Jackets*, offers more of Elton's growing vocal prowess. But though it comes from the *Ice on Fire* sessions, it is a markedly unremarkable song. Bernie is on the right track at first, using the phrase "gypsy heart" to evoke a lover whose restlessness frequently takes her out of reach ("You come and go just like the rain"). Too soon, however, the lyrics degenerate into a gray morass of love song clichés: "Your gypsy heart will never find/any arms as warm as mine." This set of *Ice on Fire* lyrics ranks with those for "Too Young" as the least distinguished of the batch.

Most affecting about the music for "Gypsy Heart," besides Elton's singing, are the throaty backing vocals of Shirley Lewis, Alan Carvell, Gordon Neville, and Davey; the waltz tempo accentuated by the Mattacks/Paton rhythm section; and Elton's gospel playing, a feature that takes the melody beyond its humdrum basics.

The last *Ice on Fire* holdover, "Angeline," threatens more misogyny of the type heard on "Don't Trust That Woman." But a closer read reveals that "Angeline"'s mate bears the markings of a nauseating villain. Poor Angeline is a slave to her lecherous man. She feeds him, brings his drugs, and has sex on demand. He thinks she likes her submissive role ("Angeline just loves it/when I treat her mean"), but his words acknowledge that, far from enjoying his advances, he makes her squirm ("Lay still honey/I can't get enough").

Elton sounds tough and rough on this song, like Angeline's nasty mate ("Well I talk tough, I act rough"), but there are aspects of the recording that overwhelm the music's self-effaced throbbing. Over the Roger Taylor/John Deacon rhythm section can be heard the thunder of motorcycles awakening and Alan Carvell's brainstorm—a series of "oh-oh-oh's" that would have been more at home on a Joan Jett record. Elton liked Carvell's idea so much that he gave him co-songwriting credit. "That whole bit made it into a much more exciting track," Elton later recalled. "There are little things like that that lift records."[119]

Leather Jackets was an album even blotchier than Elton's voice was becoming. When the album was released, the liner notes included a curious dedication from him that was almost hidden among all the other names and places listed. In it, he thanked Lady Choc Ice "for being a continued source of inspiration."

"I'VE GOTTA LAST THE NIGHT" [120]

THE AUGUST OPENING OF Elton's U.S. tour at Clarkston, Michigan's Pine Knob Music Theater was postponed due to "laryngitis." August 17 was the makeup date. For this tour, Elton returned wholeheartedly to his 1970s obsession with sartorial outrage. As USA Today's Jim McFarlin wrote, "John lit up the night all by himself, in floor-length capes of glitter and multi-colored spangles, designed by Hollywood's Bob Mackie and topped at first by a foot-high wig."[121]

While his many moments of fashion insanity a decade or more earlier had been freewheeling expressions of self-mockery, Elton carefully planned the "Look of 1986" with designer Mackie. Now, self-mockery was only part of the picture. Ever captivated by ceremony, the tour constituted his good-bye kiss to weird wardrobes. "I feel in the mood to do these sort of things once more," he said in October, once he was done searing the eyeballs of Americans and had briefly returned home. He was also interested in further cultivating the mystique surrounding his persona, believing the costumes helped attract people to his shows: "People like to see me make a fool of myself, and every time they come and see me, I do."[122]

Elton had never looked more hideous. One of his favorite costumes was a puffy-shouldered black velvet tailcoat that fastened at the abdomen and was covered with five-pronged diamanté stars. The combined effect of this, with matching trousers, a dangling star earring, and a mane of hot pink, "Tina Turner" hair was of a flashy, furry forest creature. Then there was the gold-encrusted "Aladdin" getup, complete with two-foot-high turban and squeezed by a dormant cobra (the last costume ever to expose Elton's abundant chest hair). And there were the fraternal twins: a crimson devil's outfit, its ostrich feather plume-flames shooting outward and upward from his shoulders and head; and an angel's outfit, with a halo and wings so cumbersome they had to be attached with a back brace.

Elton wasn't afraid to mix and match. He could leave off some feathers and add some spikes. He could vary the headdress, which could be as (relatively) innocuous as a standard mohawk or as comical as a wig with three fat, cone-shaped antennae. He wore glasses regularly—even if they eventually surrendered to his contacts before the show had gotten very old. The frightening Alain Mikli optical creations had claws that seemed to grab his entire head, or sometimes resembled colorfully lopsided or misshapen masks.

But the pianist didn't need the costumes to attract concertgoers. Most tickets were sold before people got wind of what they would be seeing. This was his most successful tour in years. "I'm amazed at ticket sales," he told the New York Daily News. "To have this kind of sales record without a hit single even surprised me. This is what I was doing in '76."[123] The two-month tour proved he no longer needed a hit album or single in the United States to attract throngs. In Los Angeles, he sold out seven nights at the Universal Amphitheater. The venue's general manager estimated Elton could have sold out another week.[124] Following his sold-out shows at Madison Square Garden, he was recognized for being the first rock star to play the venue more than twenty times.[125] The quietude surrounding the 1980 tour was long gone.

For these shows, Elton erased any doubt of his piano's primacy, keeping the songs interesting for himself. "Rocket Man" and "Bennie" were getting longer again, and the excitement each song generated differed from night to night. "The Bitch Is Back" was supported more by a scampering stream of piano notes than by Davey's ample electric aggression. "Burn Down the Mission" developed into a tête-à-tête between the pianist and Charlie Morgan during the rioting masses portion of the song. Sometimes, Elton played the piano while lying underneath it, no matter what headdress he was wearing. Rock critic Robert Palmer, not an Elton John fan, had this to say about the New York shows: "One had the impression that while Elton John used to emphasize the pop-song aspects of his material, thinking this would please that audience that bought his singles, he is now performing more in order to please himself. The irony of this is that he is . . . pleasing the audience more."[126]

Elton's ever more inspired playing may have also been encouraged by something else—nagging voice problems. Little was written in the press about this, except for a few mentions that he was "hoarse." But he was more than hoarse. His voice gave out at all sorts of awkward moments, disappearing as he sang "shine the light!" in "Philadelphia Freedom" or during some of the taxing portions of "Someone Saved My Life Tonight" ("This is going to be interesting," he said one night before starting it). It had become rigid and difficult to negotiate around the contours of intimate ballads like "Blue Eyes." He had little technique. Nightly, Elton apologized to his audiences for "the voice." He might slip backstage to "have a gargle" midshow, but this was no great help.

The star's dressing room was often filled with celebrity well-wishers. In New York, Mets catcher Gary Carter presented him with a team shirt. Billy Joel was there, too, but lost the chance to join Elton onstage when the latter had to finish early because of his voice. At Los Angeles's Universal Amphitheater, the fans backstage included Barry Manilow, Sting, Motley Crüe's Vince Neil, and Dynasty's Joan Collins.

Elton had to wonder what the condition of his voice meant for his upcoming tour of Australia, set to make history since it would involve a twenty-seven-date collaboration with the Melbourne Symphony Orchestra. But he still had time to worry about others. While in the United States, he befriended young AIDS sufferer Ryan White who, along with the boy's sister Andrea, was his guest at shows in Oakland and San Diego. Elton also arranged a party at Disneyland and a tour of Universal Studios for them, and pushed Ryan, who was weak after a hospital stay, through the parks in a wheelchair. Elton's support of the Whites didn't end there. Well after he'd left for Australia, he kept in touch, calling, writing, and sending gifts. When they were driven from their home in Kokomo, Indiana, by bigotry and fear and resettled in Cicero, another Indiana town, Elton paid the down payment on their house.[127]

"IT WAS THE SEASON OF LIGHT, IT WAS THE SEASON OF DARKNESS, IT WAS THE SPRING OF HOPE, IT WAS THE WINTER OF DESPAIR. . . ." [128]

THE NEXT THREE MONTHS, from October through December 1986, provided a perturbing assortment of contrasts and contradictions more unbelievable than any dime-novel writer could create. A voice brazenly persevered, was silenced, and rebounded. A wife came and went. A good friend was alienated, returned to the fold, and was alienated again. A career seemed lost, found, then lost again.

Things were pleasant enough in mid-October when Elton, with Renate in tow, presided over the unveiling of Watford's new grandstand, largely paid for with his concert proceeds. "When he held his hands above his head in a gesture of welcome, the crowd burst into spontaneous applause," observed Australian reporter Lee Wilson. "[A]mong the muffled and capped leaders of Watford, for whom popular music probably ends with Tom Jones, this sort of rapture is astonishing. It is rather like John the Baptist getting a standing ovation in a betting shop." [129]

The release of *Leather Jackets* and its first single, "Heartache All Over the World," wasn't quite as glorious. At home, the single charted on October 4 and peaked at number 45. In the United States, "Heartache" debuted at number 80 on October 18. It slid lethargically up the chart until it ran out of steam at number 55, six weeks later. In another three weeks, it was gone from *Billboard*'s Hot 100 altogether, becoming one of Elton's worst-charting American singles.

If the chart performance of "Heartache" was disheartening, the weak showing of the source album provided an even greater cause for concern. The problems were its lack of a hit single and, in the United States at least, a lack of promotion. There were some awful songs on *Leather Jackets*, but there were some awfully good ones, too.

In Britain, *Leather Jackets* debuted on November 15 and peaked at a tepid number 24—Elton's worst showing for a new studio album there since *Madman* peaked at number 41 in 1972. In the United States, the album debuted on *Billboard*'s Top Pop Albums on December 6. *The Philadelphia Inquirer*'s Ken Tucker gave the album one star out of four, complaining that "this is the worst album he's ever recorded, the first time he hasn't even written a melody that can redeem the banalities of songwriting collaborator Bernie Taupin." [130]

Leather Jackets peaked at number 91. To this day, it hasn't been certified gold in the United States.

But the rumblings of commercial eclipse were still distant in October 1986, when Elton arrived in Sydney, Australia, for "Tour de Force," his twenty-seven-date tour with his band and the Melbourne Symphony Orchestra (MSO). The first stop was Harry's Café de Wheels in the suburb of Woolloomooloo, where Elton held a press conference dressed in gray from head to toe. Only his pink ponytail seemed out of place. Switching from his regular sunglasses to ones sporting, on each lens, the Qantas logo of a leaping kangaroo, he munched on pie'n'peas (a kind of British/Australian pot pie), drank beer, and answered questions. "I'm feeling really great about the tour," he said. "I'm so excited, I've got more energy than I've had for ages."[131]

Why did Elton tour with the MSO? Nearly fifteen years earlier, William Mann of *The Times* (London) had reviewed the pianist's one-show stint with the Royal Philharmonic Orchestra, suggesting that Elton didn't need the orchestra because his "songs are basically natural and only need him to sing and play them. . . ."[132] This was still true. But when rehearsals finally began at the Brisbane Entertainment Centre, the union of the MSO's talents with Elton's perfectly constructed ballads and rock tunes proved incredibly moving.

Plans for the tour had begun in 1984, at the suggestion of Australian promoter Kevin Ritchie. Agreeing that it was an interesting idea was easy; actually making it a pleasing reality was another. Elton didn't want to do the tour unless he could be assured that the MSO would be properly amplified and sound as loud as the band.[133] Gus Dudgeon, who would be along to serve as the orchestra's sound engineer, investigated ways to "mike" the MSO, discovering a method by which each instrument could be individually amplified, using microphones as tiny as fingernails.[134]

There were other hurdles. James Newton Howard, who had been busy scoring American movies like *Wildcats* and *Tough Guys*, was recruited to adapt Buckmaster's (and his own) arrangements for a full symphony orchestra, ultimately downplaying the cello Buckmaster had favored on early albums. Then there was the reluctance of some orchestra members to do a rock tour. A few refused to participate. James, who also was to conduct the MSO, tried to assuage the musicians' fears at the Brisbane rehearsals. "I came out to meet them and let them know they weren't dealing with Ozzy Osbourne," he recalled.[135]

Principal clarinetist Philip Miechel told a television reporter that he only agreed to participate because most of the other members did. He firmly resented the orchestra's amplification, but figured the six-week tour would make a nice vacation. Although of Elton's generation, he claimed he'd never heard Elton's music prior to rehearsals.[136] Other MSO members were openly excited. Harpist Huw Jones, in his early fifties, cited "Sorry Seems to Be the Hardest Word" as his favorite Elton John song and professed to being "hypnotized by the beat" of the up-tempo numbers. Significantly younger double bassist Michelle Picker remembered enthusiastically learning Elton's songs on the piano as a girl of twelve.[137] Elton eventually won over the skeptics. Principal clarinetist Philip Green cheerily remarked when the tour was well underway that "Elton's sheer musical energy has overcome anyone's reservations."[138]

After James had worked with the orchestra in Brisbane for a week, Elton arrived for rehearsals, disarmingly clothed in shorts, sneakers, sports jersey, and ball cap, his pink ponytail poking out the back. "When we actually got together with Elton, it was one of the most emotional experiences in my life," said James. "Musically, it was *the* most satisfying moment in my life to have been involved with the orchestrations so long, and with Elton for so many years prior to that, and to really have that many components as a musician come together and work well was very gratifying."[139]

Elton agreed. He tearfully declared after his first day of rehearsals with the orchestra, "This has been the greatest day of my life." His remaining rehearsal days were long. The MSO practiced ten hours a day; Elton, thirteen.[140] The band, including Ray Cooper who, with Jody Linscott, comprised a powerhouse percussion team, joined later to review the work it would do with and without the MSO. The show's first segment was to be a twelve-song rock'n'roll set. Following an intermission, the orchestra would join the band for eighteen more songs.

Elton was mindful of the need for utmost mental acuity. Entourage member Bob Stacey, in charge of procuring the musician's backstage refreshments, said, "At the moment, the favorite drink is Diet Coca-Cola, without a doubt—and a cup of tea. In the old days it was gin, vodka, or scotch. Nowadays our attitude is: We're older and wiser and we've got to last the tour!"[141] Elton's sobriety contributed to some of the most dazzling performances of his career, despite the raspiness of his voice. The shows were also physically taxing. He was the only one among the 102 musicians who had to play and sing steadily for nearly three hours every evening.

The first half of the lively show was an abbreviated version of the one British, European, and American fans had enjoyed during the past year, with the notable addition of "Heartache All Over the World." For these first ninety minutes, Elton was at least as ridiculously dressed as he had been in the United States a month or two earlier. On opening night in Brisbane, he came out in what was described as a "pink, feathery mohawk hairdo, pink glasses, diamond teardrop earrings, and diamanté-studded tails." In the second, orchestrated half, Elton's appearance metamorphosed into a reasonable facsimile of Mozart, complete with beauty mark on his right cheek. MSO joined the band for a showcase of oldies, including six from *Elton John*, two from *Madman Across the Water*, and two from *Blue Moves*. More recent albums were represented, too, including *The Fox*, *Too Low for Zero*, and even *Leather Jackets*. Two songs that had never before been orchestrated, "Don't Let the Sun" and "Saturday Night's Alright for Fighting," were given symphonic treatment. As Christopher Beck of *TV Week* wrote, "Elton and orchestra blended perfectly to produce an exciting mix of rock and classical music which fired the enthusiasm of fans to new heights."[142]

This was the night relations between Elton and Molly Meldrum became strained. According to Meldrum, Elton "summoned" him backstage after the show to relate his opinion of the concert. The columnist told him that the first half needed more rockers, including "Crystal" and "Crocodile Rock," and that the second half should have featured "Song for Guy" and "Funeral for a Friend." His advice wasn't welcome. Meldrum later admitted that when Elton dismissed his comments, "I blew my top."[143]

The next stop was Melbourne, home of the MSO, for an eight-night stand. "There's no way I'm going to do 'Crocodile Rock,' even if Molly is in the audience!" Elton announced to concertgoers on November 10, the first night. Reviewer Brett Stavordale noticed the growing delight of "Bennie and the Jets" (writing of "a most impressive—and highly amusing—piano solo"), and how the MSO enjoyed itself during the second half. "When the eighty-eight musicians received a thunderous ovation from their home crowd, their faces showed glee," wrote Stavordale. "And their acknowledgment of Elton's performance was just as hearty as Elton's was of theirs."[144]

If some MSO members were initially reluctant to do this tour, they no longer regretted it. They realized they could attract young people to their classical concerts. Elton's professionalism helped, as did his generosity. Before the tour started, he had presented a bottle of Moët & Chandon French champagne to every musician. Attached to each bottle was a message: "Here's to a great tour."[145]

One night in Melbourne, Elton headed out to a "business meeting" at the Hilton Hotel. He just happened to be wearing a taffeta tuxedo, boater, bow tie, conservative glasses, and possibly thousands of dollars worth of jewelry. Upon entering the hotel's Decanter Room, he found the glare of television cameras and beaming MSO members. The MSO chairman of the board, Professor Peter Dennison, presented him with a plaque, which stated in part: "By public acclaim and acclaim of the critics, your 'Tour de Force' has been a triumphant success and we are deeply proud to have been involved."[146] The plaque memorialized an honorary MSO life membership for the pianist, the first such honor bestowed on any musician, let alone a rock star.

Elton acted like the average person who had just won the lottery, fists in the air, face oozing delight. "There's no need for a consolidation between me and the orchestra, it is already there," he announced (having earlier remarked to an assistant, "Lucky I got dressed up"). "But it's just confirmation of what a wonderful time we're all having together." He vowed the tour would forever impact his music, and couldn't resist a mischievous observation: "I've never had such a love affair without ever actually going to bed with anybody."[147]

Some in the classical community were incensed. Wrote *The Sun* music critic Tony Gould, "Artistically, it's rather childish. It's almost as if Elton John is one of the great musicians of the twentieth century, which he certainly is not." None of the esteemed classical musicians who had appeared with the MSO, including Aaron Copland and Igor Stravinsky, had received such an honor, Gould said. Newspaper readers called the award "phony" and an "insult."[148]

These critics, however, missed the point. Elton was spotlighting the MSO and other symphony orchestras, and enlightening rock fans. Besides, the MSO members liked and admired him. Among those coming to his defense was Molly Meldrum, who'd patched things up with Elton at a "barbie." In a column, Molly asserted that his friend's show was improving with each successive night. He quoted from Gould's protestations, then wrote, "Well, my dear man, I don't know if you went to any of the concerts. If you did you could not accuse Elton of merely 'singing pop songs and playing pop piano.' What he and the MSO have been doing is bridging a gap that I, and many others, thought would be impossible to cross."[149]

Once the long residency in Melbourne had ended, the MSO's newest member turned his sights to South Australia and Adelaide's Football Park. This was the only show at an outdoor venue, and boasted the largest crowd of the tour, twenty thousand. As he took his seat for the first number, "One Horse Town," the audience got an eyeful—silver Lurex tails and cape, dark sunglasses with a tiny fan on each lens, and Tina Turner wig. Some concertgoers retaliated with their own oversized glasses. Wrote reviewer David Sly, "The sheer power and majesty of one hundred musicians on stage bringing the diminutive Englishman's endearing melodies to life was sensational and at times overwhelming."[150] The lovefest was set to continue on the far side of the continent, in Western Australia and the city of Perth, where three concerts were scheduled.

But on Thursday, November 27, twenty minutes after show time for the last concert in Perth, fans were startled with a message that a "viral infection" would not allow Elton to perform. Fifteen minutes earlier, a specialist had examined his throat and decreed that he had better not sing.[151] The concert was ultimately canceled. Elton's doctor advised him to rest his voice for four days before the last—and lengthiest—leg of the tour began on Monday in Sydney.

As planned, Renate joined Elton in Sydney. It seemed that the "rift rumors," which had started because of her absence during the first month of the tour, were squelched.

The odds were that every concert review on the tour would not be stellar. And these odds caught up with Elton on December 1, the night of the first Sydney show. Critic Lynden Barber thought the use of the MSO effective only half the time. He also disliked Elton's purported "return" to a style favored early in his career, a "white English hybrid of gospel and New Orleans piano-led R&B," which he believed caused the musician to become "seriously unstuck." "It was easy to overlook the fact that his voice rasped terribly . . . , but less easy to feel sympathy for . . . the stolid treatment dished out to songs like 'Benny and the Jets' [*sic*] and 'Rocket Man,'" groused Barber. "The latter, in particular, was drawn out to self-indulgent extremes, the necessary sense of funk absent from John's piano technique. Hardly aided by poor sound, the whole band seemed bored. . . ."[152]

The next night saw a fuming Elton—already disturbed by increasingly irksome voice problems that had required the cancellation of a thirty-two-date American tour early the following year—start the show in his rehearsal outfit of shorts, sports jersey, ball cap, and sneakers. He made a comment about the Barber review as he began "Rocket Man" and, in the middle of the song, abruptly exited the stage as the band played. An awkward intermission ensued, followed by his surprise reappearance onstage. The band, by now backstage, hurriedly caught up with him.

But that was nothing compared to what happened on December 9. While in the middle of introducing the MSO, Elton collapsed, face first. James and some stagehands rushed to lift him up. After drinking a glass of water, he resumed the show as if nothing had happened. Rumors flew about his health. Publicist Patti Mostyn dismissed speculation of imminent disaster, saying that he had been feeling a "little tension" lately. "He has the constitution of an ox," she reassured the press.[153] It was revealed the following month that Elton's vocal cords had had episodes of spasmodic pain throughout the tour. One such episode had caused this collapse.[154]

By now, Renate was gone. Rumors again surfaced about their marriage when the pianist was accompanied by Mostyn instead of Renate to the wedding of tour manager Nick Pitts.[155]

The Sydney shows continued. The biggest night of the tour was also its last, on Sunday, December 14, when the Australian Broadcasting Corporation (ABC) was scheduled to simulcast the final show on television and radio across Australia and New Zealand. Molly Meldrum, a cohost, was to interview band members and tour participants during a live preshow segment.

Elton didn't admit it then, but it was the uniqueness of this tour that had kept him going.[156] "I'm gonna be very sad when this tour ends," he had said earlier.[157] By the last night, he knew throat surgery was in the offing. It was too early to tell whether he had growths on his vocal cords. If he did, there was a chance they were cancerous. Either way, they would have to be removed. The tour's end meant he would have to face the music, possibly very unpleasant music.

Blissfully unaware of the battleground raging in Elton's mind, Molly was befuddled when, during the live preshow that Sunday, the musician approached him (off camera) and insisted he wasn't "going on." Elton started leaving the arena for his hotel room as Molly ran after him. "I tried to convince him that it would be unfair on the people who had paid for their tickets, the eight million viewers, and on the people who had spent two years trying to put the televised concert together," Molly recounted in his column days later. Elton was unresponsive. Molly rushed to tell the show's producer of this alarming development. If they had to, they could televise the previous night's concert, which was on tape. But Molly rightly observed that that would "hardly have been the same."[158]

The pianist came through. At show time, concertgoers watched as he and his flexible band tore through the rock portion of the show. His voice, hopelessly hoarse at the beginning, loosened up as the show progressed. An innocent interpolation of Traffic's "Feelin' Alright?" in the middle of his historical survey of piano improvisation provided the only glimpse of his worries. "Rocket Man ain't feelin' too good himself," he scratchily sang.

Neither did throat pain keep him from a display of unorthodox virtuosity during "Bennie." Lowering his body onto the floor as he steadily rolled ragtime chords with his right hand, he rested on his left elbow with eyes shut and yawned while still playing. But he couldn't always keep the pain a secret. He struggled to sing "I Guess That's Why They Call It the Blues." At song's end, he puffed his cheeks and blew through his mouth, relieved it was over.

The second half with orchestra began, as always, with "Sixty Years On." Elton made his entrance in a luminous getup of white tails striped with light-reflecting silver, and a powdered white wig. The band members turned up gradually during later songs, most wearing stately matching white suits. The gruffness of Elton's voice sometimes detracted from songs that required either softness, like "Sorry Seems to Be the Hardest Word" and "Cold as Christmas," or sustained power, like "Slow Rivers," but on most, the MSO's full treatments—and Elton's playing—made up for his unbecoming singing.

The first showstopper of the evening was "Take Me to the Pilot," which included buoyant piano work reminiscent of the pianist's early 1970s shows, and a battle between band and orchestra built from a combination of the piano chord sequences heard on the original recording and James's invigoratingly bombastic reworking of the arrangements. Another delight was "Madman Across the Water." Elton's damaged voice helped convey the deranged nature of the "madman," and his dissonant playing danced around the intentionally disturbed utterances of the MSO. But the evening's most dramatic moment was the performance of "Don't Let the Sun Go Down on Me," the orchestra playing with *Gone with the Wind* style melodrama. Elton took Bernie's lyrics to heart. "I'd just allow a fragment of your life to wander free," he sang, only fragments of his voice left. His eyes looked moist, for good reason. "I was crying," he said years later. "My life was an utter disaster area."[159] He was worried about his voice, about his whole career.

The next song, "Candle in the Wind," would ensure that the sun wouldn't go down on him. A brief recess was afforded the band and the MSO as Elton performed the song solo, accompanied only by the synthesizer sounds triggered by his piano's MIDI hookup. This version was more special than any other solo versions he had played in the last year. His voice had cleared up a bit, allowing him to delicately project the song's passion while retaining the vulnerability in its message, audible in his uncomfortable timbre. His piano rang like a chorus of church bells.

During the encore, Elton dedicated "Your Song" to John Reid and Molly Meldrum "for putting up with me today," and apologized to fans for canceling the last Perth concert. "I'll be back," he said. As the ballad finished, the orchestra hummed. Familiar strains were audible from behind James's baton. The audience grew increasingly excited as it recognized the beginning of a very new "Saturday Night's Alright for Fighting." Elton leapt from his piano bench, motioning for those still seated to stand, as Davey launched into the song's expected guitar opening. Confetti, streamers, and finally, balloons fell on the band and the audience, which started dancing. Elton's only musical obstacle now was an incessant supply of streamers floating onto his keyboard, forcing him to play with one hand as he brushed them from the keys with the other. At song's end, Elton thanked everyone, including viewers in Australia and New Zealand. As the arena emptied, only the sound of popping balloons remained.

Elton hosted an end-of-tour party for four hundred people. He seemed in good spirits, noting he would be going to London for surgery but would return to hear the MSO play its customary material. "I don't think any permanent damage has been done," he said optimistically. Only Molly was in a bad mood, still shaken by Elton's near-refusal to do the last show. He told fellow *Sun* reporter Janise Beaumont that he couldn't wait to return to Melbourne. With a dig at Elton's preferred jewelers, he griped, "At least they're not impressed with Cartier jewelry there."[160] A few days later, Molly purged his feelings in a column:

I was talking to a friend who is a mad Elvis Presley fan. It started me thinking about the way in which he allowed his life to be led into a cocoon. He lost total sight of reality and allowed himself to be shuffled off to Las Vegas to play concerts that made him look like something of a parody of what he had been.

I'm not about to say that is what has happened to Elton. But the way things are going, this could almost become the case. If he had not gone on stage on Sunday night, by the next day his whole career could have been in ruins.

In my life in rock'n'roll I have seen many tragedies, the deaths of Brian Jones, Janis Joplin, Jimi Hendrix, and Jim Morrison to name a few. In this last year I have seen the decline of Boy George, someone that I would also call a friend. But I can't think of a friend in the business who is closer to me than Elton. That's why I worry.[164]

CHAPTER 9

WHIPPING
BOY[1]

(1987)

L*EATHER JACKETS* yielded no more singles in the United States, but there was another one in Britain, "Slow Rivers," which charted on November 29. It placed only one notch higher than "Heartache All Over the World" had, at number 44. By now it was clear. Elton was not on a hot streak.

"Slow Rivers" had been on the chart for a month when Elton surrendered to doctors, not in Britain but at St. Vincent's Private Hospital in Darlinghurst, Sydney. "It didn't make sense to go back to London when I was here," he explained at a Sydney press conference on Monday, January 5, 1987. He had just flown in from Perth, where, after finishing the tour in December, he and Patti Mostyn had been following international cricket matches. Elton carried with him two cricket bats autographed by England's team for good luck.[2] "I am a bit concerned about the operation, but of course we won't know exactly what the problem is until after the biopsy," Elton pluckily asserted at the press conference. "With any luck, there won't be an actual full-scale operation."[3]

Speculation accompanied his hospital admission. What would the surgeon find? If growths were found, could they be removed? If not, would the surgeon use a highly touted treatment involving a substance akin to Teflon? Some said the technique could be disastrous for a singer. And why had this happened to Elton's voice? Had he overused the top of his singing range? If there were lumps, had they developed from excessive singing or talking while he had had a cold or the flu?[4] (Later, in 1999, Elton disclosed that frequent marijuana smoking may have played a role.[5])

The surgery took place on Tuesday, January 6. It was declared a success. The surgeon had found a nonmalignant lesion on Elton's vocal cords, and removed it by laser in only fifteen minutes. A full recovery was expected, though Elton was ordered to remain in the hospital for a few more days, not to speak for a week—and not to sing for months. Elton would be staying in Australia an additional six weeks so the doctor could monitor his progress. Fortunately, he had plans for filling up the leisure time, including following cricket's World Series Cup and vacationing in the Outback. None of these activities would include Renate.[6]

Much hay was made in the tabloids of Renate's absence. The London-based, Rupert Murdoch–owned, tabloid *The Sun*, which had erroneously reported that Elton was sure to receive the Teflon-like treatment on his voice ("Elton: Fry Me!" was the headline on January 3[7]) led the pack, with an "exclusive" on January 10 that Elton and Renate's marriage was over. "Elton cannot stand our sham life together any longer," Renate had supposedly confessed.[8] Two days later, *The Sun* reported that a "best pal," described as "hunky record boss" Peter Ikin, had flown to Sydney to be with Elton in his time of need. *The Sun* gratuitously alleged that an Australian police officer once caught in a "gay sex scandal" involving "luring young boys for sex" had been "close" to Elton at one time.[9]

If the musician heard these stories, he didn't let on, making the most of his long vacation. He went on a Northern Territory safari, joined in net practice with England's cricket team, and watched the World Series Cup.[10] In February, he joined Lionel Richie onstage at the Sydney Entertainment Centre, accompanying the singer for a few songs on piano. "I'd like to introduce a new band member," Richie teased the audience. "We have been auditioning him for a few years—I think he might make it." When the crowd of twelve thousand saw that it was the man who had made history with the MSO at the same venue just two months earlier, they rose in a standing ovation.[11]

Later during his convalescence, all of Australia got to hear Elton's mended speaking voice at the first Australian Record Industry Awards, which he hosted in Sydney.[12] Gone was the pink ponytail. Now Elton was a platinum blonde, the lower half of his head shaved (leaving gleaming white stubble), the thinning top a cross between a bleached starfish and the stripe on Charlie Brown's shirt. If he couldn't sing, he could at least look like a completely different person.

Elton didn't win an award in Sydney, but, after being nominated for a Grammy seventeen times since 1971 (and vowing to *Rockline*'s Bob Coburn that if "they ever offer me a Grammy I shall offer to stick it up their whatsit"[13]), he won his first, in absentia, on February 24, 1987. It was for the AIDS benefit song, "That's What Friends Are For."

"YOU HAD A SCENT FOR SCANDAL"[14]

ON APRIL 1, Elton performed at a Wembley Arena AIDS benefit called "The Party," still sporting his zig-zagging platinum haircut. About to go onstage for his first public singing performance since the surgery, he was hopeful it would go well. "My natural voice has changed," he said from behind black sunglasses. "It's gotten lower." It had. He sounded older. On the subject of AIDS, he said, "A lot of people were pleased [about the spread of AIDS], because it meant getting rid of a lot of poofs."[15]

On stage, Elton carefully sang Carole King's haunting "Will You Love Me Tomorrow?," which he thought blended nicely with the theme of the show, and "I Guess That's Why They Call It the Blues," only reaching for his reserve of vocal strength occasionally, for emphasis. Sometimes he seemed to fear sustaining a note. Also, his singing voice, like his speaking voice, was deeper, and more commanding than even the robust, low-pitched voice he had cultivated for some years before the surgery.

Meanwhile, Elton's relationship with *The Sun* had taken a dramatic turn. On February 25, the day after he won his Grammy, *The Sun* began a full-fledged assault with a screaming front-page headline: "Elton in Vice Boys Scandal." Craig Mackenzie, brother of *Sun* editor Kelvin Mackenzie, had seen potential in the story of a ne'er-do-well twenty-year-old named Stephen Hardy, who had told of wild parties held at the English home of Rod Stewart's former manager, Billy Gaff. These parties purportedly involved drugs and underage "rent boys." Elton's name had come up tangentially. He knew Gaff, as did John Reid. But since Gaff wasn't famous, Craig Mackenzie and fellow dirt-digger Neil Wallis turned Hardy's account into a series on the supposed private habits of Elton John. For a price, Hardy became rent boy "Graham X." The first installment had Graham X claiming to have witnessed Elton snorting cocaine and engaging in sexual bondage with skinheads at Gaff's house. The date given was April 30, 1986—the day Elton was in New York to discuss his fall concert wardrobe with Bob Mackie, a trip that was well documented in the New York press.

The Sun was messing with the wrong guy. Elton immediately filed suit and emphatically informed Fleet Street competitors, like the *Daily Express*, of his whereabouts on April 30. But *The Sun* became obsessed with bringing Elton down, giving the public new Graham X stories every day. In one, Elton allegedly demanded that rent boys not be brought to his bed until they were sufficiently drugged with cocaine. In another, *The Sun* called him a liar because of his denials. In response to each sordid headline, Elton filed writ after writ in court.[16]

Finally, Elton decided to return home from Australia, via Los Angeles—where, he found out, a *Sun* reporter was shadowing him and questioning anyone who had contact with him. While in Los Angeles, Elton announced to Allan Hall of Melbourne's own *Sun* that, when he returned to London, "I will take that despicable newspaper for everything. . . . These stories have hurt all the people close to me. They have hurt me. They have hurt my wife Renate. They have hurt my family and friends." Even Watford. "What do you think the players felt when they read all that crap?" he asked.[17]

Elton was back in England for his fortieth birthday party, held at Reid's Hertfordshire home. Everyone was there, it seemed, except Renate. This led to more headlines—and not just in *The Sun*. To end the innuendo, Elton formally announced, on March 27, that they had separated.[18] This led to more grief for the couple. Rumors that Renate was a lesbian resurfaced. Their marriage was dubbed a "big lie."[19] It was getting harder for Elton to take. After performing at the Wembley AIDS benefit, he retreated from public view.

When Elton appeared on Michael Parkinson's *One-to-One* television program about three weeks later, he was barely recognizable. Otherworldly humor was gone from his wardrobe, even from his physical appearance. The stubble around his head was no longer bleached and was growing in. He scratched a new beard like an old hillbilly reflecting on the trials of hard living. Instead of a designer suit, he was clothed in a red and black jogging outfit, a Watford ball cap, and eyeglasses ordinary enough for Reg Dwight to have worn during his Bluesology days. But as plainly dressed as Elton was, he still had a lot of news for Parkinson.

Elton related that, while he was recently bedridden with the flu and during soccer's week of semifinals (to which Watford had advanced), the tabloids had trumpeted a false story that he planned to sell his beloved team. He marveled that the club's bank nearly stopped Watford's checks in response to the "news," and dismissed a rumor that he would be abandoning England altogether for the United States. "I have too many roots here," he said. But his mother and stepfather were leaving England for Spain because of *The Sun*. "My mother's had it," Elton noted calmly. "She's at the end of her tether."

He and Renate were considering reuniting, although their relationship hardly sounded romantic. "We're very, very good friends. The marriage isn't over, per se. We just separated for a little while. That happens to every marriage," he insisted, adding that *The Sun* had caused much of the strain between them. If Renate visited her doctor, a *Sun* reporter would attempt to bribe both receptionist and doctor for medical information. "They probably want to examine my sperm," Elton surmised. "According to *The Sun*, they must have packetfuls of it."[20]

Meanwhile, the rent boy stories continued to travel down new, depraved paths. When *The Sun* began losing faith in Stephen Hardy's ability to churn out tales, it turned to a Scottish rent boy pimp named John Boyce. Paid by *The Sun*, Boyce bribed a group of rent boys—as well as other youngsters who had never even been rent boys—to sign affidavits saying that, as rent boys, they had had sex and done drugs with Elton John. Later, *The Sun* reached an unprecedented low when it paid ten thousand pounds (around sixteen thousand dollars) for some old photographs of Elton in compromising positions dating back to the late 1970s and early 1980s. *The Sun* printed all but one photograph, while a nude picture with his genitals obscured was reserved for the front page.

There were problems with this strategy. Printing the pictures was an outrageous invasion of privacy. Plus, the pictures themselves were irrelevant to the rent boy allegations. Elton sued *The Sun* again.[21] But by the time he talked to Michael Parkinson on national television on April 18, the stories and pictures had already gravely undermined his sense of well-being.

Elton showed a remarkable (public) resiliency. He and Renate reunited in early May, and were seen together in the director's box in Birmingham, where Watford failed to advance to the FA Cup Final. (Watford went on to prove that, despite defeat, it had some energy left. On a return tour of China with the club, Elton joyfully watched as the team—minus manager Graham Taylor, who had just left for another club—won five games in a row and the Great Wall Cup.)[22]

"YOU KNOW YOU CAN'T HOLD ME FOREVER"[23]

AFTER MORE THAN HALF A DECADE and much dissipated acrimony, Elton was back at MCA. Words couldn't express how thrilled he was to be free of Geffen Records. "It was six years of pure hell," Elton later told *Boston Globe* reporter Brett Milano of his time under contract to Geffen. Milano, feeling the need to censor some of the musician's comments, quoted Elton as adding, "I hope I never see that bearded [bleep] again."[24]

Elton wasn't the only one who harbored such sentiments about David Geffen and his record label. Donna Summer was disappointed with her treatment as a Geffen act, as was the quirky, Jewish/African-American rhythm and blues ensemble known as Was (Not Was). After a poorly selling Geffen album, *Born to Laugh at Tornadoes*, Was (Not Was) departed the label with hard feelings, later finding a name for itself at Chrysalis with *What Up, Dog?* and the novelty hit, "Walk the Dinosaur."[25] Joni Mitchell also ended up leaving Geffen. None of her 1980s albums under the label had gone gold, even after a string of gold albums in the 1970s. Geffen contends that, to this day, Mitchell's albums still haven't recouped the advances she took.[26] But Mitchell felt cheated. "I don't make much money," she complained in 1996. "I haven't seen a royalty check in twenty years. At a certain point Geffen dammed up my only income—which is my writer's income from my publishing company—so I had *no* money coming in." When this happened, she asked to be released from her record contract, but Geffen refused, saying she couldn't get a better contract anywhere else.[27] (Mitchell has since left the label.)

One of the most bitter feuds with Geffen involved Neil Young. In 1982, Geffen had lured Young away from re-signing with Reprise by promising complete artistic freedom. But when the songwriter's first album for the label, *Trans*, made a barely perceptible dent on the charts, Geffen refused to release Young's country album, *Old Ways*, without first approving the producer and songs. Geffen instead used a chunk of Young's record advance money to buy his album *Everybody's Rockin'* from Reprise to fulfill the rest of the guitarist's contract with his former label. Released in August 1983, *Everybody's Rockin'* did even worse than *Trans*. Geffen sued

Young for failing to make "commercial" records, demanding the return of his advance money. Young counter-sued for breach of contract and fraud. Surprisingly, the suits were dropped early in 1985. Young honored his contract, and Geffen released *Old Ways*, the first of the three remaining albums. All did as badly as *Trans* and *Everybody's Rockin'*, and Young returned to Reprise.[28] Most of his albums thereafter were certified either gold or platinum.

In 1989, even after Elton and several other important artists had already experienced the grief of being a Geffen signee, David Geffen was still promoting the line he had first uttered back in 1980: "Here, people get to be exactly who they are."[29]

Elton's decision to return to MCA was a wise one. To his delight, his new-old record label was interested in releasing a double album culled from the December 14, 1986 Sydney concert. A worldwide public would soon hear his coarse, pre-surgery voice, just as it was now almost completely healed.

Not long before the new album's release, Elton made his second live singing appearance in six months, performing at the annual Prince's Trust benefit. His sartorial funny bone was back; the summer of 1987 would see him in myriad upholstered caftan-like concoctions straight out of *Alice in Wonderland*. At the Prince's Trust concert, he wore an ankle-length coat sporting exaggeratedly flared lapels, and covered with enough plump buttons to engage a sewing enthusiast for some time. His hair, short but grown in, was back to its natural color but rumored to be covered in a polymer hair spray that made it look fuller on top. He performed two songs, "Your Song" and "Saturday Night's Alright"; although he was apparently still learning about his new voice, it seemed fully healed. His reinterpretation of "Your Song" reached an unprecedented level of intimacy, and with the familiar lines "I hope you don't mind, I hope you don't mind" he seemed to be saying that he was here to stay.

Releasing *Live in Australia with the Melbourne Symphony Orchestra* at a time like this could have been a step backward. But the MSO tour had been a milestone for everyone involved, as well as an emotional crossroads for Elton. Memorializing it for the record-buying public was, in essence, a catharsis. The album included fourteen of the eighteen songs performed with the orchestra; missing were three from the Geffen years, "Cold as Christmas," "Carla/Étude," and "Slow Rivers," and one song, "Saturday Night's Alright," that had gone over nicely live but really didn't fit the album concept.

In Australia, where memories of the headline-heavy tour were still fresh, the album easily reached number 1 by the first week of August. In the United States, *Live in Australia* charted on July 25, eventually peaking at number 24. In January 1988, it was certified gold. But the American success of *Live in Australia* wasn't duplicated at home, where an unsettling commercial trend would take another three years to reverse. A limited edition box set peaked at number 70 in September. Upon re-release as a double album in early 1988, it would reach an unimpressive number 43.

The reason American record buyers embraced the album—and British record buyers should have—was a single, "Candle in the Wind," which reached the Top 10 in both countries. In Britain, Phonogram mistakenly went with "Your Song" first, a beautiful rendition, but by now the original was about as commonly heard by music fans as "Abide with Me" was by soccer fans. The single got nowhere. "Candle in the Wind," however, was a different story, even though the studio version had narrowly missed the Top 10 in 1974. On January 16, 1988, the live "Candle" debuted on the British singles chart and went on to reach number 5. Maybe the video helped. Elton had purchased twenty thousand dollars worth of vintage Marilyn Monroe footage that he had spliced in with live Sydney footage of himself.

That the album did better in the United States made the victory of "Candle" there all the sweeter. The American single started off slowly, like the album. Released in August, around the twenty-fifth anniversary of Monroe's death, it initially got airplay only on adult contemporary stations. Finally, on November 7, 1987, it entered *Billboard*'s Hot 100 at number 68. "We always knew it would have good acceptance among older listeners," said Richard Palmese, MCA's executive vice president of marketing and promotion, "but the research we've seen shows that the record did just as well among teens—which is why the record eventually crossed over from adult contemporary stations to [Top 40] stations."[30] The single did more than cross over. It hit number 6 on January 23, 1988, after twelve weeks on the chart.

A second American single from *Live in Australia*, "Take Me to the Pilot," went nowhere. By then, it was almost time for the premier single from Elton's first MCA studio album since 1980's *21 at 33.*

"DON'T IT MAKE YOU WANNA CRAWL BACK TO THE WOMB"[31]

ELTON VIEWED 1987 AS THE WORST YEAR OF HIS LIFE. Throat surgery, convalescence, and marital troubles played a part. *The Sun* played a bigger part. In a May 19 front-page story titled "My Hell," he had told London's *Daily Mirror* that it was "horrible" having to endure *The Sun*'s never-ending string of allegations.[32] On *Wogan* in June, he had confided that he was "very down in the dumps."[33]

The Sun, scrambling for more dirt after losing faith in both Stephen Hardy and John Boyce, turned from Elton's sex life to his dogs. On September 28, 1987, another *Sun* "exclusive" filled its front page: "Mystery of Elton's Silent Dogs: RSPCA probe shock claim that they had their barks removed." *The Sun*'s John Askill described the dogs as Rottweilers, although Elton owned Alsatians, and quoted an RSPCA official about the "probe." The official later protested that the quotes attributed to him were false. Elton quickly filed another writ.[34]

Three weeks before the story appeared, Elton and Bernie collected a special recognition award in Los Angeles at the MTV Video Music Awards. All was not well with the pair's musical half. He seemed to have aged ten years since he was last onstage in the United States. His clothing—a stylish trilby hat, gray suit, and conventional tie—did nothing to dispel this impression. Only his striped shirt recalled the daring sartorialism seen as recently as June.

The audience gave Elton and Bernie a standing ovation, then quieted. Elton paced. "One of the reasons why I lasted so long was that I never slept around—at least not with *him*," he said loudly, gesturing toward his songwriting partner. He briefly composed himself. "It could not have been possible without you, and all of you at home. Thank you." He exited, leaving the coherency to Bernie, who said, "I'd just like to add that I think the reason it's been so good for us for so long is because we've always remained fans, too."

Some of Elton's plans hadn't been realized. Talk of him scoring Sylvester Stallone's next Rambo movie never panned out, and plans to produce Ringo Starr's next album were pushed aside when a film acting opportunity (temporarily) beckoned, prompting him to push up his own recording schedule.[35]

In October, Elton started recording his album. It may have seemed that there was little to do. He had six or seven songs, including a number called "Heavy Traffic," left over from the prolific (if dissatisfying) *Leather Jackets* sessions. But the initial plans for the next album probably wouldn't have included those, anyway. Nine months earlier in Australia, James Newton Howard had expected to do string arrangements for a much more introspective Elton John album than *Leather Jackets*. "Elton's next album will probably use a less traditional song structure," he had said at the time. "The less accessible music is the most magical for me."[36] In fact, Elton mostly ignored the extra *Leather Jackets* songs, while coming up with tunes that weren't overwhelmingly introspective, either. He was happy about this: "I went into the studio thinking, 'I hope I don't write all these bloody slow songs,' and it turned out just the opposite."[37]

Elton went back to work to get rid of the worst depression he could remember ever having. Writing new songs made him feel useful again. He also returned to producer Chris Thomas. The former Royal Academy buddy was exultant after producing INXS's latest album, *Kick*, soon to be in the Top 10 in the United States and Britain, and contributed to the optimistic atmosphere of the sessions. Not surprisingly, then, the songs reveal a rebirth of Elton's storied joie de vivre.

The songs that would come to be known as *Reg Strikes Back* may be viewed as direct descendants of the cinematic vision of *Goodbye Yellow Brick Road*. Although Bernie still showed little interest in fashioning new characters with the staying power of hoodlum Danny Bailey or the luckless Alice, his knack for painting vignettes of life on a canvas of lively words seemed reinvigorated. The hidden colors and hues, absent from some of the more recent songs (like "Gypsy Heart," "I Fall Apart," and "Too Young"), were back in full force, informed by the more grown-up, worldly air that had become especially noticeable beginning with *Too Low for Zero*.

Like *Goodbye Yellow Brick Road*—and *Blue Moves*, for that matter—*Reg Strikes Back* both acknowledged past accomplishments and offered glimpses of the future. The ten new songs fit into most of the expansive categories that house the seventeen numbers from the celebrated 1973 double album. There are panoramic ballads, up-tempo ballads, an up-tempo (if not eccentric) song, a rock'n'roll rave-up, and, most important, adult rock songs that pick up where "Love Lies Bleeding" left off.

The nucleus of the 1985–86 touring band joined Elton and Thomas in the studio. Absent were backup singers Alan Carvell, Shirley Lewis, and Gordon Neville, percussionist Jody Linscott, and the Onward International Horns. Nigel and Dee returned (at Thomas's invitation) to sing backup alongside Davey Johnstone. Ray Cooper was on hand for several numbers. Some stellar guest musicians lent their imprint on a few tracks, including jazz trumpeter Freddie Hubbard, Pete Townsend, and some of the Beach Boys.

The first number Elton wrote, "Since God Invented Girls," provided strange words for him to sing, even if he was married. Fortunately, the finished product is neither as trying nor as improbable as "Heartache All Over the World." Bernie probably expected "Since God Invented Girls" to be up-tempo, and pieced together some mawkishly macho phrases recalling the unredeeming flavor of songs like "Li'l 'Frigerator." But Elton responded with something else, reacting to the name "Brian Wilson," which leapt up at him from a reference to "California Girls": "Now I know what Brian Wilson meant/every time I step outside." This couplet suggested a Beach Boys tribute, not the raging rocker right for other lines: "Oh! Here's a little heat boys/to straighten out them curls."

"Girls" was an ego booster for Elton. "I wrote it all the way through without stopping," he remembered. "I wrote it at home, and my engineer at the studio at home had luckily taped it. That was the first song I wrote coming out of my depression, and I went out the door of the studio and I was just punching the air."[38]

This is not, however, a punchy song. Like "Goodbye Yellow Brick Road" and "Don't Let the Sun," "Girls" possesses a sweeping, strikingly visual melodic structure. Instead of illustrating some of the more unoriginal lyric images, the melody creates a separate story of love and devotion to an asexual ideal of beauty. Elton's rejuvenated voice begins cautiously from its outer boundaries with consistently mannish tones, then breaks free, retaining its potency while scaling some intimidating heights. (He didn't use his falsetto per se on this song, though it was restored after being lost for three weeks following surgery, presumably affording him the confidence he needed to manipulate his voice once more. "Suddenly, I got it back again—I'm not telling you how!" he devilishly told Terry Wogan in June.[39]) The band, which faithfully accompanies Elton's vocal, is superfluous. He might as well have sung the song a capella, without even Bruce Johnston and Carl Wilson on backing vocals.

Bernie's lyrics for "Japanese Hands," the second panoramic ballad on *Reg Strikes Back*, may isolate some sexist or ethnocentric ideas, but they do seem inspired by traditional Japanese images. The song works as an expression of fascination and occasional passion for a foreign culture. Bernie returns repeatedly to scenes of hot and cold as his eyes absorb Asian landscapes of gilded ebony, his infatuation waxing and waning: "And the hot wind heats the bamboo blinds/and your almond eyes always shine/sitting cool behind your painted fan."

The song's arrangement is spare but effective, and as interesting as some of Elton's synthesizer work on *Too Low for Zero*. "We were trying not to go overboard with the Japanese thing," he said. "There's a mood feel to it, absolutely. But that just came about by my writing the song on a synthesizer rather than a piano. Because the synth sound is very ethereal. And that formed the shape of the song."[40] Elton's synthesizer creates a mystical, almost science fiction–like atmosphere. The other instruments are so completely swept up in the smoke of his unnatural chord changes that they, too, sound like synthesizers. Even Davey's acoustic and electric guitars and his backing vocals with Nigel and Dee seem fed through wires in an electronic keyboard. Yet all this weirdness actually seems right for Elton's pensive principal melody. He sings as if his lips are pressed against the listener's ear, so prominent are the fibers of his vocal cords. If his performance at the Prince's Trust concert in June announced that he had returned for good, his vocal on "Japanese Hands" reinforced this good news on record.

In "Poor Cow," an up-tempo ballad, Bernie improves his standing among those objecting to his seemingly misogynistic lyrics in other songs. "Poor Cow" may also contain his most English-themed story since "Saturday Night's Alright." The title represents a singularly English mode of expression, as do many of the words and phrases in the song ("lass," "us gamey lot"). Here, Bernie examines a working-class woman's dilemma. As social commentator, he observes how the main character, a young wife, only gets married because *everyone* gets married, and becomes a victim of spousal abuse.

Elton's electric piano playing on "Poor Cow" is silent movie–like. Indeed, the woman in the song might as well be tied to railroad tracks and left for the next train. The steady beat he maintains with his left hand makes the song up-tempo, giving it a greater urgency than would the soft plaints of a traditional ballad. Over silent movie strains and a persistent beat sits an engrossing melody, boasting as many paths as any of the pianist's most complex songs.

Elton makes the song a vocal editorial, raising his baritone/tenor-meshed voice to tell of unpaid bills ("the money burns") and, by the chorus, warning with clenched throat of impending violence wrought by a volatile husband ("the back of his hand"). His chameleonic vocals, a trademark throughout his career, had never before been this changeable.

The second up-tempo ballad, "A Word in Spanish," attains cinematic legitimacy with its blatant lyrical references to an imagined movie scene. Bernie becomes a tongue-tied would-be lover, who doesn't know how to tell the object of his affections of his love. He finally remembers a film he once saw: "There's a word in Spanish/I don't understand/but I heard it in a film one time/spoken by the leading man/he said it with devotion/he sounded so sincere/and the words he spoke in Spanish/brought the female lead to tears." He decides to mimic this performance in real life, hoping it will work for him, too.

The song's energy makes it an up-tempo ballad. Elton's music makes the man seem emphatic about his feelings, desperate to make clear his devotion, certain of what he must do to gain the affection of his love. Charlie Morgan's "chinka-chinka" drumming and Elton's choppy electric piano unite in a mission to loosen the man's tongue, as if to assist him in his search for words; Davey's Latin guitar-picking provides the ideal background. Amid Elton's near-shouting vocal are facile, almost imperceptible plunges to the depths, as if he is testing his voice, not unlike a young bodybuilder admiring his new muscles—a recurring feature on *Reg Strikes Back*.

The third and final up-tempo ballad is "The Camera Never Lies," which Elton wrote in James's recording studio during a Los Angeles stay.[41] Muddying the waters as he often did when asked about a song's meaning, he said in 1988, "I think it [the camera] lies all the time, especially when it takes photographs of me."[42] Actually, "The Camera Never Lies" is about a man who has exposed his two-timing wife. Bernie cleverly plays on camera-related concepts as he has the husband convince his wife he knows what she is up to: "The shutter falls each time you meet him/a negative becomes my plus."

Elton throws in Bernie's first two words ("Hey girl") as part of the song's introduction, a pounding, throbbing, soul stew that is still measured and pained enough to qualify as a ballad. More noticeable is the tone of Elton's melody. The song represents the end of the line for a troubled marriage between camera lover and camera subject, a fact audible in every phrase as Elton dives into his lower register for one punctuation after another of quavering finality. His effortless piano tinkling belies the gravity of the husband's accusations against his wife, foretelling instead a happier time once the two have gone their separate ways.

"Heavy Traffic," an up-tempo song from the *Leather Jackets* sessions, seems as if it was written with the rest of its album-mates rather than during the height of Elton's days of careless composition. Bernie, though, creates caricatures here, not memorable characters—Shakey, "Snake Hips" Joe, and others—all entangled in the seamier side of the American dream, playing out their cameos in California near the Mexican border. "Heavy Traffic" would seem at first to be about drug trafficking, but the heavy traffic subsumes many of the vices of modern-day American existence: pimping and whoring, a kind of aimlessness that leads to senseless murders and drug addiction.

This song was cowritten with Davey, who plays every manner of guitar on the recording, and whose feathery acoustic strumming is a song staple. Ray lends a Latin tang with his timbales (actually, kettledrums). Although the song's caricatures are hurtling toward self-destruction, the music is gleeful, almost comical. Elton's ironic sense is at work again. He mocks these people and their whirlwind of illicit, dead-end activities, giving them the power to recognize their path to ruin as they step back and look at themselves ("Yes, we're rollin' in heavy traffic"). His festive, scurrying, jazz-lounge piano playing completes the union of strange bedfellows.

With "Goodbye Marlon Brando," Elton and Bernie mock everything famous, notorious, or popular. Why Brando, rarely seen in films in recent years, is highlight-ed isn't certain. But there are many recognizable phenomena that Bernie targets in *Reg Strikes Back*'s sole rock'n'roll rave-up: politicians ("Say goodbye to the clowns in Congress"), New Age music ("Say goodbye to new age music/from the capa to the Coda"), pulp fiction ("Say goodbye to Jackie Collins/say goodbye to illiterate fools"), and tabloid reporting ("Say goodbye to articles/on who the senator kissed"). Even the Beach Boys, Elton's musical mentors, and Sylvester Stallone, a new friend of the musician, are bidden adieu ("Say goodbye to the Beach Boys/from the Palisades to Kona/. . . . /Say goodbye to Rocky Five,/Six, Seven, and Eight.").

For Elton, this was just a fun song. He had no complaints about Stallone or the Beach Boys (Carl Wilson and Bruce Johnston sing the word "Kona"). He may have felt varying degrees of disgust with much that was subject to his lyricist's poison pen, but the song's message, to him, was lighthearted. "It's very tongue-in-cheek, except I don't know how far Bernie's tongue is in his cheek on this one," Elton observed.[43]

Similar to "Saturday Night's Alright for Fighting," "Goodbye Marlon Brando" has a reckless sound, but still maintains a melodic harmoniousness. This makes Bernie's "goodbye" couplets, however unrelated, perfect companions: "Say goodbye to Glasnost/say goodbye to Malathion," or "Say goodbye to the tabloids/say good-bye to diet soda." Elton savagely sputters the chorus ("Don't it wanna make you crawl back to the womb . . .") as Davey's toned-down heavy-metal guitar supports his (mostly) feigned repulsion.

As inspiring as this album's panoramic ballads are, as meaty as its up-tempo bal-lads feel, and as pulse-quickening as the up-tempo song and the rock'n'roll rave-up are, the most important songs on *Reg Strikes Back* are the adult rock songs, rough descendants of "Love Lies Bleeding" and the up-tempo contemporary jazz from *Blue Moves*, like "One Horse Town" and "Crazy Water." The adult rock songs are loud and rambunctious, but possess an intangible element of restrained sophistication, cultural elevation, even occasional haughty wit.

The lyrics in "Town of Plenty" are a massaged indictment of American society in the late 1980s. At the time, Reaganomics was flouting what had previously been considered the public good, social programs were under attack, an insider trading scandal was evidencing a reckless greed not seen since the Roaring Twenties, and the media were more intent than ever on destroying the faith the public had in what remained of the communal spirit. Bernie addresses these problems with broader conceptual strokes than he used in an obvious predecessor, "Goodbye Yellow Brick Road." In the latter, a youth disgruntled with assurances of prosperity and fairness in the big city returns to the farm. In "Town of Plenty," Bernie imagines greed and avarice squeezed out by a social conscience. The youth of "Goodbye Yellow Brick Road" is now older, a stark realist who is angry that he hasn't found the dog-eat-dog world he covets. All the quintessential Americans are getting out of town: "And laid across the airstrip/were the passports and the luggage/all that once remained of the rugged individual. . . ."

"Town of Plenty," an amusing exercise in irony, opens *Reg Strikes Back*, and its opening chords provide the mirthful starting point for a Tin Pan Alley–laced rhythm and blues concoction of dream-saturated innocence. Organ and synthesizer join with child-like abandon—resembling rhythmic merry-go-round music—over the faint strains of guest Pete Townsend's guitar. Davey, Dee, and Nigel make chaste harmonies fit for the schoolyard, while David Paton establishes a bass pattern of infectious prepubescent playfulness. But despite these qualities, this isn't a kid's song. A cynical resentment is heard in the "laid across the airstrip" verse, where the melody's declarative note clusters end in a figurative sigh as resentment gives way to disillusionment. "Came looking for a town of plenty," Elton sings resignedly. His spirit perks up again as he returns to assertions of this enlightened metropolis's fail-ings: "I'll say it again/this is not my city."

A narrower examination of political and social disillusionment is found in "Mona Lisas and Mad Hatters (Part Two)." The focus here is New York City—fif-teen years after the original "Mona Lisas," also about New York, was written and recorded. Back in 1972, Bernie had been prompted to write "Mona Lisas" by a shooting beneath his hotel room window, which had given him a cold dose of Big Apple reality. He could see only the compartmentalization of New York's inhabi-tants, their single-mindedness ("they know not if it's dark outside or light"), and their oblivion to the ugliness around them ("rich man can ride, and the hobo he can drown"). By 1987, he could look back on the initial shock of that shooting ("I used to think that New York City/fell from grace with God") and make sense of things. He decides to give New York a second chance. He walks New York's streets, taking in its ambience and culture, as he looks for what had first bothered him so much ("Searching for the city that/took away the kid in me").

This may be the most maligned of Elton's songs, even by many of his own fans. Some have said that he and Bernie shouldn't revisit their earlier work, cast a subject in a different light, or reinvent themselves. But in deviating so sharply from the fifteen-year-old *Honky Chateau* track, the writers achieve something that epitomizes what can be most wonderful about songwriting—the element of surprise. The best music often comes from left field. This is what makes "Part Two" so special. "That's probably my favorite track on the album," Elton once said. "It just has a great New York feel."[44]

"Part Two" is Broadway, Swing Street, a traffic jam in the Lincoln Tunnel. It's Fifth Avenue fashion, hubbub on the floor of the New York Stock Exchange, a Battery Park breeze, a sonic explosion of the United States' most hated, loved, pursued, avoided, frightening, and exhilarating city—as if non-New Yorker Elton understood this massive urban sprawl implicitly. There are optimal performances: Davey's banjo-like picking, reminiscent of an early 1930s Hollywood take on the music of New York; Freddie Hubbard's spicy trumpet and flugelhorn solos; backing vocals by Davey, Dee, and Nigel that take some of the high-stepping, synthesized horn honking literally as they warble a Beatles reference ("Beep-beep, beep-beep, yeah!"); Elton's hustley-bustley keyboard framework that laces itself up inside the entire production; and his rippling vocal, the song's most vivid musical instrument.

The last adult rocker of the bunch is the dance-rock opus "I Don't Wanna Go On with You Like That." This song has been misnamed too many times, from the grammatically proper "I Don't Want to Go On with You Like That" to the totally wrong "I Don't Want to Go On without You." But whatever it is called, this song is thrilling from top to bottom, beginning with the vibrating cadence of the words. The subject is anything but profound—one half of a pair of lovers makes clear her wish to sleep around. Her partner comes up with elaborate objections: "I ain't no puzzle piece that needs to fit"; "Don't wanna be a feather in your cap"; "I don't want no second hand feeding me lines." The solution is simple: "You'll just have to quit 'em if you want me back."

"Philadelphia Freedom" and its scattered progeny ("Give Me the Love" and "Where Have All the Good Times Gone?") united rock, Philly Soul, and disco. "I Don't Wanna" brings rock to another musical arena—the streamlined disco known as dance music. These seemingly divergent phenomena are forged together through a whirlwind melody at least as rhythmic as Bernie's words, a lead vocal reminiscent of Big Mama Thornton singing "Hound Dog" at 78 rpm speed, and a whole new way of looking at the role of the piano in popular music. Here, Elton extracts from the percussive side of his playing the most basic rhythmic qualities, while imbuing in them decorations (pops, vibraphone-ish sweeps, and mumbling) that may individually sound mechanical, but, together, coagulate into a late twentieth-century symphony for keyboard.

Elton was pleased with his keyboard work on *Reg Strikes Back*. "There's more piano on it," he said months later, "which I think is a step in the right direction, because I think people are very fond of me when I play piano."[45] He was right about that, as well as with his initial assessment of the album. "This one sounds good all the way through," he exulted.[46] His enthusiasm would wane over time, but this was primarily a function of his ambition. Every album he did always had to be better than the previous one. Nearly three years after *Reg Strikes Back* was put to bed, Elton had a more sober view about the album that had plucked him from the doldrums: "[O]n *Reg Strikes Back*, which has some great things on it, we did so many different styles that there's no continuity."[47]

"WE HAD SOMETHING IN COMMON"[48]

A DOWNWARD BLIP on the screen of Elton's American resurgence was an album Geffen released in September 1987, *Elton John's Greatest Hits, Volume III, 1979–1987.* This completed the musician's contractual obligation to Geffen, but was a move not unlike DJM's poorly timed issuance of old Elton John songs and repackaged Elton John albums during the late 1970s in Britain. Both MCA and Elton were banking on the success of *Live in Australia*, just released in July, and didn't need the competition.

Greatest Hits III featured some glaring omissions. The only song from the late 1970s was "Mama Can't Buy You Love"; from 1980, just "Little Jeannie." Two other MCA singles were excluded, 1978's "Part-Time Love" and "Ego." Also conspicuously missing were the Geffen recordings "Nobody Wins" and "Chloe" from 1981. Though not substantial hits, these had done better than "Heartache All Over the World," which brought the album up to date. Elton's career was better represented beginning with 1982 ("Empty Garden" and "Blue Eyes"). *Too Low for Zero* was accorded the greatest honor, with four selections: "I'm Still Standing," "I Guess That's Why They Call It the Blues," "Kiss the Bride," and a song not released as a single in the United States, "Too Low for Zero." But *Breaking Hearts* was almost ignored. "Sad Songs" was included, but "In Neon" wasn't, left behind like the dream-filled woman in the song who longed to see her name in lights. "Who Wears These Shoes?," which had peaked at number 16, was also disappointingly absent, while a song from *Ice on Fire* that had only reached number 20, "Wrap Her Up," was included (along with the evergreen "Nikita").

Working against the album was a lack of new songs. Although this may not have been advisable with the live "Candle in the Wind" struggling for airplay, it had become fashionable to include new songs on greatest hits packages. Also, Elton's recent music was not considered a must-have. So *Greatest Hits III* peaked at number 82 following its October 3, 1987 chart debut. It was certified gold, eventually, on February 14, 1989.

The end of 1987 saw Elton grappling with questions not of music, but soccer. He agreed to sell his controlling interest in Watford to powerful media man Robert Maxwell for $3.5 million. With this deal, Elton looked both backward, to a year of pain when he had been unable to give Watford the attention it needed, and forward, to future crises that might take him away from the team. Some months later, after the deal had fallen through, Elton intimated to Jonathan Ross, on BBC-TV's *The Last*

Resort, that he'd tried to sell the club because he couldn't then count on himself to be reliable. "If anything happened to me," he said, tremulously, "there's no other bene-factors of the club."[49]

While the deal was pending, Elton removed ex-manager Graham Taylor's suc-cessor, Dave Bassett, replacing him with Taylor protégé Steve Harrison, in hopes of stalling the downward spiral of Watford from its former lofty heights. Nonetheless, the team was soon relegated to the second division.[50]

As Watford was relegated, the Beach Boys were elevated to the status of Rock and Roll Hall of Fame inductees. Elton ushered them in on January 28, 1988 at the third annual induction dinner held at New York's Waldorf-Astoria Hotel. "The Beach Boys were the first white band I can remember summing up America," he said in his induction speech. "If you lived in England, all you ever wanted to do was go to America. Everything you ever dreamed of was American. This band not only wrote great songs, initially writing surf music, but they did more than that. . . . This band were geniuses. They still are. They made me love America so much more, because they existed. . . . They are, for me, what America is. . . ."[51]

Later that evening, Elton and other rock stars squeezed onto the small stage together to play, sing, and mingle. Alongside Elton were Bob Dylan, the Beach Boys, Bruce Springsteen, Little Richard, Billy Joel, the Drifters, and a couple of ex-Beatles. The Pinner pianist led the group, shouting the words to "Whole Lot of Shakin' Going On" and "Hound Dog." The few remaining at their tables had achievers from rock's past, present, and future before them. Elton would continue to prove that he was firmly entrenched in all three categories.

CHAPTER 10

I

FALL

APART[1]

(1988–1990)

"**S**O IT'S OLIVIA NEWTON-JOHN produced by James Newton Howard and Elton John. How complex can you get?" Elton mused in a British ITV interview about "The Rumour," a song he cowrote with Bernie and coproduced with James for Olivia Newton-John in 1998. Maybe the three names together were too much for the gods of hit radio. Maybe the timing wasn't right. Either way, the poor commercial performance of "The Rumour" seemed to prove that Elton still couldn't write a hit for someone else.

The pianist remained more than adept, however, at writing hits for himself. On June 18, 1988, "I Don't Wanna Go On with You Like That" debuted in the United States on *Billboard*'s Hot 100 at number 60. It had a lot going for it, besides its catchiness. There was a state-of-the-art video directed by Russell Mulcahy, with images as speedily rendered as Elton's feverish melody. The video quickly became a staple of cable station Video Hits One (VH1), the mature version of MTV that had lately found its voice. There was also MCA's promotional zeal. Just as it might for any current, younger artist, MCA developed an inviting counter display for record stores across the country. Other promotional items included a *Reg Strikes Back* matchbook and a fold-open pop-up of the album cover design.

Elton's new song took off. In its third week it was in the Top 40 and, beginning on July 9, received *Billboard*'s "Power Pick/Sales" designation for two consecutive weeks. On August 27, when it reached number 2, it became the musician's highest-charting single (excluding "That's What Friends Are For") since 1980's "Little Jeannie." "I Don't Wanna" never got to the top spot, bested by the irrepressibly hot George Michael's "Monkey," but even so, Elton's dance-rock number was an essential part of the soundtrack to summer 1988.

In the United States, the album had a similarly fast start. Charting on July 9, it peaked at number 16, performing better than any album since *21 at 33*. In a month, it was certified gold. MCA was solidly behind this album. During the height of the "Candle in the Wind" phenomenon, the company couldn't wait to sell *Reg Strikes Back*. "This album [*Live in Australia*] has done its job," MCA executive Richard Palmese had said. "We want to get the new product out. Elton is a contemporary artist—and we want him to be viewed that way."[2] The contrast between this motivated attitude and the lackadaisical approach of Geffen Records was palpable.

"Elton John is creating music with the same propulsive energy of his 'Honky Cat' / 'Saturday Night's Alright for Fighting' rock phase," wrote Jonathan Takiff for the *Philadelphia Daily News*.[3] "The transformed Elton can still rock like a kid with something to prove," noted Harold Goldberg for *Rolling Stone*.[4] Mark Moses, of the culturally highbrow *New Yorker*, found the musician's latest work worthy of some discussion. Moses observed that Elton's music, once an amalgam of popular musical genres everyone knew and loved, had now graduated to a higher plane. "John has fashioned himself of bits and pieces of . . . pop-culture debris, but, just as he once slyly referred to sixties musical gems in his own songs, he is now enough of an original to refer to his own early work with the same warmth and certainty."[5]

While Elton was reentering a rarefied stratosphere of recognition in the United States, to the British public the new album and single were mere afterthoughts. Following a chart entry on June 4, the single reached number 30. The following month, the album peaked at number 18—doing better than *Live in Australia*, but not by much.

It wasn't that the British public lacked awareness of Elton's exploits. In mid-May he talked to Simon Bates on BBC Radio One. He appeared for a third year in a row at the Prince's Trust concert, playing a version of "I Don't Wanna," reconstituted for Eric Clapton's blues sensibilities. On Jonathan Ross's television show, Elton could have promoted "I Don't Wanna" to a nationwide audience. Instead, he performed Jim Reeves's "He'll Have to Go" on his new instrument of choice, a Roland piano, and later turned to pub standards, prompting a studio audience sing-along.

In the United States, too, Elton was now very visible, more so that he'd been for some time. A satellite hookup allowed him to do thirty-six ten-minute interviews for stations from coast to coast. He and Bernie met with record industry types, holding eight album-listening parties across the country.[6] And these were not staid, businesslike affairs, either. At Fantasy Studios in Berkeley, California, Elton mingled with the 150 or so guests and took a solo turn at his Roland, entertaining them with some of his more familiar tunes as well as "Get Back."[7] At Boston's Axis club, the pianist signed autographs and played a half-hour solo concert that featured "Grapevine," "Whole Lot of Shakin' Going On," and a little piano bench abuse.[8]

Whether Elton was mingling or signing autographs, he had a lot to talk about. The album's release seemed tied to another, rapidly unfolding event—preparations for the auction of many of his possessions by Sotheby's. Although seemingly a casual toss-off, the album's name cleverly related to the sale. "In a way, getting rid of all these things is a way of saying, 'I've got to get Elton out of my life and start being a little of Reg again,'" Elton said. "I used to hate Reg quite a lot, especially the name. But I think I got a little carried away with Elton. . . . I may have been a little unfair to Reg. He never had the chance to emerge properly."[9] This surprising self-analysis painted a picture few would have entertained about the coauthor and performer of so many infinitely popular songs: The unassuming and shy Reg Dwight, whose self-effacing spirit had been stamped out by the burgeoning Elton, was reborn with his alter ego's housecleaning. The *Reg Strikes Back* cover made this clear. Little Reggie stands amid flashy costumes and accessories in glorious black and white, an impish grin planted on his prepubescent face.

Did Reggie know something no one else did? Elton claimed he wanted to tone down his public image, so the costumes had to go. He could never again wear them or anything like them onstage for fear of looking like "Tina Turner's grandmother." He was also getting rid of furniture, artwork, jewelry, and knickknacks. There was no room to sit in the house, to redecorate, to appreciate what he had. And he wasn't selling it all off because he needed money. "If I needed money, I'd just go back on the road and do some shows," he assured Robert Hilburn.[10] He'd been thinking about having a massive sale for years now, he said. But the auction seemed like a purposely engineered watershed event, not unlike his marriage four years earlier, his shocking "retirement" announcement at the November 1977 benefit concert, and his statement in 1976 to Cliff Jahr that he was "bisexual." He wanted change and he made it happen, in a big way.

Elton's things went on tour in July and August—to Tokyo, Sydney, New York, Los Angeles, and London—before the big four-day sale in London in September when they would be available in to the highest bidder. It had taken Sotheby's three days to collect the items, not counting the time needed to inventory them. Elton was conveniently away in the United States while they did this, although Sotheby's had not been given carte blanche. When Elton returned from abroad, he readied himself for a bath in his emptied house, only to find an important ingredient missing: his soap dish. He marched into personal assistant Bob Halley's room, yelling, "Tell 'em to bring it back!"[11] Some more notorious costumes were also saved from the auction block, like the radioactive, Day-Glo, quasi-military uniform from 1984. His prized record collection, which numbered in the tens of thousands, was also off limits.

"If junk is worth thousands, they will sell it," sniffed Godfrey Barker in London's *The Daily Telegraph*.[12] But Sotheby's was anxious to show that Elton's collection wasn't ordinary. In preparing the four-volume catalog, the auction house interviewed the musician's longtime friend, journalist Paul Gambaccini, for each volume's preface. First there was the boring question of whether Elton was a genius. "Oh definitely," responded Gambaccini. He expounded on the musician's legendary sense of humor. Another topic was the impression Elton made on others. "When people who know Paul Macartney [*sic*] get together, they talk about him for thirty seconds and then talk about their own lives. They don't have to talk about Paul because he is an ordinary, balanced person blessed with a great gift. He fits into our understanding of the world," Gambaccini said. "But when people who know Elton get together they can't stop talking about him! I've witnessed this for years. He's a fascinating subject because he doesn't fit in to anyone's map of the world. He is his own man."[13]

Elton's taste in objects was as fascinating as his personality, and as eclectic as his taste in music. There were about two thousand lots available for sale, in four collections. Naturally, the stage costume and memorabilia collection was of particular interest to fans. Gone to private ownership come September would be gold and platinum records, *Captain Fantastic* pinball machines, vintage jukeboxes, Disney animation cels, album cover artwork, Judy Garland's camisole from the 1944 movie musical *Meet Me in St. Louis*, and tour posters and itineraries. Then there were, of course, the costumes—the fruity shoulder pads, Miss Liberty, the Pierrot's suit, the fluorescent balls, the bugle beads, the punch bowl hat, the ostrich plumes, the matador, the Ruritanian general, the fat stripes, the leviathan Pinball Wizard boots from *Tommy*, the offensive denim jacket and matching jeans that once got him in trouble in Australia ("No Entry" read a patch on the crotch). The assortment of spectacles included the mink-lined ones, the blinking "ELTON" contraption, the claws, the clouds, the stars, the diamanté, the orbiting neutrons and protons. Footwear included boots with stars, with "E" and "J," thick striped platforms, and shorter, rainbow-colored ones.

The second collection, dedicated to jewelry, was equally impressive, if less infamous. There were nineteenth- and early twentieth-century jewel-encrusted cigarette cases, clocks, and timepieces by Cartier, there were pendants, brooches, rings, and bracelets made of diamonds, amethysts, sapphires, onyx, and every other imaginable gem. Elton had worn many of the jewels in publicity photos, on the street, and at social events. Especially recognizable was the black-tasseled brooch from Elton's "Addams Family" look during the *Ice on Fire* sessions.

The third collection, called Art Nouveau and Art Deco, had to be more daunting for bidders. These included Gallé and Daum glass vases; dishes and lamps etched with mountain, stream, and forest scenes; gleaming Loetz glasswork; Tiffany lamps; icy Lalique bottles, sculptures, plates, and mirrors; and Victorian bedroom furniture, bookcases, and end tables. Best of all were an assortment of hideously seductive, turn-of-the-century Carlo Bugatti gold, black, and brown furniture pieces adorned in tassels and turrets, and a medley of graceful dancing female figures hailing from the Jazz Age and the Great Depression.

The last group of items, aptly entitled Diverse Collections, may have been what Godfrey Barker was miffed about—except that some of the art in this collection was created by the masters. But lumped together with works by Edouard Cortes, René Magritte, Pablo Picasso, Albrecht Dürer, and Rembrandt were 1920s Broadway decor and costume illustrations; Andy Warhol screenprints; a green fiberglass table supported by a mostly naked, green woman; a replica of King Tut's throne; brass palm trees; footrests sporting sunglasses and sneakered feet; the simple leather couch on which Elton was often seen in 1970s press photos; a nineteenth-century mahogany wheelchair; clothing trunks; toys; a gramophone with a human-like pair of legs; and painted Japanese screens that could have inspired Bernie to write the words to "Japanese Hands."

Sotheby's estimated that the two thousand or so lots would bring in more than five million dollars.

"YOU CAN'T ARGUE WITH THE IMAGE"[14]

NOW THAT ELTON HAD CLEANED HOUSE, he had all sorts of future plans. In July, he said, "You can never stand still. Otherwise, you'll be playing the same songs, you'll be playing in Vegas—which is the sort of thing I've always abhorred."[15] He wanted to record different kinds of albums over the next decade: one with Bonnie Raitt; an instrumental album; a country-and-western album; and, seeing as he had a new voice, an album of ballads. It was frustrating that, so far, he had had little record-company support for such ideas.[16]

He and Bernie hoped to write a Broadway musical based on an Anne Rice novel, *Interview with a Vampire*. "The subject of *Interview with a Vampire* interests me because it covers a period of two hundred years, so you've got many different sorts of music," he said excitedly. "It starts off in New Orleans, goes to the opera, Paris in the late nineteenth century, up to the present day."[17] But David Geffen, a financial backer, nixed the idea.[18]

What Elton wanted most was simply to get back onstage. This was the secret to his longevity. He said that, in the short term, he hoped to "make myself a better pianist and become a better singer."[19] As for the long term, as he said on VH1, "If I'm like a Ray Charles or Frank Sinatra in twenty years' time that goes around with a good band and sings good songs . . . , that's all I want."[20] He even had a couple of good excuses to return to the road: He had six weeks to test the strength of his voice before a world tour in 1989, and he could raise money for Watford, too.

Elton first put his voice to the test for a full ninety minutes at an Athletes and Entertainers for Kids benefit in Los Angeles on July 8, a fundraiser for "children with AIDS and other serious diseases." Ryan White was one of the night's special guests. Before the event, Elton spoke of Ryan's remarkable resolve: "He now goes and gives lectures. . . . He plays sport, he's got the most incredible attitude, which you tend to find people do have when faced with adversity."[21]

Meanwhile, Elton had assembled another new band. Although Nigel and Dee had sung on *Reg Strikes Back*, they weren't asked back for the tour. "[M]usically, you have to play with different people," Elton explained. "I'm very loyal to my musicians, but sometimes I should have chopped and changed a little more."[22] The band of the 1985–86 world tour—the one with the Melbourne Symphony Orchestra—was also torn asunder.

Elton wanted an American rhythm section and backup singers who could approximate Ray Charles's Raeletts. He got both. In fact, he looked at his whole band as "American." Davey now lived in Los Angeles and was therefore kind of American—besides, he was also the "informal musical director," so the pianist couldn't spare him. Fred Mandel, a Canadian (and therefore honorary American), was still there, too, while a second extra keyboard player, Maryland native Guy Babylon, joined the group. The band also included black musicians for the first time since Caleb Quaye—perpetually grinning New Jerseyan Romeo Williams on bass, and on drums New Orleanian Jonathan "Sugarfoot" Moffett, sweet-faced and sleek of hair, with mighty weightlifter's arms. The three quasi-Raeletts were young African-American women: Marlena Jeter (Francophile Elton pronounced her surname "Jeh-TAY") had sung for animated films, Alex Brown had gospel roots, and Natalie Jackson was classically trained.

With Marlena, Alex, and Natalie, Elton was going for a live sound that specifically recalled the soul and rhythm and blues he had been fed on as a teenager and had played with Bluesology. The imprint the band left on songs was sparer than the roof-raising tactility of the 1985–86 ensemble. Audience members were permitted more avenues from which to examine each song (even during the rockers) without the impressive web of contrary forces that had often met concertgoers' ears two years earlier. Elton also hoped to pay homage to the Australian MSO tour, relying on the teamwork of Fred Mandel and Guy Babylon to replicate on synthesizers the orchestral arrangements for a number of songs last played Down Under.

In some ways, the new band's show at the Athletes and Entertainers for Kids benefit was a disappointment. Elton's new look was a nondescript dark suit, his only glitz emanating from a cap covered with feathers and what appeared to be pieces of chandelier. Behind his tiny Roland keyboard, which was set up to face the audience ("This time I'm playing straight ahead, so I can see everyone," he told disc jockeys on New York's Z-100[23]), he flexed and preened with his voice but less so with his playing, a far cry from the thrills of the *Reg Strikes Back* parties. "Sixty Years On" was an emotional experience, yet Elton played little, in deference to the synthesized orchestrations going on behind him. "I Don't Wanna Go On with You Like That," with all of its possibilities, was perfunctory.

"It's a great privilege to play for people like you who paid so much money to see a twit like me!" he gushed.[24] The Elton of old was in evidence on such songs as "Burn Down the Mission," in which he played with his back to the Roland and his legs straddling the bench. His reliance on synths was wise for one song, when Fred and Guy faithfully interpreted the string opening to "Saturday Night's Alright," so brilliantly played in Australia by the MSO. Mindful of the reason for the gathering, Elton also premiered a song he and Bernie had just written, "Love Is Worth Waiting For," which urged teens in the age of AIDS to be sexually abstinent. But despite the good intentions of the song ("That risk you'd like to take/could be the risk that takes your life," read Bernie's lyrics) and the soulfulness of its music, it projected a preachiness not found in Elton and Bernie's other songs. Also, some of those who knew Elton must have been taken aback to hear him sing about sexual abstinence.

Elton cared about this cause, even if he didn't consider how it related to his personal life. Later in the show, he dedicated "Candle in the Wind" to the Whites, inviting Ryan and a tiny boy named Jason, who also had AIDS, to sit next to him on the bench and be personally serenaded. Afterwards, although the show was technically still in progress, Elton left the keyboard to gently escort the boys back to their tables. Sometime before the AIDS benefit, he'd filmed a public service announcement for Australian television on the subject. In liberally ad-libbing, his voice shook: "What I'm talking about tonight—drug abuse by children. . . . As adults, we can help them in life education, helping them to understand much better, and to prevent this terrible thing. . . . And if we do this, then we can sleep nights."

"I CAME LOOKING FOR A TOWN OF PLENTY"[25]

ON SEPTEMBER 3, 1988, days before the Sotheby's auction and the start of Elton's American tour, the British single "Town of Plenty" charted, peaking at a woefully inauspicious number 74. With somewhat better hopes, the Sotheby's auction began in London on September 6. The auction yielded nearly $8.5 million over four days, almost twice as much as predicted. Many lots went for double and triple the estimated high bids. The Hard Rock Cafe restaurant chain's winning bids won gold records and the "ELTON" glasses (the latter for nearly $17,000). Japanese bidders were especially interested in some of the jewelry, including a Cartier watch for $43,000. A Magritte oil painting of a blue fish draped in pearls went for more than $119,000; Stephen Griggs, of Doc Marten manufacturers R. Griggs and Company, spent more than $20,000 on the *Tommy* boots, $17,000 more than predicted. Gus Dudgeon paid $4,950 for the denim pillow used as a model for the *Madman Across the Water* album cover. It had been predicted to sell for less than $200.[26]

The raging success of Elton's auction was a pleasant way to mark the start of his first tour in more than a year and a half, launched in Miami on September 9 and 10. The consensus of critics about the tour's first couple of weeks was that both Elton's looks and performances were low-key.

Elton's hair was dyed platinum blonde, making him look prematurely gray. His clothes were described by one critic as "somewhere between a priest's frock and a Nehru jacket."[27] Another likened his new look to that of Arthur Bremer, the would-be assassin of George Wallace.[28] But generally, the musician's unimaginative suits were described less imaginatively, as "dark blue" or "gray." The hint of things to come, portended at the Athletes and Entertainers for Kids benefit, had reached fruition.

Elton engaged in few of the physical antics that had been his trademark over the years. Critics complained that he no longer used his piano as an acrobatic springboard (although if he had, the little Roland, renamed "Reg" for the tour, might have collapsed). Robert Hilburn, who noted that Elton had been "one of pop music's most . . . original figures for almost two decades," acknowledged that the first Hollywood Bowl show was marked by a "recital hall manner."[29]

It was as if sometime before the tour Elton had lost self-confidence. He had been absent for a significant period from the concert stage, had been dealt cruel abuse at the hands of the tabloids, and had suffered a terrible fright over his vocal cords. His solemnity could also have had to do with the songs. Many of those that made the final cut were serious, moody numbers from the early 1970s that had been orchestrated for the MSO in Australia—"Sixty Years On," "I Need You to Turn To," "The King Must Die," and "Have Mercy on the Criminal"—to which Elton's band gave the synth-orchestral treatment. But regardless, Elton was warmly received by audiences. The lovefest of the Athletes and Entertainers for Kids benefit was not an aberration.

As the tour unfolded, so did Elton's sense of fun and musical imagination. "The Ballad of Danny Bailey" was the show's biggest surprise. Leaving the album version in the dust, it showcased the interpretive intuition of Elton's voice and piano, an intimidating team of instruments. "Some punk with a shotgun killed young Danny Bailey, in cold blood, in the lobby of a downtown motel," Elton would whisper in anguish, as the sound of a gunshot emanated from Jonathan Moffet's drum set. The pianist's voice would rise as the story of the youthful mobster unfolded ("Killed him in anger, a force he couldn't handle helped pull the trigger that cut short his life"). At song's end, when the music reverts to the feelings of onlookers as they watch Bailey's casket ride by, the services resemble a jazzy wake on Bourbon Street.

There were other surprises, too. The pairing of "Mona Lisas and Mad Hatters, Parts One and Two" was notable for an ingenious jazz addition that flowed freely from the main portion of "Part Two." Following a bridge provided by Romeo Williams's bass and Davey's hiccuping guitar, Elton would take advantage of the Roland keyboard's versatility. At the flip of a switch, it was a vibraphone. Another flip and it sounded like an electric piano. Yet another and it was back to acoustic.

"I Don't Wanna" took on an increasingly heart-stopping aggressiveness. "Sad Songs," too, slowly became something other than a smiley, rock-tinged tune. Now, it began with temperate gospel piano playing that swiftly segued into gospel vocalizing between Elton and his backup singers. This "Sad Songs" introduction was tentative even at its most developed, although the song's principal part got its most concentrated rock'n'roll workout ever.

So even without the extended zaniness of "Bennie" and the soaring weightlessness of "Rocket Man," two songs Elton was shelving for now, the tour offered musical highlights. The waters changed a little, however, by the time Elton and the band arrived in New York on October 17 for a five-night stand at Madison Square Garden. Elton's wardrobe became a tad flashier, one night a red suit and matching plumed cap, another an elaborately tailored suit and fancy headdress suggesting a Scottish bagpipe player (despite the absence of kilts). The show, usually two hours long, threatened to break loose at two and a half hours or more. The first night included three more songs than usual, an abbreviated "Rocket Man" and two numbers—"Empty Garden" and "Lucy in the Sky with Diamonds"—played in tribute to John Lennon. "Empty Garden" sounded chewier, more sumptuously sad than when last played in 1982. "Lucy" had had a longer hiatus, last heard on tour in 1976.

On the final night at the Garden, the concert that broke a tie with the Grateful Dead for most sold-out shows at the venue (twenty-six), Billy Joel and Debbie Gibson helped with "Lucy," winding up a virtual Grand Central Station of guest stars over the five nights. On October 21, Jon Bon Jovi and Richie Sambora helped out on "Saturday Night's Alright." Bruce Hornsby joined Elton the night before that. This must have been a thrill for Hornsby, who once said, "Things sort of went full circle for me because . . . I saw this interview with Elton John, and he had said some really complimentary things about me. I got chills hearing this. It was amazing for me to hear this from the guy who—along with Leon Russell—really inspired me to get into this [playing piano] when we had a six-foot grand piano in our house."[30] Backstage visitors included Sting, Donald and Ivana Trump, Kathleen Turner, Brooke Shields, and Cyndi Lauper.

"MY GIFTS ALL LAY UNDONE"[31]

"A Word in Spanish" was the second American single from *Reg Strikes Back*. Though its success was not comparable to that of its predecessor, it was nonetheless a hit. On September 17, 1988, while "I Don't Wanna" was still in the Top 30 and the tour was a week old, "Spanish" debuted at number 86. After nine weeks on the chart, it peaked at number 19. If Elton had any complaints about this, he should have had more about what happened to "Spanish" in Britain—nothing.

By December 1988, the London *Sun*'s unsavory ranting against Elton had ended, though he still had lawsuits pending. As late as mid-1988, he was bitter about *The Sun*'s senseless attacks against him, but he did manage to joke about it. When British television's *Last Resort* host Jonathan Ross had asked him in May what he had gotten for his last birthday, Elton said with a smirk, "I've got a machine gun for Rupert Murdoch." Later, he commented, "A lot of people gave me advice such as, 'Why don't you drop it? People do forget these things.' And they do, but I'm not going to let the press get away with it. The first case that comes up is about my dogs. The headline in . . . *The Sun* said I was being investigated by the Society for the Prevention of Cruelty to Animals because I had their voice boxes torn out so they couldn't bark. They have no chance. They've written me an apology and offered to settle out of court."[32]

Elton was referring to the September 1987 "story" scheduled to be heard by the High Court ahead of the writs involving the rent boy allegations. The former was also probably the easiest to disprove. *The Sun* finally settled with Elton on December 12, 1988, paying him the highest libel settlement in British history, $1.85 million, while printing an apology to him on the front page, in the same mammoth lettering used to assassinate his character the year before. "SORRY, ELTON," read the headline. *The Sun* retracted everything it had said about him in 1987. He granted the tabloid an interview in the same issue, in which he proclaimed, "Life is too short to bear grudges and I don't bear *The Sun* any malice." Elton then talked of the twenty-eight pounds he had lost on his recent American tour.

The High Court was critical of the unseemly publicity both sides sought in the course of the unusual settlement, but Elton was pleased to be done with the matter.[33] He was a big believer in moving on. And *The Sun* had not "gotten away with it."

Meanwhile, the past was catching up with Elton's marriage. Word reached the newspapers that he and Renate had amicably divorced, which wasn't much of a surprise. They hadn't been seen together much in 1988, although Elton was still speaking positively of his marriage around the time of *Reg Strikes Back*'s release. He had then told interviewer Steve Blame: "I don't think one way and that's it. That's absolutely not the right way to think. I think some homosexuals are closed and think one way and that's it. . . . I never closed my mind to anything that could happen."[34] But now, months later, Elton realized that the marriage had failed. He bought Renate a six hundred thousand dollar country cottage. Divorce terms were not made public.

"YOU HEAR THE SOUND OF OTIS AND THE VOICE OF MARVIN GAYE"[35]

ELTON HOPED "LOVE IS WORTH WAITING FOR," the song urging teens to be sexually abstinent, would attract a star-studded lineup of vocalists, with proceeds going to AIDS education charities.[36] When the stars didn't line up, he thought of putting the song on his next album, still intending to raise money with it for AIDS awareness.[37] As a modern-day soul ballad, it might have fit the soon-to-be soul inspired album, but he and Bernie wrote so many superior songs in Denmark's Puk Studios at the end of 1988 that, true to Elton's desire to forge ahead, "Love Is Worth Waiting For" just disappeared.

Elton and Bernie chose Puk Studios in Denmark on George Michael's recommendation. It was far removed from friends who might drop in, ask how recording was going, and listen to the new tracks—over and over again. The songwriting partners needed to concentrate.

They believed the material on some of their recent albums had been too diverse, and wanted to do an album with a thematic cohesiveness. Elton had first thought of doing a soul album while touring with his new African-American–dominated band,[38] and, appropriately, he used this band on the album (with Chris Thomas again producing). In agreeing to write only soul songs, Elton and Bernie also pledged to derive their inspiration directly from 1960s soul, which they both loved.

Bernie's job was to listen to Motown, Stax, Chess, and other 1960s-era soul recordings and use them as seeds for original lyrics that recalled the songs without copying them. He immersed himself in Jackie Wilson, Otis Redding, Marvin Gaye, Aretha Franklin, Martha and the Vandellas, Sam and Dave, Percy Sledge, the Drifters, Ray Charles, and other troubadours of soul. Each time he wrote a set of lyrics, he would note at the bottom its inspiration (the name of the song or singer), and hand it to Elton. The musician kept to the soul-delving arrangement, but rarely stayed within the parameters highlighted by Bernie. The lyrics often reminded him of a different song than Bernie had noted.

Thus, although the two hadn't collaborated like this since *Captain Fantastic,* their songwriting habits hadn't really changed. They still wrote in separate rooms, although, one hopes, not the way Elton described it on *Wogan.* "He [Bernie] dresses up as a nun and hides himself in the toilet," Elton chortled. "I'm *not* going to tell you what *I* do!"[39] (Nuns were often the unhappy focus of Elton's sometimes bizarre humor. In the 1970s, he suggested to rock magazine *Creem* that his favorite hobby was "slicing up dead nuns." And he once urged the cautious Bob Halley to drive faster, as they were being overtaken by a "nun in rollerskates."[40])

The new album, *Sleeping with the Past,* was by no means a first brush with nostalgia for Elton and Bernie. *Tumbleweed Connection* had expressed a wistfulness for old Americana. And both *Honky Chateau* and *Don't Shoot Me* had looked to distant decades for inspiration. *Sleeping* was also not the first nostalgia album of the 1980s. Billy Joel had released *An Innocent Man* in 1983, which looked to roughly the same time period, give or take five or eight years. Elton didn't think of the comparison until after the *Sleeping* recording sessions had begun. "He did that brilliantly," Elton said of Joel's project. "I thought it was a superb idea. And he carried it off superbly."[41] A chief difference between Billy and Elton's albums was that while Joel faithfully imitated the doo-wop and Frankie Valli songs with which he had grown up, Elton took the Motown, Stax, and Chess numbers that had mesmerized him as a boy and rebuilt them for the late 1980s and his own free-wheeling flights of fancy.

Sleeping was also not Elton's first brush with soul. There was plenty of soul to be found on most of his albums, dating back to *Elton John*'s "Take Me to the Pilot" and *Honky Chateau*'s Al Green– and Marvin Gaye–inspired tracks. "Bennie" had enough soul credibility to go to number 1 in Detroit and lead to an appearance on *Soul Train,* and Elton engaged in passionate forays into Philly Soul in the 1970s with

"Philadelphia Freedom," "Tell Me When the Whistle Blows," and, later, the Thom Bell sessions. *Sleeping* wasn't even Elton's first soul album of the 1980s—*Ice on Fire* was, though unintentionally; at the time, Elton's main concern had been getting something unique out of his four rhythm sections. Also, *Ice on Fire* was streetwise, with sexually suggestive undertones. *Sleeping*'s songs turn inward for the introspective, cooler side of soul.

Months after *Sleeping*'s completion, Elton attributed its creative success to his state of mental and physical well-being, and the certainty that some unpleasant chapters in his life, such as his battle with *The Sun*, were drawing to a close. "This is the first album I've made where I didn't really have any pressures hanging over me," he said in 1989. "When I started it, I knew my personal life was going to be sorted out."[42] Some years later, he was more candid about his condition during the waning days of 1988: "I was sober when I recorded *Sleeping with the Past*—just."[43]

The first three songs completed for *Sleeping*—the title track, "Whispers," and "Amazes Me"—convinced Elton and Bernie that their discipline was paying off, although they wrote nearly twenty songs and, fussily, kept only ten. After each one was written, it was recorded, with all the finishing touches made the same day.[44] "When I arrived at the studio," said Elton, years later describing a day during the sessions, "I had nothing except a lyric. So I went in straight away, wrote the actual title track, 'Sleeping with the Past,' [and] by 6:30, we had the track done."[45]

The first song on *Sleeping* is the antiapartheid "Durban Deep," inspired by Lee Dorsey's chipper 1966 Top 10 American hit, the Allen Toussaint–penned and produced "Working in the Coal Mine." Bernie borrows the "down-down-down" refrain of the tune as he tells of black South African coal miners who labor to support their families with poverty-level wages while inhaling coal dust and being driven crazy day and night by the "drill an' hammer."

"Durban Deep" doesn't sound like Lee Dorsey. It is an inventive examination of a typical day in a dark, dusty South African mine, achieved through multiple layers of vaguely reggae-style rhythm and the clarity of Elton's voice. The song opens with the persistent sound of the "drill an' hammer," simulated by keyboard and Romeo Williams's bass playing, which reproduces the miners' earnest steps "down-down-down" to the recesses of the earth and their work sites. Soon this is joined by Jonathan Moffet's drumming, which imitates crumbling, tumbling rocks loosened by machinery. Then Elton's melody enters, singsongy and thoughtful, like something the miners might conjure up to pass the time (with a touch of Otis Redding's "Dock of the Bay"). He shouts it, one assumes, to make it heard over the din of the miners' pounding. The musician's voice echoes interminably, just as a miner's voice might "two miles down." These elements, and the occasional electric guitar fills by Davey and Fred, which could be the siren signaling the start of another shift, make the song hard and repetitive but also velvety and well structured.

Bernie saw the next song, "Healing Hands," as an update of the Four Tops's "Reach Out I'll Be There." The only references to "Reach Out," however, are in the phrase that urges the protagonist, who is suffering from the end of a love affair, to seek a new love interest ("Reach out for her healing hands"). More telling than the "Reach Out I'll Be There" references are the religious images, which lend themselves more to a gospel tune than a Motown dance number. "You gotta wade into the water. Touch me now and let me see again."

Elton said the Impressions were an influence on this album, and "Healing Hands" is probably where they made their mark. The civil rights–era spirituality of many of their songs, such as "Amen" and "People Get Ready," seeped into this music, which has all the markings of a church song. "Healing Hands" deviates only in its secular aura. When Elton sings, he is delivering a sermon about the power of a nonspecific kind of faith—perhaps the faith one may have in oneself—to heal wounds sustained while living life. His melody, coupled with the organ's Sunday sound and the backing vocals of Mortonette Jenkins (who had replaced Alex Brown), Marlena Jeter, and Natalie Jackson leave no doubt that this song is meant to inspire. Fittingly, by the end, the secular message reaches the heavens, with Elton's piano chords in ascension and a mounting synth-orchestral interlude.

Bernie's lyrics for the third track, "Whispers," seem more inspired by his own writing than any particular soul artist. It contains the lyricist's oft-mulled reflections on the temptation of love, in this case "whispered" by an ex-lover who the protagonist wishes would be more distant: "Whisper like cold winds/close to the bone/ save heaven for lovers/leave me alone." Despite the lyrics' Taupin-esque character, they seem also to refer to an old Benny Goodman song, "Soft Winds," recorded by Dinah Washington in 1954 ("Soft winds whisper sweet words to my love").

Just as the lyrics for "Whispers" are primarily Taupin-esque, so the music is mainly Elton-esque. It may contain hard-to-define elements of ballads by Stevie Wonder or Sam Cooke, but it is more reminiscent of the forlornly caressing "Blue Eyes" or the expression of timeless devotion in "Harmony" than a 1960s soul hit. Elton achieves this by ignoring the fear of temptation felt by the protagonist and instead focusing on the enticing memories of the long-gone love affair. The result is a comforting, feathery, Elton John keyboard ballad.

The lyrics to the next song, "Club at the End of the Street," are supposed to be a homage to the Drifters, inspired by that group's moderately successful "At the Club," a sped-up version of another Drifters song, "Up on the Roof." Funnily enough, "At the Club" was written by Carole King and Gerry Goffin, not known as soul songwriters but Brill Building composers. To ensure the song's soul authenticity, therefore, Bernie refers to the soul music everyone listens to on the jukebox as they relax at a neighborhood nightspot. Mostly, though, the lyrics mirror the images found in "At the Club." He writes: "There's a shady place/at the end of the working day/where young lovers go/and this hot little trio plays." Goffin and King wrote: "Friday night has finally come around/. . . /down at the club, everything's outasite/. . . /the band won't quit til everybody tells them to."

The Drifters' "On Broadway," written not by soulsters like Stevie Wonder or Marvin Gaye but by assembly-line writers Barry Mann, Cynthia Weil, Jerry Leiber, and Mike Stoller, may be closest to Elton's music for "Club at the End of the Street." His music is self-assured and optimistic, like the struggling musician in "On Broadway." He sings in a neon-lit voice his anthem to a night filled with good tunes. The driving tempo of "Club," though, recalls the persistent "thunk" of the Drifters' backing rhythm section in "At the Club."

The mood changes completely with the title track, "Sleeping with the Past," which has generic soul lyrics about the perils a woman faces in clinging to a man's false love. Bernie's words vaguely recall the Miracles' Smokey Robinson–penned "Shop Around." The music takes its cue from that song, too, as a fizzy, frothy concoction that has as much to say about not sleeping with the past as the Miracles tune had about being careful whom you choose—not much. "Sleeping with the Past" is a strangely cheerful song, considering its subject matter, just like "Shop Around" and countless other soul numbers with the saddest of lyrics. Like those older soul songs, "Sleeping" rejoices in life, sad tale of woe or not, and has the sort of pulse that makes music fans want to step onto the dance floor—more so than does "Club at the End of the Street." Romeo Williams's studied bass thumping plays a large part in the music's motion. The song also effectively blends old and new, with unrepentant folkie Davey Johnstone supplying some of the Miracles-style backing vocals ("Don't go sleepin'/don't go prayin'") and Elton sharing lines with Natalie Jackson.

The next song, "Stones Throw from Hurtin'," presents the same situation mourned in Breaking Hearts' "Burning Buildings," but expressed in a homier manner: A couple can't extricate itself from a doomed relationship, and things keep getting worse ("Your goodnight kiss ain't hungry/our touches don't connect/we're just a couple of kids with a broken toy/that our idle fingers wrecked"). Bernie said he was influenced here by both Sam and Dave and "I Heard It through the Grapevine." The latter is the likelier progenitor; "Soul Man," "Hold On! I'm a Comin'," and "I Thank You" don't seem relevant.

In composing the music for "Stones Throw," Elton drew from Marvin Gaye's essence—although he later jokingly referred to the recorded product as "J. J. Cale meets Canned Heat."[46] This is odd, since neither J. J. Cale nor Canned Heat was involved in the wonderful soul explosion of the 1960s to which Elton and Bernie were paying tribute. Elton probably meant his whispering, falsetto vocal, which nevertheless carries elements of Marvin Gaye. The restrained instrumentation (save Fred's blistering electric guitar solo mid-song) is also inspired by the essence of Gaye as heard in "Grapevine." In the latter, the backing musicians creep around Gaye's singing; in "Stones Throw," something similar happens. As Elton murmurs lines like "Our painted smiles are cracking" and "I know it's never gonna get no better," his keyboards effervesce from beneath the steam of Davey's electric guitar refrain and Guy's calming church organ, while the voices of Mortonette, Marlena, and Natalie hum and rumble for emphasis.

"Sacrifice" marks an abrupt shift from "Stones Throw." The former's more philosophical lyrics were inspired by Aretha Franklin's "Do Right Woman—Do Right Man." Aretha's song was a warning to men that what goes around comes around. If a man wants his woman to be faithful, he had better be faithful, too. In "Sacrifice," Bernie transforms this notion into a view of what can happen to a married couple in the wake of a husband's unfaithfulness, borrowing or adapting lines from "Do Right Woman." Like Aretha's song, "Sacrifice" also recognizes the inevitability of "temptation." Aretha's "take me to heart" becomes Bernie's "cold, cold heart." "A woman's only human," Aretha sang; Bernie has Elton sing, "It's a human sign."

Elton once said that "Sacrifice" sounds like a Percy Sledge song. Indeed, Elton's bleak melody may be a distant cousin to "When a Man Loves a Woman," and his voice's sandy timbre an amalgam of Sledge and other soul compatriots; again, Gaye and Otis Redding are audible. But more important than how "Sacrifice" fares as a soul song is how it fares as an Elton John song.

Elton has also said that "Sacrifice" is one of his fabled hymns, like "Candle in the Wind." In his eyes, it is a standard, as crucial to his repertoire as "Your Song."[47] Bernie shares this feeling. He looks at "Your Song" and "Sacrifice" as bookends of a sort. To him, "Your Song" has the naïve, hopeful outlook of pre-adulthood, while "Sacrifice" possesses no such childishness. "That song ["Sacrifice"] to me is so powerful and so meaningful," remarked Bernie some years later. "It's that sixteen-year-old twenty-five years later. It's about real pain and real life and all the things that that sixteen-year-old didn't know about."[48]

The next track, "I Never Knew Her Name," is based on another Aretha song, "I Never Loved a Man (The Way I Love You)." Lyrically, the two songs couldn't be more different. In "I Never Loved a Man," a woman moans that her man is a lying cheat. She would leave him—if she could. "I Never Knew Her Name" laments unattainable love. A man "killing time with Jesus" from a church pew in the shadows suddenly finds himself witness to a wedding ceremony between "the most beautiful woman" and a "handsome man." Immediately smitten by the woman, who "walked like a mystery" and "passed like summer rain," he suffers silently as he watches her "promise to be kept for life."

But however dissimilar "I Never Loved a Man" and "I Never Knew Her Name" are lyrically, the two are musical mates, the former defined by Aretha's hesitant tempo. Her playing, in its mysterious reluctance to choose between going forward and staying behind, and her seething vocal, combine to chill this song to the bone.

Elton purposely played like Aretha on "I Never Knew Her Name," though his shuffling interpretation of her sinister stylings sounds much less evil. True to Bernie's lyrics, which lay the groundwork for innocent fantasy, Elton stresses the dreamlike state of the hidden church worshiper.

The next-to-last song on the album is "Amazes Me," which spotlights Ray Charles and was most likely inspired by his rhythm and blues reading of a decades-old standard, "Georgia on My Mind." Instead of Georgia, Bernie focuses on humid Mississippi for a love letter to both the state and a group of African-American women, who are the subjects of a riverside reverie. The enchantment grows as mention is made of the "hoodoo" and "gri-gri" these women bring with them.

"Amazes Me," a waltz, may be the most enchanting song on *Sleeping*. It transports the listener back to the early 1960s with its Gordon Jenkins–influenced synth-string arrangement, but updates the nostalgia with a melody that teeters between a chaste love of beauty and unbridled lust. The song also includes Elton's most effective vocal on the album, as his voice changes texture to match the mood of a given line. He is the secret lover ("You're a cool little one"), a blustery bluesman ("I got no blues to preach"), and a Tin Pan Alley crooner ("What drives me crazy/is that big fat yellow moon").

"Blue Avenue" brings up the album's rear. Along with "Whispers" and "Sacrifice," "Blue Avenue" constitutes not so much a homage to old soul giants as a typical Elton John ballad. Lyrically, it is like "Stones Throw from Hurtin.'" Another relationship is on the rocks. The song's lovers find themselves entangled in a mess on Blue Avenue ("Hit and run hearts collide here/true love passes through/looks like we've got a wreck babe/up on Blue Avenue"). Musically, it is a piano-painted, folk-tinged lamentation of love's deterioration, which, judging by the song's lush contours, will soon find itself rejuvenated. As spirit-enveloping as any of Elton's most affecting ballads, "Blue Avenue" has become one of his more unsung (and less sung) masterpieces.

Even if "Blue Avenue," "Whispers," and "Sacrifice" don't have the nostalgic quality Elton and Bernie had sought, the songs have a sense of romantic reverie inherent in much soul music and fit *Sleeping* like pieces of the same puzzle. Elton and Bernie had succeeded in making an album with that one musical theme—that one emotive sense—that had so often eluded them in the past. "This is probably the strongest album we've ever made," Bernie enthused after its completion. "I think it's a 'classic' Elton John album. . . . It's incredibly accessible, but maintains great integrity and I'm very proud of that."[49]

"IT'S DAYLIGHT WHEN I HIT THE SACK"[50]

ELTON'S THREE-MONTH TOUR OF EUROPE, Britain, and Ireland opened in Lyon, France, on March 20, 1989, days before his forty-second birthday. With white hair, bloated, ashen face, and puffy eyes, Elton now *looked* like the Truman Capote figure *Rolling Stone* had called him back in 1974. As he later recalled, "I was sober when I recorded *Sleeping with the Past*—just. I went off the rails when I did the tour afterwards."[51] He was eating so much (as well as drinking excessively) that his continued bulimia was not having the expected result; his stylish Gianni Versace–designed clothing couldn't hide his substantial weight gain. Of necessity, his eyes were obscured behind black sunglasses. During the tour's first week, he collapsed onstage (although he quickly rebounded).

Not that the tour wasn't good. It was. The shows started in almost identical fashion to the American concerts the previous fall. Since Europe, like the United States, had missed Elton's Australian tour with the Melbourne Symphony Orchestra, he would bring the MSO tour to Europe. Again, the high drama of "Sixty Years On," "I Need You to Turn To," "The King Must Die," and "Have Mercy on the Criminal" were dominant. But after Elton wrenched as much all-consuming passion as he could from these diverse tales of impending death, inevitable misery, and lovelorn pleadings, the shows veered off in another direction.

"Danny Bailey" was gone. "Nikita," which Europeans had readily embraced in 1985, was back. "Kiss the Bride" had Elton jumping to the song's emphatic declaration. When he couldn't do that, since his physical talents had diminished, he would humorously slump below his bench, returning to his seat in time for the next round. Other, rarer songs also emerged, including, "Song for Guy."

A reinvigorated "Too Low for Zero" awakened the hunger of audiences for Elton's more abstract side. At first, the song sounded no different from its recorded version; one of his backup singers mimicked the interlude in which Elton's disembodied voice floats above his spare, plaintive piano solo. But making the difference here were Elton's *two* piano solos. The spare plaint from the record became fancier. Notes got caught in each other in weblike fashion. And a whole new solo, the aural equivalent of butterflies busily flitting about to a Latin beat, was tacked onto the song's end. Too soon, "Too Low for Zero" was dropped from the set list.

"Rocket Man" appeared sporadically, providing a peek at the extravaganza that would delight American audiences in the fall. After having already graduated from the spacey, discombobulated meanderings of the early 1980s tours to the more abbreviated, rhythm and blues interpretation of the 1985–86 world tour, it was now poised to incorporate the best of both, thanks to the *Sleeping with the Past* sessions. Averaging ten minutes in length, this "Rocket Man" was as ambitious as the space cadet of earlier tours, although hailing from elsewhere. As soon as Elton finished singing about space travel being his "job five days a week," he revealed his roots—an African-American community, one imagined, where he must have been reared in a church to the persistent strains of gospel music. This Rocket Man's Roland piano took on the properties of a souped-up organ. It grimaced, it tiptoed, it howled. As unfunky a line as "She packed my bags last night, pre-flight" was, it now sounded like a righteous sermon, as did the ad-libbed, "Are you gonna *Rocket* with me?"

The April 26 Verona, Italy, concert was televised across Europe and Britain, displaying the musician's grossly expanded waistline. The sweat that trickled from his white hair down his gelatinous cheeks suggested not the energy with which he played but an unattractive untidiness. The matching trilby hat and vest, a glittering festival of multiple colors, were nice to look at, but his bright yellow suit surrounded him like a tent.

Italy—not just Verona—had been good to Elton so far. Whereas *Reg Strikes Back* had been rejected in Britain, and had merely gone gold in the United States, it was certified triple platinum in Italy. Yet the countries on this long tour, including Italy, were only treated to three songs from the album: "A Word in Spanish," "I Don't Wanna," and "Mona Lisas, Parts One and Two," the latter of which had progressed considerably since its Madison Square Garden showing in October. Elton had maintained the grand piano sound with which he was most comfortable, but safety was not the watchword for his playing. His band members comprised an onstage audience for the mini-spectacle. In particular, the grinning Romeo Williams simultaneously thumped his bass, rocked to the beat, and watched the bandleader as closely as possible. There were many passages to catch. The peppery loop-de-loop. Righthanded, rolling reflections (with left hand animatedly waving in the air). Transcendent scales.

Also coming along was "Sad Songs." Elton quickly lifted the between-songs Italian chant of his affectionate Verona audience for a new piano introduction, which then evolved into something blue. A call and response with Mortonette, Marlena, and Natalie naturally ensued, giving way to vocal reflections from Elton on the virtues of sad songs, then a foghorn-like dive into the bottomless pit that his range was becoming. "Sing it, EJ!" Natalie exhorted. Even "Saturday Night's Alright" was going in new directions. The noise of Elton's premiere rock anthem was interrupted by a quiet piano segment that tricked everyone into listening intently while it mounted in volume to eventually match the ferocity of Davey's crunchy guitar chords.

"I'll never forget this night!" Elton told the Verona crowd. He had many more big nights to go, including a long-awaited return to Britain and Ireland—his first tour there in three and a half years.

Before the spring tour, Elton recorded a duet with Aretha Franklin. This was an interesting coincidence given the new album, on which Elton and Bernie had paid tribute to Aretha. "Through the Storm" was the duet, on Aretha's Arista album of the same name. It marked the tail end of The Lady Soul's commercial renaissance, which had begun with the 1985 Top 10 hit "Freeway of Love." "Through the Storm" was notable mainly for the gusto with which the duet partners sang, as well as for the technological trick of joining Elton's and Aretha's geographically far-flung voices. Although they wouldn't meet for another four years, they sounded as if they were in the same studio.

"Through the Storm" had greater impact in the United States than in Britain. The duet partners got an American Top 20 hit when it peaked at number 16 on May 27 (and at number 17 on what was then called the Hot Black Singles chart). In Britain, the song got only as far as number 41.

"I COULD FLY LIKE A BIRD SOMEDAYS"[52]

ELTON HAD ABOUT A MONTH BETWEEN THE TOUR'S FIRST LEG, which ended in Ireland, and the North American leg, which began at the end of July in New England. There was extra rehearsing to do, as the set list was to be considerably different from the one in Europe. The American shows would admirably represent most of Elton's career: old standbys, early- to mid-1980s standards, flaming rockers, two songs from *Reg Strikes Back*, new songs from *Sleeping with the Past* (the title track, "Sacrifice," "Healing Hands," and "Stones Throw from Hurtin'"), rare gems ("Come Down in Time," "Harmony," and "Island Girl"), and show-stoppers like "Levon." Most of the concerts lasted at least two and a half hours.

Health permitting, the Jammin' Piano Player (an appellation shouted out by an apparently drunken concertgoer in Pittsburgh) lived up to his name. Early on, even "Come Down in Time" got the treatment. The tempo was faster than on record, and a mystique-laden piano interlude merged New Age with Jazz Age. "I Don't Wanna" earnestly began gaining tough flesh on its brilliant flashes of teeth-clenching aggression. "The Bitch Is Back" was joined with the Rolling Stones' "Brown Sugar," one of Elton's favorites from 1971. And the two "Mona Lisas," "Sad Songs," and "Rocket Man" were each about ten minutes long. The shows were not all fire and muscle, though. At one point the band would exit, leaving Elton to interpret "Daniel," "Candle in the Wind," "Sacrifice," and "Blue Eyes" (later "Your Song") alone.

"Rocket Man" provided the best ending to an Elton John concert in recent memory. Building on the funky foundation begun in Europe, Elton added snippets of soul songs to the extended instrumental break that increasingly featured exciting interaction between the pianist, the guitarists, and the backup singers. On any given night, two or three of the following crept into the mix: the Isley Brothers' "It's Your Thing," Sly and the Family Stone's "Thank You (Falettinme Be Mice Elf Agin)," and the Temptations' "Runaway Child, Running Wild." "Rocket Man" was turning into *Sleeping with the Past, Part Two.*

The shows had an equally mesmerizing beginning. As the lights dimmed, heavy, evenly spaced drumbeats filled the air. Synthesizer chords were carefully laid on top of these. As concertgoers realized that something was sounding vaguely familiar, a figure became visible at the side of the stage, strutting to this odd pulse toward the small keyboard in the center. When the figure reached the keyboard, a guitar blasted a wonderfully premonitory chord, the lights illuminated center stage, and a roar went up as thousands of concertgoers saw Elton in a pastel Versace jacket, glittery hat, and sunglasses, his arms raised in welcome. Upon lowering his hands to the keys, the familiar strains became "Bennie and the Jets." It was shorter now, but had never before had this kind of sentient impact.

Bernie came along for the complete three-month sojourn, the first time he had done so since 1976. "I . . . wanted to do one more tour before I hang up my road shoes," he said.[53] He also wanted to be there when *Sleeping with the Past* was released, a month into the tour. "I couldn't imagine not being close to Elton while this album is out," he said.[54] But being close to Elton meant witnessing the musician's self-destruction. And, as it turned out, there was little fanfare upon the album's release.

In anticipation of the British release, Elton interrupted his American tour to fly to England for an appearance on *Wogan* at the end of August. On the show, he looked surprisingly trim and bright-eyed in a snug black suit and glinting black glengarry, the latter a variation on the caps he liked to wear in public. The conversation turned to his chart successes. He still hadn't had a solo number 1 single in Britain, and doubted *Sleeping* would yield one. "I don't think I'll ever have one now," he said, resignedly.[55] Still, it was hard to stay serious. Alluding to both the new album's title and his sexual habits, Elton mentioned that some friends had asked whether he would be issuing a "catalog" with the record.

"Healing Hands," the first single, debuted on the American Hot 100 on August 26 at number 78. Unlike the first single from *Reg Strikes Back*, "I Don't Wanna," this one crept up the chart at a snail's pace, taking months to reach its peak of number 13 on October 28. This was, however, far preferable to the single's response in Britain, where it debuted the same day but stalled at number 45.

Judging from Elton and Bernie's euphoric feelings about the album's significance and quality, its chart performance was disappointing. Upon debuting on *Billboard*'s Top Pop Albums on September 16, it failed to rise higher than number 23, although it went gold on October 30. In Britain, it peaked at number 6, a vast improvement over the number 18 apex of *Reg Strikes Back* (a terrible performance for a British release), although still far from the commercial ratification Elton and Bernie needed for a work so important to them. Presumably, the point of the album wasn't clear to the public—why it was heavy on ballads that bore strains of African-American church life, why Elton had dedicated the record to a dumbfounded but flattered Bernie.

Critics were not interested in how *Sleeping* fit in with the staggering assortment of Elton's other albums, nor how it was particularly special to him and his lyricist. A review in *People* magazine asked, if Elton had wanted to pay tribute to old soul masters, why didn't he just cover old soul songs?[56] In Britain's *Melody Maker*, Catherine Sullivan wondered why *Sleeping* was so "solemn," after Elton had delivered such romps as "Crocodile Rock." She lamented having to "come to terms with a favourite uncle suddenly wanting to bare his soul. . . ."[57] Writing for *The Philadelphia Inquirer*,

Ken Tucker grumbled, "The problem is that he hasn't written enough distinctive melodies here—too many of them merely echo his old hits."[58] *The Washington Post's* Geoffrey Grimes complained that most of the songs emphasized "mood and meaning rather than melody."[59]

If some critics, in ignoring the purpose of *Sleeping*, were unimpressed with its personal significance and sometimes understated passion, others were more positive in reviewing his live shows. For Steve Smith, Elton and the band's August 15 Los Angeles concert "delivered so many high points that to mention them all would send this review spilling over into the sports and business sections. . . ."[60] Former *Rolling Stone* reviewer Stephen Holden, now with *The New York Times,* had gotten over his outrage at what he termed the "garbage" of 1978's *A Single Man* and the unfortunate vapidity of 1979's *Victim of Love.* Now he only had kind words for Elton's third show at the Garden, astutely noticing that Elton was a one-man band: "Although Mr. John was supported by a strong pop-rock band and three soul backup singers, they were almost icing on the cake given his ability to deliver fully-fleshed renditions of his songs with just a single keyboard."[61]

It was good that many reviewers were kind about Elton's performances, because he wasn't kind to himself—and sometimes not to his audiences. From the start of what should have been his best tour yet, substance abuse was sapping his stamina. "I had a really good time taking drugs at certain times during my life, but because I have a multi-addictive personality I just didn't know when to stop," Elton remembered years later. "I used to do gigs and do the same fucking verse three times in a row. We used to stand on stage and all the band would follow me and it was like 'Philadelphia Freedom' was fifteen fucking minutes long. . . ."[62]

The ugly pattern began two weeks into the tour. Occasionally, Elton completely forgot lyrics to songs that he had played in concert for more than a decade and a half. Shows were sometimes shortened. For every few brilliant versions of "Rocket Man," there was one disappointment. Concerts were rescheduled, some canceled. Referring to this time period, Bob Halley recalled how all-consuming cocaine had become for them. "When we were on tour we would be doing it five nights out of seven," Halley said. "After a particularly heavy party you would lose a day recovering in bed."[63]

Management at the Meadowlands Arena in New Jersey, just outside New York City, had finally convinced Elton to appear there, enticing him with a flattering advertisement in *Amusement Business* magazine the previous fall. "The ad had a picture of a new hat that we said was waiting for him here, in addition to a non-New York audience of eight million that would come to see him," recounted Mike Rowe, general manager of the arena. "We get a lot of letters from Elton John fans asking us to bring him here."[64] Three nights were set—August 4, 5, and 6—although at the last minute the August 5 show was moved to August 7. By all accounts, these were spectacular shows. But something wasn't right.

The first Philadelphia show, set for September 29, was moved to October 1, becoming his second concert at the Spectrum that year, after the September 30 show. On October 2, Elton missed an appearance on radio's *Rockline*. Again, he was not well. John Reid joined Bernie in his stead. When Bob Coburn asked, "Is this just a temporary setback?" Reid explained that Elton was opening at the Garden the next night and wanted to be in "tip-top shape," noting that he'd "been on the road almost non-stop."[65] There were still two weeks to go after the four nights in New York, including several Florida dates and a return to New England, where the tour began.

Elton made all four Garden concerts, though they were about twenty minutes shorter than other shows on the tour, and received an award for being the only musician to play thirty dates at the venue. There were a couple of cancellations in Florida, due to "exhaustion and influenza."[66] When the pianist returned to New England for the final concerts, it was clear that something was wrong. On October 18, at the Veterans Memorial Coliseum in New Haven, the show was shorter than ever. Elton refused to stand up to accept applause, and, most incredibly, kept looking at his watch.

At 6:15 P.M., on Friday, October 20, Elton's tour manager telephoned the Worcester, Massachusetts Centrum to say that the shows scheduled for that night and the next—the tour's last two—were being canceled due to "nervous exhaustion and viral flu."[67] Speculation that they would be rescheduled within a couple of months, when the tour resumed in South America and Asia, bore no fruit. And the plans for concerts in those faraway places were scrapped, too.

"IT'S A HUMAN SIGN WHEN THINGS GO WRONG"[68]

ELTON KEPT A LOW PROFILE for the remainder of 1989, only emerging to surprise patrons at Los Angeles's China Club on a couple of Mondays with impromptu solo concerts, which included renditions of "Grapevine," "C.C. Rider," and "Tear It Up," as well as some of his own songs. He also helped Sting at a benefit for the ex-Police member's new Rainforest Foundation.

"Sacrifice" was on American store shelves in November. Although it was picked up by Adult Contemporary radio, it languished on the charts. In Britain, it charted on November 4, 1989, and peaked at an inglorious number 55. Consumers were missing the message hidden in the lyrics of the B-side, "Love Is a Cannibal." "Each man kills the things he loves," Elton sang in this libidinous, rock-soul amalgam. Years later, he reflected that even during his darkest days, he couldn't kill his career. "I tried my best to do that, but at the end of the day it was still there."[69]

In January 1990, Elton appeared on Arsenio Hall's television show *Night Thing*. "A lot of people think I'm ill," he started. But he failed to divulge his problems, quipping instead, "That's just because of some of the costumes they've seen me wear over the last few years." He could still make fun of himself—without being honest. Elton looked uncomfortable opposite affable Arsenio. He smiled little, which was rare for him. His fleshy neck was squeezed inside the tight-fitting collar of his dark suit, his "Boy" baseball cap providing the only jollity in his mien. He mentioned that he was selling Watford, and reminisced about the Donald Duck outfit he'd worn at the 1980 Central Park concert. "It's been a little bit slow," he said of the chart rise of "Sacrifice." There was no band in sight, but he performed the single and, later, "Sad Songs," on a grand piano.

A funny thing happened with "Sacrifice." A week before Elton's Arsenio appearance—and after two months of gathering dust in stores—the single entered the Hot 100. More than two months after that, it was in the Top 30, finally peaking at number 18. Although his guest spot on *Night Thing* didn't make the single chart, it helped the song pick up steam.

During the single's slow rise, Elton and the band (with drummer Charlie Morgan, who had replaced Jonathan Moffet) returned to Australia and New Zealand for their first shows Down Under in more than three years. He may have killed off some of the American tour and tours of Asia and South America, but nothing could make him miss Oz. "It's always a pleasure to come back," he said on an Australian radio show, *Rocksat*, on January 31, 1990. "I never need any persuasion to come here. After the last tour, I thought I'd better leave it a bit, for like two or three years, before I came back, because it was such a momentous thing that happened."[70]

The tour commenced February 1 in Melbourne, with Elton's mother, who still lived in Spain, and his Auntie Win along. The shows were similar to the American concerts, but in contrast to all of his previous Australian outings, Elton shunned media attention, except for a news program on which he announced he wanted to take a couple of years off. This time there were no performances with full symphony orchestras, no marriages, no wheelchairs, no after-hour brawls at record company parties, not even a denim jacket with offensive sayings on it. Among the few notable headlines was the Melbourne Symphony Orchestra's announcement of an MSO-Elton John scholarship, established with a "generous" sum of money from Elton, to benefit orchestra members interested in furthering their music studies. General Manager Stephen McGhee, elated at the musician's beneficence, and remembering the fruitful 1986 "Tour de Force," expressed hope that the orchestra and the "world's greatest rock star" would tour together again.[71]

"THIS ONE'S FOR RYAN"[72]

IN THE YEARS SINCE ELTON FIRST REACHED OUT to Ryan White and his family, he had managed to keep in touch with them and help in many ways. But Elton wasn't around when Ryan's health began failing in March 1990. Ryan told his mother he badly wanted to talk to his famous friend. Soon, the boy was admitted to Riley Hospital for Children in Indianapolis. Terrible infections riddled his body. His physician recommended he be rendered unconscious so essential medications could attack the infections more easily. On Sunday, April 1, the doctor put him under. Elton had returned from Australia and was in Los Angeles when he learned of Ryan's condition. The musician arrived on Monday night, finding Ryan's bloated body attached to an artificial respirator.

Although the Australia/New Zealand tour had gone well—erasing bad memories from the previous autumn in the United States—Elton was still unable to bring order to his life. He was miserable and confused. That he brought order and comfort to the Whites, and was the pillar of strength everyone needed, was astounding. During that week, the last of Ryan's life, he didn't abuse drugs or alcohol. "I was too busy organizing things and trying to help," Elton said later.[73]

The musician did little things, discarding coffee cups and sandwich wrappers and filing telephone messages, which were deluging the hospital at a rate of a thousand a day. He arranged for music to play in Ryan's room, and decorated it with get-well cards. He talked to the boy's grandparents for hours about their grandson. He became a family member, consulting with the doctor alongside Jeanne White about Ryan's condition and the treatment the boy was receiving.

On Saturday night, Elton took a break from the hospital to go to the Hoosier Dome, where Farm Aid IV was underway. To the astonishment of a crowd of forty-five thousand and host Dick Clark, he decided to briefly perform. When Clark learned who was up next, he could barely contain his excitement. "Ladies and gentlemen, there he is," he said hesitantly, from inside his broadcasting booth. "You'll recognize him . . . *Elton John!*" The musician looked fat and pasty-faced as he took the stage to an affectionate ovation. He was clad in a red and black sweat suit, with a backstage pass dangling from his neck and his white hair unusually unkempt, sprouting uneasily from the back end of a baseball cap that tightly grasped his head.

Elton played "Daniel," managing a smile at the end, as cheers rose in the Dome. He stood to acknowledge the applause, but returned to the piano for "I'm Still Standing." Forgetting the words, he quickly segued into "Candle in the Wind," blurting the sentence that became the unofficial title of Farm Aid IV: "This one's for Ryan." Elton's passion made this "Candle" his career's most touching. He seemed to ponder every last note and word as they related to the boy in the hospital bed. He then rose, thanked the enthusiastic crowd, and hastily disappeared. He was back at the hospital by nine o'clock that night. The next morning, Ryan was dead.

The Briton remained in the days that followed, helping to select a casket and make funeral plans, including selecting the songs he would sing at the service. The secularly spiritual musician chose a traditional hymn and "Skyline Pigeon." "Everybody wanted me to sing 'Candle in the Wind,' but I thought that had been overdone to death," Elton said later that spring. "Skyline Pigeon" was about the release of a bird that flies toward a "better place," he said. "'Skyline Pigeon' was written, melodically, as a hymn, anyway."[74]

On April 11, at Indianapolis's Second Presbyterian Church, a somberly dressed Elton performed "Skyline Pigeon" at a black grand piano adorned only with Ryan's high school graduation picture. Jeanne and Andrea White and the rest of their family were joined by fifteen hundred mourners, including Michael Jackson and Phil Donahue. After the funeral, Elton served as a pallbearer.

Soon after, Elton established the Ryan White Memorial Fund. As much of a help as he was to the White family, their lack of bitterness had helped him, too. "It brought me back to reality. God, I wish I could be like this. I wish I could be so forgiving and not such a nasty piece of work," Elton told David Frost a year and a half later. "I knew I wasn't a nasty piece of work, but I just—it hit home then. And it wasn't long afterwards, in fact . . . that I started to get my life together."[75]

"YOU GOTTA LEARN TO LIVE AGAIN"[76]

IN ENSUING DAYS, "Club at the End of the Street" was released as a cassette single in the United States. A cardboard cover depicted the musician as a cartoon character festooned in Versace, with the kind of winning smile associated with early 1970s American Saturday morning television. This was Elton as that missing member of the Archies.

The illustration was from the song's animated video, in which the club in question was "EJ's Club," and the hot little "trio" a quartet with "EJ" at the helm, playing a decidedly un-nostalgic electric keyboard. There was a jukebox, and happy patrons danced the night away. This was a more inviting clip than the one for "Healing Hands," which featured a plethora of hands to "reach out" for, and relay, emotional support. The video for "Club" was also more appealing than that for "Sacrifice," which had a corpulent Elton singing about marital infidelity against scenes of a guilty-looking husband who tears up a paramour's phone number and returns to his wife.

"Club" debuted on the Hot 100 on April 28, 1990, and peaked at number 28. But it was the album that provided cause for celebration. On April 2, while Elton was traveling to Indianapolis to help Jeanne White, *Sleeping with the Past* went platinum in the United States, courtesy of "Sacrifice." It was his first platinum album since 1978. Elton hadn't yet sorted out his life, but his career was, again, firmly on the rise.

Not ready to take that two-year hiatus, he continued to work. There was a long, fruitful weekend in the New York–New Jersey area that included a taping of *MTV Unplugged* on May 17. And for three nights after that, he and his band opened the Mark G. Etess Arena in Donald Trump's new altar to opulence, the Trump Taj Mahal Casino Resort in Atlantic City.

Elton's appearance on *Unplugged* was broadcast June 12, the twelfth installment of the series begun in October 1989. It was the first time the show would stretch to one hour, and although Stevie Ray Vaughan and Sinead O'Connor had performed one or two songs without accompaniment earlier in the year, the first time an *Unplugged* guest performed a full-length segment alone; it would be another five years before anyone else would do the same. Mariah Carey's 1992 appearance included three backup singers, a vocal ensemble, strings, and the Saturday Night Live Horns. Bruce Springsteen surprised producers with his full band and electric guitars (his segment was called *Plugged*). In 1993, Rod Stewart brought a cast of thirty-three.

Elton's *Unplugged* performance was a dream come true for those who had never seen him perform solo. Dressed in a hot pink sweat suit and matching baseball cap, unassuming black-framed glasses atop his nose, he proceeded to transform with thoroughly novel arrangements a mere seven songs from his daunting catalog. He did this on a lidless grand piano with microphones thrust into its guts. In a nod to the platinum-selling *Sleeping with the Past,* as well as to his musical roots, his performance was consistently rhythm and blues and gospel influenced.

It was also drama-laden. Out of some vivid piano vignettes into which he wove 1940s balladry, "Sad Songs" took form. Rather than relying on his typical steam-roller approach, he allowed the song to grow and swell. It gingerly stepped to a humorous, staccato beat. During "Tiny Dancer," Elton dissected the song into its smallest parts and improvised an idyllic piano link between verses. "Don't Let the Sun" would have worked as the musical interlude for a Sunday sermon at an African-American church. (His falsetto, too, was in full swing, proving that its disappearance from the concert stage was by choice.) During "Bennie," he threw in "Louie Louie," and threw out his modesty. After playing some red-hot chords, Elton blew imaginary smoke off his fingertips.

The next night, on Friday, May 18, Elton and his band were in Atlantic City for three shows, playing to thousands of high rollers being wined and dined by Donald Trump. Jeanne White was in attendance at all three shows, each of which Elton dedicated to Ryan. "It's been a very heavy month," the musician noted on the first night. He was, however, chattier than usual, perhaps because of the relative intimacy of the 5,200-seat venue. He was so chatty that, at one point, his statements bordered on the inflammatory. He called the coach of the Philadelphia Eagles a "pig on two legs," adding, "Great football team, shame about the coach. After a game, you should shake hands. I really mean this. I saw them play New Orleans, and they got beat. . . . Buddy Ryan is an *asshole.* If you can't shake hands after you lose, then *don't bother.*"[77]

The other notable occurrence during the Taj shows was the introduction of a new song, "Made for Me," written days earlier. "Made for Me" had the chordal toughness of the hot soul from *Ice on Fire,* with some of the introspection woven through the cooler soul of *Sleeping with the Past.* Bernie's lyrics were a rare departure from his customary romantic bent, containing equal parts love and lust. He could have been writing about a personal experience, but one wondered, upon hearing the song for the first time, whether the words held more resonance for the singer. "If I couldn't see you naked, oh, I might as well be blind. If I couldn't treat you right, wouldn't I be so unkind," Elton sang. "If I can't make love to you, this body has no use. If you believed I loved you, you wouldn't need no proof." At the time, he was in a serious relationship with a young Atlantan named Hugh Williams; they were entering a rocky phase.

"IT'S NO SACRIFICE AT ALL" [78]

"MADE FOR ME" was among four new songs Elton recorded after his shows at the Taj Mahal with producer Don Was in Los Angeles. The songs were slated for a box set due in the fall in the United States and a greatest hits package for roughly simultaneous release overseas. Another of the songs was written at the behest of David Geffen, of all people. Tom Cruise was to star in a summertime film called *Days of Thunder*, a story about a race car driver, and impresario Geffen wanted a special song for the movie ("We're still friends," Elton surprisingly announced to BBC radio's Richard Skinner some months later[79]). The song that emerged was "You Gotta Love Someone," which would first appear on the gold-selling soundtrack album for the movie in July 1990.

Another song emanating from Los Angeles was "Medicine Man," written with Bernie for the Romanian Angel Appeal, to benefit Romanian children living in squalor in hundreds of orphanages. The single appeared as part of a benefit album, *Nobody's Child*, released in midsummer 1990. With his musical mind still knee-deep in soul, Elton filled "Medicine Man" with staccato keyboard explosions and an abrupt melody sung loudly and abrasively. Thunderous programmed drumming is here, too, despite the skepticism with which he viewed such technology.

As recently as his Australian tour, the pianist had said that the "biggest change" in music had been the shift from "human beings to machines. Hopefully, it'll go back to human beings again." He had been critical of what he perceived as the prevalence of pounding click-tracks on monstrously popular albums by Paula Abdul and Janet Jackson, while admitting that he had, at times, used such things himself, on songs like "I Don't Wanna Go On with You Like That" and "Sacrifice."[80] But machines were never the basis of an Elton John song. They were just another way to get rhythm.

Also while in Los Angeles, Elton made time for an interview with Paul Gambaccini for British television's *Good Morning Britain*. Gambaccini reminded him that, in 1973, he had told filmmaker friend Bryan Forbes he hoped to become a legend someday. "Did I?" Elton asked sheepishly. He skirted the issue, talking about how fortunate he felt to still be in the music business and that he had more enthusiasm for his work than ever. Another point interested him more: Someone had just told him that he had had a Top 40 hit every year for the last twenty years. "That's not too bad," he observed.[81]

On June 6, Eric Clapton was a scheduled honoree at the second annual International Rock Awards, held in New York, and Elton was to make a laudatory statement via satellite from Los Angeles. He did, but also remarked: "I'm doing this show under protest. I'd like to congratulate Sam Kinison for being the first pig ever to introduce a rock'n'roll show." He demanded that, in the future, "decent people" host the program. His remaining comments were bleeped. Sam Kinison, who had been known for anti-gay and questionable AIDS-related lines in his routines, angrily claimed he had stopped telling such jokes. To Elton, though, AIDS was never a laughing matter.[82]

Within a week, Elton was home in time to bask in the news of a breaking hit. Steve Wright of BBC Radio One had started broadcasting "Sacrifice" persistently, every day. Public reaction dictated the song's rerelease. Elton decided that rereleasing it would be like "cheating" unless he did something else to make it meaningful, like donating all the royalties to AIDS charities.

On May 25, 1990, "Sacrifice" and "Healing Hands" were reissued on one double A-sided single to benefit the Terrence Higgins Trust, the London Lighthouse, the Jefferiss Research Wing Trust, and Body Positive. On June 9, the single debuted at number 26. In its second week, it was number 5, and in its third, number 1, staying at the top for five consecutive weeks. "It was like having my first hit record again," Elton gushed.[83] It was his first British hit since the live "Candle in the Wind" early in 1988. It was also his first solo number 1 in Great Britain.

On July 28, 1990, *Sleeping with the Past* followed suit, claiming the number 1 spot in Britain for five weeks. It was his first British number 1 since *Greatest Hits* in the long-ago year of 1974.

When "Sacrifice/Healing Hands" was at number 5, Elton decided that he wanted to do more than donate royalties from just one single to AIDS charities, announcing that royalties from all future British singles would go to AIDS charities. "My manager has now fainted in the dressing room," Elton joked after making the pledge. Months later, he explained that this commitment was better than a benefit concert because it ensured a constant flow of money to the people who needed it.[84]

Two weeks into the number 1 rank of "Sacrifice/Healing Hands," Elton made his last public performance for nearly a year when he appeared at "Knebworth—The Silver Clef Award Winners Show," a British superstar charity concert benefiting the Nordoff-Robbins Music Therapy Centre. The organizers wanted all previous Silver Clef Award winners to appear, hence the title of the show (Elton had won his in 1979). Elton wasn't looking forward to the concert at first. "I've never been on a show with so many old people on it!" he told British television host Terry Wogan, joking that George Michael decided not to participate due to "nappy rash."[85]

After Knebworth, Elton would face his personal life, and change it permanently for the better.

CHAPTER 11

MEDICINE MAN[1]

(1990–1993)

BARRY MANILOW WAS JUST AN ACQUAINTANCE OF ELTON'S, but by the fall of 1990 he was concerned about his fellow performer. "He seems sad. I wish the best for him. I wish he could pull himself together. He's a talented guy, a wonderful singer, a good songwriter, a fancy dresser. Snappy, dapper dresser! I just wish he was not sad. But I think he brings it on himself," Manilow said. "You can take your life into your hands and you can just change things if you open your eyes. I think Elton needs a little nudge, that's all."[2]

Manilow didn't know it, but Elton had already changed his life. The Pinner musician had been aware, at least since the time of Ryan White's death, that he had to change. But he had simply thrown himself back into his work, the only noticeable difference being his heartfelt support of AIDS charities. It would be the love of a good man that would provide a final push in the right direction.

Hugh Williams, Elton's twenty-something Atlantan boyfriend, suddenly entered a drug rehabilitation program in Arizona. This made Elton angry. "I was always very bad at asking for help," he reflected the following December. "I always thought I could do things myself and I thought anybody who . . . went into treatment or who asked for psychiatric help was very weak and I looked down on them."[3] He flew to Arizona to see Hugh, but things went badly. The musician returned home and tore up Hugh's pictures, sinking into a two-week period of sporadic cocaine use and overeating. Then it came to him: "I thought, 'This person tried to do something for himself and here, you are just sitting here . . . fat, haven't washed for two weeks, vomit all over your dressing gown.'"[4] He was still bulimic.

Elton returned to Arizona and Hugh. They went into couples therapy, in which they were to list complaints each had about the other. Hugh listed all the horrors he could think of about Elton—drink, drugs, promiscuity, and bulimia (the latter of which Elton had thought was still a secret). Elton's list indicated that Hugh didn't put away his CDs neatly. The musician may have still been missing the boat, but he was trying.

Finally, Elton realized he had to go into treatment, too. The only place that could treat all of his addictions, including his sex addiction, was Parkside Lutheran Hospital in Chicago. He feared the adjustment. He would have to listen to people tell him what to do, and do things for himself, including his laundry.

On July 26, before entering treatment, Elton attended a private party for the release of the latest Was (Not Was) album, *Are You Okay?*, at Los Angeles's Mayan Theater. That night, he seemed relaxed and happy, trading stories with Iggy Pop about working with Don Was. Three days later, Elton checked into Parkside Lutheran. He considered running away twice, but stayed for the duration. When he returned to London in September, he was a new man.

"I'M GOING BACK TO THE BORDER WHERE MY AFFAIRS AIN'T ABUSED"[5]

IN FALL 1990, Elton moved into a London townhouse (to be dubbed Queensdale) while Woodside underwent renovations. He found a dog, which he named Thomas, at the Battersea Dogs' Home. He also began work on a new project, himself.

Just before rehabilitation, Elton had begun taking Prozac to stabilize his moods. He would be on the antidepressant for another two or three years.[6] He was on a food plan, too, which prohibited sugar and white flour. He fended for himself, without the constant attention of Bob Halley, and wrote letters of apology to friends and associates for his pre-rehab conduct. (Elton's mother and stepfather returned to England from Spain in response to his rejuvenation.) He joined every "anonymous" group imaginable—Alcoholics Anonymous, Narcotics Anonymous, Overeaters Anonymous, and Bulimics Anonymous. He attended countless meetings. It wasn't yet public that he had gone through rehabilitation, but news filtered out that he was going to AA meetings, where he had admitted to being an alcoholic. In between meetings, caring for Thomas, and doing all sorts of little things that he might have, at another time, expected Bob Halley to do, he made some time for his career, which, in some ways, was on automatic pilot.

In August, while Elton was still in Parkside Lutheran Hospital, "Club at the End of the Street" was released as the new British single. It got no higher than number 47 following its August 18 chart debut, an inauspicious follow-up to the blockbuster "Sacrifice."

One new task for the newly sober Elton was promotional interviews for his soon-to-be-released American box set, *To Be Continued . . .* , and a corresponding double-album for the overseas market called *The Very Best of Elton John.* That spring, Elton had worked on the contents of the box set with Bernie and MCA archivist Andy McKaie.

With sixty-seven songs, *To Be Continued* . . . contains something for everyone. There is eye-popping artwork, with silk screens on the cover and inside the hinged box; a booklet containing a homage to Elton and Bernie by music-critic-turned-novelist Eric Van Lustbader, who had followed them from the beginning; and a transcript of a reminiscence-filled interview with Elton and Bernie. Scores of photographs from all periods of Elton's career are squeezed in and around the text.

Besides the expected demos, the set includes B-sides and rare live recordings that are a testament to Elton's prolific nature, plus four new Don Was–produced songs.

The new songs, all recorded in only one take,[7] didn't break new ground, but, along with the box set itself, they provide an effective cap on what the pianist regarded as the first phase of his career. They also offer an uncanny, if unintended, commentary on the transitional state of his life. The first of the four is "Made for Me," premiered at the Trump Taj Mahal in May. The song isn't much different on CD from its live rendition, although James Newton Howard helps with a string arrangement and synthesizers, and the band (except for the quasi-Raeletts) is absent, replaced by studio musicians selected by Was.

The next of the four, and the first single, is the romantic "You Gotta Love Someone." Like "Made for Me," this song seems to hold personal resonance for Elton, even if it was written with Tom Cruise in mind. "You can stop the world, steal the face from the moon," wrote Bernie. "You can beat the clock, but before high noon, you gotta love someone." Delivered in Elton's near-baritone with heaves as big as an oil tanker, "You Gotta Love Someone" examines the pitfalls of manliness as well as the challenges of courage.

The remaining new songs follow the lead of "Made for Me" and "You Gotta Love Someone" in presciently dealing with Elton's demons—before he knew he would be. "I Swear I Heard the Night Talkin'" depicts ugly streets traveled for daily doses of pleasure and pain: "This is my battleground/this is my plaything/it's the only thing I've ever known/outside of a wedding ring." He soon comes to his senses: "I swear I heard the night talkin'/cursing me for being little more than hopeless." The virility of Elton's vocal here is as striking as on "You Gotta Love Someone." He had never sounded so full of testosterone, so much as if he was singing on a "muscle car" commercial. Yet the song has more to offer than that. Within the noble framework of James's synclavier chords and Elton's galloping piano, the melody advances like a ride into uncharted territories, its chorus sliding sensibly into the hopeful future.

The last of the four songs, "Easier to Walk Away," seems to be about infidelity, like "Sacrifice." It also contains lines that fit Elton's pre-rehab denial of his problems ("Every time I look away/I find a hiding place") as well as acknowledge his new outlook ("Just release me, I can't take it/can't you see a change has come"). His singing here is at its most naked, surrounded by fewer instruments and modest backing vocals. It is also the most rhythm and blues–influenced of the new songs. Every melodic inflection is bent with a sweltering heat that melts into the kind of friendly chorus Thom Bell and the Spinners would have loved.

Only "You Gotta Love Someone" and "Easier to Walk Away" are included on the two-volume set, *The Very Best of Elton John*, which provides the best survey ever done of Elton's recording career outside North America, and within the confines of two records, CDs, or tapes. Also, fans outside the United States couldn't buy *Elton John's Greatest Hits, Volume III 1979–1987*, except on import, so now they had their own "volume three."

The overseas compilation *Best of* attracted record buyers in droves. The album was number I practically everywhere it was available for much of late 1990 and early 1991. Most important for Elton, this meant two British number I albums within one year, something he hadn't had since 1974. Unfortunately, the album-buying binge didn't translate into more hit singles at home. "You Gotta Love Someone," the first from the collection, only reached number 33. But that was much better than its fate in the United States, where it peaked at number 43 early in 1991. On the bright side, the American box set *To Be Continued . . .* did better than most expensive career retrospective packages, peaking at number 82 and being certified gold before being taken off the market.

At the end of December 1990, around the time the second British single from *Best of,* "Easier to Walk Away," hovered disappointingly at number 63, Elton guested on British television's *Tonight with Jonathan Ross.* This was one of few opportunities the public had late in 1990 to see the new, improved Elton John. His brown trilby hat cast a shadow over the upper half of his face, but he looked polished and fit, and without the desperation that had marked his appearance during the first half of the year. The platinum dye was gone, leaving graying hair visible amid his natural strawberry blonde. After the near debacle he had created for himself, he told Ross, he decided it was time to fully appreciate life. "I just want to stop a bit and smell a few roses, man."[8]

In a VHI interview broadcast that December, Elton cited "being in love with someone, and working on that" as one of those roses.[9] Both the box set and *Best of* collection included the dedication: "My old life stops with the release of this history. To the people and friends that have touched my life, thank you, you'll always be with me. A new life starts here, thanks to a willingness to change, to Hugh, and My Higher Power."

"I WON'T BREAK AND I WON'T BEND"[10]

THE FIRST HALF OF 1991 WAS QUIET for the man used to a punishing schedule of touring, recording, and partying. Early in the year, he vacationed in Hawaii. He began publicly reemerging in time for a March 10 benefit for Sting's

Rainforest Foundation at Carnegie Hall, where he performed "Your Song," his new standard, "Sacrifice," and a haunting duet with Sting of "Come Down in Time." A couple of weeks later, Elton made a surprise appearance at George Michael's opening night at Wembley Arena, duetting with him to the delight of the audience on "Don't Let the Sun." The performance was taped for possible future use.

New Elton John recordings surfaced. "Measure of a Man," written by Alan Menken for Sylvester Stallone's movie *Rocky V*, had appeared some months earlier. (Stallone was undeterred by Bernie's disapproving reference in 1988's "Goodbye Marlon Brando" to the inevitable future *Rocky* installments.) Elton's barrel-chested vocal on this song, reminiscent of *Man of La Mancha*'s "The Impossible Dream," was produced by Phil Ramone for the soundtrack and was featured in the movie as the closing credits rolled.

July found Elton at AIR Studios in London with Chris Thomas, to record newly written songs for the British version of the *To Be Continued . . .* box set. Elton hadn't anticipated doing much recording during his hiatus but, true to his word, he wanted to keep in practice.

The new songs, "Suit of Wolves" and "Understanding Women," may be harbingers of the end of Bernie Taupin's second marriage. They are certainly not endorsements of marital fealty. In "Suit of Wolves," Bernie mourns a lack of intimacy with his partner that forces him to look elsewhere for affection ("And when you can't get what you want/you take anything you can/so I wear this suit of wolves at night"). Taking a cue from the big-throated singing Elton had been offering since his 1987 surgery, the song is a voice-dominated ballad; the instrumentation, primarily Guy Babylon's keyboard programming and newcomer Olle Romo's drum programming, provides an atmospheric backdrop. Elton's voice, at the fore, forces the listener to concentrate on this first of his two most multifaceted melodies in years.

In "Understanding Women," the other new song, Bernie ponders the end of a relationship, refusing to be defined by it ("Just let me be the final word/in the book we haven't written/I won't be another page/in understanding women"). To have Elton singing "Understanding Women" isn't as peculiar as one might assume. Despite the title, it is not as transparently about women as, say, the overly macho "Since God Invented Girls," which Elton managed to turn into a tender love song. "Understanding Women" is about being jilted, and gender is irrelevant to the lyrical thrust. Here, the instrumentation is more important than in "Suit of Wolves," with a foreboding synthesized string note pattern that punctuates the quietly churning melody, and an angry electric guitar solo from guest David Gilmour of Pink Floyd. But again, Elton's voice provides the focal point of the song.

Uniting the two new songs is a liberal use of drum and keyboard programming. Neither was new to an Elton John recording, both heard on his songs as recently as

1990, nor was the programming on the new songs an overused click-track, for which he had expressed disdain. Yet programming had rarely so dominated his songs. It was far from the organic approach to which he had looked back nostalgically just half a year earlier. "In those [old] days, we went for live tracks, and that's part of the recording business I really miss," Elton had confessed in December 1990. "I like the human element. I don't mind if a song speeds up too much towards the end."[11] He was nevertheless smitten by the technology, while having no knack for it himself, since it involved computers. Did "Suit of Wolves" and "Understanding Women" provide a window onto the musical direction Elton would take?

The two new songs would replace "You Gotta Love Someone" and "I Swear I Heard the Night Talkin'" for the British counterpart to the American box set, also called *To Be Continued. . . .* Elton meant for this redone box set to be as much of a career marker, and a demarcation line for emotional rebirth, as the first.

"I'M LOCOMOTIVE STRONG"[12]

A YEAR AFTER ELTON SOLD HIS INTEREST in the Watford Football Club to businessman Jack Petchey, retaining only the title of "life president," he was back in the Watford fold. On August 5, 1991, he returned as a director.[13] Now that he had brought order to his life, he could begin to focus again on other things he cared about. Besides supporting his favorite soccer club, this included fighting AIDS, and not just through the donation of British singles royalties. In September, he headlined an AIDS walk in Atlanta, now his part-time American home, drawing about twenty-two thousand people and raising five hundred thousand dollars.

The pianist walked with the thousands alongside Mayor Maynard Jackson. Later, in Piedmont Park, he gave a pep talk. "Sometimes I get a little angry about this disease; in fact, I get a little angry about it all the time. I have so many friends who've died of it, so many friends who are dying of it." To wild applause, he continued, "I wish, sometimes, that the governments of some countries and the drug companies, especially, would show a little more compassion. To make huge, gigantic profits out of suffering people, is, I think, obscene." He punctuated the air with his fist, declaring that AIDS activists would have to return to this walk "again and again and again" to combat the disease.

Creating a big stir that fall was an album called *Two Rooms: Celebrating the Songs of Elton John and Bernie Taupin*, which recognized a remarkable fact. As of 1992 (just months away), Elton and Bernie's songwriting partnership would reach the ripe old age of twenty-five.

Two Rooms had been in the conceptual stages since the twenty-year marker. Steve Brown, an important part of the Elton John organization for the musician's first few years of stardom, returned to coordinate the project. Working with PolyGram International Music Publishing, the company that now owned the pre-1974 copyrights (having purchased them from Dick James Music), Brown assembled sixteen recording acts, collectively spanning four decades of popular music, to sing a mere sliver of the Captain and the Kid's catalog. Once the *Two Rooms* undertaking came to fruition, Brown and PolyGram planned a marketing media blitz that included a companion video, the release of some songs to radio, and a network television special.

Elton had generally been loathe to cooperate in the proper promotion of his career. To him, promoting his music meant only recording and touring. He might appear on television or radio to push new product, but this was likelier to happen at home in Britain than in the United States, and then only when he felt like it. He wore what he liked and said what he felt. He took care of his personal problems in 1990 not to pander or sell records, but because it was time he did so. Coincidentally, his career was again on the ascension just before he'd checked into Parkside Lutheran.

But Elton couldn't argue with *Two Rooms*. He and Bernie loved having other people record their songs, and a central aim of *Two Rooms* was to inspire more of this. "In the age of singing songwriters, people feel that the original version is the only one that they really want to hear," remarked David Hockman, head of PolyGram International Music Publishing. "It's a self-imposed barrier that needs to be overcome."[14] As Elton noted constantly, no one besides himself had ever had a hit with a John/Taupin tune. Aretha Franklin may have come closest, with her recording of "Border Song" going to number 37 in 1970.

Too many good John/Taupin covers had faded into unjust oblivion—Rod Stewart's "Country Comfort" and "Let Me Be Your Car," Olivia Newton-John's "The Rumour," Sandy Denny's "Candle in the Wind." Not enough superstars who could garner real exposure for these songs were recording them. Also, there was an excessive number of junk-food versions of John/Taupin songs—an American release called *The Elton John Songbook*, performed by Paul Windsor and His Orchestra, for example, and an English release called *Bobby Crush Plays Elton John*. *Two Rooms* was supposed to show that Elton and Bernie's songs could be successfully performed by major acts willing to put their imprimatur on them.

Did *Two Rooms* achieve this? As *Billboard* put it, *Two Rooms* is a "mixed bag that will delight or dismay buyers depending upon how strongly they feel about the original versions."[15] What has lent Elton's melodies their highest expression is a symbiotic relationship between his vocals and the supporting instrumentation. This symbiosis is absent from much of *Two Rooms*.

Among the failures are Jon Bon Jovi's "Levon," a rote carbon copy of the original that breaks down when he sings, in his American accent, "spends his days countin', in the *gah-RAJ* by the motorway" instead of Elton's English "GAH-ridge." Also disappointing is Bruce Hornsby's "Madman Across the Water" (a song that requires a diabolic vocal), which suffers from flaccid singing, while Phil Collins's

"Burn Down the Mission" (a song that requires riotous pianism) suffers from flaccid piano playing. If Hornsby and Collins had gotten together on either of the two songs, a brilliant cover would have been possible.

There are some bright spots. Kate Bush turns "Rocket Man" into a hazy reggae romp. Sting's bare-bones "Come Down in Time," with Elton guesting on piano as one "Nancy Treadlight," successfully evokes the surrealism of the original. The Who, with hints of "Won't Get Fooled Again" and a big slice of "Take Me to the Pilot" (in friendly retribution for Elton's interpolation of "Can't Explain" into his 1975 recording of "Pinball Wizard"), make "Saturday Night's Alright" their own brand of rock belligerence.

But despite these highlights, the album fails to showcase a fair sampling of Elton and Bernie's career. There is nothing from the Geffen years, and only six out of the sixteen songs came from Elton and Bernie's store of publishing post-1973 at Big Pig, their company that had taken up where Dick James Music left off, probably because of PolyGram's central involvement in the project.

The companion *Two Rooms* video, which entered *Billboard*'s Top Music Videos Chart at number 3 on November 23 in the United States, more fairly sampled their career. It featured the requisite rare and not-so-rare live footage, reminiscences of Elton and Bernie, and their mothers talking about the early days. Just as thought-provoking were complimentary words from an eclectic assortment of artists, including some not on the album, like Axl Rose (Elton's music was his classical music) and Neil Young (remembering Elton's 1970 Troubadour stint). The video was featured on a special December 21 prime-time edition of ABC-TV's *In Concert '91* hosted by Sylvester Stallone.

Several *Two Rooms* songs were released to radio. In the United States, the airwaves filled with Kate Bush's "Rocket Man," Oleta Adams's "Don't Let the Sun," Jon Bon Jovi's "Levon," and Wilson Phillips's "Daniel." These were played often enough to qualify for the Hot 100 had they been released as singles.[16] Rod Stewart's "Your Song," the only *Two Rooms* song released commercially in the United States, failed to reach the Top 40 but did get to number 48 in the spring of 1992. In Britain, Kate Bush's "Rocket Man" was a bona fide chart hit, nearing the Top 10 around Christmastime. Parties celebrating *Two Rooms* in London and New York generated additional press coverage.

With all of this hype, it was hard not to be aware of *Two Rooms*. That music reviewers, still blind to Elton's musical achievements, failed to use the album's release as an opportunity to reflect on the scope and breadth of his songs with Bernie or his career as a solo artist, didn't discourage record buyers. On November 9, 1991, the tribute album debuted at number 28 in the United States, on what was now called the *Billboard* 200 Top Albums chart, peaking at number 18 early the following year and going platinum. In response to the hoopla, all three of Elton's greatest hits albums rose on *Billboard*'s Top Pop Catalog Albums chart, with *Greatest Hits* going to number 1 on February 1, 1992. (*Volume III*, which had peaked at an inglorious number 84 in 1987, was certified platinum in November 1991.) In Britain, *Two Rooms* was number 1 on the Top 20 Compilation Albums chart. It was time for Elton to end his hiatus.

"LADIES AND GENTLEMEN, MR. ELTON JOHN!" [17]

THE MUSICIAN'S PUBLIC PROFILE was again prominent by late 1991. A second Diet Coke television commercial followed one he'd done with Paula Abdul early in 1990, this time showing him swapping licks with Louis Armstrong and entertaining Humphrey Bogart and James Cagney. And just as *Two Rooms* began to make waves, Elton's live duet with George Michael on "Don't Let the Sun," performed at Wembley Arena in March 1991, was released worldwide.

Days earlier, on November 24, Freddie Mercury died of AIDS. Elton, enveloped in his new, unusually calm demeanor, was limpid-eyed as he focused on his friend's legacy in a BBC One tribute to Mercury the following night. He chose his words carefully. "He was very funny, he was extremely outrageous, he was very kind, and he was a great musician and one of the great front men of rock'n'roll bands," the pianist said. "Quite simply, he was one of the most important figures in rock'n'roll over the last twenty years. I'll miss him." [18]

A couple of weeks later, as Elton adjusted to Mercury's loss, the duet with George debuted on both the American and British charts, on the heels of an emotionally charged video. Filmed that fall in an airport hangar before a live audience, it showed the two singers wildly gesticulating toward each other, and, near the end, hugging. Its dramatic reenactment of the March 1991 Wembley performance lovingly recaptured George's noisy announcement of his mentor's entrance about a third of the way into the song: "Ladies and gentlemen, Mr. Elton John!" Later in the video, the senior duet partner added to the sentimentality by mouthing "thank-you," probably in appreciation for the star treatment he received in what was, essentially, George's video.

The duet was an enormous hit. In the United States, it debuted at number 72, climbing to number 34 in its second week and number 19 in its third. By February 1, the single was certified gold and number 1—Elton's first number 1 in the United States since "That's What Friends Are For" in 1986, and his first self-penned number 1 song since "Don't Go Breaking My Heart" in 1976.

More exciting was the practical import of the single's success. The American singer who had first gotten Reggie Dwight's attention with a *Life* magazine photo spread of his slicked-back hair and gyrating hips held a record that was now threatened by the fully grown Elton John. "Don't Let the Sun," firmly entrenched in the Top 40 in 1992, enabled Elton to tie Elvis for the most consecutive years with a Top 40 hit—twenty-three. [19]

In Britain, Elton's chart rise was automatic. The single debuted on December 7, 1991 and shot to the top, quickly displacing Michael Jackson's "Black or White." For months on end, well into the spring, the duet was number 1 across Europe. Ironically, Elton had tried to dissuade George from releasing the single, thinking it would hurt his friend's career! "I said: 'George, this is a very crucial time for you. You've had this album out [*Listen Without Prejudice*], which hasn't been as successful in the States as the *Faith* album; maybe you should think twice about putting a live single out.' I left that on his answering machine and he phoned me back and said: 'No, it's going to be fine.'"[20]

It was a boon to good causes. In Britain, half the proceeds from the single went to an AIDS charity, the London Lighthouse; the other half went to the Rainbow Trust Children's Charity to benefit terminally ill children. In the United States, a portion of the proceeds went to a wider variety of causes, among them the Boys & Girls Clubs of Chicago and the San Francisco AIDS Foundation.

While the new "Don't Let the Sun" dominated European and American charts, and *Two Rooms* reminded fans of past John/Taupin triumphs, Elton began sowing the seeds for a more significant reemergence. Recording sessions for *The One* commenced in November at the Studio Guillaume Tell in Paris, broke for Christmas (which he would never have allowed pre-rehab, when the holiday season made him grumpy), and finished in March 1992.

"THE PIECES FINALLY FIT"[21]

"IT WAS SPECIAL TO GO INTO THE STUDIO FRESH AND FIT," Elton said after *The One* was done. His demons at bay and invigorated by clear-headedness, he looked forward to this latest challenge, even if he had to shake off an initial apprehension. He had written songs for benefit albums and others for box sets over the last two years, but hadn't tried putting together a whole album since the end of 1988.

"He had had a lot of fear going in to make the album because he hadn't made an album sober [in some time]," John Reid later recalled. "We went into the studio the first day, and he lasted about twenty minutes and he said he couldn't do it."[22] But Elton returned the next day, and was soon reminded that writer's block wasn't something that happened to him.

Elton would say that *The One* was his best album since *Captain Fantastic.* Bernie, too, was enthusiastic. Unlike *Sleeping with the Past,* their homage to the best in early American soul, this one "isn't a pop record," Bernie asserted. "It has real feelings and real emotions and the end product is probably one of the best things we've done, bar none, I would say."[23] This didn't mean the songwriting partners didn't have disagreements over the manner in which *The One* was recorded.

Writing against the sound of a drum machine was nothing new for Elton, except that Olle Romo was now the drummer/technician setting the tempo that the pianist requested for any given set of lyrics (after which the song would be finished as quickly as always, in fifteen to twenty minutes). During the album sessions, too, Romo's drum programming replaced the "organic" drumming that Bernie preferred. "He [Elton] knows I would have loved to hear a real drum kit somewhere on this album," the lyricist said later. His preference for a "real drum kit" symbolized the divergence of the songwriters' musical tastes. Whereas Bernie stuck to "jazz and roots music," he noticed that Elton had developed a fondness for "groups with initials for names."[24]

Extensive drum programming and some keyboard programming, two staples of groups with "initials for names," are indeed present in *The One*. The melodies, however, which are among the most supple and chewy of Elton's career, smother the sound of automation. Several even go further, turning familiar musical references upside down. His piano and keyboard playing, sometimes placed on the back burner at recording sessions in recent years, is bursting out all over. The Chris Thomas–produced *The One* "marks the return of me as a musician," he said.[25]

Besides Romo, several of the musicians on this album were either new or had only recent experience with Elton. Davey played guitar on a number of songs, but so did an unknown guitarist named Adam Seymour. Guy was back to play extra keyboards and keyboard programming, but Fred Mandel was not. In his place, Mark Taylor played keyboards. Replacing bassist Romeo Williams was Pino Palladino, a veteran of the July 1991 sessions. Most backing and harmony vocals were left to Elton, with a few sung by Davey, Kiki Dee, and, ripe for a limited reappearance, Nigel Olsson. One song featured a new trio, comprised of Jonice Jamison, Carole Fredericks, and Beckie Bell.

Among the first songs written was "The Last Song," which has confused listeners ever since *The One* was released. It actually depicts a rapprochement between a heterosexual father and his gay son, who is dying of AIDS. Despite some testosterone-laden lyrical transgressions over the years, Bernie could still be relied on to produce the right words when it counted. "It was a big subject that's never been covered in a song before and I thought somebody should deal with it," Bernie said.[26] Bernie had been "through it," as Elton put it, with a mutual friend. "It wasn't just somebody writing from an outside view. He'd been involved in someone's painful and disgusting death from AIDS."[27]

"The Last Song" begins with a graphic description of the patient's physical deterioration from his own point of view: "As light as straw and brittle as a bird/today I weigh less than a shadow on the wall." The patient regrets the youthful nonchalance that exposed him to the disease: "I only thought I'd win/I never dreamed I'd feel/this fire beneath my skin." His father's visit to his bedside and their frank talk have boosted his spirits: "The hidden truth no longer haunting me/tonight we touched on the things that were never spoken/that kind of understanding sets me free."

Bernie had originally titled the track "Song for '92," but Elton believed this would date it. AIDS and homophobia would be around a long time. "It's very hard . . . to tell your parents [about being gay]," Elton said on New York radio the following year. "I was lucky," he emphasized. "My parents [Sheila and stepfather Fred Farebrother] accepted it very well. . . . I'm . . . in a business where there are a lot of people who are creative who seem to be homosexual," he reflected. "Other people who live in small towns, or in big cities, who have had an upbringing of 'nobody in the family is homosexual'—there is a certain stigma, there's shame, there's 'why am I gay,' there's all those sorts of psychiatric things that go along with it." It is, of course, even worse when a gay man contracts AIDS and must tell his family about both his sexuality and his illness simultaneously.[28]

Elton and Bernie thus graduate from the sly hints of the long ago "All the Nasties" to the honest discussion of "The Last Song." The lyrics suggest deathbed music, and Elton instinctively came up with a funereal hymn. "I must write something that one can sing in church," he later recalled thinking.[29] But composing the music wasn't all smooth sailing. Bernie had given him the words soon after Freddie Mercury's death. "I had a hard time writing the song," Elton remembered. "I kept crying when I sang it, just putting it down on tape."[30]

The resulting recording is one of Elton's finest, as superbly lachrymose as "Sorry Seems to Be the Hardest Word," another example of a perfect hymn adapted with unerring melodic intuition. A song intimately written and sung, the only instruments audible besides Elton's voice and piano are Guy's string- and flute-mimicking keyboards. As the song opens, Guy's string simulation decrescendoes, suggesting life draining from the dying patient. This leads to Elton's lingering piano arpeggiations and hushed vocal. His singing metamorphoses through wide gradations of power within just a single phrase, from a whisper to a bright affirmation of spirit and will, while sustaining notes and vibrato at choice climactic moments.

Other songs on *The One* grapple with grave subjects, too. One is date rape, in "When a Woman Doesn't Want You." Bernie had tired of portraying male sexual conquests and women demeaned by men ("Since God Invented Girls," "Angeline," "Li'l 'Frigerator") and decided a good lecture was in order for men who, obsessed with their seeming physical superiority and perceived social supremacy, regard women as objects. Bernie thus warned men to heed women's wishes in an evolving sexual battleground ("Cause you can't take a woman/when she doesn't want you/you can't be a man/if you're blind to reason").

The seriousness of these lyrics could have invited tiresome, schmaltzy music, but the song's title, reminiscent of "When a Man Loves a Woman," meant that a ballad worthy of Percy Sledge might be in the offing. Bernie later observed that the song's message is diluted by Elton's music. "It makes it more subtle," Bernie said.[31]

"When a Woman Doesn't Want You" has country and soul elements. As Elton once hinted, country and soul are like the two sides of a split musical personality. On *Sleeping*, the country side was muted. Conversely, "When a Woman" cleverly unites both its countrified and soul-laden sides. The song is framed by Elton's gospel piano, but he sweetly sings the first verse with country inflection. The chorus bursts with rip-roaring rhythm and blues intonations, not unlike the cadences in Percy Sledge's "When a Man," which fall against a backdrop of country guitar twangs.

"On Dark Street," which discusses homelessness, involved more collaboration than usual between the songwriting partners. Bernie originally called the song "All I Ever Wanted Was You." Elton thought the title too corny and asked him to change it and rewrite the chorus. The result is a song about a family forced to live on the street during hard times. A "dark street" is where the family has figuratively settled.

Upon hearing the recording, Bernie thought the juxtaposition of images of a suffering family against the Philly Soul conceit Elton had composed was "hooky," but "incongruous."[32] Incongruity, however—or more accurately, irony—has always been one of Elton's songwriting strengths. The lively, danceable strains of Philly Soul serve to italicize the most important words, those reflecting the homeless family's lingering dreams. Elton acknowledges that "On Dark Street" may be the most "commercial" track on *The One*, but he included the song on the album to be true to music he loved.

American racism is cunningly attacked in "Whitewash County," with Bernie leaving ample clues in a lyrical game of "Name That Politician." The setting is a humid backwater in the boggy soil of the white South, where good ol' boys eagerly await the election of a candidate known for acts of racial division and hatred ("the right hand just delivered/the devil in a suit"). This leader speaks with a spurious civility, but everyone knows he's really the same guy ("Well, you've changed your face so often/but you've never changed your mind"). Who could this be but David Duke, former Ku Klux Klan leader? At the time, Duke was seeking an official platform for a racist agenda with a soft veneer.

One would expect Elton's music to recall the perspiration-filled, bitter drawl of "Slave" from *Honky Chateau*. With jocularity, the musician instead drew from the scrappier aspects of "Burn Down the Mission" to construct a tune of faux innocence, a playful hoedown led by malcontents in the shadows of a foul-smelling back alley. Elton bends his voice around the country curves, avoiding a loss of composure that could have betrayed the real intentions of the politician who "talks big in Whitewash county."

The song opens with strains of synthesized square-dance fiddles that shrewdly link tradition to modernity (as Duke tried to mask his old white hood and robe with a modern designer suit). Halfway through, Davey's scratchy guitars ("Get on down," Elton urges) and Elton's yodeling piano tear through the petticoats and denim overalls. But the song's thunderous fade-out, lent its character by Elton's bulky chords, gives the listener pause. "Whitewash County" turns into a rocking melee that washes the county not in white paint, but strokes of danger.

More pressing subjects surface in "Sweat It Out," an all-purpose protest song. It addresses almost every problem not found in "The Last Song," "When a Woman," "On Dark Street," and "Whitewash County." Elton saw Bernie's words as an indictment of 1980s selfishness, describing the song as critical of people who don't care about the world. The musician also thought it was a bit like Bob Dylan's "Subterranean Homesick Blues,"[33] which creates a montage of disparate images. Among the problems cited in "Sweat" are the tendency for U.N. forces in the world's hot spots to attract further conflict ("Peace keepers keep on breathing/can't deny eye for eye/it's open season"); the futility of superstar charity songs and concerts ("Band aids on dead doorways"); environmental tragedies like the Exxon Valdez disaster ("Oil slicks put us on the ropes"); and the failure of American savings and loan institutions ("Man it's hard to handle/when the bank's broke").

The musician took a chance with this song. Although he disliked rap, he raps his way through "Sweat It Out," influenced by the similarities he perceived between Bernie's lyrics and those for "Subterranean Homesick Blues." Like Dylan's rap, Elton's doesn't abandon melody, straying sparingly but effectively from a central tonality. The chorus—"when your back's up, sweat it out"—encompasses a proper melody, a singsongy, childlike refrain so scornful as to make even an adult shudder with apprehension. Embracing Elton's rap-like vocal are Romo's industrial drum claps and discomfiting keyboard playing by Guy and Mark Taylor. Davey accents Elton's wry chord structure with acoustic picking, and later mockingly leans his electric guitar against the pianist's rap pattern. The pièce de résistance is a lengthy coda that Elton composed and recorded while Guy was indisposed.[34] This surprising introduction of Elton's acoustic piano at what would otherwise be the end of the song provides an appetizing jazz interlude. Elton's merciless splashes of sound and spiraling closing chords manage a cynical commentary on interminable strife.

Unlike the real-world concerns in "Sweat It Out," the ballad "Emily" is poised for the next world. After years of avoiding the creation of new mythical characters, Bernie introduces an old woman named Emily who is preparing to meet her maker. Bernie sets the scene with the changing of the seasons, signifying a fate still unknown to Emily as she visits her sisters' graves. She also converses with a picture of her late husband, a war veteran whose grave she can't reach ("Emily prays to a faded hero/in a little frame clutched to her gown"). Emily is painfully alone, but death is coming for her, too.

Elton makes "Emily" an optimistic death song, like "Song for Guy." His midtempo melody, evangelical in shape but worldly in mood, celebrates the familial companionship Emily craves and will soon get; a rosy piano passage represents Emily's longed-for passage to the Hereafter.

Four other songs on *The One* are neither social commentaries nor, like "Emily," touching sagas. Rather, they are celebrations of Elton's renewal. "The North" is one of these. On one level, "The North" ponders Bernie's Americanization, in which he left the gray North of England for sunny Los Angeles ("The North was my mother/but I no longer need her/you trade your roots and your dust/for a face in the river/and a driven rain that washes you/to a different shore"). However, the words could also symbolize Elton's newfound sobriety. For Elton, the North is the dark, wintry seclusion that drugs and drink had held for him and the seeming insurmountability of his addictions before rehabilitation ("Have you seen the North/that cold grey [*sic*] place/don't want its shadow anymore/on my face. . . ./some of us never get to see/a better place").

Elton makes "The North" a contemplative, arpeggiated piano ballad lubricated by the glistening fibers of his voice. Its three-part melody takes the listener through different stages of the musician's recovery, from resigned defeat to gradual self-awareness, and, finally, an affirmation of renewal.

A self-awareness for two is at work in "Runaway Train." Before Elton began *The One*, negotiations were underway for a series of double-billed concerts with Eric Clapton. Anticipating these shows, Elton asked Bernie to write lyrics for a John/Clapton duet. "A lot of it has to do with the pain of losing," Bernie said of the song. "That sort of ties in with both Elton and Eric. . . . There's a redemptional quality about it. . . . They've both been through the mill and come back stronger than ever."[35] Clapton had had his share of tragedy (the freakish death in 1991 of his son Conor) and drug dependency. "Runaway Train" depicts a chaotic underworld of runaway trains that Elton and Eric must dodge. They incrementally reach sunlight and safety: "And I've poured out the pleasure and dealt with the pain/standing in a station waitin' in the rain/I'm starting to feel a little muscle again."

The stars alternate vocals and engage in an instrumental/vocal call and response. When Elton sings the first verse, Eric's wailing guitar rises up in rejoinder; when Eric sings the second, Elton's organ responds. In the shared chorus, blues guitar and strident organ share top billing. The song ends as they battle over the last note. The persistent tempo of "Runaway Train" evokes their dogged determination to reach a positive end as the ferocious runaway train won't quit in its pursuit of them.

Two other songs, "Simple Life" and the title track, represent different ways of saying the same thing. If "Runaway Train" examines the quest of Elton and Eric for redemption, in "Simple Life" and "The One," the pianist has found it.

Bernie said that "Simple Life," the album opener that sets the tone for and imparts the album's message, is about "coming to terms with yourself and . . . about being born again, but not in a religious sense, just within the confines of your own mind."[36] In getting his songwriting partner back to the simple life, Bernie has him abandon the excesses of youth. The lyricist alludes to a song that predates Elton's downward spiral of substance abuse, "Rocket Man," in which the musician sings, "It's lonely out in space, on such a timeless flight." In "Simple Life," he sings, "There's a breakdown on the runway, and the timeless flights are gone." But if Bernie thought Elton's rehabilitation meant a retreat into peaceful solitude or a fading hunger for greater achievements—as suggested by the disappearance of the timeless flights—the lyricist was wrong.

The music for "Simple Life" means something else entirely. In "Runaway Train," Elton is being chased by a renegade locomotive. In the stunning, Gershwin-cum-Bo Diddley symphony of "Simple Life," Elton *is* the locomotive—a strong and disciplined one, intent on letting nothing stand in its way. Romo's most inspired drum programming on the album is a viscerally satisfying shuffle of metal wheels against metal tracks, with Elton's descending piano chords and Mark Taylor's synth strings and harmonica resembling the voice of the train as it announces its arrival. There is a powerful "clickety-clack" in Elton's melody, too, and Bernie's line, "I'm locomotive strong," seized upon by the musician as the song's linchpin, inspires his steely vocal.

The locomotive in "Simple Life" pulls right into "The One," which, as Elton said, is a "song about finding yourself, finding what you're looking for, and being very happy about it."[37] For him, "the one" is a spiritual awakening, which Bernie's lyrics describe like a meeting between soon-to-be lovers. This liberating awakening allows Elton to look askance on past reckless living ("Drunken nights in dark hotels/when chances breathe between the silence/where sex and love no longer gel").

"The One" is one of Elton's most intrinsically romantic songs. It sounds like a love affair everyone would want to have, while illustrating the simple joys of spiritual rebirth. Melodically and vocally, it traces a slow but sure transformation from initial awe at the discovery of a welcome truth, to realization that its promise is there for the taking, to the pronouncement of a promise fulfilled. The emotional/intellectual progression works convincingly for both the initiation of a loving relationship and the acceptance of a fresh perspective. The newness of the relationship—or the perspective—is heard in Elton's classically tinged piano playing, too, evocative of precious droplets of clear, refreshing water dashed on a parched surface.

The One, filled out with an eleventh track, "Understanding Women," from the 1991 summer sessions, explains better than the *To Be Continued . . .* box sets how Elton had gotten where he was by 1992. Though he didn't choose the songs' subjects, *The One* expresses his restored ability to devote time and energy to the things he cared about; the songs of redemption explain how turning inward enabled him to comfortably turn outward.

"IF YOUR FRIENDS ARE THERE, EVERYTHING'S ALRIGHT"[38]
ON JANUARY 15, 1992, forty-five-year-old Nashville resident Dee Murray died of a massive stroke related to the skin cancer he had been fighting for eight

years. Although his career with Elton had ended in 1984, except for an appearance on *Reg Strikes Back*, he'd kept busy, playing bass on tours with country artists like Johnny Rodriguez. Dee left behind a wife and three children, including a toddler. Elton issued a statement acknowledging Dee's contributions to his career and expressing admiration for the bassist's musicianship. He added, "His courage, his humor, and his determination in his fight against his illness is something that will stay with me forever. I loved him dearly and will miss him."[39]

Dee's family needed help with medical and other bills that had piled up during his illness. Toward the end of February 1992, tickets went on sale for a March 15 Dee Murray benefit and tribute concert at the Grand Ole Opry, in which Elton would perform solo. All 4,300 tickets were sold in ten minutes; another show for the same day was quickly added, also rapidly selling out.[40]

That week, Elton won his first Grammy for songwriting. In Britain he was no stranger to such awards. As early as 1974, he received an Ivor Novello award for "Daniel," voted the best song musically and lyrically. Most recently, in 1991, he had won two Ivor Novellos for "Sacrifice." He had also been named best British male at the Brit Awards that year.

The long overdue 1992 Grammy for best instrumental composition was for a little-known, weeping instrumental called "Basque," recorded by flutist James Galway for Galway's 1991 album, *The Wind Beneath My Wings*. Elton had first played the song to Paul Gambaccini in a 1980 BBC-TV interview, the same one in which he turned John Donne's "No Man Is an Island" into a modern song. Galway was the first to record "Basque."

Awarded off camera, Elton's Grammy made little news. He wasn't in New York when the ceremonies were held, although he arrived about three weeks later for Sting's Rainforest Foundation benefit on March 12, three days before the Grand Ole Opry shows. Called *An Evening of Gershwin and Porter and Coward and . . .*, contemporary music was not on the benefit's agenda. Neither, for Elton, were hats. His first live performance of 1992 was marked by a full head of hair. Audience members had to wonder: Had one of those painful hair transplants finally worked? Or had Elton forsworn torturing his scalp and bought a toupee?

The thick, lustrous mop on his head was neither the product of follicular seeds sown into his skin nor a glued-on hairpiece. It was a twenty-seven thousand dollar "weave," created by sewing strands of human hair into the filaments left on his head. The weave wasn't a perfect solution; on a windy day, it was obvious that the thatch hanging over his forehead didn't come from the top of his scalp but from the back. But along with his weight loss and renewed energy, the weave took years off Elton's appearance. He loved it. Later in the year, he smirked, "The *Independent* came out and said, 'Elton John has a dead cat on his head.' It's better than having a dead *cap* on your head!"[41] If hair had been miraculously restored to his head, it had vanished from the rest of his body. Over the next year and a quarter, concert audiences around the world would notice Elton's newly waxed, baby-soft skin. While in New York for Sting's benefit, Elton caught cold. He still hadn't shaken it by March 15, the day of the Dee Murray benefits, but his two ninety-minute performances were still potent. He and his two pianos (an acoustic grand and the Roland) were accompanied only by a MIDI synthesizer hookup. These shows were his biggest challenge since the 1979 tour with Ray Cooper. He was energized by them.

Elton didn't have to do much to get the audiences riled up. Just walking onstage and bowing brought each set of 4,300 concertgoers to its feet. Still, the pianist didn't rest on his laurels. "Sixty Years On," not played since the 1988 *Reg Strikes Back* tour, hadn't been so satisfying since 1979, now played with a breezy, campestral intermezzo. "Philadelphia Freedom," too, won its first notable transformation since birth. Played on the Roland, the 1975 single was preceded by a wry, bubbly introduction, with "Stones Throw from Hurtin'" references that reappeared and changed during a long mid-song solo. "I Guess That's Why They Call It the Blues" strutted and stomped during its first major reinterpretation. "Sad Songs," which, in recent tours, had fused gospel with rock, now sounded like a jocose relative of "Bennie and the Jets." And the extended end of "Burn Down the Mission" ran like a contestant in a hundred-yard dash, evoking memories of the mayhem he had squeezed out of it in 1970.

Elton also unveiled "The North," announcing that his next album was almost done. And he performed sentimental oldies, like Jim Reeves's "He'll Have to Go." ("It would be a sacrilege to come to the Grand Ole Opry and not do a country song," Elton explained.) But it was the last number that really raised emotional levels. "That's What Friends Are For," which the musician had never sung in a full-length concert, was the soundtrack for a commemorative slide show that flashed nostalgic images behind him. Where the recorded version had seemed like a vocal competition among Elton and his compatriots, his voice at the Opry was closer to the loving, flexible timbre he mustered in hymns like "Candle in the Wind" and "The Last Song." At the end of both performances, he walked to the side of the stage and embraced Dee's widow, Maria, and the Murrays' baby girl, Jenna. "Dee used to complain about everything; that was Dee on tour. But when Dee got ill, I never heard him complain once," Elton said. "I've seen so much courage. Dee will always be with me."[42]

Elton found himself singing for yet another lost friend on April 20, when he announced to a crowd of seventy-two thousand at Wembley Stadium, "I'd like to do a song, one of my favorites from the *Innuendo* album. . . . It's a great privilege for me to be here tonight to pay homage to someone I love very much." Elton then sang "The Show Must Go On," one of Freddie Mercury's last compositions for Queen. Television viewers in seventy countries tuned in to see Elton and others perform at this AIDS benefit and Mercury tribute, called "A Concert for Life." Many of the performers never knew Mercury. Some were influenced by him and wanted to acknowledge that. For Elton, this was a chance to show his affection for Queen's front man.

George Michael sang Queen's "Somebody to Love." David Bowie and Annie Lennox collaborated on the Queen/Bowie duet, "Under Pressure." Elton's selection, "The Show Must Go On," peered into Mercury's mind as he unwillingly succumbed to disease. It was the perfect motto to which any musician facing adversity, or anyone facing a scourge, could relate: "Inside my heart is breaking. My make-up may be flaking, but my smile still stays on."

Like those lyrics, Elton's physical appearance was optimistic. His devotion to the designs of Gianni Versace, who had by now become a close friend, had led to a tantalizingly gaudy look that allowed the forty-five-year-old musician to boldly shimmer and sparkle in sense-heightening colors and cuts. That night, he wore an oversized crimson jacket with gold-plated collar and pockets and leatherette fringes dangling from the sleeves. Underneath were a matching vest held together with a vertical row of eight golden buckles and, beneath that, a red shirt that dripped gold from the collar corners. Even his tight-fitting black leather pants shone. This outfit was a preview of the wardrobe for his upcoming world tour. There would be black, reds, yellows, blues—as well as simulated leopard skin—all with the requisite jangling, gold-encrusted accents covering him from head to toe.

Elton's voice glided forcefully across Mercury's melody as he comfortably strode the huge stage with his cordless microphone, often gesturing for emphasis. One doubted whether, had he come from behind the piano during the last world tour, when his face was hidden by a trilby hat and charcoal sunglasses and his body obscured inside a tent-like suit, he could have exhibited such self-assurance.

Before "The Show Must Go On," Elton shared the stage with Axl Rose, the bad boy of Guns 'N' Roses, for an unorthodox rendition of "Bohemian Rhapsody." Elton sang the ballad portion of this short rock opera, while Axl whirled into public view in his dark football jersey, black skirt, and red bandana-wrapped flaxen hair to screech the "head-banging" section. Overcome by a rock'n'roll seizure, Axl's body jerked uncontrollably. As the music wound down, his body relaxed, and the members of the oddest temporary pairing in rock history took a deep breath of relief, smiled at each other in an expression of mutual satisfaction, and, arm in arm, joined voices for the final verse. "Nothing really matters to me," they sang sweetly.

Elton had once been critical of Guns 'N' Roses; one of the group's songs, "One in a Million," contained seemingly bigoted lyrics penned by Axl Rose. But the pianist eventually forgave Axl's transgression. With the Gunner's involvement in "A Concert for Life," in which he paid tribute to one gay man and sang with another (calling his duet with Elton a "humbling experience"[43]), he could probably be viewed less disapprovingly. "I thought if he was willing to come on the show that we should make him feel at home," Elton later told Robert Hilburn. "We all say and do things we regret. I met him before the show and he seemed quite gentle, and I very much like some of his music."[44]

Elton left before the show was over, missing the grand finale, "We Are the Champions." He felt bad Freddie Mercury wasn't there, too.

"REALITY RUNS UP YOUR SPINE"[45]

IN MARCH 1992, Elton signed a new recording contract for North America, again leaving MCA, although any complaints he had with the company weren't openly aired. PolyGram, which had released *Two Rooms*, bid for his services and won, in an arrangement an official described as more lucrative than his MCA contract. The company had been marketing Elton's new product in the rest of the world for a decade and a half through its subsidiary, Phonogram.

In North America, Elton would be obligated to deliver up to six albums for PolyGram (the catch being that he still owed MCA two studio albums—including *The One*—and a greatest hits package). At an undisclosed future date, PolyGram would acquire the rights to his post-1975 back catalog, including the Geffen albums then marketed by MCA, and to the three albums the musician still owed MCA. This complex agreement was preceded by a separate arrangement in which PolyGram acquired the rights to Elton's pre-1976 output, following a period during which MCA would sell off existing stock.[46]

In the meantime, Elton's career forged ahead. Band rehearsals for his 1992 world tour began in Paris on May 10 with the now official musical director, Davey Johnstone. Davey had recruited Bob Birch to play bass. Mark Taylor, from *The One* sessions, joined as the extra keyboardist/guitarist, replacing Fred Mandel. Guy Babylon and Charlie Morgan were back. So were the quasi-Raeletts, Mortonette, Marlena, and Natalie. Elton joined the band two days later for eleven days of practice, four of them in Oslo, the tour's first stop.

The pianist, listed as Sir Tarquin Budgerigar IV (occupation: "Artiste") in the European tour itinerary, was a diminutive ball of electricity. He believed he had never been more fit, committing himself to between sixty and ninety minutes of tennis several mornings a week. "I regret going on stage sloshed and not delivering the best of my abilities to people who've paid the money," he said. "I've got a chance now to make up for that, and I intend to do that."[47] His ticklish anticipation for the tour threatened to explode through an unassuming outfit of short-sleeved black shirt and jeans.

The first challenging task was selecting the songs for the tour, which was getting harder with the release of each new album. Elton regarded this process as a "delicate balance" between old and new. An old song, "Don't Let the Sun," would have to open the show, due to the duet's current high profile. Also rehearsed were many from the last three albums, including *The One*. Elton would take his Freddie Mercury tribute across the continent, too, with "The Show Must Go On."

Elton enlisted Versace, who had designed for opera, to outfit the tour—clothes, staging, and lights. "Gianni's not a dull man," the musician deadpanned. "I adore him."[48] Of course, Versace conceived of his designs with Elton's patently un-dull personality in mind.

Opening night of the Coca-Cola Light–sponsored tour provided a first glimpse into Versace's creations. The first song alone was an aural and visual stunner. Central to its visual success wasn't just Versace's artistry, but a technological wonder the road crew dubbed the "riser of doom."[49] Elton's Roland piano and a set of surpassingly loud speakers—which enabled him to hear every last guitar crackle, vocal quirk, piano resonance, and drumbeat—were carefully positioned on a monstrosity fit for a soundstage at NASA. This thing could move forward, backward, rise up eight feet, and rotate 360 degrees, all while Elton performed.

In Oslo, as the first synthesizer strains of "Don't Let the Sun" were heard, the lights illuminated a translucent, gold-patterned curtain. Through a white oval near the top appeared Elton in silhouette at his Roland, a convincing "sun" shining from behind him. He began the song's well-known piano preamble, and as he sang the first few measures, the curtain slowly rose as the riser descended, the "sun" vaporizing. Within seconds, concertgoers could see the Briton as clear as day, resplendently framed in tapered golden-yellow Versace tails and snug black pants that, together, made him look tall and thin.

From Stockholm Stadium to Vienna's Praterstadion, from Copenhagen's Osterbro Stadium to Dortmund's Westfalenhalle, the "New Elton John" came to call. Some songs began to emerge, cocoonlike, from infusions injected as recently as March or as long ago as 1988, finally tapping into their true potential. "Sad Songs" surpassed its blithe Grand Ole Opry examination, as well as formative versions heard live in 1988 and 1989. Elton opened the song with an ever-longer gospel sonata that segued into the "sad" ruminations of Mortonette, Marlena, and Natalie, which he accompanied with an emotional, seemingly church-born instrumental. Mid-song, he amazed audiences when he plunked a still-muscular leg on top of the Roland and played around it. The heart-stopping piano passages in "Mona Lisas and Mad Hatters Parts One and Two," as heard in 1989, were now full-fledged movements that climaxed with bass and treble punctuations demanding the utmost concentration and stamina. "Philadelphia Freedom," only just rethought in March, now included those wry bubbles that his Tennessee audiences had enjoyed.

Eric Clapton and his band joined Elton for a limited tour throughout Western Europe. "[W]e thought, 'Let's join forces,'" recalled Clapton. "Musically, Elton and I are both at the peak of our powers, and our styles complement each other. It's a lot of fun to play together."[50] At these shows, and at the newsmaking three sell-outs at Wembley Stadium from June 26 to 28, Elton and Eric alternated opening and closing spots. They also jointly performed "Runaway Train." The pianist must have felt a little strange: Ray Cooper, with whom he shared so much history, was touring with Clapton.

It had been three years since Elton had played any English dates. He started off with two shows at the Sheffield Arena on June 21 and 22; after Wembley, he played Birmingham's National Indoor Arena before returning to the Continent. "Elton John is back in Brum!" exclaimed local journalist Paul Cole, writing for the *Birmingham Evening Mail.* "And it's all because he loves the city and his West Midland fans so much."[51]

The Wembley shows attracted most of the headlines. Elton was atypically nervous for these, especially the first night, when many concertgoers were stuck in traffic and late getting to the stadium during his set. "I felt awkward," he said a year later. "I didn't feel as if it was my show." He figured Clapton felt the same way.[52] Yet Elton wrung the Roland dry, and gave his microphone an earful as well. He grimaced, he grunted. He kicked over his piano bench and played spread-legged, crouched over the keyboard. He tunefully lectured the hundreds of thousands that the "show must go on." He tore his elegant Versace tails off to make a point, grinned at his improvisations, and shared toothy snarls with Davey.

Missing all of this, *Billboard* reviewer Hugh Fielder complained that the pianist's performance was "lackluster" and "surprisingly bereft not just of showmanship but of a proper regard for one of the greatest songwriting heritages in popular music."[53] Fielder seemed to suggest that Elton was slumped, motionless, against the Roland, barely eking out notes from a well-worn script.

Nonsensical reviews like Fielder's caused nary a ripple as the tour proceeded. Among Elton's last shows in Europe was a concert at Barcelona Stadium on July 21, on the eve of the Olympic Games, beamed to Britain via BBC Radio One in celebration of that station's twenty-fifth anniversary and taped for commercial video release. Elton, in modest jacket and taut bicycle shorts, ended the concert with a union of "Song for Guy" and "Your Song," the latter assuming some properties of the instrumental to become an elegy.

"LIKE FREEDOM FEELS WHERE WILD HORSES RUN"[54]

THE ONE was not the only new Elton John recording released in 1992. There was also "Up the Revolution," a charming, calypso-spiced ditty from a Bee Gees project for BBC television called *The Bunbury Tails,* recorded during Elton's trilby days. He also recorded a song cowritten with Bruce Roberts, "Some Other World," for the soundtrack to the 1992 animated film, *Fern Gully: The Last Rainforest.* He turned Roberts's sermon about humankind's destruction of the world's natural habitats into a punchy dance tune whose serious message was housed in the frenzied overtones of his vocal. "Runaway Train," from *The One*, was also on a movie soundtrack, *Lethal Weapon 3*.

The One was released in June 1992, in the middle of Elton's European/British tour. Issued only on CD and cassette in the United States, it was the first non-vinyl Elton John release there. Critics offered both praise and derision for the album, in both cases uninformed by what it meant for Elton to record clean and sober for the first time in ages. On the positive end, the *Los Angeles Times*'s Mike Boehm liked the album's topicality: "This may be the most insightful and alert-to-its-times album that composer John and lyricist Taupin have ever done."[55] On the negative end, clever Robert Christgau was still at it, skewering the musician from his perch at *The Village Voice* in his periodic "Consumer Guide" column. "Fun automaton, floundering has-been, or unnoticed fixture, he hung in there so that 1992 was the *twenty-third consecutive year* he put a single in the Top 40," he shrugged, giving the album a C+,[56] the same rating he'd given *Goodbye Yellow Brick Road* about eighteen years earlier.

But no matter what Christgau said, *The One* was a hit. In Britain, it shot in at number 2, its chart peak, right behind Lionel Richie's greatest hits album, *Back to Front*. The album took a little longer to catch on in the United States, but when it did, its sales figures surprised everyone. It debuted on The Billboard 200 on July 11 at a discouraging number 31. Over the course of the summer, however, it rose steadily until, by September 5, it nosed into the Top 10, stopping at number 8. It was Elton's first Top 10 album in the United States since 1976's *Blue Moves*. (Within the year, *The One*, unlike *Blue Moves*, would go double platinum.) The album reached number 1 throughout Europe.

To what could this album's American success be attributed? MCA Records, which Elton had evicted from his future when he signed with PolyGram in the spring, didn't lavish much attention on publicity, which accounts for its tepid chart debut. But the album had other things going for it. The *Two Rooms* tribute helped pique interest in the Elton John phenomenon, given its effect on sales of his back catalog. The number 1 duet with George Michael, "Don't Let the Sun," heightened the pianist's public profile. And anticipation for new product, after Elton's three-year hiatus from album making, probably helped fuel interest in *The One*, also. The lead single, the title track, was all over the airwaves throughout the summer, still rising on the Hot 100 even as the album peaked at number 8.

The single "The One" peaked at number 10 in Britain on June 27, and at number 9 in the United States on September 19, when it became Elton's twenty-fifth Top 10 hit there. It was not the biggest hit of the summer in the United States; that feat was accomplished by Boyz II Men's "End of the Road," which stayed at number 1 for months. But the popularity of "The One" ensured that it would be an American concert staple for years to come. The song also remained in the Top 5 throughout the summer across much of the Continent.

"This has been a great year for John, who landed his first Top-10 album since 1976; scored a number 1 single with George Michael; was saluted on the platinum *Two Rooms* album; and has performed in concert with such top stars as Michael, Eric Clapton, and Axl Rose," read a *Billboard* magazine commentary as "The One" hit number 9.[57]

"FIRE FLYING FROM YOUR HANDS" OR, "PLAY THE PIANO, BOY!"[58]

IN AUGUST, Elton took his tour to the United States, again double-billing with Clapton for selected cities. The two's concerts in New York's Shea Stadium on August 21 and 22 and Los Angeles's Dodger Stadium on August 29 and 30 attracted huge throngs, with tens of thousands of fans jamming the cities' roads and public transportation systems. Among the audience members in New York was Elizabeth Taylor, who remarked afterward, "'Candle in the Wind' is my favorite Elton John song. I just hope when I die Elton writes a song like that for me."[59]

On the whole, the U.S. tour received excellent notices. Among the most enthusiastic was the review by *Baltimore Sun* critic J. D. Considine, who carefully placed superlatives one on top of the other to illustrate how Elton had outdone himself at the September 20 concert in Columbia, Maryland. Considine gave due credit to the band, but said that it was Elton who had made the show unbearably thrilling: "[W]hat truly put this concert over the top was the star himself, whose performance was nothing short of stunning. . . . Strong as his singing was, . . . it paled in comparison to his playing. . . . Excessive? Maybe. Exciting? Absolutely. Consider it proof that some stars really do improve with age."[60] At forty-five, the pianist did indeed seem to be improving, harkening back to a more innocent, fresh-faced time. With a full head of longish strawberry-blonde hair, "granny" glasses, and a thinner countenance, he looked much as he had when first taking the United States by storm back in 1970.

The U.S. tour, which stretched to November, combined Elton's bottomless store of adrenaline with each audience's affectionate, persistently off-key sing-along accompaniment. At the September 22 Philadelphia Spectrum concert, the pianist instructed himself mid-show to "Play the piano, boy!" before launching into a hair-raising section of "I Don't Wanna Go On With You Like That." His body shook, recoiling from imaginary sparks that scrappy playing sent flying from the keys. During "Saturday Night's Alright," he positioned one leg on his bench and the other in the air, comically kicking in the direction of the derrieres of Davey and Bob Birch, who had jumped behind him on the riser.

"THE HIDDEN TRUTH NO LONGER HAUNTING ME"[61]

"I WANT YOU TO MEET SOMEBODY who is an inspiration to me and the person that has directly influenced me the most when it comes to doing fundraising for

AIDS," Elton told fifteen thousand Madison Square Garden concertgoers on October 11, at a concert benefiting the Elizabeth Taylor AIDS Foundation during a seven-night stand at the Garden. "She spoke out at a time when it was not fashionable to say anything, because it was a 'homosexual disease.' And she had the balls to say, 'Fuck you.'"

What a way to talk about Elizabeth Taylor! To an ovation, Taylor emerged from backstage and credited Elton with the idea for the benefit, and for putting it all together. The night had begun with an abridged, hour-long set by Elton and his band. Also performing was a small but illustrious group he had amassed, including host Whoopi Goldberg and Bruce Hornsby, who accompanied Elton on his song "Lost Soul" (a song, Elton said, that had gotten him through some of his darkest days of substance abuse) and sang with Lionel Richie on "Imagine." Later, Elton accompanied George Michael on "Candle in the Wind" and on an uncommon treat, "Ticking." The showstopper was a duet with Whoopi Goldberg on "Jumpin' Jack Flash." As strange as it was to see Elton sing "Bohemian Rhapsody" with Axl Rose at the Freddie Mercury benefit, even stranger was the vision of the pianist serenading a hopping Elizabeth Taylor with Mick Jagger's lyrics ("But it's alright now! In fact, it's a gas!").

The Garden was also the scene of a celebration, on October 9, when Elton became the first entertainer to be honored with a spot on the Madison Square Garden Walk of Fame, which already contained the names of twenty-five sports figures. "As people know, this is probably my favorite place to play in the whole world," Elton said, in accepting the honor. "I've been playing here for a long time. Every time I come back, it seems to get better."[62]

At that night's show, a security guard named Robert Simms claimed he was minding his own business checking VIP passes by the stage when Elton left his Roland piano, walked over, struck him in the back of the head and neck, and returned to the piano. Simms later checked himself into a hospital, where he was listed in satisfactory condition, although he complained of dizziness and headaches. An examination by a Garden physician cast doubt on Simms's story. Elton's position was that he saw Simms bothering a woman in the audience and walked over to get the guard's attention by tapping him on the shoulder. But how had a mere tap on the shoulder, even by one of the pianist's formidable fingers, resulted in serious injury? Simms threatened a lawsuit.[63] Much hay was made of the alleged incident in the local press.

Nothing came of Simms's allegations. The week would be better remembered for the series of knock-out shows, the AIDS benefit concert, and a pledge by Elton to donate all royalties from sales of his American singles to AIDS charities, as he'd been already doing in Britain for two years.

This pledge was precipitated by MCA representatives, who had approached the musician about making "The Last Song" a charity single. In the United States, the promotion of "The Last Song" centered around a cassette single that people could purchase by calling a toll-free number. A two-hour radio program called "The Elton John Music Special," set to air across the United States on three hundred radio stations in late October, was another part of the promotional venture. Hosted by Leeza Gibbons, the show included an interview with Elton and public service announcements by Whoopi Goldberg, Richard Gere, Arsenio Hall, Billy Crystal, and Sting, asking listeners to make donations. MCA contributed a one hundred thousand dollar advance against royalties to six of the designated AIDS charities: AIDS Project Los Angeles, Hollywood Supports, the Gay Men's Health Crisis, Project Open Hand/Atlanta, the Pediatric AIDS Foundation, and the Ryan White Children's Fund.

People could also buy a video of "The Last Song," filmed the day after Elton's August 30 concert with Eric Clapton at Los Angeles's Dodger Stadium. "I decided that I definitely wanted a gay director," the musician told a reporter for the gay magazine *Ten Percent*. "I wanted to be sure that it [the video] wouldn't come across as too mushy because I wanted anyone with any bigotry, or hatred, or fear about this to be touched and, hopefully, encouraged to be more compassionate." He approached Russell Mulcahy, director of his early videos and the romantic clip for "The One," but Mulcahy was making a feature film. Then he asked Gus Van Sant, who agreed. Elton told him he wanted the video to depict a young, gay man with AIDS (but not in the last, horrifying stages, which might have looked too unpleasant).[64] The director set the scene in a hospital, where a father visits his son. A picture of the son with his male lover sits on a night table. Elton narrates the scene through song. In the touching ending, father and son embrace and all past differences are resolved.

Sales of the American single didn't accelerate until Elton appeared with Bernie on Arsenio Hall's November 16 installment of *Night Thing*, where he performed the song. It reached number 23 on December 19, 1992 and stayed in the Top 40 through the turn of the year. By 1993, then, Elton had had a Top 40 song every year for twenty-four years, breaking the tie with Elvis. The song did a little better in Britain, reaching number 21 by November 14.

More American Elton John releases were issued that fall. No new songs were among them, yet there was almost a glut of product, just as at other moments in Elton's career—though this time it didn't appear to harm sales of his current album. The overabundance stemmed from PolyGram's acquisition of his pre-1976 recordings. The centerpiece of the new offerings was *Rare Masters*, a two-CD collection of rare old singles, demos, B-sides, and alternate versions of familiar songs dating back no later than 1975. If it weren't for the fact that the last seventeen years of Elton's career were completely ignored by this retrospective, it would have been the ideal replacement for the *To Be Continued . . .* box set, which, despite its name, MCA had discontinued.

The release of *Rare Masters* was the signal that PolyGram's Polydor label was reissuing all of Elton's pre-1976 albums as well as *Elton John's Greatest Hits Volume II*, which now featured only songs from the pre-1976 period. A more radical change came from MCA. Since the company now owned Geffen Records, it deleted the 1987 album, *Elton John's Greatest Hits, Volume III 1979–1987*, and replaced it with *Greatest Hits 1976–1986*. Neither *Rare Masters* nor *Greatest Hits 1976–1986* charted, though the latter was eventually certified platinum.

In October, Elton and Bernie signed a subpublishing deal with Warner-Chappell, which had been administering the duo's post-1973 Big Pig publishing. Under this contract, the songwriters received an advance of thirty-nine million dollars, vastly eclipsing the ten million Prince had received for his new Warner-Chappell agreement. "Because we get so many covers of their songs, John and Taupin are, to me, the George and Ira Gershwin of our time," said Les Bider, the CEO of Warner-Chappell. "Their earnings are so high that the deal is justified." The deal included overseas publishing, too.[65]

November saw a different kind of milestone—the establishment of the Elton John AIDS Foundation.

"I ONLY THOUGHT I'D WIN"[66]

"I WANT TO GET MORE INVOLVED in raising money for AIDS. I need something else to focus my attention on other than my career," Elton explained to Paul Gambaccini in a 1993 BBC Radio One interview at his Atlanta home. While he passionately cared about helping people living with the disease, the cause also offered *him* continued therapy. "I don't want to raise money and say, 'Here you are, there you are, thank you very much, aren't I doing a great job?' That's not the point. This is something for me, too. . . . It helps me to see people, to be with people, who live with this disease. . . .We all need to look at people's courage, sometimes, to get it for ourselves." He feistily added: "Being a gay man, being someone surrounded with a lot of people with HIV, it's something I have to do. . . . I'm sure people are gonna send me up. Sod them."[67]

The foundation was codirected in the United States by Elton and friend John Scott, with a governing board that included Bernie Taupin, MCA's Al Teller, John Reid, and publicist Sarah McMullen. In the UK, the Elton John AIDS Foundation would have five codirectors. Patrons included Sir David Frost, Annie Lennox, PolyGram's Alain Levy, Sting, and Gianni Versace. Elton hoped to raise at least two million dollars annually in both the United States and Britain for AIDS education and patient care.[68]

Elton participated in various high-profile AIDS charity events, happily summoning an androgynous image when his showman's sense called for it. He bent his gender at a November 18 AIDS Project Los Angeles (APLA) benefit, the Commitment to

Life Awards, honoring David Geffen and Barbra Streisand. Bernie was the producer and was aiming for an "anti-benefit benefit," as he told Arsenio Hall, in which incompatible singers and musicians would perform unusual interpretations of ill-fitting songs from *West Side Story*. That night, Billy Joel and Eddie Van Halen reinterpreted "Jet Song." Natalie Cole and Patti LaBelle duetted on "America." These performances didn't raise an eyebrow, but Elton's song did. "I feel pretty, oh so pretty, I feel pretty, and witty, and gay!" he belted, prancing about the stage in a heavy woman's coat and string of pearls. "And I pity, any girl who isn't me today!"[69]

"THERE'S A BREAKDOWN ON THE RUNWAY,"[70] PART ONE

"IT WOULD HAVE BEEN VERY DISAPPOINTING to come to South America for the first time and not give my best," Elton said, referring in a May 1992 Brazilian television interview to the South American dates he'd canceled after his aborted 1989 American tour. This time, however, he couldn't wait to go to Latin America. The first stop was Mexico City, for shows on November 13 and 14 at El Estadio Azteca, where he drew crowds of ninety thousand and eighty-six thousand, respectively.

Five fans on the stadium field, each wearing a white sweatshirt bearing a letter of Elton's first name, assumed a cheerleading role. But the enormous crowds didn't need cheerleaders. The percolating "Philadelphia Freedom" got everyone dancing. When the lights onstage dimmed for "Funeral for a Friend," thousands feared he was leaving and chanted, "Elton! Elton!" as the synthesizer opening began. During "Rocket Man," they were effective backing vocalists, with Elton conducting their interjections of "long, long time." A fifteen-minute "Sad Songs," whose piano instrumental opening included a romp through idyllic meadows, a session in an African-American church, and a Keystone Kops thriller, prompted Natalie Jackson to exhort, "Sing a sad song, Elton John, for Mexico City!"

Before these dates, Elton's record sales in Mexico had been paltry. He had sold 280,000 albums in his entire career as of two weeks before the shows. After the concerts and a television special with radio simulcast, Elton sold another 120,000 albums. Sixty-one thousand of those were *The One*, certified gold in January.[71]

After these concerts, the pianist was due back in Los Angeles for Arsenio's *Night Thing* and the APLA benefit, but would be flying to South America for a November 21 concert at Buenos Aires's River Plate Stadium before a throng of fifty thousand. "I'm just about to leave for Argentina," he excitedly said in a telephone interview on New York radio. "Would you believe it?"[72]

Unfortunately, the River Plate concert was a debacle. Elton was always fussy about his onstage sound. The monitors around him were the key to whether he could hear himself and the band, and thus whether he felt comfortable about performing. If something was off, he might get a bit exasperated, mouthing "more piano" or "more voice" to a backstage hand. He might leave the stage so an assistant could fix a problem. On this night, they probably should have stopped the show until things could be righted.

The show began calmly enough. A look of genuine pleasure on his face, Elton waited behind the Roland for his cue to begin "Don't Let the Sun." But soon there were trouble signs. Elton mouthed "louder" and "more piano" toward stage left, as he glared at someone. The first song was peppered with these exclamations; he would smile, absorb the audience's positive response, and, within seconds, scowl, "More piano, now!"

By "Philadelphia Freedom," the situation worsened. Elton stopped playing and sang with only band accompaniment, exposing the hole left in the arrangement without the juicy meat of his Roland. At song's end, he waved over an assistant and emphatically told him something. The assistant nodded. But whatever the assistant did, it didn't save "Burn Down the Mission." Elton was angry, his neck a relief map of pulsing veins. Mid-song, a monitor was replaced. But he stopped singing and impatiently stood while the band played the ending, as he jerkily waved his right arm like an irascible conductor. "Mission" done, he yelled at someone; as "Tiny Dancer" started, an assistant crawled around him to check on the monitors.

The concert proceeded uneventfully again until the end of "The One," when the pianist walked over to Davey and, arms flailing, complained bitterly. Davey patted his back. The pianist stepped onto the platform where his Roland and the faulty monitors sat and finished his Diet Coke, deliberately dropping the can on the floor and kicking it hard. Not surprisingly, the next song, "I Don't Wanna," received spotty treatment. Sometimes Elton played and sometimes he sang, but he didn't do a lot of both. "From bad to worse" is how he introduced "Sorry Seems to Be the Hardest Word."

As the show wore on, Elton finally seemed placated; if he couldn't hear the bass in his piano, he'd have to accept that. The show ended raucously with "Saturday Night's Alright," the pianist stripped down to an oversized turtleneck and skintight bicycle shorts. But his obvious frustrations for most of the show prevented him from connecting with his large audience, as well as from improved Argentinian album sales,[73] and he canceled his other South American dates. Elton may have conquered drink, drugs, and bulimia, but he still had to work on his temper.

"THEM 'SKEETAS BIT ME ONE TOO MANY TIMES"[74]
IN JANUARY 1993, Elton resigned as a director of Watford, saying that touring conflicted with the post's duties.[75] Left unspoken were his growing devotion to the AIDS fight and his involvement in the newly formed Elton John AIDS Foundation. In early February, he found time to present Gianni Versace with the 1992 International Award at the twelfth annual Council of Fashion Designers of America Awards held at Manhattan's Lincoln Center, before flying to Australia to continue his

world tour. "I am . . . deeply grateful that I can afford his [Gianni's] clothes," Elton quipped.[76]

Upon arriving Down Under, he was met with unwelcome public accusations by former lover Gary Clarke about the musician's pre-rehab conduct. Clarke said he was writing a book, although for now anyone who wanted to know his story would have to read the two interviews he gave the Australian supermarket tabloid, *Woman's Day.* Elton had already talked about most of Clarke's recollections in the press—the substance abuse, the mood swings, the sexual promiscuity. What *Woman's Day* readers now learned were specifics of what supposedly happened in bed between Clarke and Elton. But as shocking as Clarke tried to be, he couldn't hide Elton's human side. The two articles clearly described the musician's physical insecurities, his all-pervasive craving for loving companionship, and his hugely generous nature.[77]

"He'll always be special to me," said Clarke of Elton on a tabloid television program, *A Current Affair,* timed to coincide with Elton's Australian appearances. "It's not an act of vengeance," he insisted. Clarke established a phone number people could call to hear about his affair with Elton and gossip about famous people he had apparently met in his travels with the musician. (Elton took legal action to halt this last enterprise.)[78]

The musician refused to be interviewed by *A Current Affair,* so instead the program aired clips from an interview done with David White for the show *Real Life.* More revealing, however, were portions of the *Real Life* interview not aired by *A Current Affair.* "I personally find it disappointing that Gary's done it, but I'm not going to let it destroy my life," Elton told White. "My life back then was pretty damned bad. It was a box full of maggots in many ways. . . . I can't change it. But what I have to do now is get on with the future and make sure it doesn't happen again."[79]

The musician forged onward, keeping ahead of the past that was breathing down his neck. "It's always good to be back in Oz no matter what the circumstances," he told the opening night crowd at Flinders Park, Melbourne. "We're just going to shut up and get on with it." Charitable fund-raising was the goal at all Australian concert stops, which offered "bucket drops" where concertgoers could donate money to the fight against AIDS and pick up red AIDS ribbons.[80]

Though Elton had left his past in the shadows where it belonged, countless winged, six-legged creatures stealthily caught up with him, emerging from their dank abodes on Elton's third night in Flinders Park to cover the stage, the Roland, and the pianist's hair. Davey dutifully brushed the bugs, known as black field crickets, off his employer's back between guitar licks as Elton played with one hand, flicking bugs away with the other. Mortonette, Marlena, and Natalie slipped on crushed exoskeletons. This went on for nearly two hours until one bug lodged itself in Elton's mouth just as he inhaled. The squeamish musician walked offstage. The band followed. After five minutes, an announcement came over the public address system that the show was over.[81] According to a local entomologist, Elton couldn't have been harmed by swallowing one of the crickets, nor would his diet have been ruined. These bugs were fat-free. Fortunately, the fourth Flinders Park show was bug-free, following a thorough fumigation.[82]

The Australian tour drew to a close in Sydney, where a seventh show at the Entertainment Centre was added for March 11 as a combination AIDS benefit and telethon. "It's going to be a day about compassion, about gratitude, about awareness and generosity," Elton said. He hoped the telethon would raise at least $500,000 (Australian), but viewers lost no time in phoning in $677,000 early in the show. He earmarked the concert proceeds, the telethon money, and everything collected at the bucket drops for AIDS charities in Australia.[83]

Another cause in which Elton still held a strong interest was the scholarship he'd helped set up in 1990 for Melbourne Symphony Orchestra members. While in Melbourne, he met MSO violinist Deborah Fox, the latest recipient of the ten thousand dollar award, who would be studying in New York and Britain for three months.[84]

The rest of March 1993 was taken up by concert stops in Hong Kong and Singapore, where, to Elton's delight, audiences knew—and sang—all the words to his songs. Then he flew to Los Angeles for the Academy Awards on March 29, hosting an Oscar night party at the Maple Drive Restaurant in Beverly Hills to benefit his foundation. Elton was competing with established hosts accustomed to attracting the biggest names in Hollywood, but among the two hundred Maple Drive attendees were Chris Rock, Mike Meyers, Whoopi Goldberg, Marisa Tomei, Sharon Stone, Dennis Quaid, William Baldwin, and old friend Billie Jean King. "I'm the new kid on the block," Elton fretted. "I don't know too many actors." Still, he raised $125,000. And he would be back next year.[85]

"WE COULD WALK PROUD AFTER MIDNIGHT"[86]

"SIMPLE LIFE" wasn't much of a hit. Following a February 27, 1993, Hot 100 debut, it peaked in April at number 30. In Britain, the song debuted and peaked at number 44 in May. But "Simple Life" was Elton's new anthem. More than "The One," it showed where he'd been and where he was going.

During an April–May 1993 American tour sponsored by Hard Rock Cafe, "Simple Life" was an essential ingredient in a stage show that shocked fans with its unpredictability. The only similarity between these shows and the 1992 summer–fall tour was in Elton's gold-accented Versace tails, and alert fans noticed a difference even before the concert started. There was no hint of "Don't Let the Sun" in Guy's pre-recorded synthesizer theme. Instead, *Tommy* came to mind. When the pianist appeared to deafening applause and mounted the riser, the contraption turned counterclockwise for dramatic effect as he sprinkled the broken chord introduction of "Pinball Wizard" over his Roland. He had last played his 1975 turntable hit live in 1984. In a one-two punch, the song was followed with the more commonly played "The Bitch Is Back," but the surprises kept coming, since the United States had last heard song number three, "Take Me to the Pilot," way back in 1979. It was now dressed up in a synthesizer version of the Buckmaster orchestrations adapted for the 1986 MSO tour.

In more than one city, Elton was a guest of the tour sponsor, which donated money to his AIDS Foundation. At Washington, D.C.'s Hard Rock Cafe, he posed for pictures with an unlikely likeness of himself, a grinning self-portrait on the back of the Hard Rock signature t-shirt. A portion of the t-shirts' sales proceeds went to AIDS organizations, raising half a million dollars.

Then it was on to London and Earl's Court for two more AIDS benefit concerts on May 12 and 13, to kick off a month-long tour of Europe and the Near East, this tour leg sponsored by Revlon. Elton donated the cosmetics company's fee to his foundation, too.

The Earl's Court shows marked a culmination in the development of "Rocket Man," "Bennie," and "Sad Songs." The latter, which had been temporarily eviscerated earlier in the spring to make room for some rarely heard songs, gradually grew its insides back. By May 12, it was again in a league with the pianist's other adventurous examinations. "Watch my right hand go!" was his cry on the second night, about six minutes into the eight-minute "Sad Songs" introduction.

During his European jaunt, Elton received a high French honor, becoming an officer of arts and letters on June 1. French Minister of Culture Jacques Toubon decorated him in a private ceremony, at which Toubon remarked that Elton had "greatly influenced our artistic and musical world for the last twenty-five years."[87]

THERE'S A BREAKDOWN ON THE RUNWAY,"[88] PART TWO

A JUNE 16 CONCERT WAS SCHEDULED for Tel Aviv's HaYarkon Park, Elton's first Israeli concert appearance since May 1979. The flight from Singapore to Tel Aviv left him spent and eager to slip through Israeli customs quickly, but he got the same treatment Bob Dylan had days earlier, being moved from room to room at the airport for more than an hour before being cleared to enter the country.

Local promoters were amazed by the public response to Elton's upcoming concert. Some Israeli fans were traveling more than two hundred miles, and a nearby high school canceled its graduation ceremony so that students could attend the show.[89] Outside the Tel Aviv Hilton, about one hundred photographers and reporters, and about as many fans, awaited the musician's arrival from the airport, mobbing him as he exited his limousine. His bodyguard attempted to clear room for him to enter the hotel, touching off a fracas that left several injured. But Elton never got farther than the elevators. Deciding he'd rather leave than face more chaos, he turned around and fled—leaping over a couch and rushing into his limousine, which he ordered back to the airport. A member of the Knesset, Avraham

Burg, tried to convince him to stay, but the musician returned to England that night, canceling the concert.[90]

The next day, the incident was the talk of the nation. Israelis were split in their reaction to Elton's abrupt departure. Some were angry, some embarrassed. Distraught fans sued for damages.[91] Several Knesset members appealed to Elton to return, as did Israeli Health Minister Haim Ramon, who sent a fax telling him how much Israel loved him. But Israeli President Ezer Weizman was uninterested in mollifying Elton. "I can't change my people," he said. "Elton is replaceable."[92]

Britain's ambassador to Israel finally secured an agreement that Elton would perform in Israel one day late, in return for assurances that he would be whisked through customs and, more important, that his time of arrival would be kept secret and that security would be provided. His impending return was met with relief. "It's important for Israel's reputation that he come," said concert promoter Zeev Eizek. "We don't have a beautiful image abroad, and I hope this helps repair the situation a little."[93]

Elton was all smiles in a polka-dot jacket and windswept hair weave as he disembarked from his plane at Ben Gurion Airport for the second time in forty-eight hours. He went through customs without a hitch and was at HaYarkon Park in time for the show's scheduled start. Just before performing the aptly titled "The Bitch Is Back," he told the vociferously cheering crowd: "I am sorry for any inconvenience. It was regrettable. I do apologize for my part in it. Thank you for your understanding, patience, and your tolerance."[94]

"FEEL LIKE LIFE HAS JUST BEGUN"[95]

"I WOULD CRAWL OVER MOUNTAINS TO RECORD WITH HER," Elton had said of Bonnie Raitt in 1990.[96] In the summer of 1993, he got his wish. He had just come off the road in June after playing Tel Aviv, Athens, and Istanbul. Instead of taking a rest, he returned to the studio. His non-North American record company, Phonogram, was considering issuing an album of his previously released duets in time for the Christmas season. Instead, Elton preferred to record new duets. He started with Raitt, k.d. lang, and Tammy Wynette, but had such a good time he decided to make a whole album of new duets, in a multiplicity of studios and with numerous producers.[97]

"It's quite amazing—the energy that shows in the album took place virtually by putting together a track a day for the first couple of weeks," John Reid noted.[98] *Duets* was finished in eight weeks, during July and August, an almost instantaneously completed album by 1993 standards. "The reason I wanted to do it quickly is because there's not much spontaneity anymore in music," Elton explained. "I wanted it to be done quickly so that we could have fun and the fun would translate into the CD."[99]

The first thing Elton did was come up with a list of performers with whom he'd like to sing. Unavailable were U2's Bono, James Taylor, Neil Young, Axl Rose, and Steve Winwood, who were either in the studio themselves or touring. But he sang with everyone else he'd wanted—an eclectic bunch, consistent with his wide taste in music and unrelenting fan mentality. Besides Raitt, lang, and Wynette, there were Leonard Cohen, Don Henley, Chris Rea, Gladys Knight, and Marcella Detroit. And RuPaul, the transvestite comic. "When I first found out about doing a duet with Elton John I was in a hotel in Los Angeles, and after putting the phone down I screamed nonstop," RuPaul remembered later.[100] There were also Paul Young, Nik Kershaw, Little Richard, and P.M. Dawn, a rhythm and blues–tinged hip-hop group. P.M. Dawn's singer, Prince Be, didn't know that Elton, as famous as he was, could be so down to earth. "He was funny, man," Prince Be laughed later. "I thought it was going to be like, 'How you doin', sir?'. . . but it didn't end up that way." They ate Japanese food and chili together during their session.[101]

Elton also wanted to sing with Kiki Dee. "She's just an angel, I love her," he said. "She's such a sweet lady." He wanted her to get back into recording on her own, too.[102] Not much had happened in Kiki's recording career since a little-known 1981 duet with Elton, "Loving You Is Sweeter than Ever." In 1987, she recorded an album, *Angel Eyes*, then looked toward other musical outlets, like theater, starring in the London production of *Blood Brothers*. In 1991, she learned that she had uterine cancer, but regained her health with surgery and radiation treatments.

The song Elton and Kiki recorded for his duets project was the Cole Porter standard, "True Love," which Elton fondly remembered from childhood. He had first heard it sung by Bing Crosby and Grace Kelly in *High Society*, the 1956 movie musical.[103] Recorded across two continents, the Elton/Kiki duet was produced by Narada Michael Walden, veteran of Elton and Aretha's "Through the Storm." Walden put so much chintz and tinsel into the one-two-three waltz of "True Love," one would have thought the song destined for the Christmas charts.

Most pleasing about the duet is the new vocal relationship between Elton and Kiki. In "Don't Go Breaking My Heart," they charmed listeners with a clean, pure vocal texture. For "True Love," the post-surgery Elton summons a husky tenor that joins the gruffer side of Kiki's voice to create a dense blanket of sound wrapped warmly around Porter's rock-a-bye melody.

How must Kiki have felt about RuPaul working with Elton on a remake of "Don't Go Breaking My Heart?" Was RuPaul treading on sacred ground? Some may have felt that way. Although the original is considered one of Elton's less profound efforts, the lighthearted chemistry between his melody and his infectious piano chords make it a minor masterpiece of giddiness. But, in the summer of 1993, with RuPaul singing along and famed disco technician Giorgio Moroder producing, "Don't Go Breaking" was just high camp with a heavy beat. To be fair, Elton didn't see the RuPaul duet as a major departure from the original. "It was a very tongue-in-cheek song when Kiki and I did it in 1976," he said.[104]

He and Don Henley reached back to the 1970s, too, with their remake of the Temptations' 1975 American Top 30 hit, "Shaky Ground." The recording is chiefly a Henley band effort, with drumming and organ work reminiscent of Santana's early days. The vocals are stray bones, meaty enough with the Four Tops' Levi Stubbs soul of Elton's voice and the tart consistency of Henley's to ward off hunger pangs, but so sparsely distributed as to leave a listener unsatisfied, begging for more. One can't help chuckling over the unlikely lyrics Elton sings: "My car got repossessed this morning/harder times I haven't seen in years."

Better results were obtained when Elton reached back to the 1960s with Marcella Detroit to remake the 1968 Marvin Gaye and Tammi Terrell hit, "Ain't Nothing Like the Real Thing." Detroit, an American expatriate and one-half of female duo Shakespear's [sic] Sister, played most of the instruments, including Stevie Wonder–style harmonica. Elton and Detroit have more to sing than Elton and Henley on "Shaky Ground," the pianist's rippling romance blending seamlessly with, while tempering, Detroit's nimble but shrill technique.

Elton again delved into the 1960s on a track with Paul Young, who suggested a cover of James and Bobby Purify's "I'm Your Puppet," a 1966 American Top 10 hit. A man after Elton's musical heart, Young enjoyed doing old soul covers; his renditions of "Oh Girl" and "What Becomes of the Brokenhearted" were successful singles in the early 1990s. Elton and Young substantially improved on the original "I'm Your Puppet," which sounded more like an incomplete demo than a real song. Here, Elton takes the high end of the harmony. Especially exciting is their ad-libbing. With their voices teasingly sliding off each other, the men make a convincing duo.

The Briton revisits the 1960s yet again with Bonnie Raitt in an update of the 1962 Ketty Lester hit, "Love Letters" (also a hit for Dick Haymes in 1945). The opening notes alone make "Love Letters" one of Duets' most memorable tracks, as Elton and Raitt duet in both voice and instrument. From the gospel chord progression to the chortling broken chords that invariably end in a bell-like chorus of "brrringg! dingg!," Elton's acoustic piano touch is as welcome as the familiar greeting of an old friend. Sometimes his piano keys bump up against and join Raitt's fiery slide guitar. Notwithstanding the sex-filled suggestiveness of their vocals, "Love Letters" would have made a nice instrumental.

"Love Letters," a hit in both the 1940s and 1960s, naturally gives way to "Born to Lose," a hit in those decades, too, first for Ted Daffan's Texans and later for Ray Charles. Leonard Cohen selected this one to sing with Elton. Cohen's own music is eminently listenable (he gets raw admiration from his peers, including Elton and Billy Joel), and his one-note vocal tones are filled with wry wit. Still, the blatant contrast between Cohen's gravelly, almost nonexistent voice and Elton's makes for the album's funniest duet. Cohen's bottom-of-the-barrel singing gives the down-and-out professions he describes in the song an authenticity that Elton's vocal, which fluctuates between a Sinatra-esque dreaminess and a Ray Charles–inspired yelp, cannot attain.

Key to the album's eclecticism is Elton's ability to shift easily between musical styles and eras. Moving up a couple of decades, he chose to sing "Teardrops," a 1988 British hit for the soul duo of Womack and Womack, with k.d. lang. The recording begins promisingly with a nostalgic disco string arrangement by Arif Mardin. Elton's percussive playing drives a four-piece band that includes Clapton veteran Nathan East on bass. Expectations are kept aloft as Elton and k.d. launch into song together so easily that they might as well be one person. "Teardrops" is an attractive album opener, even if it provides no clue as to what lies ahead.

Song number two is the undisco-ish "When I Think About Love (I Think About You)," a P.M. Dawn creation not unlike the duo's eerie 1992 Top 5 American hit, "I'd Die Without You." The voices of Elton and Prince Be are almost as ill-matched as those of Elton and Leonard Cohen, the difference being that Prince Be can carry a tune, offering the nasal qualities of Stevie Wonder's singing (albeit without Wonder's might or range). Prince Be's vocal limitations lend a welcome vulnerability to this odd coupling, while mystery man Etienne Lytel (Elton himself) adds a weepy piano interlude.

Stevie Wonder is on a song, too, although not officially a duet partner. He wrote, produced, played all the instruments, and sang some of the backing vocals on "Go On and On," coaching lead singers Elton and Gladys Knight. The song showcases the two's friendly sparring. They think of as many ways to sing "on and on," "yeah," and "oh" as there are colors in a rainbow. For these unplanned throwaways alone, "Go On and On" is one of *Duets'* most stimulating songs.

Other musicians also contributed their own songs to *Duets*. Chris Rea, a British singer-songwriter best known for his 1978 single "Fool (If You Think It's Over)" and for guitar playing that recalls indigenous Hawaiian music, wrote "If You Were Me." Rea also produced the song, using a bare-bones ensemble. As with the RuPaul, P.M. Dawn, and Leonard Cohen collaborations, the difference in vocal prowess between duet partners is striking. Rea's cloudy voice floats pleasantly around Elton's weighty delivery, helping to illustrate the endearing incompatibility of the song's two friends.

Nik Kershaw, whose talents Elton had been touting for nearly a decade, wrote and duetted on a song called "Old Friend," a story about buddies who are devoted even when separated by distance. Kershaw's voice, though slighter than Elton's, is still tunefully accessible. This is a sentimentally radiant, mid-tempo composition, music that perennial fan Elton had to be impressed with, too.

Elton and Bernie also wrote new songs for *Duets*. One was "The Power," for a duet with Elton's childhood idol, Little Richard. "The Power" is nothing like the racy Little Richard ditty "The Girl Can't Help It," which Sheila Dwight wouldn't let her son listen to back in 1957, nor any of the Georgia Peach's other signature tunes. It is more like something Little Richard would have heard growing up in Macon, Georgia. "The Power" acknowledges life's adversities but insists that these can be overcome by a strong will and love of a higher force. If the words seem church-spawned, the music seems more so, with its marching beat that a gospel choir could clap to, the preacher inflections of Elton's melody, which seems tailor-made for Little Richard's latter-day spirituality, and the song's finale, an extravagant mix of energetic backing vocals from the Andrae Crouch singers and shuffling piano playing from Elton.

A second John/Taupin collaboration, and another songwriting apex for them, is "A Woman's Needs," a duet they wrote with Tammy Wynette in mind (it would also appear on her album, *Without Walls*). The song's conceptual chauvinism (the title suggests a benevolent male paternalism) is overcome by Bernie's adeptness at capturing regional dialect and black-eyed peas–flavored cliché. The woman in the song forces the man in her life to sit down and have a heart to heart about the slow progress of their relationship. She finds that he seems out of reach because of his fears; she isn't the only one with needs. Both of their needs bring them together in the end, developed in the form of a dialogue.

Although the song has a standard waltz underpinning, there is nothing standard about the melody, nor Elton's fluid, arpeggiated playing; both fit the lyrics like a glove. The give and take of the conversation between man and woman can be heard in the melody's ebb and flow. The chorus, which brings the couple to an understanding, is noticeably more hopeful than the verses and is filled with thoughts of a good future. And the vocal dynamic between Elton and Wynette transforms the words and melody into a drama of real life for real people.

The pianist cowrote one more new song for the album, "Duets for One," this time with Chris Difford of Squeeze. The only song on *Duets* in which Elton sings by himself, it expresses his new outlook on life, much as "Simple Life" does. True, Difford wasn't one of Elton's best friends. Elton, in his fan-frenzied benevolence, would try to get Squeeze's 1993 album *Some Fantastic Place* a British chart position by buying up all copies of the CD in a store near home soon after his own album was completed.[105] Difford couldn't have foreseen this unbridled generosity when he wrote the lyrics for "Duets for One," but does manage to describe Elton's newfound contentment as precisely as if he were in Woodside's inner circle: "You and I have come so far, with shaken faith/from the pit of a broken heart, to feeling great/feels like life has just begun/there'll be no more singing duets for one." While not chugging away like the "locomotive strong" survivor in "Simple Life," "Duets for One" has the gentler clickety-clack of a train a passenger has been waiting for all his life, finally pulling into the station.

Also included is Elton's number 1 song with George Michael, "Don't Let the Sun Go Down on Me," the sole concession to Phonogram's original idea of issuing an album of previously released duets. Elton figured it hadn't been on an album before, so now it would be.[106]

When Elton finished *Duets* in August, it constituted further evidence of his renewed zest for life as well as his never-abating, awe-stricken admiration for the abilities and music of others. But the pianist's agenda was brimming with other endeavors that would have to be finished before *Duets* could be released.

"NEVER LETTING THE LIGHT SLIP AWAY"[107]

"WE'RE PLANNING A FUN-FILLED TWO-DAY BENEFIT that will take you from the tennis courts to the concert stage—all for a very crucial cause: the fight against AIDS," read a June 24, 1993 letter signed by Elton and Billie Jean King. The letter invited potential benefactors to attend the first ever World Teamtennis All-Star Smash Hits event to benefit the Elton John AIDS Foundation, scheduled for September 22 and 23, 1993, in Los Angeles.

The piano player and tennis star had continued to be in touch since the 1970s, though their friendship seldom received the publicity it had when his tribute to her, "Philadelphia Freedom," became an American number I in 1975. "She's been there at the worst moments of my life," Elton, with typical post-rehab frankness, informed Jay Leno on the musician's second *Tonight Show* appearance in thirteen years. "And she's been there at my best moments." "How's he doing now?" Leno asked Billie Jean, also a guest. She gave her English friend of twenty years an approving thumbs-up as Elton looked on, embarrassed.[108]

Elton gave the founder of the Philadelphia Freedoms credit for coming up with the event concept. Billie Jean gave Elton credit. Either way, what would become an annual partnership of the tennis and music worlds to help people living with AIDS and spread AIDS awareness was as much a product of Elton's talent for striking up worthwhile friendships as it was of the tennis world's recent awakening from Arthur Ashe's death from AIDS.

The tennis tournament portion of Smash Hits, held at the Forum, included names synonymous with the game: Martina Navratilova, Chris Evert, John McEnroe, and Jimmy Connors, as well as the notorious (but now aged seventy-five) Bobby Riggs. One of the biggest attractions of the evening was a King/Riggs "rematch" during mixed doubles, with Elton and Billie Jean on one side and Riggs (relieved by Connors halfway through) and Navratilova on the other.

The musician's name, collegiality, and goodwill also helped attract big names and big money to an auction held at the Regent Beverly Wilshire Hotel the night before, part of the two-day Smash Hits event. Some of the fun included a ninety-minute, thirteen-song set with his band. Sylvester Stallone, George Foreman, Lily Tomlin, and Pierce Brosnan were among the celebrities who attended. Altogether, the event raised a total of four hundred thousand dollars.

This was not Elton's only big fundraiser of the year. On July 29, he sold his gigantic record collection through Sotheby's—25,000 albums and 23,000 singles. He didn't listen to or look at them anymore (he was now a major CD collector), and believed they could be put to better use elsewhere. The lucky buyer acquired Elton's vast warehouse of music for about $269,000. Included in this mountain of vinyl, which could have filled a two-bedroom home from floor to ceiling, were mint copies of all of James Brown's albums, almost every single released in Britain between 1963 and 1974, and demos of the Beatles' "Day Tripper." It was estimated that some of the rarer singles were worth about $500 each. Elton gave the money raised to the Terrence Higgins Trust, a favorite British AIDS charity.[109]

"SOME SOULS GET RESTLESS"[110]

"Guess her bus broke down."

"She's not here—'less she's hidin'.'"

"As you can see, she's not here tonight, but never fear. I'm gonna sing her part, as well as mine."[111]

Tammy Wynette wasn't at any of Elton's U.S. shows that fall (nor was she supposed to be), and he playfully referred to that fact night after night when introducing his solo piano version of "A Woman's Needs." "All you've got to do is figure out which part is which—which, with my sexual history, is gonna be a little bit hard for you," he kidded his Providence audience on October 23. The distraction of guitar and other traditional band instruments was gone. The muted strife of the woman and her errant boyfriend was brought to life through Elton's rocketing vocals and the grandeur of his playing. He was alone, behind a black Yamaha grand with MIDI hookup.

"[T]his new show is an innovative mix of acoustic whispers and sonic bursts, a sparsely arranged mix of old hits, beloved rarities, emotional ballads, and snappy Top 40 confections recast with a devilish bent," wrote Deborah Wilker for the *Fort Lauderdale Sun-Sentinel* after seeing "An Evening with Elton John and Ray Cooper" at Fort Lauderdale's Sunrise Musical Theater.[112] Ray Cooper was back for a three-week stint, as the two men revisited a concert format for which fans had clamored since the end of the 1979 world tour.

Elton's return to this "naked" setup had been stewing for a while. The two solo Dee Murray tribute shows in March 1992 had shown he was again testing the waters, much as he had with his September 1976 outing in Edinburgh. In September 1992, he told Whoopi Goldberg on her talk show that he expected his next tour to be simple and stripped down. It was.

"An Evening with Elton John and Ray Cooper" was the rightful heir to the 1979 tour. American audiences in both 1979 and 1993 were treated to a show about two hours and forty-five minutes long, beginning with Elton's unostentatious appearance onstage and a simple bow. The first seventy-five minutes were taken up by Elton's stint at the piano, with Ray joining him, as in 1979, halfway through "Funeral for a Friend"—lights ablaze, mallets flying, cymbals crashing. The remainder of the show found Elton and Ray enthusiastically pushing the boundaries of rock as the percussionist played off the electricity surging from his cohort's piano. Also as in 1979, only a third of the thirty-odd songs were bona fide hits or reasonably successful Top 40 singles. From here, however, the shows diverged.

In 1979, the venues tended to be smaller, with capacities of no more than a few thousand. Now, Elton brought his stripped-down show to venues that held ten to twenty thousand people. In 1979, the set list included concert staples like "Rocket Man" and "Goodbye Yellow Brick Road." In 1993, these were gone, along with songs current in 1979, like "Mama Can't Buy You Love." Added were several more recent songs, such as "The Last Song," "I Don't Wanna Go On Like with You Like That," "Sacrifice," and the as-yet-unreleased "A Woman's Needs." The first two 1993 shows also included two songs Elton hadn't performed live since 1976—"We All Fall in Love Sometimes" and "Curtains." These differences, plus Elton's reinterpretation of some of the more aged numbers, made the 1993 tour a whole new ballgame. Added to the mix was sobriety. Elton's lack thereof had been a topic of his concert banter in 1979, while adorned in colorful, crinkly suits, narrow ties, and no glasses. Now, wearing a simple, white ruffled shirt, black Versace jeans, and plain, wire-rimmed glasses, he sang about healthful living and spiritual cleansing in "The North" and "The One."

Then there was "Crocodile Rock." In 1979, Elton had rendered the song as faithfully to the original recording as possible without a full band. It was cute, fun, and nostalgic. By 1993, he hadn't played the song on tour in nine years. At one time, he'd expected to lay it to rest for good. And even as late as May 1993 he was insisting he'd never play it again.[113] But his experience playing, as he once put it, a "cabaret version" of the song at a Milan AIDS benefit in June 1992—at Sting's suggestion—led to its return from exile in the fall of 1993.

"This is a song that I said I would never, ever, ever, ever sing again," he told his audience in Providence. "A dear friend of mine by the name of Sting said, 'Well, you should do it slowly instead of quickly.'" Elton did it slowly *and* quickly. The verses were reflective, pondering a more innocent time long gone. "I remember when rock was young," he sang with the savory consistency of warm jam sliding across a few granules of fine sand. The chorus then picked up the tempo just enough to evoke a more carefree era, as if through a time warp. But Elton didn't try to sing the song like Del Shannon, Dion—or Speedy Gonzales. His performance took the song back a few decades further, to the 1920s. One expected the intrusion of hot trumpets and trombones evoking a house of ill repute where patrons drank shots of bootleg whiskey.

Audiences heard not just the reworking of "Crocodile Rock," but also other, singular renderings of songs. If a music fan was lucky enough to follow the tour between, say, Fort Lauderdale and New Haven, he or she would have heard the growth, from infancy to adulthood, of some provocative reinterpretations, as if Elton were testing musical ideas in front of thousands of people. Old Mad Joe in "Talking Old Soldiers" benefited from the musician's more seasoned, worldly singing, highlighting the disillusionment of the old veteran. "Indian Sunset" benefited from concerto-inspired piano flourishes and the cannon fire of Ray's tribal timpani, neither of which is heard on the original *Madman Across the Water* version.

"Take Me to the Pilot" explored territories still uncharted in 1979, becoming saturated with particles both fragile and muscular during its near fifteen-minute duration. Most significant in this bombardment of classic gentility and gospel celebration was the traversal of humorous jazz expressions, begun during Elton's Los Angeles concerts in November 1992, during the "Sad Songs" introduction. When Elton first happened upon the gestating riff back in 1992, he must have been tickled with delight. An unlikely union of a cat's combined purr-meow with the resonance of a plaintive violin somehow caught up in the machinery of an organ, it grew and took shape in the fall of 1993 until the poor cat had gotten stuck in the organ with the violin and the whole combination was buffeted about in a violent windstorm.

All this physicality taxed Elton little. Concertgoers who surged toward the stage during the "Crocodile Rock" and "Bennie" encores were close enough to observe the dryness of the pianist's furrowed brow. Just as he might have in 1975, he threw his head in the direction of the audience, glaring, lips pursed, like a testy headmaster with eyebrows in a mock frown, as he listened to the crowd answer his all-important "Pinball Wizard" question:

"How do you think he does it?"

"I don't know!"

"THE LEGAL BOYS HAVE WON AGAIN" [114]

"IT JUST SHOWS that songs are the most precious things a musician can have—unless you sell them," Elton said in London at the American Society of Composers, Authors, and Publishers' (ASCAP) annual Performing Right Society tribute dinner on September 17, 1993. He had just won three ASCAP statues for his work in 1992: song of the year (for "The One"), publisher of the year (for Big Pig Music), and songwriter of the year (for himself). He was the first to receive all three awards at once.[115]

After his brief American tour, Elton picked up another "award" in London, this one for $518,000, bestowed on him by a majority of jurors who found that London's *Sunday Mirror* had libeled him and deserved to be punished. In December 1992, the newspaper had printed a front-page story called "Elton's Diet of Death," in which the musician's alleged "bizarre" dietary habit was supposedly witnessed by a freelance journalist at a Los Angeles party. Elton was said to have spit his food into a napkin, explaining to other guests that he kept his weight down this way. This suggested he was still bulimic. But he wasn't, nor was he in Los Angeles on the night at issue.

Back in England, Elton's mother saw the *Sunday Mirror* headline and, distressed, called him in Atlanta. He was mortified. He had talked and talked publicly of his various addictions and eating disorder and his triumph over them, and had presented himself as a role model for others battling such demons, and now the *Sunday Mirror* was implying he was a liar. He believed his reputation had been seriously harmed. The story's publication wasn't limited to the *Sunday Mirror*, either. It was picked up by wire services and published throughout the United States.

Elton challenged the story. The newspaper eventually acknowledged that it wasn't true, offering a printed apology and a charitable gift in his name. He rejected the settlement because of the paper's explanation for what happened—that it had been a case of mistaken identity. So he took the matter to trial. "I would have accepted an apology much earlier in the case if they had said the story was fictional," he said.[116] Scoffing at the claim that someone else had been mistaken for Elton, his barrister argued, "I suspect the face and voice of Elton John is rather better known than that of the prime minister."[117] On November 4, the majority of jurors agreed. Only one-fifth of the award they fashioned was for actual damages. The rest was a punishment. Elton gave most of the money to charity.

The pianist believed in a free press. Since the *Sun* nightmare in 1987, however, he had felt compelled to ensure that newspapers acted with greater restraint. When asked by British ITV talk show host Des O'Connor to comment on the verdict, the musician said, "I have to be careful here, because I'm also an advocate of free speech. . . . [But] free speech for me doesn't mean you make up stories or you print things that aren't true. . . . I think that's irresponsible, and I think it lowers the standards of the press. . . . I think it has gone a little too far."[118]

"I LIE AWAKE AND DREAM ABOUT YOU"[119]

ON OCTOBER 30, days before the jury's verdict, Elton met someone who would become very important in his life very quickly. David Furnish was twenty-seven years old when he left the Toronto offices of Ogilvy & Mather for London, where he successfully built the advertising agency's health care division. Four years later, Furnish was elected to the firm's international board of directors. Tall, dark, and handsome, with a reedy speaking voice and a sincere demeanor that made him more approachable than his good looks suggested, he was surprised by the message a friend left on his answering machine, inviting him to dinner at Elton John's house. David didn't know Elton, and wasn't currently a fan, although he'd grown up with Elton's music. He felt apprehensive about going, fearing Elton would be a bore or the evening unpleasant. After some thought, he decided to go, but planned to drive himself instead of arriving via Elton's chauffeur, in case he had to make a speedy getaway.[120]

Elton hoped to make new friends in London and enjoy a night of good food and conversation. Several guests were invited. When David got to Woodside and met his host, he noticed that, contrary to his expectations, Elton was warm, friendly, and genuinely interested in the lives of his guests. Almost as immediately, David noticed his attraction to the host. It appeared that Elton was attracted to him, too. His suspicions were borne out when, at the end of the evening, Elton rather indiscreetly asked for his phone number. The musician, whose relationship with Hugh Williams had long since ended and who was unattached following a relationship with Elton John AIDS Foundation codirector John Scott, wasted no time, calling David the next day for a date. The Canadian returned to Woodside that night for a supper of Chinese take-out. There was no looking back.[121]

The pianist's career marched on. *Duets* was released in November, just a couple of weeks after Frank Sinatra's own *Duets*. Despite their similar format and identical titles, the two albums couldn't have been more different. Frank Sinatra, for many the century's premier male vocalist, stuck to songs he had already recorded at least once, as early as 1955—all standards written by songwriters of a different era. They included "I've Got a Crush on You," "I've Got the World on a String," "In the Wee Small Hours of the Morning," "Witchcraft," and "One for My Baby." Most of his duet partners were known as balladeers, and a good many—Barbra Streisand, Liza Minelli, Tony Bennett, and Natalie Cole—were known for their interpretations of the standards. Virtually all of them seemed selected for their name recognition, and none of the duets were recorded in the same room. The singer who had broken new vocal ground and had been immeasurably influential over legions of vocalists wasn't breaking any new ground here. It seemed more like a publicity move by his management, although it only served to divert attention from all of Sinatra's much better work that preceded it.

By contrast, Elton refused to retread the familiar. He looked at his *Duets* as another opportunity to broaden his musical experiences while also having fun. Some of the singers he selected were notably popular; more were underappreciated. With the exception of "Don't Go Breaking My Heart" and the live duet of "Don't Let the Sun," the songs were new or had never before appeared on an Elton John release.

There was no common thread among the songs. Some were old, some new, all were stylistically diverse. Most of the vocals were recorded in the same room. The cover of Elton's *Duets* album exemplified its collegial atmosphere with a pair of gilded late eighteenth-century chairs from one of the rooms at Woodside. These suggested two people sitting side by side, trading ideas. Elton's *Duets* deserved greater attention than Frank Sinatra's, particularly in the United States, where it was comparatively overlooked.

Sinatra's *Duets* debuted on the Billboard 200 at number 2 on November 20 and was certified triple platinum in the United States. Elton's album, released by MCA on November 23, debuted on the U.S. chart at number 25 on December 11 and was certified platinum. Elton had better success in Britain, where his album entered at number 5, becoming the sixth best-selling album for the month of December, something Sinatra's album didn't achieve.[122]

The Briton's *Duets* received mixed reviews. Peter Kane of *Q* observed a "distinct and disappointing lack of spontaneity and, indeed, fun about the whole exercise."[123] Oddly enough, the album was also skewered in a *Request* column by Mike Lehecka as *too* spontaneous. The pianist "actually recorded these songs at the same time and place as his partners, rather than going the fiber-optic route like Sinatra. Part of the fun of Sinatra's album is the clinical, cut-and-paste sound of the vocal cameos, while the emotional tension John & Co. feign is unbearable."[124] Conversely, *The New York Times's* Stephen Holden declared Elton the "closest that a modern pop performer has come to developing a distinctive voice for all seasons."[125]

Elton's *Duets* singles did better than Sinatra's. The Sinatra/Bono duet of "I've Got You Under My Skin" was relegated to B-side status in both Britain and the United States behind a U2 song from the group's *Zooropa* album. The first single from Elton's *Duets*, the Kiki Dee collaboration "True Love," peaked at number 56 in the United States. In Britain, "True Love" found a wider audience, reaching number 2. It was Kiki's biggest hit since "Don't Go Breaking My Heart," seventeen years earlier.

"GUESS LIFE JUST BUGGED HIM"[126]

ELTON AND RAY HAD FOUR SHOWS at South Africa's Sun City resort, on December 6 through 10, 1993. It had been ten years since Elton last played South Africa. The cultural boycott had lifted, Nelson Mandela was president, and one assumed no controversy would accompany his shows this time.

The concerts, grouped under the moniker "Under African Skies," were the first at the Valley of the Waves, an outdoor site located between the Sun City and Lost City hotel complexes. The venue had some grandstand seating but it offered mostly unreserved field seating. It was an uncomfortable-looking place in a surreal setting, marked by an Art Deco tower housing a giant flame.

The concerts gave executives of South African Phonogram licensee Teal-Trutone a chance to present Elton with a number of gold and platinum awards: a triple platinum for *The Very Best of Elton John*, a platinum for *Sleeping with the Past*, and one gold each for *The One* and *Duets*. One record company official pointed out that the acoustic format of the Elton/Ray shows, which included a large number of old and rare songs, wasn't ideal for promoting *Duets*,[127] though Elton's career was peppered with instances in which he neglected commercial considerations. Still, there were good feelings. On December 7, before going onstage for his second show, Elton met with seventeen-year-old Paul Gleeson, a leukemia patient and self-professed huge Elton John fan.[128]

The last concert, on December 10, was simulcast on television and radio. Many in the mostly standing crowd of fifteen thousand, which included both white and black South Africans, held sparklers aloft. Blood-curdling screams ripped through the air as Elton sang even the quietest songs, like "I Need You to Turn To" and "The Greatest Discovery." During the piano-only "I Don't Wanna," most audience members were clapping and frantically dancing. Insects materialized and flew crazily around Elton, but didn't get in his way. At song's end, he leapt up from his bench, smiled, and bowed.

During "Mona Lisas and Mad Hatters," the insects became bolder. A large insect landed on the left side of Elton's frilly shirt and clung determinedly. The pianist disgustedly glanced at it several times as he played and sang until a stagehand appeared, placed his hand over the winged creature, and removed it with surgical precision. Elton couldn't help chuckling. But soon he was waving at his head between piano chords in response to butterflies and moths circling above. By the end of "Where to Now, St. Peter?" the bugs were so plentiful that a stagehand had to come out again and brush them off the keys.

A wind then kicked up as Elton launched into "The North." By "The One," he was forced to bow his head to evade the gusts, sometimes missing his singing cues. During Ray's entrance for "Funeral for a Friend/Tonight," Elton was still flicking away bugs and ducking. Half jokingly, he introduced his Gilbert and Sullivan style number: "It's called 'Better off Dead,' which is a good description of this place."

"Daniel" suffered from missed lines as the wind picked up and eerily amplified itself through the stage equipment. Finally, after "Sorry Seems to Be the Hardest Word," a stagehand helped Elton don a windbreaker and a long-brimmed ball cap that shielded much of his face. The show continued, but the solos were shorter. "Take Me to the Pilot" was a mere seven minutes. Before the pianist returned to the stage for the final encore of "Candle in the Wind," the audience, unperturbed by the weather, shouted, "We want Elton! We want more!" "It was my decision to come and play in this swimming pool and it was the wrong decision. I apologize," he said, before starting his Marilyn Monroe elegy. "This place is really a water park, and that's about it. When I come back, I'll play somewhere decent, okay?"[129]

"THANK YOU FOR THE YEAR,"[130] TWENTY YEARS ON

FOUR DAYS LATER, Elton had a garage sale for his jewelry collection, through Sotheby's. He was acquiring beautiful things at a feverish rate, and, as in 1988, wanted to clear room for more. He also liked the thought of instant cash with which to buy more jewelry. When asked by Des O'Connor which charity the sale was benefiting, Elton replied, "*My* charity."[131]

The funny thing was that some of the jewelry had been treasured parts of his collection well before the 1988 auction. No matter how many things he sold, there was still more back at the house. Some pieces going this time tickled the funny bone, such as an Alfred Hitchcock–profile pendant and a tie clip that read "EXPEN$IVE," featuring circular diamonds in the dollar sign. Some pieces he probably shouldn't have given up, like a ruby, sapphire, and diamond brooch depicting him wearing a boater and surrounded by a victory ribbon, specially made for him as a Watford commemoration; and a Cartier brooch celebrating his 1989–90 world tour designed as a flattened globe of the world, with concert sites marked by tiny diamonds. A tortoiseshell cane with a Napoleonic head, which he'd been seen clasping in the mid-1980s, was also slated for auction—until he pulled it at the last minute for "sentimental reasons."

The remaining ninety-four lots raised nearly £1 million (about $1.7 million).[132] Had Elton lost his charitable urges? No. His singles sales in the United States and Britain were still raising money for his Foundation, and he continued to plan fundraising events. A couple of weeks earlier, he had participated at opening ceremonies for a sexual health clinic at King's College hospital in South London, in time for World AIDS Day on December 1.[133]

On January 19, 1994, Elton's music was on his mind—twenty-five years' worth of music. Back on October 19, the Rock and Roll Hall of Fame had announced their new inductees. Solo and group acts were eligible twenty-five years after their first recording. Elton's 1968 single, "I've Been Loving You," was enough for the nominating committee, which included journalists known to be friendly to Elton and his music, like Robert Hilburn, Lisa Robinson, and Timothy White, as well as one in particular, Dave Marsh, who had never been a fan. (The makeup of the board was just as mixed, including MCA executive Al Teller as well as *Rolling Stone* editor and publisher Jann Wenner.) Apparently, "I've Been Loving You" was also enough for the several hundred music industry types who voted on the nominations.

Elton was preceded into the Hall of Fame by so many he'd idolized as a child that being inducted himself was a daunting notion. In 1986 alone, the first year of the Hall's existence, such rhythm and blues and rock piano pioneers as Ray Charles, Fats Domino, Jerry Lee Lewis, and Little Richard had been swept into history. In succeeding years, Elton had watched as some of his favorite soul stars, such as Aretha Franklin, Marvin Gaye, Otis Redding, the Temptations, and the Drifters, were also inducted. The Beach Boys, to whom he had paid tribute at the 1988 induction, the Beatles, and the Rolling Stones followed. In 1993, in addition to Elton, honors went to his friend Rod Stewart, idol and friend John Lennon, favorites of his like the Band and Bob Marley, the Animals, countercultural icons the Grateful Dead, and early rocker Duane Eddy.

"His latest album, *Duets*, is his thirty-fifth . . ., as his creative energy and prodigious output remain undiminished in the 1990s. He is, and promises to remain, one of the brightest stars in the rock firmament," wrote Parke Puterbaugh in the program for the Rock and Roll Hall of Fame's Ninth Annual Induction Dinner.[134] The induction ceremony was held at the Waldorf-Astoria's Grand Ballroom. Elton, who arrived with RuPaul (David Furnish had professional commitments in London) with bejeweled fingers, a white suit, and tinted glasses, was anxious.[135] He had expected his guests to be seated at adjacent tables. When the tables weren't set up this way, he left the ballroom and didn't return until they were.[136]

Seymour Stein, president of the Hall of Fame's Board of Directors and also president of Sire Records, was the first to speak about Elton. Stein recalled how John Reid, whom he knew as a young record industry go-getter, had invited him to one of the November 1970 concerts at New York's Fillmore East, at which Reid's "flatmate" was on the bill with Leon Russell. Stein remembered being floored by Elton's performance. In ensuing years, Elton and Reid became Stein's family friends and godfathers to his daughters. When Stein finished, and after a film was shown hailing Elton's career, Axl Rose made the induction speech:

> . . . For myself and for many others, no one has been there more for inspiration than Elton John. Also, when we talk of great rock duos, like Jimmy Page and Robert Plant, John and Paul, Mick and Keith, I like to think of Elton John and Bernie Taupin. But also tonight, I think Elton should be honored for his great work and contribution in the fight against AIDS and also his bravery in exposing all the triumphs and tragedies in his personal life. The knowledge of these things helps us get through things every day.
>
> When I first heard "Bennie and the Jets," I knew at that time that I had to be a performer, so now a man who's responsible for more things than he ever planned on, Elton John.

To an ovation, Elton stepped up to the podium and accepted his statue. "I had a really boring fucking childhood," he reminisced to laughter. "If it wasn't for the fact that I suddenly heard rock'n'roll for the first time—in England, we had nothing." One of the few pianists who influenced him during pre-rock days, he said, was "a lovely lady named Winifred Atwell, and she was fabulous. She was from Barbados." He continued:

> . . . I'd like to pay tribute to the people who were my biggest influences. Little Richard, Jerry Lee Lewis, Ray Charles, George Shearing, anybody who played the piano, and played rock'n'roll. Also, there are so many people on the bill tonight I used to pay to go and see: Duane Eddy, the Animals. Alan Price, who played for the Animals, played the Vox Continental organ. Organs have been the downfall of my life somewhat, or the upswing of my life. I don't know. . . .
>
> I wasn't very good with words and I'm not very good with words. I let all my expressions and my love and my pain and my anger come out in my melodies. I had someone to write my words for me. Without him, the journey would not have been possible. I feel cheating standing up here. Without Bernie, there wouldn't have been any Elton John at all.

The cheers from the floor were passionate, almost guttural. "I would like him to come up and I would like to give this [statue] to him," Elton concluded. "We've been together for a very long time. I love him dearly." Bernie, present despite a Southern California earthquake days earlier, joined Elton, who handed the award to him.

On this night, Elton could explain, for those who still didn't realize it, how much of a starry-eyed fan he still was. He also had the chance to express his feelings about his achievements, old, new, and yet to come. Most of this happened backstage at an informal press gathering. "I feel so young and that I have a lot to do," he declared.

Some of the questions from the press demonstrated a fundamental lack of education about Elton John. One woman asked how many pairs of glasses he now owned. Politely, he replied, "I've probably got about two thousand pairs somewhere." Another reporter asked, "Considering you've never been a critic's darling, is this sort of your official membership to the club?" Elton remembered those heady months following his Troubadour debut, and said, "I used to be a critic's darling, then I started wearing funny clothes and dressing up." He changed the subject to what really mattered. "The most important thing to me is to be able to play my music live like the Grateful Dead said [in their induction acceptance speech]. That is the greatest thing for me, the biggest kick. . . . It still gives me a thrill."

Another reporter asked, "Rock'n'roll came out of rebellion against the establishment. Your thoughts on being inducted into an establishment Hall of Fame?" The pianist, who had been criticized over the years for being anything but rebellious, responded candidly and good-naturedly, "I've always been an establishment sort of guy—aren't I, really? The boy next door, the over—, chubby kid who made the grade." He stopped before describing himself by the judgmental "overweight," opting for the more positive "chubby." "I was never David Bowie or Mick Jagger or Axl. I just sat at the piano and put my feet up on the piano and danced on it. You know, anyone can make it if they try."[137]

CHAPTER 12

BLESSED[1]

(1994–1995)

*D*UETS LINGERED IN THE PUBLIC CONSCIOUSNESS with the release in February 1994 of its second single, the "Don't Go Breaking My Heart" remake with RuPaul. Although Elton seldom chose his singles, this time he did.[2] It remained to be seen whether this was for better or worse. For those in love with remixes, the release was for better. Elton's voice would be heard in the dance clubs, to his certain delight.

The video was the single's strong suit. A comic chemistry existed between pianist and drag queen as they mugged for the cameras. Elton beat his chest playing Antony to RuPaul's demure Cleopatra, looked somber as the farmer in *American Gothic* (RuPaul was a little too lovely for a Dust Bowl wife), grinned in Sonny Bono–like fake black hair and mustache as RuPaul "out-Cher'd" Cher, squirmed in his Little Bo Peep/Marie Antoinette outfit alongside RuPaul's Louis XIV, and leered and squinted as *Grease*'s Danny Zuko while primping RuPaul became the newly transformed Sandy-as-biker-chick.

Elton and RuPaul lip-synched to the song on the Brit Awards, on German television, and at the San Remo Music Festival. In Britain, the single went to number 7 on March 5. In the United States, it broke the Top 5 on *Billboard*'s Hot Dance Music Club Play chart and the Top 10 on the Hot Dance Music Maxi-Singles Sales chart, competing for attention with such unwholesome songs as "Why Is It? (Fuk Dat)" by Sagat and "Bump 'n' Grind" by R. Kelly. After "bubbling under" for a few weeks, on March 26 the duet finally reached the Hot 100—peaking at number 92—then disappeared after two weeks. The remix had the same chart success as the infinitely more sublime "Border Song" in August 1970.

A third song from *Duets* was released in Britain only. "Ain't Nothing Like the Real Thing," with Marcella Detroit, was actually a single from Detroit's own album, *Jewel.* Hence, the billing was "Marcella Detroit & Elton John." The pianist didn't have the fit of pique he had had when Cher insisted on being listed first in the "Don't Trust That Woman" credits—a good thing, too, since "Marcella Detroit & Lady Choc Ice" would have confused many record buyers. On May 21, 1994, the song peaked at number 24 on the British singles chart.

"MORE TO DO THAN CAN EVER BE DONE"[3]

In 1991, the Walt Disney Company, under the stewardship of Michael Eisner and Jeffrey Katzenberg, recruited Tim Rice to write lyrics for an animated musical about the tumultuous life of a lion. "They said to me, very kindly, 'Who would you like to do the music?'" Rice said later. "And Elton was my first choice. . . . I didn't think they could get him, to be honest, but they did."[4]

"I actually jumped at the chance," Elton remembered,[5] although he later admitted John Reid had admonished: "If you don't do this, I'll kill you." When an agreement was finally reached, Elton's fee wasn't disclosed, but he felt fortunate enough to buy a new Bentley.[6]

Disney producer Don Hahn was instantly persuaded by the idea of using Elton. "Here's someone who's kind of the tunesmith for the late twentieth century," he observed, "So we thought, 'Of course, why don't we take his songs, his melodies, and pair him with Tim Rice and come up with this truly extraordinary songwriting team?'"[7]

Well, that's not exactly the way it would end up working. After years, during the late 1970s and early 1980s, of being amenable to writing music before any lyrics were penned, Elton had decided he wanted to stick to the method he found most comfortable and that brought him the most success—writing music to lyrics. Rice, who back in 1981 had assumed that Elton would set his "Legal Boys" lyrics to music, not realizing that Elton already had the music written, waiting to be mated with those words, was now surprised that the musician insisted on having the lyrics first.

Both songwriters believed Elton had the easier job. The movie went through all sorts of changes. Initially, it was to be called *King of the Jungle*, but since lions don't live in the jungle, they settled on *The Lion King*.[8] The story line underwent numerous phases, as did actors' lines and therefore the lyrics. Once Elton wrote his melodies, however, he was done.

Studio time was booked for a Thursday at London's Oxford Street. Tim Rice telephoned Elton on Monday, saying he would have the lyrics for "Circle of Life" that afternoon, giving Elton three days to compose. Rice later admitted that the lyrics weren't quite done; perhaps he had given himself this deadline as motivation to work faster. Fortunately for Rice, Elton didn't want or need the lyrics then. He asked Rice to bring them with him on Thursday. When the day came, the lyricist watched as Elton swiftly composed the music that would become the movie's spectacular opener.[9]

Hans Zimmer, recruited to score *The Lion King*, gave "Circle of Life" an overpowering African sensibility. But Rice believed it wouldn't have made sense for Elton and him to incorporate African themes in the music or lyrics during the songwriting process. "I always felt quite strongly that one shouldn't try and ape a style of music or lyrics we weren't naturally able to do," he said. "We should write a great song or songs and a nice score and give it the flavor of Africa, but I think it would have been a mistake to try to have done something that was completely African because it wouldn't have been right, it wouldn't have been honest."[10]

Elton had no reservations about giving Zimmer complete freedom to play with his songs. "Hans is one of the top score writers for the movies in the world," the pianist noted. "You don't tell somebody like that what to do."[11] Zimmer's credits included the scores for *Driving Miss Daisy*, *Thelma & Louise*, and *Rain Man*. (He was also coproducer of the Buggles' 1979 hit "Video Killed the Radio Star," the song that unwittingly heralded the rise of the music video.)

In addition to scoring, and arranging two of the John/Rice songs, Zimmer arranged vocals on all five of their production numbers, well after Elton wrote the music. Despite Zimmer's Africanization of "Circle of Life," it remained fundamentally the same. The appealing vocal solos of Lebo M. and Mbongeni Ngema, and the triumphant South African chorus, gave the song its proper setting, yet it was still an Elton John song. Carmen Twillie, a veteran of the *21 at 33* sessions, sang the lead. Elton did, too, on the alternate version for the soundtrack.

Both the Lebo M.–flavored, Hans Zimmer–arranged version and the Elton John rendition of "Circle of Life" successfully set the spiritual tone of the movie. The saga of the lion cub, Simba, begins here. He is the newest member of the circle, or cycle, of life, as his father, King Mufasa, proudly presents him shortly after birth to the kingdom's subjects, the reverential animals of the wild. Later, the young Simba's self-imposed banishment following the murder of his father by the treacherous Scar must come to an end so that Simba can take his rightful place in the circle of life. The self-anointed King Scar has tried to thwart this cycle with the assistance of the pillaging hyenas; the ecological balance, essential in the circle of life, has also been rent asunder under Scar's malevolent rule.

Rice, who believed in writing not simply to entertain children but also to stimulate their minds,[12] hints in his lyrics at the story to come. He foreshadows the wildebeest stampede, orchestrated by Scar, that kills Mufasa ("But all are agreed as they join the stampede/you should never take more than you give"), as well as the challenge Simba faces in Scar ("And some of us sail through our troubles/and some have to live with the scars"). An example of the rewrites Rice did is found in these plot twists, omitted from Carmen Twillie's version. As the movie opens, filmgoers contemplate only the potential of the newborn Simba. Twillie thus sings about how the "circle of life . . . moves us all/through despair and hope/through faith and love." On the soundtrack, however, Elton reflects on the whole story, in a voice fit for King Mufasa.

The combination of Elton's voice and the instrumental backing would have given the movie as uplifting, if less African, an opener as that finessed by Zimmer. Elton's heraldic piano notes, Davey Johnstone's soaring, heaven-bound guitar playing, and percussion programming by Matthew Vaughn that is reminiscent of distant, tribal drums give the song all the authenticity it needs.

Simba is overcome by cockiness when told he's in line for the throne—hence, the movie's Busby Berkeley–inspired production number, "I Just Can't Wait to Be King." In the film, singing is shared by Michael "Never Can Say Goodbye" Jackson sound-alike Jason Weaver (as Simba) and comedic personality Rowan Atkinson (as Zazu, King Mufasa's all-purpose, horn-billed servant). Simba's cockiness spills into Elton's melody, which charges full speed ahead with the youthful energy and uninhibited nature of a child just told of a great destiny. The film rendition was arranged by Mark Mancina (known for his scores for *Twister* and *Con Air*), who Africanized the song more than Hans Zimmer did "Circle of Life," with tribal drums, chanting, and a danceable flute pattern unrelated to Elton's composition.

Sung solo, rather than as a duet, Elton's version sports better lyrical imagery than that heard in the film ("Way beyond the water hole/a little down the line/the jungle and the plains and peaks/are scheduled to be mine") as well as clever wordplay ("It's easy to be royal/if you're already leonine/it isn't just my right/even my left will be divine"). Meant less for the brat Simba and more for an adolescent with delusions of grandeur, Elton's "I Just Can't Wait to Be King" is a wiry rocker shaped by party-style piano chords and dressed up in Davey's bounding guitar.

The ambitions of the wild Simba are no match for those of his evil Uncle Scar, whose dastardly plans are outlined in "Be Prepared" (originally titled "Thanks to Me"[13]). Here, Scar plots insurrection with the hyenas. Tim Rice's theatrical insight is in full bloom, matching snide asides with quick quips and having the devilishly smart Scar imply that, even with the hyenas' help, Scar will reap the bulk of the reward ("The future is littered with prizes/and though I'm the main addressee/the point that I must emphasize is/you won't get a sniff without me"). In one of his two Broadway-esque efforts for *The Lion King*, Elton links a facile melody worthy of *Mary Poppins* to Rice's theatrical lyrics for an unlikely soundtrack highlight. Jeremy Irons, as Scar, with limited pipes but villainous delivery, wrings special meaning from Elton's melody, which makes one cringe even without Zimmer's sounds of hell rising up.

Elton's other Broadway-esque effort is "Hakuna Matata." But before there was a "Hakuna Matata," there was a "Warthog Rhapsody." When Simba leaves home, wracked with guilt after Scar convinces him he caused his father's death, the cub wanders until he finds two friends—a meerkat, Timon, and a warthog, Pumbaa—who rear him to lionhood.

Timon and Pumbaa instruct Simba on their philosophy of life. In "Warthog Rhapsody," they advise Simba of the virtues of laziness ("Now if you want a role model/of a life most blissfully led/then look no further than Pumbaa here/than this laid-back quadruped"). Elton gave these words a Tin Pan Alley tune, reminiscent of *Kiss Me, Kate*–era composing and suitable for the Rockettes. The song almost made the film. It was recorded for this purpose by Nathan Lane (Timon) and Ernie Sabella (Pumbaa), with an arrangement by Zimmer and Bruce Fowler, but, when nixed from the soundtrack, was relegated to *Rhythm of the Pride Lands*, a compilation released a year later and described as "inspired by" *The Lion King*.

The movie's creators believed the movie needed something more to the point than the exaltation of laziness sung in "The Warthog Rhapsody." Accordingly, Rice perused a Swahili phrase book and found "hakuna matata," which means "no worries."[14] He built new lyrics around it, offering a reason for the warthog's philosophy—namely, that working hard in anticipation of a better future gets one nowhere.

Tim Rice had to insert a farting reference in "Hakuna Matata," since flatulence was the warthog's major vice. In "The Warthog Rhapsody," Pumbaa notes, "Let my lifestyle be your reference frame, as long as you stand upwind." In "Hakuna Matata," he laments the pain he felt as a "young warthog" when he realized he had an embarrassing problem ("I'm a sensitive soul though I seem thick-skinned/and it hurt that my friends never stood downwind"). But it's the "hakuna matata" mantra that carries the song, in the movie's lyrical and musical modern-day counterpart to "Bare Necessities," from 1968's *The Jungle Book*, another acclaimed Disney movie.

The most famous song from *The Lion King*, "Can You Feel the Love Tonight," is evidence of both Elton's ease in making music and his involvement in the movie. "They didn't just hire me to write the songs—'Thank you very much, goodbye,'" he said. "I was very much a part of it."[15] He saw the storyboards and suggested a romance between the exiled Simba and childhood friend-cum-lioness Nala, who, in the movie, seeks help against the treacherous King Scar and finds the future king lounging in the lush tropics with Timon and Pumbaa.[16] But when, in the course of animation, "Can You Feel the Love Tonight" went from romantic to mocking, Elton had some words about that, too. "I wrote it to be sung by the two lion cubs, who were in love with each other," he remembered. "I was horrified when I heard it being sung by the warthog."[17]

Elton insisted the song's romance be restored, and it was, requiring Tim Rice to do yet another rewrite. In the film, although Timon and Pumbaa are permitted to express their distress at the burst of feelings between Simba and Nala ("They'll fall in love and here's the bottom line/our trio's down to two"), the two lions—singing voices provided by Joseph Williams and Sally Dworsky—ponder their passion ("So many things to tell her/but how to make her see/the truth about my past? Impossible!/She'd turn away from me").

Mark Mancina had sole arranging duties for the song's film version. His understated African rhythms are ill matched to Elton's warm, fuzzy melody. The pianist sings the original, vastly superior, version on the soundtrack, which also makes the film's closing credits. His recording accentuates the song's gem-like construction, placing it on the same rarefied level as, among others, "Daniel" and "Nikita."

Elton could look back on his experience with Disney fondly. "It's probably been the most pleasurable experience of my career, dealing with these [Disney] people," he remarked, once the film and the soundtrack were out. "They've been absolutely fabulous. I can't say one bad word about the experience."[18]

"IT'S THE BAND OF HOPE"[19]

MARCH 21, 1994 WAS OSCAR NIGHT. Elton granted Barbara Walters his first interview with her, for her annual "Barbara Walters Special." It was his most candid, high-profile interview on American television yet. He had already talked at length about his drug and alcohol problems in a 1991 . . . *Talking with David Frost* segment for public television, and, the following year, had chatted freely with Whoopi Goldberg about his homosexuality on the comedienne's talk show, but Walters reached millions more households. In case any Americans still thought Elton was bisexual, she had the musician clarify his sexual orientation. "I am a homosexual man," he asserted, also mentioning his new, loving relationship with the as-yet-unnamed David Furnish.

The night of the telecast, Elton was hosting his second annual Academy Awards party, to benefit his AIDS Foundation, at the Maple Drive Restaurant. The Cartier-sponsored benefit's star power was much brighter than in 1993. On the party's fund-raising committee were Neil Young, Bonnie Raitt, and Don Henley. Whoopi Goldberg, who was hosting the Oscars, rushed to Maple Drive straight from the ceremonies. And three of the night's biggest Oscar winners, Steven Spielberg (who won for directing *Schindler's List*), Tom Hanks (named best actor for the AIDS drama *Philadelphia*), and Bruce Springsteen (honored for his song, "Streets of Philadelphia"), showed up at Maple Drive together. Oscar Night pundits saw this jackpot of winners as a "coup" for Elton's party. The proud host shared some time with them in a private booth. By the end of the party, more than two hundred thousand dollars had joined the AIDS Foundation's coffers.

"WHAT'S LEFT TO PROVE?"[20]

ELTON WAS REGRESSING. In 1992, he had resembled a slightly older version of the young Briton who had stormed American shores in August 1970. Now, in late winter 1994, he resembled Linus Van Pelt, Lucy's younger, blanket-wielding brother from *Peanuts*. But this older version of the wise and resourceful Linus had, at times, a heavy growth of beard, and always wore a pair of eyeglasses. The security blankets of drugs and alcohol were long gone.

When he returned to the recording studio—a former church now known as George Martin's AIR Studios in Hampstead, London—in February 1994, Elton was determined to make his best album in nearly twenty years. This meant he had to vanquish his recent accomplishments—the adrenaline-charged *Reg Strikes Back*, his tribute to soul music in *Sleeping with the Past*, his homage to sobriety in *The One*. He wanted to sound young again, to remind people of his 1970s successes by evoking them with new material, even if he had long ago moved beyond the innocence of those days. Seeing the world with knowing eyes, all he could really do was build on past achievements, not go back. But go back is what he wanted to do.

The musician was so bent on creating the right atmosphere to get those creative juices flowing that he tried to replicate the past with some of the old cast. He recruited Paul Buckmaster to do orchestral arrangements. Bernie flew in from California to write lyrics in the studio, just as he had in the early days. Chris Thomas, with whom the pianist had just worked in January (on the *Lion King* soundtrack), was gone from the picture for now. "I just wanted to change the waters a little bit," Elton said.[21] He brought in Greg Penny, who had been a young observer at the Chateau d'Hierouville while the musician made *Goodbye Yellow Brick Road*.

Elton decided to be in the studio for everything and not "tune out," as he had on recent albums when the agenda was drum programming, a technology he often liked but couldn't work. So the *Made in England* sessions had no drum programming, just his band: Davey Johnstone, Guy Babylon, Charlie Morgan, Bob Birch, and, once again, Ray Cooper. The pianist wanted "150 percent" of himself on the album, to involve himself with keyboard and guitar parts. He believed he'd been too easygoing in the recent past. He insisted that, sometimes, he'd left problems with the sound unresolved, or had stuck with songs he shouldn't have. Now, he was poised with his editing pen.

Buckmaster noted a marked difference between Elton's attitude now and what it was when Dick James allotted only twelve thousand dollars to a production that would include elaborate orchestral arrangements. Back then, the budding star had made a conscious decision not to get involved in the arrangements. "Elton, at that time, was very quiet. He had a tremendous sense of humor when we were off the 'set'. . . . We would just be like crazy schoolboys, saying silly things and joking," he recalled in 1996. "During the work periods, he was very quiet, almost shy, a reticent, quiet person. And recently, he's involved in everything. He takes a directorial role in every part of the production. . . . That's the way we did it for *Made in England*."[22] This is why Elton was credited as coproducer.

Over a three-month period, beginning in February 1994 and culminating in May—with writing and recording squeezed in around a busy schedule—the *Made in England* sessions produced twenty songs. AIR Studios was conducive to prolific behavior. "The sun was shining through the windows," Elton said. "[It was] a very inspiring place to write."[23] Yet only eleven songs of the twenty made the album.

Everything seemed wrong at first. During the initial weeks at Air Studios, "I was a bear," said Elton. "Nothing seemed to be taking shape until I wrote the music for 'Believe'. . . . With 'Believe,' I thought, 'That's the benchmark for this album.' Even though the song is a ballad, it has an edge. . . ." Nothing else measured up to "Believe"—for a while. His companion, David, listened to many a complaint after Elton returned from the studio at night.[24]

The album's benchmark, "Believe," is a song about love, but not a love song. Bernie had found love again, with his third wife, Stephanie Haymes, and her two daughters in the Santa Ynez Valley. He was raising horses and helping Stephanie run their highly acclaimed Hollywood restaurant, Cicada. But his father, whom he had moved to California some time before, was dying.[25] This fact provided the lyrics' cornerstone: "Cancer sleeps/curled up in my father/and that means something to me." Out of the helplessness that comes from watching a loved one die emerged a recognition of what is important. Without love, nothing has meaning. It is the reason for living, having principles, fighting for a cause. Love transcends movements and institutions. "Churches and dictators/politics and papers/everything crumbles/sooner or later/but love," Bernie wrote.

Elton has said that his music for the song is "Lennon-ish" (Bernie had suggested writing a song like "Imagine"). This influence aside, "Believe" is mournfully grand. The dark beauty of its desperate optimism and hopeful pessimism is far more intense than the simple chords that support peace and brotherhood in Lennon's "Imagine."

"Believe" starts with a rush of sound, as sudden as the inflation of an airbag, which recurs throughout the song and is strangely comforting due to its recurring core parts, Elton's dirge-like piano chords and Buckmaster's swooping strings. These, along with Davey's sitar, unite for a John-composed, Far East–inflected jazz line that embodies life's dichotomous quality as seen through Bernie's emphatic words, a bleakness constantly overtaken by love-fueled inspiration. The song "ends" tentatively, with Buckmaster's orchestral coda, an orderly dropping of notes into a musical well that wouldn't reveal itself for another five songs.

Buckmaster's fading coda is overcome by metallic factory noises that become "Made in England," which Elton called a "four-minute précis of my life"[26] (though the song is actually more than five minutes long). It took no less a biographer than Bernie to get it right. "We've known each other for over twenty-seven years," said the lyricist. "In that time, I've learned everything there is to know about him, about his childhood and whatever loneliness he may have existed in, and also that it's the music that's always kept him alive and kept him going. . . . It's always been the music that's kept him afloat."[27] But "Made in England" is about more than the music in Elton's life. It is also about his brushes with fate and his resilience.

What did Reggie Dwight have as a child? Bernie's answer: Stanley and Sheila Dwight ("I had a quit-me father/I had a love-me mother") and early idols ("that sweet Georgia Peach/and the boy from Tupelo"). Stanley's intolerance for contemporary music had frustrated Reggie, this only child's solitude a source of despair ("Face down on a playground/crying God send me a brother/not a bloody nose/for rock'n'roll"). Who is Reggie's brother? Bernie. A leap is taken to the momentous summer of 1970 and another, to six years later, when candor almost finished Elton's career ("A Yankee summer/had a way about her/you had a scent for scandal/well here's my middle finger"). Homophobes thought they would have the last laugh ("You can still say homo/and everybody laughs"), but Elton outsmarted them all. Made of "cadillac muscle," he was "built to last."

Despite all the nose-thumbing, "Made in England" isn't a bitter tune, but a celebration. As the metallic factory noises give entry to the song, a Beatles-esque guitar chord à la "A Hard Day's Night" is heard, which, in turn, opens up to Davey's dancing guitar pattern. Like the chugging perseverance of the "locomotive strong" Elton in "Simple Life," "Made in England" musically demonstrates his indomitability. This stamina is audible first in Davey's unflinching guitar playing, since the melody's singsong structure represents not victory over adversity but Elton's childlike awe of music's magic. As the pace picks up near the close, the pianist breaks into Little Richard piano phrases and Jerry Lee Lewis–inspired vocal ejaculations ("I was made in England! Yeah, yeah!"). Like its indestructible subject, "Made in England" goes out with a blast of rock'n'roll that doesn't stop. It merges with Buckmaster's orchestral vision for the beginning of "House," which in turn provides a context for the pride celebrated in "Made in England."

For Elton, "House" is also autobiographical, but turns to the middle of the story to find him struggling from day to day. Whether touring before adoring throngs, recording the last notes for his next, "best" album, or picking up awards for longevity or a memorable melody, he could often barely stand after downing his daily bottle of scotch. But what he really lived for was cocaine. The white powder sharpened his wit (which didn't need sharpening), enhanced his sex drive, and made him feel omnipotent—until it wore off. Then he would have to sniff more, even lick it from a mirror or off the floor. Ultimately, it dulled his appreciation of the adulation he received regularly, his judgment, and his love of life. Although "House" is open to multiple interpretations, cocaine addiction is the one that resonates for the musician.

Bernie's lyrics find a desolate soul nestling in his room, gazing dully at whatever is visible from his window ("This is my house. . . . /Those are the trees/I can hear them breathe/this is my bed"). As he sees what he has, he thinks of what he doesn't have ("Where is my tired heart?/That is the question/where is the answer?"). Unwilling or unable to leave the security of home, he opts for the easy answer ("Where is the answer?/Inside my house"). "As soon as I read the lyrics, I thought of when I used to do cocaine and wouldn't come out of my room for two weeks at a time," Elton told Robert Hilburn. "I would creep around my own house so slowly that it would take me fifteen minutes to walk across my bedroom floor. I didn't want the floorboards to creak because I didn't want anyone to know I was still up."[28]

But even "House" holds hope for the future. Elton is at his weakest, and yet, as he gazes out the window, he thinks: "I wish I was rain/I want to fall from the sky/I want to get wet all over again." "To me, that line is like the baptism—the reemergence," Elton later explained. "It's about looking out of the window and then finding the strength to follow through."[29] And he did find that strength. The vividly told battles against personal demons in "Made in England" and "House," and the sentiments in "Believe," make this new album *Captain Fantastic II.*

"House" is a waltz, with Elton's delicate piano lines culminating in broken chord flourishes, augmented by his harp-imitating synthesizer. Unlike "Made in England," it is sad—in fact, it is depressing. To Elton, the room-dweller lacks friends, love, and an interest in living. But the melody also communicates an uncertain love affair. The musician's vocal gently questions what went wrong, supported by Charlie Morgan's patient, slow-dancing percussion and sentimental countermelodies from Davey's guitar and Bob Birch's bass. What emerges is a trip to Eisenhower-era lovelorn songs—"A Teenager in Love," "Tears on My Pillow"—that Reggie Dwight could have been listening to in his room, sitting on his bed and studying his cherished 45s, loathe to open the door lest he hear his parents argue. "These are my dreams," he might have thought, as he imagined his name on a record label. "They belong to me."

Whereas "Believe," "Made in England," and "House" are connected by Buckmaster's orchestral bridges, the fourth song, "Cold," begins abruptly, almost as a continuation of "House." If "House" examines loneliness and seclusion, "Cold" goes a step further, providing a commonplace, nonautobiographical framework: the end of one love affair and the possible resuscitation of its predecessor. Bernie refrains from describing these events in commonplace terms, instead using sexually ambiguous language to identify the participants in this mini-soap opera. "Cold" thus signifies a change in emphasis in Bernie's writing, from the man/woman melodrama to lyrical motifs not limited to the heterosexual experience. Elton had depended on other lyricists for homosexual outlooks during the days of his commercial downturn, with Tom Robinson and the straight Gary Osborne. But now Bernie had to eventually acknowledge and portray gay love, too, in view of Elton's stature as the most prominent openly gay man in music. This happened at Elton's urging. "[H]e likes the material to be ambiguous," Bernie said recently. "No 'he' or 'she.' The references are important to him. He wants people to believe that what he is singing about is true, that it's honest."[30]

Like "House," the music for "Cold" is depressing, but the depths to which its melancholia plunges hadn't been seen since 1981's "Chloe." "Cold" has a more complex melody, framed in a thin layer of tear-stained rhythm and blues, with Elton's piano weaving in and out of gospel and blues and Davey's many guitars interjecting light blues references. Buckmaster's strings paint a blues pastiche recalling Artie Shaw's 1941 adaptation of "Dancing in the Dark" and the warm, twilight sparkles of Gershwin's "Rhapsody in Blue." But Elton's repeated utterances of "Baby, I'm cold, I'm so cold," and the drawn out, falsetto-hooked enunciations of "cold," give the song its greatest torment, much as his lengthened vocalization of the name "Chloe" lent that song its supreme misery.

What better song to follow "Cold," but "Pain"? The semiautobiographical "Pain" isn't about a fictional relationship, nor is it specific to Elton and Bernie, but it is generally applicable to everyone. There was the real pain Bernie's ailing father felt. There was also Bernie's emotional pain, watching him suffer. There was the pain of Elton's insecurities that, over the years, he had tried to hide with costumes, alcohol, and drugs. And there was the pain that existed everywhere and in everything, much like the pantheistic view of God's existence.

The lyrics to "Pain" are written as an interview between a journalist and "Pain," a solitary creature instantly constructed of its billions of worldwide components, just for this occasion. Bernie reveals Pain's pervasiveness in couplets that could literally go on forever: "Pain is love/Pain is pure/Pain is sickness/Pain is the cure." Pain is the captor of humanity ("My name is pain/You belong to me/You're all I ever wanted/I'm all you'll ever be"), its mission facilitated by its great age, "nineteen hundred and ninety-four years" (a line that, though it could have served to date the song, Elton wisely left in, thus retaining its rhythmic quality).

Is "Pain" a sad song, like "House" and "Cold"? Interestingly, no. Elton once said that "Pain" marries Rolling Stones guitar riffs to a David Bowie-esque vocal. "It just moves," he crowed happily.[31] Like other exercises in Eltonian irony, the song's meaning is subverted, in this case by a vigorous pace and blithe melody. Instead of reflecting on the turmoil caused by pain, the song exults in pain's power. Its main guitar riff harkens back, much more faithfully than did "Saturday Night's Alright," to Stones songs like "Can't You Hear Me Knocking" and "Brown Sugar." Conversely, the uplifting counter riff Elton composed doesn't refer to the Stones, nor does the melody, which sports glittering forays up, down, and sideways—not something Mick Jagger's voice could have easily handled.

Pain is also relevant to the next song, "Belfast," which tells of intra-ethnic conflict. "Belfast" is linked musically to "Believe," through Buckmaster's sonic droplets, which fall into the musical well of this sixth song on the album.

To Elton, "Belfast" didn't have to be about Belfast. "You can substitute Belfast for Chechnya," Elton said. "It could be . . . any place where human beings are being subject to intolerable pressure and pain. It's about the human spirit . . . and being able to battle through those conditions, and being stronger than all of that."[32] But inasmuch as "Belfast" presents the universal themes Elton explained, the lyrics also conjure up fanciful Irish scenes depicting the impact of endless war on Belfast's inhabitants: "No more enchanted evenings/the pubs are closed/and all the ghosts are leaving." And then there is the most image-laden of Bernie's lines: "And so say your lovers/from under the flowers/every foot of this world/needs an inch of Belfast."

Elton's music is soaked in Irish themes. Not known for his grasp of ethnic music, he evokes the lilt in both Irish speech and traditional music in the upward slant of the melody toward the end of each verse, and in his piano prologue that follows Buckmaster's wistful movie-soundtrack beginning. Most affecting, though, is Elton's vocal, his most disciplined since "The Last Song," which manages, through a refreshing swing in a vocal hammock, to capture the melody's Irish lilt.

"Belfast" almost didn't make the album. "[After] . . . we wrote the song and recorded it, the cease-fire [in Northern Ireland] was announced and I thought, 'Should we still put the song on the album?,'" Elton later recalled on Danish television. He decided "Belfast" was still worthy of inclusion. "It's about hope; it's about the positive side of Belfast rather than the negative side," he explained.[33] Besides, it could apply equally to the Chechnyas of the world. Sadly, unlike "Nikita," "Belfast" hasn't become outdated.

The brief respite from autobiographical themes ends with the first notes of "Latitude," when *Captain Fantastic II* resumes. Elton's take on "Latitude" is simple. "It's about being away from someone," he said.[34] It is also a 1994 lyrical follow-up to "I Guess That's Why They Call It the Blues." The spouse from whom Bernie was separated geographically this time was Stephanie Haymes, not Toni Russo. Bernie wrote the words because of his lovesick, homesick feelings after talking to Stephanie on the telephone.[35] Latitude is what separated them, a "straight line of distance/a cold stretch of black across blue."

According to producer Greg Penny, Bernie gave Elton the lyrics to "Latitude" as soon as the musician, experiencing his own dose of latitude, returned to London and David from Los Angeles after his Oscar night AIDS benefit. Elton didn't try to adapt to the time difference, beginning work on the song immediately, and, again in little time, finishing a complete song on his instrument of choice that afternoon, a harmonium.[36] He saw "Latitude" as another Beatles-influenced song. A lot of this has to do with the arranger on the track—George Martin. It is "Penny Lane" all over again as Martin's strings and French horns hover over the musical landscape. It is also a seamless Elton John waltz, with his harmonium sighing wistfully, playfully stabbed by Davey's banjo licks. "Latitude" doesn't sound cloudy and dreary, as one would imagine from reading the lyrics. The music succeeds in doing what Bernie, stuck in London, couldn't: drenching the scenery with sun instead of rain while erasing the distance between loved ones, paving the way for a happy reunion.

Elton saw the next song, "Please," as vindication, an acknowledgment that he had found the loving relationship he'd been waiting for all his life. "I have always been the person who wanted the white picket fence and the happy marriage and the wonderful American kind of 'Ozzie and Harriet' story, and I think this song says it all," he remarked to Robert Hilburn. "I feel very happy . . . that I can actually sing that and have someone in my life that I want to spend the rest of my life with."[37] Bernie had reason for contentment now, too. "Please," he wrote, thinking of Stephanie, "let me grow old with you."

Couldn't this also have been a goal for the Captain and the Kid, an update of "Two Rooms at the End of the World"? In 1979, Bernie had reflected on their escapades: "Well we've both ridden the wagon, bit the tail off the dragon/borne our swords like steel knights on the highway." Since then, each had battled personal troubles, withstood the lean Geffen years, and still managed to churn out a nice supplement to their back catalog. This is reflected in "Please": "We've been crippled in love/shortchanged hung out to dry/we've chalked on the walls/a slogan or two about life/. . . /we've been flipped like a coin/both of us landing face down." While this was happening, the Captain and the Kid had grown up. They no longer needed that "healthy time apart," as Elton once called their brief professional separation. They didn't have to compete to feel fresh. "After everything we've been through," Bernie wondered, "what's left to prove?"

Elton had tried recording "Please" at least twice, and at least one of those times with piano. The mild undercurrent of his harmonium and Davey's twelve-string guitar that made the final cut echoes the Beatles (and the Byrds). Still, "Please" comes across as the album's sole country tune. Elton accents every syllable sharply, like a singer from the U.S. heartland, helping the frisky, cowboy-saloon melody climb a pleasant hill to the top, where one may discern earnest messages that tout settling down and growing old together. Guy Babylon and Bob Birch, in their sole vocal outing on an Elton John album, join Davey for backing vocals. They don't evoke the unique vocal blending of Davey, Dee, and Nigel, but they do demonstrate camaraderie and add to the number's casual, country air.

One could easily mistake the next song, "Man," for a tribute to the Promise Keepers, the American movement of churchgoing men intent on reclaiming the nobility, chivalry, and responsibility once supposedly subscribed to by men of old, but lost with the decline of religion and traditional values. "I'm a man working on the living part of life," Bernie has Elton sing. "You see through me, I understand. Don't lose hope, if you can have a little faith in man." But Bernie was skeptical of the normative male view of self. "Man stands in all his glory," he wrote, paradoxically adding: "Man breathes his own deceit/Man worships his own defeat."

For Elton, "Man" is not so much a criticism of man's heightened view of himself as a celebration of a particular group of men. "It's very important for me, being gay, to say I'm a man, too," he said. "It's just affirming I'm proud to be a gay male."[38] "I'm a man. I know what it feels like," read the lyrics. Not quite "we're here, we're queer, get used to it," but the sentiments are similar. Antigay bigotry often denies gay men and lesbians their humanity. Male gay-bashing also denies gay men their masculinity.

"Man" is among the most masculine of Elton John songs. A brawny, gospel number with plenty of church piano, it has the Pinner pianist boldly declaring his manhood, passing a test of vocal stamina rarely heard on his albums. Most of the lyrics concern man's fallibility, but if that's what it means to be accepted as a man, then Elton and other gay men want that, too. Elton's rumbling, multitracked backing vocals ("I'm a man! I'm a man!" and "Ye-eah!") during the chorus further proclaim his male identity. Wending its way through the macho pronouncements is a string arrangement, dripping with the bravado one might have expected from the original *Superman* television series. The arrangement is notable also for its coauthors, the pianist and Guy Babylon.

"Lies," the next song, propounds something that so rarely occurs: a satisfaction with self, imperfections and all, and comfort in one's identity, even if unacceptable to others. The song recalls, in Elton's case, his pre-rehab habit of denying his alcohol and drug abuse while at the same time using them to mask his insecurities ("I've lied for a drug or two"). It also touches on Elton's sexuality, which first became a public issue in 1976 and continued as a topic—and subject of confused discussion—through an ill-chosen marriage and his eventual rehabilitation from substance abuse. "Some lie about who they love," Elton sings.

Musically, "Lies" is what you get from fusing the James Bond-like swagger of Johnny Rivers's 1966 "Secret Agent Man," the wilderness cries from the theme to the 1968 movie *The Good, the Bad, and the Ugly,* and classical chord progressions. The trip back to the 1960s in "Lies" befits an era when Elton—and, before him, Reg—strove for recognition and endured disappointments, not with "lies" but with perseverence. "Lies" embodies the incorruptible charm of those days and nights when Elton/Reg dreamed of success but couldn't imagine it would ever actually happen.

The official interpretation of the last song on *Made in England,* "Blessed," is that it expresses Bernie's belated desire to have children. "Until now, I was never around kids, didn't think I had the time for them," he said, months after the album's completion. "But your eyes open up. I love getting up and taking kids [his stepdaughters] to school. It is a great feeling. . . ." The lyrics for "Blessed" give voice to this desire: "I need you before I'm too old/. . . /to walk with you and watch you grow/and know that you're blessed." That his offspring would be "blessed" is repeated throughout, a promise that his child will have only good things. In another verse, Bernie anticipates his child before he or she is even conceived: "Hey you, you're a child in my head/you haven't walked yet/your first words have yet to be said." Here, a sense that "Blessed" has a dual meaning begins to take shape: "I know you're still just a dream/your eyes might be green/or the bluest that I've ever seen." One is suddenly reminded of an older song: "So excuse me forgetting, but these things I do./You see I've forgotten,/if they're green or they're blue./Anyway the thing is, what I really mean/yours are the sweetest eyes I've ever seen."

"Your Song" was the first hit for Elton and Bernie, and the first to be universally accepted as evidence of their songwriting talent. Writing it, seeing it blossom into a hit, and savoring its growth and maturation over time was like watching the birth of a child and its flowering into a distinct human being over many years. Elton and Bernie had had many such children. With "Blessed," they disclose that they hope to have more.

"Blessed" may lyrically recall "Your Song," but musically they couldn't be more dissimilar. "Blessed" is in a league with *Sleeping with the Past*'s "Blue Avenue": piano-painted, folkish, and spirit-enveloping. "Blessed" also picks up where "Blue Avenue" left off, digging more deeply into the mystical side of romance with its emphatic tone ("I'll pick a star from the sky/pull your name from a hat"), set against Elton's twinkling broken piano chords, Guy's cavernous synthesizer breaths, Ray's rattlesnake tambourine, Davey's Spanish guitar, and some studio trickery that distorts Elton's voice, trapping it in an imaginary megaphone as he sings, "I promise you that."

The title for *Made in England* came when, after months of prerelease publicity, Elton decided *Believe* wasn't the right name. "I thought, 'I can't call it that, it's a bit bleeding mystic,'" he divulged on the eve of the album's release.[39] And, although he and Bernie had determined to experiment with one-word titles for all the songs, "England" didn't express the fact of Elton's birth and evolution nearly as well as "Made in England." The addition of the two words made sense, and sounded more sensible as an album title, besides. It also communicated Elton's sense of national pride, something he found lacking in the English, as opposed to the Scottish, Irish, and Welsh. "I find that a shame," he noted. "I live here, I'm proud of my country. . . . I'm proud to be English."[40]

Whether this album was Elton's best in nearly twenty years isn't important. After more than a quarter century of John/Taupin compositions, there was too much to evaluate, too much to treasure, too much that was brushed with fond reflections of adolescence for some, the toils of early adulthood for others, and the challenges of grown-up living for still others. Yet the appeal of *Made in England* is automatic. It is an outgrowth of the past triumphs of one of England's most prominent songwriting duos.

One song Elton left off *Made in England* was "Live Like Horses," but it wouldn't vanish. It would sneak into live shows, be retooled for a special single, and, later, take its proper place on a new studio album.

"RESPECTED, SALUTED, AND SEEN FOR THE WONDER I AM"[41]

WHO KNEW HOW BIG IT WOULD BE? There was an early sense of the dominance *The Lion King*—Disney's thirty-second animated feature—would have on American movie screens during the summer of 1994, but what really happened was too good to be true.

The first commercial skirmish took place in March 1994, when *The Lion King* clawed at Universal Pictures' live-action *The Flintstones!* at the ShoWest motion picture exhibitors' convention in Las Vegas. Disney and Universal each had a night to woo exhibitors. The maker of *Cinderella* and *Aladdin* had conventioneers on the edge of their seats with 100 dancers, 150 robed singers singing "Circle of Life," and appearances by James Earl Jones, Whoopi Goldberg, Cheech Marin, and other *Lion King* stars. A carnival with live animals and food capped off the festivities. Universal, however, didn't produce *Flintstones* star John Goodman, leaving script-reading to some of the supporting cast. The B-52s (the "BC-52s" for the occasion) failed to excite the crowd with their "(Meet) the Flintstones" theme. And the movie clips shown were also scheduled to be aired on television's *Entertainment Tonight*, depriving the convention of an exclusive.[42] In the first battle of the studios, it was King Mufasa 1, Fred Flintstone 0.

Walt Disney Records also won over merchants at the National Association of Recording Merchandisers (NARM) convention with what *Billboard* magazine described as a "song-and-dance revue." Product tie-ins were planned for both the film and the soundtrack, there would be children's "play-along," "read-along" and "sing-along" releases,[43] and then there were Elton's music and performances, which automatically garnered radio programmers' interest. Patience had worn thin with big movie ballads of late. "Going to Elton John was an ideal audience-broadening move for Disney. He has the perfect combination of wide popularity and artistic credibility," said *Radio & Records* staff researcher Ken Barnes.[44]

As *Duets* faded from the American charts and Elton and Bernie were named ASCAP songwriters of the year (for 1992–93), "Can You Feel the Love Tonight" was released to American radio and, soon, to retail. On May 28, 1994, the song was at number 50 in its second week on the Hot 100, winning *Billboard*'s designation of "greatest gainer/airplay." The following week, at number 28, *Billboard* awarded it the double whammy of "greatest gainer/sales & airplay." And the movie wasn't even out yet. A couple of weeks after the animated feature bared its friendly teeth in theaters, "Can You Feel the Love Tonight" was in the Top 10. It would stay there for the summer, peaking at number 4 on August 6 and going gold that month, becoming Elton's second gold single of the 1990s. In Canada, the single debuted at number 1, a peak position it held for three months.

The soundtrack followed a similar upward path, debuting on *Billboard*'s album chart on June 18 at number 13, well before the movie's release on June 24. Four weeks later, *The Lion King* would be the number I album in the United States for nine weeks straight; within coming months it would be certified for shipments of ten million.

The story of King Mufasa and Prince Simba was also well on its way to being the summer's number one movie, as well as the most popular animated feature of all time, grossing forty-six million dollars its first weekend. This was the third-highest opening for any movie, placing Mufasa and Simba right behind *Jurassic Park* and *Batman Returns*. The Flintstone brood, those likable stone-age buffoons, had amassed more than one hundred million dollars in about a month's time, just as the strains of "Hakuna Matata" began emitting from theater speakers. But from here on, Universal Studios would need more than Bedrock to combat the Pride Lands.

"PIANO MAN MAKES HIS STAND IN THE AUDITORIUM"[45]

"IS THIS A COOL IDEA, OR WHAT?" Billy Joel, in dark beard stubble and plain tweed jacket, asked more than fifty thousand screaming fans night after night in stadium after stadium across the United States. Joel was referring to a brainchild of his that had come true—touring with Elton for six weeks during the summer of 1994. Of *course* this was a cool idea. Those who were fans of both musicians could finally see them in one place. Fans of just one could enjoy at least half the show. Elton's plan to resume the tour with Ray Cooper that summer had to be pushed back to September.

The Elton/Billy tour, officially named the "Summer of 1994" tour, but variously dubbed the "Piano Men" tour, the more confrontational "Face to Face" tour, even the "Heart and Soul" tour, seemed to some in the press an ideal union of like-minded musicians. Although Billy Joel insists Elton never influenced his music, the Pinner pianist's influence can be heard in many a Joel tune: among them, "Rosalinda's Eyes" ("Tiny Dancer"), "Pressure" ("Ego"), "The Stranger" ("I've Seen That Movie Too," "Funeral for a Friend"), "Ballad of Billy the Kid" ("Burn Down the Mission"), and "Miami 2017" ("Love Lies Bleeding").

It is understandable that Joel wouldn't readily embrace the connection. Early in his career, he was repeatedly questioned about the similarity between his music and Elton's. Comparisons plagued him all the way to Australia, where he was included in a feature called "The Elton John Mystique" in the September 4, 1976 issue of *Juke* magazine. "Elton has definitely repopularized the piano as a lead rock instrument," Joel was quoted as saying. "It used to be only a backup instrument, but I think it's a beautiful instrument. I've been blatantly compared with Elton, whom I like a lot, but I don't like the comparison. It's almost as if people are trying to get [me] to say something bad about him."[46]

Not long after Joel gave this interview, the news broke of Elton's "bisexuality." While the Briton's American fan base dwindled and he took a hiatus from touring and recording, Joel's career ascended. The Long Islander had his first major hit with

"Just the Way You Are" in February 1978 and a blockbuster album with *The Stranger*. During this same period, Elton's "Ego" foundered at number 34, and "Part-Time Love" missed the Top 20. *Elton John's Greatest Hits Volume II* went platinum, as did *A Single Man* a year later, but neither neared the Top 10 or had much longevity. Billy Joel filled the void left by Elton's retreating career—unwittingly becoming his heterosexual alternative. It would be years before Elton would repair his stature, while Joel's star shone ever brighter.

Elton noticed this switch in fortunes. At the August 1980 Hollywood party where MCA celebrated his ten years of success in the United States, a very large, very muscular man playing "the Incredible Hulk" had joined Elton onstage to present him with a commemorative plaque. The pianist was dwarfed in the shadow of this herculean model. "Oh my God, it's Billy Joel!" Elton had quipped.[47]

To this day Joel continues to draw distinctions between himself and his sometime English tour mate. Writing music to lyrics, Billy recently said, means the "music is secondary to the lyric. In other words, the music isn't the motivational beginning of the song being written. That's how Elton does it. . . . I'm the opposite."[48] He has painted a limited picture of Elton's playing, describing it as "more rhythmic and maybe gospel, rhythm and blues, and blues based," while his own playing, he has said, "tends to come more from jazz and even classical music." Joel has described Elton's singing as having remained the same over the years, while his has demonstrated versatility. "[S]inging-wise, Elton has always remained Elton," he posited. "He can shade his voice darker and he can brighten his voice, but he's always remained true to his singing style. . . . I tend to want to change my voices as much as possible because I get bored with my own voice."[49]

At the core, Joel was a fan. But as strongly influenced as his music has been by Elton John, and as much as the American has touted their "mutual admiration society," it was a simple desire to fill stadiums that led to his idea for the double billing. "Billy feels the consumer gets ripped off in a stadium unless they can be delivered a bang for their buck," said his agent, Dennis Arfa of the QBQ Agency in 1996. "[W]e wanted Billy to play some stadium shows. To play stadiums, he wanted another artist, and the artist he chose was Elton John."[50]

In late winter 1994, Joel broke the news to CNN's Larry King. But King had some questions: Whose set would come first, Elton's or Billy's? Would they alternate the coveted second spot? Joel was reluctant to answer, saying only that those details hadn't been worked out yet.

Larry King's question wouldn't be answered until the first trio of shows, all at Philadelphia's Veterans Stadium on July 8, 9, and 12. In the interim, Elton and Billy got to know each other a little and became more accustomed to paying each other public tributes. At his May concert at Wembley Arena, Joel covered "The Bitch Is Back." Then Elton emerged from backstage to lead the crowd in a "Happy

Birthday" sing-along for Joel's forty-fifth. A big bash in his honor followed, thrown by Elton, and attended by, among others, Sting, Joan Collins, and Tim Rice. The English pianist later gave his American counterpart a first edition of *Moby Dick*. Days before opening night in Philadelphia, Elton hosted Billy and their respective bands for rehearsals at Atlanta's Georgia Dome.

The tour program captured the congenial mood. A photograph had the part-time Atlanta resident affectionately mushing his nose into Billy's, the tops of their eyeglass frames touching. In the program's centerfold, Elton, with his Yamaha grand and Union Jack, and Billy, with his Steinway grand and Stars and Stripes, flanked a compelling statement: "[T]his event is a clear indication that the piano is, and has always been a seminal instrument for rock and roll."

Philadelphia on July 8, 1994 was excruciatingly hot, in the upper nineties with humidity so dense the air seemed like a live, unmoving being. Come concert time, eight o'clock that evening, it was still 93 degrees. On the field, covered with a tarmac and a few thousand seats, it was 102 degrees. The specter of dehydration prompted stadium staff to break with policy and encourage fans to bring in water. Ice, water, and cups were made available.

A lack of physical comfort didn't deter excitement from building as showtime approached. Early arrivals not interested in tailgating parties could sit in their seats, unload the water from their backpacks and tote bags, and gaze at the mammoth staging. The eighty-foot stage was furnished with two grand pianos facing each other, perched above two lower oval tiers (the higher painted with giant piano keys, the lower basic black) that jutted into the audience. Framing the stage was a mural, evoking old British gentility on the left and the American Revolution on the right. A modest banner stated simply, "Heart and Soul." On either side, two twenty- by thirty-foot video screens hung at the ready, to bring every last onstage antic to people sitting in the farthest reaches—once the sun went down.

At eight o'clock, with the sun hot and bright enough for midday, the sounds of eighteenth-century pomp and circumstance filled the air. First, it was "Yankee Doodle Dandy." Billy Joel materialized in gray and strolled about the stage to wild applause. Then the music turned regal, and Elton emerged, wearing a creamy white suit over a gold vest. The two took in the ovations, approached each other with greetings and embraced. Taking their respective places—at left, Elton, on a pincushion bench at his Yamaha; at right, Joel, on a revolving stool at his Steinway—they traded off the verses and choruses of "Your Song," Billy's "Honesty," and, with Elton's band and the guest appearance of two of Billy's backing vocalists, "Don't Let the Sun Go Down on Me."

After "Don't Let the Sun" came to a rousing conclusion, Joel left with a "see you later." Elton opened the show for the next seventy-five minutes. The sun was still shining brightly enough to render the huge video screens useless. For the first half hour, most concertgoers could barely see Elton and his band. "Philadelphia Freedom" began with the sizzle of a simulated electric piano solo reminiscent of renditions on *The One* tour. "Take Me to the Pilot," unknown to most in the audience, included an abbreviated version of the witty, purr-meow expressions that had opened the song for fans the past fall. "Levon" blew by in blustering majesty. "Rocket Man" was stretched into a survey of blues and early rock'n'roll that included snatches of "Working in the Coal Mine."

The Philadelphia critics loved that. Wrote *The Philadelphia Inquirer*'s Tom Moon: "Once-idyllic chords took on the urgency of a feverish sermon, and before long, John was singing 'Working in a Coal Mine' [*sic*] and uncorking intricate New Orleans–style solo riffs."[51] Jonathan Takiff of the *Philadelphia Daily News* was equally delighted, writing: "A three stage 'Rocket Man' spun off into a New Age instrumental noodle between John and acoustic guitar-picking Johnstone, then into a sly quote from Lee Dorsey's 'Working in the Coal Mine.' I found the mix a happy surprise. . . ."[52]

It wasn't until a quarter to nine, and the song "Simple Life," that dusk set in and the video screens lit up. Finally able to see the onstage goings-on, almost everyone in the stadium stood, something few had done for "Rocket Man." After "The One," Elton's supple version of Billy's "New York State of Mind," and the inevitable "Funeral for a Friend/Love Lies Bleeding," Billy joined his fellow pianist for "I Guess That's Why They Call It the Blues" to a rush of appreciation and a hearty sing-along. Next was "Can You Feel the Love Tonight," with *Lion King* clips on the video screens, and the double-fisted finale—"Pinball Wizard" and "Saturday Night's Alright"—during which concertgoers got an eyeful of Elton in all his rock'n'roll crazed glory, kicking away the piano bench and playing on his knees, his head thrown back and mouth open wide.

As thrilling as Elton's performance was, it didn't get the reception of Billy's set. After a twenty-minute intermission, Joel's entrance was signaled by a tape of Gershwin's "Rhapsody in Blue." By now the sweltering night was pitch black, the only light provided by the staging and video screens. The crowd greeted the American musician and his band as if he were the headliner, and he gave them mainly his hits.

Despite that quote in the program about the piano's seminal place in rock, and the unofficial "Piano Men" tour monicker, Billy knew better than Elton that piano playing wasn't what had drawn tens of thousands to Veterans Stadium that night. They wanted spectacle. Accordingly, Billy did little soloing and actually left his Steinway for extended periods to stand, center stage, with a guitar around his neck, or to dance with a microphone stand, or traverse the eighty-foot stage, even venturing to the lower tier (Elton hadn't) to shake hands, accept flowers, and let fans touch his legs as he sang.

Joel covered "Goodbye Yellow Brick Road." Later, Elton joined him for "My Life," which markedly swelled an already tremendous audience response. Once Billy's set was over, the half-hour–long grand finale, a virtual battle of the bands, ensued. Here, it was obvious that the two "piano men" enjoyed playing with each other, although Billy again neglected the piano in favor of a microphone stand for "The Bitch Is Back" and his own "You May Be Right," while Elton dutifully pounded the keys. It wasn't until "Bennie" that a special musical moment happened between them as the two traded riffs against the syncopated beat. The Beatles' "A Hard Days' Night" followed, but was merely a prelude to the most hair-raising part of the show, the joint tribute to Little Richard and Jerry Lee Lewis. Predictably, Elton led with the homosexual, African-American Georgia Peach's "Lucille," for which he served up 1940s boogie-woogie chords. Joel chose raging heterosexual Lewis's "Great Balls of Fire," the better known of the two songs.

A joint John/Joel "Piano Man" ended the evening, turning Veterans Stadium into a colossal piano bar and encouraging the most spirited sing-along of the night. "Philadelphia, we broke your 'cherry,'" Billy said tastelessly, eager to let the crowd know it was the first to experience the pleasures of the "Summer of 1994" tour.

Local television news coverage, broadcast before the show was finished, focused on contrasts between Elton and Billy. "I happened to be backstage when they were just coming out," reported Gerald Kolpan for Fox-29's *The Ten O'Clock News.* "Elton John was nervous, and it looked like he was going to his own funeral. Billy Joel was driving his own golf cart, looked like he was on his way to his birthday." He described Joel as a "macho man, tough guy, supermodel's ex-husband," while Elton was a "self-confessed gay man and child classical prodigy."[53]

Throughout the tour, which took Elton and Billy through much of the eastern United States, journalists found more contrasts between the two. *USA Today* reporter David Zimmerman noted Billy's "absolutely bare" dressing room, the opposite of Elton's, which was "decorated to the nines" with flowers, candles, and *Lion King* memorabilia.[54] Of the third night at Giants Stadium in New Jersey, *Rolling Stone's* Elysa Gardner wrote, "[I]t was Joel who gave the more musically in-your-face performance. The crowd was his; their obvious affection for John notwithstanding, most related more to the Long Island, N.Y., native and embraced his New Yawk [sic] shtick more readily than John's droll British charm."[55]

Backstage before the first Giants Stadium concert, Elton told a radio interviewer, "He's [Billy's] the wild one. He just struts around. He's great fun to work with. I'll tell you, he just cracks me up. And Billy is so revered in this country. . . . The crowd loves his stuff. You know, he's kind of like an American institution. So it's really been fun for us, for a Brit like me to come over and play on his home turf."[56]

Musically, there were plenty of challenges and changes on the tour. "Candle in the Wind" was slotted into the set list, just before "Piano Man," by the July 12 Philadelphia concert. "Bennie" often turned into an "I'll-show-you" display of piano fireworks, in which Elton would surprise Billy with shifts in tempo, mood, or style. The Briton's "Lucille" was dressed in a Swing Era zoot suit on some nights, hammered by the brazen rock'n'roll chops of 1957 on others. During his set, Elton continued to explore and lengthen his amusing introduction to "Take Me to the Pilot." He danced on the piano keys that decorated the staging's upper tier to rouse the audience for "Simple Life."

Competition or not, the camaraderie between the two "camps" was evident. When, at the July 9 Philadelphia show, Billy's drummer Liberty DeVitto took ill from shellfish poisoning, Charlie Morgan filled in without a moment's rehearsal. On numerous evenings, Elton chatted with Billy in the latter's dressing room. He counseled Billy on substance abuse after the Long Islander came onstage drunk one night. At lunch the next day, Elton embraced him, proclaimed, "I care about you," and offered his help. He also felt comfortable enough with the friendship to joke at Billy's expense. When asked on Atlanta radio whether the American was shorter, Elton said, "He would kill me if I said yes, [but] just a fraction." Then, mischievously linking the size of his cohort to tiny Herve Villechaize of television's *Fantasy Island*, he added with a wink, "He keeps going, 'Da plane! Da plane!'"[57] At the August 18, Detroit-area concert at the Pontiac Silverdome, Billy apologized for the show's rescheduled date. "I was really sick," he explained to the audience. "You've always been sick," Elton replied.

"GREAT AND SMALL ON THE ENDLESS ROUND"[58]

THE AMERICAN "CIRCLE OF LIFE" single was out by the end of the "Summer of 1994" tour, but Elton didn't add it to his set list. *The Lion King* didn't need any more publicity, though the song could have used help in grabbing attention away from "Can You Feel the Love Tonight," which was still in the Top 10. "Circle of Life" charted on August 27, peaking at number 18 nearly two months later, on October 15. The song was a big hit, though not a Top 10, receiving substantial airplay as a Top 5 entrant on *Billboard*'s Hot Adult Contemporary chart.

The European *Lion King* singles preceded the release of the soundtrack and movie in the fall. In Britain, the movie opened nationwide on October 14. Perhaps Britons were bucking all the American-generated hype (though the singer and both composers were countrymen), as "Can You Feel" got no higher than number 14, on July 23. Or maybe there was too much of a wait between the single and the movie. The greater success of "Circle of Life" lends credence to this view. It was released in October and got closer to the Top 10 than had "Can You Feel," peaking at number 11 on October 8.

Both songs did better elsewhere in Europe, reaching the Top 10 or higher in many countries. In France, "Can You Feel" was number 1 for months. The soundtrack, too, gradually reached the Top 5 of the Eurochart Hot 100 albums. These successes extended well into 1995 (in March, the French "Can You Feel" single was still in the Top 10). Because of *The Lion King*'s impact, the release of *Made in England* was pushed back to the new year.

Late summer 1994 saw the release of a Larry Adler tribute album, issued for the American expatriate's eightieth birthday and titled *The Glory of Gershwin*. During the *Made in England* sessions, Elton had recorded two songs for the project, "Someone to Watch Over Me" and "Our Love Is Here to Stay." As usual in these affairs, Elton got in on the ground floor. Adler had played harmonica on Sting's 1993 album *Ten Summoner's Tales*, and then appeared at the 1994 Rainforest Benefit, where Elton sang "Someone to Watch Over Me." Adler had initially favored working with classical musicians for his birthday album, but after being exposed to the talents of Sting and Elton, had asked them to join him on an LP of popular performers. George Martin gladly assumed the reins of producer, recruiting sixteen others to lend their voices, including Elvis Costello, Carly Simon, Lisa Stansfield, and Peter Gabriel.

Adler and each guest recorded live with an orchestra. Elton sounded like an entirely different singer from the one burning up the airwaves with "Can You Feel the Love Tonight" and "Circle of Life." Over the years and, especially lately, his voice had become startlingly malleable. Who could have imagined that the Philly Soul enthusiast of "Philadelphia Freedom" could also be the torch singer of "Blue Eyes"? That he could sing with equal credibility on P.M. Dawn's "When I Think About Love" and the Kiki Dee duet "True Love"? George Martin's production focused the listener on Elton's voice. Every susurration, crescendo, throaty utterance, and soaring note was given its due. As Adler noted, "Elton John's people said they'd never heard him sing like that."[59]

Though *The Glory of Gershwin* wasn't done for charity, much of what Elton did after his tour with Billy Joel was. There was the second annual World Teamtennis All-Star Smash Hits benefit for his AIDS Foundation. The exhibition match, which this time boasted Gigi Fernandez, John McEnroe, Gabriela Sabatini, Martina Navratilova, and coorganizer Billie Jean King, was held in Chestnut Hill, Massachusetts on August 25, 1994. The night before, a celebrity dinner and auction offered up such choice items as a *Lion King* songbook autographed by Elton and Tim Rice, which went for $9,300.

"I MAY BE JUST AN OLD SOLDIER TO SOME"[60]

THE WESTERN UNITED STATES, which had been deprived of the Elton/Ray shows in 1993, finally got their turn in the fall of 1994, with a short string of concerts that started in Phoenix and ended with four nights at Los Angeles's Greek Theater. The set list was nearly identical to that of the fall 1993 tour, with the addition of, among others, the brand-new "Believe" and "Can You Feel." "Pinball Wizard" was freed from the environs of "Bennie," its partner in 1993. Both now had to fend for themselves.

Paul Buckmaster, who attended one of the Greek Theater performances, was moved by the progression of Elton's musicianship since the early days, and was especially overwhelmed by "Take Me to the Pilot." "He started playing this long intro. I didn't know what it was," remembered Buckmaster two years later. "Then, little by little, it started tickling my memory, and I realized after—this must have been eight minutes of intro . . . not at all boring, very interesting and very full of surprises—I began to recognize what it was. It had elements of 'Take Me to The Pilot' in it. In fact, it was an extended intro to 'Take Me to the Pilot.' And he displayed such humorously brilliant inventiveness on that piano intro, I was just overjoyed to hear it. . . . That means he's very committed to his musical development, which is a wonderful thing."[61]

There was also the element of charity. Elton and Ray were playing to approximately six thousand people a night, netting the AIDS Foundation $750,000. The Disney Channel was filming every performance for a television special to be aired in 1995. And Walt Disney Records feted Elton and Tim Rice before the first performance, presenting the songwriters an award for the six million units shipped of *The Lion King* soundtrack.

The pianist had ever new ideas for fund-raising. New items for sale included a line of china, eyeglasses, watches, and, available in time for Christmas 1994, a set of secular Christmas cards depicting a painting Elton owned, *Putti Blowing Bubbles,* and an "In Memory" ring to commemorate the life and untimely death of a loved one to AIDS or other diseases.

There was also the "'Out' the Closet" sale at a shop on Fulham Road in London. A fan of Elton's music or clothing could snap up his used designer suits, shoes, vests, shirts, belts, t-shirts, bathing trunks, ties, underwear, and hats for a fraction of what the star had paid. This may have been Elton's most pleasing fund-raiser; he could clean out his well-stocked closets at Woodside and Queensdale to make room for more clothing while watching fans—who flew in from around the world—buy items they would treasure forever, all the while raising money for AIDS. After only one month, the shop raised $240,000 for Elton's foundation. There would have to be more sales like this in the future; Elton's closets were always bulging with his latest purchases.

In a special edition of *48 Hours* in November, Dan Rather pointed out that eighty-three to eighty-five percent of monies raised for the Foundation went where it was supposed to. "That's really high!" Rather exclaimed in amazement to Elton, who replied, "Either you run a proper business or you don't. And it is a business." Rather told viewers, "Elton John is steadfast in making sure that the checks get to the right places." In the United States, this was done through an arrangement with the Washington, D.C.–based National Community AIDS Partnership. Had he ever thought of lending his name to a cause for publicity's sake?, Rather asked. Elton was honest. "I've done a lot of things in the past for publicity, like 'Don't drink and drive and don't take drugs' when I was the biggest alcoholic and drug addict going, so, I mean, I've been a hypocrite in my time."[62]

"THERE'S MORE WAYS THAN ONE
TO REGAIN YOUR SENSES"[63]

THE 1993 AND 1994 CONCERTS with Ray did for Elton the same thing they had in 1979. "It's very good for a musician to go back to the . . . basics and find himself again. . . . It proves to me that I can still play. . . . With just a piano and a voice, you go back and find your confidence again and believe that you are at least a reasonably talented musician."[64]

But a series of sold-out Elton/Ray shows that followed at the Royal Albert Hall, from November 27 to December 12, exacted an emotional toll. "It's so draining, doing twelve shows in sixteen days, which was really too much for me, I think," he admitted months later. "By the end, I was a complete and utter mess. I was drained. I didn't have anything else to give. But at least I felt good that all of the performances were of a relatively high standard. The audience in Britain appreciated those shows a lot. . . . I got so much feedback from it."[65] Any positive feedback, however, was apparently evident only in hindsight. After his last night at the Albert Hall, all Elton could think about was dissatisfaction with his performance. He smashed a commemorative plaque he'd been presented with that night into smithereens backstage and, just as Princess Margaret was taking an elevator to visit him, left the building in a fit of pique.[66]

The pianist wore a multitude of Versace vinyl suits during his Albert Hall stint, some light and polite like the pale pink getup, others as unsubtle as the waxen sheen of a fire engine. For an AIDS Foundation benefit concert on World AIDS Day, December 1, his jacket was canary yellow, his trousers a calm blue. The show was largely indistinguishable from the others, except that several songs were omitted to make time for special guests Kiki Dee, Boy George, Lisa Stansfield, and George Michael.

The night's cause didn't deter Elton from commenting on his least favorite sector of British society. He was perturbed by the concert reviews he'd been getting. "We will be lining up the whole of the British press and machine gunning them to death," he fantasized aloud. True to form, he spent the evening showing the press up with his playing. During "I Don't Wanna," his powerful hands scurried over the piano keys like fleshy spiders. His newly long bangs bounced uncontrollably as he tore through that song and "Levon." The longer hair weave, rootless and lacking lift since it emanated from natural strands growing from the back of his head, transformed his forehead into a steep slope. But it was the hair that impressed Paul Gambaccini, who was on hand to say laudatory words about Elton before the show was turned over to the guests. "I never thought I would see the night where Elton has more hair than I do," he jokingly began.[67]

The Albert Hall shows saw Elton resume a technique he had mostly abandoned for some years—that of constructing musical witticisms while lying on the floor, his right arm stretched to the keys as his thick fingers hopped between the whites and blacks. He also performed not only "Believe," but "Live Like Horses." Thus began a love affair between fans and the unrecorded "Live Like Horses" that would grow stronger every day.

"THERE'S A LOT MORE LIFE IN THE OLD GIRL YET"[68]

IT IS COMMON FOR THE PRESS to cite Elton's Oscar acceptance speech of March 27, 1995 as the day on which he publicly announced his affection for his partner in life, David Furnish, but this really happened at the Golden Globes on January 21. Seated between Diana Ross and David at a table of Disney heavy hitters, he looked embarrassed when his name was read along with Tim Rice's for "Can You Feel the Love Tonight," named the best movie song. Clutching his award at the microphone, Elton got through his obligatory thank-you's and then blurted out, "and to David, love you very much, too." The camera zoomed in on the pleased young Canadian, who had recently left Ogilvy & Mather to pursue his dream of filmmaking (and had that month started filming his lover at work and play for a "warts and all" documentary).

During the first quarter of 1995, Elton received a flurry of awards nominations. A couple were guaranteed. One was the statue he picked up on January 19 for his AIDS fund-raising, at the Bernie Taupin–produced AIDS Project Los Angeles's (APLA) annual Commitment to Life benefit, which also honored Tom Hanks (for his role as an AIDS-afflicted lawyer in the movie *Philadelphia*) and Creative Artists Agency President Ron Meyer. Calling himself APLA's "official gay recipient" as he shimmered in aluminum foil–styled vinyl, Elton informed more than six thousand benefactors, "This [America] has been my second home for many, many years. This is where I 'came out,' in this country. I slept with half of it, and I came out HIV negative. I was a lucky, lucky person. It's my job to repay that debt."[69]

The other guaranteed statue was a Brit Award for outstanding contribution to popular music, which Sting presented to him on February 21. "He's a musician of commanding authority," Sting said of the pianist. "He's a man also with an outrageous sense of humor as well as a great sensitivity. . . . I'm proud to be a friend of his."[70]

Rod Stewart delivered the less reverential, filmed speech for the awards show, which harkened back to the public insults of the late 1970s. "You are a tremendous singer, songwriter, and performer—but not quite as good as me," Rod grinned. "The award you're getting tonight is long overdue. I've got mine here," he said, holding up the trophy he'd gotten two years earlier. But he also got sentimental. Displaying a 1978 photograph of himself, Elton, and John Reid, he said, "I leave you with this wonderful thought: 'Where did the years go'?" It was enough to get misty-eyed.[71]

The outlook for the Grammys was less certain, and less warm and fuzzy. It should have been Elton's year. He'd been in the Rock and Roll Hall of Fame for twelve months, in the Songwriters Hall of Fame for three years, and a recipient of numerous Ivor Novello awards since the 1970s. But he only had two Grammys, both in minor categories. Elton had admonished onlookers at the Brit Awards that there was "a lot more life in the old girl yet," but would the Grammys finally acknowledge all the "life" he showed in the past year alone, with *The Lion King* and a gold-selling Top 5 single?

It looked that way at first. On January 5, 1995, Grammy voters unveiled five nominations for Elton, more than he'd ever received in one year (he'd had three nods each in 1970 and 1974). The nominations were skewed; four (for "Can You Feel" and "Circle of Life") were in two categories, song of the year and song written for motion picture or television. The fifth was in the category for which he'd been nominated the most over the years, best pop vocal performance, male, this time for "Can You Feel."

Upon hearing of his nominations, the rock press was annoyed. The *New York Post*'s Lisa Robinson, supportive in the past, called him a "perennial winner."[72] The *New York Daily News*'s Jim Farber lumped Elton's music with what he called other "mush," such as Boyz II Men's "I'll Make Love to You," which was contaminating what he viewed as an otherwise intelligent slate of choices.[73] Even the music industry's unofficial house organ took to editorializing. Writing for *Billboard*, Craig Rosen complained that the Grammys continued to favor "past winners" like Elton in its nominations process.[74]

They needn't have been so indignant. For Elton, the Grammys came and went uneventfully. In the end, he won one more Grammy to add to his two others, for best pop vocal, male, in an untelevised presentation.

The Oscars were better. And by the time he got his bulky, faceless Academy Award for "Can You Feel," he had a new single and album out, and was in the middle of a second tour with Billy Joel.

"LOVE HAS NO BOUNDARIES"[75]

"I DECIDED WHEN THIS ALBUM WAS COMING OUT that I should make my peace with the press, especially in England, because I think if you sustain that for too long, you get bitter about it and you harbor grudges," Elton told an Australian interviewer on April 14, backstage at Miami's Joe Robbie Stadium, the site of his last gig with Billy Joel on the American mainland. So he had cover stories in Britain's *Q*, *New Musical Express*, and *Telegraph Magazine*. He was also on the cover of a lesser-known vestige of Andy Warhol's artistic vision, *Interview*, and the subject of a feature in *Time*. Like never before, Elton was spilling his guts about past substance abuse, excessive sex, and, sometimes, his music.

All of this was intended to trumpet the release of *Made in England* and its debut single, "Believe." *Made in England* was to have been Elton's last studio album for MCA, but PolyGram, impatient to start working with the artist whom it had signed in 1992 before the release of *The One*, wisely purchased rights to the album. The release of *Made in England* under PolyGram's auspices also represented the American kickoff of a label that had fallen by the wayside in the last decade: Rocket Records. For the first time since *Blue Moves*, Elton would have an American release on Rocket, this time through the PolyGram subsidiary, Island. Also, he would now be on the same label globally.

By the time Elton won his third Grammy, "Believe" was out. It bowed on the British singles chart on March 4 at number 16, moving up one space to its peak of number 15 a week later, when the single debuted in the United States at number 52. The Top 15 showing at home hurt Elton's morale; he had had lofty hopes for the first public taste of *Made in England*. In the United States, conversely, he was thrilled with the single's performance. It leaped to number 26 in its second week and reached its apex of number 13, just missing the Top 10 but still besting its British performance and sticking around longer.

The Marcus Nispel–directed video for "Believe" had been filmed in New York in late January. It managed to hide the "tantrum" that had immediately preceded it, immortalized by David Furnish in the documentary he was shooting. The tirade, triggered when Elton's chauffeur accidentally drove away with his video wardrobe, was fueled by the star's deep-seated fear of performing on film due to insecurities about his looks. It didn't matter that he had countless videos to his name in which he always looked stylish, even if he didn't have movie-star features or a washboard stomach. Happily, the driver returned with the musician's clothing, and Elton acquiesced to the task at hand.

All he had to do in filming, whether he was angry or not—and an on-site interview by television's *Entertainment Tonight* suggested he was still a mite peeved—was lipsynch on a platform that became, in the video, the inside of a 1930s dirigible moving above what appeared to be Gotham City. Computers took care of the rest: a group of identical, umbrella-carrying men hanging off a bridge, the spitting image of an open-armed Lady Samantha in a Grand Central Station setting, a newsboy flinging papers from a skyscraper, a giant cat that dwarfed its urban surroundings. All the while, the dirigible surveyed the scene. What all this had to do with believing in love wasn't certain, but it sure was great cinema. *Entertainment Weekly* selected Nispel's work for the magazine's "It's cooler than the song!" citations.[76] As fun as the video was to watch, the collage of strange images wouldn't have had a clear impact without the emotional pull of Elton's music.

Elton's new album was released worldwide on March 21. It had a significant commercial impact on Southern California that day because of a staged event, something Elton wouldn't have done pre-rehab. In a nationally publicized gesture, he and Bernie appeared at Tower Records in West Hollywood just before midnight to sign autographs for eager fans, some of whom had driven hundreds of miles for the privilege. In a way, the signing was a page ripped out of the annals of Elton's 1970s stardom. The name "Tower Records" was changed to "Elton John Records" for the occasion. Many standing in line had brought old vinyl albums for the songwriters to sign; many more bought *Made in England* for the same purpose.

Autograph hunters ranged in age from two to forty-something. One young woman, clutching her autographed items, wept. An awestruck father, hoping to impress Elton any way he could, assured the musician he would be buying *The Lion King* on laser disc soon, having watched it with his tiny son on the video umpteen times. Liza Minnelli suddenly appeared, cutting in line so she could give the man with whom she'd almost costarred in a Blake Edwards movie a big peck on the cheek.

As scintillating as the signing was, it gave music analysts the wrong impression about the new album's probable success. West Hollywood's Tower Records reported strong pre-sales of *Made in England*, and this was taken as reflecting demand for the album nationwide.[77] The hard truth was, although the release of *Made in England* had been delayed by six months to avoid competition with *The Lion King* soundtrack, the two albums were still going head to head.

"I'D LIKE TO DEDICATE THIS AWARD TO MY GRANDMOTHER"[78]

AS USUAL, THE CRITICS WERE SPLIT on the new Elton John album. *Entertainment Weekly* had a good review: ". . . *Made in England* acts as a refresher course in Eltonia; it recapitulates virtually every phase of his career and compels a listener to appreciate just what the man . . . is capable of doing."[79] *Out* magazine also provided its stamp of approval: "He sings love songs to men, not the gender-free ditties we've come to expect from our out pop stars."[80] (Actually, the love songs on *Made in England* did tend to be gender free, but considering Elton's openness about his sexuality, they made sense as love songs sung to men.)

But *Made in England* was panned, too. New Jersey's *Star-Ledger* described it as full of "[p]lodding rhythms, unimaginative string-cushioned arrangements, and toothless lyrics. . . ."[81] Jim Farber of the *New York Daily News* wrote, "Elton offers yet another synthetic-sounding, ballad-heavy bore."[82]

What really mattered to sales of the album, however, were not the reviews, but extraneous factors—chiefly the Academy Awards, as it pertained to *The Lion King*, and the release of that movie on video.

On the eve of *Made in England*'s release, as the second half of his tour with Billy loomed, Elton's grandmother, Ivy Sewell, passed away. Mrs. Sewell had lived well into her nineties, and had spent her last years in a cottage on Woodside's grounds, within close view of her grandson's larger manse. "I knew she was gonna die," Elton said. "It wasn't a shock, because she had had a stroke. And she died peacefully at home, near her garden, which she loved."[83] The relationship between Elton and his "Nan" had been marked by exchanges of affection. He visited to see how she was doing; from the road, he sent flowers and postcards. He saw her for the last time before traveling to the United States for the Billy Joel tour and the Academy Awards, David Furnish filming their embrace. She said she hoped her grandson would get a "half dozen" Oscars.

Although his grandmother died during the third week of March, Elton couldn't properly commemorate her life until he returned home in April. Then he would join his mother, aunt, and uncle in scattering her ashes on her garden.

On Oscar night, March 27, 1995, while others assumed the task of hosting his fund-raising party, Elton spent hours backstage with David and Bob Halley, watching the biggest night in Hollywood on television. He and Tim Rice had been nominated for three Oscars each, a rare feat, for "Can You Feel," "Circle of Life," and "Hakuna Matata." Late in the proceedings, it was time for the musician to perform "Can You Feel."

The pianist was nervous. "Halfway through my performance, I started getting the jitters, thinking about, 'Well, the announcement's gonna be fairly soon,' and I was shaking in my seat."[84] Gossip columnist Cindy Adams surmised he knew he'd win, since he and David had already exchanged "his and his" Oscar earrings.[85] But the musician still looked stunned when, finally sitting in the audience, he heard presenter Sylvester Stallone call his name.

Stallone looked pleased. "Elton befriended me about ten years ago for no reason," the movie actor said the following summer. "Here's a man who has been on an extraordinary roller coaster . . . and is one of the great artists. So I wanted to be there for Elton, even though the Oscars, if you're not receiving one, can be a real tour de force in testing your patience."[86]

Elton and David refrained from a public display of affection, but did pat each other on the back as the musician stood to retrieve his award with Tim Rice.

"This is such an exciting night," Elton gloated upon taking the microphone. "I'd like to thank the Academy for this incredible honor, to Hans Zimmer, who did a wonderful job with the songs, to everybody at Disney, to my parents who are here tonight, to David, to John Reid, to my friends in Utah, and everybody else who worked on this incredible project." By thanking his "friends in Utah," he avoided any ill feelings that could have resulted from mentioning Utah vacationer and Disney expatriate Jeffrey Katzenberg.

Elton continued, "I'd like to dedicate this award to my grandmother, Ivy Sewell. She died last week. She was the one who sat me down at the piano when I was three and made me play, so I'm accepting this in her honor."

Meanwhile, *The Lion King* album was about to start a second life. Spurred by the February 28 release of *The Lion King* video (twenty million were sold the first week), the seven-time-certified platinum soundtrack briskly climbed back up the Billboard 200. On April 8, 1995, when *Made in England* debuted, and peaked, at number 13, the soundtrack was number 5. A week later, the new album fell to number 15 and the soundtrack, whose sales were encouraged by *The Lion King*'s Oscar wins (Zimmer had also won for best original score), bulleted at number 2. "Believe," now at number 17 on the Hot 100, didn't help *Made in England* nearly as much as the Oscar helped the soundtrack. This fact was more apparent by April 29, when "Believe" reached number 14, *Made in England* slipped to number 17, and the soundtrack again reached the pinnacle. Elton was competing with himself, and the victor was clear.

In Britain, *Made in England* peaked at 3 its first week on the chart, on April 1. Despite its name, it only spent a couple of weeks in the Top 10. Elsewhere, it was a Top 10 staple, and a solid number 3 for some time on the Eurochart Hot 100. But "Believe" was hampered by the long run of *The Lion King*'s singles. In France, it struggled in the Top 20 alongside the indestructible "Can You Feel," stumbling from number 14 and soon disappearing. In Europe, as in Britain and the United States, the impact of *The Lion King* thwarted Elton's ambitions for another huge hit.

"YOU'LL HAVE THE BEST, I PROMISE YOU THAT"[87]

REGARDLESS OF CHART PERFORMANCE, Elton believed that live performing gave him the greatest charge. He knew he was at his best onstage. Though he'd just learned of his grandmother's death, he still had to go through with the March 22 Billy Joel show in San Diego.

During this second string of concerts together, the piano playing pair hit a number of towns they'd missed the previous summer. The tour was interrupted only by Oscar night, the New York launching of the Oliver Peoples line of eyeglasses to benefit Elton's AIDS Foundation, and an April 12 Rainforest Benefit to which Elton dragged Billy, who might otherwise have had a night off during a heavy touring week.

The third week of May saw Elton kick off his own band tour, in Europe. But before that, on May 9 in Stockholm, he got another award, the Polar Music Prize, which he shared with cellist/conductor Mstislav Rostropovich, a couple of decades his senior but soon to be a new chum. The two artists' music worlds were radically different, yet each was honored for excelling in his own—Rostropovich, from the "serious" world, for being possibly the greatest cellist of the twentieth century, and Elton, from the "popular" world, for his "unique feeling for melody," being among the "foremost popular artists of the late twentieth century" and for his "fascinating capacity for detachment" that enabled his amusing, self-parodying persona. Apportioned between the two of them was $274,000. Both received a plaque and a bouquet of flowers. During the ceremony, each was also paid a musical tribute.[88] In

Elton's case, this was a mainly orchestral suite of some of his songs, arranged and conducted by Paul Buckmaster.

The project was a revelation for Buckmaster. In preparing to write the orchestral suite, Buckmaster had listened to some of the old albums and was struck by the evolution of Elton's vocals. Since working with the pianist as recently as 1994 on *Made in England* (and attending one of Elton's Greek Theatre concerts), Buckmaster remembered only his "new" voice. When Buckmaster listened to the early albums, he was shocked. "I was amazed to hear this boy, like a schoolboy's voice, this high, fragile, delicate voice," Buckmaster said in 1996. "His voice is now very strong, very powerful. It's clear he's worked very hard on mastering the vocal technique and he has incredible power and stamina," he said. "Now, he's so confident and powerful in his vocal delivery, it's just effortless. It seems like he's got a ceiling above that that he's not even tapping into."[89]

A week after the Swedish ceremony, Elton's voice would soar in performances across Europe. There was a new band member, John Jorgenson, a tall American with lots of auburn hair and a Nordic profile, whom Elton would dub "the Viking." A multi-instrumentalist who played flute and saxophone but specialized in guitars like Davey, Jorgenson was also a member of the instrumental group the Hellecasters. Elton had first discovered him around 1988, when Jorgenson, along with former Byrd Chris Hillman, was part of the Desert Rose Band, which the pianist raved about at the time. In the past, Jorgenson had also played rockabilly, new wave, bluegrass, swing, and show music. "On the new album, there's so much guitar, Davey would have to be an octopus to play everything on stage," Elton said of adding Jorgenson to the lineup. "It's good to add somebody fresh, as well."[90] Jorgenson's resume showed versatility, a necessary quality in an Elton John band member.

The European leg of the *Made in England* tour commenced in Lievin, France, on May 20 and then proceeded to Rotterdam's Maaspop Festival. Soon, the tour reached Moscow, where they played two nights at the six-thousand-seat Kremlin Palace. Unlike the last time the pianist toured Russia, when it was part of the Soviet Union, all tickets were on sale to the public. The shows promptly sold out, even though ticket prices reportedly ranged from thirty to two hundred dollars, and scalpers' prices ran as high as one thousand dollars. These concerts were not groundbreaking like the 1979 shows with Ray; then, Elton and the percussionist were among the first Western acts to play anywhere in the Soviet Union. The earlier concerts were credited with influencing the performing style of Soviet (now Russian) acts.[91]

Ten days, several concerts, and a handful of countries later, Elton and the band were in Hamburg for the Luneberg portion of the Rock Over Germany festival. The sober musician, off Prozac for a while now, still faced occasional depression and a mercurial temper. At the show's start, he wore his final encore clothing—charcoal coveralls—intimating that something was amiss. What followed was almost as disquieting as the 1992 Argentina blowup. Opening, some would say quite rightly, with "The Bitch Is Back," Elton looked utterly miserable and within seconds began yelling at a sound assistant. Miraculously, all the teeth-gnashing didn't affect the vibrancy of his playing or singing, but at song's end, he shared his anger with concertgoers, who were happy to see him no matter what. "Welcome to paradise!" he yelled. The crowd cheered. "Thank you for coming out and standing in the rain," he bellowed, "but I ain't playing any of these *fucking* festivals again!"

The tour continued through other German cities, as well as Spain, France, and Poland. European audiences were witness to perhaps the best band tour Elton had ever done. The concerts typically lasted more than two and a half hours, sometimes approaching two hours and forty-five minutes. They contained both old, seldom-heard nuggets ("Dixie Lily" and "Come Down in Time") and five songs from *Made in England* (the title track, "Pain," "Lies," "House," and "Believe").

This was a big band with a big sound, though it still managed to avoid the "wall of sound" that his 1975–76 band had mustered. No matter how big his band's sound got, Elton's piano playing stood out. On "I Don't Wanna," he berated every audience, mercilessly throttling every note, shaking every chord from complacency. In the joyously resurrected "Honky Cat," nightly reinventions of candied honky-tonk phrases, hot flourishes steaming out of the humid French Quarter of New Orleans and giggly chords caused conflicting feelings: Should one laugh or dance? On "The One," the pianist filled in theretofore unperceived melodic gaps with Victorian civility.

Elton made sure to spend some time underneath the piano for every "Bennie" performance. He was on top of the piano, sort of, for "Saturday Night's Alright," one leg on the piano bench, his body balanced precariously against the lid with the support of just his left hand, punching out stormy splashes of rock'n'roll with the other as Davey, John, and Bob Birch encircled him with their guitars.

Guy Babylon played the synthesizer introduction to "Funeral for a Friend" live for the first time in the twenty-two years that the song had been a concert staple, giving the number's opening bars a much-needed, spontaneous dynamic. His synthesized, melodic wind tunnel at the end of "Made in England," lifted from an undercurrent on the recording, embellished Elton's English pride.

Ray added a fine measure of insanity to every song, whether banging a gong to herald the start of "Pinball Wizard," or spraying sweat from his bare pate during "Someone Saved My Life Tonight," the wet pellets darting between his mallets as he thumped the timpani.

The tour was occasionally interrupted by duty. Elton raised another $160,000 for his AIDS Foundation in June at a London benefit to promote Versace's book, *Men Without Ties,* which was filled with portraits of attractive, nearly nude young men. And of course he watched the progress of the new single, "Made in England," on the charts.

In the United States, "Made in England" debuted on the Hot 100 at number 76 on July 15, but never got past 52. Sales seriously lagged behind airplay. Airplay lagged, too. The song did best, in a butchered dance state, on the Hot Dance Music's Club Play chart, where it was a Top 15 commodity.

Maybe the American public's failure to embrace "Made in England," at a time when few British acts were having hits in the United States, had to do with the title or theme of the song. Or maybe it was its up-tempo music. Since the late 1980s, Elton's up-tempo singles had tended to do less well than the slower songs or ballads. The snappy "Club at the End of the Street" made it to number 28 in 1990; "Sacrifice" reached 18. In 1993, "Simple Life," a bluesy throbber, had barely reached the Top 30, while its slower compatriots from *The One*, the title track and "The Last Song," reached the Top 10 and Top 25, respectively.

In Britain, the fast-paced "Made in England," released a month earlier than in the United States and perhaps aided by its patriotic veneer, reached number 18 on May 27.

"IF YOU'RE MADE IN ENGLAND, YOU'RE BUILT TO LAST"[92]

ELTON'S NEXT U.S. TOUR was a two-and-a-half-month journey, hitting both major cities that he visited every year or two and urban areas not played in over a decade. It was a tour filled with tales of broken records, ill humor tempered by prompt remorse, an awful accident that would temporarily cripple a band member, and an unseemly amount of energy radiating from a forty-eight-year-old man.

The tour was sponsored by Visa Gold, and Elton, one of the biggest spenders of them all, gladly starred in a commercial for the credit card. He was shown confidently producing his trusty piece of plastic and assuring a hotel clerk that he would be using it to pay for an entourage of about three hundred.

Concertgoers were treated to a rich, full show that almost never wavered from its standard length of two hours and forty-five minutes. Toward the end of the tour, the shows were closer to three hours long. The pianist, nearly unhinged in his musical enthusiasm, modeled his new line of Versace wear. First unveiled in Europe, the suits were checkered in pale pink, light blue, or, more commonly, blazing red or pitch black. The checks were big or small, mixed or matched. For the encores, he liked to come out in glittery jackets of gold, sea blue, or multiple miniature mirrors. In Atlanta, he surprised his Lakewood Amphitheater audience with a polka-dot skirt that showed off his legs.

San Jose Mercury News critic Brad Kava compared the stamina-filled pianist to baseball's iron man, Cal Ripken.[93] A month later, the raves were still coming. "John's nearly three-hour concert at [Cleveland's] Gund Arena Sunday night was a vivid reminder of the man's immense skills as an earthy balladeer, as a consummate honky-tonk pianist, and a give-until-it-hurts entertainer," gushed Dan Kane for Canton, Ohio's local newspaper, *The Repository*.[94] Other critics weren't quite so impressed. Reviewing the same show Brad Kava liked so much—one of Elton's most sweat-inducing of the tour—the *San Francisco Examiner's* Barry Walters wrote: "You had to either let the mediocrity wash over you like lukewarm flavorless soup, or set your mind into denial and pretend you're having a wonderful time."[95]

Fortunately, Elton was focusing on other things, even in the heat of the most blazing version of "Levon" ever to come from the concert stage. In Mansfield, Massachusetts, he dedicated "Rocket Man" to Boston Red Sox pitcher Roger Clemens and said he hoped the Red Sox would play the Atlanta Braves in the upcoming World Series. In Chicago for a couple of shows before the playoffs, he went to a Cubs/Braves game and took to advising Braves manager Bobby Cox about the team's revised batting order (he wasn't pleased with it). In Cleveland once the playoffs had started, he periodically updated his appreciative audience with the score of that night's Yankees/ Mariners game.

Sports wasn't the only nonmusical subject on his mind. He reminded concertgoers in the Tacoma Dome about AIDS walks coming up in Tacoma and Seattle. While in Boston, he boosted the confidence of a local rock group, Division Street, with a listening party for the band's latest CD that benefited his AIDS Foundation. In September, he was back in Chicago, just three weeks after his Windy City shows, for the annual round of Smash Hits. And on September 30, he repaid Andre Agassi's participation in the benefit tournament by performing at Agassi's first Grand Slam Concert for the Children in Las Vegas.

On September 22 and 23, Elton played at the Hollywood Bowl, breaking the record for the most shows at the venue. The shows didn't start off very auspiciously. At first, the only sign of this was the muddy sound mix, apparent to many in the audience and undoubtedly to Elton, too, since he was notoriously fussy about such things. But the show plowed ahead. After the pianist introduced the band members, a routine affair, he added some thoughts: "We've just had a band vote onstage, and we've decided this is probably the worst gig we've had to play, a goddamn miserable place to play at," he said, laughing a little, which prompted members of the audience to laugh. "Never mind—we'll continue." He paused. "Oh Christ, what a miserable dump." Pausing again, he grunted, "Ugh! Never again!"[96] Amazingly enough, the show would turn out to be as good as most of the others on the tour, even if he dropped three songs that night. Robert Hilburn chose to ignore the musician's grumblings. "The audience wasn't just saluting stardom, but appeared to be acknowledging what has become a family tie," he wrote afterward.[97]

The next night, Elton regretted his petulance. The whole show was reinstated and he sprang a lengthy apology on his audience. "I had a tough night last night up here," he explained. "If any of you were here last night, I said some really derogatory things about this place, which I'd like to apologize for. I was so pissed, I just wanted to get my aggravation out. It *happens*, what can I tell you? You say things when you're pissed that you don't mean. . . . I'd like to thank the people at the Bowl. They've been so nice to us and for me to say that was completely out of line."[98]

He didn't always let technical difficulties get to him. Nights earlier, in Salt Lake City, assistants had had to change his monitors several times. He was dissatisfied enough with the sound to shave twenty minutes off the set list and rearrange the order of some songs. Still, he mostly kept his concerns private, simply apologizing to the audience for the sound, which, to the untrained ear, didn't seem affected.

Elton had a real crisis, however, at the end of September. The night he was at Andre Agassi's benefit, Bob Birch was walking down a Montreal sidewalk when a truck spun out of control and ran up onto the pavement. The bass player's legs were crushed, his lower back broken. He was out for the season. For the Montreal shows, John Jorgenson put down his electric guitar, pedal steel, and saxophone, and took up the bass. An emergency signal went out for a replacement bass player. David Paton answered it. He abruptly left the band he was in and boarded the next plane from Scotland to Detroit, where he joined Elton's tour for the first time since 1986.

There wasn't much left to do in the United States. Besides Detroit, there were Cleveland and six shows at Madison Square Garden. The last one, on October 20, was Elton's forty-fourth show at the venue, a record for a solo act. Two Garden executive officers presented him with a number 44 New York Rangers jersey.

The Garden shows offered a wild time. In other places, Elton was generous with autographs and handshakes and received a multitude of flowers and gifts. At the Garden, he was a virtual between-song autograph factory, also receiving a mother lode of choice goods from fans and dispensing so many handshakes he could have been campaigning for public office. Security, at which Elton always looked askance, was remarkably lax; early and often, concertgoers piled up in the small space between the front row and the stage. On October 12, opening night, a woman who was crammed into this space got the musician to sign her jacket. She also got pulled onstage, hugged, and kissed. Young *Lion King* fans tended to get special attention. It was obvious, from the way his eyes lit up as stuffed animals, balloons, and messages were thrust into his hands, that Elton genuinely appreciated this outpouring of love. His vigor never seemed to flag, either. After giving the piano keys a savage pounding, he could approach a fan waiting to give him a gift, lean way over to receive the item, and deliver, in return, a bone-crushing handclasp that left the concertgoer happily in pain.

"I SWEAR YOU'LL BE BLESSED"[99]

ELTON REPLACED "HOUSE" WITH "BLESSED" in New York, since "Blessed" was the new American single. It debuted on the Hot 100 at number 87 on November 4, 1995. Elton performed the song on David Letterman's show and the otherwise abysmal first annual VH1 Fashion Awards, facilitating the single's number 34 peak, a far preferable fate than that of the under-appreciated "Made in England" single. More impressive was the new single's long stay on the Hot Adult Contemporary chart—nearly a year, from its inception in mid-October 1995.

Overseas, the next single was billed as representing a forthcoming greatest hits compilation called *Love Songs*, rather than *Made in England*. "Blessed" was one of two *Made in England* tracks also on *Love Songs*, and was supposed to be that next single, but was stopped in its tracks by British radio programmers' poor reaction. Market research, that ugly strategy employed all too often in the music industry, suggested that "Please" would do better, so "Please" was the single in Britain and Europe.[100]

"Please" entered the British singles chart at number 33, which was also its peak, on February 3, 1996. *Love Songs* did a lot better, peaking at number 4 in Britain on December 16, 1995. Almost everywhere, this quasi-greatest hits collection was in the Top 10, if not the Top 5. In some countries, like Chile and New Zealand, it was number 1.

The success of *Love Songs* was surprising. It didn't have a single new song—although it did have some recent ones, like the Kiki Dee duet "True Love," the two *Lion King* hits, and two *Made in England* selections. The timing of *Love Songs* wasn't propitious, either, coming on the heels of the moderately best-selling *Made in England*, and only five years after the multi-multi-platinum *The Very Best of Elton John*, which featured ten of the seventeen songs on *Love Songs* and had been number 1 all over the globe outside the United States and Canada.

There had been other Elton John *Love Songs* compilations over the years. A 1982 Rocket Records *Love Songs* combined then-contemporary hits with album tracks and reached number 39 in Britain. Then there was a 1991 Dick James Records/PolyGram *Love Songs* with old ballads, most of them obscure, including the seldom heard "Sweet Painted Lady," "First Episode at Hienton," and "Pinky." Also in 1991 was a Pickwick Music *Love Songs*, about half of which were post-Dick James compositions or recordings. Proving the remarkable variety in Elton's back catalog, even "Warm Love in a Cold World" from *Victim of Love* had a spot on the Pickwick album.

The 1995 *Love Songs* outsold all of its other namesakes. And while it couldn't eclipse *Very Best of*, it showed that, when given the opportunity, and without extraneous distractions like *The Lion King* soundtrack, people around the world still wanted to buy Elton's music. A lot.

"I'M A ROCKET MAN IN RIO"[101]

ELTON WAS AN AWARD-WINNER AGAIN THAT FALL, named songwriter of the year at ASCAP's October 27 London dinner honoring Performing Right Society (PRS) songwriters and publishers. Along with Tim Rice, he received an award in absentia at the Broadcast Music, Inc. November 9 London dinner for PRS members, which recognized "Can You Feel" as the most performed song of 1994.

Beginning on November 16 in Bogotá, Colombia, Elton toured South America. The tour included about a half dozen dates, with Sheryl Crow as his supporting act. Besides Colombia, they toured Chile, Uruguay, and Brazil. Elton almost regretted Bogotá. The high altitude may have contributed, at the end of "Saturday Night's Alright," to his loss of breath for a worrisome period backstage while Ray engaged the crowd with an extended percussion solo.

The November 20 Parque Central concert in Montevideo, Uruguay, went more smoothly. "Innovator of an entire creative style and aesthetic presence, the small Englishman appeared and began to rise up the audience from the first few seconds . . . ," wrote Leandro Delgado. "[H]e makes them stand up or sit down with just a chord whenever it occurs to him. . . ."[102] To fellow critic Alejandro Espina, the evening revealed the depth of Elton's back catalog, judging by how many hits the pianist and his band *didn't* play. "[W]hat can be said of an artist who played almost two and a half hours of well-known songs (and still has the luxury of leaving out various hits like 'Nikita,' 'Little Jeannie,' 'Sorry Seems to Be the Hardest Word,' 'Don't Go Breaking My Heart,' or many others) without for one moment breaking rhythm?" Espina asked. "The public, the highest judge, gave their answer, applauding on their feet each time one of the songs was sung." Espina also noted the centrality of the piano to this music. "[I]n spite of Elton John remaining seated at his piano for almost the entire concert, he's the one you notice because of his intelligent music and ability to conduct," he wrote. "He's impulsive, in charge of the scene, and when it's his turn to be soloist, he devours the rest."[103]

The Santiago, Chile, concert two days later wasn't a sell-out like Montevideo. *Billboard*'s John Lannert wrote that the Estadio Nacional de Santiago was just a little over half full, with forty thousand of the seventy thousand seats taken. He also reported that the show suffered from sound problems and that Elton's performance was "less-than-sparkling."[104] These assessments are not borne out by footage from the Television Nacional de Chile, however, which broadcast an edited version of the concert. The show was marked by numerous standing ovations, and Elton and the band seemed to be enjoying themselves immensely, too. Davey Johnstone and John Jorgenson had their choreographed guitar picking down to a fine art. David Paton, again accustomed to playing Elton John songs, grinned constantly. And Elton whipped himself into a lather from the beginning, leaping from his piano bench (when it wasn't toppled over, or awkwardly stuck between his straddling legs) to accept applause, and teasing the crowd with the unexpected direction of some chords, sweat-matted hair flopping.

Questions about the tour's success were erased by the time it reached Brazil, for concerts in São Paolo and Rio de Janeiro. The final show, in Rio, attracted a vast sea of standing onlookers who cheered, chanted, and played with what must have been the biggest beach ball in the Southern Hemisphere. They gladly followed Elton's

"Rocket Man" from his Martian Jazz Lounge to an African-American church in the United States, and then back to their native city before the song was over, prompting Elton's exclamation, "I'm a rocket man in Rio!"

Some concertgoers were so happy to be there that they got as close to the stage as they could. At Elton's invitation, two lucky young men even got onstage. One, wearing an Elton/Billy t-shirt, presented him with flowers. The other got his attention with a handmade sign that read, in English, "Please hold me, Elton John." Face to face with Elton, he kissed the musician on the cheek.

"SOME LIE IN WORDS AND SPEECHES" [105]

THE END OF 1996 BROUGHT BOTH GOOD NEWS AND BAD. The bad news was a December 12 decision of Britain's Court of Appeal, which sliced off most of the damages Elton had won against the *Sunday Mirror* for its report in 1992 that he'd been seen at a party chewing food and then spitting it out. Elton was left with about $115,000, which didn't even cover his legal costs. Since he had refused a settlement offer from the newspaper, he was responsible for half the cost of the appeal, too. The appellate judges contended that the original award of more than $500,000 was "manifestly excessive." Although the offending story was false, the judges said, it hadn't harmed Elton's personal image or artistic reputation. [106]

Elton protested that the decision effectively allowed newspapers to print "whatever lies they want." He was concerned that the decision would discourage other, less wealthy, people from suing in similar situations. [107]

The good news, however, was that Elton was on the Queen's New Year's Honors List. He was being made a Commander of the Order of the British Empire (CBE) for "services to music and for charitable services." Thus began rumors that he was in line for a knighthood.

Elton infiltrates his guitarists' line dance in Philadelphia, September 1986. Left to right: Fred Mandel, Davey Johnstone, Elton, and David Paton. ©Nannette M. Bac

Jammin' in Philadelphia, September 1989. Davey Johnstone is at Elton's left, while Jonathan "Sugarfoot" Moffett is behind the drum kit. ©Nannette M. Bac

Opening the Mark Etess Arena at the Taj Mahal in Atlantic City, May 1990. ©Nannette M. Bac

In the 1990s and today, Elton continues to grace the covers of magazines, although rarely in the United States. Clockwise from top left: *Paris Match* (France), *Smash Hits* (UK), *Radio Times* (UK), *Il Venerdi* (Italy), *Revista Teclado* (Brazil), and *New Weekly* (Australia).

Image of magazines by Lori Sears

Upon his induction into the Rock and Roll Hall of Fame in January 1994, Elton invites longtime lyricist Bernie Taupin to the podium to share the applause.

©Gene Shaw/Star File Photo

A grand finale at the April 1996 Rainforest Benefit in Carnegie Hall, New York. Left to right: Diana Ross, Mstislav Rostropovich, Elton, Sting, Andrea Griminelli, Trudie Styler, and James Taylor. ©Nannette M. Bac

Auctioning off a pair of his platform shoes from the 1970s for the Elton John AIDS Foundation, Houston, September 1996. ©Nannette M. Bac

An avid tennis player, Elton has played with tennis stars of the past and present to benefit his AIDS Foundation. *ABOVE,* With friend Billie Jean King in Orlando, September 1997; *LEFT,* Playing in the Orlando benefit.
©Nannette M. Bac

John Jorgensen (left) and Davey Johnstone (top) corner Elton during "Saturday Night's Alright for Fighting" in Ann Arbor, Michigan, April 1998. ©Sharon Kalinoksi, Hercules USA

Swept away. Atlanta, May 1998. ©Lisa Macdonald

Bernie Taupin performs with his own group, Farm Dogs,
in Alexandria, Virginia, June 1998. ©Judith A. McArthur

Taming the eighty-eights from below at Madison Square Garden, October 1998. ©Nannette M. Bac

Elton at the Broadway Cares/Equity Fights AIDS benefit honoring him, April 2000. *ABOVE,* Being manhandled during a rendition of "Diamonds Are a Girl's Best Friend"; *LEFT,* Singing "Somewhere"; *BELOW,* Acknowledging the applause with Nathan Lane (left) and Betty Buckley (right).

Above and left, ©Lynn Sykes; Below, ©Nannette M. Bac

Displaying keyboard prowess and the glint of Versace in Wilkes-Barre, Pennsylvania, April 2000. ©Nannette M. Bac

Elton and Kiki reprise their number 1 of yesteryear, "Don't Go Breaking My Heart," for a wildly enthusiastic audience at Madison Square Garden, October 2000. ©Lori Sears

Elton kindly poses with two fans (the author at left, friend Lori Sears at right) in Atlanta, his U.S. "hometown," December 2000.
©Elizabeth J. Rosenthal

CHAPTER 13

WRITING[1]

(1996–1997)

THE YEAR 1996 WAS ONE ELTON WAS SUPPOSED TO BE TAKING OFF. And it was, relatively speaking. He didn't tour.

But he did write. Some of the music Elton wrote that year was destined to go a long way. Why take time off when there was work to be done? "I'm a very driven person," he'd admitted to Bob Costas the previous fall. "Rock'n'roll per se is a young man's business," he'd continued. "I don't consider myself a rock'n'roll artist. I mean, we play rock'n'roll onstage, [but] I consider myself now a singer-songwriter who plays the piano, which is probably always what I've been."[2]

There were three new songs to write with Tim Rice for the stage version of *The Lion King*, and many more than that for an update of Giuseppe Verdi's nineteenth-century opera *Aïda*, another Disney project slated for Broadway. Elton and Tim were supposed to write all new songs for this modernized *Aïda*; the only relationship the new musical would bear to Verdi's opera was the story line, a love triangle between an Egyptian general, a princess, and an Ethiopian (later, Nubian) slave. Disney gave Elton the project because he hadn't wanted to follow up *The Lion King* with another cartoon. He'd told Disney's executives, "Give me something dangerous."[3] He wanted a challenge, and took to it with relish. Once Rice gave him the lyrics, he wrote nineteen songs in nineteen days.

It was not yet certain which show, the as-yet-unnamed *Aïda* or the Broadway adaptation of *The Lion King*, would open the renovated New Amsterdam Theater on 42nd Street. As it soon became clear that *The Lion King* would do the honors, there was time for a half dozen more songs to be written for the Verdi update, bringing the total to more than two dozen.

Although Elton didn't want to do another Disney cartoon right away, he didn't hesitate to accept Jeffrey Katzenberg's invitation to write songs with Rice for DreamWorks's animated musical, planned for 1999, tentatively titled *El Dorado: City of Gold.* The enterprise would be the musician's first with Katzenberg's partner David Geffen since the 1980s.

There were also nonmusical projects on the agenda during the first half of 1996. A February 22, 1996 news conference highlighted Elton's influence in soccer. As the lifetime president of Watford, he announced Graham Taylor's return. Although Elton was no longer actively involved in the club, he had talked the former manager, responsible for the team's glory days, into renewing his affiliation after eight years away. The team, currently on the bottom of the first division, was in dire need of help. "A lot of dead wood needs to be cleared out and Graham Taylor is the only manager I can think of frightening enough to do that," Elton said. "To be honest, I didn't come to games because it broke my heart. The club had lost its heart and soul and that hurt me a lot."[4]

Taylor had been enjoying time away from the soccer cauldron after being fired by Wolverhampton. He hoped for an executive position with Watford in the future, but would be down in the trenches with the team for the season's remainder. "I would not have come back to Watford Football Club without talking to Elton," Taylor explained. "There is a respect we have for one another."[5] He didn't mention a not yet public fact: A key to his return was Elton's own return. The former Watford chairman was working on a way to reclaim his position.

As usual, charity was also on the agenda. Oscar night fell on Elton's forty-ninth birthday. He celebrated by returning his AIDS Foundation benefit to the Maple Drive Restaurant after one year at the Four Seasons. As in previous years, moviemakers and musicians accepted invitations, including Whoopi Goldberg, Laurence Fishburne, Steven Spielberg, Prince, Stevie Wonder, and Herbie Hancock. At night's end, the Foundation's coffers were $250,000 richer. In another two weeks, Elton was at Sting's annual Rainforest benefit in New York.

As expected, the benefit concert was an eclectic one. Performers included Elton, Sting, Don Henley, James Taylor, Spanish guitarist Paco Peña, the Institutional Radio Choir, Branford Marsalis, flutist Andrea Griminelli, pianist sisters Katia and Marielle Labeque, and one of Elton's new friends, cellist Mstislav Rostropovich. The grand finale brought a surprise guest, Diana Ross, who sang a medley of some of her hits sans the Supremes. Elton, Sting, Don Henley, James Taylor, and unbilled guest Robin Williams then emerged to much audience laughter as the super backing group's latest incarnation, in matching black trousers and t-shirts—and elegant elbow-length gloves. Elton, whose gloves were hot pink (the other men's were white) to complement his tambourine and fluorescent green-rimmed spectacles, retrieved the shy, sixty-nine-year-old Rostropovich from the wings to join them onstage for "You Can't Hurry Love." The cellist eventually relaxed, delightedly singing and dancing arm in arm with England's most daring man of fashion.[6]

For many fans that night, the show's highlight wasn't Elton's love of color or his collegiality, but his unveiling of a song as yet unrecorded and never before heard live in the United States, "Live Like Horses." A "magnificent ballad," reacted *People's* Mitchell Fink, reporting that Elton would be recording the song with Luciano Pavarotti for the tenor's "Bosnian relief" charity. Fink was referring to War Child,[7] for which Pavarotti, himself once a "war child," organized benefit concerts featuring international names. The events raised money for food and medical supplies for Bosnian children, and to finance a children's music center in Mostar.

Pavarotti had invited Elton to perform at his benefit three years in a row, although in previous years the pianist had had to decline due to scheduling conflicts. Now that he had time off, he could accept. He approached Pavarotti, sometimes called the "Voice of God," with a proposal to sing a duet of "Live Like Horses" at the 1996 benefit. "I was delighted when he said yes," Elton recalled. "It's a very classical kind of song with a beautiful melody."[8]

The music of "Live Like Horses" grips the majesty of life's dreams filtered through the most simple of pleasures. A rush of soaring melody brushes the senses like a cool, flower-scented breeze on an early spring day. Visions engage the mind's eye of snow-capped mountains, blossom-filled meadows, anything that encourages feelings of quietude instead of everyday stress.

Bernie's lyrics for the song appear to have been written about himself, an autobiographical story left off *Made in England.* Here, he returns to his aimless boyhood: "I can't control this flesh and blood/that's wrapped around my bones/it moves beneath me like a river/into the great unknown." His fascination with American music propelled his sights beyond the Northern English farm country: "Pried a harp out of the fingers of a renegade/who lived and died the blues." The message he culled from these interests ("There's more ways than one/to regain your senses") brings him to the United States, and the place he would soon call home ("Claimed a spoke in the wheel of the wagon train/on the road to the golden gate/on the flat dry desert I jumped ship").

Elton and Pavarotti recorded their duet during the first week of May, under Chris Thomas's supervision.[9] The pianist also recorded a solo version. Anne Dudley, a newcomer to Elton John sessions, provided orchestrations for both, accompanying Guy Babylon's computer arrangements and backing vocals from the Angel Voices Choir.

Guy's technology doesn't render the song any less organic. One can imagine his computerized heartbeat played by a real instrument, and the freshness of Elton's melody overwhelms the sounds of modernity. Still, the fluid piano arpeggios heard during his live performances, a favorite aspect of "Live Like Horses" for those lucky enough to be in the audience, are missing from the studio recordings.

On June 20, 1996, the Modena, Italy, audience at Parco Novi Sad, site of the fifth War Child benefit, enjoyed a star-studded event, broadcast live on Italian television network RAI UNO. Guests included Eric Clapton, Sheryl Crow, Liza Minnelli, Jon Secada, Zucchero (Italy's answer to Joe Cocker), and Italian rock groups Ligabue and Litfiba. Elton and "Live Like Horses" were pegged to close the show, as an encore.

During Elton's first performance of "Live Like Horses" with Pavarotti that day, the pianist stood in white tails, hair mussed, coat flapping in the wind. As the opera singer took his turn with the chorus in Italian, Elton pretended to conduct the orchestra and the East London Gospel Choir, his dramatic gesticulations sometimes drawing his hands to his heart. He was genuinely moved, as was Pavarotti, who smiled broadly when Elton, in turn, tackled the chorus.

Songs later, the pianist reemerged from backstage in an electric blue suit and yellow turtleneck for "I Guess That's Why They Call It the Blues." This was an important performance, too, because it signaled a different direction for the song. As a remote band played in the background, it became a barrel-house blues examination, which stood out all the more in the absence of Guy's synthesized adaptation of Stevie Wonder's harmonica solo. "Alright!" Elton yelled, just out of microphone range. He knew it was good.[10]

The grand finale immediately followed, with all those performing earlier returning to the stage. Again duetting with Pavarotti, Elton this time remained at his piano, affording "Live Like Horses" the arpeggiated flourishes the song deserved. Clapton noodled on his guitar. The other guests supplemented the choir's accents. Pavarotti delivered the vocal coup de grace.

"IF I COULD ONLY HEAR SOMETHING THAT SOUNDS LIKE THE TRUTH"[11]

SOME FOUR THOUSAND PIECES OF ELTON'S WARDROBE went on sale in Atlanta's Lenox Square shopping mall on June 4, 1996. The men's sportswear department at Neiman-Marcus had been emptied for the occasion. Like the London "'Out' the Closet" sale in December 1994, this one, called "Elton's Closet," also benefited the AIDS Foundation. Boots, hats, bathrobes, all manner of streetwear, and some 1990s Versace stagewear—even the red jacket Elton had worn at the Freddie Mercury benefit—were available at a fraction of their original prices. Only 1970s and 1980s stage costumes that had missed the 1988 Sotheby's call were priced beyond the average consumer's reach. Like the 1994 London sale, this one attracted fans from far and wide.

Soon, the first round of items was gone. But there were twenty more racks of clothing waiting in storage![12] "I buy lots of clothes," Elton said, a major understatement. "I get a lot of clothes given to me. I have a lot of stage clothes. And while it's nice, they just sit there in the garage, sit there in the closet. Now that's stupid. I'd rather see people wearing them and give the money to people who need it."[13] The sale raised half a million dollars.[14]

Even more personal than the opening of his closets to the public was the airing of *Tantrums and Tiaras*, David Furnish's unnervingly honest look at the life, lifestyle, and temperament of his companion, on Britain's ITV a month later. "I don't want any dissection of melodies. I don't want any retrospectives," Elton tells David at the film's start, first broadcast on July 7. "I don't want a documentary to come across as holier than thou. I don't want a sycophantic one. I just want people to see how I am."

Elton had chosen David to do the documentary because of his lover's lifelong ambition to be a filmmaker and because he knew he would feel comfortable if the camera following him was held by the man he loved. What resulted was a film far superior to *Elton John and Bernie Taupin Say Goodbye to Norma Jean and Other Things*, the 1973 Bryan Forbes documentary that had caught Elton everywhere *except* in his most candid moments. The musician in *Goodbye Norma Jean* was funny, fun-loving, and as scarily talented as he was overly modest. But viewers were cut off from the after-hours Elton, the depressed Elton, the crabby Elton. His sexuality was hidden. Reid was just his manager. While the limits of Forbes's film comported with the star's wishes at the time, *Goodbye Norma Jean* simply crumbled under the weight of the new, multidimensional *Tantrums and Tiaras*.

Most of what Furnish filmed in 1995 was left on the cutting-room floor. Bits spared the cold linoleum were pieced together for an hour of revelatory footage. A couple of tantrums made the final cut. One of them, when the musician cursed and stomped because an assistant had driven away with his wardrobe the day the "Believe" video was to be filmed, opens the documentary. "They're fucking loathsome!" Elton shrieks, talking about music videos in general, as creative director Steve Brown tries to calm him.

The other tantrum appears midway through the film. Elton and David are vacationing in the South of France in July 1995. The musician is playing his morning tennis when an uninhibited woman greets his ears with "Yoo hoo!" His privacy violated and his tennis game ruined, he violently hurls his racket to the pavement and storms back to the hotel suite. In the next scene, they are in the suite. Unsuccessfully holding back tears, the musician is on the telephone, trying to arrange the earliest possible flight back to England. "I have had it here," he murmurs when he gets off the phone, stalking into a separate room and slamming the door behind him.

Tantrums and Tiaras impresses the viewer with the uneasiness of Elton's sometimes desperate quest for a normal existence. The "tiaras" aspect of the film highlights the duality of the musician's life. Taking David on a tour of his vacation closet in France, he shows viewers rack after rack of suits, jackets, silk shirts, about two dozen pairs of shoes, countless pairs of eyeglasses ("all prescription, of course") organized by the color of their frames, and two tiaras. "You never know when you're going to be invited to something formal," Elton explains about the tiaras. The sheer volume of things in this closet shows his mixed feelings about being an extremely busy star. When he isn't home, he takes his home with him, he says, to keep "sane."

Also graphically evident is the frantic pace of the star's life. Sharp editing has viewers breathlessly following him from interview to interview for *Made in*

England—now in France, then in Spain, now back to England. He meets the press in Russia. He rushes around Japan. He meets fans. He hurriedly shops for photography (a new passion), clothing (especially Versace), hats (even women's hats). He makes speeches about AIDS. He performs a lot, even when it seems life-threatening, such as when he lost his breath in Bogotá.

With all the activity, it is a good thing Elton can write the music for a song in only fifteen minutes. In the film, he meets singer Lulu at AIR Studios in Hampstead, where she excitedly hands him lyrics. "No one does this but you!" she squeals. At four o'clock in the afternoon, he sits at an electric piano. At 4:15, the song, a muscular ballad, is mostly done. By 4:30, Elton and a still ecstatic Lulu are singing the new song in an impromptu duet. "Tea break!" Elton announces when they finish.

There are plenty of funny moments in the film. Backstage at the 1995 Brit Awards, the pianist teases Madonna by unbuttoning the top of his coveralls to display the nipples on his waxed chest, recalling one of her notorious fashion moments when she wore a gown with her breasts completely exposed.

There are also serious and sad moments. Elton seeing his Nan for the last time before his flight to the United States for the Oscars. Elton and his mother, who weeps at memories of his drug dependency. Elton's therapist, Beauchamp "Beechy" Colclough, who describes his patient's obsessive-compulsive behavior and skepticism at the level of his public adulation. Elton reflecting on the death of a young member of his entourage from AIDS, saying he knew "too fucking many" people who had died from the disease. Elton expressing his thoughts on sexual openness: "Living a lie is not worth it. You only get one attempt on this earth. It's far better to be yourself. If others don't like it, tough shit."

Beechy Colclough, brutally honest about his patient in the film, gave the finished product a good review—in *The Sun,* no less. He was proud of Elton. "How many other stars of his caliber would expose themselves to such scrutiny?" Colclough asked. "Elton hasn't just stopped drinking and thought that's it. He's continually working at it."[15]

"YOU COULD LOOK AT ME IN THE SCHEME OF THINGS"[16]

BERNIE'S LATEST PROJECT, after a 1987 solo outing called *Tribe,* was Farm Dogs, a real band, and their album debut, *Last Stand in Open Country.* It wasn't enough that he was already a cowboy of sorts in the Santa Ynez Valley. "I write songs [for Farm Dogs] about desert nights and horses and guns because I'm around them," he said. "I spend most of my life on a horse. Elton doesn't. He spends most of his life in designer clothes." Bernie knew Elton had passed the fanciful *Tumbleweed Connection* days. The musician was well beyond the limits of "tabacky," warm leather, and smoking metal, and had long since evolved into the musical reference point he had always wanted to become. "He wouldn't feel honest doing it [a *Tumbleweed*-type album], because his personality has developed into something larger than life," Bernie said.[17]

The larger-than-life star's "Live Like Horses" sessions also yielded two songs for the September 24, 1996 North American *Love Songs* release, "You Can Make History (Young Again)" and "No Valentines."

"You Can Make History" seems like a love song, sung by someone resisting the specter of aging, whose love interest makes him or her feel young again. The protagonist may also be viewed as Elton singing about himself to his audience. The musician's career fluctuations had often been undetectable to American popular music watchers, who either saw him as never having lost the popularity of his youth, or as having never quite regained it. Tied to this dichotomy were questions: Was his music still worth buying? Were his shows still worth going to? Millions of people were increasingly answering "yes" to both, but an undercurrent of doubt still persisted. "You Can Make History" was a way of telling the doubters that, though times had changed, he was still the same man, the same musician, the same songwriter. If people wanted to, they could look at his career as a continuum of accomplishments and rethink their misconceptions about the permanency of his stardom. As Bernie wrote: "You could look at me in the scheme of things."

Elton's music caters to the love angle of "You Can Make History." In a strong whisper, he sings words into the ear of a lover that are only for him to hear. The record buyer feels like an eavesdropper. The overall sound, however, seems processed. There are too many layers between the lovers' intimacy and what the outside world hears. Multiple strata unnecessarily fatten Elton's vocal, and his piano is absent. He may have succeeded in evoking the cloudiness of the Stylistics' sound,[18] particularly in John Jorgenson's sitar opening, but the song would have benefited from the simpler approach heard in a rough mix obtained by some American radio stations and record collectors in the fall. In this, only some of Guy's synthesized strings and none of the drum loops Thomas added are audible. The piano underpinning, which provides the sitar outlines, slows the tempo but makes it more suitable for a scene between lovers. Elton's vocal is untouched, except for the occasional interjection of a harmony fragment. Even better than the rough mix were Elton's solo interpretations of the song on the *Rosie O'Donnell Show* and *Late Night with Conan O'Brien* in November, in which the Stylistics' influence was gone but references to "Sacrifice" and "You Gotta Love Someone" crept into the piano arrangement.

The other new *Love Songs* track, "No Valentines," examines the heartbreak of an ended love affair: "No more Valentines day/no more Christmas cards/I've thrown 'em all away/no more sequined stars."

None of the lines in "No Valentines" are as steeped in imagery as those in "You Can Make History," which boasts verses about encroaching age like, "I can feel the time closing in/I can feel the years crawling through my skin/and if I doubt myself/I can count on the rain/to cover the tears of this aging game." What "No Valentines" lacks in verbal imagination, however, it makes up for in a shifting melody, sporting four separate progressions in the first verse alone. Thus, it is a more exciting song—despite Bernie's pessimistic, lovelorn line, "No reason to get excited." The active musculature of Elton's voice seems inconsistent with the vulnerability of the lovelorn character until one realizes that his singing represents a loud, impassioned mourning. The loneliness absent from his vocal takes up residency in his synthesizer solo, which mimics a French horn.

MCA released the North American edition of *Love Songs*, with little fanfare, to fulfill Elton's obligations for one last MCA album. In some deference to regional preferences, five songs from the overseas version—"I Guess That's Why They Call It the Blues," "Nikita," "True Love," "Song for Guy," and the moderate 1995 British hit, "Please"—were replaced with the two new songs, plus "Believe." The North American compilation also passed over the 1973 version of "Candle in the Wind" in favor of the live recording from 1986.

On October 12, 1996, *Long Songs* debuted at number 24 on the *Billboard* 200. Although it would enjoy a flurry of interest following some television appearances, two months into sales the album had sold only just over two hundred thousand copies.[19] By mid-December, though, it was certified gold, and by mid-April 1997, MCA had shipped enough copies for it to go platinum.

Minimal Top 40 airplay for the single "You Can Make History" did little to help; the song peaked at number 70 on the Hot 100. For now, *Billboard* columnist Melinda Newman seemed right about her year-old observation that solo male artists were having trouble getting Top 40 airplay vis-à-vis their female counterparts, even if, back when she'd noted this phenomenon, Elton was having Top 40 success with "Blessed"—though singers like Joshua Kadison, Michael Bolton, and Sting were getting most of their airplay on Adult Contemporary stations. Now, in 1996, it seemed that Elton's latest song was following suit. "I don't know if some great music industry cabal had a secret meeting and decided that solo men aren't hip anymore," Newman had wondered.[20]

It was a little different overseas. In December, the Elton/Pavarotti duet, "Live Like Horses," reached number 9 in Britain. The song had a lot going for it, not the least of which was a high profile, live performance by its two singers on the *National Lottery* variety program on November 30, and division of the single's proceeds between the AIDS Foundation and Pavarotti's charity.

Even in this less active year, in which his music wasn't soaring on the charts, Elton was still collecting trophies. For the second year in a row, he was ASCAP's songwriter of the year, on the strength of American airplay for "Believe," "Blessed," and "Made in England." A similar BMI/PRS dinner honored him for "Daniel," which had reached a landmark number of performances in the United States, and also awarded him humanitarian of the year accolades. On November 23, in honor of his sexual openness, he received the Rand Schrader Distinguished Achievement award from the Los Angeles Gay & Lesbian Center at its twenty-fifth anniversary ball. The week of the ball, Tom McCormick, the coexecutive producer of the Gay/Lesbian American Music Awards, lauded Elton's public candor in a letter to *Billboard* magazine: "While artists such as Melissa Etheridge and Elton John do not sing specifically of gay themes, their choice to be 'out' professionally has far-reaching positive effects that are arguably as important as the contributions of more politically driven artists."[21]

Elton's fashion sense was lauded in October at the otherwise inconsequential VH1 Fashion Awards, where he was selected by viewers as most fashionable artist. His friend Gianni Versace gave him the biggest cheer in the crowd as he walked onstage to receive his award. Dressed in a plush quilted suit and red, rectangular glasses, he said, "For me, fashion has always been about Dennis Rodman, people who like to take a chance," he told the audience, his voice rising. "It's not about shops that look like hospitals full of beige suits. It's about people who've got the *balls* to make a difference!"[22]

The musician gave a private concert that week in New York for Versace and partygoers like actress Elizabeth Hurley, television journalists Matt Lauer and Forrest Sawyer, and model Naomi Campbell. The concert was held at Versace's midtown Manhattan townhouse, where Elton and David were guests. Such was the closeness between Elton and Versace (indeed, Elton and David were wont to vacation with Versace and the designer's lover, Antonio D'Amico), that Elton had his own suite. It featured a painted ceiling imported from Italy and wall murals by Versace's friend, Julian Schnabel.

Throughout the year, Elton continued to work with his AIDS Foundation. There was now an MBNA Visa card linked with it; Lalique had designed and begun marketing a crystal cherub with twenty-four-karat gold enamel to benefit the foundation (a singing angel would follow by March 1997); and there were a line of Boy London watches with Elton's engraved autograph, and a new series of Oliver Peoples eyewear. The charitably minded could enjoy live entertainment, too. Elton and Billie Jean hosted the fourth annual Smash Hits in September, this time at the Houston Summit. And in commemoration of World AIDS Day on December 1, the musician donated nearly $170,000 to a new AIDS clinic in Britain. He urged people to remember that safe sex was crucial to fighting AIDS. "There is no cure for AIDS and there is a danger that people believe there is a cure," he warned.[23]

For pure drama, no AIDS event of 1996 matched opera star Jessye Norman's benefit at Riverside Church, in New York City. The beneficiary, the Balm in Gilead, Inc., worked to spread AIDS awareness in African-American churches and mosques. Fittingly, the benefit was conducted like a nondenominational church service. Every performer, from actress Anna Deavere Smith to choreographer Bill T. Jones, had a clear role to play in the service, which began with an operatic celebration of that "ol' camp meetin' in the promised land." Later, Elton sang and accompanied himself on "Border Song" with the Opera Ebony, a treat in light of the few times he'd performed this gospel reflection live since the 1970s.

The pianist was the only Briton, and the only white person, to perform at the talent-heavy event. Before he took a spot behind his piano, Whoopi Goldberg introduced him: "Although he was not raised in a black church," she said, as many in the interracial audience chuckled, "there are questions about that. And I'd like to investigate." Why? Because of what his music revealed. "He carries within him," she declared, "not just the spirit of people, but the spirit of black people and our music."[24]

"I CAN WATCH THE WEEKS SWEEPING BY"[25]

THE BEGINNING OF 1997 offered no inkling of the unusual. Elton planned to record another album and embark on another concert tour in the fall. The only outstanding milestone was his impending fiftieth birthday, which he expected to celebrate with appropriate, over-the-top gusto.

Billboard chart watchers wondered whether Elton could keep his Top 40 streak alive. In January 1996, "Blessed" had reentered the Top 40, extending his string of Top 40 hits to at least one a year for twenty-seven consecutive years. Could he do it for a twenty-eighth? *Billboard*'s Fred Bronson was sanguine in a February 8, 1997 column: "[E]ven though 'You Can Make History (Young Again)' peaked at No. 70 in November 1996, Elton has the rest of 1997 to extend his unprecedented Top 40 streak to a twenty-eighth year."[26]

Elton "soldiered on," as he would have put it, doing what he liked and what had meaning for him. For one thing, he proved he wasn't just an "out" gay male star whose art and persona were otherwise "straight." In January he came out as never before, when newspapers and magazines all over the world printed photos from a Richard Avedon photo session, shot in late 1996, that featured Elton in drag, modeling a new Versace evening dress made of metal mesh and lace. In eyeliner and gelled hair weave, Elton was demure in some poses, aggressive in others. He didn't make a pretty picture, but that wasn't his intention.

On February 8, Elton hosted and performed at his Foundation's biannual dinner, live auction, and concert, held at New York's Waldorf-Astoria. In return for his participation in the War Child and Balm in Gilead fund-raisers, both Pavarotti and Jessye Norman were on hand to sing opera, with and without their host. Elton also put on a freshly tailored solo show during the concert segment. That night, more than one million dollars were raised, bringing the total collected for the Foundation since its inception in 1992 to an astounding fourteen million.

Also in February, Elton's name fell into the center of an unlikely controversy, leading to the cancellation of a February 18 AIDS Foundation fund-raising party to launch Gianni Versace's new book, *Rock and Royalty*. Princess Diana, friend to both

Elton and Versace, had written a foreword for the book—upon assurances that the book would contain nothing to cause "offence"—and had agreed to appear at the launch party. There was talk that she would auction some of her dresses at the function. But on the eve of the book's release, Diana finally saw its contents, in which well-proportioned, skimpily clad men faced stiff portraits of members of the Royal Family (there were also several camp shots of Elton, fully dressed in neon vinyl). The portraits of barely clothed men were similar to those appearing in Versace's 1996 book, *Men Without Ties*, which Diana might have expected more of in the new book. But the princess issued a formal statement pulling her support from the project: "I am extremely concerned that the book may cause offence to the Royal Family. For this reason I have asked for my foreword to be withdrawn and I will now not attend the dinner intended to mark the book's launch."[27]

Versace canceled the party to "protect Diana," giving the money he would have spent on it to the AIDS Foundation. A chill beset the friendship of the princess and the pianist. Later, Elton wrote to Diana, saying he was sorry about the course their relationship had taken. He received a formal reply instructing him to send correspondence through Buckingham Palace.[28] After all they had shared over the years—the enjoyment of "dishing," the serious reflections on their respective bouts with bulimia, and their joint interest in fighting AIDS—they were at an impasse.

For now, Elton turned to other fund-raisers to make up for the loss of the canceled *Rock and Royalty* party. At his fifth annual Oscar night party on March 24, actors and makers of some of the year's best independent films, including *Shine* and *Fargo*, were on hand. Elton posed for pictures with everyone from Jonathan Lipnicki, child star of *Jerry Maguire*, to Gillian Helfgott, wife of the inspiration for *Shine*, David Helfgott. And when the clock struck midnight, he was fifty.

But Elton wasn't ready to celebrate yet. On March 27, he surprised Mstislav Rostropovich at a seventieth birthday extravaganza for the cellist held at the Théâtre des Champs-Élysées in Paris. Some of the world's most renowned classical musicians were there to pay tribute, but it was Elton's unbilled appearance to sing "Happy Birthday" that brought tears to Rostropovich's eyes.[29]

That week, the pianist joined the ranks of Franz Liszt and Felix Mendelssohn in receiving honorary membership in the Royal Academy of Music, the school he attended as a boy. "When I went there as a little boy . . . , I was so afraid of going," he reminisced months later. "You walked into the building and there was the smell of fear, and it was very intimidating." Now, it was different, he said. The Academy offered classes in songwriting. Students could join rock bands.[30]

The Academy's current principal, Dr. Curtis Price, explained Elton's honor. "Elton was a prodigiously gifted child. Had he chosen to, he would certainly have progressed to our senior academy." Honorary membership was the Academy's "highest accolade."[31]

CHAPTER 14

HERE'S TO
THE NEXT
TIME[1]

(1997–1998)

"**I**F PUNK HAD BEEN AROUND WHEN I had started off, I would have had to be taken around in a furniture lorry," Elton said in 1990. "My hair would have been nine foot tall."[2]

When Elton and David Furnish arrived in a van at the Hammersmith Palais in London on the evening of April 6 to celebrate his fiftieth, they looked like the Sun King and his courtier. Elton astonished onlookers in a three-foot-high silver wig splashed in jewels, sequins, and glitter and topped with a silvery eighteenth-century Spanish galleon in miniature. His fifteen-foot train of ostrich feathers was carefully toted by two male "servants," whose slight garb more closely resembled that of ancient Greece than Louis XIV-era France. Underneath was a costume that matched David's—a square-cut coat covered in diamanté and lace, complemented by shimmering breeches, stockings, and silver shoes with oversized buckles. The two were lowered onto the pavement via a hydraulic platform, camera shutters snapping, flashes firing.

Despite this getup, nowadays Elton's dress tended to be interesting, sometimes daring, occasionally sensible, but seldom shocking. Perhaps the passage of time had made him wary of outrageousness. Yet he still had a craving for a flamboyant explosion of color and light—and girth—that had to be satisfied now and then. He'd worn a similarly styled outfit at his forty-seventh birthday party, but the half-century mark begged for more.

As Elton turned fifty, the pundits turned to the seeming absurdity of over-fifty musicians continuing to perform and write rock music. One commentator in the London *Sunday Mirror* warned that Elton would be "unwise" to sing "Saturday Night's Alright" at his party, since "there's nothing the cynics like more than the incongruity of rebel rousing lyrics and paunches and balding pates."[3] The likelihood that Elton would sing at his party was dim. And regardless, Elton no longer considered himself a rocker, even if he played (and wrote) some rock music. He had an advantage over many other rock front men, like Mick Jagger and Rod Stewart, who strutted their stuff before audiences no matter what they looked like. Elton, who at twenty-three had wanted to have Jimi Hendrix's mobility even while playing the piano (thereby precipitating his use of the instrument as a prop for handstands), was now grateful that he could sit behind the eighty-eights instead of trying to act like a boy.

The birthday party was planned by Bob Halley, who had kept as many of the details a secret from his employer as possible.[4] It hadn't been easy. Weeks before the affair, it was leaked that six hundred people from all over the world had received invitations embossed with a gold crest and a thoughtful motto, "Eltono Es Bueno." It was reported that guests were being asked to dress up. Music for dancing would be provided by Boy George as disc jockey. Cabaret acts and a ballroom dancing troupe from South Wales were on the bill. Apart from these leaks, Australian Prime Minister John Howard announced he would be sending an emissary to present Elton with a uniquely Australian gift at taxpayers' expense.[5]

The van that transported the heavily clothed musician doubled as a drawing room, carpeted and furnished with thrones, paintings, mirrors, and a mock fireplace. Once inside the Hammersmith Palais, Elton and David found the nightclub transformed into an Italian garden. Fountains, Roman busts, ice sculptures, and floral arrangements were in abundance, tables hidden under faux leopard- and giraffe-skin cloths. While they were still dressing back at their London home, representatives of *The Sun* had arrived, also dressed in period costumes, to present a birthday cake. How times had changed!

Many friends of longer standing awaited the guest of honor at the Palais. Some, like REM's Michael Stipe, came in street clothes. Bryan Forbes and Nanette Newman wore smart attire, Forbes in black tie, Newman in a bright red gown with matching sash in her hair. Billy Joel appeared in a staid American military officer's uniform. Others dressed more imaginatively. David Frost was the Phantom of the Opera, Andrew Lloyd Webber a soccer player, the Viscount Linley the Cowardly Lion, designer Jean-Paul Gaultier a suggestively dressed French maid. Shirley Bassey dressed as Cleopatra, Paul Young a swashbuckler. Molly Meldrum was a sorceress or fairy godmother, depending on one's perspective. Graham Taylor and his wife were the King and Queen of Hearts. Laurence Fishburne was an Arab sheik, Chris Rea a bishop with enhanced chest nipples, Lulu a 1920s vamp, John Reid a swan. Elton's mother was the Queen of England, his stepfather the Duke of Edinburgh.

There were superheroes, a pope, a Michael Jackson impersonator accompanied by a human Bubbles the chimp. And then there was Elton who, to enjoy the festivities, had discarded his ostrich train and galleon-bearing wig, but still struck a regal figure as he observed one of the biggest surprises of the night, a multitiered birthday cake on a Styrofoam swan lit by electric candles. He cut the confection with a sword and saluted his mother: "I am an old queen and I have been difficult to live with, but I have to say that I have had a brilliant upbringing."[6] Later, Billy Joel summed up the evening: "It was pretty wild in there . . . like being back in the Sixties again."[7]

BBC news presenter Jon Snow lauded the fact that Baby Boomer Elton could celebrate his fiftieth birthday in such style. Snow saw the Palais party as evidence that the day's middle-aged adults were much younger at heart than their parents had been.[8] Elton would be the first to agree with this statement. As he'd been asserting for years, through lifetime achievement recognition and the pursed eyes of skeptics who believed his time had passed, "There's a lot more life in the old girl yet."

"LET THE PEOPLE KNOW YOU GOT WHAT YOU NEED"[9]

IN APRIL, it was announced that Elton was returning as chairman of Watford. Instead of being majority owner and single-handedly keeping the team's finances afloat, Elton bought Watford back from Jack Petchey with the help of a consortium of businessmen. Coincidentally, a short time later a comedy opened at the Palace Theatre in Watford called *Elton John's Glasses.* The main character, Bill, was still obsessed with Watford's loss to Everton at the 1984 FA Cup Final. He was certain Everton had won because Watford's goalie had been distracted by the sunny glint of the glasses Elton was wearing that day, and spent his life replaying a videotape of the unfortunate game.

Also coincidental was Elton's recent recording of "Abide with Me," the hymn that had made him cry at that FA Cup Final, for the Rainforest Foundation's first album, *Carnival!.* The album featured an interpretation of the Saint-Saëns composition *Le Carnaval des Animaux* by Katia and Marielle Labeque, as well as other music that had meant something to the album's guest artists as children. "As a kid growing up and loving football, every year I would watch the FA Cup Final and everyone would sing 'Abide with Me' before the teams came out," Elton said in the liner notes.

He also sang "Abide with Me" at the April 30 Rainforest benefit in New York, a concert that was the *Carnival!* album come to life. On CD, he was backed by the Black Dyke Mills Brass Band; at Carnegie Hall, it was the Salvation Army Band, which paraded through the hall's aisles in red uniforms brilliant enough for Elton's wardrobe. But the show wasn't as solemn as one would have expected from this song, or from *Carnival!* selections like "If I Loved You" and "All through the Night," sung by Bonnie Raitt and Shawn Colvin, respectively. Elton also sang the Temptations' "My Girl," following it with Mary Wells's "My Guy," drawing much laughter as he declared his allegiance in Mae West fashion to the man of his dreams.

Ten days later, Elton was in Melbourne, Australia, with Billy Joel, helping to open the multipurpose Crown World of Entertainment center. They each received one million dollars (Australian) to appear there in shows on May 9 and 10 before an invitation-only audience. While in town, they filmed a television interview with

Richard Wilkins, showering each other with compliments. "He'll do things with his left hand, these bass substitutions, which I never thought of," said Billy of Elton, calling his colleague's left-hand playing "cool." Elton replied that Billy was an "excellent" musician who challenged him. "If you play with someone who's substandard, you're on cruise control." Peering into television cameras, the two let viewers know they would be back next year for a major Australian tour.[10]

"I'LL SHOW YOU WHERE THE BEST OF ME HAS BEEN"[11]

WHY ANOTHER ALBUM? asked *Le Figaro* reporter François Délétraz not long after *The Big Picture*, Elton's twenty-fifth album of original material, was completed. Down on the French Riviera, musician and writer were sitting on a balcony of Elton's new *palais Niçoise*, which combined modernity with classicism. "Simply because I love to write," Elton answered. "It's a personal need to write songs, record them and play them in public."[12]

It wasn't enough that he had written about two dozen songs for the upcoming musical based on *Aïda*, seven songs (so far) for the DreamWorks *El Dorado* project, or three additional ones for Broadway's *The Lion King*. "I'm a prolific kind of guy," Elton immodestly proclaimed.[13] The side projects had made up for the relative deficiency in the number of his studio albums in the 1990s, which were piling up at a slower rate than in the 1980s—which even then had been only about half his output in the 1970s. But no matter how Elton's productivity was evaluated, it was substantial, especially in comparison to most of his contemporaries. Billy Joel's last album had come out in 1993; the album before that, 1989. Before 1996, Lionel Richie hadn't put out an album of new material in ten years. Paul Simon hadn't had one since 1990 (although he was then working on his Broadway musical-in-development, *The Capeman*). Eric Clapton had released no regular studio album since 1989.

Sessions for Elton's new album, at Townhouse Studios in London, were split up as they had been in 1994 when he did *Made in England*. One session yielded four songs by mid-February 1997. He resumed recording in spring 1997, after various events, like the Oscar night party and the Rainforest benefit, were out of the way. Except for Ray Cooper, the whole band was back—including the recovered Bob Birch and relative newcomer John Jorgenson. Paul Carrack and the East London Gospel Choir made guest appearances. Replacing Paul Buckmaster were Guy Babylon and Anne Dudley. Chris Thomas returned as producer.

Despite what some might have thought of his work with Greg Penny on *Made in England*, Elton had never said his professional relationship with Thomas was over. He admired Thomas's wide range of musical tastes. The producer could coax an album out of the group Pulp, or the Pretenders, or INXS, or Paul McCartney, or Roxy Music. And each of those albums would sound different. "He brings that experience, listening to other sounds and listening to how other musicians play things,"

Elton said admiringly. He also valued Thomas's facility with drum loops and programming, important elements in the recording process to the pianist, even if he had mostly abandoned these for *Made in England*. Elton asserted, "You have to *acknowledge* technology. It can be very exciting and it can be very helpful. So he [Thomas] manages to merge the actual ambient, live playing with the electronic side of things."[14]

What kind of album would this be? Elton wasn't going to copy the styles of young acts he liked—the rock groups Oasis and Blur, or electronica proponents the Chemical Brothers, the Prodigy, and Underworld. Of electronica, he effused, "It's the sound that will take us into the next millennium. That's what excites me."[15] But Elton was just as likely to listen to Billie Holiday, and his music was more likely to be closer to the songs she sang sixty years ago than to the Prodigy's songs. Moreover, Elton's songwriting method had always been to make music that came naturally. His writing tended to draw inspiration from older, grounded sources, while referring to modern influences that complemented his sense of melody. When he didn't follow that calling, he came out with mistakes like *Victim of Love*.

A clue to Elton's direction could be found in the two new songs he'd written for the North American *Love Songs*. Bernie liked the idea of an album of new love songs—standards, like the ones Frank Sinatra and Tony Bennett sang. "I love that shit," he rhapsodized.[16]

"When I got the first batch of lyrics to this album and I went into the studio . . . I looked at the lyrics and picked the ones I liked," Elton remembered, but it seemed that almost none of the lyrics would work as up-tempo songs. This worried him. "I talked to my producer, Chris Thomas, and asked him, 'Do you think that matters?'" the pianist recalled. "He said that as long as the songs are good, it doesn't matter at all."[17] Indeed, the songs' mostly slow tempos have little bearing on their levels of excitement and ingenuity; tempo has never been the defining quality of Elton's music. Neither is *The Big Picture* composed of Sinatra/Bennett standards, as Bernie had envisioned, although most tracks are love songs. "I chose the songs lyrically basically because they're mostly about relationships," Elton explained. "Some of these relationships are good, some are rocky, some are—you know—questionable. But I think people like any kind of song like that, and they are easy to sing."[18]

Rather than echo the standards, the love songs on *The Big Picture* follow in the footsteps of earlier Elton John progeny by breaking stimulating new ground in the wake of older accomplishments, as had *Goodbye Yellow Brick Road* and *Blue Moves*. But *The Big Picture* is more unified in concept and sound than those albums, with mood-shifting tunes of deception, anxiety, lovesickness, and sexual passion that can as easily make the listener white with fear as red with lust (or blue with pain).

Initially, Elton thought the song order on *The Big Picture*, chosen, as always, by the producer, was poor, fretting that "Long Way from Happiness" shouldn't come first. Eventually, he came to accept the song sequence, which he concluded gave the album the "full" sound he wanted.[19] A preliminary hearing does give the impression that the first three songs are too slow and introspective to engage the listener's interest in the remaining eight songs. But their slow tempo is only one quality of many that those tracks possess. They are otherwise markedly different.

"Long Way from Happiness" had a more difficult birth than the usual Elton John song, and provides a good example of Elton and Bernie's consultative process, which they were now proudly describing in interviews. They still wrote in separate rooms, but Elton would now ask him what he thought of a just-written song. Elton was also more likely to ask for a lyric rewrite than just delete lines that he didn't like or that made the song too long. He explained, "I had the verse written. I couldn't get a melody 'round the chorus. It was too long and kind of uneven, so I rang Bernie up and said, 'Listen, I've got a great verse. I need you to rewrite the chorus more simply,' which he did. As soon as he did, the song fell into place."[20]

The result is a composition that evokes the piano-painted, spirit-enveloping characteristics of "Blessed" and "Blue Avenue," and reaches toward unknown boundaries of reality like a floating spacecraft. Bernie's lyrics are the words of a kind soul obliged to mop up the distress in which a friend wallows, in the wake of yet another failed relationship. The song unites a deliberate drum loop, a breathy synthesizer pattern, a Spanish guitar (which, in its staccato-stumped fluidity, could be a "Blue Avenue" outtake), clumps of nervous, teardrop-laden piano notes, and a melody that alternates between miserable (distressed friend) and optimistic (encouraging friend). Elongated phrases, especially Elton's utterance of the song's title in the rewritten, simpler chorus, lends "Long Way from Happiness" an aural distance. The melody thus sounds like the friend, who, in ruminating over the latest doomed love affair, is suspended, far from tranquility, on the fragile limb of a disappointing body of relationships.

"Live Like Horses" is the second track on *The Big Picture* and the only non-relationship song, as well as the only *Made in England* leftover. Why was it included? Elton noticed his fans' passion for the song, both before and after he'd turned it into a single in 1996. "I got fans with placards [at concerts] saying, 'Please play "Live Like Horses."' . . . Fans had written to me saying, 'Please put it on the [next] album.'"[21] Putting it after "Long Way from Happiness" makes for odd pacing, the wide-open sound of freedom in "Live Like Horses" posing a distinct contrast to the seclusion of the love-ravaged friend in the other song.

"The End Will Come," the third track, evokes the nagging feeling a couple detects as they embark on their journey of love. One half of the couple spends the song attempting to refute a prediction of their relationship's demise ("And so they say, the end will come for us/and so the world slows down to let us off/just hang it up and let it go, accept it if I must/but I don't believe, I don't believe that the end will come for us").

"The End Will Come" is the first of several songs on *The Big Picture* to herald a complete departure from the musical forms Elton had nurtured for three decades. While its pace is deliberate, like "Long Way from Happiness" and "Live Like Horses," its apocalyptic tones are what distinguish the song. Initially, one is misled to think "The End Will Come" is Beatles influenced, because of the Lennon-esque echo treatment Thomas administered to Elton's singing for the first two verses. But even during those verses, the melody's restlessness sounds less Lennon-esque and more like Elton John tweaking unfamiliar chord changes into fearful configurations, as John Jorgenson is heard on faint, guitar brushstrokes. The chorus is the real surprise, and assures the song's place in a rare musical slot: jazz-soaked folk. A choppy, near-linear melody descends into a dark abyss of portentous strings where the love, so fiercely protected by the song's couple, seems to disappear. A piano interlude, with responsive commentary by Davey's guitar, is more neurotic than the piano notes winding through "Long Way from Happiness." Elton's chords in "The End Will Come" sport tics of nervous insecurity, as if to say, "They say the end will come. They couldn't be right, could they?"

The fourth track, "If the River Can Bend," expresses two major thoughts. One is a testament to the faithfulness of lovers through thick, thin, and the winding paths of fate. Bernie writes: "Come and embrace the struggle/but win or lose we live here/build a new beginning on an old rock/breathe deep of the sweet fresh air." Elton said the song is "about all the possibilities if you're willing to change. Never give up, there's always hope. And there's so much more to do. But you have to be true to yourself, because you're creating your own future."[22]

The other major thought, not acknowledged by Elton, is an allusion to the John/Taupin songwriting partnership through a reference to 1973's "Harmony": "If the river can bend/I'll find you waiting/home at last from the wild sea/all the twists and turns/we've made together/all the boats you rocked/with your harmony." For *Goodbye Yellow Brick Road*'s "Harmony," Bernie had written: "Harmony and me/we're pretty good company,/looking for an island/in our boat upon the sea."

"Harmony" can be read as the story of Elton's courtship with melody. With "If the River Can Bend," the story in "Harmony" broadens to embrace the enduring artistic union between Elton and Bernie ("All the boats you rocked/with your harmony"), just as *Made in England*'s "Please" served as a postscript to *21 at 33*'s "Two Rooms at the End of the World." Unlike "Please," however, "If the River Can Bend" doesn't plead for fidelity. The song assumes it and is certain it will continue.

"If the River Can Bend" is the first up-tempo song on *The Big Picture*, its rock gospel signifying a get-up-and-testify marriage between Elton's soul-enriching duet with Little Richard, "The Power," and the spiritual raving of *Blue Moves*'s "Bite Your Lip." From the opening notes, in which Elton's monosyllabic excitations hang in the air and Bob Birch's bass calmly foreshadows the blood-pumping inspiration to come, the song tingles with a tension that frequently bursts into simple explosions. A thrilling, full band effort, "If the River Can Bend" frees the listener from complacency, so he or she can embrace the powerful sparks with which the senses are showered. The danceable string arrangement, the happy voices of the East London Gospel Choir, and John Jorgenson's wincing guitar all add zest to Elton's exuberant melody, a forward-looking, brave exercise in attitude and nonspecific faith.

The album moves from the bravery that unity and loyalty produce, to rejection. In "Love's Got a Lot to Answer For," Bernie remembers what it was like to be out of love and rejected by romance. The protagonist wanders the streets on a cold night to rue the day he (or she) entered into a relationship that has left him (or her) achingly alone. "Is loneliness the same as being free?" the protagonist asks, concluding: "Freedom's like the stars in the sky/alone and cold and burning/each one keeps its distance/if only we were stars you and I."

Beginning like a hymn with thoughtfully apportioned arpeggiated piano patterns, "Love's Got a Lot" proceeds carefully to the doleful first part of a three-part melody. This is one of four songs on the album to boast such an abundance of tunefulness, making *The Big Picture* one of Elton's few albums dominated by multi-part melodies. Each submelody in "Love's Got a Lot" contains numerous melodic progressions, each of which takes the listener through several dimensions of lovelorn despair in the modest span of six lines, before effortlessly segueing to the next verse and a new set of dimensions. Elton adds a fourth melody with his organ solo, dissimilar from the rest except for its tempo and mood. Superimposed over the ever-changing musical focus of the song is an evocative vocal, in which Elton sounds extremely sorry for himself, much as he did in "Sorry Seems to Be the Hardest Word." But the self-pity in "Love's Got a Lot" isn't drawn from the falsetto, so common in his 1970s recordings. It comes from the breadth and depth of his singing.

The next song, "Something About the Way You Look Tonight," is more than just a ballad, blurring the line between the softness of balladry and the physicality of rock. The music suggests that love is in the air, purposely attaching itself to the two people involved, and that sex between them is just around the corner—sex imbued with love, of course.

Bernie's lyrics express this love, but by themselves are surprisingly dull, as if he'd tried too hard to write the kind of love song to which most people are accustomed. There are few twinges of imagery. The love interest has saved the protagonist from "feeling like a cloud across the sun" by lighting "up every second of the day." Then the words degenerate into a paraphrase of ordinary words of love, as heard in the 1970s Clapton prom song "Wonderful Tonight" and the cloying 1980s Chris de Burgh ballad "Lady in Red."

Elton rescues the banality from itself and turns "Something About the Way" into a love epic. The song's buildup serves as foreplay for the love-struck couple, aided by many stirring elements, which, taken together, make it unlike anything else Elton has written. There are the strategically placed synthesized horn decrescendoes, as dreamy as their slower soul mates on "Goodbye Yellow Brick Road" and as instilled with rhythm and blues as the "white soul" of *Sleeping with the Past*; the gospel-inspired note bundles that tickle the libido, outlined by the equally gospel-inspired backing vocals of guests Carol Kenyon and Jackie Dawes; and Davey's elated guitar solo. The most sensual and important of the song's components are the melodic waves heralding the couple's promising infatuation and sexual arousal, which buoy otherwise unremarkable phrases such as "I can't explain" and "I can't describe. . . ."

The song following "Something About the Way" is the title track, which, far from expressing the certainty of true love, has the protagonist asking the monumental question, "Am I in your future?" Bernie's imagination is revived as he uses the movies as metaphor for eternal fidelity and togetherness. By contrast, in 1973's "I've Seen That Movie Too," the movies were a metaphor for infidelity ("I'm not the blue-print/for all of your B films" and "So keep your auditions for somebody/who hasn't got so much to lose"). In "The Big Picture," the protagonist seems to be proposing matrimony: "I've got some good lines for my big star." In the earlier song, deceit is the theme: "you can tell by the lines I'm reciting/I've seen that movie, too." "The Big Picture" offers a greater variety of movie-related themes ("happy endings," "a part like this," "brightest star"). All are more naturally related to the song's main question, in this case whether the lovers are right for each other.

The song begins with a retiring sweetness, as the listener hears just Elton's voice and piano with the slightest synthesizer interpolation and upended acoustic guitar statements. For the initial verse, "The Big Picture" is a polite ballad of gentle reflection that recognizes the length—and directionlessness—of the couple's life together. In the chorus, the song turns theatrical, with equal parts assertiveness and bombast insisting on an answer: Does the protagonist have a part in the big picture? Heavy metal without the metal, shades of the Fifth Dimension singing Laura Nyro, a symmetrical reworking of the title song in *Jesus Christ, Superstar*—the chorus is all of these things and more, as Elton's voice turns from music-box innocence to sharp and cutting instrument. Before falling back on the verse's message, a third melody releases the pressure of the chorus while retaining its urgency. "The Big Picture" is a musical roller coaster that ends like an amusement park ride when the operating switch is turned off—quietly, but not completely. The question about fitting into the "big picture" still hasn't been fully reconciled, to the protagonist's distress.

"The Big Picture" is followed by "Recover Your Soul," the only song, Elton says, whose music he has ever rewritten. Its lyrics are another vignette of lost love, not unlike those for "Long Way from Happiness." This time, someone tries to shake the heartbroken subject out of a malaise: "So spare your heart save your soul/don't drag your love across the coals/find your feet and your fortune can be told."

Like "The End Will Come," "Recover Your Soul" is that rare amalgam of jazz and folk. Unlike "The End Will Come," it moves along at a contented clip, as if the song's subject has already recovered his (or her) soul and the listener gets to enjoy its rebirth. Contributing to this feeling are Elton's light-stepping piano and chuckling organ and an artfully muscle-bound vocal that ripples, swells, and pulsates around an anthem of hope and aspiration.

In the ninth track, "January," the lyrics are more obscure than those for most of Bernie's recent work. "January" seems to refer to an epochal moment, which Bernie expresses in many ways: counting clouds or blades of grass or smiles or sounds, drinking wine, rolling in the "ashes," lounging in heaven. The month of January holds special significance in the moment. That the enigmatically appealing phrase, "January is the month that cares," means that January is the subject couple's favorite month, or the month in which they met, seems doubtful. Every part of the year is special to them, as Bernie shows their tight bond (a "love's knot," "tied together," "wrapped up," "bound together") continuing through summer, winter, spring, and autumn. January, as the year's first month, is symbolic of the couple's first discovery of their love.

"January" is one of Elton's weirdest songs—not as weird as "Bennie," but similarly constructed of off-kilter material not reminiscent of anything else in his back catalog. As cryptic as the lyrics, the multipart melody progresses from a tight-lipped, sensual beginning (Guy's warbly synthesizer sitting atop Elton's coolly concocted piano) to an emphatic revelation (the guitars of Davey and John highlighting Elton's near-shouting vocal), then lowering onto a more measured plateau of anticipation for every passing season (Elton's minty fresh singing punctuated mainly by Bob Birch's low-frequency bass plucking). The unorthodox ending, in which Davey and John employ guitar licks plucked from the song's musical line of intrigue ("January is the month that cares"), backed by the Guy/Elton keyboard team, trails off to silence. The happy couple in the song will be bound, tied, knotted, and wrapped up forever.

The next-to-last song on the album, "I Can't Steer My Heart Clear of You," may be the closest Elton and Bernie have come to writing a song that Frank Sinatra or Tony Bennett might have sung. The protagonist views life as a shiplike vessel that is hard to control in the face of temptation—the temptation being another person, whose presence leads only to anguish for the protagonist. Like the lyrics for "The Big Picture," the lyrics for "I Can't Steer" take a central theme (in "Picture," it is movies, in "Steer," a ship on the sea) and represent it in various ways. Here, a neat collection of high-seas visions floats to the surface: "rough seas," "cold front," "compass," "sailed out of a storm and into view."

"I Can't Steer" is what the ill-fated "I Fall Apart" from *Leather Jackets* could have been if Elton had been clearheaded while writing that stump of a song. While the latter got no further than melodic clichés, "I Can't Steer" uses these clichés as a springboard for new paths. The song has, as Elton said, "one of the most complex melodies I've ever written."[23] Against a background of acoustic and electronic percussion by Charlie Morgan and guest Matthew Vaughn (who lent a similar sound to "Circle of Life" years earlier) and a swirling, stormy string arrangement, the melody rises, then drops when least expected, then suddenly breaks into an incongruously enchanted chorus to which early 1950s pre-rock'n'roll adolescents could have necked.

The last song, "Wicked Dreams," almost didn't make the album. Elton decided at the last minute to tack it on at the end. Among the less obvious of Bernie's lyrics, "Wicked Dreams" portrays someone engaged in a fantasy life who invites an imaginary guest to join in undisclosed revelry. "And you appear as I descend, a soft outline all poised in feather light," says the dreamer. "Join me if you have the nerve. . . . Behind my eyes I'll wait for you. Imagine just what we could do!" This is not a love song, but it could be an invitation to kinky sex or a hedonistic game.

Elton's melody for "Wicked Dreams" is the simplest of all those on *The Big Picture*, offering little variation between verse and chorus. No matter. An exercise in irony, it jogs along like a happy dance, exhibiting complete disregard for the implications of twisted fantasy. One of only two blatantly up-tempo numbers on the album (the other being "If the River Can Bend"), it provides a rousing vehicle for band interplay. Everyone paints a sprightly dream sequence behind Elton's positive melody. After so many songs of despair and uncertainty, *The Big Picture* ends with a grin.

Naturally, Elton couldn't predict whether the public would embrace the new album or any of its singles. So unlike most of what he had done before, it posed a risk to his commercial success. Worse, during the first half of 1997, the "big picture" for male solo artists in the United States remained grim. In a January 18, 1997 article entitled "Pop Music Is Looking for a Few Good Men," *Billboard* noted that, although many male solo artists dominated the country and rap fields, few were enjoying mass appeal.[24] Only a newcomer, Duncan Sheik, with his song "Barely Breathing," was having momentary success.

Another strike against male solo artists was that they tended to be older, with an already substantial body of work that distracted the radio listening and record buying audience. In May, *New York Daily News* columnist David Hinckley noted that both Paul McCartney and former Creedence Clearwater Revival lead singer John Fogerty had new albums out, but that radio program directors believed listeners only wanted to hear their old songs.[25] Against that background, what could happen with Elton's uncommercial effort, *The Big Picture*?

"I DON'T KNOW WHERE THE LIGHT SHINES"[26]
ELTON WASN'T WORRIED. Whatever happened, he had plenty of music left in him, even after he was through with the upcoming musical based on *Aida*, and with

DreamWorks's *El Dorado* project. After so many years and much talk, an instrumental album was still possible. "It's just a matter of the right time in the right place," Elton told Gambaccini early in the summer. "It's something that's unfulfilled. . . . There are so many things on the horizon."[27]

In the meantime, he had reevaluated his "midget boxer's hands," as he had disparagingly called them in the 1973 Bryan Forbes documentary. Rarely since then had he said much about his musicianship, although he nearly misplaced his humility in a 1986 interview ("I'm a fuckin' good piano player," he'd insisted[28]). Now, he realized his "chipolata fingers" were useful tools. "I've got really powerful hands," he admitted. They made him a "good rhythm piano player." He looked forward to using them on the upcoming October–November band tour of the United States and his British tour in December, the first British dates since his 1994 stint with Ray Cooper at the Royal Albert Hall.[29]

As expected, the musician's career had already taken off in new directions. In July, *The Lion King* musical opened in Minneapolis, to standing ovations and rave reviews. On the charitable front, the focus of the Elton John AIDS Foundation was readjusting. New drugs for AIDS patients meant many in Western Europe and North America who had thought they were going to die would now live. Money was needed for these drugs, as well as for counseling, to help patients cope with having a future.[30]

The political scene at home had changed as well. Elton was pleased that, after eighteen years, the Labour Party, led by Tony Blair, a man several years his junior, had returned to power. "I think this country desperately needed the change. I think John Major was a very honorable man, and I had a lot of time for him, but the Conservative Party as a whole just kind of self-destructed and I think people didn't have respect for them at all," Elton said. "Everything . . . [the Labour government] is doing at the moment makes a lot of sense. It's given this country a lot of hope and made everybody feel good."[31]

Elton was enjoying summer in Nice and anticipated vacationing with Gianni Versace, although he and his band did perform live on July 8 at an open-air concert in Aschaffenburg, Germany, a UNICEF benefit. "Border Song" was in the set list, as was the brand-new "Something About the Way You Look Tonight," which, Elton announced, would be the first single from *The Big Picture.* Local fans noticed that the band lineup had again changed. Ray Cooper was gone. In his stead were two relative youngsters, John Mahon (who had played in former Three Dog Night singer Chuck Negron's band) on percussion and backing vocals, and Billy Trudel (who sang with Davey Johnstone's side group, Warpipes), also on backup singing.

Exactly one week later, on a sunny morning in Miami's South Beach, Versace went out for a short walk to buy magazines. When he returned to his magnificent home and neared the steps to the main gate, he was shot dead by Andrew Cunanan, who would evade apprehension for another nine days, despite being among the nation's ten most wanted for brutal killings across the country. From behind the gate, a young man, thought by witnesses to be a Versace employee, ran about frantically and yelled for help as the designer lay dying. The distraught young man was actually Antonio D'Amico, Versace's longtime companion.

At first, nothing was heard from Elton, who was still in Nice. The following day, *USA Today* reported that Elton had been "too upset" to issue a statement.[32] After some hours, he did: "I am devastated to have lost one of my closest friends, who I loved so much and who I had been looking forward to seeing again on holiday very soon. We were so close that it's like a large part of my life has died with him."[33]

In another, more composed, statement, Elton recalled, "Gianni and I were like brothers. We were very similar. We had the same taste. He taught me about art, and I taught him about music. He was someone on my level of thinking. We were continually trying to improve our creativity. You never left him without being stimulated about some aspect of fashion or art or life."[34]

Career retrospectives immediately filled newspapers all over the world. Versace was credited with pioneering the use of the "supermodel," being the first designer to court stars of Hollywood and music, and turning the fashion runway show into a major event. If his innovation had made him extraordinarily rich and successful, it had also ensured that his work got the broadest, most visible exposure, that his clients expressed themselves as they wished. He had admired his friend Elton, who had the desire and the nerve to wear some of his more eye-popping creations. "I make clothes for the soul, as well as for the body," Versace once said. "They have both chic and shock."[35]

Many press accounts pointed to the music Versace commissioned for his runway shows. Most often, Prince was mentioned as a runway composer. Elton had written and recorded a few instrumentals for Versace's shows, too—expressions of affection for his friend so clever and moving they could have been on a regular album. He wrote "lyrics" for them, mainly exclamations that supplemented or gave context to the music. In the Latin-esque, percussive "Into the Jungle," he'd proclaimed his regard for the Versace line and affection for his friend: "Deep in the jungle, a story's unfolding—exotic, sexy, classic, Gee-AH-nee!"

Now that the Versace empire was left to Gianni's sister Donatella and brother Santo to run, Elton would no longer be celebrating the name of "Gee-AH-nee!" the same way. As a devoted family friend, he was poised to support Donatella's lone efforts. But first, he had to mourn Gianni's death.

The funeral was held in Milan on July 22. Elton arrived with David, going first to a family shrine, where Gianni's ashes were temporarily kept in an urn. There the musician stood silently for fifteen minutes before convulsing in sobs. He had to be led away. Later, he was seen looking skyward in disbelief, David by his side, as they walked toward the entrance to the centuries-old Duomo. Inside, the two thousand mourners included Sting, Naomi Campbell, Carolyn Bessette Kennedy, and fashion colleagues Giorgio Armani and Karl Lagerfeld. Princess Diana approached Elton and David and sat with them for the services. Here, the musician and the princess reconnected, after a months-long standoff. Seated between David and Diana, Elton wept terribly, speaking about his grief through tears, taking his glasses off to wipe his eyes. David, at his left, put his arm around him, gently leaning his head against his companion's. Diana stroked the musician's right arm and uttered comforting words. It was this scene that would make the front pages of newspapers around the globe. Later, Elton steadied himself for a walk near the pulpit where he and Sting sang the twenty-third Psalm.

The rest of the summer was difficult for Elton. He spent it in Nice (where he had received a key to the city and been named a Freeman), often surrounded by friends, including the bereft Antonio D'Amico, and reflected on what had happened. He listened to a Beth Nielsen Chapman album released on the day of Gianni's death, *Sand and Water*, which Chapman had written to deal with her husband dying of cancer.

As for the future, he planned on appearing at a Versace memorial on September 8 at New York's Metropolitan Museum of Art. He also agreed to participate in a September 15 benefit concert organized by George Martin for the volcano-stricken island of Montserrat. Nearly two dozen residents had been killed by the erupting volcano, and about fifteen hundred were left homeless. Martin's AIR Studios, where Elton had recorded *Jump Up!*, *Too Low for Zero*, and *Breaking Hearts*, destroyed in a hurricane years earlier, was buried for good.[36]

Days before the end of August, Elton was still in Nice, making a serious effort to rehearse for his upcoming tour. He was bouncing back from the loss of Gianni. Journalist Nigel Farndale, who met the musician at a local rehearsal hall, found an Elton John still very much like the man *Tantrums and Tiaras* had portrayed—impatient, with a quick temper (when a piano pedal stuck, he demanded a technician's immediate attention), eager to talk about the days of drugs and drink, and, as the writer put it, "really, really funny—and he can really, really laugh at himself." Once the piano pedal was fixed, Farndale enjoyed a mini-Elton John concert, featuring "Bennie" and a "hauntingly introspective 'Long Way from Happiness.'" Elton was satisfied. "Come the second half of the rehearsal, I was really getting into it and enjoying it," he remarked. "First half, it wasn't there."[37]

In a little over a week, "Something About the Way" was to be released as a single in Britain, with various dates planned for other countries. It was already getting airplay in the United States. On September 10, *The Big Picture* would see an early release in Japan. On September 22, Europeans would get the album; a day later, so would Americans. A week after that, it would finally be out in Britain. To promote the album, Elton was going to host a British television special, "An Audience with. . . ." In the United States, *Tantrums and Tiaras* was scheduled to premiere on

Cinemax on September 3. Elton was also going to be the VH1 artist of the month, with several specials in the works, including the first ever live (and ninety-minute-long) *Storytellers* concert since VH1 had launched the series years earlier. He also had a string of American television appearances scheduled for the week of the album's release, something he had never done, with one more following in early October, as well as a guest spot on the Fran Drescher sitcom, *The Nanny*. The October 4 issue of *Billboard*, a celebration of the thirtieth anniversary of the John/Taupin partnership, was collecting advertisements from well-wishers at a record pace. It was shaping up to be the biggest tribute issue for a solo artist ever. After all that, Elton would be on the road again.

Still in Nice, he learned on Sunday, August 31, that another friend was dead: Diana, the Princess of Wales.

"FLAGS OF MANY NATIONS FLYING
HIGH ABOVE HER HEAD"[38]

WAKING UP THAT MORNING, anywhere in the world, it was hard not to feel a sense of loss. For Elton, the pain was real. Among the statements of sorrow uttered by scores of celebrities were his simple words: "The world has lost one of its most compassionate humanitarians and I have lost a special friend. My thoughts and deepest sympathies are sent out to her sons, family, and friends."[39] He added separately, "This is the most tragic and senseless death."[40]

Diana had died while being chased by paparazzi at high speed on a Parisian street, when the chauffeur-driven car in which she and her boyfriend Dodi Al-Fayed were riding crashed into a wall. Soon after the accident, the famous and infamous united in a call for a crackdown on paparazzi photographers. From Tom Cruise to George Clooney and Madonna, celebrities decried these purveyors of exclusive film. The stars said that, like Diana, they suffered miserably at the hands of the press.

One who didn't join in condemning the paparazzi was Elton, who probably had more reason to complain about the press than most of the indignant stars. In the days following the princess's death, he did little to draw attention to himself. His dignified, thoughtful conduct—not a surprise to any who knew him or had observed his public demeanor over three decades—carried him through the autumn, ultimately engendering the admiration and reawakening the interest of millions across the globe.

It didn't seem, at first, that Elton would have any role to play in the fast-approaching Saturday, September 6 funeral. Many reporters, especially in the United States, had little idea that Elton had a special relationship with the Royal Family, let alone with Diana. A *New York Post* correspondent, Steve Dunleavy, figured that Queen Elizabeth had been angry at Diana for knowing rock star Elton.[41] *Goldmine*, an American magazine for record collectors, reported that the princess's favorite song had been Phil

Collins's "Groovy Kind of Love"; Elton was just one of many British musicians who had performed at a series of Prince's Trust benefits during the 1980s.[42]

The more grieving Britons of all ages and races laid flowers, stuffed toys, notes, and cards at all the palaces, and the more they lined up at St. James Palace to pay their respects, the more "Candle in the Wind" was played on radio and television as a sort of theme for British news programs about Diana, and the more Elton's name began to surface. It was reported that Pavarotti had been asked to sing at Diana's funeral, but, being too upset, declined. Rumors grew that Elton would be invited to sing instead. Regardless of his status in the eyes of the Royal Family, the idea of a "pop" singer performing at Westminster Abbey at what was practically a state funeral was novel, if not downright heretical. As the week wore on, the British press played up a perceived conflict between the Royal Family and their subjects about the funeral plans. The tabloids made Elton, symbol of Diana and the people, an unwitting player in the conflict.

Wheels turned behind the scenes. On Tuesday, September 2, Elton got a call from wealthy businessman Richard Branson indicating that the princess's sister, Lady Sarah McCorquodale, wanted him to sing at the funeral. The musician should be prepared in case this was approved.[43] Elton called Bernie to say he needed something to sing at the funeral, just in case. The musician mentioned the ubiquitousness of "Candle in the Wind" in British press coverage of Diana's death. Bernie thought Elton was requesting a rewrite of the lyrics, so that's what he did, over the course of two hours. Anxious, Elton called again as Bernie was writing. Bernie then realized Elton hadn't asked for a "Candle" rewrite, but for a new set of lyrics in the vein of "Candle." In the interest of time, and because the familiarity of the song would help people identify with it, the two agreed to go with what they had.[44]

"I tried to write it from a nation's standpoint and not as a singular person paying tribute," Bernie explained later. "I felt it was very important that it sounded like it was coming from the people."[45] American citizen Bernie reverted to a method he'd employed many times, stepping into someone else's shoes to express certain feelings.

The original lyrics to the song were about Marilyn Monroe, who was also a beautiful, young thirty-six when she died, but were specific to her Hollywood travails. "They set you on the treadmill, and they made you change your name," Bernie had written about her life as a star in old Hollywood. "Hollywood created a superstar, and pain was the price you paid." The press's role in her unhappiness ("Loneliness was tough, the toughest role you ever played") was laid bare: "Even when you died, Oh, the press still hounded you." In death, her humanity shone through: "Goodbye Norma Jean, from the young man in the twenty-second row, who sees you as something more than sexual."

As much as these lyrics resonated for Princess Diana, they weren't sufficient for a figure on the world stage who had raised more issues and touched more lives than

Monroe's ever could. Yes, Diana's marriage to Prince Charles had put her on a "treadmill" of steely smiles and stiff upper lips. Her royalty—and beauty—had made her a "superstar." As biographers and friends said, she could get desperately lonely. Certainly, the press "hounded" her to her last moment. But Bernie captured the rest of her story in new lyrics, in a positive light. He didn't want, for example, to leave in any press reference. "I think it would have taken away the emphasis on the sympathy that people have for her and the love that people have for her," he said.[46]

In the song that would begin "Goodbye, England's rose," Bernie omitted the line that could have been construed as a slight against the Royal Family: "You had the grace to hold yourself, while those around you crawled." He kept the "grace" in the context of her work with children, AIDS patients, and land mine victims: "You were the grace that placed itself where lives were torn apart." "Crawling" by others became a "calling" for Diana to raise consciousness: "You called out to our country." The treadmill operators who "whispered" into Monroe's "brain" were gone; in their stead, Diana "whispered to those in pain." The lyrics also didn't portray Diana as the fragile person Monroe appeared to have been ("never knowing who to cling to when the rain set in"). The Princess may have been a "candle in the wind," but of the sturdy variety: "And it seems to me you lived your life like a candle in the wind: never fading with the sunset when the rain set in." Some new lines were a trifle corny: "Now you belong to heaven, and the stars spell out your name." Others were better, invoking both Diana's legacy and the beauty of England: "And your footsteps will always fall here, along England's greenest hills."

By Wednesday, September 3, anticipation had mounted, though Elton's role at the funeral was still unconfirmed. Just before boarding a plane at London's Heathrow Airport to New York, where he would be a presenter at the MTV Music Video Awards, he told reporters, "It is really up in the air at the moment."[47] Confusion was still so great among some American radio outlets about Elton's standing in British society that Trenton, New Jersey's Top 40 radio station, WPST, reported that whether Elton would be *invited* to the funeral was unresolved. Finally, on Thursday, September 4, the word was out: He was invited to sing, and the song would be a revised "Candle in the Wind."

Thursday evening, the musician made his scheduled appearance to present the award for best new artist in a music video at the MTV Music Video Awards. He emerged from backstage to the tune of "Bennie and the Jets" in an electric blue suit and matching eyeglasses, exceeding some of the honorees and presenters in age by as much as three decades. "To add a little age to the evening, I've come out here," he smiled into a microphone. He announced that MTV would be donating a portion of the evening's proceeds to a new charity, the Diana, Princess of Wales, Memorial Fund, and that one hundred thousand dollars had been set aside for AIDS charities the princess had liked.

After the nominees for best new artist were announced, Elton revealed the winner, twenty-year-old Fiona Apple. Elton waited with Apple's statue as the small, skinny singer slowly mounted the stage. She looked down as she approached the fifty-year-old legend, who handed her the award and kissed her cheeks. Still looking down, she said nothing to him, and took the microphone to thank no one, quoting Maya Angelou for the proposition that you create your own opportunities. Apple posed a contrast to the young Elton John, who could never get enough of thanking everyone for anything he achieved. "It's Steve Brown as much as me, Gus Dudgeon as much as me, Paul Buckmaster as much as me," he had said at a party to launch *Tumbleweed Connection* in October 1970, when he was twenty-three.[48]

The day after the awards show, Elton was back in England and did his first run-through of "Candle" with the new lyrics,[49] which by then were reprinted in every newspaper. In Glasgow, numerous disgruntled people telephoned the *Glasgow Herald* to protest that the song should not call Princess Diana "England's Rose," since she was princess to the people of Scotland and Wales, too. "Some English people are wondering why the Scots and Welsh may vote for increased political power later this month," said one caller. "After this, is it surprising?" The national parties of Scotland and Wales took no position, focusing on their sorrow over Diana's death.[50]

The new lyrics remained as written. Word leaked out that the song, called "Candle in the Wind 1997," would be recorded right after the funeral, and commercially released to benefit Diana's new charity. The allure of this possibility was so overwhelming that, if anyone knew that another Elton John song, "Something About the Way You Look Tonight," was already supposed to be released (and actually had been in some parts), no reporters let on. The pundits predicted that "Candle in the Wind 1997" would be the biggest single of all time. "When you consider the reaction that has existed in the U.S. and Europe, and you have a major international artist singing, then this record could break records," said Gennaro Castaldo of HMV Records, a music store chain. "It is very rare that a single has such a global appeal, as this evidently will have."[51]

A new Barbara Walters interview with Elton was televised in the United States that night on *20/20*. "I'm not scared about it," Elton said, of singing at the funeral. "She kept her cool for me at Gianni's funeral. . . . I've got to do the same for her." He confirmed that he planned to record the revised song and put it on his single, which he didn't identify, to benefit Diana's charity.[52]

"THE CELLOPHANE STILL ON THE FLOWERS"[53]

ON SEPTEMBER 6, an estimated one billion people watched as London paid its respects to Princess Diana. Fifty million people in the United States tuned in; for Americans, it was still the middle of the night, or close to it. In Britain, nearly sixty percent of the population watched.[54]

Crowds lined the streets as the funeral cortege made its way to Westminster Abbey. Thousands congregated in Hyde Park to watch the service on giant screens. All of these people made barely a sound. Only the lone pealing of a bell in the Abbey tower was audible. Funeral guests streamed into the Abbey: American entertainers Tom Cruise, Tom Hanks, and Diana Ross; entertainment mogul Steven Spielberg; British singers Cliff Richard, Sting, Shirley Bassey, and Chris de Burgh; Donatella and Santo Versace; Luciano Pavarotti; representatives of foreign countries, including First Lady Hillary Rodham Clinton; former prime ministers John Major and Margaret Thatcher; a grandson of a prime minister, himself named Winston Churchill.

Applause broke out across the street as spectators saw Elton and David Furnish walking sternly toward the entrance. Once inside, Elton unsmilingly blew a kiss to someone in the pews. Within the hour the funeral began. Midservice, Prime Minister Tony Blair read a New Testament passage, I Corinthians 13 ("and now abideth faith, hope, love"). As he concluded, the familiar opening notes to "Candle in the Wind" were heard from the other side of the Abbey. Although he later acknowledged using a teleprompter to help with the new lyrics ("I'm not gonna mess this one up on such a big occasion," he later told David Frost he'd been thinking), Elton often leaned back, gazing at the vaulted ceiling, or closed his eyes.

Outside, as people listened over a public address system or watched in Hyde Park, the weeping was unabashed. During the last verse, Elton nearly lost his composure, his voice slipping momentarily. "Goodbye, *English* rose," he sang hesitantly (consistent with an early draft of the lyrics), lending the performance the merest hint of emotional uncertainty. As he finished, the throngs outside applauded.

Immediately after the funeral, the musician met George Martin at the Townhouse Studios to record the song. Martin suggested Elton do the piano and voice live. "I did two takes, and the second take was really, really good," Elton would recount. He sang harmony with himself, he said. Then Martin added a string quartet and woodwind. The pianist added, "I just thought people would want a reminder of this." He hoped the single would raise between five and ten million pounds.[55]

The recording's drawback was that it wasn't the funeral performance. The recording was beautiful and moving, but lacked the unpredictability of raw emotion audible in Elton's live rendering. The harmonies on the recording, though flawless, tended to distract the listener from the pure lead, and the string quartet and woodwind, which might have lent intimacy on any other song, rendered Elton's uncomplicated piano and voice interpretation less intimate.

Firestorms were brewing. On Sunday morning, Elton rejected the notion of legally restraining the press, even in light of the paparazzi's invasiveness. "It would be nice to have a little more privacy, but how do you do that?" Elton asked. "How do you legislate what is private and what is public?" Replayed in the press would be comments about his celebrity brethren. "We've had all this wailing and caterwauling from people in show business, Madonna and people like that, who have manipulated the press to suit their own ends." He insisted his experience at the hands of the press and paparazzi and the experience of Madonna and others, despite claims to the contrary, were unlike what Diana had suffered. "They [the paparazzi] are intrusive and it would be nice if they weren't intrusive," Elton said. "But I think it's part and parcel of what we are [as celebrities]."[56]

Within days, syndicated columnist Liz Smith leapt to the Material Girl's defense. "What is Elton's problem?" she complained. "*He* has certainly made considerable hay out of Diana's death, giving interviews, revamping songs, singing at the funeral, giving *more* interviews, telling the world of his 'falling out' with Diana, etc."[57]

Liz Smith had to know she was exaggerating. There was just one interview before the funeral (with Barbara Walters) and one after (with David Frost), with a few words also uttered to a VH1 camera since he was their artist of the month. Smith also knew that Elton (and Bernie) had only revamped one song, to sing at the funeral and pay tribute to his friend. Smith's bewilderment may have been due to her lack of significant exposure to an Elton John trademark—his bluntness. Neither she nor much of the American press and public were used to this.

In ensuing weeks, more of that bluntness would surface—in reaction to the words of a member of one of Elton John's favorite bands, the Rolling Stones. In an interview with *Entertainment Weekly*, Keith Richards was asked what he thought of Elton singing for royalty. "Yeah, it did jar a bit. Songs for dead blondes," said Richards, referring to the old and new versions of "Candle in the Wind." "But he was a personal friend, after all," Richards allowed, adding, "I'd find it difficult to ride on the back of something like that myself, but Reg is showbiz."[58]

At a press conference, Elton responded: "I have great respect for Mick Jagger and Charlie Watts and the Rolling Stones, actually, as a group. I just think if they had thrown Keith Richards out of the band ten years ago they would have made better records. I think he's held them back." Elton said he was glad he had kicked drink and drugs, or he might be like Richards. "He's so pathetic, poor thing, like a monkey with arthritis trying to go onstage and look young," he said.[59]

Elton was also the subject of religious criticism for his role in the funeral. A minister of the Free Presbyterian Church of Scotland, the Reverend Neil Ross, criticized the way Diana's funeral was conducted, saving his most stinging words for Elton. "Such is the spiritual darkness that pervades the country that the singer was center stage during the funeral," said the minister, asserting that the musician's "immorality is public knowledge." Moreover, it was "offensive," asserted the clergyman, for the musician to perform a secular song at a funeral service.[60]

The pianist had also offended rock purists. In an article titled "Stop the Madness: Why 'Candle in the Wind' is the Death of Rock," *New Musical Express* writer John Mulvey argued that, once again, a member of the rock establishment had taken the focus away from newer and ostensibly more worthy acts—and this was the fault of the charitable impulse of rock's so-called "*ancien regime.*"[61] Other commentators focused on the curious fact that Elton had revised one of his old songs, instead of writing a new one in Diana's memory. "Admittedly, there comes a point in every performer's career when they begin to recycle their work, but this was just crude," wrote Emma Forrest in *The Guardian.* "You can't give a song to a tragic, misunderstood beauty and then take it back because someone more tragic, misunderstood, and beautiful has died."[62]

Elton received a more welcome reception at a Watford match the day after the funeral, where he was met with a tremendous ovation. Two rows behind him, his mother beamed proudly, while his stepfather sized up the enormousness of the affection. The musician delightedly stood and waved.

"BOUND TOGETHER IN THE AUTUMN"[63]

IN NEW YORK ON SEPTEMBER 8, Elton attended a memorial service for Gianni Versace at the Metropolitan Museum of Art's Temple of Dendur, and sang "Live Like Horses" in tribute to his friend. On September 10, he was in Orlando for the fifth annual Smash Hits benefit. During the usual benefit press conference, he took a moment to urge people to move past mourning for Diana and concentrate on what she believed in. "Life has to go on, you know? I've had a tough two months. I've lost two great friends," Elton, seated next to Pete Sampras, said. "The human spirit is very tough. . . . You just have to carry on."[64]

As Elton spoke, PolyGram and merchants around the world were gearing up for a campaign that would enable people to both mourn and do something in the princess's name. As the record company withdrew "Something About the Way," orders for "Candle in the Wind 1997" neared astronomical levels, days before its release in countries outside the United States. In Britain, orders reached the 1.5 million mark as of September 10, which meant it was guaranteed quintuple platinum certification.[65]

In the absence of the single, there was a stampede for almost any other recording that had the original "Candle" on it, which seemed to indicate that people really liked the song, independent of the Diana connection. In the United States, sales of *Greatest Hits,* which included the 1973 song, ballooned from 4,300 units to more than 15,000 in sales. The sales increase was equally dramatic for *Love Songs,* which contained the live "Candle" played in Australia. Off the album chart for weeks, it reentered the stakes at number 99. Sadly, the attention of consumers didn't turn to *Live in Australia,* the album the live "Candle" had originally come from, although *Goodbye Yellow Brick Road,* which included a studio version of the song, enjoyed an appreciable bump. Puzzlingly, *Greatest Hits 1976–86,* which had nothing remotely approaching "Candle," was suddenly doing almost as well. A similar story played out overseas where, as far away as Singapore, people were cleaning the shelves of Elton John albums.[66]

Elton benefited greatly from the "Candle" frenzy. *New York Daily News* writer Jim Farber waxed cynical about the commercial effect of Elton's performance at Princess Diana's funeral: "[N]o matter how you play it, mourning pays."[67] But if this meant more people would come to appreciate the musician's talent, Diana herself couldn't have objected. Elton hoped that, if people were buying *Goodbye Yellow Brick Road* for "Candle," they would get their money's worth and hear the whole album. "It's a great double album," he said in a call to a New York radio station.[68]

While it seemed Elton was benefiting from unprecedented global exposure, he was also doing what he could to separate his steeply climbing career trajectory from the voracious appetite of the public for everything Diana. He announced that he would never again play "Candle in the Wind 1997" live (except at her family's request), nor would he play the original song for quite some time. He refused the BBC and Independent Television News permission to include his funeral performance in a commercially released video of the service, because only one-quarter of the proceeds was pegged for Diana's fund. He did, however, allow its inclusion in the official BBC recording of the funeral, as all profits were to go to the fund.

The continual broadcast of the performance on VH1 provoked Elton in another way. Until he'd sung in Westminster Abbey, the sum total of VH1's artist of the month programming for him had been his new video for "Something About the Way," played about once a day, and previews of a few specials. But as the last notes of "Candle in the Wind 1997" evaporated into London's morning air on September 6, VH1 slapped together a soppy segment titled *Candles in the Wind.* Featuring his funeral performance, the program examined Elton's charitable nature and asked some sentimental fans what his music meant to them personally. The musician asked VH1—and MTV—to stop playing the funeral footage, as he wanted it restricted to news programming, and *Candles in the Wind* vanished.

"YOU JUST SHINE LIKE A BEACON ON THE BAY"[69]

WHILE EVERYONE WAS TALKING ABOUT "Candle in the Wind 1997," "Something About the Way" gained ground on radio. In the United States, the news was especially heartening. By September 13, when, in its second week of Hot 100 airplay, the song leapfrogged from number 71 to number 56, it was already doing better than "You Can Make History" had a year earlier.

Initially, airplay was nothing compared to that of "Candle," which had debuted in the United States on the Hot 100 Airplay Chart at number 35 on September 20. Elton had two songs ascending both the Airplay Chart and the Adult Contemporary Chart simultaneously, with "Something About the Way" leading on the latter. The week after the funeral, airplay of "Candle in the Wind 1997" was aided considerably by efforts on the part of the BBC and PolyGram to electronically distribute it to broadcasters around the world in advance of its release. Stations far and wide were "play listing" the song immediately.

On September 13, the first day the single (containing "Something About the Way," "Candle," and "You Can Make History") was officially available in Britain, Paul Gambaccini astutely observed, "Everything that Elton John has ever done has been temporarily eclipsed by the identification of the song 'Candle in the Wind' with the mourning of Diana, Princess of Wales." People had lined up at midnight for the first shipment—three hundred outside the Tower Records in Piccadilly Circus alone. After nearly an hour and a half, a thousand singles were sold at that store. Come Saturday morning, extra production shifts at PolyGram boosted the initial, grossly inadequate shipments projection of 250,000 singles to 650,000.[70]

On Saturday morning, throngs of people congregated in the chill outside every record shop, and, when the doors opened, engaged in a mad rush, pressing toward the singles display. People bought as many copies as they could grab. An unprecedented sign at a check-out in the Piccadilly Circus Tower Records read: "Express till for customers *not* buying the Elton John single."[71] At day's end, all 650,000 British copies of the single had been sold. It was already double platinum and set to enter the singles chart at number 1 on the strength of only one day of sales. It was also the fastest selling single in British history. A minor point, perhaps, was the single's status as only the second British solo number 1 of Elton's career. In an additional triumph for Diana's fund, Finance Minister Gordon Brown decreed that all sales taxes on the single would be forgiven. That much more would go to charity.

France had gotten the single two days earlier, before everyone else. The Virgin MegaStore on the Champs Élysées, just a short walk from the site of Princess Diana's death, was selling five hundred singles an hour. By the next day, 500,000 singles were sold in France. "Something About the Way/Candle" was platinum and number 1.[72] Within days, similarly astounding sales figures were racked up across Europe. In Germany, PolyGram's beleaguered European plants slowly filled two million advance orders. In Holland, the 155 stores of the Free Record Shop chain asked for 150,000 singles, but only got 100,000. Almost all the "Candle" singles in Dutch shops—including Ear & Eye in Emmen, Studio 2000 in Appingedam, and De Cirkel in Groningen—were reserved in advance by eager buyers, many of whom were elderly and had never purchased a single before.[73] In Portugal, a lone shipment of 5,000 CDs sold out in less than fifteen minutes.

The single overpowered most European charts in a massive domino effect. By the end of September, it was number 1 not just in Britain and France, but also in Holland, Germany, Italy, Ireland, Switzerland, Belgium, Austria, and Norway (where the single was certified seven times platinum). In South Africa, the single went platinum twelve times. In Israel, it was the first gold single ever. Days after most of Europe got the single, Canada did, too; as it had in several other countries, "Candle" entered the chart there at number I.[74] In Australia, where the single wasn't released until September 22, the full initial shipment was quickly sold, with almost as many orders waiting to be filled. "Candle" was soon certified seven times platinum there.[75] In Japan, the single wasn't released until September 27. When it was, it entered the combined international and domestic music chart at number I, only the second foreign single to do so since 1976.[76]

In the United States, retailers and consumers had been anxiously waiting for the single's arrival since September 16, which had been prematurely announced as the release date. They finally got what they wanted a week later, the delay due to the belated availability of the single's artwork (the rose), since it had been designed in England, and of the "Candle" recording's master tape, which had been recorded in London. Getting the single out in the United States was also a daunting task. PolyGram enlisted the help of rival record companies like Sony to manufacture the needed millions.[77]

The extra week didn't dampen interest. News reports kept trumpeting the expected release date. Retail orders kept rising. People kept calling to reserve the single. At midnight, September 22, when many stores coast-to-coast opened early, the purchasing spree began. Hollywood's Tower Records sold five hundred copies in ninety minutes; at HMV on New York's Broadway, nearly one hundred were sold in an hour. At the same store, 1,000 copies were sold by mid-afternoon of the official release day, with 2,500 copies going during that same period at an HMV store on Fifth Avenue.[78]

By the end of the day, the single had been certified multi-platinum for eight million in shipments. By the end of the week, actual sales at stores hooked up to *Billboard*'s Soundscan system were tallied at 3.4 million, the biggest figure for one-week sales ever in the United States. This translated into 20,833 singles an hour sold during the first week, or 5.8 a *second.*[79]

A&M, the Polygram subsidiary through which Elton's music was now released in the United States, figured that another half a million in actual sales that week could be attributed to outlets not known for selling music: Ace Hardware, 7–11 convenience stores, Kroger groceries, Walgreen drugstores, Avon salespersons, and W.H. Smith, a newsstand/gift shop found in airports.[80] The single was also being sold at Bloomingdale's. And Boscov's. As if Boscov's really needed to entice people, a September 23 newspaper advertisement read, "This special recording—1997 version—will never be performed again live by Elton John!"[81] Overseas, the single was available at greeting card stores, gas stations, drugstores, and, in London, at Harrods, the department store owned by Dodi Al-Fayed's father.[82]

Sometimes, the single brought out the best in American retailers. St. Louis–based Venture Stores announced before its release that the "family value" store chain would be donating all of its profits from sales of the single to the Pediatric AIDS Foundation. Dayton, Ohio–based CD Connection announced that all of its profits would be going to a local AIDS charity. Philadelphia-based music store chain The Wall declared that fifty cents from every purchase of the single made through October 1 would go to Diana's fund. Other stores said they would be sharing profits with various charities, but didn't say how much. This was also happening overseas. In Australia, the Coles-Myer group, which owned 850 stores throughout the country, pledged all profits to charities, including those favored by Princess Diana.[83]

The single went on to be certified for shipments of eleven million in the United States, and spent fourteen weeks at the top of the Hot 100 before commencing its molasses-like slide down the chart. It had gone to number 1 in twenty-two of the forty countries in which it was released. And only thirty-seven days after hitting stores in September, "Candle" bested Bing Crosby's "White Christmas" as the world's best-selling single of all time, with thirty-one million copies shipped. "Candle" was now in *The Guiness Book of World Records.*

Elton received three awards for all this at the December 8 Billboard Music Awards: single of the year, singles artist of the year, and singles sales artist of the year. "The only positive thing that has come out of Diana leaving us is that, thanks to people who bought the single, Diana's work will continue," Elton said in a taped statement.[84] Two days later, with Lady Sarah McCorquodale and Finance Minister Gordon Brown looking on, he presented a check for twenty million pounds (thirty-two million dollars) to the Diana, Princess of Wales Memorial Fund. This was the first installment of money from sales all over the world, and already twice what Elton had anticipated.

"Something About the Way," which many mistook for a B-side (the single was double A-sided), didn't do badly, either, surpassing and strongly outlasting airplay of "Candle" on both Top 40 and adult contemporary radio. "Certainly, ['Something'] wouldn't have sold three million pieces without 'Candle,' but it still would've been the biggest Elton John single in years," said Jim Ryan, program director for New York's adult-contemporary station WLTW.[85] The song reached the pinnacle of the Adult Contemporary chart on November 22, and stayed there for ten weeks. It had enormous staying power on the Hot 100 Airplay chart, where it peaked at number 18 in November 1997 and again in January 1998.

"JOIN ME IF YOU HAVE THE NERVE" [86]

ELTON'S NEWLY MONUMENTAL STATURE didn't generally translate into similar sized sales for *The Big Picture.* Dedicated to Gianni Versace, it debuted on the Eurochart and Italy's albums chart at number 1, where it remained on top for, respectively, two and four weeks. It also went to number 1 in Denmark, Austria, and Switzerland. It debuted at number 3 in Britain, and in the Top 10 in Holland, Germany, France, and Australia. It had a certain longevity in Scandinavia, but fell precipitously in other countries, such as the aforementioned Holland, Germany, and Australia. In Canada, the album debuted less impressively at number 14 before falling. In the United States, it debuted at number 9 with more than 101,000 units sold, Elton's best start since the 1970s, but declined sharply with each week, to numbers 17, 26, 34, and so on.

It was easy to see why the album didn't mimic the single's gargantuan success. The single was, of course, number 1 everywhere and had debuted on the charts, in most cases, contemporaneously with, just before, or just after *The Big Picture*. In Australia, the week the album debuted at number 5, it competed not only with the frighteningly popular single, but also with *The Very Best of Elton John*, at number 36, and *Love Songs*, at number 41. In Germany, when the album debuted at number 8, *Love Songs* was at number 15. In Holland, when *The Big Picture* debuted at number 8, *Love Songs* was number 9.

One might have expected a better outcome for the album in the United States. On September 19, just days before its release, Elton premiered "Something About the Way" and "Long Way from Happiness" during a solo performance at the House of Blues in New Orleans, broadcast live on a VH1 *Storytellers* segment. He joked with Jay Leno on September 22, Oprah Winfrey on September 24, and Conan O'Brien on September 25, playing "Something About the Way" each time. He bantered with Rosie O'Donnell on October 1, again performing the song. In his first guest role on an American sitcom, he played himself on *The Nanny*, broadcast on October 8. *The Big Picture* was worked into the plot. "Live Like Horses" could be heard in the background.

Elton clearly wanted people to know about this album, but his various plugs were a little unfocused. In a slip on *Storytellers*, Elton introduced "Long Way from Happiness" as another song "from the album," but didn't say which album. *The Big Picture* was mentioned on all the other shows, but not discussed, and the only song he played from the album was the one people were already able to get on the single. By the time Oprah plugged the single, on September 24, it had just floored the competition the day before.

The *New York Daily News*'s Jim Farber came close to admitting that the reason for *The Big Picture*'s plummeting sales was that Elton was competing with himself. "[T]he whole Diana connection actually may have *harmed* him on one level," he wrote, "siphoning off sales from his profit-making product to the charity single."[87] Farber didn't mention that, due to the public's infatuation with "Candle in the Wind," *Love Songs* and *Greatest Hits* were selling huge amounts, and, for several weeks in mid-autumn, were close behind *The Big Picture* in sales, with *Goodbye Yellow Brick Road* not far off. Elton was competing not only with himself in the United States, but with himself, himself, and himself, similar to when *Made in England* was forced to compete with the *Lion King* soundtrack.

Overall, *The Big Picture* could have done worse. By February 1998, it had sold well over five hundred thousand copies, enough for a gold certification. The following August, it received gold and platinum certifications simultaneously.

"YOUR SPIRIT'S POUNDING LOUD AND CLEAR"[88]

THE "CANDLE IN THE WIND" phenomenon may not have helped *The Big Picture*, but it did help *The Big Picture Tour*, the collection of dates in mostly small U.S. towns—where Elton had rarely, or never, played before—that he undertook beginning on October 10, 1997 for six weeks. Many of these gigs broke sales records. More than 14,350 tickets for the October 10 Winston-Salem, North Carolina date were sold in a record-breaking three hours. Twenty thousand tickets for the October 11 concert in Virginia Beach sold in thirty-six minutes. In an hour and seven minutes, 12,700 tickets went for the October 17 Charleston, West Virginia show. And in Moline, Illinois, 10,960 tickets sold out in a record-breaking eighteen minutes.

Elton had ample opportunity to sharpen his chops and lubricate his vocal cords prior to the tour. In Britain, he and his band filmed the "An Audience with Elton John" ITV television special on September 13, in which he and the band played, among others, "If the River Can Bend" and "Something About the Way." He also duetted with Sting on "Come Down in Time," with the Pet Shop Boys on a preternatural "Song for Guy" and "Believe" medley, and with the Spice Girls on "Don't Go Breaking My Heart." On September 15, he was at the Royal Albert Hall for the Montserrat benefit, performing chest-busting solo versions of "Your Song," "Live Like Horses," and "Don't Let the Sun," and doing a piano tête-à-tête with Paul McCartney on "Hey Jude."

There were only about one thousand general admission tickets available for the pre-tour concert at Atlanta's tiny Roxy.[89] One concertgoer who didn't have to worry about a ticket was Beth Nielsen Chapman. The job of the Nashville-based singer-songwriter was to rewrite the third verse of one of her songs, "Sand and Water," so Elton could sing the song on tour.

Elton and Chapman had first had contact in 1990, when Elton was moved enough by her self-titled album to send flowers. In September 1991, they met at the From All Walks of Life AIDS walk in Atlanta.[90] Then, prior to the death of Gianni Versace, Chapman gave Elton an advance copy of her new album, *Sand and Water*.[91] Less than three months later, following Versace's murder, Elton found himself relying on the album as an emotional release. In late summer, when it was time to draw up a set list, he knew he wouldn't be singing any version of "Candle in the Wind," but still wanted a vehicle for expressing his feelings on the deaths of Gianni and

Diana. Chapman's gorgeous title track—her way of dealing with the impending death of her husband from cancer—was just the cathartic song Elton wanted.

He called Chapman to say how much the song had moved him, and that he wanted to sing it. But he needed a new third verse—something of universal application. In the lyrics to that verse, Chapman reflected on having to raise her young son alone. She asked her now sixteen-year-old's permission to revise the words. He unhesitantly replied, "Sure!"[92] When Elton mentioned the song to Robert Hilburn, and again to Oprah, the new lyrics had not yet been written, and weren't finished until Chapman's car was practically pulling onto the street where Elton was rehearsing in Atlanta. "The syllables were kind of falling through the sun roof just in time," she said. "He [Elton] was actually the first person to sing it. I hadn't even tried singing it."[93]

Chapman did succeed in universalizing the message: "All alone I hear this heart of sorrow/I can only live this day/flesh and bone, my world's bursting towards tomorrow/and the love you send my heart still finds its way." She said, on the eve of Elton's Roxy concert, that the revised third verse "could be Diana, Versace, Ryan White, your mother, or your lover."[94]

For Chapman, all this meant that her album sales would triple and that her record label, Reprise, would be persuaded to release "Sand and Water" as a single. The song would not chart on the Hot 100, but eventually "bubbled under," and received substantial Adult Contemporary airplay. Chapman had a distinct way of looking at her sudden good fortune. "I can't help but believe that in some way those who go beyond this world have something to do with the energy that comes back," she said.[95]

Elton played "Sand and Water" as an encore, one of many highlights of his fall shows. Despite the challenge he again faced in selecting a fair sampling from his long career, the songs spanned decades. The show began with earthshaking percussion and charged guitars that turned into "Simple Life." As the audience roared, three triangular curtains decorated with Versace-inspired Medusa's heads, which had concealed most of the stage, abruptly flew up into the ceiling to reveal wheels, waves, and etchings reminiscent of Egyptian and Aztec hieroglyphics. More striking was the brightly dressed Elton, his body already divided between the piano and audience, his face broken into a ridiculous smile, leading the band through the song's powerfully chugging tempo.

There seemed no hint of the trauma he'd endured, no trace of pain, fear, or despair. Instead, he pushed and teased his audience. A big surprise early on was "Goodbye Yellow Brick Road," a song he had once suggested he would never play again. He assigned his voice to the high notes with a mellower, mature phrasing, leaving the boyish falsetto to harmonizer Billy Trudel. An unknown delicacy for many was the lovingly played "We All Fall in Love Sometimes" and "Curtains" pairing, dedicated to the John/Taupin thirty-year partnership.

One-third of the songs, of varying familiarity, hailed from the pianist's recent output, in tribute to his continued creative inspiration. The 1992 contingent, in addition to "Simple Life," included the expected "The One" and "The Last Song." The *Lion King* remained relevant with "Can You Feel the Love Tonight." *Made in England*, though, seemed slighted, with only two of its songs played night after night, the title track and "Believe." *The Big Picture* was better represented, with "Something About the Way," "Love's Got a Lot to Answer For," and "If the River Can Bend."

Some concertgoers in the small communities that were getting Elton for the first time in twenty-five years (such as Charleston, West Virginia), or for the first time ever (like Fargo, North Dakota), hoped he would forget what he said and play "Candle in the Wind 1997" one more time. "Just imagine—Elton John is right inside . . . and he knew Princess Diana," said one woman before the October 18 show in Louisville, Kentucky, a city Elton hadn't visited in twenty-one years.[96] A fan at the November 5 Amherst, Massachusetts show was more to the point. "I'd like to see him play it [the song] one more time," he said.[97] But Elton didn't.

The concerts routinely aroused the most vociferous responses, which John Jorgenson, during the tour's first week, called "amazing." "Davey Johnstone says [they are] as good as in the 1970s, at Elton's peak then," John noted in wonderment.[98]

"ALL THE BEASTLY NEWS"[99]

BETWEEN THE KNOXVILLE AND OKLAHOMA CITY CONCERTS, Elton was presented with an award not meant for rock stars—the CARE USA Oliver Kiss International Humanitarian Award, for "his extraordinary dedication to improving the lives of those living with HIV/AIDS." The ceremony was part of a benefit dinner held on November 17 at the Ritz-Carlton in Atlanta. Elton noted in his speech that AIDS cases in Third World countries were increasing at an alarming rate: "More and more, we're going to have to fund efforts overseas. As long as there's breath in my body, I will continue the fight."[100] In 1998, the AIDS Foundation would fund programs in Thailand, Lesotho, and Niger.[101]

There were other charity events, too, once the tour's fall leg ended on November 22 in Memphis. The most publicized was the second London "'Out' the Closet," which opened on November 28. It was estimated that Elton had spent about four million dollars on the ten thousand pieces of clothing being resold.

Days later, on December 1 in New York, he was at a different sort of benefit, for the Venetian opera house La Fenice, which had burned down. Versace, an opera fan, had asked him to participate in the Carnegie Hall fund-raiser. Elton kept his pledge to his departed friend, performing "Live Like Horses" in a primarily operatic show.[102] A persistent standing ovation couldn't persuade him to return for an encore.[103]

Meanwhile, the new musical *The Lion King* had been playing at the renovated New Amsterdam Theater on 42nd Street since October, having officially opened on

November 13. In a break between tour stops, Elton and Tim Rice attended the opening, which attracted myriad names: Mary Tyler Moore, Julie Andrews, theater-touter Rosie O'Donnell, Francis Ford Coppola, Regis Philbin, even former Texas governor Ann Richards. "After the astonishing 'Circle of Life' opening number, the audience began applauding and crying 'Bravo!'" observed Liz Smith. "I think they would be sitting there still if the play had not continued over the noise." At the curtain call, she noted, every person who had had a hand in the show was called up for a bow, including Tim and Elton.[104] The pianist held avante-garde director Julie Taymor's right arm determinedly aloft as the applause continued.

Taymor later said she had been nervous about meeting Elton because of her decisions to cut and slice some of his songs. "But he was very gracious about what we'd done to the score," she said. "He really adored it."[105] Elton understood why he and Rice were only asked to write three additional songs—while five from the Lion King–inspired album, Rhythm of the Pride Lands, were added. "I think they wanted to accentuate the African, which was a very clever move on their part," Elton reflected. "In fact, some of the African things work better than some of my things."[106]

Director Taymor and arranger Mark Mancina did justice, overall, to Elton's original songs, especially "Can You Feel the Love Tonight" and "Circle of Life," which, along with the elephant, giraffes, and gazelles (thespians on stilts or inside human-propelled costumes), had so overwhelmed theatergoers. The love song, insubstantial in the movie, was fattened up in the production to a level worthy of the fanciful melody, featuring a dream ballet sequence. But the three new John/Rice songs were, as Taymor admitted, sliced up. Hard to appreciate, they functioned as mere comic relief. This would explain critics' lukewarm reaction to them. Yet they, more than the first five Elton wrote, possess intriguing split personalities.

"The Morning Report" is equal parts Gilbert and Sullivan—staccato and country twang. Mainly sung by Zazu, King Mufasa's trusty hornbill, its midsection is trounced by dialogue related to Mufasa's "pouncing" class for his son. Another new song was "Chow Down," which Elton half-seriously dubbed the "Hyena Slobber Song" not long after he wrote it, as it was meant for the hyenas, licking their chops over the prospect of eating young Simba and Nala, who were lost in the terrifying elephant graveyard. A hard rock song with a dainty filling, it is less diluted by dialogue. Not so for the final new John/Rice song, "The Madness of King Scar," a combination of 1930s pizzazz and sad, 1990s introspection so pockmarked by talking it is possible to miss. Every couple of bars is succeeded by the nonmusical fretting of the guilt-ravaged Scar, the hyenas' complaints of hunger, and Zazu's wisecracks.

Audiences responded enthusiastically to the music as well as to the unparalleled staging and costumes. The day the reviews were out, people lined up for tickets. Over the following weekend, the show became the biggest and fastest selling in Broadway history.[107] Elton now had a name on the Great White Way.

"I PROUDLY REPRESENT YOU IN THIS WORLD" [108]

IT HAD BEEN AN INCREDIBLE YEAR FOR ELTON. In the United States, he made year-end lists in *People* and *Entertainment Weekly* of celebrities with the most impact in 1997, and was featured on the December 2 Barbara Walters television special, "The Ten Most Fascinating People of 1997." In Britain, the December 1997 issue of the magazine *Gay Times* named him man of the year. The tribute inside oversimplified Elton's struggles, but rang true:

> *Man of the Year? Well, obviously. But Elton John is the man of all our years. His life story has neatly mirrored that of all gay men: repressed in the Sixties, a model of Seventies hedonistic excess, a victim of the Right's homophobic backlash in the Eighties, then fighting his way forward to something approaching sainthood today.*
>
> *And he's done it all on pretty much his own terms. He's said "fuck you" and "love me" in equal measure. But is Elton John an example of gay men's liberation or merely our assimilation?*
>
> *I guess the answer is "a bit of both."* [109]

Elton's commercial, artistic, and public profiles were continuing to rise. And the weekend that his British tour started, a rumor began circulating—he was going to be knighted. In light of all this, one review of the December 11 Glasgow concert came as quite a shock. Barbara Ellen of *The Observer* did have some good things to say: "Elton's genius is that, when he is on form, his music can make you feel that past hurt is just future joy in disguise. . . . If, like me, you think that a talent for playing the piano is proof positive that God has favourites, Elton is up there with the cosseted best. Not only can he play the piano brilliantly, he can play it brilliantly lying on the floor, with his back to the keyboard, and even, at one notable point, with one leg stuck up in the air as if it had been caught in an invisible stirrup." But Ellen also asserted that Elton's jawline reminded her of a "beach ball with air hissing out of a very small puncture. . . ." She insisted the pianist would sometimes "scowl at the piano like someone had just urinated all over the keys." Acknowledging his large catalog of songs, she nevertheless criticized the length of the show: "I thought that this tour was meant to be for Christmas, not for life." [110]

All very entertaining to read, but upsetting enough to Elton to make him swear that he would never tour Britain again. Innocent fans at the December 14 Manchester show were immediate victims of the musician's anger. In a petulant response to the review, he shortened the concert by half an hour and dropped, among other songs, "Made in England."

By the first Birmingham concert, the next night, he'd restored most of the deleted songs to the show. And by the time he played two nights at Wembley Arena, less than two weeks later, he reached a performing peak. John Jorgenson noticed that on both nights the "crowd greeted Elton like a returning conqueror, on their feet from the beginning, stamping and cheering to show their approval." At the second show on December 20, the pianist "added some new riffs to 'Bennie' and 'Philadelphia Freedom' and even incorporated 'White Christmas' into his solo piano intro to 'Take Me to the Pilot,'" Jorgenson said. "After the show, Elton told me that he felt he couldn't play or sing any better than he did that night. A great show to end a tour on."[111] Elton bade farewell to the audience with a "see you next year." He would be back after all.

Ten days later, Elton's name was on Queen Elizabeth's New Year's Honors List. As the rumors hinted, he was going to become Sir Elton John. After a second American leg of the *Big Picture Tour* in January and February 1998, he went home to receive his knighthood at a February 24 ceremony. He was accompanied by David, his mother, and his stepfather. "To be knighted by the Queen with my mum and dad here is fantastic," he said after the investiture, holding up for reporters' cameras the medal he got at Buckingham Palace. "I am extremely proud. I love my country, and to be recognized in such a way—I can't think of anything better."[112]

Queen Elizabeth feared the investiture had interfered with his "busy" schedule, he said, but how could he have stayed away? Sir Elton John was always going to have a busy schedule.

EPILOGUE

I'M
STILL
STANDING
AFTER
ALL THIS
TIME[1]

O N GRAMMY NIGHT, FEBRUARY 21, 2001, the normally noisy back-stage area at Los Angeles's Staples Center hushed to silence as a giant video screen lit up with images of rain and lightning, while florid, broken chords emanated pessimistically from a hidden electric piano. A slender, blonde-complexioned, pinch-nosed, twenty-something man in ball cap and comfortable, baggy clothes began rhythmically narrating, with urban African-American inflection, an imagined fan letter to a big pop star. The electric piano self-effacingly rumbled in the background, until the young man stopped his narration and a semi-circular partition slid smoothly aside to reveal Elton John, in fuchsia polka-dotted orange suit, dangling earring, and rectangular sunglasses, standing behind the keyboard. He sang in the thick tenor through which, in his live shows, he might summon the sounds of a gentle balladeer, a country troubadour, or, on a night like this, a hard-bitten soul man.

The singing done, the spindly Eminem continued his rap about "Stan," an unhinged fan so obsessed with the star that when his admiring letters weren't returned, he drove his car off a bridge with his pregnant girlfriend tied up in the trunk. As Stan's anger increased with each verse, so did the volume of Elton's play-ing, peppered with staccato chord accents reminiscent of his work on *A Single Man*, recorded some twenty-three years earlier. Between each verse, he would soulfully sing the chorus, taken from the slight-voiced English singer Dido's song "Thank You," his earring swinging as his body subconsciously rocked to the song's only other accompaniment, some percussion.

Elton's full-bodied playing had found its way into a genre not known for embrac-ing the sounds of piano, so rarely heard even in rock'n'roll. As the most visible propo-nent of the piano in modern popular music, he had surprised his audience again.

The Briton's performance with Eminem was not done—as some in the gay community, angered at Eminem's seemingly homophobic, violent lyrics, charged—

simply to seem current. Elton had been touting Eminem's latest album, *The Marshall Mathers LP,* since the summer.[2] Not normally one to easily get through a rap album, he'd found this one musically interesting—"intelligent, hardcore stuff," provocatively shocking like Oliver Stone's film, *Natural Born Killers.* He rejected the charge that Eminem was bigoted. Through the fall of 2000, he publicly praised the rapper's music every chance he got. In December, Matt Lauer asked him with whom he'd like to duet next. "I'd love to do something with Eminem," Elton replied, after initially struggling for an answer. "But we come from two different stratospheres of music."[3]

Few had taken notice of his admiration for Eminem. Then, the National Academy of Recording Arts and Sciences announced the Grammy nominations. *Marshall Mathers* was up for, among other awards, album of the year. Gay and women's advocates protested vociferously, becoming more enraged when word leaked that Elton would be performing with Eminem on the Grammy telecast.

Representatives of the Gay and Lesbian Alliance Against Defamation (GLAAD), which had honored Elton in April 2000 for his gay advocacy, were "shocked," "flabbergasted," "appalled," and "disgusted."[4] Not all gays joined in GLAAD's condemnation. Some hoped Elton's work with Eminem would reform the rapper,[5] others argued that antigay expressions should not be stifled but rebutted.[6]

Elton certainly hadn't forgotten about his gay brethren and the hate crimes committed against them. "I've got a picture of Matthew Shepard in my kitchen to remember how lucky I am and that, around the corner, someone, because of their sexuality, because of their religion, because of their color, someone is going to be taken to task for it," he told Matt Lauer.[7] He and Bernie had written "American Triangle" in tribute to Shepard, the gay Wyoming college student killed because he was gay, for their new album, eventually dubbed *Songs from the West Coast,* due in 2001.

The pianist's own fans were often critical of his sexual openness. "While being gay is nothing to be ashamed of, it is also nothing to be *proud* of," wrote one on an Internet newsgroup. "No reason to go around turning off more than ninety percent of your audience by constantly discussing your sexuality over and over and over!"[8] This viewpoint wouldn't keep Elton from talking about it, nor would gay critics of Eminem keep him from performing with the former Marshall Mathers.

Since being knighted, Elton's life and career had done anything but wind down. Retirement wouldn't have worked for one still so full of energy and ambition. Yet, during the first half of 1998, as he blanketed the world with live performances, a man not so smitten with his work might have wanted to hide. He was besieged by rumors of financial insolvency that culminated in the shocking firing of John Reid.

It happened during the second week of May 1998. Fans and celebrity watchers had assumed that the two men were inseparable. But around the same time that the Fleet Street tabloids got wind of some documents suggesting Elton was spending more than he was taking in, the musician himself became suspicious of the man he had once considered his most trusted associate. For the first time, he had accountants do an independent audit of his books, and was mortified to discover a money drain attributable to Reid.[9]

To Elton, it was bad enough that Reid had taken out mortgages secured with his client's assets and sold off others at a loss, or that while the 1980 tour had supposedly lost Elton money, it had made Reid more than one million dollars richer. But the pianist hated the betrayal most of all. "I pride myself on the loyalty and friendship of the people that work with me and that's why John Reid hurt me so much," he said in 1999.[10]

Now managed by former chief attorney Frank Presland through a new enterprise, 21st Artists, Elton dismissed further rumors of financial woes, ignited by news of a forty million dollar bank loan, which, the gossipmongers insisted, would be used to pay off his substantial debts. "Frank has borrowed [the money] to buy my assets back and we are planning to expand," Elton said.[11]

Meanwhile, Elton had continued to perform. By February 1999, he had begun what would become a more than two-year solo tour, without even Ray Cooper behind his trusty timpani. Dusting off rarely heard songs like "Carla/Étude," "Friends," "Elton's Song," "Sweet Painted Lady," "Amazes Me," "Harmony," and "Nikita," he played mostly small American cities, Canadian arenas, and, in Europe, castle grounds and stately homes. Interrupted by what was officially described as a "minor imbalance of the heart" that necessitated an operation to fit the musician with a pacemaker, he continued on as if nothing had happened. Seeing Elton manically roll riotous chords during "Burn Down the Mission" just a couple of months later, it was easy to forget he had an ailment that could have killed him had it not been caught soon enough.

Elton still loved connecting with other talent, as he did at the "One Night Only" gigs at Madison Square Garden in October 2000. These shows were supposed to pay tribute to his back catalog, as well as provide material for a live album, television special, and video. Joining him for various songs were old veterans (Billy Joel, Bryan Adams, and Kiki Dee), a star of recent vintage (Mary J. Blige), and rising stars (Anastacia, a hip-shaking throwback to Janis Joplin adorned with modern-day glitz, and heartthrob Ronan Keating, late of Boyzone). Elton also saluted departed friend Lennon with a brash "Come Together" that combined the pianist's abstract chord changes and bluesy growling, set against harsh electric assertions from the band (including the returning Nigel Olsson), as images of the ex-Beatle flashed on video screens in the background.

That weekend in October seemed to be a self-actualized *Two Rooms II*, another bridge between older accomplishments and things yet to come. But older accomplishments were streaming into the future. Some projects—such as a classical score for Albert Brooks's 1999 comedy *The Muse*—suggested a new direction, scoring films for a John/Furnish enterprise, Rocket Pictures. Other projects, including the under-appreciated John/Rice songs in DreamWorks's *The Road to El Dorado*, and the wildly appreciated, epochal John/Rice compositions for the second most popular (next to *The Lion King*) musical on Broadway, *Aida*, whose soundtrack had earned him another Grammy, hinted that there were more musicals in the offing. At least some of these were expected to eventually blossom on the big screen, like an adaptation of Rudyard Kipling's *Just So Stories*, through a joint venture between Rocket Pictures and Disney.

The only thing missing from Elton's never-ending activity was another major hit. He'd had a U.S. Top 40 in 1999, thanks to his duet with LeAnn Rimes on "Written in the Stars," from the all-star *Aida* album, part of the carpet-laying for the eventual Broadway debut of the musical. But the song had only reached number 29, mainly on the strength of singles sales. A year later, his deliciously textured "Someday out of the Blue," from *The Road to El Dorado*, didn't quite made it into the U.S. Top 40. The song and soundtrack disappointingly sank with the cartoon. The failure meant little, though, with all the projects and ideas Elton was nurturing. He would always be back with something else—a new album, tour, musical, score, or duet.

He would love every minute of the work. He would relish anticipating the results. And there would always be people to line up for it.

Prologue

1 Lyric from "Tiny Dancer," 1971.

2 Gary Cee, *Classic Rock*. (New York: MetroBooks, 1995.)

3 Bob Doerschuk, "Elton John," *Contemporary Keyboard*, February 1981.

Chapter One

1 Song title, B-side to U.S. "Goodbye Yellow Brick Road," 1973.

2 Fred Hauptfuhrer, "Bio: Elton John No Longer Views Life through Crazy Glasses, Darkly: He's a New and Different Man," *People*, 16 January 1978.

3 Elton John, radio interview with Dick Clark, "Dick Clark Presents Elton John," Mutual Broadcasting System, 4 July 1981.

4 Unknown author, "The Rock Family Affair," *Life*, 24 September 1971.

5 Tony Norman, "Elton the Embarrassed 'Genius,'" unknown publication and date.

6 Philip Norman, *Elton John: The Biography*. (New York: Harmony Books, 1991.)

7 Lyric from "Made in England," 1995.

8 Liner notes, *To Be Continued. . .* box set (U.S.), MCA Records, 1990.

9 Philip Norman, liner notes, *To Be Continued. . .* box set (U.K.), Rocket Records, 1991.

10 P. Norman, *Elton John*.

11 Elton John, Bernie Taupin, Gus Dudgeon, and others, radio interview with Paul Gambaccini, "The Elton John Story," WKRQ (Cincinnati), fall 1976.

12 Liner notes, *To Be Continued . . .* (U.S.).

13 P. Norman, *Elton John*.

14 Elton John, radio interview with Steve McCoy and Vikki Locke, Star-94 (Atlanta), 19 August 1994.

15 P. Norman, *Elton John*.

16 Ben Edmonds, "Elton John, Prisoner of Wax," *Creem*, February 1974.

17 Eugenie Ross-Leming and David Standish, "Playboy Interview: Elton John," *Playboy*, January 1976.

18 Roy Carr and Charles Shaar Murray, "The Life and Times of Elton John (Part One: The Early Years)," *Rock Australia Magazine* (RAM), 5 April 1975.

19 Lyric from "Captain Fantastic and the Brown Dirt Cowboy," 1975.

20 John Tobler, "Part One: Paying Dues," *Zig Zag 25*, No. 25, 1972.

21 Carr and Murray, "The Life and Times of Elton John (Part One)."

22 P. Norman, *Elton John*.

23 Carr and Murray, "The Life and Times of Elton John (Part One)."

24 Ibid.

25 Tobler, "Part One: Paying Dues."

26 Gerald Newman and Joe Bivona, *Elton John*. (New York: New American Library, 1976); ibid.

27 Patti LaBelle with Laura B. Randolph. *Don't Block the Blessings: Revelations of a Lifetime*. (New York: Riverhead Books, 1996.)

28 Tobler, "Part One: Paying Dues."

29 Carr and Murray, "The Life and Times of Elton John (Part One)."

30 Charles "Dr. Rock" White, *The Life and Times of Little Richard*. (New York: Pocket Books, 1984.)

31 Tobler, "Part One: Paying Dues."

32 Lyric from "Captain Fantastic and the Brown Dirt Cowboy," 1975.

33 Bernie Taupin, *A Cradle of Haloes: Sketches of a Childhood*. (London: Aurum Press, 1988.)

34 Lyric from "Captain Fantastic and the Brown Dirt Cowboy," 1975.

35 Liner notes, *To Be Continued . . .* (U.S.).

36 Kirk Duncan, letter to the editor, "Elton: The Apprentice," *Record Collector*, February 1998.

37 Carr and Murray, "The Life and Times of Elton John (Part One)."

38 Lorna Dickinson and Claudia Rosencrantz, *Two Rooms: Elton John and Bernie Taupin in Their Own Words*. (London: Boxtree Limited, 1991.)

39 Carr and Murray, "The Life and Times of Elton John (Part One)."

40 Dickinson and Rosencrantz, *Two Rooms*.

41 Elton John, radio interview with Bob Coburn, *Rockline*, the Global Satellite, 3 October 1988.

Chapter Two

1 Song title, late 1960s (never released).

2 Unknown author, "The House that James Built," *Billboard*, 18 September 1971.

3 Bernie Taupin, liner notes for *Rare Masters* (box set), Polydor, 1992.

4 Ibid.

5 Elton John, Bernie Taupin, Gus Dudgeon, and others, radio interview with Paul Gambaccini, fall 1976.

6 Unknown author and title, *Goldmine*, November 1993.

7 Ken Garner, *In Session Tonight: The Complete Radio I Recordings*. (London: BBC Books, 1993.)

8 Lyric from "Someone Saved My Life Tonight," 1975.

9 Marc Kirkeby, "Bill Martin Recalls an Early Elton Tune," *Record World*, 31 January 1976.

10 Carr and Murray, "The Life and Times of Elton John (Part One)."

11 Cliff Jones, "Sound Your Funky Horn: Elton John," *Mojo*, October 1997.

12 Lyric from "We All Fall in Love Sometimes," 1975.

13 Elton John, radio interview with David Symonds, *Symonds on Sunday*, BBC, 20 July 1969.

14 Lyric from "Writing," 1975.

15 Elton John, radio interview with Andy Peebles, *BBC Rock Hour*, American broadcast, 28 December 1980.

16 Elton John, Bernie Taupin, Gus Dudgeon, and others, radio interview with Paul Gambaccini, fall 1976.

17 Elton John, radio interview with Andy Peebles, 28 December 1980.

18 Richard Cromelin, "The Elton John Career: For the Love of Him Make Him Your Reason for Living," *Phonograph Record*, November 1973.

19 P. Norman, *Elton John*.

20 C. Jones, "Sound Your Funky Horn: Elton John."

21 Carr and Murray, "The Life and Times of Elton John (Part One)."

22 David White, "Corporal Loudmouth," *RAM*, 28 June 1975.

23 Elton John, Bernie Taupin, Gus Dudgeon, and others, radio interview with Paul Gambaccini, fall 1976.

24 Carr and Murray, "The Life and Times of Elton John (Part One)."

25 Liner notes, *To Be Continued . . .* (U.S.).

26 Carr and Murray, "The Life and Times of Elton John (Part One)."

27 Question and answer session (Q&A), Elton John Expo, Cleveland, Ohio, 26 July 1996.

28 P. Norman, *Elton John*.

29 Elton John, Bernie Taupin, Gus Dudgeon, and others, radio interview with Paul Gambaccini, fall 1976.

30 Murray M. Silver, Jr., "Interview with: Nigel Olsson," *Modern Recording*, June 1979.

31 Penny Valentine, "The Sounds Talk-In: Elton John," *Sounds*, 26 December 1970.

32 Vic Lewis, "Vic Lewis: Aiding Elton's Breakout," *Record World*, 31 January 1976.

33 Lyric from "Country Comfort," 1970.

34 Elton John, Bernie Taupin, Gus Dudgeon, John Reid, Steve Brown, and Paul Buckmaster, radio interview, "The Elton John Story," WBBM-FM (Chicago), 1974.

35 Robert Hilburn, "John, Taupin Go Back Years," *The Times* (Trenton, New Jersey), 29 September 1989.

36 Roy Carr and Charles Shaar Murray, "The Life and Times of Elton John (Part Two: The First Sweet Thrill of Lady Success)," *RAM*, unknown date.

37 Garner, *In Session Tonight*.

38 Lyric from "(Gotta Get a) Meal Ticket," 1975.

39 P. Norman, *Elton John*.

40 Taupin, *Rare Masters*.

Chapter Three

1 Song title, 1970.

2 Cromelin, "The Elton John Career."

3 Ibid.

4 Ingrid Sischy, "Elton John: 150% Involved," *Interview*, April 1995.

5 Philip Norman, "The Night Timid Reg of Pinner Transformed Himself into Elton John and Rocked the World," *Daily Mail*, 26 November 1994.

6 Cromelin, "The Elton John Career."

7 David Felton, "Elton John: After Three Gold Albums and the Praise of Dylan, Leon and Millions, What Can He Say but Thank You and Occasionally Fuck off, Norman," *Rolling Stone*, 10 June 1971.

8 P. Norman, "The Night Timid Reg of Pinner Transformed Himself."

9 Robert Hilburn, "Elton John New Rock Talent," *Los Angeles Times*, 27 August 1970.

10 Ibid.

11 Ellen Mandell, "The Many Faces of Elton John," *Good Times*, originally printed late 1970 or early 1971, reprinted 21 June 1988.

12 Brian Wilson with Todd Gold, *Wouldn't It Be Nice: My Own Story*. (New York: HarperCollins Publishers, 1991.)

13 Lyric from "Made in England," 1995.

14 Robert Greenfield, "Elton John Steams 'em Up," *Rolling Stone*, 12 November 1970.

15 Robert Hilburn, "Elton John: A Super Rock Star Arrives on Scene," *Los Angeles Times*, 13 September 1970.

16 Norma McLain Stoop, "John Reid: The Right Way In," *After Dark*, March 1976.

17 Leslie Bennetts, "Still Captain Fantastic," *Vanity Fair*, November 1997.

18 Roy Carr, "A Single Man: The Elton John Interview," *New Musical Express*, 28 October 1978.

19 Cromelin, "The Elton John Career."

20 Greenfield, "Elton John Steams 'em Up."

21 Karl Dallas, "Fotheringay: Albert Hall," *The Times* (London), 3 October 1970.

22 Lyric from "Friends," 1971.

23 Paul Gambaccini, "The Rolling Stone Interview: Elton John," *Rolling Stone*, 16 August 1973.

24 Liner notes, *To Be Continued . . .* (U.S.).

25 Gambaccini, "The Rolling Stone Interview: Elton John."

26 Greenfield, "Elton John Steams 'em Up."

27 Audience cries heard on 11-17-70, 1971.

28 Elton John, Bernie Taupin, Gus Dudgeon, John Reid, Steve Brown, and Paul Buckmaster, radio interview, 1974; Alan Finch, discography, and Chris Charlesworth, short biography, *Elton John: 'Only the Piano Player': An Illustrated Discography*. (London: Omnibus Press, 1983.)

29 Robert Hilburn, "Hello, Yellow Brick Road," *Los Angeles Times*, 19 February 1998.

30 Eliot Tiegel, "Odetta, John, Coorder [*sic*]: 1 Plus & 2 Maybes," *Billboard*, 28 November 1970.

31 Fred Kirby, "Talent in Action: Leon Russell Elton John," *Billboard*, 5 December 1970.

32 Mike Jahn, "Elton John Reveals Rich Song Talents," *The New York Times*, 22 November 1970.

33 Lyric from "Burn Down the Mission," 1970.

34 William Bender, "Handstands and Fluent Fusion," *Time*, 14 December 1970.

35 *An Open-End Interview: Friends*, promotional record, Paramount, 1971.

36 Unknown author, "Radio One DJs Pop Opinion Poll," *Disc and Music Echo*, 2 January 1971.

37 Jon Landau, "Tumbleweed Connection: Elton John," *Rolling Stone*, 18 February 1971.

38 Robert Hilburn, "John Disc Something to Shoot At,"

Los Angeles Times, 17 January 1971.

39 Albert Goldman, "Copycat in Wild Threads," *Life,* 5 February 1971.

40 Chris Van Ness, "Elton John." *Los Angeles Free Press,* 21 May 1971.

41 Mike Flood Page and Chris Salewicz, "Elton John: Renaissance Man of Pop," *Let It Rock,* September 1973.

42 Andrew Means, "Magna Carta and the Gentle Sound," *Melody Maker,* 23 January 1971.

43 Lyric from "Holiday Inn," 1971.

44 Author and title unknown, *Zig Zag,* issue unknown, 1972.

45 Gambaccini, "The Rolling Stone Interview: Elton John."

46 Elton John, Bernie Taupin, Gus Dudgeon, and others, radio interview with Paul Gambaccini, fall 1976.

47 P. Norman, *Elton John.*

48 Lyric from "Holiday Inn," 1971.

49 Felton, "Elton John: After Three Gold Albums and the Praise of Dylan, Leon and Millions."

50 Michael Wale, "Garden Party: Crystal Palace," *The Times* (London), 2 August 1971.

51 Elton John, radio interview with Andy Peebles, 28 December 1980.

52 Unknown author and title, *Q,* July 1995.

53 Nik Cohn, "I'm a Mess but I'm Having Fun," *The New York Times,* 22 August 1971.

54 Robert Hilburn, *Five Years of Fun.* (Boutwell Enterprises, Inc., 1975.)

55 Cohn, "I'm a Mess but I'm Having Fun."

56 Margaret English, "Twinkle Twinkle Superstar Do We Know Who You Are?" *Look,* 27 July 1971.

57 Neil Spencer, "As Elton Backs Government, Labour Rock Ads Spark RAR [Rock Against Racism] Protest," unknown publication, *c.* 1979.

58 Carr, "A Single Man: The Elton John Interview."

59 Lyric from "Holiday Inn," 1971.

60 Unknown author, "Dick James in Finland," *Billboard,* 18 September 1971; Michaelway, "Elton a Hit in France," *Billboard,* 18 September 1971; unknown author, "Dick James in Scandinavia," *Billboard,* 18 September 1971.

61 Stephen MacLean, "Elton Arrives with a Flash Bang," *Go-Set,* 23 October 1971; unknown author, "Feds 'Censor' Star," unknown publication, October 1971.

62 Unknown author, "Wild Little Man in Flowing Cloak," unknown Australian publication, October 1971; Ian Meldrum, "The Weather Was Nothing! It Was Elton, Nigel and Dee Who Blew Everyone's Cool," unknown publication (probably *Go-Set*), 1971.

63 Lyric from "All the Nasties," 1971.

64 Jose Manuel Nunes, "Lisbon," *Billboard,* 28 August 1971 and 2 October 1971.

65 Jon Tiven, "Elton John's 'Captain Fantastic and the Brown Dirt Cowboy': The Story of a Million $ Friendship," *Circus Raves,* August 1975.

66 Elton John, radio interview with Andy Peebles, 28 December 1980.

67 Thomas Ryan, *American Hit Radio.* (California: Prima Publishing, 1996.)

68 Doerschuk, "Elton John."

69 Eric Van Lustbader, "The Songs of Elton and Bernie: A Musical Monument to the '70s," *Record World,* 31 January 1976.

70 Patrick Snyder, "Taupin Speaks through Elton John's Mouth," syndicated *Rolling Stone* article in unknown newspaper, fall 1977.

71 Elton John, Bernie Taupin, Gus Dudgeon, and others, radio interview with Paul Gambaccini, fall 1976.

72 Page and Salewicz, "Elton John: Renaissance Man of Pop."

73 Elton John, television interview, *Old Grey Whistle Test,* BBC-TV, 7 December 1971.

74 Lyric from "Hercules," 1972.

75 Barbara Graustark, "Elton Shoots Back on 'Piano Player,'" *Circus,* April 1973.

76 Peter Buckley, "Is Elton John Obsolete?" *Circus,* 1972.

77 Julie Webb, "Elton John: Undedicated Performer," *Hit Parader,* October 1972.

78 Michael Wale, "Elton John," *The Times* (London), 8 June 1972.

79 Page and Salewicz, "Elton John: Renaissance Man of Pop."

80 Elton John, Bernie Taupin, Gus Dudgeon, and others, radio interview with Paul Gambaccini, fall 1976.

81 Unknown author and title, *Goldmine,* 28 October 1994.

82 Webb, "Elton John: Undedicated Performer."

83 Lyric from "Honky Cat," 1972.

84 Author and title unknown, *Zig Zag,* issue unknown, 1972.

85 William Mann, "Elton John: Festival Hall," *The Times* (London), 7 February 1972.

86 Neil Tennant, "It's Him!" *Interview,* January 1998.

87 Michael Wale, "Elton John: Shaw," *The Times* (London), 29 February 1972.

88 Elton John, Bernie Taupin, Gus Dudgeon, and others, radio interview with Paul Gambaccini, fall 1976.

89 Andrew Tyler, "Davey Johnstone, Straight Man in Elton's Camp," unknown publication, *c.* 1973.

90 Lynn Van Matre, "Superstar in Shining Splendor," *Chicago Tribune,* 9 May 1972.

91 Mike Ledgerwood, "Everything Stops for Baldry," *Disc,* 3 June 1972.

92 Lyric from "Rocket Man (I Think It's Going to Be a Long, Long Time)," 1972.

93 Unknown author, "Rocket Elton," unknown Houston publication, 1972.

94 Jon Landau, "Elton John Gets into Fantasy on 'Chateau,' 'Blue River' Is Eric's Finest Hour," *Rolling Stone,* 17 August 1972.

95 Robert Hilburn, unknown title, *Los Angeles Times,* 9 July 1972.

96 Dave McAleer, *The All Music Book of Hit Albums.* (San Francisco: Miller Freeman Books, 1995.)

97 Lyric from "I'm Going to Be a Teenage Idol," 1973.

98 Graustark, "Elton Shoots Back with 'Piano Player.'"

99 Elton John, radio interview with Scott Mitchell, "Shades of Elton John," Westwood One, week of 17 May 1993.

100 Dickinson and Rosencrantz, *Two Rooms.*

101 Paul Gambaccini, "Singles: Daniel: Elton John," *Rolling Stone,* 7 June 1973.

102 Elton John, radio interview with Jim Conley, *Startrak*, Westwood One, 1983.

103 Elton John, radio interview with Andy Peebles, 28 December 1980.

104 Gambaccini, "The Rolling Stone Interview: Elton John."

105 Elton John, radio interview with Dave Charity, "The Elton John Story," United Stations Programming Network, 16–18 June 1989.

106 Song title, 1973.

107 Eric Van Lustbader, "Elton John: He's Only Just Begun," *Contemporary Music,* September 1974.

108 Edmonds, "Elton John, Prisoner of Wax."

109 Robert Hilburn, "Elton Rolls with the Punches and Keeps on Rockin'," *Los Angeles Times,* 22 October 1972.

110 Lyric from "I Think I'm Going to Be a Teenage Idol," 1973.

111 Cathi Stein, *Elton John: Rock's Piano Pounding Madman.* (New York: Popular Library, 1975.)

112 Hilburn, "Elton Rolls with the Punches and Keeps on Rockin'."

113 Penny Valentine, "Elton: Earthquake in LA," *Sounds,* 4 November 1972.

114 Kirb., "Elton John (18), Family (5)," *Variety,* 29 November 1972.

115 Nat Freedland, "Talent in Action: Elton John, Family," *Billboard,* 23 December 1972.

116 Lyric from "Crocodile Rock," 1972.

117 Paul Gambaccini, *A Conversation with Elton John and Bernie Taupin.* (New York and London: Flash Books, 1975.)

118 Gambaccini, "The Rolling Stone Interview: Elton John."

119 Robert Hilburn, "Top Rock Artists for 1972 Named," *Los Angeles Times,* 2 January 1973.

120 Lyric from "Daniel," 1973.

121 Unknown author, "That Single," *Go-Set,* 27 January 1973.

122 Elton John, Bernie Taupin, Gus Dudgeon, and others, radio interview with Paul Gambaccini, fall 1976.

123 McAleer, *The All Music Books of Hit Albums.*

124 Lyric from "Jamaica Jerk-Off," 1973.

125 Carr and Murray, "The Life and Times of Elton John (Part Two)."

126 Dickinson and Rosencrantz, *Two Rooms.*

127 Liner notes, *To Be Continued. . .* (U.S.).

Chapter Four

1 Part of a song title, from "I'm Going to Be a Teenage Idol," 1973.

2 Unknown author, "Now Elton's a Teen Idol!" *Melody Maker,* 31 March 1973.

3 Lyric from "Harmony," 1973.

4 Elton John, Bernie Taupin, Gus Dudgeon, John Reid, Steve Brown, and Paul Buckmaster, radio interview, 1974.

5 Elton John, radio interview with Bob Coburn, 3 October 1988.

6 Van Lustbader, "Elton John: He's Only Just Begun."

7 Elton John, radio interview with Bob Coburn, 3 October 1988.

8 Steve Demorest, "'Goodbye Yellow Brick Road'— Elton John Rockets Over the Rainbow," *Circus,* December 1973.

9 Gambaccini, *A Conversation with Elton John and Bernie Taupin.*

10 Arthur Levy, "Elton John: The Leaving of America: Beau Brummel Meets Yogi Berra," *Zoo World,* 6 December 1973.

11 Ibid.

12 Ibid.

13 Ibid.

14 Dickinson and Rosencrantz, *Two Rooms.*

15 Demorest, "'Goodbye Yellow Brick Road'—Elton John Rockets Over the Rainbow."

16 Elton John, Bernie Taupin, Gus Dudgeon, and others, radio interview with Paul Gambaccini, fall 1976.

17 Demorest, "'Goodbye Yellow Brick Road'—Elton John Rockets Over the Rainbow."

18 Gambaccini, "The Rolling Stone Interview: Elton John."

19 Van Lustbader, "Elton John: He's Only Just Begun."

20 Gambaccini, *A Conversation with Elton John and Bernie Taupin.*

21 Lyric from "Saturday Night's Alright for Fighting," 1973.

22 Bart Mills, "Kiki Dee's Career Hits High Notes Under Elton John's Wing," *Chicago Tribune,* 9 January 1977.

23 Kiki Dee, "My Mate Elton," *Rock World,* December 1993.

24 Elton John, radio interview with Dennis Elsus, WNEW-NY (New York), 29 November 1974.

25 K. Dee, "My Mate Elton."

26 Lyric from "Bennie and the Jets," 1973.

27 Al Martinez, "The Vision They Create Is Most Spectacular," *Los Angeles Times,* 23 September 1973.

28 Dickinson and Rosencrantz, *Two Rooms.*

29 Mary Anne Cassata, "Elton John: The Balance Brings Happiness," *Music Paper,* November 1988.

30 Lynn Van Matre, "Flashy Elton's Varied Sound Is in the Pink," *Chicago Tribune,* 27 August 1973.

31 Linda Lovelace announcing Elton John at the Hollywood Bowl, 7 September 1973.

32 Robert Hilburn, "Elton John and that Good Time Spirit," *Los Angeles Times,* 11 September 1973.

33 Jerry Gilbert, "The Bernie Taupin Talk-In," *Sounds,* 10 November 1973.

34 Steve Ditlea, "Offstage with Elton John," *New Ingenue,* March 1974.

35 Newman and Bivona, *Elton John.*

36 Tom Zito, "Boring Music, Bad Attitude," *The Washington Post,* 1 October 1973.

37 Lyric from "Love Lies Bleeding," 1973.

38 Stephen Davis, "Goodbye Yellow Brick Road: Elton John," *Rolling Stone,* 22 November 1973.

39 Robert Christgau, "The Christgau Consumer Guide," *Creem,* February 1974.

40 Elton John, radio interview with Andy Peebles, 28 December 1980.

41 Lyric from "Step into Christmas," 1973.

42 Gambaccini, *A Conversation with Elton John and Bernie Taupin.*

43 Levy, "Elton John: The Leaving of America."

44 Jerry Gilbert, "Christmas Crackers!" unknown publication (possibly *Sounds*), 1973.

45 Lyric from "Step into Christmas," 1973.

46 Elton John, Bernie Taupin, Gus Dudgeon, and others, radio interview with Paul Gambaccini, fall 1976.

47 Tony Wilson, "Elton John," unknown publication, 1973.

48 Author unknown, letter to the editor, unknown publication, 1973.

49 Elton John, John Walters, and others, radio interview with Andy Peebles, "Elton John at the Beeb," BBC, 7 December 1985.

50 Ibid.

51 Robert Hilburn, "Most Popular Record Artists of 1973," *Los Angeles Times*, 1 January 1974.

52 Lyric from "Don't Let the Sun Go Down on Me," 1974.

53 Gambaccini, *A Conversation with Elton John and Bernie Taupin.*

54 D. White, "Corporal Loudmouth."

55 Charles Shaar Murray, "The Short Hello," *New Musical Express*, 6 July 1974.

56 Tiven, "Elton John's 'Captain Fantastic and the Brown Dirt Cowboy.'"

57 Hilburn, "John, Taupin Go Back Years."

58 Elton John, Bernie Taupin, Gus Dudgeon, and others, radio interview with Paul Gambaccini, fall 1976.

59 Adam Block, "Undeniably Elton," *Ten Percent*, summer 1993.

60 Dave Marsh, *The Heart of Rock and Soul: The 1001 Greatest Singles Ever Made.* (New York: New American Library, 1989.)

61 Doerschuk, "Elton John."

62 Steven Gaines, "'Caribou'—Elton John's Rocky Mountain Orgasm," *Circus*, September 1974.

63 Gambaccini, *A Conversation with Elton John and Bernie Taupin.*

64 Lyric from "Bennie and the Jets," 1973.

65 Unknown author, "Elton: Any Night's All Right for Fightin'," *Rolling Stone*, 9 May 1974.

66 Unknown author, "'Bennie and the Jets' Goes Soul," *Record World*, 31 January 1976.

67 Pat Pipolo, "Elton's Chart Challenge," *Record World*, 31 January 1976.

68 Elton John, radio interview with Andy Peebles, 28 December 1980.

69 Cliff Jahr, "Elton John: It's Lonely at the Top," *Rolling Stone*, 7 October 1976.

70 Lyric from "The Bitch Is Back," 1974.

71 Ian Meldrum, "To: Mr. Reg Dwight, Alias Elton John," unknown publication and date (probably *Go-Set*, January 1973).

72 Ian Meldrum, "Ian Meldrum's Keyhole News," *Go-Set*, 2 March 1974.

73 Bruce Guthrie, "Extravaganza of Sight and Sound," unknown publication, February 1974; Ian Meldrum, unknown title, *Go-Set*, probably 9 March 1974.

74 Tony Wilson, "Genius with Feathers," unknown Australian publication, February 1974.

75 Unknown author, "Elton's $200,000 Wardrobe and $6500 Overweight Baggage" and "Cassidy Tour a Flop?" *Go-Set*, 16 March 1974; unknown author, "Elton Was Out of This World—and Looked It,"

unknown Australian publication, February/March 1974; Mitch, "Front Row Reviews: Elton John, Randwick Racecourse," unknown Sydney publication, February/March 1974.

76 Staff writer, "Random Notes," *Rolling Stone*, 11 April 1974.

77 Staff writer, "Elton John Scandal," *Go-Set*, 16 March 1974; Ian Meldrum, "Ian Meldrum's Keyhole News," *Go-Set*, 16 March 1974.

78 Lyric from "Hard Luck Story," 1974.

79 Liner notes, *To Be Continued . . .* (U.S.).

80 Elton John, Bernie Taupin, Gus Dudgeon, and others, radio interview with Paul Gambaccini, fall 1976.

81 Nickname for members of the Watford Hornets football club.

82 Unknown author, "Elton Kicks Football Debt," unknown U.S. publication, spring 1974.

83 Edmonds, "Elton John, Prisoner of Wax."

84 Lyric from "The Bitch Is Back," 1974.

85 Joel Whitburn, "Joel Whitburn's Record Research Report," *Billboard*, 13 July 1974.

86 Robert Hilburn, "Elton John—the $8 Million Man," *Los Angeles Times*, 25 June 1974.

87 Len Epand, "Madman Across the Net," *Zoo World*, 21 November 1974.

88 Hilburn, "Elton John—the $8 Million Man."

89 Ibid.

90 Stoop, "John Reid: The Right Way In."

91 Nat Freedland, "Record-Setting Pact Ups Superstar Ante," *Billboard*, 13 July 1974.

92 Stoop, "John Reid: The Right Way In."

93 Freedland, "Record-Setting Pact Ups Superstar Ante"; Hilburn, "Elton John—the $8 Million Man."

94 Paul Gambaccini, "Elton Says No to U.S.A.," *Disc*, 14 December 1974.

95 Lyric from "Captain Fantastic and the Brown Dirt Cowboy," 1975.

96 Elton John, Bernie Taupin, Gus Dudgeon, and others, radio interview with Paul Gambaccini, fall 1976.

97 Ibid.

98 Elton John, recorded press interview, *Telltales* [CD], Tell 08, 1975.

99 Elton John, radio interview with Andy Peebles, 28 December 1980.

100 Elton John, radio interview with Timothy White, "Poet of the Piano," *Timothy White's Rock Stars*, unknown U.S. network, 18 June 1990.

101 Elton John, Bernie Taupin, Gus Dudgeon, and others, radio interview with Paul Gambaccini, fall 1976.

102 Epand, "Madman Across the Net."

103 John Lennon, 1974 radio interview, featured in "The Elton John Story," KOPA-FM (Scottsdale, Arizona), fall 1982.

104 Epand, "Madman Across the Net."

105 Elton John, radio interview with Dennis Elsus, 29 November 1974.

106 Lyric from "Captain Fantastic and the Brown Dirt Cowboy," 1975.

107 Tiven, "Elton John's 'Captain Fantastic and the Brown Dirt Cowboy.'"

108 Elton John and Bernie Taupin, radio interview, *Classic Album Series*, BBC, 24 February 1990.

109 D. White, "Corporal Loudmouth."

110 Elton John and Bernie Taupin, radio interview, *Classic Album Series*, 24 February 1990.

111 Ibid.

112 Ibid.

113 D. White, "Corporal Loudmouth."

114 Elton John, television interview with David Frost, American public television, 22 November 1991.

115 Elton John, Bernie Taupin, Gus Dudgeon, and others, radio interview with Paul Gambaccini, fall 1976.

116 Elton John and Bernie Taupin, radio interview, *Classic Album Series*, 24 February 1990.

117 Ben Fong-Torres, "The Four-Eyed Bitch Is Back," *Rolling Stone*, 21 November 1974.

118 Elton John and Bernie Taupin, radio interview, *Classic Album Series*, 24 February 1990.

119 Ibid.

120 Ibid.

121 D. White, "Corporal Loudmouth."

122 Ibid.

123 Lyric from "Philadelphia Freedom," 1975.

124 Elton John, Bernie Taupin, Gus Dudgeon, and others, radio interview with Paul Gambaccini, fall 1976.

125 Elton John, as quoted in *Elton John and Bernie Taupin Say Goodbye Norma Jean and Other Things*, documentary by Bryan Forbes, ABC-TV, 12 May 1974.

126 Gaines, "'Caribou'—Elton John's Rocky Mountain Orgasm."

127 Epand, "Madman Across the Net."

128 Elton John, television interview with Paul Gambaccini, *The Other Side of the Tracks*, BBC-TV, 24 March 1984.

129 Bernie Taupin, radio interview with Dick Lillard, WMOD-FM (Washington, D.C.), 16 May 1976.

130 Dickinson and Rosencrantz, *Two Rooms*.

131 Lyric from "The Bitch Is Back," 1974.

132 Elton John, Bernie Taupin, Gus Dudgeon, and others, radio interview with Paul Gambaccini, fall 1976.

133 John Biggs, "Where Were You in 1974? Part One: Goldmine Readers: Radio Ramblings," *Goldmine*, 14 October 1994.

134 Elton John, Bernie Taupin, Gus Dudgeon, and others, radio interview with Paul Gambaccini, fall 1976.

135 Elton John, radio interview with Dennis Elsus, 29 November 1974.

136 Elton John, Bernie Taupin, Gus Dudgeon, and others, radio interview with Paul Gambaccini, fall 1976.

137 Elton John and Neil Sedaka, radio interview with Dick Clark, 4 July 1981.

138 Elton John, radio interview with Dennis Elsus, 29 November 1974.

139 Lyric from "The Bitch Is Back," 1974.

140 Lynn Van Matre, ". . . And in Elton's Case It's Framed in Feathers, Finery, and Frenzy," *Chicago Tribune*, 10 November 1974.

141 Gambaccini, "Elton Says No to U.S.A."

142 Robert Hilburn, "Christmas Comes Early for Elton John," *Los Angeles Times*, 6 October 1974.

143 Epand, "Madman Across the Net."

144 Gambaccini, "Elton Says No to U.S.A."

145 Robert Hilburn, "Elton John, Superstar—and Still a Fan," *Los Angeles Times*, 1 October 1974.

146 Toy., "Elton John Kiki Dee Band," *Variety*, 9 October 1974.

147 Jack McDonough, "Talent in Action: Elton John Kiki Dee," *Billboard*, 2 November 1974.

148 Unknown author, "Elton Braves Arrest to Save Fans," *Circus Raves*, unknown date (probably early 1975).

149 Lyric from "Your Song," 1970.

150 Elton's greeting to the Madison Square Garden audience on November 28, 1974.

151 Liner notes, *To Be Continued . . .* (U.S.).

152 Elton John, radio interview with Dennis Elsus, 29 November 1974.

153 Lenny Kaye, "Live on Stage in New York: Elton John Lennon," *Disc*, 14 December 1974.

154 Elton John, Bernie Taupin, Gus Dudgeon, and others, radio interview with Paul Gambaccini, fall 1976.

155 Lyric from "Made in England," 1995.

156 Hilburn, "Christmas Comes Early."

157 Van Matre, ". . . And in Elton's Case."

158 Fong-Torres, "The Four-Eyed Bitch Is Back."

159 Ed McCormack, "Elton's Tour Ends: Tears, Lennon and Whatever Gets You through the Night," *Rolling Stone*, 2 January 1975.

160 Elton's remarks about "Lucy in the Sky with Diamonds" at a December 24, 1974 Hammersmith Odeon concert.

161 Unknown author, letter to the editor, *Record Mirror*, 30 November 1974.

162 Live television broadcast of concert at Hammersmith Odeon, BBC-TV, 24 December 1974.

163 Robert Hilburn, "Denver, John and Reddy Top Sales," *Los Angeles Times*, 28 December 1974.

164 Robert Hilburn, "Elton John—Wire-to-Wire Artist of the Year," *Los Angeles Times*, 5 January 1975.

165 Lyric from "Philadelphia Freedom," 1975.

166 Unknown author, "John, Elton (Hercules)," *Current Biography*, 1975.

167 Lyric from "Philadelphia Freedom," 1975.

168 David DeVoss, "Elton John: Rock's Captain Fantastic," *Time*, 7 July 1975.

169 Elton John, television interview with Michael Parkinson, BBC, late spring 1975.

170 Joyce Haber, "Million-Dollar Mansion for Elton," *Los Angeles Times*, 22 April 1975.

171 Unknown author, "Making Tommy," *Rock Scene*, July 1975.

172 Elton John, Bernie Taupin, Gus Dudgeon, and others, radio interview with Paul Gambaccini, fall 1976.

173 Elton John, recorded press interview, *Telltales*, 1975.

174 Elton John, radio interview with Richard Skinner, "Reg on the Radio," BBC, 14 and 29 December 1990.

175 Gambaccini, "Elton Says No to U.S.A."

176 Nigel Olsson, promotional interview with Radio and Records AOR Director Mike Harrison, *Drummers Can Sing Too!* MCA/Rocket Records Company, PIG-1932, 1975.

177 Ibid.

178 Lyric from "I Feel Like a Bullet (In the Gun of Robert Ford)," 1975.

179 Elton John, television interview with Conan O'Brien, *Late Night with Conan O'Brien*, NBC-TV, 15 November 1996.

180 DeVoss, "Elton John: Rock's Captain Fantastic."

181 Elton John, Bernie Taupin, Gus Dudgeon, and others, radio interview with Paul Gambaccini, fall 1976.

182 Paul Gambaccini, "Elton & Company Seduce Wembley," *Rolling Stone*, 31 July 1975.

183 Unknown author, "After the Budget: Up, Up, Up!" *Melody Maker*, 1975.

184 Robert Hilburn, "Paul Never Better; Elton Still Best," *Los Angeles Times*, 8 June 1975.

185 Greg Shaw, "Captain Fantastic and the Brown Dirt Cowboy: Elton John," *Phonograph Record*, June 1975.

186 Dave Marsh, "Captain's Latest Feat Is Not So Fantastic," *New Orleans Times-Picayune*, 16 June 1975.

187 Lyric from "Someone Saved My Life Tonight," 1975.

188 Elton John, Bernie Taupin, Gus Dudgeon, and others, radio interview with Paul Gambaccini, fall 1976.

189 Bob Doerschuk, "Elton John's Multi-Keyboard Sideman: James Newton Howard," *Contemporary Keyboard*, February 1981.

190 Sue Byrom, "Captain Fantastic Marshals His Troops," *Record Mirror*, 21 June 1975.

191 Geoffrey Wansell, "Elton John, a Long Way From a Pound a Night, Plus Tips, in Northwood," *The Times* (London), 21 June 1975.

192 Gambaccini, "Elton & Company Seduce Wembley."

193 Ibid.

194 Elton John, recorded press interview, *Telltales*, 1975.

195 Philip Norman, "Playing It the Way It Was at the Top," *The Times* (London), 23 June 1975.

196 Lyric from "I Feel Like a Bullet (In the Gun of Robert Ford)," 1975.

197 Craig Rosen, *The Billboard Book of Number One Albums.* (New York: Billboard Books, 1996.)

198 Robert Hilburn, "Elton John's Menagerie of Demons," *Los Angeles Times*, 23 August 1992.

199 Stephen P. Wheeler, "Bernie Taupin: The Brown Dirt Cowboy Rides Again," *Music Connection*, 30 October–12 November 1989.

200 Elton John, television interview with David Frost, 22 November 1991.

201 Doerschuk, "Elton John's Multi-Keyboard Sideman."

202 Gus Dudgeon, "Introduction," *Rock of the Westies: Songs from the Album by Elton John and Bernie Taupin.* (Melville, NY: Big Pig Music Ltd., 1975.)

203 Bernie Taupin, radio interview with Dick Lillard, 16 May 1976.

204 Elton John, recorded press interview, *Telltales*, 1975.

205 Lyric from "I'm Going to Be a Teenage Idol," 1973.

206 Unknown author, "Elton John Honored by 'The Rock Music Awards,'" *Los Angeles Times*, 12 August 1975.

207 Mark Goodman, "Trimmed Down, Megamillionaire Elton John Says He Also Wants to Tone Down His Image," *People*, 18 August 1975.

208 Robert Hilburn, "Elton John Returns to Troubadour," *Los Angeles Times*, 27 August 1975.

209 Ibid.

210 Ibid.

211 Unknown author, "John at Troubadour Brings $150,000 Net," *Billboard*, 6 September 1975.

212 Hilburn, "Elton John Returns to Troubadour."

213 Lyric from "Island Girl," 1975.

Chapter Five

1 Song title, 1970.

2 John Wendeborn, "Rock Singer Justifies Full House," *The Oregonian*, October 1975.

3 Robert Hilburn, "Elton John Rocks and Audience Rolls," *Los Angeles Times*, 4 October 1975; Hanford Searl, "John Gig 'Best Rock Show to Play Vegas in Memory,'" *Billboard*, 25 October 1975.

4 Robert Hilburn, "Elton Booked into Dodger Stadium," *Los Angeles Times*, 5 July 1975; Robert Hilburn, "It Was Quite a Double-Header," *Los Angeles Times*, 28 October 1975.

5 Will., "Elton John (6) (Convention Center, L.V.)," *Variety*, 15 October 1975; Searl, "John Gig 'Best Rock Show to Play Vegas in Memory.'"

6 Elton John, television interview with Michael Parkinson, Network 10 (Australia), summer 1982.

7 Ross-Leming and Standish, "Playboy Interview: Elton John."

8 Adrian Deevoy, "Nobody's Perfect," *Q*, April 1995.

9 Julia Orange, ". . . And a Star on Hollywood Boulevard," *Rolling Stone*, 4 December 1975.

10 Staff writer, "Elton John Corrals Over $1-Mil in Dodger Stadium Concert Gigs," *Variety*, 29 October 1975.

11 Sheila Farebrother, as quoted in *Tantrums and Tiaras*, documentary by David Furnish, Cinemax, 21 September 1997.

12 Elton John, television interview with Michael Parkinson, summer 1982.

13 John F. Higgins, "Interview: Caleb Quaye, Part II: After the Drugs, the Tours and the Fame, EJ Guitarist/Friend Finds Peace in His Faith," *East End Lights*, No. 23, summer 1996.

14 Lyric from "Island Girl," 1975.

15 Robert Christgau, "Elton John: The Little Hooker that Could," *The Village Voice*, 24 November 1975.

16 Peter Delacorte, "Sound Track," *Modern Screen*, December 1975.

17 Ross-Leming and Standish, "Playboy Interview."

18 Elton John, recorded press interview, *Telltales*, 1975.

19 Lyric from "I Feel Like a Bullet (In the Gun of Robert Ford)," 1975.

20 Unknown author, "John Is Mil Tape Seller in England," *Billboard*, 22 November 1975.

21 Associated Press, "Elton the Biggest Money-Maker," *San Francisco Chronicle*, 13 February 1976.

22 Elton John, Bernie Taupin, Gus Dudgeon, and others, radio interview with Paul Gambaccini, fall 1976.

23 Edmund White, "My Life as a Man," *Rolling Stone*, 10–24 July 1997.

24 P. Norman, *Elton John*.

25 Lyric from "Bite Your Lip (Get Up and Dance!)," 1976.

26 Elton John, radio interview, "Christmas from Barbados," WRKO (Boston), December 1975.

27 Liner notes, *To Be Continued* . . . (U.S.).

28 Phil Sutcliffe, "Elton John Mk II," *Juke*, 15 April 1977 (reprinted from *Sounds*).

29 Elton John, Gus Dudgeon, Kiki Dee, and others, radio interview with Paul Gambaccini, "The Elton John Story," BBC, 3 October 1982.

30 Elton John, television interview with David Frost, 22 November 1991.

31 Bill Dahl, "Fats Domino: The King of Blueberry Hill," *Goldmine*, 29 June 2001.

32 P. Norman, *Elton John*.

33 Sutcliffe, "Elton John Mk II."

34 Elton John, Gus Dudgeon, Kiki Dee, and others, radio interview with Paul Gambaccini, 3 October 1982.

35 Ibid.

36 Lyric from "Pinball Wizard," 1975.

37 Sutcliffe, "Elton John Mk II."

38 Ibid.

39 P. Norman, *Elton John*.

40 Barry Toberman, *Elton John: A Biography*. (London: Weidenfeld and Nicolson, 1988.)

41 P. Norman, *Elton John*.

42 Andy Polack, "Remember David's Mum? Say Hello to Reggie's Dad," *New Musical Express*, 29 May 1976.

43 Lyric from "Don't Go Breaking My Heart," 1976.

44 Elton John, radio interview with Dick Clark, 4 July 1981.

45 Jahr, "Elton John: It's Lonely at the Top."

46 Unknown author, "Elton John: The Elton John Mystique," *Juke*, 4 September 1976.

47 Unknown author, "Kiki Dee: The Elton John Mystique," *Juke*, 4 September 1976.

48 Lyric from "Don't Go Breaking My Heart," 1976.

49 Marian Burros, "Elton, Mum . . . and Yum," *The Washington Post*, 30 June 1976.

50 Elton John, television interview with David Frost, 22 November 1991.

51 Nat Freedland, "At Arena Concerts, John Champ Grosser," *Billboard*, 23 October 1976.

52 Al Cunniff, "The Beatin' Path: How Elton Spent His Days in D.C.," *The News American*, 11 July 1976.

53 Staff writer, "Random Notes," *Rolling Stone*, 7 October 1976.

54 Larry Rohter, "Elton John: The Music Machine," *The Washington Post*, 1 July 1976.

55 Chris Charlesworth, "He's Got the Whole World in His Hands," *Melody Maker*, 14 August 1976.

56 Van Matre, "All that Glitters in Elton John's Act Is Not Gold . . . but It Dazzles the Faithful," *Chicago Tribune*, 18 July 1976.

57 John Rockwell, "Elton John in a Smooth Show at Garden," *The New York Times*, 12 August 1976.

58 Cliff Jahr, "Hurricane Elton Is 'Fee-urious' in New York," *Rolling Stone*, 23 September 1976.

59 Elton John, television interview with Tom Snyder, *Tomorrow Show*, NBC-TV, fall 1976.

60 Lyric from "Don't Go Breaking My Heart," 1976.

61 Mike Greenblatt, "Elton John Is Back! Rock's Most Elusive Aristocrat Breaks the Silence," *Aquarian Weekly*, 18–25 October 1978.

62 Chris Salewicz, "The Rise and Fall of Reginald Dwight," *Q*, December 1986.

63 Lee Winfrey, "A Look at Sex in Film Is Not So Satisfying," *The Philadelphia Inquirer*, 22 September 1996.

64 Jahr, "Hurricane Elton Is 'Fee-urious' in New York."

65 Ibid.

66 Jahr, "Elton John: It's Lonely at the Top."

67 Ibid.

68 Lyric from "Sorry Seems to Be the Hardest Word," 1976.

69 Sutcliffe, "Elton John Mk II."

70 Salewicz, "The Rise and Fall of Reginald Dwight."

71 Carr, "A Single Man: The Elton John Interview."

72 Correspondence between the author and the following individuals: Daryl Treger, Farmington Hill, Michigan, e-mail dated 15 July 1996; Anthony Dodd, Brooklyn, New York, e-mails dated 17 and 18 July 1996; Tim Fitzpatrick, Batavia, Illinois, e-mail dated 12 July 1996; Andy Geisel, Orlando, Florida, e-mail dated 15 July 1996; Leonard Herman, Springfield, New Jersey, e-mail dated 15 July 1996; Sharon Kalinoski, LaGrange, Illinois, letter dated 16 August 1996.

73 Randi Reisfeld and Danny Fields, *Who's Your Fave Rave?* (New York: Boulevard Books, 1997.)

74 Live television broadcast of concert at Edinburgh Playhouse Theatre, Edinburgh, Scotland, BBC-TV, 17 September 1976.

75 Lyric from "Sorry Seems to Be the Hardest Word," 1976.

76 Sutcliffe, "Elton John Mk II."

77 Lyric from song of same name, 1976.

78 Elton John, television interview with Tom Snyder, fall 1976.

79 Elton John, television interview with David Frost, 22 November 1991.

80 Elton John, Gus Dudgeon, Kiki Dee, and others, radio interview with Paul Gambaccini, 3 October 1982.

81 Josh Mills, "The Fall of the Somewhat Mighty," *New York Daily News*, 10 July 1977.

82 Lyric from "Crazy Water," 1976.

83 Johnny Black, "Eyewitness," *Q*, February 1995.

84 Swan., "Elton John (2), (Rainbow, London)," *Variety*, 18 May 1977.

85 Robin Smith, "Star Spangled Piano," *Record Mirror*, 7 May 1977.

86 P. Norman, *Elton John*.

87 Lyric from "Nice and Slow," 1977 (not released until 1989).

88 Van Lustbader, "Elton John: He's Only Just Begun."

89 Paul Gregutt, "Elton John's Next Album," *The Weekly of Metropolitan Seattle*, 26 October–1 November 1977.

90 Liner notes, *To Be Continued* . . . (U.S.).

91 Gregutt, "Elton John's Next Album."

92 Ibid.

93 Irwin Stambler, *The Encyclopedia of Pop, Rock and Soul.* (New York: St. Martin's Press, 1989.)

94 Liner notes, *To Be Continued . . .* (U.S.).

95 Elton John, radio interview with Andy Peebles, 28 December 1980.

96 Patrick MacDonald, "Elton John Begins New Album Here," *Seattle Times,* 22 October 1977.

97 Lyric from "Philadelphia Freedom," 1975.

98 P. Norman, *Elton John.*

99 Elton John, Bernie Taupin, and David Nutter, *Elton: It's a Little Bit Funny.* (New York: The Viking Press, 1977.)

100 Unknown author, "Elton John Conquers New York," *Rock Scene,* March 1978.

101 Television broadcast of November 3, 1977 concert at the Empire Pool, Wembley, North London, HBO, 1978.

102 Charley Crespo, "P.T. Barnum, Muhammad Ali and Elton John?" *Circus,* 8 December 1977.

103 Television broadcast of November 3, 1977 concert, HBO, 1978.

104 Colin Irwin, "Elton Quits—and Wembley Weeps," *Melody Maker,* 12 November 1977.

105 Brian Glanville, "The Thoughts of Chairman Elton," *The Times* (London), 16 April 1978.

106 Author unknown, "Elton John Says He's Quitting Road," *Variety,* 9 November 1977.

Chapter Six

1 Song title, 1984.

2 Elton John, radio interview with Dennis McNamara, WLIR-NY (New York), fall 1978.

3 Ellen Farley, "Hype Night for Elton John," *Los Angeles Times,* 31 March 1978.

4 P. Norman, *Elton John.*

5 Nigel Goodall, *Elton John: A Visual Documentary.* (London: Omnibus Press, 1993.)

6 Ed Harrison, "Elton John's New Confidence and Appearance Spark His Return to Records After a 2 Year Hiatus," *Billboard,* 4 November 1978.

7 Robert Hilburn, "Elton John: Breaking the Silence," *Los Angeles Times,* 22 October 1978.

8 Lyric from "Big Dipper," 1978.

9 Harrison, "Elton John's New Confidence."

10 Carr, "A Single Man: The Elton John Interview."

11 Deevoy, "Nobody's Perfect."

12 Ian Parker, "Annals of Pop: He's a Little Bit Funny," *The New Yorker,* 26 August–2 September 1996.

13 Elton John, radio interview with Scott Muni, WNEW-NY (New York), 10 October 1978.

14 Ibid.

15 Ibid.

16 Ibid.

17 Elton John, radio interview with Andy Peebles, 28 December 1980.

18 Greenblatt, "Elton John Is Back!"

19 Lyric from "Georgia," 1978.

20 Harrison, "Elton John's New Confidence."

21 Robert Hilburn, "Elton John—'Just Me and the Piano,'" *Los Angeles Times,* 17 October 1978.

22 Elton John, radio interview with Andy Peebles, 28 December 1980.

23 Kelly Tucker, "Record Reviews: Elton Gets Some Sense," *New Orleans Times-Picayune,* 12 November 1978.

24 Harry Doherty, "Elton Kicks off Again," *Melody Maker,* 21 October 1978.

25 Stephen Holden, "Elton John: No Future?" *Rolling Stone,* 25 January 1979.

26 Associated Press, "Elton John Collapses—Chest Pains," *San Francisco Chronicle,* 8 November 1978; Gary Lockwood and Tracy Mitchell, "A Stricken Elton John Is Taken to a London Hospital in the Midst of a Promotion Tour," *Seattle Post-Intelligencer,* November 1978; Goodall, *A Visual Documentary.*

27 Staff writer, "Random Notes," *Rolling Stone,* 8 February 1979.

28 Elton John, radio interview with Andy Peebles, 28 December 1980.

29 Martin Cerf, "The New Elton," *Phonograph Record,* January 1978.

30 Staff writer, "Random Notes," *Rolling Stone,* 24 August 1978.

31 Joel Whitburn, *Joel Whitburn's Bubbling Under the Hot 100: 1959–1985.* (Menomonee Falls, Wisconsin: Record Research Inc., 1992.)

32 Lyric from "Shooting Star," 1978.

33 Geoffrey Giuliano, *Rod Stewart: Vagabond Heart.* (New York: Carroll & Graf Publishers, Inc., 1993.); Toberman, *Elton John: A Biography.*

34 Staff writer, "Random Notes," *Rolling Stone,* 10 February 1977.

35 Staff writer, "Random Notes," *Rolling Stone,* 8 February 1979.

36 Daisann McLane, "Someone Saved His Life Tonight," *Feature,* January 1979.

37 Lyric from "Nikita," 1985.

38 Unknown author, "Elton May Tour U.S., U.S.S.R.," *Rolling Stone,* 17 May 1979.

39 Associated Press, "Elton John Wows Muscovites," *New Orleans Times-Picayune,* 21 May 1979.

40 *To Russia with Elton,* ITC Live Home Video, 69994, 1979.

41 Robert Hilburn, "Elton John Tour: Rock's Revolution in Russia," *Los Angeles Times,* 27 May 1979.

42 Robert Hilburn, "Rock Star Rises Over Russia," *Los Angeles Times,* 23 May 1979.

43 Ibid.; Jim Gallagher, "Elton John Wows 'em—to Put It Mildly—Back in the USSR," *Chicago Tribune,* May 1979.

44 Gallagher, "Elton John Wows 'em."

45 Robert Hilburn, "Moscow: 12 Days that Shook a Rock Critic's World," *Los Angeles Times,* 10 June 1979.

46 Robert Hilburn, "Elton John—Rock Star Rolls into Moscow," *Los Angeles Times,* 28 May 1979; Robert Hilburn, "Strong Response to Elton John in Moscow," *Los Angeles Times,* 29 May 1979.

47 Elton John, John Walters, and others, radio interview with Andy Peebles, "Elton John at the Beeb," BBC, 7 December 1985.

48 Hilburn, "Moscow: 12 Days that Shook a Rock Critic's World."

49 Robert Hilburn, "Is There Rock in Russia's Future?"
  Los Angeles Times, 1 June 1979.
50 Lyric from "Mama Can't Buy You Love," 1979.
51 Elton John, radio interview with Andy Peebles,
  28 December 1980.
52 Lester Bangs, "Elton John After the Fact," *The Village
  Voice*, 29 October 1979.
53 Bob Claypool, "Rock: Victim of Love, Elton John,"
  Houston Post, 18 January 1980.
54 Finch and Charlesworth, "Elton John: 'Only the
  Piano Player.'"
55 Name of Elton John's fall 1979 U.S. tour.
56 Lynn Van Matre, "Smaller-Scale Rocking Makes It
  Fun Again for Elton John," *Houston Post*, 3 October
  1979.
57 Ed Harrison, "Elton John: Universal Amphitheatre,
  Universal City, Calif.," *Billboard*, 13 October 1979.
58 *Opening Night*, bootleg vinyl album of seven songs from
  September 26, 1979 Los Angeles performance.
59 Pat Bowring, "A Genius with Guts," unknown
  Melbourne publication, December 1979.
60 Unknown author, "Elton's Tight Schedule," unknown
  Australian publication, c. November 1979.
61 Janet Hawley, "A Pianist Who Hasn't a Leg to Stand
  On," unknown Sydney publication, c. November 1979;
  Peter Young, "Jinx and Hi-Jinx Put Elton on Wheels,"
  unknown Sydney publication, c. November 1979;
  Craig McCarthy, "Elton Wrestles with a Problem,"
  unknown Sydney publication, c. November 1979;
  unknown author, "Elton Wheels in . . . ," unknown
  Sydney publication, c. November 1979.
62 Bowring, "A Genius with Guts"; Ross Gardiner,
  "The Night Elton John Ran Hot," *The Herald*,
  1 December 1979.
63 Hawley, "A Pianist Who Hasn't a Leg to Stand On."
64 Gary Clarke, *Elton, My Elton.* (London: Smith Gryphon
  Publishers, 1995.)
65 Hawley, "A Pianist Who Hasn't a Leg to Stand On."
66 Elton John, "Elton John: Storytellers Live," VH1,
  19 September 1997.
67 Johnny Dee, "Specs and Drugs and Drugs and Drugs
  and Rock'n'Roll," *New Musical Express*, 25 February
  1995.
68 Deevoy, "Nobody's Perfect."
69 Lyric from "Two Rooms at the End of the World,"
  1980.
70 Elton John, radio interview with Jim Ryan, WDRQ
  (Detroit), September 1980.
71 Pat Bowring, "Will the Real Ray Cooper . . . ?"
  unknown Melbourne publication, December 1979.
72 Sal Manna, "Riding the Tiger," *Illinois Entertainer*,
  August 1980.
73 Elton John, interview with Andy Peebles,
  28 December 1980.
74 Jaan Uhelszki, "Bernie Taupin: The Cheese Stands
  Alone," *Creem*, September 1976.
75 Elton John, radio interview with Andy Peebles,
  28 December 1980; unknown author and title, *Rolling
  Stone*, 17 April 1980.
76 Elton John, television interview with Paul Gambaccini,

24 March 1984.
77 Elton John, radio interview with Dave Charity,
  16–18 June 1989.
78 Doerschuk, "Elton John."
79 Elton John, television interview with Paul Gambaccini,
  24 March 1984.
80 Translation from French by Normand Bérubé.
81 Elton John, television interview with Paul Gambaccini,
  24 March 1984.
82 Ibid.
83 Lyric from "Little Jeannie," 1980.
84 Uhelszki, "Bernie Taupin: The Cheese Stands Alone."
85 Lyric from John Lennon's "Imagine" modified by
  Elton John at September 13, 1980 Central Park
  concert, New York City.
86 Robert Hilburn, "Elton John Celebrates a Big 10th
  Anniversary," *Los Angeles Times*, 30 August 1980.
87 Silver, "Interview with: Nigel Olsson."
88 Robert Hilburn, "Elton: Like Old Times," *Los Angeles
  Times*, 4 November 1980.
89 Bill Farrell, "Free Parking for Weekend," unknown
  New York City publication, September 1980;
  unknown author, "Elton John Bash Benefits Park,"
  unknown New York City publication, 1980.
90 *Elton John in Central Park, New York*, laser disk, VCL
  Communications, Inc., Pioneer Artists, PA-83-057,
  1982.
91 Unknown author, "Crowd of 400,000 Sets Record
  for Park," *The New York Times*, 14 September 1980.
92 Elton John, television interview with Tom Snyder,
  Tomorrow Show, NBC-TV, September 1980.
93 Parker, "Annals of Pop: He's a Little Bit Funny."
94 Lyric from "Saturday Night's Alright for Fighting,"
  1973.
95 Fred Goodman, *The Mansion on the Hill.* (New York:
  Times Books, 1997.)
96 Unknown author, "David Geffen Announces New
  Record Company," *Rolling Stone*, 15 May 1980.
97 Patrick Goldstein, "Elton John Signs with David
  Geffen," *Los Angeles Times*, 26 September 1980.
98 Doerschuk, "Elton John."
99 Ibid.
100 Claude Bernardin and Tom Stanton, *Rocket Man:
  The Encyclopedia of Elton John.* (Westport, CT: Greenwood
  Press, 1995.)
101 Lyric from "Love So Cold," B-side, 1980.
102 Ross Gardiner, "Elton Sings for John," *The Herald*,
  December 1980.
103 Unknown author, "The News Stuns Elton John,"
  unknown Australian publication, December 1980.
104 Unknown author, "Elton Plans to Say Hello to the
  Mellow Pick Mode," unknown Australian publication,
  December 1980; Carolyn Parfitt, "Elton John Has
  New Directions in Mind for His Music," unknown
  Australian publication, December 1980.
105 Unknown author, "Reg and Bette—Oh, What a
  Divine Double," unknown Australian publication,
  December 1980.
106 Unknown author, "Elton Gets Kill Threat,"
  unknown publication, 1980; United Press Inter-

national, "A Police Bodyguard for Elton John," *San Francisco Chronicle*, 24 December 1980; unknown author and title, *St. Louis Post-Dispatch*, 24 December 1980.

Chapter Seven

1 Song title, 1983.
2 Robert Hilburn, "Spunky Elton John Tries Again," *Los Angeles Times*, 12 May 1981.
3 Elton John, radio interview with Scott Muni, WNEW-NY (New York), 15 June 1981.
4 Geffen Records teleconference for *The Fox*, broadcast via satellite, April 1981.
5 Elton John, radio interview with Scott Muni, 15 June 1981.
6 Ibid.
7 Elton John, radio interview with Andy Peebles, 28 December 1980.
8 Randy Alexander, "Elton's Other Lyricist," *East End Lights*, No. 8, summer 1992.
9 Elton John, radio interview with Scott Muni, 15 June 1981.
10 Ibid.
11 Lyric from "The Fox," 1981.
12 Michael Martinez, "Elton John Files $11 Million Breach Suit Against MCA," *Cash Box*, 28 March 1981.
13 Patrick Goldstein, "Pop Eye: New Old Albums," *Los Angeles Times*, 29 March 1981.
14 Lane Maloney, "MCA Sues John, Geffen, WB for Infringement of Copyright; Tries to Stop Release of Album," *Variety*, 13 May 1981.
15 Goldstein, "Pop Eye: New Old Albums."
16 Lyric from "Nobody Wins," 1981.
17 Geffen Records teleconference, April 1981.
18 Hilburn, "Spunky Elton John Tries Again."
19 Colin Irwin, "Elton John: The Fox," *Melody Maker*, 6 June 1981.
20 Steve Pond, "Elton John Almost Back," *Los Angeles Times*, 5 July 1981.
21 Robert Palmer, "Two Icons of Rock Music," *The New York Times*, 31 May 1981.
22 Unknown author and title, *The Washington Post*, 14 June 1981.
23 Cary Darling, "John's *Visions* Tells a Story," *Billboard*, 30 October 1982.
24 Paul Roland, *Elton John*. (New York and London: Proteus Books, 1984.)
25 Elton John, radio interview with Scott Muni, 15 June 1981.
26 Lyric from "The Man who Never Died," B-side, 1985.
27 Elton John, radio interview with Scott Muni, 15 June 1981.
28 Ibid.
29 Elton John, television interview with Barbara Walters, "A Farewell to a Princess," *20/20*, ABC-TV, 5 September 1997.
30 Elton John, radio interview, *Rolling Stone Magazine Rock Review*, unknown network, April 1982.
31 Ibid.
32 Lyric from "Empty Garden," 1982.
33 Elton John, radio interview, *Rolling Stone Magazine Rock Review*, April 1982.
34 *Jump Up! Down Under* tour program, Pan Enterprises, Victoria, Australia, 1982.
35 Bernie Taupin, interview with ROKRITR, America On-Line (AOL) Elton John Bulletin Board (most likely taken from an interview conducted by Stephen P. Wheeler, from which excerpts appeared in *Music Connection*, 30 October–12 November, 1989), posted 14 April 1995.
36 Elton John, television interview with Paul Gambaccini, 24 March 1984.
37 Ryan, *American Hit Radio*.
38 Elton John, radio interview, *Music Star Special*, unknown network, 4 September 1982.
39 Michael Walsh, *Andrew Lloyd Webber: His Life and Works*. (New York: Harry N. Abrams, Inc., 1989.)
40 Gerald McKnight, *Andrew Lloyd Webber: A Biography*. (New York: St. Martin's Press, 1984.)
41 Walsh, *Andrew Lloyd Webber: His Life and Works*.
42 Elton John, television interview with Paul Gambaccini, 24 March 1984.
43 Elton John, radio interview with Jim Conley, 1983.
44 Elton John, radio interview, *Star Sessions*, unknown network, 25 July 1982.
45 Dickinson and Rosencrantz, *Two Rooms*.
46 Liner notes, *To Be Continued . . .* (U.S.).
47 Ibid.
48 Elton John, television interview with Paul Gambaccini, 24 March 1984.
49 Lyric from "Blue Eyes," 1982.
50 Brett Stavordale, "Elton's Just Feuding in Fun," unknown Australian publication, March/April 1982; Jeff Coltrane, "Elton John Sets the Machine on 'Recycle,'" unknown Australian publication, March/April 1982; Allan Webster, "Mentals in Clover or Elton Goes Mental," unknown Australian publication, March/April 1982.
51 Ed Harrison, "Elton John Judie Tzuke," *Billboard*, 22 November 1980.
52 Brett Stavordale, "Knock-Out Gig Ruffled Elton's Feathers," unknown Australian publication, March/April 1982.
53 Steve Kulak, "Elton John/Moving Pictures," unknown Sydney publication, March/April 1982.
54 Michael Morris, "Elton John, Venue: Hordern Pavilion, Sydney," unknown Sydney publication, March 1982.
55 Kulak, "Elton John/Moving Pictures."
56 Dan Formento, "Elton John: Lust for Life," *Hit Parader*, September 1982.
57 Clarke, *Elton, My Elton*.
58 Lyric from "Empty Garden," 1982.
59 Salewicz, "The Rise and Fall of Reginald Dwight."
60 Lynn Van Matre, "All That Glitz and Glitter Is Elton John," *Chicago Tribune*, 12 July 1982.
61 Richard Harrington, "Elton John," *The Washington Post*, 23 July 1982.
62 Ken Tucker, "Elton John Back on the Track with 'Jump Up!' Album," *The Philadelphia Inquirer*, 25 July 1982.

63 Robb., "Elton John (4), (Hollywood Bowl)," *Variety*, 30 June 1982.

64 Dick Richmond, "Elton John's Fans Willing to Suffer for Star," *St. Louis Post-Dispatch*, 6 July 1982; Tommy Robertson and Phyllis Breach, "Elton John Plays Decoy to Duck Fair Admirers," *St. Louis Post-Dispatch*, 6 July 1982.

65 Scott Mitchell, "Shades of Elton John."

66 Unknown author, "Elton John Celebrates His Friend John Lennon and Gets a Visit From Yoko and Godson Sean," *People*, 20 August 1982; Ira Mayer, "Even Subdued Elton Is Still a Knockout," *New York Post*, 6 August 1982.

67 Lyric from "I'm Still Standing," 1983.

68 Paul Grein, "Taupin, John Happily Reunited," *Billboard*, 18 June 1983.

69 Robert Hilburn, "Elton Live: Crowd Is One for the Record," *Los Angeles Times*, 22 June 1982.

70 Elton John, radio interview, *The Hot Ones*, RKO Radio Networks, June 1983.

71 Ibid.

72 Liner notes, *To Be Continued . . .* (U.S.).

73 Elton John, *The Hot Ones*, June 1983.

74 Elton John, radio interview with Andy Peebles, BBC, 30 May 1983.

75 Elton John, *The Hot Ones*, June 1983.

76 Salewicz, "The Rise and Fall of Reginald Dwight."

77 Nancy Malitz, "Oh, That Elton! He's in the Pink Again," *USA Today*, 17 June 1983.

78 Elton John, radio interview with Scott Muni, WNEW-NY (New York), 14 May 1983.

79 Walsh, *Andrew Lloyd Webber: His Life and Works.*

80 Julia Phillips, *You'll Never Eat Lunch In This Town Again.* (New York: Signet, 1992.)

81 Lyric from "All Quiet on the Western Front," 1982.

82 Live television broadcast of concert at the Hammersmith Odeon in London, BBC-TV, 24 December 1982.

83 Unknown author, "From Reg to Riches," unknown U.K. publication, 18–24 December 1982.

84 Associated Press, "Elton John's Unique 'Gift,'" *San Francisco Chronicle*, 25 December 1982.

85 Audience recording of concert at the Hammersmith Odeon in London, 15 December 1982.

86 Elton John, radio interview with Simon Bates, BBC Radio One, 22–25 April 1985.

87 P. Norman, *Elton John.*

88 Lyric from "I'm Still Standing," 1983.

89 Christopher Connelly, "1982 in Review: Who Won, Who Lost," *Rolling Stone*, 17 February 1983.

90 Unknown author, "Rockin': Praise for Bowie," *Rolling Stone*, 10 June 1982.

91 Roy Trakin, "Elton John: Staying in Touch," *Hit Parader*, November 1983.

92 Elton John, radio interview with Andy Peebles, 30 May 1983.

93 Chris Charlesworth, "The Second Coming of Elton John," unknown publication and date.

94 Unknown author, "Elton John to Visit China," *The Times* (London), 1 June 1983.

95 Martin Amis, *Visiting Mrs. Nabokov and Other Excursions.* (New York: Vintage Books, 1995.)

96 Ibid.

97 Lyric from "I'm Still Standing," 1983.

98 Unknown author, "Elton and Bernie Together," *Rolling Stone*, 14 April 1983.

99 Robert Hilburn, "Elton John: New Quest For No. 1," *Los Angeles Times*, 17 May 1983.

100 Malitz, "Oh, That Elton! He's in the Pink Again."

101 Trakin, "Elton John: Staying in Touch."

102 Unknown author, "*Too Low for Zero:* Elton John," *People*, August 1983.

103 Don Shewey, "*Too Low for Zero:* Elton John," *Rolling Stone*, 9 June 1983.

104 Trakin, "Elton John: Staying in Touch."

105 Lyric from "I Guess That's Why They Call It the Blues," 1983.

106 Ian Meldrum, "Elton and Rod—It's On!", unknown publication (probably *The Sun* (Melbourne)), 1983.

107 Ian Meldrum, "Rod and Elton Tour Latest," unknown publication (probably *The Sun* (Melbourne)), 1983.

108 Elton John and Rod Stewart, television interview with David Frost, unknown Australian network, 1983.

109 Elton John, radio interview, Capital Radio, December 1983.

110 Lyric from "Sad Songs (Say So Much)," 1984.

111 Elton John, Bernie Taupin, John Reid, and others, television interview, *Cinemax Album Flash*, Cinemax, October 1984.

112 Ibid.

113 Unknown author, "On the Road to Wembley," *Radio Times*, 30 June–6 July 1984.

114 Elton John, Bernie Taupin, John Reid, and others, *Cinemax Album Flash*, October 1984.

115 Ibid.

116 Ibid.

117 Ibid.

118 Candace Sutton, "Time Gentlemen, Please, It's Mr. John," unknown Australian publication, 1984.

Chapter Eight

1 Title of alternate version of B-side, "Lonely Boy," 1984.

2 Parker, "Annals of Pop: He's a Little Bit Funny."

3 Unknown author and title, *Q*, July 1995.

4 Elton John, radio interview with Scott Muni, WNEW-NY (New York), 9 May 1983.

5 Carr, "A Single Man: The Elton John Interview."

6 Deevoy, "Nobody's Perfect."

7 Sutton, "Time Gentlemen, Please, It's Mr. John."

8 Lynda Gray, "Member of the Wedding . . . ," unknown Australian publication, February 1984.

9 Melanie Whitehouse, "Elton's Wedding Plan in Court," unknown Australian publication, February 1984; Stephen Rice and Robert Thomson, "Elton's Getting Married This Morning, Thanks to Mr. Landa and 'Good, Cogent' Reasons," unknown Sydney publication, 14 February 1984.

10 John Grant, "Elton: Bizarre Wedding Twist," unknown Australian publication, February 1984.

11 Unknown author, "Bride-to-Be Tells: 'My Love for Elton,'" *Sunday Telegraph*, February 1984.

12 Richard Shears, "Elton's Marriage Plans Run into Last-Minute Hitch," unknown Australian publication, 13 February 1984.

13 Staff writer, "How Elton Wooed and Won His Bride," *The People*, February 1984.

14 James Oram, "Elton Jokes Way Through $80,000 Party," *Daily Mirror*, 15 February 1984; Ian Meldrum, "Elton Weds," *The Sun* (Melbourne), February 1984; unknown author, "Elton Weds in Style," *Watford Observer*, 17 February 1984.

15 Kevin Sadlier, "What a Bash!" *The Sun* (Melbourne), 15 February 1984.

16 Nick Ferrari, "Good on Yer, Poofter!" *The Sun*, February 1984; Nick Ferrari, "My Joy, by His Mum," *The Sun*, February 1984; Oram, "Elton Jokes Way."

17 Nick Ferrari, "Elton's Tough Minder Beats up Sun Man," *The Sun*, February 1984.

18 Garry Maddox, "The Church and THAT Marriage," unknown Australian publication, February 1984.

19 Wensley Clarkson and Tony Bushby, "Elton Jilted Me," *Sunday Mirror*, 19 February 1984.

20 David Jones, "I Lived with Elton's Bride," *News of the World*, 19 February 1984.

21 Lyric from "Crystal," 1983.

22 Unknown author, "Race Row Greets Elton John," unknown Adelaide publication, March 1984.

23 Peter Dean, "Elton's Non-Stop Magic," unknown Brisbane publication, March 1984.

24 Kevin Sadlier, "Hey Hey It's Elton John," *The Sun* (Melbourne), March 1984.

25 Lyric from "One More Arrow," 1983.

26 Elton John, television interview, unknown network (probably BBC), April 1984.

27 Roger Boyes, "Elton, in Stetson and Earring, Calls on Lech," *The Times* (London), 30 April 1984.

28 Roger Boyes, "Elton John to Meet Walesa," *The Times* (London), 26 April 1984; Boyes, "Elton, in Stetson and Earring."

29 Unknown author, "On the Road to Wembley."

30 Elton John, radio interview with Bob Coburn, *Rockline*, WNEW-NY (New York), 20 August 1984.

31 Lyric from "Burning Buildings," 1984.

32 John Sadler, "Elton Has Found His Perfect Partners," *The Sun*, 13 April 1984.

33 Elton John, live television interview, "Elton's Journey," BBC-TV, 18 May 1984.

34 Lyric from "Sad Songs (Say So Much)," 1984.

35 Ibid.

36 Unknown author, "On the Road to Wembley."

37 Lyric from "Passengers," 1984.

38 Lyric from "Who Wears These Shoes?" 1984.

39 Michael Goldberg, "Elton John: A Commercial Success," *Rolling Stone*, 11 October 1984.

40 David Fricke, "Touring's a Drag, Says Elton John, Who Wants to Play Hubby Instead," *People*, 12 November 1984.

41 Liner notes, *Two Rooms: Celebrating the Songs of Elton John and Bernie Taupin*, Polydor 845 750-2, 1991.

42 Elton John, radio interview with Scott Muni, WNEW-NY (New York), 25 October 1984.

43 Boo Browning, "Elton John Wows Packed House," *Phoenix Gazette*, 18 August 1984.

44 Robert Hilburn, "Elton John's Tour: A Goodby [*sic*] to the Road?" *Los Angeles Times*, 21 August 1984.

45 Ibid.

46 Peter Stack, "Elton John's Fire-Breathin' Rock," *San Francisco Chronicle*, 30 August 1984.

47 Iain Blair, "Elton John Displays Talent That Made Him Popular, at L.A. Forum," *Hollywood Reporter*, 24 August 1984.

48 Browning, "Elton John Wows Packed House."

49 Blair, "Elton John Displays Talent."

50 Stack, "Elton John's Fire-Breathin' Rock."

51 Bob Claypool, "Music: Elton John," *Houston Post*, 15 October 1980.

52 Elton John, radio interview with Scott Muni, 25 October 1984.

53 Mary Anne Cassatta, "Concert Comments: Elton John," *The Music Paper*, October 1984.

54 Elton John, radio interview with Scott Muni, 25 October 1984.

55 Steve Morse, "Amazing Elton John Far from Over the Hill," *The Boston Globe*, 5 November 1984.

56 Lyric from "In Neon," 1984.

57 Elton John, television interview, "Pop Profile," *Saturday Picture Show*, BBC-TV, 15 June 1985.

58 "Best of Friends," Columbia Records press release for Wham!, spring 1985.

59 Elton John, "Pop Profile," 15 June 1985.

60 Lyric from "Nikita," 1985.

61 Elton John, radio interview with Scott Muni, WNEW-NY (New York), 22 May 1985.

62 Elton John, Bernie Taupin, John Reid, and others, *Cinemax Album Flash*, October 1984.

63 Elton John, "Pop Profile," 15 June 1985.

64 Elton John, radio interview with Scott Muni, 22 May 1985.

65 Elton John and Nik Kershaw, radio interview with Andy Peebles, BBC, 29 November 1985.

66 Ibid.

67 Ibid.

68 Dickinson and Rosencrantz, *Two Rooms*.

69 Ibid.

70 Elton John, radio interview with Andy Peebles, 29 November 1985.

71 Ibid.

72 Elton John, radio interview with Scott Muni, 22 May 1985.

73 Elton John, radio interview with Andy Peebles, 29 November 1985.

74 John F. Higgins, "Dudgeon on the Record," *East End Lights*, No. 13, winter 1993.

75 John F. Higgins, "Out from Behind the Kit: Rapping with Charlie Morgan," *East End Lights*, No. 18, spring 1995.

76 Elton John, radio interview with Andy Peebles, 29 November 1985.

77 Ibid.

78 Lyric from "Act of War," 1985.

79 Elton John, radio interview with Scott Muni, 22 May 1985.

80 Elton John, radio interview with Andy Peebles, 29 November 1985.

81 Statement by George Michael at Live Aid, Wembley Stadium, London, 13 July 1985.

82 Elton John, radio interview with Andy Peebles, "Elt for Leather," BBC Radio One, 17 October 1986.

83 Peter Hillmore, *Live-Aid: World-Wide Concert Book.* (New Jersey: The Unicorn Publishing House, 1985.)

84 Toberman, *Elton John: A Biography.*

85 Elton John and George Michael, radio interview with Andy Peebles, 29 November 1985.

86 Song by Marvin Gaye, played by Elton John as encore during his 1985–86 world tour.

87 Associated Press, "Elton John Sues Over Song Rights," *San Francisco Chronicle,* 5 June 1985.

88 Simon Garfield, "Rock in the Dock: The Trials of Elton John," *Time Out London,* unknown date; P. Norman, *Elton John.*

89 P. Norman, *Elton John.*

90 Various BBC and ITV television reports concerning Elton John/Bernie Taupin court action against Dick James, November 1985.

91 Ibid.

92 Liner notes, *To Be Continued . . .* (U.S.).

93 Lyric from "Nikita," 1985.

94 Unknown author, "The Years in Music," *Billboard,* 28 December 1996.

95 Elton John, television interview with Paula Yates, *The Tube,* BBC-TV, November 1985.

96 Lyric from "Shoot Down the Moon," 1985.

97 Elton John, television interview with Terry Wogan, *Wogan,* BBC-TV, 25 December 1984.

98 Damian Corless, Dermot Stokes, Fiona Looney, and Niall Stokes, "Desperately Seeking Elton," *Hot Press,* 5 December 1985.

99 Caroline Sullivan, "Flip Yer Wig!" *Melody Maker,* 21–28 December 1985.

100 David Sinclair, "Rock: Elton John," *The Times* (London), 15 December 1985.

101 Corless, et al., "Desperately Seeking Elton."

102 Lyric from "Cry to Heaven," 1985.

103 Brian Woolnough, "Angry Elton Fires a Rocket," *The Sun,* 13 December 1985.

104 Elton John, television interview, *60 Minutes* (Australia), unknown network, fall 1986.

105 Elton John, radio interview with Andy Peebles, 17 October 1986.

106 Elton John, television interview with Terry Wogan, *Wogan,* BBC-TV 24 February 1986.

107 William Norwich, "Elton Homes in on Manhattan," *New York Daily News,* 1 May 1986.

108 Ibid.

109 "Prince's Trust All-Star Rock Concert," MGM/UA Home Video, M301089, 1986.

110 Lyric from "Leather Jackets," 1986.

111 Fred A. Bernstein, "Elton John Is Still a Class Act, but with New Hits, Hair and Friends—Andrew & Fergie," *People,* 8 September 1986.

112 Elton John, radio interview with Andy Peebles, 17 October 1986.

113 C. Jones, "Sound Your Funky Horn: Elton John."

114 Gus Dudgeon, television interview, "Elton John: Behind the Music," VH1, 19 March 2000.

115 Elton John, radio interview with Andy Peebles, 17 October 1986.

116 Unknown author and title, *Goldmine,* 15 May 1992.

117 Elton John, radio interview with Andy Peebles, 17 October 1986.

118 Ibid.

119 Ibid.

120 Lyric from "Paris," 1986.

121 Jim McFarlin, "Elton John Is Back, with More Flash than Fire," *USA Today,* 19 August 1986.

122 Elton John, television interview with Esther Rantzen, *Wogan,* BBC-TV, October 1986.

123 Unknown author, "Talk Show: Guest Star: Elton John," *New York Daily News,* 9 September 1986.

124 Robert Hilburn, "It's Party Time Again for John," *Los Angeles Times,* 5 October 1986.

125 Staff writer, gossip column, *New York Daily News,* 15 September 1986.

126 Robert Palmer, "Rock: Elton John Performs," *The New York Times,* 13 September 1986.

127 Ryan White and Ann Marie Cunningham, *Ryan White: My Own Story.* (New York: Dial Books, 1991.)

128 Charles Dickens, *A Tale of Two Cities.* (Philadelphia: T. B. Peterson, c. 1859.)

129 Lee Wilson, "Superstar's Other Goal," *The Sun Weekend* (Melbourne), 29 November 1986.

130 Ken Tucker, "Pop Albums," *The Philadelphia Inquirer,* 23 November 1986.

131 Chris Blanche, "Elton's Changed His Tune about Clothes," unknown Australian publication, October 1986.

132 William Mann, "Elton John: Festival Hall," *The Times* (London), 7 February 1972.

133 Liner notes, *To Be Continued . . .* (U.S.).

134 "Tour de Force" television preshow, Australian Broadcasting Corporation (ABC), 14 December 1986.

135 Pat Bowring, "First Note Sounds in Tour de Force," unknown Melbourne publication, 1986.

136 Philip Miechel, television interview, "Tour de Force" documentary, Australian Broadcasting Corporation (ABC), summer 1987.

137 Sally McDonnell, "Michelle Hits a Different Note," *The Sun* (Melbourne), 29 November 1986.

138 Philip Green, television interview, "Tour de Force" documentary, Australian Broadcasting Corporation (ABC), 1987.

139 James Newton Howard, television interview, "Tour de Force" preshow, Australian Broadcasting Corporation (ABC), 14 December 1986.

140 Suzanne Pekol, "Piano-Man Elton Hits Right Chord," unknown Australian publication, c. October 1986; Brad Forrest, "Is Elton Playing Our Song?" unknown Australian publication, c. October 1986;

Pat Bowring, "Change of Tune," unknown Melbourne publication, 1986.

141 Unknown author, "Elton's Favorite Things," *New Idea*, 13 December 1986.

142 Christopher Beck, "Extravagantly Elton!" *TV Week*, 22 November 1986.

143 Ian Meldrum, "Concert that Nearly Wasn't," *Sun Leisure* (Melbourne), 18 December 1986; Ian Meldrum, "Molly Tells the Truth," unknown Melbourne publication, 1986.

144 Brett Stavordale, "Elton at His Blazing Best," unknown Melbourne publication, November 1986.

145 McDonnell, "Michelle Hits a Different Note."

146 Patrick McDonald, "Kisses Seal Elton's Love for Symphony," unknown Australian publication, November 1986.

147 Helen Ballard, "Elton Gets Life in a Musical Love Affair," unknown Melbourne publication, November 1986.

148 Bob Crimeen, "Award Is off Key, Says Critic," unknown Melbourne publication, *c.* November 1986.

149 Ian Meldrum, "Elton and Orchestra in Harmony," *The Sun* (Melbourne), *c.* November 1986.

150 David Sly, "A Memorable Harmony of Orchestra and Rock'n'Roll," unknown Adelaide publication, November 1986.

151 Kent Acott, "Sick Elton John Cancels Concert: Angry Fans Abuse Staff," unknown Perth publication, November 1986.

152 Lynden Barber, "Elton, the Latent Liberace," unknown Sydney publication, December 1986.

153 Peter Kogoy, "Elton Collapse: But the Show Goes On," unknown Sydney publication, December 1986.

154 Unknown author, "Elton John Satisfactory after Throat Surgery," *The New York Times*, 7 January 1987.

155 Mike Safe, "Party Fuels Elton Rift Rumors," unknown publication, December 1986.

156 Elton John, television interview with Michael Parkinson, *One-to-One*, ITV, 18 April 1987.

157 Elton John, television interview, "Tour de Force" documentary, Australian Broadcasting Corporation (ABC), summer 1987.

158 Ian Meldrum, "Concert that Nearly Wasn't."

159 Liner notes, *To Be Continued . . .* (U.S.).

160 Peter Coster and Mike Safe, "Mozart Would Have Rocked in His Grave," *The Herald*, 15 December 1986; Janise Beaumont, "Goodbye Elton," *The Sun* (Melbourne), 15 December 1986.

161 Meldrum, "Concert that Nearly Wasn't."

Chapter Nine

1 Song title, 1983.

2 Annette Witheridge, "Tell Me If It's Cancer, Says Plucky Elton," *News of the World*, 4 January 1987.

3 Brad Crouch, "I'm OK Says Brave Elton Before Vital Op," unknown Sydney publication, 5 January 1987.

4 Richard Shears, "Silent Year for Elton," *Daily Mail*, 3 January 1987.

5 Elton John, television interview, *One on One with David Frost*, A&E, 15 August 1999.

6 Unknown author, "Elton John's Surgery 'Success,'" *The Times* (London), 7 January 1987; unknown author, "Elton John Gets Cancer All Clear," *The Times* (London), 8 January 1987; Peter Game, "Elton Can't Talk to Wife," *Daily Express*, 9 January 1987; Chris Blanche, "Elton to Recuperate in Outback," unknown Australian publication, January 1987.

7 John Murphy, "Elton: Fry Me!" *The Sun*, 3 January 1987.

8 Nick Ferrari, Craig Mackenzie, and David Jones, "Elton and Renate: It's All Over," *The Sun*, 10 January 1987.

9 David Jones, "Elton Cries on His Old Pal's Shoulder," *The Sun*, 12 January 1987.

10 Unknown author, "At Least Our Ian's on Song," *Daily Mirror*, 7 February 1987; unknown author, "Elton Score Makes a Hit with England," *Daily Mail*, 7 February 1987.

11 Philip McLean and Fiona Manning, "It's Quite an Achievement!" unknown Sydney publication, February 1987.

12 Philip McLean, "Whispering Jack Makes a Big Noise," unknown Sydney publication, 1987.

13 Elton John, radio interview with Bob Coburn, 20 August, 1984.

14 Lyric from "Made in England," 1995.

15 Elton John, television interview, *The Party*, unknown U.K. network, 1 April 1987.

16 John Sweeney, "How Elton Won His Million," *The Independent Magazine*, 11 February 1989.

17 Allan Hall, "Furious Elton to Fight Sex Claims," *The Sun* (Melbourne), 11 March 1987.

18 Jill Rowbotham, "Elton, Renate Call It Quits," unknown publication, March 1987.

19 Patrick Hill, "Stories About Sylvia and Me Are Disgusting, Says Renate," *Daily Mail*, 28 March 1987.

20 Elton John, television interview with Michael Parkinson, 18 April 1987.

21 Sweeney, "How Elton Won His Million."

22 Phil Taylor, "Elton and Renate Make Up," *Sunday Today*, 10 May 1987.

23 Lyric from "Goodbye Yellow Brick Road," 1973.

24 Brett Milano, "Elton Gives a Surprise Performance," *The Boston Globe*, 17 June 1988.

25 Jeffrey Ressner, "Geffen's Coming of Age," *Rolling Stone*, 13–27 July 1989.

26 Joe Dolce, "David Geffen Q & A," *Details*, July 1996.

27 Brantley Bardin, "Joni Mitchell Q & A," *Details*, July 1996.

28 Goodman, *The Mansion on the Hill*.

29 Ressner, "Geffen's Coming of Age."

30 Robert Hilburn, "The Recycled Hits: Some Are Bigger the Second Time Around," *Los Angeles Times*, 9 January 1988.

31 Lyric from "Goodbye Marlon Brando," 1988.

32 John Jackson, "My Hell," *Daily Mirror*, 19 May 1987.

33 Elton John, television interview with Terry Wogan, *Wogan*, BBC-TV, June 1987.

34 Sweeney, "How Elton Won His Million."

35 Elton John and Bernie Taupin, radio interview, *Rockline*, WNEW-NY (New York), August 1987.

36 Lesley Hetherington, "Honeymoon at Last," unknown Australian publication, *c.* November 1986.

37 MCA press release for *Reg Strikes Back*, 1988.

38 Dave Sholin, "Back to the Songs," *Playing Keyboards*, April/May 1989.

39 Elton John, television interview with Terry Wogan, June 1987.

40 MCA press release for *Reg Strikes Back*, 1988.

41 Ibid.

42 Elton John, radio interview, NRG (France), spring 1988.

43 MCA press release for *Reg Strikes Back*, 1988.

44 Sholin, "Back to the Songs."

45 Cassata, "Elton John: The Balance Brings Happiness."

46 MCA press release for *Reg Strikes Back*, 1988.

47 Liner notes, *To Be Continued . . .* (U.S.).

48 Lyric from "Town of Plenty," 1988.

49 Elton John, television interview with Jonathan Ross, *The Last Resort*, BBC-TV, May 1988.

50 Barry Flatman, "Elton's Dream Is Fading," *Daily Express*, 2 April 1988; Harry Harris, "Elton Gone!" *Daily Mirror*, 5 April 1988.

51 Videotape of Rock and Roll Hall of Fame induction ceremony, 28 January 1988.

Chapter Ten

1 Song title, 1986.

2 Hilburn, "The Recycled Hits."

3 Jonathan Takiff, "Elton John: A Makeover. It's out with the Outrageous and in with the Conservative for the Superstar of the '70s," *Philadelphia Daily News*, 4 October 1988.

4 Harold Goldberg, "Reg Strikes Back: Elton John," *Rolling Stone*, 6 October 1988.

5 Mark Moses, unknown title, *The New Yorker*, 14 November 1988.

6 Sholin, "Back to the Songs."

7 Sheila Rene, "San Francisco: Elton Charms Bay Area Music Vets," *Pulse*, September 1988.

8 Milano, "Elton Gives a Surprise Performance."

9 Robert Hilburn, "Goodbye to Elton John's Yellow Brick Road," *Los Angeles Times*, 5 June 1988.

10 Ibid.

11 Elton John, radio interview with Simon Bates, BBC Radio One, 17–20 May 1988.

12 Godfrey Barker, "Why Sotheby's Will Never Be the Same after Elton," *The Daily Telegraph*, *c.* August 1988.

13 Paul Gambaccini, "Elton John," from *Sotheby's: Elton John* (four-volume catalog auction set). (London: Sotheby's, 1988.)

14 Lyric from "The Camera Never Lies," 1988.

15 Elton John, television interview with Steve Blame, MTV-UK, July 1988.

16 Elton John and Bernie Taupin, radio interview, *Rockline*, 3 October 1988; Stephen Holden, "Coping with a Bad Year," *The New York Times*, 19 October 1988.

17 Unknown author, "Talking to Elton John," unknown U.S. publication, 1988.

18 Phillips, *You'll Never Eat Lunch*.

19 Elton John, television interview with Steve Blame, July 1988.

20 Elton John, television interview, "Elton John Weekend," VH1, summer 1988.

21 Elton John, television interview with Steve Blame, July 1988.

22 Cassata, "Elton John: The Balance Brings Happiness."

23 Elton John, radio interview, WHTZ-NY (New York), 19 October 1988.

24 Videotape of Athletes and Entertainers for Kids benefit, held in Los Angeles on July 8, 1988.

25 Lyric from "Town of Plenty," 1988.

26 Nick Robertshaw, "Mobbed Elton John Raises $8 Mil. in London," *Billboard*, 24 September 1988; Terry Trucco, "Pop Ephemera Auction: Elton John's Collection," *The New York Times*, 7 September 1988.

27 Claudia Jannone, "Alive: And Now for Something Completely Different," *East Coast Rocker*, 12 October 1988.

28 Jim Sullivan, "A Down-to-Earth Elton John," *The Boston Globe*, 10 October 1988.

29 Robert Hilburn, "Turning Back the Clock on British Invasion," *Los Angeles Times*, 26 September 1988.

30 Unknown author, "Bruce Hornsby's Top Ten Elton John Songs," *Rolling Stone*, 20 September 1990.

31 Lyric from "A Word in Spanish," 1988.

32 Lisa Robinson, "Elton John: Pop Superstar Tones Down His Act as He Cleans House," *Chicago Sun-Times*, 27 November 1988.

33 Gordon McKibben, "Elton John Wins Record-Setting Suit," *The Boston Globe*, 13 December 1988.

34 Elton John, television interview with Steve Blame, July 1988.

35 Lyric from "Club at the End of the Street," 1989.

36 Unknown author, "Elton's Safe Sex," *Rolling Stone*, 25 August 1988.

37 Elton John, radio interview, WHTZ-NY (New York), 19 October 1988.

38 Elton John and Bernie Taupin, radio interview with Roger Scott, BBC Radio One, 26 August 1989.

39 Elton John, television interview with Terry Wogan, *Wogan*, BBC-TV, 28 August 1989.

40 Unknown author, "My Amazing Years with the Show Prince of Pop," *Daily Mirror*, 17 March 1997.

41 Elton John and Bernie Taupin, radio interview with Roger Scott, 26 August 1989.

42 Ibid.

43 Elton John and Bernie Taupin, radio interview, "Two into One," BBC Radio One, 31 August 1992.

44 Iain Blair, "Glitter and the Beat," *Chicago Tribune*, 20 August 1989.

45 Elton John, television interview with David Frost, 22 November 1991.

46 Elton John, radio interview with Roger Scott, 26 August 1989.

47 Ibid.

48 Elton John and Bernie Taupin, "Two into One," 31 August 1992.

49 Elton John, radio interview with Roger Scott, 26 August 1989.

50 Lyric from "Too Low for Zero," 1983.

51 Elton John and Bernie Taupin, "Two into One," 31 August 1992.

52 Lyric from "Healing Hands," 1989.

53 Wheeler, "Bernie Taupin: The Brown Dirt Cowboy Rides Again."

54 Bernie Taupin, interview, *Sleeping with the Past* promotional film, Phonogram, summer 1989.

55 Elton John, television interview with Terry Wogan, 28 August 1989.

56 Ralph Novak, "*Sleeping with the Past:* Elton John," *People*, 6 November 1989.

57 Catherine Sullivan, "Elton John: *Sleeping with the Past*," *Melody Maker*, 16 September 1989.

58 Ken Tucker, "A Rapping Duo, n'Dour and Debussy," *The Philadelphia Inquirer*, 12 October 1989.

59 Geoffrey Grimes, "Masters of the Hook," *The Washington Post*, 18 October 1989.

60 Steve Smith, "Add Elton John to List of Great Shows," *San Gabriel Valley Tribune*, 17 August 1989.

61 Stephen Holden, "Elton John, Still Colorful and Popular," *The New York Times*, 9 October 1989.

62 J. Dee, "Specs and Drugs."

63 Unknown author, "My Amazing Years with the Show Prince of Pop."

64 Candice Carmel, "Officials Pleased: Elton Finally Books N.J. Meadowlands," *Amusement Business*, 1 July 1989.

65 Bernie Taupin and John Reid, radio interview, *Rockline*, WNEW-NY (New York), 2 October 1989.

66 Paul Rochibeau, "Elton John Cancels Local Dates," *The Boston Globe*, 21 October 1989.

67 Ibid.

68 Lyric from "Sacrifice," 1989.

69 Elton John, radio interview with Johnnie Walker, BBC, 25 March 1995.

70 Elton John, radio interview, *Rocksat*, unknown Australian network, 31 January 1990.

71 Steve Dow, "Elton Reaches out—to Help," unknown Australian publication, *c.* February 1990.

72 Elton John, Farm Aid, Indianapolis Hoosier Dome, 7 April 1990.

73 Hilburn, "Elton's Menagerie of Demons."

74 Elton John, radio interview with Timothy White, 18 June 1990.

75 Elton John, television interview with David Frost, 22 November 1991.

76 Lyric from "Healing Hands," 1989.

77 Elton John concert at Trump Taj Mahal Casino Resort, Mark G. Etess Arena, Atlantic City, 18 May 1990.

78 Lyric from "Sacrifice," 1989.

79 Elton John, radio interview with Richard Skinner, 14 and 29 December 1990.

80 Elton John, *Rocksat*, 31 January 1990.

81 Elton John, television interview with Paul Gambaccini, *Good Morning Britain*, BBC-TV, May 1990.

82 Television broadcast of International Rock Awards, ABC-TV, 6 June 1990.

83 Elton John, radio interview with Richard Skinner, 14 and 29 December 1990.

84 Ibid.

85 Elton John, television interview with Terry Wogan, *Wogan*, BBC-TV, 15 June 1990.

Chapter Eleven

1 Song title, 1990.

2 Unknown author and title, *Rolling Stone*, 1 November 1990.

3 Elton John, television interview, *VH1-One*, VH1, 16 December 1990.

4 Hilburn, "Elton John's Menagerie of Demons."

5 Lyric from "Border Song," 1970.

6 Deevoy, "Nobody's Perfect."

7 Elton John, radio interview with Richard Skinner, 14 and 29 December 1990.

8 Elton John, television interview with Jonathan Ross, *Tonight with Jonathan Ross*, BBC-TV, December 1990.

9 Elton John, television interview, *VH1-One*, 16 December 1990.

10 Lyric from "Simple Life," 1992.

11 Elton John, radio interview with Richard Skinner, 14 and 29 December 1990.

12 Lyric from "Simple Life," 1992.

13 Dennis Signy, "John Returns to Watford as a Director," *The Times* (London), 6 August 1991.

14 Thom Duffy, "Guest Set Fetes John/Taupin Songs," *Billboard*, 28 September 1991.

15 Unknown author, "Various Artists: Two Rooms," *Billboard*, 26 October 1991.

16 Michael Ellis, "Hot 100 Singles Spotlight," *Billboard*, 18 January 1992.

17 From "Don't Let the Sun Go Down on Me," live recording with George Michael, 1991.

18 Televised tribute to Freddie Mercury, BBC One, 25 November, 1991.

19 Paul Grein, "Elton Matches Elvis in Top-40 Tenure," *Billboard*, 4 January 1992.

20 Martin Townsend, "I Took a Lot of Drugs and I Drank a Lot . . . ," *Vox*, August 1992.

21 Lyric from "The One," 1992.

22 Hilburn, "Elton John's Menagerie of Demons."

23 Elton John and Bernie Taupin, "Two into One," 31 August 1992.

24 Robert Sandall, "Him Indoors," *Q*, July 1992.

25 Elton John and Bernie Taupin, "Two into One," 31 August 1992.

26 Sandall, "Him Indoors."

27 Elton John, radio interview with Paul Gambaccini, "Rocket Man and the Chipolata Fingers," *Kaleidoscope*, BBC Radio Four, 19 September 1997.

28 Elton John, radio interview, WPLJ-NY (New York), 6 October 1992.

29 Ibid.

30 Elton John and Bernie Taupin, "Two into One," 31 August 1992.

31 Ibid.

32 Ibid.

33 Elton John, radio interview with Steve Wright, BBC, 12 June 1992.

34 John F. Higgins, "Babylon on Touring, Recording with Elton," *East End Lights*, No. 11, spring 1993.

35 Elton John and Bernie Taupin, "Two into One," 31 August 1992.

36 Ibid.

37 Elton John, radio interview with Steve Wright, 12 June 1992.

38 Lyric from "Friends," 1971.

39 Unknown author, "Dee Murray 1946–1992," *Rolling Stone*, 5 March 1992.

40 Unknown author, "Newsmakers: One More Time," *The Philadelphia Inquirer*, 23 February 1992.

41 Elton John, radio interview with Steve Wright, 12 June 1992.

42 Robert K. Oermann, unknown title, *Tennessean*, 16 March 1992.

43 Isolated quote, *Rock World*, December 1993.

44 Hilburn, "Elton John's Menagerie of Demons."

45 Lyric from "The One," 1992.

46 Chris Morris, "The Big Switch: Elton Likely to Join P'Gram," *Billboard*, 22 February 1992; unknown author, "P'Gram Says Elton's on Board," *Billboard*, 4 April 1992; Irv Lichtman and Chris Morris, "MCA Losing Elton to P'Gram, Petty to Warner Bros., in U.S.," *Billboard*, 11 April 1992.

47 Elton John, radio interview with Steve Wright, 12 June 1992.

48 Elton John, television interview with Cara Cara, *Internacional*, unknown Brazilian network, May 1992.

49 Unknown author, "Live Sounds: Elton John," *Mix*, February 1993.

50 Randy Alexander, "Mega-Show Joins Rock Giants in Separate Sets," *The Times* (Trenton, New Jersey), August 1992.

51 Paul Cole, "Brum's Big Fan!" *Birmingham Evening Mail*, 30 June 1992.

52 Elton John, radio interview with Paul Gambaccini, BBC Radio One, 11 May 1993.

53 Hugh Fielder, "Artists in Concert," *Billboard*, 18 July 1992.

54 Lyric from "The One," 1992.

55 Mike Boehm, "Elton Gets Warm," *Los Angeles Times*, 12 July 1992.

56 Robert Christgau, "Consumer Guide," *The Village Voice*, 1 December 1992.

57 Unknown author and title, *Billboard*, 19 September 1992.

58 First quote, lyric from "The One," 1992; second quote, Elton's exclamation during live "I Don't Wanna Go On with You Like That," 1992.

59 Unknown author, "Elton John and Eric Clapton Concert: New York," *Us*, October 1992.

60 J. D. Considine, "Elton John Delivers Knock-'em, Sock-'em Rock and Roll Show," *Baltimore Sun*, 21 September 1992.

61 Lyric from "The Last Song," 1992.

62 Audience recording of Hall of Fame induction speech, Madison Square Garden, 9 October 1992.

63 Nadine Brozan, unknown title, *The New York Times*, 13 October 1992.

64 Adam Block, "Undeniably Elton."

65 Irv Lichtman, "Elton and Bernie Renew Pub Tie," *Billboard*, 14 November 1992.

66 Lyric from "The Last Song," 1992.

67 Elton John, radio interview with Paul Gambaccini, 11 May 1993.

68 Elton John, radio interview, WMXV-NY (New York), 20 November 1992.

69 From *A Current Affair*, syndicated U.S. television program, 19 November, 1992.

70 Lyric from "Simple Life," 1992.

71 John Lannert, "Elton John: PolyGram," *Billboard*, 13 February 1993.

72 Elton John, radio interview, WMXV-NY (New York), 20 November 1992.

73 Lannert, "Elton John: PolyGram."

74 Lyric from "Dixie Lily," 1974.

75 Unknown author, "Guentchev May Stay After FA Inquiry," *The Times* (London), 12 January 1993.

76 Unknown author and title, *New York Daily News*, 3 February 1993.

77 Michael Sheather, "Elton's Lover Tells All," *Woman's Day*, 18 January 1993; Michael Sheather, "Elton's Sex Secrets," *Woman's Day*, 25 January 1993.

78 Ian Dougall, "Elton Phone Tapes Fury," *Truth*, 20 February 1993.

79 Elton John, television interview with David White, *Real Life*, unknown Australian network, February 1993.

80 David Brown, "Exclusive Interview: Man with a Mission," *TV Week*, 6 March 1993.

81 Denise Ryan, "Elton Bugged, but Pests Get the Flick," unknown publication, February 1993; unknown author, "Elton Venue Sprayed," *Herald-Sun*, 21 February 1993.

82 Nui Te Koha, "It's Not Cricket for Poor Elton," *Herald-Sun*, February 1993.

83 Brown, "Exclusive Interview: Man with a Mission."

84 Unknown author, "Elton Helps Music Play," unknown publication, February 1993.

85 Jeannie Williams, "A Screaming Good Time for Clint," *USA Today*, 31 March 1993.

86 Lyric from "Simple Life," 1992.

87 Unknown author, "Vive Elton," unknown U.S. newspaper, June 1993.

88 Lyric from "Simple Life," 1992.

89 Unknown author, "I'm Special," *Time*, 28 June 1993.

90 John Vincent, "Elton John Abandons Israel Tour," *The Times* (London), 16 June 1993.

91 Ethan Bronner, "For Israel, Elton's Act Is Hard to Follow," *The Boston Globe*, 17 June 1993.

92 Uri Dan and Leo Standora, "Elton's Going Back to Israel," *New York Post*, 17 June 1993.

93 Associated Press, "Mobbed by His Fans, Elton John Flees Israel," *The New York Times*, 17 June 1993.

94 Unknown author, "Elton Says Sorry to Israeli Fans," *Star-Ledger*, 18 June 1993.

95 Lyric from "Duets for One," 1993.

96 Elton John, *Rocksat*, 31 January 1990.

97 Robert Hilburn, "Having a Go at 'Indifference, Intolerance,'" *Los Angeles Times,* 22 September 1993.

98 Elton John, John Reid, and others, television interview, *The Beat File,* unknown Japanese network, 1994.

99 Elton John, radio interview, 105 Network (Italy), November 1993.

100 RuPaul, *Lettin It All Hang Out.* (New York: Hyperion, 1995.)

101 Elton John, John Reid, and others, *The Beat File,* 1994.

102 Ibid.

103 Hilburn, "Having a Go at 'Indifference, Intolerance.'"

104 Elton John, radio interview, 105 Network (Italy), November 1993.

105 Chris Difford, "Some Fantastic Days," *Q,* December 1993.

106 Hilburn, "Having a Go at 'Indifference, Intolerance.'"

107 Lyric from "The Power," 1993.

108 Elton John and Billie Jean King, television interview with Jay Leno, *The Tonight Show,* NBC-TV, 20 September 1993.

109 Michael Goldberg, "Record High," *Rolling Stone,* 16 September 1993.

110 Lyric from "A Woman's Needs," 1993.

111 Audience recordings, "An Evening with Elton John and Ray Cooper" in Fort Lauderdale, Florida on 30 September 1993; New Haven, Connecticut on 20 October 1993; and Providence, Rhode Island on 23 October 1993.

112 Deborah Wilker, "Elton John Is Hardly Resting on His Laurels," *Ft. Lauderdale Sun-Sentinel,* October 1993.

113 Elton John, radio interview with Paul Gambaccini, 11 May 1993.

114 Lyric from "Legal Boys," 1982.

115 Dominic Pride, "A Sweep for Elton at ASCAP Awards," *Billboard,* 2 October 1993.

116 Richard Duce, "Jury Awards £350,000 Damages to Elton John," *The Times* (London), 5 November 1993.

117 Televised news reports on BBC Four, BBC One, and ITV, 4 November 1993.

118 Elton John, television interview with Des O'Connor, *Des O'Connor Tonight,* ITV/Thames, 17 November 1993.

119 Lyric from "Elton's Song," 1981.

120 Constance Droganes, "Captains Courageous," *Images,* spring 1996.

121 Ginny Dougary, "My Life with Captain Fantastic," *The Times* (London), 23 June 1996; Colin Wills, "My Life with Elton," *Sunday Mirror Magazine,* 23 June 1996.

122 McAleer, *The All Music Book of Hit Albums.*

123 Peter Kane, "Mangled," *Q,* January 1994.

124 Mike Lehecka, "Geezers," *Request,* March 1994.

125 Stephen Holden, "For Elton John, One Voice Fits All Seasons," *The New York Times,* 21 November 1993.

126 Lyric from "The Ballad of Danny Bailey (1909–34)," 1973.

127 Arthur Goldstruck, "The British Abroad: Elton John," *Billboard,* 12 February 1994.

128 Jesse Nash, "Losing Elton in the Lost City," *Creem,* March 1994.

129 Television broadcast of Elton John/Ray Cooper concert, M-Net (South Africa), 10 December 1993.

130 Lyric from "Step into Christmas," 1973.

131 Elton John, *Des O'Connor Tonight,* 17 November 1993.

132 Emma Wilkins, "Elton John Sells Jewels for £1m," *The Times* (London), 15 December 1993.

133 Unknown author, "Star Opens Sex Clinic," *The Times* (London), 1 December 1993.

134 Parke Puterbaugh, "Elton John," program for Rock and Roll Hall of Fame Annual Induction Dinner, 1994.

135 Lisa Robinson, "Rockers Rolled in Revelations," *New York Post,* 21 January 1994.

136 Ibid.; Edna Gundersen, "Musicians Sing Praises of Those They Call Heroes," *USA Today,* 21 January 1994.

137 Audience recording of Rock and Roll Hall of Fame Ninth Annual Induction Dinner and backstage press conference, 19 January 1994.

Chapter Twelve

1 Song title, 1995.

2 RuPaul, *Lettin It All Hang Out.*

3 Lyric from "Circle of Life," 1994.

4 Larry Nager, "Singing Animals Are Only Human," *Philadelphia Daily News,* 6 July 1994.

5 Elton John and others, television interview, "The Lion King: A Musical Journey," ABC-TV, 15 June 1994.

6 Gill Pringle, "The Mane Event!" *Sunday: News of the World Magazine,* 2 October 1994.

7 Elton John and others, "The Lion King: A Musical Journey," 15 June 1994.

8 Pringle, "The Mane Event!"

9 Elton John and others, "The Lion King: A Musical Journey," 15 June 1994.

10 Nager, "Singing Animals Are Only Human."

11 Elton John and others, "The Lion King: A Musical Journey," 15 June 1994.

12 Dan DeLuca, "Disney Is Lord of the Pop Charts," *The Philadelphia Inquirer,* 26 June 1994.

13 Elton John, radio interview with Steve McCoy and Vikki Locke, 19 August 1994.

14 Tom Green, "Not to Worry: Film Sires Fun Phrase," *USA Today,* 27 June 1994.

15 Elton John and others, "The Lion King: A Musical Journey," 15 June 1994.

16 DeLuca, "Disney Is Lord of the Pop Charts."

17 Elton John, television interview, *The Lion King* telecast, ABC-TV, 3 November 1996.

18 Elton John, radio interview, unknown New York City network, 22 July 1994.

19 Lyric from "Circle of Life," 1994.

20 Lyric from "Please," 1995.

21 Elton John, radio interview with Johnnie Walker, 25 March 1995.

22 Q & A, Elton John Expo, 26 July 1996.

23 Elton John, radio interview with Johnnie Walker, 25 March 1995.

24 Sischy, "Elton John: 150% Involved."

25 Unknown author, "Books," *East End Lights,* No. 17, winter 1995.

26 Elton John and Bernie Taupin, interview, *Made in England* promotional video, Rocket/Mercury, 1995.

27 Ibid.

28 Robert Hilburn, "Get Back, Honky Cats," *Los Angeles Times*, 2 April 1995.

29 Ibid.

30 Paul Zollo, "Bernie Taupin's Words of Wisdom," *Musician*, January 1998.

31 Elton John, radio interview with Simon Mayo, BBC, 20–24 March 1995.

32 Elton John and Bernie Taupin, interview, *Made in England* promotional video, 1995.

33 Elton John, television interview with Axel Boisen, Denmark, from *Made in England* promotional interactive CD ROM, Rocket/Mercury, 1995.

34 Elton John, radio interview with Simon Mayo, 20–24 March 1995.

35 John F. Higgins, "Made in England; Dissected in LA," *East End Lights*, No. 22, spring 1996.

36 Ibid.

37 Hilburn, "Get Back, Honky Cats."

38 Elton John, radio interview with Johnnie Walker, 25 March 1995.

39 J. Dee, "Specs and Drugs."

40 Elton John, radio interview with Johnnie Walker, 25 March 1995.

41 Lyric from "Be Prepared," 1994.

42 David Poland, "The Flintstones v. the Lion King," *The Philadelphia Inquirer*, 15 March 1994.

43 Poland, "The Flintstones v. the Lion King," *Billboard*, 16 April 1994; Craig Rosen, "New Disney Soundtrack Fit for a 'King,'" *Billboard*, 16 April 1994.

44 DeLuca, "Disney Is Lord of the Pop Charts."

45 Lyric from "Tiny Dancer," 1971.

46 Roland Stone, "Billy Joel: How a Blue-Blooded Star Studded Boy Got the Label 'America's Elton John,'" *Juke*, 4 September 1976.

47 Robert Hilburn, "Elton John Celebrates Big 10th Anniversary," *Los Angeles Times*, 30 August 1980.

48 Unknown author and title, *Performing Songwriter*, January–February 1996.

49 Steve Morse, "Not a Duel, but a Duet," *The Record* (New Jersey), 22 July 1994.

50 Unknown author and title, *Performance*, 12 July 1996.

51 Tom Moon, "Elton John, Billy Joel at the Vet," *The Philadelphia Inquirer*, 9 July 1994.

52 Jonathan Takiff, "A Duel of Piano-Men," *Philadelphia Daily News*, 9 July 1994.

53 Gerald Kolpan, *The Ten o' Clock News*, WTXF Fox-29 (Philadelphia), 8 July 1994.

54 David Zimmerman, "Joel, John Keyed to Each Other," *USA Today*, 11 July 1994.

55 Elysa Gardner, "Performance: Billy Joel/Elton John," *Rolling Stone*, 8 September 1994.

56 Elton John, radio interview, 22 July 1994.

57 Elton John, radio interview with Steve McCoy and Vikki Locke, 19 August 1994.

58 Lyric from "Circle of Life," 1994.

59 Unknown author and title, *Baltimore Sun*, 1994.

60 Lyric from "Talking Old Soldiers," 1970.

61 Q & A, Elton John Expo, 26 July 1996.

62 Elton John, television interview with Dan Rather, *48 Hours*, CBS-TV, 23 November 1994.

63 Lyric from "Live Like Horses," 1996.

64 Elton John, radio interview with Johnnie Walker, 25 March 1995.

65 Ibid.

66 Dougary, "My Life with Captain Fantastic."

67 Audience videotape of "World AIDS Day Concert: An Evening at the Royal Albert Hall with Elton John and Ray Cooper," London, 1 December 1994.

68 Television broadcast of the Brit Awards, BBC-TV, 21 February 1995.

69 News report from *Show Biz Today*, CNN, 20 January 1995.

70 The Brit Awards, 21 February 1995.

71 Ibid.

72 Lisa Robinson, "Newcomer Sheryl Crow Tops Grammy Nominations," *New York Post*, 6 January 1995.

73 Jim Farber, "Grammy's Ayes Still out of Focus," *New York Daily News*, 6 January 1995.

74 Craig Rosen, "Grammy Offers Open Arms to a New Generation of Talent," *Billboard*, 14 January 1995.

75 Lyric from "Believe," 1995.

76 Unknown author and title, *Entertainment Weekly*, 28 April 1995.

77 Adam Sandler, "Fans Queue Up for John Disc," *Reuters/Variety News Service*, 19 March 1995.

78 Television broadcast of the 67th Annual Academy Awards, ABC-TV, 27 March 1995.

79 Ken Tucker, "Art in the Right Place," *Entertainment Weekly*, 31 March 1995.

80 Unknown author, "Music: Elton John Made in England," *Out*, May 1995.

81 Unknown author and title, *Star-Ledger*, 31 March 1995.

82 Jim Farber, "Record Reviews," *New York Daily News*, 4 April 1995.

83 Elton John, television interview with Ray Martin, *Ray Martin Presents*, unknown Australian network, April 1995.

84 Elton John, television interview, *Extra*, WCAU-TV (Philadelphia), 28 March 1995.

85 Cindy Adams, unknown title, *New York Post*, 30 March 1995.

86 Unknown author and title, *Interview*, July 1995.

87 Lyric from "Blessed," 1995.

88 Keith Foster, "Polars Warm Hearts of John, Rostropovich," *Billboard*, 20 May 1995.

89 Q & A, Elton John Expo, 26 July 1996.

90 Elton John and Bernie Taupin, *Made in England* promotional video, 1995.

91 Vadim Yurchenkov, "Elton John Performs in Russia for 2nd Time," *Billboard*, 24 June 1995.

92 Lyric from "Made in England," 1995.

93 Brad Kava, "Elton John Captivates with Hits of His Career at Shoreline Concert," *San Jose Mercury News*, 17 September 1995.

94 Dan Cane, "Elton John Yields Three Hours of Hit After Hit at Gund Arena," *The Repository*, 10 October 1995.

95 Barry Walters, "Elton Gives New Meaning to 'Sad Songs,'" *San Francisco Examiner*, September 1995.

96 Audience recording, concert at the Hollywood Bowl, Los Angeles, 22 September 1995.

97 Robert Hilburn, "Elton John Shines as a Favorite Son of L.A. at Hollywood Bowl," *Los Angeles Times*, 25 September 1995.

98 Concert at the Hollywood Bowl, 23 September 1995.

99 Lyric from "Blessed," 1995.

100 Unknown author, "Why 'Blessed' Was Not Released as a Single in the UK," *Hercules*, No. 34, March 1996.

101 Elton John sang this as part of "Rocket Man," Rio de Janeiro, November 1995.

102 Leandro Delgado, "El Triunfo del Idolo Pop" ("Triumph of the Pop Idol"), unknown Montevideo publication, 25 November 1995 (English translation by Judith A. McArthur).

103 Alejandro Espina, "Alguien Salvo Mi Juventud Esa Noche" ("Someone Saved My Childhood Tonight"), *El Observador*, November 1995 (English translation by Judith A. McArthur).

104 John Lannert, "Elton, Soda Play Chile," *Billboard*, 16 December 1995.

105 Lyric from "Lies," 1995.

106 Helen Smith, no title, Reuters, 13 December 1995; Frances Gibb, "Elton John Award Cut by Libel Ruling," *The Times* (London), 13 December 1995.

107 H. Smith, no title.

Chapter Thirteen

1 Song title, 1975.

2 Elton John, television interview with Bob Costas, *The Today Show*, NBC-TV, 5, 6, and 12 September 1995.

3 Ingrid Sischy, "Sing It Again Now," *Interview*, April 1999.

4 Andrew Longmore, "Watford's Greatest Hits Back in Harmony," *The Times* (London), 23 February 1996.

5 Graham Taylor, televised press conference, BBC One, 27 February 1996.

6 Elizabeth J. Rosenthal, "Elton Goes Pinky," *Hercules*, No. 35, June 1996.

7 Mitchell Fink, unknown title, *People*, 20 May 1996.

8 Tim Cooper, "Elton and the 'Voice of God' Are a Big Hit," unknown London publication, June 1996.

9 Unknown author, "News," *Hercules*, No. 35, June 1996.

10 Television broadcast of "Pavarotti and Friends," RAI UNO (Italy), 20 June 1996.

11 Lyric from "Lies," 1995.

12 A. Scott Walton, "John Hosts Eye-Popping Rummage Sale," *Atlanta Journal-Constitution*, 4 June 1996.

13 Margaret Hall, "Going for a Song," unknown publication, 1996.

14 Dawn Eden, "Interview: Elton John Talks About Grieving, Diana's Death, and How He Keeps His Faith Alive," *Good Housekeeping*, February 1998.

15 Beechy Colclough, "My Pal's Been to El and Back," *Sun TV*, 8 July 1996.

16 Lyric from "You Can Make History (Young Again)," 1996.

17 Zollo, "Bernie Taupin's Words of Wisdom."

18 Dale Berryhill, "An Old Producer Returns to Elton Team for Latest Tracks, Impressing the New Guitarist," *East End Lights*, No. 24, fall 1996.

19 David Sprague, "New Sets Offer 'Greatest Ballads,'" *Billboard*, 23 November 1996.

20 Melinda Newman, "Equal Opportunity on Pop Charts?" *Billboard*, 18 November 1995; "For Petty's Sake: Another Boxed Set," *Billboard*, 18 November 1995.

21 Tom McCormick, letter to the editor, *Billboard*, 30 November 1996.

22 Television broadcast of VH1 Fashion Awards, VH1, 29 October 1996.

23 Staff writer, "Newsmakers," *The Philadelphia Inquirer*, 2 December 1996.

24 Elizabeth J. Rosenthal, "Elton Brings Down the Roof in Benefit at Church," *East End Lights*, No. 26, spring 1997.

25 Lyric from "You Can Make History (Young Again)," 1996.

26 Fred Bronson, unknown title, *Billboard*, 8 February 1997.

27 Robert Jobson, "Diana's Fury Over Nude Photographs," *International Express*, 11–17 February 1997.

28 Unknown author, "Dear John," unknown newspaper, July 1997.

29 Craig R. Whitney, "Rostropovich at 70, Con Brio & 700 Friends," *The New York Times*, 29 March 1997.

30 Elton John, interview, *Big Picture* promotional CD, Rocket Records, 1997.

31 Associated Press, "Royal Academy Honors John," *The Record Herald* (Waynesboro, PA), 25 March 1997

Chapter Fourteen

1 Song title, B-side, 1968.

2 Elton John, radio interview with Richard Skinner, 14 and 29 December 1990.

3 Unknown author, "Too Old at 50?" *Sunday Mirror*, March 1997.

4 Unknown author, "My Amazing Years."

5 Unknown author, "Elton to Have a Ball," *Mail on Sunday*, 1997; Emma Wilkins, "Elton John Steps Lightly into Sixth Decade," *The Times* (London), 5 April 1997.

6 Staff writer, "Elton John Celebrates His 50th Birthday with a Showbiz Extravaganza," *Hello!* 19 April 1997.

7 Ibid.

8 Jon Snow, "Still Not Grown up at 50," unknown publication, 1997.

9 Lyric from "Friends," 1971.

10 Elton John and Billy Joel, television interview with Richard Wilkins, Nine Network (Australia), conducted May 1997, broadcast summer 1997.

11 Lyric from "Wicked Dreams," 1997.

12 François Délétraz, "Elton John: J'ai Enfin Changé de Vie," *Le Figaro*, 23 August 1997.

13 Elton John, radio interview with Paul Gambaccini, *Kaleidoscope*, BBC Radio Four, 13 and 19 September 1997.

14 Elton John, *Big Picture* promotional CD, 1997.

15 Ibid.

16 Craig Rosen, "Bernie Taupin: The Billboard Interview," *Billboard*, 4 October 1997.

17 Bobbie Katz, "Sir Elton John on 'The Big Picture,'" *Los Angeles Times*, 1 February 1998.

18 Ibid.

19 Ibid.

20 Elton John, *Big Picture* promotional CD, 1997.

21 Ibid.

22 Timothy White, "Elton John: The *Billboard* Interview."

23 Elton John, *Big Picture* promotional CD, 1997.

24 Dominic Pride et al., "Pop Music Is Looking for a Few Good Men," *Billboard*, 18 January 1997.

25 David Hinckley, "Veteran Rockers Gasping for Airplay," *New York Daily News*, 22 May 1997.

26 Lyric from "If the River Can Bend," 1997.

27 Elton John, radio interview with Paul Gambaccini, 13 and 19 September 1997.

28 Salewicz, "The Rise and Fall of Reginald Dwight."

29 Elton John, radio interview with Paul Gambaccini, 13 and 19 September 1997.

30 Ibid.

31 Elton John, *Big Picture* promotional CD, 1997.

32 Elizabeth Snead, "Designer Brought Star Power to Fashion," *USA Today*, 16 July 1997.

33 Jenifer Braun and Susain Alai, "Fashion Kind Flourished on the Edge," *Star-Ledger*, 16 July 1997.

34 Amy M. Spindler, "Gianni Versace, 50, the Designer who Infused Fashion with Life and Art," *The New York Times*, 16 July 1997.

35 Andy Geller, "Outrageousness Turned Versace into a Superstar," *New York Post*, 17 July 1997.

36 Leonard Boasberg, "Rock Royalty Will Come to Aid of Ravaged Island," *The Philadelphia Inquirer*, 31 July 1997.

37 Nigel Farndale, "As 'Candle in the Wind '97' Becomes the Best Selling Record Ever, a Candid Interview with the Man Whose Song Is a Hymn to Diana," *Daily Mail*, 16 September 1997.

38 Lyric from "Cage the Songbird," 1976.

39 Unknown author, "Fashion and Show Business," *International Express*, 3 September 1997.

40 Bill Hoffmann, "Celebrity Pals Are Stunned," *New York Post*, 1 September 1997.

41 Steve Dunleavy, "The Queen Has Lost Her Flock Forever," *New York Post*, 5 September 1997.

42 Dave Thompson, "Diana, Princess of Wales: The 'Rock'n'Roll Princess,'" *Goldmine*, 26 September 1997.

43 Robert Hilburn, "Amid All of His Sorrows, He's Still Standing," *Los Angeles Times*, 26 September 1997; Tim Cooper, "Tribute to Top of the Charts in Only Eight Days," unknown London publication, September 1997.

44 Robert Hilburn, "Relighting 'Candle' for Di," *Los Angeles Times*, 14 September 1997.

45 Ibid.

46 Ibid.

47 Sue Leeman, "Royals OK a Longer Funeral Procession," *Philadelphia Daily News*, 4 September 1997.

48 Greenfield, "Elton John Steams 'em Up."

49 Cooper, "Tribute to Top of the Charts."

50 Ian Smith and Craig Watson, "Elton Hit Rewritten as Tribute to Diana," *Glasgow Herald*, 5 September 1997.

51 Associated Press, unknown title (news report from London concerning hit potential of "Candle in the Wind 1997"), 5 September 1997.

52 Elton John, *20/20*, 5 September 1997.

53 Lyric from "Cage the Songbird," 1976.

54 Kim Willis, "1 Billion Watched Around the Globe," *USA Today*, 8 September 1997.

55 Elton John, television interview with David Frost, *Breakfast with Frost*, BBC-TV, 7 September 1997.

56 Ibid.

57 Liz Smith, unknown title, *New York Post*, 10 September 1997.

58 Unknown author, "Glimmer of Youth: A Nice Chat with Keith Richards," *Entertainment Weekly*, 3 October 1997.

59 Television news clip, *Extra*, WCAU-TV (Philadelphia), 8 October 1997.

60 Shirley English, "Wee Wee Frees Attack Funeral for 'Superstition,'" unknown UK publication, September 1997; Rev. Neil Ross, unknown title, *Free Presbyterian Magazine and Monthly Record*, October 1997.

61 John Mulvey, "Stop the Madness: Why 'Candle in the Wind' Is the Death of Rock," *New Musical Express*, 20 September 1997.

62 Emma Forrest, "The Singer, Not the Song," *The Guardian*, 10 September 1997.

63 Lyric from "January," 1997.

64 Television news clip, *Access Hollywood*, WCAU-TV (Philadelphia), 11 September 1997; television news clip, *Show Biz Today*, CNN, 11 September 1997.

65 Chris Hughes, "Elton: Time to Move On," unknown London publication, September 1997.

66 Dominic Pride et al., "'Candle' Ignites Globally," *Billboard*, 20 September 1997.

67 Jim Farber, "Bullets & Bombs: Oasis' Sales Dry Up and It's Not Alone," *New York Daily News*, 22 September 1997.

68 Elton John, radio interview, WPLJ-NY (New York), 10 October 1997.

69 Lyric from "Something About the Way You Look Tonight," 1997.

70 Associated Press, unknown title, 13 September 1997.

71 Elton John, radio interview with Paul Gambaccini, 13 and 19 September 1997.

72 Jeff Clark-Meads et al., "'Candle' Lights a Fire in Stores Globally," *Billboard*, 27 September 1997.

73 Peter Blom, "Enorme Vraag Naar Single-CD Elton John" ("Many People Want Elton John CD Single"), unknown Dutch publication, September 1997 (English translation by Gerda Bosscher).

74 Rocket Records/A&M Associated Labels press release, America On-Line (AOL), 2 October 1997.

75 Patricia Germani, "'Candle' Burns Toward the Million," unknown publication, *c.* September 1997; Lyall Johnson, "CD Stores Get Set for Diana's 'Candle,'" unknown publication, 21 September 1997.

76 Rocket Records/A&M Associated Labels press release, 2 October 1997.

77 Don Jeffrey, "PolyGram Burns 'Candle' at Both Ends to Ship Single," *Billboard*, 25 October 1997.

78 Unknown author, "'Candle' Buyers Tend the Flame," unknown Los Angeles newspaper, September 1997; David M. Halbfinger, "Elton John's 'Candle' Anthem for Diana Sells Briskly in Its U.S. Debut," *The New York Times*, 24 September 1997.

79 Unknown author, "Diana: Let Us Count the Ways," *Entertainment Weekly*, 26 December 1997–2 January 1998.

80 Jeffrey, "PolyGram Burns 'Candle' at Both Ends."

81 Newspaper advertisement, *The Philadelphia Inquirer*, 23 September 1997.

82 Jeffrey, "PolyGram Burns 'Candle' at Both Ends."

83 Unknown author, "CD to Boost Charity," unknown Australian newspaper, 1997.

84 Television broadcast of *Billboard* Music Awards, WTXF Fox-29 (Philadelphia), 8 December 1997.

85 Tom Sinclair, "Hear and Now: This Week on the Music Beat," *Entertainment Weekly*, 17 October 1997.

86 Lyric from "Wicked Dreams," 1997.

87 Jim Farber, "Stones & Elton Get PR Hoopla, Not LP Moolah," *New York Daily News*, 24 November 1997.

88 Lyric from "If the River Can Bend," 1997.

89 Russ DeVault, "Elton: Opens at Roxy," *Atlanta Journal-Constitution*, 3 October 1997; Miriam Longino, "700 Lucky Fans Take Home Prizes in the Elton John Sweepstakes," *Atlanta Journal-Constitution*, 7 October 1997.

90 Jerry Crowe, "This Is Their Song," *Los Angeles Times*, 19 October 1997.

91 Unknown author, "Sand and Water: Beth Nielson [*sic*] Chapman's Opus of Grief and Healing," *Inside Borders*, March 1998.

92 Unknown author, "Sand, Water & Son," *Atlanta Journal-Constitution*, 10 October 1997.

93 Gary Graff, unknown title, *Reuters/Variety*, 12 November 1997.

94 Richard L. Eldredge, "Peach Buzz: Chapman Revises Song for John," *Atlanta Journal-Constitution*, 8 October 1997.

95 Crowe, "This Is Their Song."

96 Leslie Scanlon, "To Legions of Fans, No One Can Hold a Candle to Elton," *Louisville Courier-Journal*, 19 October 1997.

97 Patrick Johnson, "Elton John Rocks Mullins Center," *Union-News*, 6 November 1997.

98 John Jorgenson, *Reports from the Road*, www.hellecasters.com, 15 October 1997.

99 Lyric from "The Morning Report," 1997.

100 Richard L. Eldredge, "Peach Buzz: Elton John Honored by CARE," *Atlanta Journal-Constitution*, 18 November 1997.

101 Reuters, unknown title, America On-Line (AOL), 18 November 1997.

102 Jeannie Williams, "News & Views: An Opera Overture for JFK Jr. and Wife," *USA Today*, 3 December 1997.

103 Dr. Stephen J. Matlaga, personal communication with author, December 1997.

104 Liz Smith, unknown title, *New York Post*, 17 November 1997.

105 Staff writer, gossip column, *New York Daily News*, 19 November 1997.

106 Barry Singer, "On an Assembly Line of Hits," *The New York Times*, 21 December 1997.

107 David Patrick Stearns, "'Lion King' Crowned Broadway's Fastest Seller," *USA Today*, 20 November 1997.

108 Lyric from "The Big Picture," 1997.

109 Richard Smith, "Elton John: Man of the Year," *Gay Times*, December 1997.

110 Barbara Ellen, "It's a Little Bit Funny—How People Love Elton," *The Observer*, December 1997.

111 Jorgenson, *Reports from the Road*.

112 Sara Marani, "Proud Elton John Knighted for Music and AIDS Work," Reuters, 24 February 1998.

Epilogue

1 Lyric from "I'm Still Standing," 1983.

2 Elton John, "Elton John's Tip Sheet: The Rocket Man Says What's Rocketing," *Interview*, August 2000.

3 Elton John, television interview with Matt Lauer, *The Today Show*, NBC-TV, 27 December 2000.

4 Renee Graham, "Elton John-Eminem Teaming Stirs Outcry Among Gays, Lesbians," *The Boston Globe*, February 2001.

5 Christopher Heredia, "Elton John's Decision to Appear with Eminem at Grammys Angers Gay Community," *San Francisco Chronicle*, February 2001.

6 Richard Johnson with Paula Froelich and Chris Wilson, "Page Six: Gays Split on Elton–Eminem Act," *New York Post*, 13 February 2001.

7 Elton John, *The Today Show*, 27 December 2000.

8 Madhatter, "Elton and the Gay Thing," alt.fan.Elton-John (Internet newsgroup), 9 February 2001.

9 Matthew Wright, "Fleeced: Elton Tells Mirror: My Lying Cheat Manager Cost Me £20m," *Daily Mirror*, 16 July 1999.

10 Ibid.

11 Ibid.

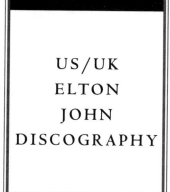

US/UK
ELTON
JOHN
DISCOGRAPHY

THIS DISCOGRAPHY is intended to examine the breadth and scope of Elton John's recorded output in his two most important markets: the United States and the United Kingdom. It includes all of his singles and albums released in both countries, with the exceptions of most promotional items and reissued singles and albums that are no different from the originals.[1] In focusing chiefly on the music, I have also omitted reference to special features such as picture sleeves, gatefold sleeves, postcards, posters, booklets, and other collectible things that were included with many of these releases. The reader should be aware, though, that numerous Elton John U.S. and U.K. vinyl singles from the 1970s, and virtually all from the 1980s and 1990s, have been available in picture sleeves, while for his audiocassette and CD singles, cover art has been the norm.

This discography also traces the evolution of Elton's record company affiliations. His American label is now Universal. He has, in a sense, returned to the place that first took a chance on him in the United States: Uni, or the parent company in 1970, MCA. But he is a Universal artist now only because of the 1999 takeover of PolyGram by Seagram, which had previously purchased MCA. It was Seagram's acquisition of PolyGram that ultimately led to the demise of Rocket Records.

All songs listed in this discography are performed by Elton John unless otherwise noted or marked with an asterisk (*). The discography also includes one album on which Elton only cameos—*Two Rooms: Celebrating the Songs of Elton John & Bernie Taupin*—due to the album's significance in laying the groundwork for his post-rehabilitation comeback in 1992. Finally, all of the songs and albums listed are Elton John/Bernie Taupin compositions unless followed by one of the letters listed under the Songwriters Key on pages 500–501.

---

[1] *Elton's US radio-only singles, which are promotional items, are included starting in 1999 since* Billboard *magazine, as of December 1998, began assigning a Hot 100 chart impact to singles that were not available at retail but received significant airplay.*

SONGWRITERS KEY

a – Elton John

b – Reg Dwight

c – Caleb Quaye, Reg Dwight, Bernie
  Calvert, and Chris Jackson

d – Lord Choc Ice (Elton John pseudonym)

e – Dinah Card/Carte Blanche (Elton John
  pseudonyms)

f – Ann Orson/Carte Blanche
  (John/Taupin pseudonyms)

g – Elton John, Bernie Taupin, and
  Davey Johnstone

h – Elton John, Bernie Taupin, Davey
  Johnstone, and Phineas McHize

i – Elton John, Bernie Taupin, Davey
  Johnstone, and Caleb Quaye

j – Elton John, Bernie Taupin, Davey
  Johnstone, Caleb Quaye, and James
  Newton Howard

k – Elton John, Bernie Taupin, Davey
  Johnstone, Kiki Dee, and David Nutter

l – Elton John, Bernie Taupin, Charlie
  Morgan, Paul Westwood, Davey
  Johnstone, and Fred Mandel

m – Elton John, Bernie Taupin, and James
  Newton Howard

n – Elton John, Bernie Taupin, and
  Alan Carvell

o – Elton John, Bernie Taupin, and
  Thom Bell

p – Elton John and James Newton Howard

q – Elton John and Paul Buckmaster

r – Elton John and Gary Osborne

s – Elton John, Gary Osborne, and
  Tim Renwick

t – Elton John and Tom Robinson

u – Elton John and Tim Rice

v – Elton John, Tim Rice, and Hans Zimmer

w – Elton John, Tim Rice, and
  Patrick Leonard

x – Elton John and Judie Tzuke

y – Elton John and Chris Difford

z – Cher and Lady Choc Ice (latter is Elton
  John pseudonym)

aa – Bernie Taupin and Michel Berger

bb – Gary Osborne and Jean-Paul Dreau

cc – Paul Buckmaster

dd – Caleb Quaye

ee – Kiki Dee

ff – Kiki Dee, Gary Osborne, and
  Reid Kaelin

gg – Hans Zimmer

hh – John Powell

ii – Cole Porter

jj – John Lennon

kk – Paul McCartney

ll – John Lennon and Paul McCartney

mm – Chuck Berry

nn – Stevie Wonder

oo – Stevie Wonder and Ivy Hunter

pp – Stevie Wonder and Yvonne Wright

qq – Stevie Wonder, Lee Garrett, Syreeta
  Wright, and Lula Mae Hardaway

rr – Mick Jagger and Keith Richards

ss – Pete Townsend

tt – Burt Bacharach and Carole Bayer Sager

uu – Victor Young and Edward Heyman

vv – John Fogerty

ww – Roger Cook and Roger Greenaway

xx – Roger Cook, Roger Greenaway,
  Albert Hammond, and Mike
  Hazelwood

yy – Cat Stevens

zz – Norman Greenbaum

aaa – Nicholas Ashford and
  Valerie Simpson

bbb – Dionne Warwick

ccc – Francis Lai and Hal Shaper

ddd – John Chatman (aka Memphis Slim)

eee – Huddie Ledbetter (aka Lead Belly)

fff – Jimmy Witherspoon

ggg – Arthur Crudup

hhh – Jack Conrad and Don Goodman

iii – Leroy Bell and Casey James

jjj – Thom Bell, Leroy Bell, and Casey James

kkk – Peter Bellotte and Michael Hofmann

lll – Peter Bellotte and Geoff Bastow

mmm – Peter Bellote, Stefan Wisnet, and
Gunther Moll

nnn – Peter Bellotte, Sylvester Levay, and
Jerry Rix

ooo – Freddie Mercury, Brian May,
Roger Taylor, and John Deacon

ppp – Albert Hammond and Diane Warren

qqq – Bruce Roberts and Andy Goldmark

rrr – Bruce Roberts and Donna Weiss

sss – Marcella Detroit

ttt – Attrell Cordes

uuu – Willard Eugene Price

vvv – Jeffrey Bowen, Eddie Hazel,
and Alphonso Boyd

www – Chris Rea

xxx – Nik Kershaw

yyy – Linden Oldham and Dan Penn

zzz – Ted Daffan

aaaa – Andy Fairweather Low

bbbb – Tony Hiller and John Goodison
(aka Peter Simons)

cccc – Guy Fletcher and Doug Flett

dddd – Weldon Irvine, Jr. and Nina Simone

eeee – Ray Dorset

ffff – Ken Howard and Alan Blaikly

gggg – Kevin Godley, Lol Creme, and Eric
Stewart

hhhh – Lou Christie and Herbert Twyla

iiii – John Hurley and Ronnie Wilkins

jjjj – Charles G. Dawes and Carl Sigman

kkkk – Jeff Christie

llll – Byrne and Kenny Lynch

mmmm – Shuman and Kenny Lynch

nnnn – George Michael

oooo – George Michael, B. Romeo,
C. Wheeler, N. Hooper, and S. Law

pppp – Edwin Hawkins

qqqq – Michael Bolton, Jennifer Rush, and
M. Radice

rrrr – P. Sawyer, C. MacMurray, and
G. Jones

ssss – Charles Williams

tttt – Jean-Paul Dreau

uuuu – Norman Whitfield and
Barrett Strong

vvvv – Dave Williams and Sunny David

wwww – Phil Medley and Bert Berns
(aka Bert Russell)

xxxx – Leon Russell

yyyy – Jack Bruce and Pete Brown

zzzz – Lesley Duncan

aaaaa – Joseph B. Jefferson

bbbbb — Zekkariyas and Zeriiya Zekkariyas

The Singles

FORMAT KEY

7VS – 7-inch vinyl single   12VS – 12-inch vinyl single   ACS – audio cassette single

7DVS – 7-inch double vinyl single   CDS – CD single   PD – picture disc

RELEASE DATE & COUNTRY	SINGLE (A-SIDE/B-SIDE)	FORMAT	LABEL
February 1965 (UK)	*Bluesology:* Mr. Frantic (b)/Every Day (I Have the Blues) (ddd)	7VS	Fontana
July 1965 (UK)	*Bluesology:* Come Back Baby (b)/Times Getting Tougher than Tough (fff)	7VS	Fontana
October 1967 (UK)	*Stu Brown & Bluesology:* Since I Found You Baby (llll)/Just a Little Bit (mmmm)	7VS	Polydor
March 1968 (UK)	I've Been Loving You[2] (a)/Here's to the Next Time (a)	7VS	Philips
January 1969 (UK)	Lady Samantha/All across the Havens	7VS	Philips
January 1969 (US)	Lady Samantha/All across the Havens	7VS	DJM
February 1969 (UK)	*The Bread and Beer Band:* The Dick Barton Theme (The Devil's Gallop) (ssss)/Breakdown Blues (c) *(both instrumentals)*	7VS	Decca
May 1969 (UK)	It's Me That You Need/Just Like Strange Rain	7VS	DJM
January 1970 (US)	Lady Samantha/It's Me That You Need	7VS	Congress
March 1970 (UK)	Border Song/Bad Side of the Moon	7VS	DJM
April 1970 (US)	Border Song/Bad Side of the Moon	7VS	Congress
April 1970 (US)	From Denver to LA[3] (ccc)/*The Barbara Moore Singers (non-Elton group):* Warm Summer Rain (ccc)	7VS	Viking
June 1970 (UK)	Rock and Roll Madonna/Grey Seal	7VS	DJM
August 1970 (US)	Border Song/Bad Side of the Moon	7VS	Uni
October 1970 (US)	Take Me to the Pilot/Your Song	7VS	Uni
January 1971 (UK)	Your Song/Into the Old Man's Shoes	7VS	DJM
March 1971 (US)/ April 1971 (UK)	Friends/Honey Roll	7VS	Uni, DJM
November 1971 (US)	Levon/Goodbye	7VS	Uni
February 1972 (US)	Tiny Dancer/Razor Face	7VS	Uni
April 1972 (UK)	Rocket Man (I Think It's Going to Be a Long, Long Time)/Holiday Inn & Goodbye	7VS	DJM
April 1972 (US)	Rocket Man/Susie (Dramas)	7VS	Uni
July 1972 (US)	Honky Cat/Slave	7VS	Uni
August 1972 (UK)	Honky Cat/Lady Samantha & It's Me That You Need	7VS	DJM
October 1972 (UK)/ November 1972 (US)	Crocodile Rock/Elderberry Wine	7VS	MCA, DJM
January 1973 (UK)/ March 1973 (US)	Daniel/Skyline Pigeon (*1972 rerecording*)	7VS	MCA, DJM
June 1973 (UK)/ July 1973 (US)	Saturday Night's Alright for Fighting/Jack Rabbit & Whenever You're Ready (We'll Go Steady Again)	7VS	MCA, DJM
September 1973 (UK)	Goodbye Yellow Brick Road/Screw You	7VS	DJM
October 1973 (US)	Goodbye Yellow Brick Road/ Young Man's Blues (*same as "Screw You"*)	7VS	MCA

[2] *Elton John and Bernie Taupin are the credited songwriters, but this was actually written by Elton alone.*
[3] *Elton was erroneously credited on this single as "Elton Johns."*

RELEASE DATE & COUNTRY	SINGLE (A-SIDE/B-SIDE)	FORMAT	LABEL
November 1973 (US, UK)	Step into Christmas/Ho! Ho! Ho! (Who'd Be a Turkey at Christmas?)	7VS	MCA, DJM
February 1974 (UK)	Candle in the Wind/Bennie and the Jets	7VS	DJM
February 1974 (US)	Bennie and the Jets/Harmony	7VS	MCA
May 1974 (US, UK)	Don't Let the Sun Go Down on Me/Sick City	7VS	MCA, DJM
August 1974 (UK)/ September 1974 (US)	The Bitch Is Back/Cold Highway	7VS	MCA ,DJM
November 1974 (US, UK)	Lucy in the Sky with Diamonds (ll)/ One Day at a Time (jj)	7VS	MCA, DJM
February 1975 (US, UK)	Philadelphia Freedom/I Saw Her Standing There[4] (ll)	7VS	MCA, DJM
May 1975 (UK)/ June 1975 (US)	Someone Saved My Life Tonight/House of Cards	7VS	MCA, DJM
September 1975 (US, UK)	Island Girl/Sugar on the Floor (ee)	7VS	MCA, DJM
January 1976 (US, UK)	Grow Some Funk of Your Own (g) & I Feel Like a Bullet (In the Gun of Robert Ford) (double A-sided single)	7VS	MCA, DJM
March 1976 (UK)	Pinball Wizard (ss)/Harmony	7VS	DJM
June 1976 (US, UK)	Don't Go Breaking My Heart (f)/ Snow Queen (k) (both duets with Kiki Dee)	7VS	Rocket/MCA, Rocket/EMI
September 1976 (UK)	Benny and the Jets [sic]/Rock and Roll Madonna	7VS	DJM
October 1976 (UK)/ November 1976 (US)	Sorry Seems to Be the Hardest Word/Shoulder Holster	7VS	Rocket/MCA, Rocket/EMI
January 1977 (US)	Bite Your Lip (Get Up and Dance!) (Tom Moulton remix)/Chameleon	7VS	Rocket/MCA
February 1977 (UK)	Crazy Water/Chameleon	7VS	Rocket/EMI
April 1977 (UK)	The Goaldiggers Song (a)/Jimmy, Brian, Elton & Eric[5]	7VS	Rocket
May 1977 (UK)	"Four from Four Eyes": Your Song & Rocket Man/ Saturday Night's Alright for Fighting & Whenever You're Ready (We'll Go Steady Again)	7VS	DJM
June 1977 (UK)	Bite Your Lip (Get Up and Dance!) (Tom Moulton remix) & Kiki Dee: Chicago (hhh) (double A-sided single)	12VS	Rocket/EMI
March 1978 (US, UK)	Ego/Flinstone Boy (a)	7VS	MCA, Rocket/ Phonogram
September 1978 (UK)	Elton John Special 12-Record Pack[6]: Lady Samantha/Skyline Pigeon (1972 rerecording); Your Song/Border Song; Honky Cat/Sixty Years On; Country Comfort/Crocodile Rock; Rocket Man (I Think It's Going to Be a Long, Long Time)/Daniel; Sweet Painted Lady/Goodbye Yellow Brick Road; Don't Let the Sun Go Down on Me/Someone Saved My Life Tonight; Candle in the Wind/I Feel Like a Bullet (In the Gun of Robert Ford); The Bitch Is Back/Grow Some Funk of Your Own (g); Island Girl/Saturday Night's Alright for Fighting; Philadelphia Freedom/Lucy in the Sky with Diamonds (ll); Pinball Wizard (ss)/Benny and the Jets [sic]	7VS	DJM

[4] Live with John Lennon at Madison Square Garden, 11/28/74.
[5] The B-side of this limited-edition soccer charity single includes banter among Elton, television soccer commentators Jimmy Hill and Brian Moore, and comedian Eric Morecambe.
[6] Merchants were encouraged to sell these individually or as a set.

RELEASE DATE & COUNTRY	SINGLE (A-SIDE/B-SIDE)	FORMAT	LABEL
September 1978 (UK)	Funeral for a Friend—Love Lies Bleeding/ We All Fall in Love Sometimes & Curtains	12VS	DJM
October 1978 (US, UK)	Part-Time Love (r)/I Cry at Night	7VS	MCA, Rocket/ Phonogram
November 1978 (UK)/ March 1979 (US)	Song for Guy (a) *(instrumental)*/Lovesick	7VS	MCA, Rocket/ Phonogram
April 1979 (UK)	"The Thom Bell Sessions '77": Are You Ready for Love (jjj)/Three Way Love Affair (iii) & Mama Can't Buy You Love (iii)	12VS	Rocket/ Phonogram
April 1979 (UK)	Are You Ready for Love (Part 1) (jjj) & Are You Ready for Love (Part 2) (jjj)	7VS	Rocket/ Phonogram
June 1979 (US)	"The Thom Bell Sessions": Mama Can't Buy You Love (iii)/Three Way Love Affair (iii) & Are You Ready for Love (jjj)	12VS	MCA
June 1979 (US)	Mama Can't Buy You Love (iii)/ Three Way Love Affair (iii)	7VS	MCA
August 1979 (UK)	Mamma Can't Buy You Love [*sic*] (iii)/Strangers (r) *(withdrawn single)*	7VS	Rocket/ Phonogram
September 1979 (US, UK)	Victim of Love (nnn)/Strangers (r)	7VS	MCA, Rocket/ Phonogram
December 1979 (UK)	Johnny B. Goode (mm)/Thunder in the Night (kkk)	7VS, 12VS	Rocket/ Phonogram
December 1979 (US)	Johnny B. Goode (mm)/Georgia (r)	7VS	MCA
May 1980 (US, UK)	Little Jeannie (r)/Conquer the Sun (r)	7VS	MCA, Rocket/ Phonogram
August 1980 (UK)	Sartorial Eloquence (t)/White Man Danger & Cartier (e)	7VS	Rocket/ Phonogram
August 1980 (US)	Don't Ya Wanna Play This Game No More? (Sartorial Eloquence) (t)/Cartier (e) & White Man Danger	7VS	MCA
November 1980 (UK)	Harmony/Mona Lisas and Mad Hatters	7VS	DJM
November 1980 (UK)	Dear God (r)/Tactics (a) *(instrumental)*	7VS	Rocket/ Phonogram
November 1980 (UK)	Dear God (r)/Tactics *(instrumental)* & Steal Away Child (r) & Love So Cold	7DVS	Rocket/ Phonogram
March 1981 (UK)	"28th November 1974": I Saw Her Standing There (ll)/Whatever Gets You thru the Night (jj) & Lucy in the Sky with Diamonds (ll) *(all live with John Lennon)*	7VS	DJM
May 1981 (US, UK)	Nobody Wins (bb)/Fools in Fashion	7VS	Geffen, Rocket/ Phonogram
July 1981 (UK)	Just Like Belgium/I Can't Get Over Getting Over Losing You (r)	7VS	Rocket/ Phonogram
July 1981 (US)	Chloe (r)/Tortured	7VS	Geffen
November 1981 (UK)	Loving You Is Sweeter Than Ever (oo) *(duet with Kiki Dee)*/Kiki Dee: 24 Hours (ff)	7VS	Ariola
March 1982 (UK)/ July 1982 (US)	Blue Eyes (r)/Hey Papa Legba	7VS	Geffen, Rocket/ Phonogram
March 1982 (US)/ May 1982 (UK)	Empty Garden/Take Me Down to the Ocean (r)	7VS, PD (UK)	Geffen, Rocket/ Phonogram

RELEASE DATE & COUNTRY	SINGLE (A-SIDE/B-SIDE)	FORMAT	LABEL
September 1982 (UK)	Princess (r)/The Retreat	7VS	Rocket/ Phonogram
November 1982 (UK)	All Quiet on the Western Front/ Where Have All the Good Times Gone?	7VS	Rocket/ Phonogram
1982 (US)	Ball and Chain (r)/Where Have All the Good Times Gone?	7VS	Geffen
April 1983 (UK)	I Guess That's Why They Call It the Blues (g)/ Choc Ice Goes Mental (d) *(instrumental)*	7VS	Rocket/ Phonogram
April 1983 (US)	I'm Still Standing/Love So Cold	7VS	Geffen
July 1983 (US)	Kiss the Bride/Choc Ice Goes Mental (d) *(instrumental)*	7VS	Geffen
July 1983 (UK)	I'm Still Standing *(remix)*/ Earn While You Learn (d) *(instrumental)*	7VS, 12VS, PD	Rocket/ Phonogram
October 1983 (US)	I Guess That's Why They Call It the Blues (g)/ The Retreat	7VS	Geffen
October 1983 (UK)	Kiss the Bride/Dreamboat (s)	7VS	Rocket/ Phonogram
October 1983 (UK)	Kiss the Bride *(extended version)*/Dreamboat (s) *(extended version)*	12VS	Rocket/ Phonogram
October 1983 (UK)	Kiss the Bride/Dreamboat (s) & Ego & Song for Guy (a) *(instrumental)*	7DVS	Rocket/ Phonogram
November 1983 (UK)	Cold as Christmas (In the Middle of the Year)/Crystal	7VS	Rocket/ Phonogram
November 1983 (UK)	Cold as Christmas (In the Middle of the Year)/ Crystal & Don't Go Breaking My Heart (f) & Snow Queen (k) *(last two, duets with Kiki Dee)*	7DVS	Rocket/ Phonogram
November 1983 (UK)	Cold as Christmas (In the Middle of the Year)/ Crystal & J'Veux de la Tendresse [*sic*] (tttt)	12VS	Rocket/ Phonogram
May 1984 (US, UK)	Sad Songs (Say So Much)/A Simple Man (r)	7VS, 12VS (UK), PD (UK)	Geffen, Rocket/ Phonogram
July 1984 (UK)	Passengers *(remix)*/Lonely Boy (r)	7VS	Rocket/ Phonogram
July 1984 (UK)	Passengers *(extended remix by Julian Mendelsohn)*/ Lonely Boy & Blue Eyes	12VS	Rocket/ Phonogram
August 1984 (US)	Who Wears These Shoes?/Lonely Boy (r)	7VS	Geffen
October 1984 (UK)	Who Wears These Shoes?/Tortured	7VS	Rocket/ Phonogram
October 1984 (UK)	Who Wears These Shoes?/Tortured & I Heard It through the Grapevine (uuuu) *(live, Wembley Pool, 11/3/77)*	12VS	Rocket/ Phonogram
November 1984 (US)	In Neon/Tactics (a) *(instrumental)*	7VS	Geffen
February 1985 (UK)	Breaking Hearts (Ain't What It Used To Be)/ In Neon	7VS	Rocket/ Phonogram
June 1985 (US, UK)	Act of War (Part 1)/Act of War (Part 2) *(duet with Millie Jackson)*	7VS	Geffen, Rocket/ Phonogram
June 1985 (US, UK)	Act of War (Part 3)/Act of War (Part 4) *(duet with Millie Jackson)*	12VS	Geffen, Rocket/Phonogram

RELEASE DATE & COUNTRY	SINGLE (A-SIDE/B-SIDE)	FORMAT	LABEL
June 1985 (UK)	Act of War (Part 5)/Act of War (Part 6) *(duet with Millie Jackson)*	12VS	Rocket/ Phonogram
September 1985 (UK)	Nikita/The Man Who Never Died (a) *(instrumental)*	7VS	Rocket/ Phonogram
September 1985 (UK)	Nikita/The Man Who Never Died (a) *(instrumental)* & Sorry Seems to Be the Hardest Word & I'm Still Standing *(last two live, Wembley Stadium, 6/30/84)*	7VS, 7DVS, 12VS	Rocket/ Phonogram
October 1985 (US)	Wrap Her Up (l)/The Man Who Never Died (a) *(instrumental)*	7VS	Geffen
October 1985 (US, UK)	*Dionne & Friends (Elton John, Gladys Knight, and Stevie Wonder):* That's What Friends Are For (tt)/*Dionne Warwick:* Two Ships Passing in the Night (bbb)	7VS	Arista
October 1985 (UK)	*Dionne & Friends (Elton John, Gladys Knight, and Stevie Wonder):* That's What Friends Are For (tt)/same song* *(instrumental)* & *Dionne Warwick:* Two Ships Passing in the Night (bbb)	12VS	Arista
November 1985 (UK)	Wrap Her Up (l)/Restless *(live, Wembley Stadium, 6/30/84)*	7VS, PD	Rocket/ Phonogram
November 1985 (UK)	Wrap Her Up (l)/Restless *(live, Wembley Stadium, 6/30/84)* & Nikita & The Man Who Never Died (a) *(instrumental)*	7DVS	Rocket/ Phonogram
November 1985 (UK)	Wrap Her Up (l)/Restless *(live, Wembley Stadium, 6/30/84)* & Nikita & Cold As Christmas (In the Middle of the Year)	12VS	Rocket/ Phonogram
January 1986 (US)	Nikita/Restless *(live, Wembley Stadium, 6/30/84)*	7VS	Geffen
February 1986 (UK)	Cry to Heaven/Candy by the Pound	7VS	Rocket/ Phonogram
February 1986 (UK)	Cry to Heaven/Candy by the Pound & Rock and Roll Medley Live (Whole Lotta Shakin' Going On [vvvv]/ I Saw Her Standing There [ll]/Twist & Shout [wwww]) & Your Song *(last two, live, Wembley Stadium, 6/30/84)*	7DVS, 12VS	Rocket/ Phonogram
September 1986 (UK)/ **October 1986** (US)	Heartache All over the World/Highlander (a)	7VS, 12VS (US)	Geffen, Rocket/ Phonogram
September 1986 (UK)	Heartache All over the World/Highlander (a) & I'm Still Standing & Passengers (h)	7DVS	Rocket/ Phonogram
September 1986 (UK)	Heartache All over the World *(remix)*/Highlander (a) & Heartache All over the World *(single version)*	12VS	Rocket/ Phonogram
October 1986 (US)	Heartache All over the World *(Mega-mix)*/Highlander (a) *(instrumental)* & Heartache All over the World *(standard cut)*	ACS	Geffen
November 1986 (UK)	Slow Rivers *(duet with Cliff Richard)*/ Billy and the Kids	7VS, PD	Rocket/ Phonogram
November 1986 (UK)	Slow Rivers *(duet with Cliff Richard)*/ Billy and the Kids & Lord of the Flies	12VS	Rocket/ Phonogram
November 1986 (UK)	Slow Rivers *(duet with Cliff Richard)*/ Nikita & Blue Eyes (r) & I Guess That's Why They Call It the Blues (g)	ACS	Rocket/ Phonogram
May 1987 (US)/	Flames of Paradise (qqq) *(duet with Jennifer Rush)*/ *Jennifer Rush:* Call My Name (qqqq)	7VS	Epic, CBS
May 1987 (US)/ **June 1987** (UK)	Flames of Paradise (qqq) *(duet with Jennifer Rush)*/ same song* *(instrumental)* & *Jennifer Rush:* Call My Name (qqqq)	12VS	Epic, CBS
July 1987 (UK)	Your Song/Don't Let the Sun Go Down on Me *(both live, Sydney, 12/14/86)*	7VS	Rocket/ Phonogram

RELEASE DATE & COUNTRY	SINGLE (A-SIDE/B-SIDE)	FORMAT	LABEL
July 1987 (UK)	Your Song/Don't Let the Sun Go Down on Me & The Greatest Discovery & I Need You to Turn To *(all live, Sydney, 12/14/86)*	12VS	Rocket/ Phonogram
July 1987 (UK)	Your Song/I Need You to Turn To & The Greatest Discovery & Don't Let the Sun Go Down on Me *(all live, Sydney, 12/14/86)*	ACS	Rocket/ Phonogram
August 1987 (US)/ January 1988 (UK)	Candle in the Wind/Sorry Seems to Be the Hardest Word *(both live, Sydney, 12/14/86)*	7VS, PD (UK)	MCA, Rocket/ Phonogram
January 1988 (UK)	Candle in the Wind/Sorry Seems to Be the Hardest Word & Your Song & Don't Let the Sun Go Down on Me *(all live, Sydney, 12/14/86)*	7DVS, 12VS, CDS	Rocket/ Phonogram
January 1988 (UK)	Candle in the Wind/Sorry Seems to Be the Hardest Word/Your Song/Don't Let the Sun Go Down on Me *(all live, Sydney, 12/14/86)*	ACS	Rocket/ Phonogram
1988 (US)	Take Me to the Pilot/Tonight *(both live, Sydney, 12/14/86)*	7VS	MCA
May 1988 (UK)/ June 1988 (US)	I Don't Wanna Go On with You Like That/ Rope Around a Fool	7VS, ACS (US)	MCA, Rocket/ Phonogram
May 1988 (UK)	I Don't Wanna Go On with You Like That/Rope Around a Fool & Elton John Interview with Simon Bates, on BBC Radio One Broadcast, 17– 20 May 1988	7VS	Rocket/ Phonogram
May 1988 (UK)	I Don't Wanna Go On with You Like That/ Rope Around a Fool & I Don't Wanna Go On with You Like That *(The Shep Pettibone Mix)*	CDS	Rocket/ Phonogram
May 1988 (UK)	I Don't Wanna Go On with You Like That *Tthe Shep Pettibone Mix)*/same song *(single version)* & Rope Around a Fool	12VS	Rocket/ Phonogram
June 1988 (US)	I Don't Wanna Go On with You Like That *(The Shep Pettibone Mix)*/same song *(Pub Dub)* & same song *(Just Elton and His Piano Mix)* & same song *(Just for Radio Mix)*	12VS	MCA
August 1988 (UK)	Town of Plenty/Whipping Boy	7VS	Rocket/Phonogram
August 1988 (UK)	Town of Plenty/Whipping Boy & Saint & I Guess That's Why They Call It the Blues (g)	CDS	Rocket/ Phonogram
August 1988 (UK)	Town of Plenty/Whipping Boy & Saint	12VS	Rocket/ Phonogram
September 1988 (US)/ November 1988 (UK)	A Word in Spanish/Heavy Traffic (g)	7VS, ACS (US)	MCA, Rocket/Phonogram
November 1988 (UK)	A Word in Spanish/Heavy Traffic (g) & Medley: Song for You *[sic]* (xxxx), Blue Eyes (r), I Guess That's Why They Call It the Blues (g) & Daniel *(last two, live, Sydney, 12/14/86)*	CDS	Rocket/ Phonogram
November 1988 (UK)	A Word in Spanish/Daniel & Medley: Song for You *[sic]* (xxxx), Blue Eyes (r), I Guess That's Why They Call It the Blues (g) *(last two, live, Sydney, 12/14/86)*	12VS	Rocket/ Phonogram
1988 (US)	Mona Lisas and Mad Hatters (Part Two) *(The Renaissance Mix)* & same song *(The Da Vinci Version)*/ A Word in Spanish & Mona Lisas and Mad Hatters (Part Two) *(The Self-Portrait instrumental)*	12VS	MCA
April 1989 (UK)/ May 1989 (US)	Through the Storm (ppp) *(duet with Aretha Franklin)*/ *Aretha Franklin:* Come to Me (uuu)	7VS, PD (UK), ACS (UK)	Arista

RELEASE DATE & COUNTRY	SINGLE (A-SIDE/B-SIDE)	FORMAT	LABEL
April 1989 (UK)	Through the Storm (ppp) *(duet with Aretha Franklin)*/ *Aretha Franklin:* Come to Me (uuu) & *Aretha Franklin and Mavis Staples:* Oh Happy Day (pppp)	12VS, CDS	Arista
August 1989 (US, UK)	Healing Hands/Dancing in the End Zone (g)	7VS, ACS	MCA, Rocket/ Phonogram
August 1989 (UK)	Healing Hands *(extended remix)*/same song *(single version)* & Dancing in the End Zone (g)	12VS	Rocket/ Phonogram
August 1989 (UK)	Healing Hands/Sad Songs (Say So Much) *(live, Verona, Italy, 4/26/89)* & Dancing in the End Zone (g)	CDS	Rocket/ Phonogram
October 1989 (UK)/ **November 1989** (US)	Sacrifice/Love Is a Cannibal (g)	7VS, ACS	MCA, Rocket/ Phonogram
October 1989 (UK)	Sacrifice/Love Is a Cannibal (g) & Durban Deep	12VS, CDS	Rocket/ Phonogram
April 1990 (US)	Club at the End of the Street/*(no B-side)*	ACS	MCA
April 1990 (US)	Club at the End of the Street/Sacrifice	7VS	MCA
June 1990 (UK)	Sacrifice & Healing Hands *(double A-sided single)*	7VS, ACS	Rocket/ Phonogram
June 1990 (UK)	Sacrifice & Healing Hands/Durban Deep *(double A-sided single)*	12VS, CDS	Rocket/ Phonogram
August 1990 (UK)	Club at the End of the Street/Whispers	7VS, ACS	Rocket/ Phonogram
August 1990 (UK)	Club at the End of the Street/Whispers & I Don't Wanna Go On with You Like That	12VS, CDS	Rocket/ Phonogram
October 1990 (US)	You Gotta Love Someone/*(no B-side)*	ACS	MCA
October 1990 (UK)	You Gotta Love Someone/Medicine Man	7VS, ACS	Rocket/ Phonogram
October 1990 (UK)	You Gotta Love Someone/Medicine Man & same song *(with Adamski)*	12VS, CDS	Rocket/ Phonogram
October 1990 (UK)	You Gotta Love Someone & Sacrifice *(double A-sided single)*	7VS	Rocket/Phonogram
December 1990 (UK)	Easier to Walk Away/I Swear I Heard the Night Talkin'	7VS	Rocket/ Phonogram
December 1990 (UK)	Easier to Walk Away/I Swear I Heard the Night Talkin' & Made for Me	12VS, CDS	Rocket/ Phonogram
December 1990 (UK)	"Elton John's Christmas E.P.": *Christmas Side:* Step into Christmas/Cold as Christmas (In the Middle of the Year. *New Side:* Easier to Walk Away/I Swear I Heard the Night Talkin'	7VS	Rocket/ Phonogram
February 1991 (UK)	Don't Let the Sun Go Down on Me/ Song for Guy (a) *(instrumental)*	7VS, ACS	Rocket/ Phonogram
February 1991 (UK)	Don't Let the Sun Go Down on Me/ Song for Guy (a) *(instrumental)* & Sorry Seems to Be the Hardest Word	12VS, CDS	Rocket/ Phonogram
November 1991 (US, UK)	Don't Let the Sun Go Down on Me *(live duet with George Michael, Wembley Arena, 3/91)*/*George Michael:* I Believe (When I Fall in Love It Will Be Forever) (pp)	7VS, ACS	Columbia, Epic
November 1991 (UK)	Don't Let the Sun Go Down on Me *(live duet with George Michael, Wembley Arena, 3/91)*/*George Michael:* I Believe (When I Fall in Love It Will Be Forever) (pp) & Last Christmas (nnnn)	12VS	Epic

RELEASE DATE & COUNTRY	SINGLE (A-SIDE/B-SIDE)	FORMAT	LABEL
November 1991 (UK)	Don't Let the Sun Go Down on Me *(live duet with George Michael, Wembley Arena, 3/91)/George Michael: I Believe (When I Fall in Love It Will Be Forever)* (pp) & If You Were My Woman (rrrr) & Fantasy (nnnn)	CDS	Epic
November 1991 (US)	Don't Let the Sun Go Down on Me *(live duet with George Michael, Wembley Arena, 3/91)/George Michael: I Believe (When I Fall in Love It Will Be Forever)* (pp) & Freedom *(Back to Reality Mix)* (oooo) & If You Were My Woman (rrrr)	CDS	Columbia
May 1992 (US, UK)	The One/Suit of Wolves	7VS, ACS	MCA, Rocket/Phonogram
May 1992 (US, UK)	The One/Suit of Wolves & Fat Boys and Ugly Girls	CDS	MCA, Rocket/Phonogram
May 1992 (UK)	The One/Your Song & Don't Let the Sun Go Down on Me & Sacrifice	CDS	Rocket/Phonogram
July 1992 (UK)/ **August 1992** (US)	Runaway Train *(duet with Eric Clapton)/* Understanding Women *(remix and additional production) (single withdrawn in US)*	7VS, ACS	MCA, Rocket/Phonogram
July 1992 (UK)	Runaway Train *(duet with Eric Clapton)/*Understanding Women *(remix and additional production)* & Made for Me	CDS	Rocket/Phonogram
July 1992 (UK)	Runaway Train *(duet with Eric Clapton)/* Through the Storm (ppp) *(duet with Aretha Franklin)* & Don't Let the Sun Go Down on Me *(live duet with George Michael, Wembley Arena, 3/91)*	CDS	Rocket/Phonogram
August 1992 (US)	Runaway Train *(duet with Eric Clapton)/* Easier to Walk Away & Understanding Women *(remix and additional production) (withdrawn single)*	ACS, CDS	MCA
October 1992 (UK)	The Last Song/The Man Who Never Died (a) *(instrumental) (remix with additional production)*	7VS, ACS	Rocket/Phonogram
October 1992 (UK)	The Last Song/The Man Who Never Died (a) & Song for Guy (a) *(last two, instrumentals, and remixes with additional production)*	CDS	Rocket/Phonogram
October 1992 (UK)	The Last Song/Are You Ready for Love (jjj) & Three Way Love Affair (iii) & Mama Can't Buy You Love (iii)	CDS	Rocket/Phonogram
October 1992 (US)	The Last Song/The Man Who Never Died (a) & Song for Guy (a) *(last two, instrumentals)*	ACS	MCA
February 1993 (US)	Simple Life *(Hot Mix)*/The North	7VS, ACS	MCA
May 1993 (UK)	Simple Life/The Last Song	7VS, ACS	Rocket/Phonogram
May 1993 (UK)	Simple Life/The Last Song & The North	CDS	Rocket/Phonogram
November 1993 (US)	True Love (ii) *(duet with Kiki Dee)*/Runaway Train *(duet with Eric Clapton)*	7VS, ACS	MCA
November 1993 (UK)	True Love (ii) *(duet with Kiki Dee)*/The Show Must Go On (ooo) *(live, Wembley Stadium, 6/92)*	7VS, ACS	Rocket/Phonogram
November 1993 (UK)	True Love (ii) *(duet with Kiki Dee)*/The Show Must Go On (ooo) *(live, Wembley Stadium, 6/92)* & Runaway Train *(duet with Eric Clapton)*	CDS	Rocket/Phonogram

RELEASE DATE & COUNTRY	SINGLE (A-SIDE/B-SIDE)	FORMAT	LABEL
November 1993 (UK)	True Love (ii) *(duet with Kiki Dee)*/Wrap Her Up (l) & *Dionne & Friends (Elton John, Gladys Knight, and Stevie Wonder):* That's What Friends Are For (tt) & Act of War *(duet with Millie Jackson)*	CDS	Rocket/ Phonogram
February 1994 (UK)	Don't Go Breaking My Heart (f) *(duet with RuPaul)*/ Donner Pour Donner (aa) *(duet with France Gall)*	7VS, ACS	Rocket/ Phonogram
February 1994 (UK)	Don't Go Breaking My Heart (f) *(duet with RuPaul)*/ Donner Pour Donner (aa) *(duet with France Gall)* & A Woman's Needs *(duet with Tammy Wynette)*	CDS	Rocket/ Phonogram
February 1994 (UK)	Don't Go Breaking My Heart (f) *(duet with RuPaul)* *(Moroder 7" Mix)*/same song *(Moroder 12" Mix)* & same song *(Serious Rope 7" Mix)* & same song *(Serious Rope 12" Mix)* & same song *(Serious Rope Instrumental)* & same song *(Serious Rope Dirty Dub)*	CDS	Rocket/ Phonogram
February 1994 (US)	Don't Go Breaking My Heart (f) *(duet with RuPaul)*/Same song *(edited 12" remix)*	ACS	MCA
February 1994 (US)	Don't Go Breaking My Heart (f) *(duet with RuPaul)* *(remix)* & same song *(Don't Go Dubbing My Heart Mix)* & same song *(album version)*	ACS, 12VS	MCA
February 1994 (US)	Don't Go Breaking My Heart (f) *(duet with RuPaul)* *(remix)* & same song *(MK Mix)* & same song *(Serious Rope 12" Mix)* & same song *(Roger's Dub Mix)*	CDS	MCA
April 1994 (UK)	Ain't Nothing Like the Real Thing (aaa) *(duet with Marcella Detroit)*/Marcella Detroit: Break the Chain (sss)	7VS, ACS	London
April 1994 (UK)	Ain't Nothing Like the Real Thing (aaa) *(duet with Marcella Detroit)*/Marcella Detroit: Break the Chain (sss) & I Feel Free (yyyy)	CDS	London
April 1994 (UK)	Ain't Nothing Like the Real Thing (aaa) *(duet with Marcella Detroit)* *(Kenny Dope Extended Mix)* & same song *(Troopa Mood Mix)*/Marcella Detroit: I Feel Free (yyyy) *(Full Cream Mix)* & same song *(Cry Out Loud Mix)*	CDS	London
May 1994 (US)	Can You Feel the Love Tonight (u)/same song	ACS, CDS	Hollywood
June 1994 (UK)	Can You Feel the Love Tonight(u)/same song *(instrumental)*	7VS, ACS	Mercury
June 1994 (UK)	Can You Feel the Love Tonight (u)/same song *(instrumental)* & Hakuna Matata (u) (Lion King *movie cast version*) & Under the Stars* (gg) *(instrumental)*	CDS	Mercury
August 1994 (US)	Circle of Life (u)/same	ACS, CDS	Hollywood
September 1994 (UK)	Circle of Life (u)/same song *(Lion King movie cast version)*	ACS	Mercury
September 1994 (UK)	Circle of Life (u)/same song *(Lion King movie cast version)* & I Just Can't Wait to Be King (u) *(cast version)* & This Land* (gg) *(instrumental)*	CDS	Mercury
February 1995 (US, UK)	Believe/The One *(live, Greek Theater, Los Angeles, 9/94)*	7VS (US), ACS	Rocket/Island, Rocket/Mercury
February 1995 (UK)	Believe/Sorry Seems to Be the Hardest Word *(live, Greek Theater, Los Angeles, 9/94)*	ACS	Rocket/ Mercury

RELEASE DATE & COUNTRY	SINGLE (A-SIDE/B-SIDE)	FORMAT	LABEL
February 1995 (UK)	Believe/Believe & Sorry Seems to Be the Hardest Word *(last two, live, Greek Theater, Los Angeles, 9/94)*	CDS	Rocket/ Mercury
February 1995 (UK)	Believe/The One & The Last Song *(last two, live, Greek Theater, Los Angeles, 9/94)*	CDS	Rocket/ Mercury
February 1995 (US)	Believe/The One & Believe *(last two, live, Greek Theater, Los Angeles, 9/94)*	CDS	Rocket/ Island
February 1995 (US)	Believe/The One & The Last Song & Sorry Seems to Be the Hardest Word & Believe *(last four, live, Greek Theater, Los Angeles, 9/94)*	CDS	Rocket/ Island
May 1995 (UK)	Made in England/Whatever Gets You thru the Night (jj) & Lucy in the Sky with Diamonds (ll) & I Saw Her Standing There (ll) *(last three, live duets with John Lennon, Madison Square Garden, 11/28/74)*	CDS	Rocket/ Mercury
May 1995 (UK)	Made in England/Can You Feel the Love Tonight (u) & Your Song & Don't Let the Sun Go Down on Me *(last two, live, Greek Theater, Los Angeles, 9/94)*	CDS	Rocket/ Mercury
May 1995 (UK)	Made in England/Can You Feel the Love Tonight (u) & Daniel *(live, Greek Theater, Los Angeles, 9/94)*	ACS	Rocket/ Mercury
May 1995 (US)	Made in England/same song *(edited version)*	ACS	Rocket/Island
May 1995 (US)	Made in England/Lucy in the Sky with Diamonds (ll) *(live duet with John Lennon, Madison Square Garden, 11/28/74)*	7VS	Rocket/ Island
May 1995 (US)	Made in England *(radio edit)*/same song *(Junior's Sound Factory Mix)* & same song *(Junior's Factory Dub)* & same song *(Junior's Joyous Mix)*	CDS	Rocket/ Island
May 1995 (US)	Made in England *(edit)*/Whatever Gets You thru the Night (jj) & Lucy in the Sky with Diamonds (ll) & I Saw Her Standing There (ll) *(last three, live duets with John Lennon, Madison Square Garden, 11/28/74)* & Believe *(Hardkiss Mix)*	CDS	Rocket/ Island
May 1995 (US)	Made in England *(Junior's Sound Factory Mix)* & same song *(Junior's Factory Dub)* & same song *(Junior's Joyous Mix)* & Believe *(Hardkiss Mix)*	12VS	Rocket/ Island
September 1995 (US)	Bruce Roberts Featuring Elton John: When the Money's Gone (rrr) *(edit)*/same song *(E-Smoove Club Remix edit)*	ACS	Atlantic
October 1995 (US)	Blessed/Latitude	7VS, ACS	Rocket/Island
October 1995 (US, UK)	Blessed/Honky Cat & Take Me to the Pilot & The Bitch Is Back *(last three, live, Royal Festival Hall, 5/18/74)* *(single withdrawn in UK)*	CDS	Rocket/ Island, Rocket/Mercury
October 1995 (UK)	Blessed/Made in England *(Junior's Sound Factory Mix)* & same song *(Junior's Joyous Mix)* *(withdrawn single)*	CDS	Rocket/ Mercury
October 1995 (UK)	Blessed/Honky Cat & Take Me to the Pilot & The Bitch Is Back *(last three, live, Royal Festival Hall, 5/18/74)* *(withdrawn single)*	CDS	Rocket/ Mercury
1995 (UK)	Reg Dwight: United We Stand (bbbb) *(duet with Kay Garner)* *(1995 remix)*/same song* *(Instrumental 1995 Mix)* & same song *(original mix)* & Neanderthal Man (gggg) *(all songs are dime store covers Elton recorded in 1970)*	CDS	DeeJay
January 1996 (UK)	Please/Latitude	7VS, ACS	Rocket/ Mercury

RELEASE DATE & COUNTRY	SINGLE (A-SIDE/B-SIDE)	FORMAT	LABEL
January 1996 (UK)	Please/Made in England *(Junior's Sound Factory Mix)* & same song *(Junior's Joyous Mix)*	CDS	Rocket/ Mercury
January 1996 (UK)	Please/Honky Cat & Take Me to the Pilot & The Bitch Is Back *(last three, live, Royal Festival Hall, 5/18/74)*	CDS	Rocket/ Mercury
September 1996 (US)	You Can Make History (Young Again)/ Song for Guy (a) *(instrumental)*	ACS	MCA
December 1996 (UK)	Live Like Horses *(duet with Luciano Pavarotti)*/ same song *(duet with Luciano Pavarotti, live finale version, Modena, Italy, 6/20/96)*	ACS	Rocket/ Mercury
December 1996 (UK)	Live Like Horses *(duet with Luciano Pavarotti)*/Live Like Horses *(duet with Luciano Pavarotti)* & I Guess That's Why They Call It the Blues (g) *(last two, live, Modena, Italy, 6/20/96)* & Live Like Horses *(solo version)*	CDS	Rocket/ Mercury
December 1996 (UK)	Live Like Horses *(duet with Luciano Pavarotti)*/ Live Like Horses *(live duet with Luciano Pavarotti, Modena, Italy, 6/20/96)* & Step into Christmas & Blessed	CDS	Rocket/ Mercury
September 1997 (UK)	Something About the Way You Look Tonight *(edit)*/I Know Why I'm in Love & No Valentines & Something About the Way You Look Tonight *(withdrawn single)*	CDS	Rocket/ Mercury
September 1997 (US, UK)	Candle in the Wind 1997 & Something About the Way You Look Tonight *(double A-sided single)*	7VS (US), CDS (US) ACS	Rocket/A&M, Rocket/Mercury
September 1997 (UK)	Candle in the Wind 1997 & Something About the Way You Look Tonight/You Can Make History (Young Again) *(double A-sided single)*	CDS	Rocket/ Mercury
February 1998 (UK)	Recover Your Soul *(single remix)*/ I Know Why I'm in Love	ACS	Rocket/ Mercury
February 1998 (UK)	Recover Your Soul *(single remix)*/Big Man in a Little Suit & I Know Why I'm in Love & Recover Your Soul *(album version)*	CDS	Rocket/ Mercury
February 1998 (UK)	Recover Your Soul *(single remix)*/No Valentines/ Recover Your Soul *(album version)* *(PC-enhanced CD single)*	CDS	Rocket/ Mercury
February 1998 (US)	Recover Your Soul *(radio mix)*/ I Know Why I'm in Love	ACS	Rocket/ A&M
February 1998 (US)	Recover Your Soul *(radio mix)*/I Know Why I'm in Love & Big Man in a Little Suit	CDS	Rocket/ A&M
June 1998 (UK)	If the River Can Bend *(edit)*/Bennie and the Jets	ACS	Rocket/Mercury
June 1998 (UK)	If the River Can Bend *(edit)*/Bennie and the Jets & Saturday Night's Alright for Fighting & If the River Can Bend *(album version)*	CDS	Rocket/ Mercury
June 1998 (UK)	If the River Can Bend *(edit)*/Don't Let the Sun Go Down On Me & I Guess That's Why They Call It the Blues (g) & Sorry Seems to Be the Hardest Word *(last three, live, Paris, 1/14/98)*	CDS	Rocket/ Mercury
February 1999 (US)	Written in the Stars (u) *(duet with LeAnn Rimes)*/ same song *(duet with LeAnn Rimes, alternate version)* & *Aida* Album Sampler *(Spice Girls: My Strongest Suit [u]; Boyz II Men: Not Me [u]; and Elton John, Heather Headley, and Sherie Scott: A Step Too Far [u])*	ACS, CDS	Rocket/ Island

RELEASE DATE & COUNTRY	SINGLE (A-SIDE/B-SIDE)	FORMAT	LABEL
February 1999 (UK)	Written in the Stars (u) *(duet with LeAnn Rimes)*/ same song *(duet with LeAnn Rimes, alternate version)* & Recover Your Soul *(live, Paris, 1/14/98)*	CDS	Rocket/ Mercury
February 1999 (UK)	Written in the Stars (u) *(duet with LeAnn Rimes)*/ *Aida* Album Sampler (*Spice Girls:* My Strongest Suit [u]; *Boyz II Men:* Not Me [u]; and *Elton John, Heather Headley, and Sherie Scott:* A Step Too Far [u]) & Your Song *(live, Paris, 1/14/98)*	CDS	Rocket/ Mercury
February 1999 (UK)	Written in the Stars (u) *(duet with LeAnn Rimes)*/ same song *(duet with LeAnn Rimes, alternate version)*	ACS	Rocket/ Mercury
May 1999 (US)	A Step Too Far (u) *(Elton John with Heather Headley and Sherie Scott)*/ *(no B-side)* *(radio-only single)*	CDS	Rocket/ Island
April 2000 (US)	Someday Out of the Blue (w)/Cheldorado*(gg) *(instrumental)*	ACS, CDS	DreamWorks
August 2000 (US)	Friends Never Say Goodbye (u) *(radio edit)*/ same song *(album version)* *(radio-only single)*	CDS	DreamWorks
September 2000 (US)	Tiny Dancer *(edit)*/*Almost Famous* movie edit with dialogue from the movie & Tiny Dancer *(album version)* *(radio-only single)*	CDS	DreamWorks
November 2000 (US)	I Guess That's Why They Call It the Blues (g) *(live duet with Mary J. Blige, Madison Square Garden, 10/21/00)*/ same song *(studio duet with Mary J. Blige)* *(radio-only single)*	CDS	Universal
February 2001 (US)	Stan *(live duet with Eminem from 2001 Grammy Awards, radio edit)* *(radio-only single)*	CDS	Interscope Records
February 2001 (US)	Stan *(live duet with Eminem from 2001 Grammy Awards, new radio mix)* *(radio-only single)*	CDS	Interscope Records

Albums

FORMAT KEY	V – vinyl	AC – audio cassette	CD – CD	PD – picture disc

RELEASE DATE & COUNTRY	ALBUM	FORMAT	LABEL
June 1969 (UK)	*Empty Sky:* *Side One:* Empty Sky/Val-Hala/Western Ford Gateway/ Hymn 2000. *Side Two:* Lady What's Tomorrow?/Sails/ The Scaffold/Skyline Pigeon/Gulliver's Gone/ Hay Chewed (a) *(instrumental)*/Reprise.	V	DJM
April 1970 (UK)/ **July 1970** (US)	*Elton John:* *Side One:* Your Song/I Need You to Turn To/Take Me to the Pilot/No Shoe Strings on Louise/First Episode at Hienton. *Side Two:* Sixty Years On/Border Song/ The Greatest Discovery/The Cage/The King Must Die.	V, AC	Uni, DJM
October 1970 (UK)/ **January 1971** (US)	*Tumbleweed Connection:* *Side One:* Ballad of a Well-Known Gun/Come Down in Time/Country Comfort/Son of Your Father/ My Father's Gun. *Side Two:* Where to Now, St. Peter?/ Love Song (zzzz)/Amoreena/Talking Old Soldiers/ Burn Down the Mission.	V, AC	Uni, DJM

RELEASE DATE & COUNTRY	ALBUM	FORMAT	LABEL
March 1971 (US)/ April 1971 (UK)	*Friends* (movie soundtrack): *Side One:* Friends/Honey Roll/Variations on Friends Theme (The First Kiss) (q) *(instrumental)*/Seasons/ Variations on Michelle's Song (A Day in the Country) (q) *(instrumental)*/Can I Put You On? *Side Two:* Michelle's Song/ I Meant to Do My Work Today (A Day in the Country) (q) *(instrumental)*/Four Moods (cc) *(instrumental)*/Seasons Reprise.	V, AC	Paramount
April 1971 (UK)	*17-11-70* (recorded live on New York radio on 11/17/70): *Side One:* Take Me to the Pilot/Honky Tonk Women (rr)/Sixty Years On/Can I Put You On. *Side Two:* Bad Side of the Moon/Burn Down the Mission/Medley: My Baby Left Me (ggg)/Get Back (ll).	V, AC	DJM
May 1971 (US)	*11-17-70* (same album as above, with date transposed)	V, AC	Uni
November 1971 (US, UK)	*Madman across the Water*: *Side One:* Tiny Dancer/Levon/Razor Face/Madman across the Water. *Side Two:* Indian Sunset/Holiday Inn/ Rotten Peaches/All the Nasties/Goodbye.	V, AC	Uni, DJM
May 1972 (US, UK)	*Honky Chateau*: *Side One:* Honky Cat/Mellow/I Think I'm Going to Kill Myself/Susie (Dramas)/Rocket Man (I Think It's Going to Be a Long, Long Time). *Side Two:* Salvation/ Slave/Amy/Mona Lisas and Mad Hatters/Hercules.	V, AC	Uni, DJM
January 1973 (US, UK)	*Don't Shoot Me, I'm Only the Piano Player*: *Side One:* Daniel/Teacher I Need You/Elderberry Wine/Blues for Baby and Me/Midnight Creeper. *Side Two:* Have Mercy on the Criminal/I'm Going to Be a Teenage Idol/Texan Love Song/Crocodile Rock/High Flying Bird.	V, AC	MCA, DJM
October 1973 (US, UK)	*Goodbye Yellow Brick Road*: *Side One:* Funeral for a Friend—Love Lies Bleeding/ Candle in the Wind/Bennie and the Jets. *Side Two:* Goodbye Yellow Brick Road/This Song Has No Title/ Grey Seal *(1973 rerecording)*/Jamaica Jerk-Off/I've Seen That Movie Too. *Side Three:* Sweet Painted Lady/ The Ballad of Danny Bailey (1909–34)/Dirty Little Girl/All the Girls Love Alice. *Side Four:* Your Sister Can't Twist (But She Can Rock'n'Roll)/Saturday Night's Alright for Fighting/Roy Rogers/Social Disease/Harmony.	V, AC	MCA, DJM
June 1974 (US, UK)	*Caribou*: *Side One:* The Bitch Is Back/Pinky/Grimsby/Solar Prestige a Gammon/You're So Static. *Side Two:* I've Seen the Saucers/Stinker/Don't Let the Sun Go Down on Me/Ticking.	V, AC	MCA, DJM
September 1974 (UK)	*Lady Samantha* (collection of B-sides and rare tracks): *Side One:* Rock and Roll Madonna/Whenever You're Ready (We'll Go Steady Again)/Bad Side of the Moon *(B-side version)*/Jack Rabbit/Into the Old Man's Shoes/ It's Me That You Need/Ho! Ho! Ho! (Who'd Want to Be a Turkey at Christmas?) [*sic*]. *Side Two:* Skyline Pidgeon [*sic*] *(1972 rerecording)*/Screw You/Just Like Strange Rain/ Grey Seal *(1970 version)*/Honey Roll/Lady Samantha/Friends.	AC	DJM

RELEASE DATE & COUNTRY	ALBUM	FORMAT	LABEL
November 1974 (UK)	**Greatest Hits:** *Side One:* Your Song/Daniel/Honky Cat/Goodbye Yellow Brick Road/Saturday Night's Alright for Fighting. *Side Two:* Rocket Man/Candle in the Wind/ Don't Let the Sun Go Down on Me/Border Song/ Crocodile Rock.	V, AC	DJM
November 1974 (US)	**Greatest Hits** (same tracks as above, but "Bennie and the Jets" was included instead of "Candle in the Wind")	V, AC	MCA
January 1975 (US)	**Empty Sky** (same songs as 1969 UK release)	V, AC	MCA
May 1975 (US, UK)	**Captain Fantastic and the Brown Dirt Cowboy:** *Side One:* Captain Fantastic and the Brown Dirt Cowboy/Tower of Babel/Bitter Fingers/Tell Me When the Whistle Blows. *Side Two:* (Gotta Get a) Meal Ticket/Better Off Dead/Writing/ We All Fall in Love Sometimes/Curtains.	V, AC PD (1978, UK)	MCA, DJM
October 1975 (US, UK)	**Rock of the Westies:** *Side One:* Medley: Yell Help, Wednesday Night, Ugly (g)/Dan Dare (Pilot of the Future)/Island Girl/ Grow Some Funk of Your Own (g)/I Feel Like a Bullet (In the Gun of Robert Ford). *Side Two:* Street Kids/ Hard Luck Story (f)/Feed Me/Billy Bones and the White Bird.	V, AC	MCA, DJM
April 1976 (UK)/ May 1976 (US)	**Here and There** (live album): *Side One ("Here," Royal Festival Hall, 5/18/74):* Skyline Pigeon/Border Song/Honky Cat/Love Song (zzzz)/Crocodile Rock. *Side Two ("There," Madison Square Garden, 11/28/74):* Funeral for a Friend— Love Lies Bleeding/Rocket Man/Bennie and the Jets/ Take Me to the Pilot.	V, AC	MCA, DJM
October 1976 (US, UK)	**Blue Moves:** *Side One:* Your Starter For . . . (dd) *(instrumental)*/ Tonight/One Horse Town (m)/Chameleon. *Side Two:* Boogie Pilgrim (i)/Cage the Songbird (g)/ Crazy Water/Shoulder Holster. *Side Three:* Sorry Seems to Be the Hardest Word/Out of the Blue (a) *(instrumental)*/ Between Seventeen and Twenty (i)/The Wide-Eyed and Laughing (j)/Someone's Final Song. *Side Four:* Where's the Shoorah?/If There's a God in Heaven (What's He Waiting For?)/Idol/Theme from a Non-Existent TV Series (a) *(instrumental)*/Bite Your Lip (Get Up and Dance!).	V, AC	Rocket/MCA, Rocket/EMI
September 1977 (UK)	**Elton John's Greatest Hits, Volume II:** *Side One:* The Bitch Is Back/Lucy in the Sky with Diamonds (ll)/Sorry Seems to Be the Hardest Word/ Don't Go Breaking My Heart (f)/Someone Saved My Life Tonight. *Side Two:* Philadelphia Freedom/Island Girl/ Grow Some Funk of Your Own (g)/Bennie and the Jets/ Pinball Wizard (ss).	V, AC	DJM
October 1977 (US)	**Elton John's Greatest Hits, Volume II** (same tracks as above, but "Levon" was included instead of "Bennie and the Jets")	V, AC	MCA

RELEASE DATE & COUNTRY	ALBUM	FORMAT	LABEL
January 1978 (UK)	*Candle in the Wind* (compilation of rare and album tracks sold in Marks and Spencer stores): *Side One:* Skyline Pigeon *(1969 version)*/Take Me to the Pilot/Burn Down the Mission/Teacher I Need You/ Rocket Man (I Think It's Gonna Be a Long, Long Time) [*sic*]/Don't Let the Sun Go Down on Me/ Elderberry Wine. *Side Two:* Bennie and the Jets/Midnight Creeper/Dan Dare (Pilot of the Future)/Someone Saved My Life Tonight/Better Off Dead/Grey Seal *(1970 version)*/ Candle in the Wind.	V, AC	St. Michael
March 1978 (UK)	*Elton John Live 17-11-70* (repackaged version of original *17-11-70*)	V	Pickwick
September 1978 (UK)	*London & New York Live!* (repackaged version of original *Here and There*)	V	Pickwick
October 1978 (US, UK)	*A Single Man*⁷: *Side One:* Shine on Through/Return to Paradise/ I Don't Care/Big Dipper/It Ain't Gonna Be Easy. *Side Two:* Part-Time Love/Georgia/Shooting Star/ Madness/Reverie *(instrumental)*/Song for Guy *(instrumental)*.	V, AC	MCA,Rocket/ Phonogram
February 1979 (UK)	*The Elton John Live Collection* (repackaged versions of original *17-11-70* and *Here and There* as double album)	V	Pickwick
August 1979 (UK)	*Elton John* (5-LP box set retrospective of Elton's DJM recording career): RECORD ONE: *EARLY YEARS* *Side One:* Lady Samantha/Skyline Pigeon *(1969 version)*/ Empty Sky/Border Song/I Need You to Turn To/ Sixty Years On. *Side Two:* Country Comfort/Burn Down the Mission/Where To Now, St. Peter?/Levon/Madman across the Water/Friends. RECORD TWO: *ELTON ROCKS* *Side One:* Saturday Night's Alright for Fighting/ (Gotta Get a) Meal Ticket/Screw You/Teacher I Need You/ Grow Some Funk of Your Own (g)/Grey Seal *(1973 rerecording)*/The Bitch Is Back. *Side Two:* Crocodile Rock/The Cage/Elderberry Wine/Whenever You're Ready (We'll Go Steady Again)/Street Kids/Midnight Creeper/Pinball Wizard (ss). RECORD THREE: *MOODS* *Side One:* I Feel Like a Bullet (In the Gun of Robert Ford)/ Mona Lisas and Mad Hatters/High Flying Bird/ Tiny Dancer/The Greatest Discovery/Blues for Baby and Me. *Side Two:* Harmony/I've Seen That Movie Too/Pinky/ It's Me That You Need/Indian Sunset/Sweet Painted Lady/ Love Song (zzzz). RECORD FOUR: *SINGLES* *Side One:* Your Song/Rocket Man (I Think It's Going to Be a Long, Long Time)/Honky Cat/Daniel/ Goodbye Yellow Brick Road/Candle in the Wind/ Don't Let the Sun Go Down on Me.	V	DJM

⁷ *All songs written by Elton John/Gary Osborne except for the instrumentals, which were composed by Elton.*

Elton John (continued):
Side Two: Lucy in the Sky with Diamonds (ll)/
Philadelphia Freedom/Someone Saved My
Life Tonight/Island Girl/Bennie and the Jets.
RECORD FIVE: *CLASSICS*
Side One: Funeral for a Friend—Love Lies Bleeding/
The Ballad of Danny Bailey (1909–34)/Ticking.
Side Two: Texan Love Song/Captain Fantastic and the
Brown Dirt Cowboy/We All Fall in Love Sometimes/
Curtains.

October 1979 (US, UK)	*Victim of Love:* *Side One:* Johnny B. Goode (mm)/Warm Love in a Cold World (mmm)/Born Bad (lll). *Side Two:* Thunder in the Night (kkk)/Spotlight (mmm)/Street Boogie (mmm)/ Victim of Love (nnn).	V, AC	MCA, Rocket/ Phonogram
February 1980 (UK)	*Lady Samantha* (reissuance and repackaging of 1974 tape-only compilation)	V, AC	DJM
May 1980 (US, UK)	*21 at 33:* *Side One:* Chasing the Crown/Little Jeannie (r)/Sartorial Eloquence (t)/Two Rooms at the End of the World. *Side Two:* White Lady White Powder/Dear God (r)/ Never Gonna Fall in Love Again (t)/Take Me Back (r)/ Give Me the Love (x).	V, AC	MCA, Rocket/ Phonogram
October 1980 (UK)	*The Very Best of Elton John* (compilation of hits and album tracks): *Side One:* Your Song/Goodbye Yellow Brick Road/ Daniel/Song for Guy (a) *(instrumental)*/Candle in the Wind/Friends/Tiny Dancer/Rocket Man (I Think It's Going to Be a Long, Long Time). *Side Two:* Sorry Seems to Be the Hardest Word/ Border Song/Someone Saved My Life Tonight/ Mona Lisas and Mad Hatters/Harmony/ High Flying Bird/Don't Let the Sun Go Down on Me.	V, AC	K-Tel
November 1980 (US)	*Elton John Milestones* (greatest hits compilation): *Side One:* Don't Go Breaking My Heart (f) *(duet with Kiki Dee)*/Island Girl/The Bitch Is Back/ Honky Cat/Bennie and the Jets/Someone Saved My Life Tonight/Don't Let the Sun Go Down on Me/ Sorry Seems to Be the Hardest Word. *Side Two:* Mama Can't Buy You Love (iii)/Philadelphia Freedom/Crocodile Rock/Rocket Man (I Think It's Going to Be a Long, Long Time)/Daniel/Lucy in the Sky with Diamonds (ll)/ Your Song/Goodbye Yellow Brick Road.	V, AC	K-Tel
May 1981 (US, UK)	*The Fox:* *Side One:* Breaking Down Barriers/Heart in the Right Place (r)/Just Like Belgium/Nobody Wins (bb)/Fascist Faces. *Side Two:* Carla-Étude (a) *(instrumental)*/Fanfare (q) *(instrumental)*/Chloe (r)/Heels of the Wind/Elton's Song (t)/The Fox.	V, AC	Geffen, Rocket/ Phonogram

RELEASE DATE & COUNTRY	ALBUM	FORMAT	LABEL
	Elton John (continued): *Cassette Two, Side Two:* Crocodile Rock/The Ballad of Danny Bailey/High Flying Bird/Burn Down the Mission/ Love Song (*zzzz*)/Goodbye Yellow Brick Road.		
May 1983 (US)/ **June 1983** (UK)	*Too Low for Zero:* *Side One:* Cold as Christmas (In the Middle of the Year)/I'm Still Standing/Too Low for Zero/ Religion/I Guess That's Why They Call It the Blues (g). *Side Two:* Crystal/Kiss the Bride/Whipping Boy/ Saint/One More Arrow.	V, AC	Geffen, Rocket/ Phonogram
June 1983 (UK)	*The New Collection* (compilation of hits and album tracks): *Side One:* Crocodile Rock/Don't Let the Sun Go Down on Me/Saturday Night's Alright for Fighting/It's Me that You Need/Someone Saved My Life Tonight/ Whatever Gets You thru the Night (jj) (*live duet with John Lennon, Madison Square Garden, 11/28/74*)/Lucy in the Sky with Diamonds (ll). *Side Two:* The Bitch Is Back/ High Flying Bird/Elderberry Wine/Candle in the Wind/ Your Sister Can't Twist (But She Can Rock'n'Roll)/Daniel.	V, AC	Everest
June 1983 (UK)	*The New Collection, Volume Two* (compilation of hits and album tracks): *Side One:* Your Song/Benny and the Jets [*sic*]/Harmony/ Take Me to the Pilot/Island Girl/Rocket Man. *Side Two:* Good Bye Yellow Brick Road [*sic*]/Honky Cat/ Philadelphia Freedom/Skyline Pigeon/Roy Rodgers [*sic*]/ I Think I'm Going to Kill Myself.	V, AC	Everest
May 1984 (UK)	*Seasons: The Early Love Songs* (withdrawn collection of album tracks and rarities): *Cassette One, Side One:* First Episode at Heinton [*sic*]/ Amoreena/I Need You to Turn To/Sweet Painted Lady/ The Tide Will Turn for Rebecca (*previously unreleased late 1960s recording*)/Amy/Where to Now, St. Peter? *Side Two:* Don't Let the Sun Go Down on Me/Someone Saved My Life Tonight/Writing/We All Fall in Love Sometimes/Curtains. *Cassette Two, Side One:* Candle in the Wind/It's Me That You Need/I've Seen that Movie Too/Mellow/ Empty Sky. *Side Two:* Funeral for a Friend—Love Lies Bleeding/Susie (Dramas)/Sails/Come Down in Time/Rock'n'Roll Madonna [*sic*]/Goodbye.	AC	Cambra
June 1984 (UK)/ **July 1984** (US)	*Breaking Hearts:* *Side One:* Restless/Slow Down Georgie (She's Poison)/ Who Wears These Shoes?/Breaking Hearts (Ain't What It Used to Be)/Li'l 'Frigerator. *Side Two:* Passengers (h)/In Neon/Burning Buildings/Did He Shoot Her?/Sad Songs (Say So Much).	V, AC, CD	Geffen, Rocket/ Phonogram
November 1985 (US, UK)	*Ice on Fire:* *Side One:* This Town/Cry to Heaven/Soul Glove/ Nikita/Too Young. *Side Two:* Wrap Her Up (l)/Satellite/ Tell Me What the Papers Say/Candy by the Pound/ Shoot Down the Moon/Act of War (*duet with Millie Jackson*) (*last song, AC and CD only*).	V, AC, CD	Geffen, Rocket/ Phonogram

RELEASE DATE & COUNTRY	ALBUM	FORMAT	LABEL
November 1986 (US, UK)	*Leather Jackets*: *Side One:* Leather Jackets/Hoop of Fire/Don't Trust That Woman (z)/Go It Alone/Gypsy Heart. *Side Two:* Slow Rivers *(duet with Cliff Richard)*/ Heartache All over the World/Angeline (n)/ Memory of Love (r)/I Fall Apart.	V, AC, CD	Geffen, Rocket/ Phonogram
1986 (US)	*Your Songs* (hits and album tracks compilation): *Side One:* Your Song/Country Comfort/Tiny Dancer/ Burn Down the Mission/Friends. *Side Two:* Take Me to the Pilot/Candle in the Wind/Elderberry Wine/ Razor Face/Harmony.	V, AC, CD	MCA
July 1987 (US)/ September 1987 (UK)	*Live in Australia with the Melbourne Symphony Orchestra* (recorded live in Sydney, 12/14/86): *Side One:* Sixty Years On/I Need You to Turn To/ The Greatest Discovery/Tonight. *Side Two:* Sorry Seems to Be the Hardest Word/The King Must Die/Take Me to the Pilot/Tiny Dancer. *Side Three:* Have Mercy on the Criminal/Madman across the Water/Candle in the Wind. *Side Four:* Burn Down the Mission/Your Song/ Don't Let the Sun Go Down on Me.	V, AC, CD	MCA, Rocket/Phonogram
September 1987 (US)	*Elton John's Greatest Hits, Volume III, 1979–1987*: *Side One:* I Guess That's Why They Call It the Blues (g)/Mama Can't Buy You Love (iii)/Little Jeannie (r)/ Sad Songs (Say So Much)/I'm Still Standing/Empty Garden (Hey Hey Johnny). *Side Two:* Heartache All over the World/Too Low for Zero/Kiss the Bride/Blue Eyes (r)/Nikita/Wrap Her Up (l).	V, AC, CD	Geffen
June 1988 (US)/ July 1988 (UK)	*Reg Strikes Back*: *Side One:* Town of Plenty/A Word in Spanish/Mona Lisas and Mad Hatters (Part Two)/I Don't Wanna Go On with You Like That/Japanese Hands. *Side Two:* Goodbye Marlon Brando/The Camera Never Lies/ Heavy Traffic (g)/Poor Cow/Since God Invented Girls.	V, AC, CD	MCA, Rocket/Phonogram
February 1989 (US)	*The Complete Thom Bell Sessions* (reissuance of 1979 EP with remixed versions of three original tracks and featuring three previously unreleased tracks): *Side One:* Nice and Slow (o)/Country Love Song (aaaaa)/ Shine on Through (r). *Side Two:* Mama Can't Buy You Love (iii)/Are You Ready for Love (jjj)/Three Way Love Affair (iii).	V, AC, CD	MCA
August 1989 (US, UK)	*Sleeping with the Past*: *Side One:* Durban Deep/Healing Hands/Whispers/ Club at the End of the Street/Sleeping with the Past. *Side Two:* Stone's Throw from Hurtin'/Sacrifice/I Never Knew Her Name/Amazes Me/Blue Avenue.	V, AC, CD	MCA, Rocket/Phonogram
October 1989 (UK)	*The Collection* (compilation of hits and album tracks): *Side One:* Funeral for a Friend—Love Lies Bleeding/ Sweet Painted Lady/Elderberry Wine/Come Down in Time/Border Song/Crocodile Rock. *Side Two:* Mona Lisas and Mad Hatters/The Greatest Discovery/ Blues for My Baby and Me [*sic*]/Ballad of a Well Known Gun [*sic*]/Teacher I Need You.	V, AC, CD	Pickwick

RELEASE DATE & COUNTRY	ALBUM	FORMAT	LABEL
October 1990 (UK)	**The Very Best of Elton John** (different from the 1980 UK K-Tel release): *CD One:* Your Song/Rocket Man (I Think It's Going to Be a Long, Long Time)/Honky Cat/Crocodile Rock/ Daniel/Goodbye Yellow Brick Road/Saturday Night's Alright for Fighting/Candle in the Wind *(1973 version)*/ Don't Let the Sun Go Down on Me/Lucy in the Sky with Diamonds (ii)/Philadelphia Freedom/ Someone Saved My Life Tonight/Pinball Wizard⁸ (ss)/ The Bitch Is Back⁸. *CD Two:* Don't Go Breaking My Heart (f) *(duet with Kiki Dee)*/Bennie and the Jets/Sorry Seems to Be the Hardest Word/Song for Guy (a) *(instrumental)*/ Part Time Love [*sic*] (r)/Blue Eyes (r)/I Guess That's Why They Call It the Blues (g)/I'm Still Standing/ Kiss the Bride/Sad Songs/Passengers (h)/Nikita/ I Don't Wanna Go On with You Like That⁸/Sacrifice/ Easier to Walk Away⁸/You Gotta Love Someone.	V, AC, CD	Rocket/ Phonogram
November 1990/ October 2000 (US) (limited reissue)	**To Be Continued . . .** (4-volume box set retrospective of Elton's career): *CD One: Bluesology:* Come Back Baby (b)/Lady Samantha/It's Me That You Need/Your Song *(demo)*/ Rock and Roll Madonna/Bad Side of the Moon/ Your Song/Take Me to the Pilot/Border Song/Sixty Years On/Country Comfort/Grey Seal [*sic*] *(1970 version)*/ Friends/Levon/Tiny Dancer/Madman across the Water/ Honky Cat/Mona Lisas and Mad Hatters. *CD Two:* Rocket Man/Daniel/Crocodile Rock/Bennie and the Jets/Goodbye Yellow Brick Road/All the Girls Love Alice/Funeral for a Friend—Love Lies Bleeding/Whenever You're Ready (We'll Go Steady Again)/Saturday Night's Alright for Fighting/ Jack Rabbit/Harmony/Young Man's Blues/Step into Christmas/The Bitch Is Back/Pinball Wizard (ss)/Someone Saved My Life Tonight/Philadelphia Freedom/One Day at a Time (jj)/Lucy in the Sky with Diamonds (ll)/I Saw Her Standing There (ll) *(live duet with John Lennon, Madison Square Garden, 11/28/74)*/Island Girl/Sorry Seems to Be the Hardest Word/Don't Go Breaking My Heart (f) *(duet with Kiki Dee)*/I Feel Like a Bullet (In the Gun of Robert Ford) *(live, London, May 1977)*/Ego. *CD Three:* Song for Guy (a) *(instrumental)*/Mama Can't Buy You Love (iii)/Cartier (a)/ Little Jeannie (r)/Donner Pour Donner (aa) *(duet with France Gall)*/Fanfare (p) *(instrumental)*/Chloe (r)/The Retreat/ Blue Eyes (r). *CD Four:* Empty Garden (Hey Hey Johnny)/ I Guess That's Why They Call It the Blues (g)/I'm Still Standing/Sad Songs (Say So Much)/Act of War *(duet with Millie Jackson)*/Nikita/Candle in the Wind/Carla-Étude (a) *(instrumental)*/Don't Let the Sun Go Down on Me *(last three live, Sydney, 12/14/86)*/I Don't Wanna Go On with You Like That *(12" Shep Pettibone Remix)*/Give Peace a Chance (jj) *(rare B-side)*/Sacrifice/Made for Me/You Gotta Love Someone/I Swear I Heard the Night Talkin'/Easier to Walk Away.	AC (1990), CD	MCA

⁸ *Not available on vinyl.*

RELEASE DATE & COUNTRY	ALBUM	FORMAT	LABEL
October 1991 (US, UK)	*Two Rooms: Celebrating the Songs of Elton John & Bernie Taupin* (album of John/Taupin covers, with name of artist covering song in parentheses): Border Song (Eric Clapton)/Rocket Man (I Think It's Going to Be a Long, Long Time) (Kate Bush)/Come Down in Time (Sting)/Saturday Night's Alright (for Fighting) [*sic*] (the Who)/Crocodile Rock (the Beach Boys)/Daniel (Wilson Phillips)/Sorry Seems to Be the Hardest Word (Joe Cocker)/Levon (Jon Bon Jovi)/ The Bitch Is Back (Tina Turner)/Philadelphia Freedom (Daryl Hall & John Oates)/Your Song (Rod Stewart)/ Don't Let the Sun Go Down on Me (Oleta Adams)/ Madman across the Water (Bruce Hornsby)/Sacrifice (Sinead O'Connor)/Burn Down the Mission (Phil Collins)/ Tonight (George Michael).	CD, AC, V (UK)	Polydor
November 1991 (UK)	*To Be Continued . . .* (repackaged 4-volume box set): Same tracks as above, except for the deletion of "You Gotta Love Someone" and "I Swear I Heard the Night Talkin" and the addition of "Suit of Wolves" and "Understanding Women"	CD, AC	Rocket/ Phonogram
February 1992 (UK)	*Love Songs* (different from 1982 compilation): Are You Ready for Love? [*sic*] (jjj)/Little Jeannie (r)/ I've Seen That Movie Too/High Flying Bird/Heartache All over the World/Warm Love in a Cold World (mmm)/ Cry to Heaven/Sorry Seems to Be the Hardest Word/ I Need You to Turn To/Harmony/Never Gonna Fall in Love Again (t)/Candle in the Wind *(1973 version)*/It's Me That You Need/Give Me the Love (x)/We All Fall in Love Sometimes/Curtains.	CD	Pickwick
June 1992 (US, UK)	*The One:* Simple Life/The One/Sweat It Out/Runaway Train/ Whitewash County/The North/When a Woman Doesn't Want You/Emily/On Dark Street/ Understanding Women/The Last Song.	CD, AC, V (UK)	MCA, Rocket/ Phonogram
October 1992 (UK)	*Songbook* (compilation of hits and rare tracks): All Quiet on the Western Front/Tiny Dancer/Where to Now, St. Peter?/Ego/Shooting Star (r)/Wrap Her Up (l)/Texan Love Song/Nobody Wins (bb)/Empty Garden/Lady What's Tomorrow/Who Wears These Shoes?/Just Like Belgium/Empty Sky/Crazy Water/ Island Girl/Friends.	CD, AC	Pickwick
October 1992 (US)	*Greatest Hits 1976–1986* (replaces *Elton John's Greatest Hits, Volume III, 1979–1987*): I'm Still Standing/Mama Can't Buy You Love (iii)/ Sorry Seems to Be the Hardest Word/Little Jeannie (r)/ Blue Eyes (r)/Don't Go Breaking My Heart (f) *(duet with Kiki Dee)*/Empty Garden (Hey, Hey Johnny)/Kiss the Bride/I Guess That's Why They Call It the Blues (g)/ Who Wears These Shoes?/Sad Songs (Say So Much)/ Wrap Her Up (l)/Nikita.	CD, AC	MCA

RELEASE DATE & COUNTRY	ALBUM	FORMAT	LABEL
October 1992 (US)/ January 1993 (UK)	*Rare Masters* (remastered *Friends* soundtrack, B-sides, demos, early singles, and previously unreleased tracks): *CD One:* I've Been Loving You[9] (a)/Here's to the Next Time (a)/Lady Samantha/All across the Havens/It's Me That You Need/Just Like Strange Rain/Bad Side of the Moon/Rock and Roll Madonna/Grey Seal *(1970 version)*/Friends/Michelle's Song/Seasons/Variation [*sic*] on Michelle's Song (A Day in the Country) (q) *(instrumental)*/Can I Put You On/Honey Roll/Variation on Friends [*sic*] (q) *(instrumental)*/I Meant to Do My Work Today (A Day in the Country) (q) *(instrumental)*/Four Moods (cc) *(instrumental)*/Seasons Reprise. *CD Two:* Madman across the Water *(1970 version)*/Into the Old Man's Shoes/Rock Me When He's Gone/Slave *(fast version)*/Skyline Pigeon *(1972 rerecording)*/Jack Rabbit/Whenever You're Ready (We'll Go Steady Again)/Let Me Be Your Car *(demo)*/Screw You (Young Man's Blues)/Step into Christmas/Ho! Ho! Ho! (Who'd Be a Turkey at Christmas) [*sic*]/Sick City/One Day at a Time (jj)/I Saw Her Standing There (ll) *(live duet with John Lennon, Madison Square Garden, 11/28/74)*/House of Cards/Planes/Sugar on the Floor (ee).	CD, AC	Polydor, Rocket/ Phonogram
October 1992 (US)	The following were reissued as remasters, with track changes as noted: *Empty Sky/Elton John/Tumbleweed Connection/11-17-70/Madman across the Water/Honky Chateau/Don't Shoot Me, I'm Only the Piano Player/Goodbye Yellow Brick Road/Caribou/Greatest Hits[10]/Captain Fantastic and the Brown Dirt Cowboy/Rock of the Westies/Here and There/Elton John's Greatest Hits, Volume II[11]*	CD, AC	Polydor
November 1993 (US, UK)	*Duets* (duet partner listed in parentheses): Teardrops (bbbbb) (k.d. lang)/When I Think About Love (I Think About You) (ttt) (P.M. Dawn)/The Power (Little Richard)/Shakey Ground (vvv) (Don Henley)/True Love (ii) (Kiki Dee)/If You Were Me (www) (Chris Rea)/A Woman's Needs (Tammy Wynette)/Don't Let the Sun Go Down on Me (George Michael, *live, Wembley Stadium, 3/91*)/Old Friend (xxx) (Nik Kershaw)/Go On and On (nn) (Gladys Knight)/Don't Go Breaking My Heart (f) (RuPaul)/Ain't Nothing Like the Real Thing (aaa) (Marcella Detroit)/I'm Your Puppet (yyy) (Paul Young)/Love Letters (uu) (Bonnie Raitt)/Born to Lose (zzz) (Leonard Cohen)/Duets for One (y) (Elton John).	CD, AC, V (UK)	MCA, Rocket/ Phonogram
June 1994 (US)/ October 1994 (UK)	*The Lion King* (movie soundtrack): Circle of Life (u)/I Just Can't Wait to Be King (u)/Be Prepared (u)/Hakuna Matata (u)/Can You Feel the Love Tonight (u) *(last five cast version)*/This Land (gg)/ . . . To Die For (gg)/Under the Stars (gg)/King of Pride Rock (gg) *(last four instrumentals, not performed by Elton John)*/Circle of Life (u)/ I Just Can't Wait to Be King (u)/Can You Feel the Love Tonight (u) *(last three Elton John version)*.	CD, AC	Walt Disney Records, Mercury

[9] *Elton John and Bernie Taupin are the credited songwriters, but this was actually written by Elton alone.*
[10] *Contains both "Bennie and the Jets" and "Candle in the Wind" (1973 version).*
[11] *Replaces "Sorry Seems to Be the Hardest Word" and "Don't Go Breaking My Heart" (f) (duet with Kiki Dee) with "Tiny Dancer" and "I Feel Like a Bullet (In the Gun of Robert Ford)."*

RELEASE DATE & COUNTRY	ALBUM	FORMAT	LABEL
October 1994 (UK)	*Reg Dwight's Piano Goes Pop* (rereleased 3/95 as *Chartbusters Go Pop*; includes many of Elton's dime store covers, including lead vocals and/or harmonies, from 1969 and 1970): My Baby Loves Lovin' (ww)/Cottonfields [*sic*] (eee)/ Lady D'Arbanville (yy)/Natural Sinner (aaaa)/ United We Stand (bbbb)*(duet with Kay Garner)*/ Spirit in the Sky (zz)/Travellin' Band (vv)/ I Can't Tell the Bottom from the Top (cccc)/ Good Morning Freedom (xx)/Young Gifted & Black (dddd)/In the Summertime (eeee)/Up Around the Bend (vv)/Snake in the Grass (ffff)/Neanderthal Man (gggg)/She Sold Me Magic (hhhh)/Love of the Common People (iiii)/Signed Sealed Delivered [*sic*] (qq)/It's All in the Game (jjjj)/Yellow River (kkkk).	CD	RPM
November 1994 (US)	*Greatest Hits* (remastered by Steve Hoffman in 10/94; issued on 24-karat gold; same as 1974 release, except that "Candle in the Wind" is added at the end)	CD	DCC Compact Classics/Polydor
March 1995 (US, UK)	*Made in England*: Believe/Made in England/House/Cold/Belfast/ Latitude/Please/Man/Lies/Blessed.	CD, AC V	Rocket/Island, Rocket/ Mercury
May/July/October 1995 (UK), **February/ March 1996** (US)	*The Classic Years* (1970s albums remastered by Gus Dudgeon and rereleased with bonus tracks. Only bonus tracks are listed, where applicable, unless otherwise noted): *Empty Sky:* Lady Samantha/All across the Havens/ It's Me that You Need/Just Like Strange Rain. *Elton John:* Bad Side of the Moon/Grey Seal *(1970 version)*/Rock 'n Roll Madonna [*sic*]. *Tumbleweed Connection:* Into the Old Man's Shoes/ Madman across the Water *(1970 version)*. *11-17-70* (US) and *17-11-70* (UK) (tracks were reordered[12]): Bad Side of the Moon/Amoreena *(bonus track)*/Take Me to the Pilot/Sixty Years On/Honky Tonk Women (rr)/Can I Put You On/Burn Down the Mission/Medley: My Baby Left Me (ggg)/Get Back (ll). *Madman across the Water:* no bonus tracks. *Honky Chateau:* Slave *(fast version)*. *Don't Shoot Me, I'm Only the Piano Player:* Screw You (Young Man's Blues)/Jack Rabbit/Whenever You're Ready (We'll Go Steady Again)/Skyline Pigeon *(1972 rerecording)*. *Goodbye Yellow Brick Road:* no bonus tracks. *Caribou:* Pinball Wizard (ss)/Sick City/Cold Highway/ Step into Christmas. *Captain Fantastic and the Brown Dirt Cowboy:* Lucy in the Sky with Diamonds (ll)/One Day at a Time (jj)/Philadelphia Freedom. *Rock of the Westies:* Don't Go Breaking My Heart (f) *(duet with Kiki Dee)*.	CD, AC	Rocket/Island, Rocket/Mercury

[12] *This remastered album is not recommended. The piano is downplayed in the mix, many of Elton's vocal exclamations have been erased, and most sounds of audience excitement have been obliterated. Fans should seek out the 1992 Polydor remaster instead, even at the expense of the bonus track.*

RELEASE DATE & COUNTRY	ALBUM	FORMAT	LABEL
	The Classic Years (continued): *Here and There* (expanded from nine tracks to 25; original tracks are noted with the symbol "†"): *CD One* (Royal Festival Hall, London): Skyline Pigeon†/Border Song†/ Take Me to the Pilot/Country Comfort/Love Song† (zzzz)/ Bad Side of the Moon†/Burn Down the Mission/Honky Cat†/ Crocodile Rock†/Candle in the Wind/Your Song/Saturday Night's Alright (for Fighting) [sic]. *CD Two* (Madison Square Garden, New York): Funeral for a Friend—Love Lies Bleeding†/Rocket Man (I Think It's Going to Be a Long, Long Time)†/Take Me to the Pilot†/Bennie and the Jets†/Grey Seal/ Daniel/You're So Static/Whatever Gets You thru the Night (jj)/ Lucy in the Sky with Diamonds (ll)/I Saw Her Standing There (ll) *(last three, duets with John Lennon)*/Don't Let the Sun Go Down on Me/Your Song/The Bitch Is Back.		
Summer 1995 (US)	*Visa Gold Presents Elton John's Gold* (available for purchase by phone order for Visa Gold cardholders): Your Song/Someone Saved My Life Tonight/ Philadelphia Freedom/Come Down in Time/Rocket Man/Honky Cat/I Guess That's Why They Call It the Blues (g)/Sad Songs (Say So Much)/Sorry Seems to Be the Hardest Word/I'm Still Standing/The Bitch Is Back/Saturday Night's Alright for Fighting.	CD	Rocket/Poly-Gram Special Markets/Visa
September 1995 (US)	*Classic Elton John* (charity release available for purchase at McDonald's fast food restaurants): Take Me to the Pilot/Burn Down the Mission/Friends/ Saturday Night's Alright (for Fighting) [sic]/Madman across the Water *(1970 version)*/Tiny Dancer/Honky Cat/Crocodile Rock/Mona Lisas and Mad Hatters/Levon.	CD, AC	PolyGram Special Markets
November 1995 (UK)	*Love Songs* (different from other *Love Songs* compilations): Sacrifice/Candle in the Wind *(1973 version)*/I Guess That's Why They Call It the Blues (g)/Don't Let the Sun Go Down on Me*(live duet with George Michael, Wembley Arena, 3/91)*/Sorry Seems to Be the Hardest Word/Blue Eyes (r)/Daniel/Nikita/Your Song/The One/Someone Saved My Life Tonight/True Love (ii) *(duet with Kiki Dee)*/ Can You Feel the Love Tonight (u)/Circle of Life (u)/ Blessed/Please/Song for Guy (a) *(instrumental)*.	CD, AC, V	Rocket/ Mercury
June 1996 (UK)/ **August 1997** (US)	*Blue Moves* (remastered by Gus Dudgeon with the following tracks restored after being left off the original 1980s US and/or UK CD releases): Cage the Songbird (g)/Shoulder Holster/The Wide Eyed and Laughing (j)/Where's the Shoorah?/Out of the Blue (a) *(instrumental)*.	CD	MCA, Rocket/ Mercury
September 1996 (US)	*Love Songs* (similar to 1995 compilation with two newly written songs indicated with the symbol "†"): Can You Feel the Love Tonight (u)/The One/Sacrifice/ Daniel/Someone Saved My Life Tonight/Your Song/ Don't Let the Sun Go Down on Me *(live duet with George Michael, Wembley Arena, 3/91)*/Believe/Blue Eyes (r)/ Sorry Seems to Be the Hardest Word/Blessed/Candle in the Wind *(live, Sydney, 12/14/86)*/You Can Make History (Young Again)†/No Valentines†/Circle of Life (u).	CD, AC	MCA

RELEASE DATE & COUNTRY	ALBUM	FORMAT	LABEL
September 1997 (US, UK)	*The Big Picture*: Long Way from Happiness/Live Like Horses/ The End Will Come/If the River Can Bend/ Love's Got a Lot to Answer For/Something About the Way You Look Tonight/The Big Picture/ Recover Your Soul/January/I Can't Steer My Heart Clear of You/Wicked Dreams.	CD, AC	Rocket/A&M, Rocket/ Mercury
April 1998 (US)	*16 Legendary Covers from 1969/70 as Sung by Elton John* (similar to 1994 *Reg Dwight's Piano Goes Pop* release): Natural Sinner (aaaa)/United We Stand (bbbb)/ Spirit in the Sky (zz)/Travellin' Band (vv)/ I Can't Tell the Bottom from the Top (cccc)/ Good Morning Freedom (xx)/Up Around the Bend (vv)/She Sold Me Magic (hhhh)/Come and Get It (kk)/ Love of the Common People (iiii)/Signed Sealed Delivered [*sic*] (qq)/It's All in the Game (jjjj)/ Yellow River (kkkk)/My Baby Loves Lovin [*sic*] (ww)/ Cottonfields [*sic*] (eee)/Lady D Arbanville [*sic*] (yy).	CD	Purple Pyramid
1998 (UK)	*The Classic Years* (1980s and 1990s albums remastered by Gus Dudgeon and rereleased with bonus tracks. Only bonus tracks are listed, where applicable): *A Single Man:* Ego/Flinstone Boy (a)/I Cry at Night/ Lovesick/Strangers (r). *Too Low for Zero:* Earn While You Learn (d) *(instrumental)*/Dreamboat (s) *(extended version)*/ The Retreat. *Ice on Fire* [13]: The Man Who Never Died (a) *(instrumental)*/Restless *(live, Wembley Stadium, 6/30/84)*/ Sorry Seems to Be the Hardest Word *(live, London, 5/77)*[14]/ I'm Still Standing *(live, Wembley Stadium, 6/30/84).* *Live in Australia with the Melbourne Symphony Orchestra:* no bonus tracks. *Reg Strikes Back:* Rope around a Fool/I Don't Wanna Go On with You Like That *(12" Shep Pettibone Mix)*/same song *(Just Elton and His Piano Mix)*/Mona Lisas and Mad Hatters (Part Two) *(Renaissance Mix). Sleeping with the Past:* Dancing in the End Zone (g)/Love Is a Cannibal (g). *The One:* Suit of Wolves/ Fat Boys and Ugly Girls.	CD	Rocket/Mercury
March 1999 (US, UK)	*Elton John and Tim Rice's Aida*[15] (14 songs from various versions of the stage production; artists performing songs indicated in parentheses): Another Pyramid (Sting)/Written in the Stars (Elton John and LeAnn Rimes)/Easy as Life (Tina Turner featuring Angelique Kidjo)/My Strongest Suit (Spice Girls)/ I Know the Truth (Elton John and Janet Jackson)/Not Me (Boyz II Men)/Amneris' Letter (Shania Twain)/A Step Too Far (Elton John, Heather Headley, and Sherie Scott)/ Like Father Like Son (Lenny Kravitz)/Elaborate Lives (Heather Headley)/How I Know You (James Taylor)/ The Messenger (Elton John and Lulu)/The Gods Love Nubia (Kelly Price)/Enchantment Passing Through (Dru Hill)/Orchestral Finale *(includes "Written in the Stars" [prelude], "I Know the Truth," "Easy As Life," and reprise of "Written in the Stars").*	CD, AC	Rocket/Island, Rocket/Mercury

[13] *"Act of War" was omitted from remastered rerelease.*
[14] *Liner notes mistakenly state year as 1984.*
[15] *All songs by Elton John/Tim Rice.*

RELEASE DATE & COUNTRY	ALBUM	FORMAT	LABEL
March 1999 (US)	*Live at the Ritz: Limited Edition* (live, Paris, 1/14/98[16]; sold at Target stores to coincide with release of *Elton John and Tim Rice's Aida*): Daniel/Don't Let the Sun Go Down on Me/Sorry Seems to Be the Hardest Word/Something About the Way You Look Tonight/Take Me to the Pilot/The Last Song.	CD	Rocket-Island/ Universal Music Special Markets/ Target
August 1999 (US)	*The Muse*[17] (movie soundtrack; noninstrumentals indicated with the symbol "✝"): Driving Home/Driving to Universal/Driving to Jack's/ Walk of Shame/Better Have a Gift/The Wrong Gift/ The Aquarium/Are We Laughing?/Take a Walk with Me/What Should I Do?/Back to the Aquarium/ Steven Redecorates/To the Guesthouse/The Cookie Factory/Multiple Personality/Sarah Escapes/Back to Paramount/Meet Christine/The Muse✝/The Muse✝ *(remixed by Jermaine Dupri)*.	CD	Rocket/Island
March 2000 (US)/ April/August 2000 (UK)	*Elton John's the Road to El Dorado* (songs written for and inspired by the movie): El Dorado (u)/Someday Out of the Blue (Theme from El Dorado) (w)/Without Question (u)/Friends Never Say Goodbye (u)/The Trail We Blaze (u)/16th Century Man (u)/The Panic in Me (v)/It's Tough to Be a God (u) *(duet with Randy Newman)*/Trust Me (u)/My Heart Dances (u)/Queen of Cities (u)/Cheldorado* (gg)/The Brig* (gg)/ Wonders of the New World* (hh) *(last three, instrumentals)*/ Perfect Love[18] (u)/Hey, Armadillo[19] (u).	CD, AC	DreamWorks
May 2000 (US, UK)	*Live at Madison Square Garden* (from solo shows recorded on 10/15 and 10/16/99; available only as part of membership on eltonjohn.com, Elton's official Web site): Your Song/Skyline Pigeon/The Greatest Discovery/ Harmony/Honky Cat/Rocket Man/Philadelphia Freedom/Elton's Song (t)/Sweet Painted Lady/Ticking/ Empty Garden/Crocodile Rock.	CD	eltonjohn.com
November 2000 (US, UK)	*One Night Only: The Greatest Hits* (from band shows recorded at Madison Square Garden on 10/20 and 10/21/00): Goodbye Yellow Brick Road/Philadelphia Freedom/ Don't Go Breaking My Heart (f) *(duet with Kiki Dee)*/ Rocket Man/Daniel/Crocodile Rock/Sacrifice/Can You Feel the Love Tonight (u)/Bennie and the Jets/ Your Song *(duet with Ronan Keating)*/Sad Songs (Say So Much) *(duet with Bryan Adams)*/Candle in the Wind/The Bitch Is Back/Saturday Night's Alright (for Fighting) [*sic*] *(duet with Anastacia)*/I'm Still Standing/Don't Let the Sun Go Down on Me/I Guess That's Why They Call It the Blues (g) *(duet with Mary J. Blige)*.	CD, AC	Universal, Mercury

[16] *Date of concert is given mistakenly as 1/15/98.*
[17] *All songs by Elton John, except "The Muse," which is by Elton John/Bernie Taupin.*
[18] *Extra track available only on bonus CD in the United States at Best Buy stores.*
[19] *Extra track available only on bonus CD in the United States at Best Buy stores.*

RELEASE DATE & COUNTRY	ALBUM	FORMAT	LABEL
March 2001 (US)	*The Remasters* (same as *The Classic Years* series released in the UK in 1998. All bonus tracks are identical to those on the UK releases): *A Single Man, Too Low for Zero, Ice on Fire, Live in Australia with the Melbourne Symphony Orchestra.*	CD, AC	Universal/Island
May 2001 (US)	*The Remasters* (same as *The Classic Years* series released in the UK in 1998. All bonus tracks are identical to those on the UK releases): *Reg Strikes Back, Sleeping with the Past, The One.*	CD, AC	Universal/Island
June 2001 (US, UK)	*Live at Madison Square Garden, Volume 2* (from solo shows recorded on 10/15 and 10/16/99; available only as part of "Year Two" Rocket membership on www.eltonjohn.com, Elton's official Web site): Border Song/Daniel/Tiny Dancer/Better off Dead/ I Guess That's Why They Call It the Blues (g)/ Carla-Étude [*sic*] (a)/Tonight/Burn Down the Mission/ The One/Levon/Don't Let the Sun Go Down on Me/ Bennie and the Jets.	CD	www.eltonjohn.com
October 2001 (US, UK)	*Songs from the West Coast*: The Emperor's New Clothes/Dark Diamond/Look Ma, No Hands/ American Triangle/Original Sin/ Birds/I Want Love/The Wasteland/Ballad of the Boy in the Red Shoes/Love Her Like Me/Mansfield/This Train Don't Stop There Anymore.	CD, AC	Universal/Island, Mercury